(Continued on back endsheets)

American Magazine Journalists, 1900-1960
1900-1960
First Series

American Magazine Journalists, 1900-1960
First Series

Edited by
Sam G. Riley
Virginia Polytechnic Institute & State University

A Bruccoli Clark Layman Book
Gale Research Inc.
Detroit, New York, London

Advisory Board for
DICTIONARY OF LITERARY BIOGRAPHY

John Baker
William Cagle
Jane Christensen
Patrick O'Connor
Peter S. Prescott

Matthew J. Bruccoli and Richard Layman, *Editorial Directors*
C. E. Frazer Clark, Jr., *Managing Editor*

Manufactured by Edwards Brothers, Inc.
Ann Arbor, Michigan
Printed in the United States of America

Copyright © 1990
Gale Research Inc.
835 Penobscot Bldg.
Detroit, MI 48226-4094

Library of Congress Cataloging-in-Publication Data

American magazine journalists, 1900-1960. First series/
    edited by Sam G. Riley.
      p. cm.–(Dictionary of literary biography; v. 91)
    "A Bruccoli Clark Layman book."
    ISBN 0-8103-4571-4
    1. Journalists–United States–Biography–Dictionaries. 2.
Authors, American–20th century–Biography–Dictionaries.
3. Journalism–United States–History–20th century. I.
Riley, Sam G. II. Series.
PN4871.A475 1990
070'.92'273–dc20
[B]
                                                89-48356
                                                CIP

Dedicated to Daniel Blalock Riley, matchless son, by your dad, who takes great delight

in your wit and talent

Contents

Plan of the Series

. . . Almost the most prodigious asset of a country, and perhaps its most precious possession, is its native literary product—when that product is fine and noble and enduring.

Mark Twain*

The advisory board, the editors, and the publisher of the *Dictionary of Literary Biography* are joined in endorsing Mark Twain's declaration. The literature of a nation provides an inexhaustible resource of permanent worth. We intend to make literature and its creators better understood and more accessible to students and the reading public, while satisfying the standards of teachers and scholars.

To meet these requirements, *literary biography* has been construed in terms of the author's achievement. The most important thing about a writer is his writing. Accordingly, the entries in *DLB* are career biographies, tracing the development of the author's canon and the evolution of his reputation.

The purpose of *DLB* is not only to provide reliable information in a convenient format but also to place the figures in the larger perspective of literary history and to offer appraisals of their accomplishments by qualified scholars.

The publication plan for *DLB* resulted from two years of preparation. The project was proposed to Bruccoli Clark by Frederick G. Ruffner, president of the Gale Research Company, in November 1975. After specimen entries were prepared and typeset, an advisory board was formed to refine the entry format and develop the series rationale. In meetings held during 1976, the publisher, series editors, and advisory board approved the scheme for a comprehensive biographical dictionary of persons who contributed to North American literature. Editorial work on the first volume began in January 1977, and it was published in 1978. In order to make *DLB* more than a reference tool and to compile volumes that individually have claim to status as literary history, it was decided to organize volumes by topic, period, or genre. Each of these freestanding volumes provides a biographical-bibliographical guide and overview for a particular area of literature. We are convinced that this organization—as opposed to a single alphabet method—constitutes a valuable innovation in the presentation of reference material. The volume plan necessarily requires many decisions for the placement and treatment of authors who might properly be included in two or three volumes. In some instances a major figure will be included in separate volumes, but with different entries emphasizing the aspect of his career appropriate to each volume. Ernest Hemingway, for example, is represented in *American Writers in Paris, 1920-1939* by an entry focusing on his expatriate apprenticeship; he is also in *American Novelists, 1910-1945* with an entry surveying his entire career. Each volume includes a cumulative index of subject authors and articles. Comprehensive indexes to the entire series are planned.

With volume ten in 1982 it was decided to enlarge the scope of *DLB*. By the end of 1986 twenty-one volumes treating British literature had been published, and volumes for Commonwealth and Modern European literature were in progress. The series has been further augmented by the *DLB Yearbooks* (since 1981) which update published entries and add new entries to keep the *DLB* current with contemporary activity. There have also been *DLB Documentary Series* volumes which provide biographical and critical source materials for figures whose work is judged to have particular interest for students. One of these companion volumes is entirely devoted to Tennessee Williams.

We define literature as the *intellectual commerce of a nation:* not merely as belles lettres but as that ample and complex process by which ideas are generated, shaped, and transmitted. *DLB* entries are not limited to "creative writers" but extend to other figures who in their time and in their way influenced the mind of a people. Thus the series encompasses historians, journalists, publishers, and screenwriters. By this means readers of *DLB* may be aided to perceive litera-

---

*From an unpublished section of Mark Twain's autobiography, copyright © by the Mark Twain Company.

ture not as cult scripture in the keeping of intellectual high priests but firmly positioned at the center of a nation's life.

DLB includes the major writers appropriate to each volume and those standing in the ranks immediately behind them. Scholarly and critical counsel has been sought in deciding which minor figures to include and how full their entries should be. Wherever possible, useful references are made to figures who do not warrant separate entries.

Each *DLB* volume has a volume editor responsible for planning the volume, selecting the figures for inclusion, and assigning the entries. Volume editors are also responsible for preparing, where appropriate, appendices surveying the major periodicals and literary and intellectual movements for their volumes, as well as lists of further readings. Work on the series as a whole is coordinated at the Bruccoli Clark Layman editorial center in Columbia, South Carolina, where the editorial staff is responsible for accuracy of the published volumes.

One feature that distinguishes *DLB* is the illustration policy–its concern with the iconography of literature. Just as an author is influenced by his surroundings, so is the reader's understanding of the author enhanced by a knowledge of his environment. Therefore *DLB* volumes include not only drawings, paintings, and photographs of authors, often depicting them at various stages in their careers, but also illustrations of their families and places where they lived. Title pages are regularly reproduced in facsimile along with dust jackets for modern authors. The dust jackets are a special feature of *DLB* because they often document better than anything else the way in which an author's work was perceived in its own time. Specimens of the writers' manuscripts are included when feasible.

Samuel Johnson rightly decreed that "The chief glory of every people arises from its authors." The purpose of the *Dictionary of Literary Biography* is to compile literary history in the surest way available to us–by accurate and comprehensive treatment of the lives and work of those who contributed to it.

The *DLB* Advisory Board

Foreword

This volume of the *Dictionary of Literary Biography*, the first of two devoted to American magazine journalists during the period 1900-1960, focuses on publishers and editors. The most striking feature of the American magazine evolution during this period was the emergence of the magazine as a truly *mass* medium. In 1900 perhaps two hundred thousand households subscribed to one or more magazines; by 1950 the number had soared to around thirty million, a remarkable growth, especially considering it took place in the face of competition from new media–film, radio, and television.

The surging growth and increased importance of magazines cannot be explained without taking note of overall changes in the American economy. By the turn of the twentieth century the effects of the Industrial Revolution were such that mass production had done away with the shortage of domestic consumer goods that had previously characterized the American market. In its place an unfamiliar new specter had arisen: overproduction, or, looked at from the other side, underconsumption. The economics of scarcity had been converted into an economics of abundance. At a time when standardized, branded goods were coming to dominate the consumer market, department stores were becoming common, and retail chains were about to proliferate, a need had arisen for sellers of goods to reach the great mass of the American public through some medium more national than even the largest newspapers. National advertising became vastly more important, and in 1900 the only available answer was the magazine.

The old-style literary magazine with its elitist appeal and limited circulation would not serve the purpose, nor would religious magazines or other periodicals that were aimed at a segmented audience. In an economy that had become more industrial and less agriculture-based, the farm magazine also would not suffice. The nation's marketing needs demanded, instead, affordably priced magazines that appealed to a mass audience via easy to understand, varied editorial content.

The stage had been set prior to 1900. New postal regulations had been passed that allowed cheaper distribution of magazines, and America's rail system had linked the nation. Magazines, like all mass-produced goods, could now more easily reach national markets. A few magazines, such as *The Ladies' Home Journal* (established in 1883), *Munsey's* (1891), and *McClure's* (1893), had anticipated the trend and were showing the way to popularized content and vastly larger circulations.

By the turn of the century, most of the larger magazines had begun actively soliciting advertisers, rather than passively waiting for advertisers to come to them, and ads were moved from the last pages of magazines to occupy more prominent space throughout issues. In the early 1900s roughly half the space in a popular monthly was filled with ads; by the end of World War II, ad content outstripped editorial content, and a 65/35 ratio became common. Magazine ad revenues continued to advance throughout the period, were slowed by the Depression, but remained essentially unharmed even by the powerful new competition of radio. By 1950, television, which would soon cause great changes in the magazine industry, was still too new a medium to have cut severely into periodical ad revenues. By 1960, however, it was a different story. The newer visual medium, with its immediacy and enormous reach, cut deeply into the ad base and readership of mass magazines. The *American Magazine* succumbed in 1956, and *Collier's* in 1957. These deaths would soon be followed by *Coronet* in 1961, *Saturday Evening Post* in 1969, *Look* in 1971, and *Life* in 1972.

As these economic changes occurred, magazine publishers came to see subscribers less as readers and correspondingly more as consumers. Magazines grew less literary and became more an integral part of the marketing process. Attempting to boost circulation so as to be able to justify higher ad rates, magazine publishers gave more thought to what the public at large wanted. In the process, magazines gradually changed from an elitist medium to a popular one, from leaders to followers of public taste. Industry leaders such as Frank Munsey, S. S. McClure, and George Horace Lorimer showed that it was possible for a publisher to slash per-copy price (often by more than half), drive up circulation, and make a great deal more profit via ad sales than earlier magazine owners or editors had ever dared imagine.

In selecting editorial content, magazine editors had to pay increased attention to the likes and dislikes of the business community from whence their advertising revenue would come. Certainly this was a strong force for dictating practical, safe, conservative article content. While some large, profitable magazines made defensive pronouncements about the separation of the editorial and advertising functions, many newer or smaller magazines readily agreed to run puff pieces in their editorial columns in exchange for the placing of paid ads. Clearly article content came to be more closely geared to ad content, and much editorial space was used, sometimes blatantly, sometimes subtly, to stimulate consumer purchases–a phenomenon economist Thorstein Veblen called "devout consumption."

Magazines themselves are, of course, also consumer products and must be marketed. Prior to 1900 most magazines were sold by single copy in bookstores, newsstands, and railway stations. Subscription sales increased greatly after World War I as publishers vigorously sought subscribers, often by the efforts of door-to-door salesmen. Soliciting subscriptions by direct mail did not really come into its own until after World War II, by which time better prospect lists had become more available. In the meantime, the 1930s saw supermarkets and drugstores become important outlets for single-copy sales.

Magazines differ from competing media because they depend so much on what is now called "positioning"–the need for a concept that distinguishes a magazine from other similar magazines and makes it simultaneously attractive to subscribers and to advertisers who hope to reach those subscribers. A magazine publisher with a good concept also has other advantages not shared by newspapers and radio stations. Most of the editorial copy written for magazines comes from free-lance writers rather than full-time employees, and the magazine publisher can contract out printing and distributing rather than having to make large capital investments in these areas. During the period covered in this volume most national magazines were distributed by the American News Company, a situation that changed in 1957 because of antitrust action.

By 1900 New York City was in firm control as the nation's magazine capital, having long since surpassed Boston and Philadelphia in this regard. As early as the 1920s, however, publishers had realized they could save money by locating their printing and distribution operations more centrally, usually in the Midwest.

Increasing affluence, higher education levels, redistributed buying power, and increases in leisure time helped the magazine industry's growth. Even in wartime, both circulation and the total number of magazines continued to grow; especially dramatic was the explosive growth following World War II. By this time, well over two-thirds of adult Americans were magazine readers, a situation very different from magazine readership in 1900.

Looked at from the point of view of the sociologist rather than the economist, the newly popularized magazines of the first half of the 1900s, along with film and the new broadcast media, assumed a major role in setting the national agenda. Magazines read in every corner of the nation by persons from all walks of life began to help replace America's regionalism with a new nationalism. With their widely dispersed reading publics, magazine editors could not look at events or ideas from a local angle, as newspaper editors necessarily do, and surely this influence has caused a subtle, long-term cultural leveling process to occur. The ability of magazines to showcase American life has given the medium a role in teaching Americans what to want, how to live, which of their fellows to admire. As magazines have a tendency to push needs and wants that can be gratified by purchasing the products advertised in their pages, the values so imparted tend to be material values. Magazine historian Theodore Peterson has written of the "directory function" of magazines. Through magazines, readers could discover where to look for various commodities, whom to go to for advice, how to build or repair things, where to travel, and the like. By 1960 an immense number of specialized magazines and other non-newspaper periodicals were being published to satisfy an enormous variety of specialized public interests, from coin collecting to knowledge about scientific advances to sports to public affairs.

Overviews of magazine history sometimes err in making it appear as though the first half of the 1900s produced only periodicals aimed at amorphous mass audiences, and that specialized periodicals did not appear in significant numbers until the late 1950s. In reality, of course, specialized magazines have been published in America since the 1700s, and by 1950 thousands of these periodicals existed. True, the specialization trend intensified after 1955, when television became an established medium, but it had originated much earlier.

Numerous quality magazines founded during this era never tried to reach mass audiences. Many of these periodicals fall into two categories: literary magazines and magazines devoted to public affairs. Both categories were edited for better educated and more sophisticated elements of the population and offered an outlet for new ideas, commentary that would not appeal to a wider public, unpopular stands, and literary experimentation.

Almost always in a delicate financial condition were the "little magazines," literary periodicals that had very short subscription lists, and that were either subsidized by universities or depended upon the generosity of wealthy supporters. Examples of notable literary periodicals founded within this period are *South Atlantic Quarterly* (1902-current), *Poetry* (1912-current), *Little Review* (1914-1929), *Texas Review* (1915-1924, later retitled *Southwest Review*, 1924-current), *Midland* (1915-1933), *Reviewer* (1921-1925), *Double Dealer* (1921-1926), *Fugitive* (1922-1925), *Prairie Schooner* (1926-current), *Partisan Review* (1934-current), *Southern Review* (1935-1942), *Kenyon Review* (1939-1970), and the *Quarterly Review of Literature* (1943-current).

Except for those having university affiliation, these literary magazines tended to disappear almost as quickly as they had been established. Offering a mix of creative prose and poetry, plus literary commentary, they greatly expanded America's body of belles lettres, small as most of the publications were and are individually. They have been a training ground for some of the nation's best writers and have kept the literary waters stirred. Of the hundreds of small literary periodicals–probably at least a thousand–published in this period, some, such as the *Double Dealer* and *Prairie Schooner*, were mainly regional in orientation. Others, such as the *Partisan Review*, had radical political underpinnings. In general, the 1920s and 1930s were the heyday of literary experimentation in these journals, whereas the 1940s were more distinguished by literary criticism.

Occupying a literary middle ground between the serious literary journal and the popular weeklies and monthlies were two magazines that had rich literary traditions going back well into the nineteenth century–*Harper's*, dating from 1850, and *Atlantic Monthly*, founded in 1857. Both these monthlies recovered from circulation slumps in the early 1900s and continued throughout the period of this volume to offer content less strictly literary than what they had carried in the 1800s, but still of considerable literary merit.

Neither as radical nor as literary, yet out of step with the mainstream of American thought, and with the optimistic commercialism of the mass magazines, were the more intellectually oriented journals of opinion and commentary. *Nation*, founded in 1865, was a liberal, pacifist voice, and one that many in the twentieth century came to view as soft on communism. Another liberal voice was that of the *New Republic* (1914-current). More iconoclastic and derisive was the *American Mercury* (1924-1979), which frequently aimed its barbs at those George Jean Nathan and H. L. Mencken considered boobs. The 1930s brought in *Common Sense* (1932-1946), a progressive journal, and the 1940s the anticommunist *Plain Talk* (1946-1949) and the one-world spokesman *Freedom and Union* (1946-1978). Common threads running through these opinion journals were their lack of profitability and the frequent ideological splits that developed among their editors, writers, and owners.

Notable magazine deaths occurred during the years encompassed by this volume. *Puck* perished in 1918, *Leslie's Weekly* and *Munsey's* during the 1920s. The list of failed magazines during the 1930s was long and included *Smart Set, Century, McClure's*, the old *Life, Literary Digest, Delineator, Town Topics, Ballyhoo, Pictorial Review*, and *Country Home*. Perishing in the 1940s were such magazines as the *North American Review, Current History, Living Age, Scribner's Commentator*, and *St. Nicholas*. Noteworthy magazine deaths of the 1950s, as already mentioned, were the *American Magazine* and *Collier's*.

Many mergers and absorptions took place as older magazines began their declines. *World's Work* was absorbed by *Review of Reviews*, which later merged with *Literary Digest* to form the *Digest*. The *Literary Digest* reappeared under new ownership and was absorbed by *Time*. A leader in circulation and advertising in the late 1800s, *Century* was bought by *Forum* in 1930; in turn *Forum* was bought by *Current History* in 1940.

Other magazines that had been founded in the nineteenth century managed to adapt to new demands and have lasted long past the period of this volume: the *Atlantic, Nation, Ladies' Home Journal, Good Housekeeping, National Geographic, Vogue,* and *McCall's.* Noteworthy magazine births occurred: the *New Republic* in 1914; *Reader's Digest, Time,* the *Saturday Review of Literature,* and the *New Yorker* in the 1920s; *Fortune, Esquire, Newsweek,* and *U.S. News* in the 1930s; and *Mad, Playboy,* and *Sports Illustrated* in the 1950s–all of which survive at this writing.

Looking at trends in magazine content, perhaps the most dramatic single development came just after the turn of the century when in 1903 *McClure's* ushered in a period of investigative journalism that came to be known as "muckraking." *Collier's, Everybody's, Hampton's, Cosmopolitan, Ladies' Home Journal,* and other magazines joined *McClure's* for a sustained period of reform-oriented journalism and assumed briefly the role of newspapers, the more likely medium for such endeavors. This period of muckraking lasted until 1912. This "literature of exposure" provided by "periodicals of revolt" appealed to the public's desire for justice, and also to Americans' traditional irreverence toward authority. It was a period in which magazines achieved a new importance by tackling difficult social and economic problems, and in which magazine circulations surged.

In the 1920s and 1930s many farm magazines disappeared. During the decade of the 1920s, the number of these periodicals declined by more than half. By this time farmers had at their disposal new sources of information such as university agriculture programs and government extension services, and the farm magazines that remained in business tended to broaden their content accordingly.

In a land that could claim "the business of America is business," success-oriented copy was highly valued during the early years of the new century. After the stock market crash of 1929, however, success articles diminished in number. Similarly, humor magazines enjoyed sunny times in the 1920s, but many of them, notably *Life, Judge,* and *Ballyhoo,* became casualties of the Great Depression. In the 1940s and 1950s many magazines de-emphasized fiction.

It might be said that a trend toward brevity characterized this era in American magazine history. As content was popularized to appeal to a wider audience, article length was gradually reduced to make for easier reading. Article length varies so greatly that generalizations are hard to make, but in the 1840s, sixteen-thousand-word articles in *Graham's* were common, as were eighteen-thousand-word articles in *Harper's Monthly* in the 1860s, and ten-thousand-word features in *Atlantic Monthly* during the 1880s. By the 1920s, many magazines had shortened average article length to something more like five-thousand words, though there were many exceptions, such as *National Geographic,* which in the 1920s regularly carried twelve-thousand-word stories that meandered through sixty or so heavily illustrated pages. The new attraction of brevity was readily apparent in the success of *Reader's Digest,* with its condensed copy; *Time,* with departmentalized articles of 250-700 words; and the new picture magazine *Life,* in which the written copy mainly existed to serve its pictorial content.

Another magazine trend of this period, and one that has been so thoroughly documented elsewhere that it will only be acknowledged here, is the use of more and better photography to illustrate articles and to provide rich pictorial content independent of articles. *Life* and *Look* may be remembered as having exhibited the full potential of magazine photography.

Also, a trend toward concentrating on personalities developed, placing more attention on people, less on abstract ideas. Essay-style articles of the 1800s on such subjects as introversion, superficial attainments, advice giving, and disinterested friendship, gave way to stories based on people, real or imagined. The cover girl on women's magazines, the portrait covers of *Time,* and the personality profiles in the *New Yorker* are all manifestations of this trend.

In the early years of the century, the magazine industry itself remained highly personal; a magazine's own "personality" was still strongly linked to the personality of its editor, many of whom remained in the editorial chair for extended periods. By 1960 this situation had, for the most part, changed, with editors coming and going far more frequently. Magazines, like almost every other facet of American life, came to be run in a more impersonal, corporate manner.

Despite this loss of the personal touch, and despite a de-emphasis of literary quality of most magazines, the magazine industry ended this period as a fully democratized medium able to offer practical information as well as entertainment to a vast audience.

–Sam G. Riley

Acknowledgments

This book was produced by Bruccoli Clark Layman, Inc. Karen L. Rood is senior editor for the *Dictionary of Literary Biography* series. J. M. Brook was the in-house editor.

Production coordinator is James W. Hipp. Systems manager is Charles D. Brower. Photography editor is Susan Todd. Layout and graphics supervisor is Penney L. Haughton. Copyediting supervisor is Bill Adams. Typesetting supervisor is Kathleen M. Flanagan. Typography coordinator is Sheri Beckett Neal. Information Systems Analyst is George F. Dodge. Charles Lee Egleston and Laura Ingram are editorial associates. The production staff includes Helen Baucum, Rowena Betts, Anne L. M. Bowman, Teresa Chaney, Patricia Coate, Sarah A. Estes, Willie M. Gore, Cynthia Hallman, Susan C. Heath, David Marshall James, Kathy S. Merlette, Laura Garren Moore, John Myrick, Laurrè Sinckler, and Betsy L. Weinberg. Jean W. Ross is permissions editor.

Walter W. Ross, Jennifer Toth, and Parris Boyd did the library research with the assistance of the reference staff at the Thomas Cooper Library of the University of South Carolina: Lisa Antley, Daniel Boice, Faye Chadwell, Cathy Eckman, Gary Geer, Cathie Gottlieb, David L. Haggard, Jens Holley, Jackie Kinder, Marcia Martin, Jean Rhyne, Beverly Steele, Ellen Tillett, Carol Tobin, and Virginia Weathers.

American Magazine Journalists, 1900-1960
First Series

Dictionary of Literary Biography

Robert S. Abbott
(28 November 1868-29 February 1940)

Harry Amana
Clark Atlanta University

See also the Abbott entry in *DLB 29: American Newspaper Journalists, 1926-1950.*

MAJOR POSITIONS HELD: Publisher, *Abbott's Monthly* (1930-1933), *Abbott's Weekly and Illustrated News* (7 October 1933-3 March 1934).

No account of Robert S. Abbott's life could be made without mention of the *Chicago Defender,* a weekly newspaper published by Abbott as a tool to champion the cause of black people in the United States. During the years between World War I and World War II, the heyday of the black press, the *Defender* was the single most influential national black newspaper in America. At its peak during that period it had a paid circulation in excess of 230,000, and most black-press researchers agree that its readership was anywhere from two to five times that number.

Abbott, through the *Defender,* is credited with being one of the major influences in persuading tens of thousands of blacks to migrate from the South to Chicago during the period between the world wars. Moreover, his crusading stories, bold red headlines, slashing editorials against segregation and discrimination, and innovations in creating, among other things, a children's section establish the *Defender* as one of the great influences on black newspapers. The relationship of the *Defender* to the black press is frequently compared to the Hearst papers' relationship to the daily press of their time. Lawrence D. Hogan in *A Black National News Service: The Associated Negro Press and Claude Barnett, 1919-1945* (1983) quotes a black reporter in 1928 who worked for a white

Robert S. Abbott

daily in Boston: "The *Defender* may be justly blamed for Negro journalism as it is known today. Robert Abbott was the pioneer for the Negro press as Hearst was for the white metropolitan press." Gunnar Myrdal in his two-volume study of black Americans–*An American Dilemma* (1944)–wrote that Abbott's *Defender* "was destined to revolutionize Negro journalism." The newspaper has published continuously since its founding, and in 1956, in the hands of Abbott's nephew, John H. H. Sengstacke, it became and remains one of only a handful of black dailies. The success of the *Defender* enabled Abbott to publish *Abbott's Monthly,* the most successful mass-circulation black magazine of its time.

Robert Sengstacke Abbott was born on St. Simons Island, Georgia, on 28 November 1868, almost six years after the issuance of the Emancipation Proclamation and three years after the Civil War–events whose consequences for blacks would mold, shape, and determine his destiny. (Obituaries and many early biographical accounts list his birth as 24 November 1870, a date Abbott himself believed to be correct, but biographer Roi Ottley says the parish register [1868-1900] of St. Stephens Episcopal Church, Savannah, where Abbott was baptized, records his birth as the above date.) His parents, Thomas and Flora Butler Abbott, were former slaves. His father died months after the boy was born. Abbott was reared and greatly influenced by his stepfather, half-German-half-black John Hermann Henry Sengstacke, who lived his developing years in Germany before returning to the United States to marry, settle, and become a store owner, teacher, publisher of the short-lived *Woodville Times,* and Congregational minister. It was he who developed in Abbott a sense of racial pride, group unity, and the importance of newspapers for blacks. Abbott grew up in Savannah and attended school at Beach Institute before enrolling at Claflin College in Orangeburg, South Carolina, and Hampton Institute (now Hampton University) in Virginia, where he was trained as a printer and was graduated in 1896. During the summers he held odd jobs at the *Echo* in Savannah. After graduation he helped his stepfather publish the *Woodville Times.* In 1899 he was graduated from the Kent College of Law in Chicago with an LL.B. degree but was discouraged from pursuing a law career because, in the words of a black Chicago attorney, he was "a little too dark to make any impression on the courts in Chicago." He stayed in Chicago, however, inspired by a deep need to speak to the masses of blacks through the medium with which he was most familiar, and dreamed of publishing a newspaper. Finally, on 15 May 1905, with twenty-five cents, borrowed resources, and an agreement to pay printing costs after sales, he published from his living quarters three hundred copies of a four-page, sixteen-by-twenty-inch *Chicago Defender.* The paper grew sufficiently in its first twenty-five years to make its founder a millionaire who was able not only to travel to Latin America and Europe (and write, respectively, ten-part and thirteen-part series about the trips in the *Defender*) but also to survive the Great Depression, during which time he experienced a costly and embarrassing divorce, a financial crisis at his newspaper, the onset of a long fight with tuberculosis, and a failed excursion into the world of magazine publishing with the three-year run of *Abbott's Monthly.*

On 13 September 1930 the *Chicago Defender* ran an advertisement that said in part: "On Sept. 25, 1863, Abraham Lincoln signed the Emancipation Proclamation and on September 25, 1930, the first issue of Abbott's Monthly, a magazine that's different, will appear on the news stands and in the book stores. . . ." Actually, the freedom document was issued on 1 January 1863, but it was not unlike Abbott to bend the truth for the sake of making a splash in the *Defender.* The advertisement further stated that the editor had been begged so long by friends to give them "a high class magazine," that he finally agreed, "not only to satisfy the reading public, but to open avenues of employment for artists, writers and others." The magazine, the ad continued, would be of interest to "lawyers, scholars, churchmen, students, travelers, the housewife, the musician, the workman." Furthermore, it would have a "vivid four-color outside cover" and sell for only twenty-five cents. Twelve days later, eleven months into the Great Depression, Abbott lived up to his word and launched for the first time in United States journalism history a substantial, well-illustrated, well-edited, four-color-cover magazine produced by a black American.

The first issue, dedicated to the Reverend Mr. Sengstacke, carried in the masthead what would be the continuing motto: "A Magazine That's Different," and true to Abbott's *Defender* boast, it was of "high class" and had something of interest to everyone. It contained eight poems; four lengthy, illustrated romance stories; fifteen well-written "Special Features" articles of varying lengths; and numerous photographs, illustrations, news items, book reviews, and bawdy jokes. There also was a full-page photograph of the publisher and his mother. And though subsequent issues would drop in size from the initial ninety-eight pages to a standard sixty-six pages, each would carry even more romance stories (generally six or seven) and five to eight feature arti-

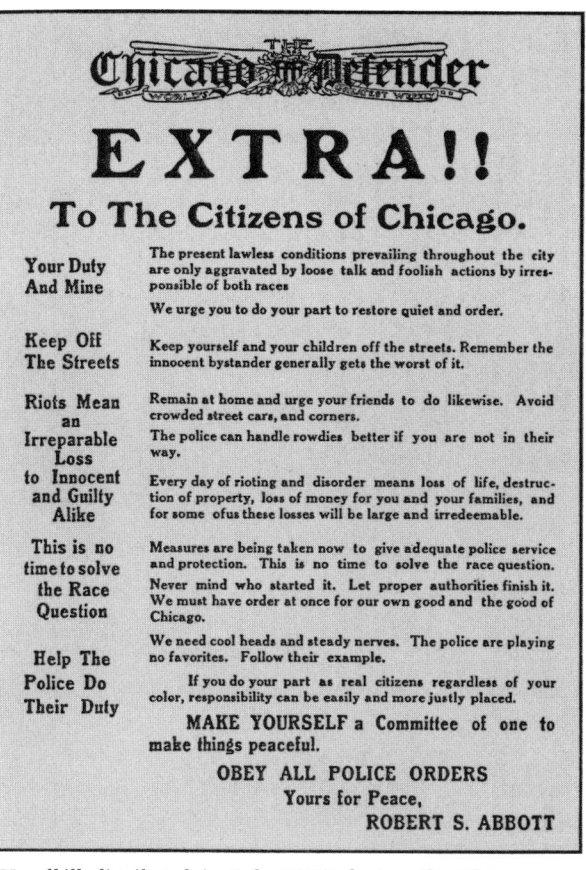

Handbill distributed in July 1919 during the Chicago race riot. Abbott founded the Chicago Defender *newspaper in 1905.*

cles. With the exception of the reduction in pages, subsequent issues of the magazine for its entire three-year life span would resemble the original and continue to be of high quality. The *New York Amsterdam News,* another national black weekly of the period, stated in its 8 October 1930 edition that the magazine "compares favorably with the magazines got out by the larger publishing companies; the coloring and makeup of the cover are artistic and tasteful." Even more significant, however, was the newspaper's further comment, which probably coincided with the way the monthly was perceived by middle-class or striving-to-be-middle-class black Americans: "One of the sure-fire things about Abbott's Monthly is that it will be welcomed in the home. More than any other magazine of recent years it strikes the common denominator of normal, healthy Negro life." Biographer Ottley quoted from the *Detroit Independent,* another black weekly: "It has outstripped the imagination of all and upon perusal proves to surpass any other endeavor. . . . Mr. Robert S. Abbott and his staff of efficient co-workers are to be complimented on blazing the

trail in this field of journalism."

Ottley called the monthly "the forerunner of today's eminently successful *Ebony* magazine, owned and edited by John H. Johnson," but Roland E. Wolseley in *The Black Press, U.S.A.* (1971) noted that *Ebony,* as a picture magazine, "owes as much to *Life* and *Look* as to any other [magazine]." Actually there are parts of *Abbott's Monthly* that resemble two of Johnson's publications—*Ebony* and *Jet.* In truth, Abbott was probably trying to appeal to all segments of the black community with a combination of news, fiction, jokes, and scholarly researched articles. That may have been a mistake. Perhaps an *Amsterdam News* columnist quoted by Ottley correctly describes what was wrong with the magazine. "Probably it will be an interesting magazine when it makes up its mind just what type . . . it wants to be. . . . Its first issue is a mongrel affair."

Eventually the bawdy jokes would disappear, but photographs and illustrations would continue as a part of the format, and noted writers, scholars, and historians would continue to appear regularly in the monthly. In the first issue, for example, are articles written by J. A. Rogers, a well-known history buff who would cover World War II in Europe and write a much-read column on black history and culture, and Arthur A. Schomburg, for whom a black research branch of the New York Public Library is named. Others who would appear in *Abbott's Monthly* include attorney Clarence Darrow, poet Langston Hughes, and novelist and short-story writer Chester Himes.

The covers of the magazine would also become standard. Ottley describes them as "The red, yellow and lavender cover (carrying) the picture of a pretty girl." These illustrations depicted mulattoes for the first several issues. By the fifth issue browner women would appear, but not with distinctly Negroid features. To be sure, the emphasis on mulattoes and non-Negroid features was a trend of the times, but it was also something with which Abbott may have had some psychological peculiarity. Ottley noted that Abbott, a dark man, was regularly tormented by mulattoes during his childhood in Georgia, as a young man at Hampton, and in later life by some of the inner circles of the so-called black aristocracy in Chicago. "Abbott's own color became a cross for him to bear within his own race," Ottley wrote. Twice he married mulatto women who could pass for white, neither of whom bore him children or treated him with much affection. In 1918 Abbott married a widow named Helen Thornton Morri-

Abbott's home (top), and the Chicago Defender *offices, formerly a synagogue (bottom)*

son, who was thirty years younger than he and who "passed" regularly in order to travel first-class on the railroad. He met her when she worked as a salesgirl, a job she had secured by "passing." She, like the women on the cover of his magazine, became his showpiece. Ironically, one of the bitterest disagreements they would have would be over his refusal to correct a misconception that occurred when they traveled in Europe. "She never forgave him," Ottley wrote, "for his extraordinary behavior in London, when she had objected to being disparagingly labeled the 'white wife of a black millionaire' by the newspapers and he had refused to seek a retraction in her behalf." It was as if he enjoyed the thought that she had been mistaken for white. Ottley wrote that Abbott "came to hate the color black . . . I suspect he was afflicted with a case of self-hate."

Certain types of articles in the monthly would become standard also. Though the editor was listed as Lucius C. Harper, Abbott's *Defender* foreign editor and longtime friend, articles generally carried a racial slant with a point of view similar to those expressed by Abbott in the pages of the *Defender*. This would not have required Abbott's constant supervision since the bulk of the writing for the magazine was done by the *Defender* staff. Also, it is unlikely that Abbott would discontinue spending most of his energies with his first love, the *Defender*. Ottley noted that Abbott was insistent that the print facility be spotlessly clean and that he was frequently seen visiting the building during off hours, putting things in place. Hogan quotes a friend of Abbott who often went to the theater with him: "But before Mr. Abbott would go home nights, he always passed by the plant and looked at it admiringly, as if he were surprised it were still there."

But his hand could be seen plainly in the monthly. Two articles in the first issue, for example–"Uncle Sam's Inequality Policy in the Virgin Islands" and "Will Great Britain's Dark Subjects Crumble her Empire?"–examined issues about which Abbott had become increasingly interested since his twelve-day trip to Latin America in 1923 and his five-month trip to Europe in 1929. After each trip he took the opportunity to compare in print the race problems in other countries with the race problem in the United States. In many instances he closed his eyes to some of the obvious examples of racism abroad in order to provide a better contrast to the discrimination and segregation that characterized his homeland.

Abbott's mother, Flora Abbott Sengstacke, at the dedication of Abbott's printing plant in 1921

The country outside the United States he found to be the most racist, he said, was Great Britain. Metz T. P. Lochard, who became editor in chief of the *Defender* after Abbott's death, wrote in the second quarter 1947 edition of *Phylon*: "Abbott's tendency was to make a special problem of the Negro's subjugation to discrimination, and, almost without exception, he failed to point out the related problems of minority elements in the population which, if united, would have wielded far greater power. He occasionally ascribed the same stereotype notions about the economic solidarity of Jews as the most rabidly anti-Semitic metropolitan dailies."

It was also during his European trip to Belgium and France that Abbott became impressed with the esteem given to African artifacts and jazz musicians. Typical headlines from his "My Trip Abroad" European-tour series read: "All Races Welcomed in Belgium, Editor Abbott Finds" and "Congo Museum Called Most Interesting Spot in Belgium." Thus, it is no surprise to find in his magazine such articles as "Where Uncle Remus Got His Inspiration," "From Africa's Tom-Tom," "Ignatius Sancho," and "Alexandre Dumas Missed Military Greatness by One Hour." The first two articles establish the African links to black Americans through their folktales and their music and spirituals; the latter two emphasize the greatness of black men from other countries. For the rural grass-roots readers the October 1929 issue carried an article entitled "Some Facts About the Black Farmer," in which a subhead stated: "He Cultivates More Than Forty-Five Million Acres of Soil, and the Value of His Property Is Over Two Billion Dollars." The copy, like the author, seems obsessed with race.

The lengthy romance stories presumably were for the housewife mentioned in the *Defender* ad. Abbott, according to Lochard, "insisted that women should study the arts, attend finishing schools, and not attempt to compete with men."

Other articles which appeared as parts of a debate in the first and third issues of the monthly may have reflected the publisher's ambivalence about traditional religion. In October and December articles appeared bearing the same title: "Is It Possible for the Church to Serve the Modern Youth?" The October author decided "no," the December author decided "yes." Ottley noted that Abbott's caste abuse by mulattoes extended to the church when he turned to and was rejected by both the Episcopal and Presbyterian black churches. Later he would withdraw from the Christian Science religion when it established separate worship places for blacks and whites. Lochard wrote that Abbott "judged the value of religion by the degree to which racial equality was practiced, and the only religious sect that sanctioned and encouraged full equality in every aspect of life, not excluding intermarriage, was Baha'ism." Before he died Abbott became a Baha'i.

Another recurring element is the up-from-slavery theme that has some biographical implications and was consistent with Abbott's overall philosophy about the black race. Since his days at Hampton he had been greatly influenced by Hampton alumnus Booker T. Washington and vigorously endorsed Washington's theory of industrial education. Thus, while Abbott was persistent in his criticism of the white power structure in the United States, he was equally, if not more, persistent in his criticism of "the race," as he referred to black people. Abbott, according to Lochard, was credited with the remark: "When I consider the whole range of our social behavior,

Abbott, circa 1930

I am almost tempted to say that we are just a little more than educated apes."

In an essay published in the February 1919 edition of Hampton's *Southern Workman* Abbott stated: "Our future hinges on our making good—not good for colored people—there must not be two standards. . . . Our whining, baby, dependent days are over . . . if anything, we must be a shade the better to get equal credit." It is not surprising, then, that the magazine regularly featured articles on individuals who dared to dream beyond the norm and who succeeded in spite of opposition. The first three issues include the following: "This Man Made a Fortune Out of What People Laughed At," "An Idea That Grew from a Shanty Into a Million Dollar Project," and "He Left a Jungle to Become an Artist Model."

Other features that appeared regularly include a photo page on coeds at a different black college each month, a photo story on blacks in entertainment, and annual features on the black All-American football team, the All-American track and field athletes, and the stars in the Negro baseball leagues. A promotional contest was publicized in 1931 whereby readers were to find six pictures of "our greatest presidents carefully hidden" in a picture for prizes totaling $12,500.

Advertising in *Abbott's Monthly* was never more than a small percentage of the publication and most assuredly was not enough to support it. Indeed, it was circulation and subscription that produced the majority of wealth accumulated by black publishers during this period. During the first year a full-page ad for the "Hupmobile" automobile ran fairly consistently, as did an ad for a Chicago insurance company. The most consistent ads, however, were the same small ads that appeared in the *Defender*–skin lighteners, hair straighteners, beauty aids, and bogus health remedies and ointments. Even the Listerine ad that appeared throughout the life of the publication was for use of the mouthwash as an astringent. Abbott had been criticized for carrying ads for skin lighteners and hair straighteners by Marcus Garvey, the militant back-to-Africa Jamaican who mobilized tens of thousands of blacks throughout the country under his Universal Negro Improvement Association. His weekly, the *Negro World,* excluded such ads, for Garvey saw no future for blacks who engaged in assimilation and compromise. And though both men exhibited a passion and sense of mission on behalf of "the race," Abbott was color sensitive, while Garvey reveled in his blackness. Both also used their papers to scorn and ridicule each other. Hogan notes the irony inherent in their hostility for one another, however, in that they both gained initial following by noting the contradictions in World War I of blacks fighting for freedom abroad when they did not experience freedom at home. Moreover, Hogan writes: "When Abbott trumpeted his *Defender* as a 'Race paper for Race people,' exaggerated the accomplishments of Afro-Americans, and sensationalized the injustices (most notably lynching) that blacks faced, he was striking the chord that Garvey touched in launching [his programs]."

Circulation for *Abbott's Monthly,* according to Ottley, reached about 100,000. Soon, however, the Depression would catch up to the magazine and its readers. Blacks were unemployed in record numbers and no longer could afford the twenty-five cents for such a lavish publication. In addition, the *Defender* circulation was dropping by more than two-thirds from about 230,000 to 73,000 by 1935. The last year of the magazine's existence was probably the most difficult single period for the publisher. Besides the falling circulations of the newspaper and the magazine, he also

was stricken with tuberculosis, an illness that, with a later attack of Bright's disease, would lead to his death, and he had to be cared for by private nurses. Moreover, he was having internal financial difficulties with the paper, and his difficult divorce proceedings that lasted for almost a year were exposed publicly by some of his fiercest competitors in the black press. Rival papers, using the exaggerated style they copied from the *Defender,* told in bold headlines that the black millionaire was being sued by his mulatto wife. Typical headlines in the *Pittsburgh Courier,* Abbott's strongest national competitor, stated: "SOCIETY WIFE FILES NEW CHARGES, Nurse is Named as Abbott's 'Friend' " and " 'WHY NOT A MILLION?' ASKS MRS. ABBOTT WHEN INFORMED NURSE HAS SUED HER FOR $100,000." Stories told in detail of Helen Abbott's intimation that her husband was somehow involved with one of his nurses, and her claim that he had threatened her, used vile language, and struck her. She asked for his removal as publisher and asserted that the paper was on the verge of ruin. Her lawyer called for a divorce, receivership for the paper, a property settlement, and $100,000.

On 26 June 1933, three months before the demise of *Abbott's Monthly,* Helen Abbott was awarded $50,000, plus $5,000 for lawyers' fees, a Pierce Arrow automobile, and home furnishings from the couple's mansion. One cannot be certain to what extent this settlement caused or helped to hasten the death of the magazine, but it surely could not have helped. Thus, in September 1933, exactly three years after it first appeared, the last edition of the monthly was published. Irregular volume numbers help distort the figures, but thirty-six issues were published. Still Abbott was not ready to give up on the magazine entirely. On 7 October 1933 a twenty-eight-page, five-column publication entitled *Abbott's Weekly and Illustrated News* appeared. It was run on standard newsprint paper and sold for five cents. It featured many of the writers and feature articles previously found in the magazine. On 14 October 1933 a sixteen-page edition appeared, and, the periodical would continue to be published in that format every week thereafter until 3 March 1934, when it, too, ceased publication.

Finally, Abbott's dream of a "high class" magazine for blacks of all walks of life had perished. In early 1934 he wrote, with Lochard's assistance, another lengthy series of articles, entitled "The

Search for Culture," ostensibly written as a program of racial improvement, but which was primarily a personalized commentary on his disastrous marriage. On 7 August 1934 he married Edna Brown Dennison, a widow twenty-two years his junior with four grown children, and spent the remainder of his life crusading against the ills of the Depression and fighting to keep himself and his beloved *Defender* vital. He died in 1940 at seventy-one.

Lest he be perceived as a tragic hero, it should be noted that in spite of the hard times he faced the last seven years of his life, Abbott was by no stretch of the imagination a man without means. A better perspective on the "hard times" Abbott faced may be made when one considers the revelations made during his divorce proceedings. Many in the court and many who read newspaper accounts of the proceedings were astonished when it was disclosed that Abbott—in the midst of the Depression and with a declining *Defender*—possessed a Rolls Royce, a Pierce Arrow, a Cunningham, a fleet of Fords, real estate including the mansion, some stocks and bonds, and in excess of $335,000 cash in two banks.

Abbott is remembered little, if at all, for *Abbott's Monthly* and very little as a personality, but rather as the founder and publisher of the *Chicago Defender*. The paper has assumed an identity of its own and is mentioned in every major work on the black press. More recent research into the lives and personal papers of other black publishers and "race" leaders of Abbott's time reveals more about the man as a personality. When he is mentioned he is usually described as a hardworking, determined man who was obsessed with race and his major love, the *Defender*. Only rarely is the monthly mentioned, and then only in subsections of black press histories reserved for magazines and periodicals. And then it pales considerably under the descriptions and space usually given W. E. B. Du Bois's *Crisis* and A. Philip Randolph's *Messenger*. Because of its short existence, the monthly is seldom described as a magazine with as much substance as it had.

A final look at *Abbott's Monthly* reveals perhaps that, like Abbott, the magazine tried to be too many things to too many people. " 'Polite society,' 'fine manners' and 'correct usage' were to him of great importance in the progress of the 'race,' " Lochard wrote. And these were the things Abbott attempted to put into the monthly. At the same time he tried to be a man of the masses, and many remember him as a humble man close to the people. Others viewed his attempts at culture as snobbery, Lochard wrote, and they remember him as a "pompous, conspicuous spender, having a baronial home with a corps of servants and three automobiles." That sense of paradox extended to his magazine and contributed to its failure.

Biography:
Roi Ottley, *The Lonely Warrior: The Life and Times of Robert S. Abbott* (Chicago: Regnery, 1955).

References:
Langston Hughes, *Famous American Negroes* (New York: Dodd, Mead, 1954);

Metz T. P. Lochard, "Robert S. Abbott—'Race Leader,' " *Phylon*, 8 (Second Quarter 1947): 124-132;

Mary White Ovington, *Portraits in Color* (New York: Viking, 1927);

Jay Saunders Redding, *The Lonesome Road* (Garden City, N.Y.: Doubleday, 1958);

Roland E. Wolseley, *The Black Press, U.S.A.* (Ames: Iowa State University Press, 1971).

Papers:
The majority of Robert S. Abbott's papers are held at the archives of the *Chicago Defender*, Chicago, Illinois. Other collections exist at the University Archives, Hampton University, Hampton, Virginia; the National Newspaper Publishers Association Collection, the Black Press Archives, Moorland-Spingarn Research Center, Howard University, Washington, D.C.; and the Schomburg Research Center in Black Culture, Lenox Avenue Branch, New York City Public Library. Some significant mention of him is made in the Claude A. Barnett Papers, Chicago Historical Society.

Charles Alexander

(7 March 1868-5 September 1923)

Cathy Packer
University of North Carolina

MAJOR POSITIONS HELD: Editor and publisher, *Monthly Review* (1894-1896), *Alexander's Magazine* (1905-1909).

BOOKS: *One Hundred Distinguished Leaders* (Atlanta: Franklin Printing & Publishing Co., 1899);
Under Fire With the Tenth U.S. Cavalry, by Alexander, Herschel V. Cashin, William T. Anderson, Arthur M. Brown, and Horace W. Bivins (New York & London: F. Tennyson Neely, 1899);
Battles and Victories of Allen Allensworth (Boston: Sherman, French, 1914).

SELECTED PERIODICAL PUBLICATIONS: "The Garrison Centenary Celebration," *Alexander's Magazine*, 1 (January 1906): 11-15;
"Negro Journalism," *Alexander's Magazine*, 1 (March 1906): 19-20;
"Down in Mississippi," *Alexander's Magazine*, 7 (December 1909): 177-181.

Charles Alexander

Charles Alexander was an editor and publisher of black magazines and newspapers and a pioneering black literary critic during the first quarter of the twentieth century. Although his publications were plagued by the financial difficulties typical of black publications of that period, they were praised for the high quality of their literary content and editing.

Alexander was born in Natchez, Mississippi, to James and Angerline Thompson Alexander. He grew up in New London, Connecticut, and was educated in that city's public schools. He studied literature under private tutors and completed the Chautauqua Literary and Scientific Circle course in 1893. The four-year, home-reading course covered European and American history and literature. Alexander then moved to Boston, where he entered the merchant tailoring business and became a journalist, working on the *Reflector* newspaper.

When the *Reflector* failed in 1894 Alexander launched the *Monthly Review* magazine and founded the Monthly Review Press. Published in Boston in 1894 and 1895, the *Monthly Review* covered a wide variety of topics, including "science, art, literature, biographies, history, politics, religion, Masonic orders, Odd Fellow news, great speeches, serial stories, short stories, poetry, sports, sociology." In the magazine's first issue, Alexander said in an editorial that the magazine "will listen to all conflicting opinions, no matter by whom expressed, so long as sincerity and dignity prevails. Radicals and conservatives alike will be given a fair hearing." He continued: "We are independent in politics because we are not inclined to believe that every man who professes to be a Republican is a saint, or that every individual who claims himself to be a Democrat is a sinner. We are independent in religion because we are not inclined to believe that Heaven is a celestial apartment house the choice suites of which are leased for eternity by any certain religious denomination."

Contemporary writers praised the *Monthly Review* as a quality literary magazine. In *Evidences of Progress Among Colored People* (1896), G. F. Richings commented, "The *Monthly Review* is beyond all doubt the most worthy undertaking of its kind in the history of the race. This magazine represents to the colored people what the *Forum*, the *North American Review*, the *Century*, and the *Arena* represent to the white people of America. It contains matter that cannot be found in newspapers, and it should, by all means, receive the hearty support and endorsement of the entire race. It is a high type of the literary possibilities of the race. It is ably edited, well managed, and the contributors include some of the ablest writers in America." Richings credited Alexander with assisting him in compiling his book and wrote about Alexander in the chapter entitled "Colored Editors and Journalists." In addition to his comments on the *Monthly Review*, Richings said, "I regard Mr. Alexander as one of the most fluent speakers, one of the most versatile writers, and one of the sweetest poets the race has thus far produced."

By 1896 Alexander had moved to Philadelphia, where he was publishing the magazine and operating a bookstore. However, the magazine folded a few months after the move, the first of a string of financial failures that would mar Alexander's journalism career. Richings noted in a later edition of his book that the magazine failed because "the masses of the race have not as yet acquired a taste for that sort of literature."

After the demise of the *Monthly Review* Alexander moved south to teach printing. He taught eight years, first at the Alabama Agricultural and Mechanical College in Huntsville. While in Huntsville, Alexander, along with Herschel V. Cashin, operated the Cashin and Alexander printing establishment. Cashin, a native Georgian, was the receiver of public moneys at the United States Land Office in Huntsville from 1898 to 1904 and an influential Republican campaign orator. In addition to their printing venture, the two men authored, with three other men, *Under Fire With the Tenth U.S. Cavalry* (1899), the story of a black cavalry regiment that fought in Indian campaigns in the American West but received its greatest distinction during the Spanish American War.

In Huntsville, Alexander again operated a bookstore, as he later would in Boston, and

served as editor of the *Normal Index* newspaper and as chief of the local fire company. He also began to contribute articles and poetry to the *Philadelphia Times*, the *Washington Colored American*, the *Indianapolis Freeman*, and other black newspapers, as well as the *Educator*, the official publication of the teachers' association of the state of Alabama, and the *National Baptist Magazine*. On 1 August 1897 Alexander married Fanny Worthington of Washington, D.C.

From 1899 to 1901 Alexander was an instructor of printing at the Tuskegee Institute. As he would throughout his life, Alexander also pursued his cultural interests. In 1900 the *Tuskegee Student* newspaper reported that he was appearing as Montano and Lodivico in a school production of Shakespeare's *Othello* for the benefit of the school's Cemetery Fund. Then Alexander moved to Ohio, where for two years he taught printing at Wilberforce University.

In 1904 Booker T. Washington, who had founded the Tuskegee Institute in 1881, called Alexander back to Boston to help counter growing opposition to Washington's conciliatory approach to race relations. Washington advocated economic progress for blacks through self-help and racial cooperation. He believed prejudice and discrimination would diminish in the face of economic prosperity. That position was under attack by W. E. B. Du Bois and other radical blacks who advocated political action to counter injustice.

One of Washington's sources of power during this period was his control over the black press. He used cash, advertising revenues, and canned news releases and editorials from the Tuskegee Institute to influence editorial policy. He summoned Alexander to edit the failing *Colored Citizen* newspaper to combat the influence of William Monroe Trotter's *Boston Guardian*, one of Washington's harshest critics. The previous editor of the *Colored Citizen*, Peter J. Smith, had proven incompetent.

Despite the fact that Washington called on Alexander for help, Washington's assessment of Alexander's abilities is unclear. In 1899 Washington wrote about Alexander to a friend at the *New York Age*: "I hardly know what to say about Alexander. He is a good fellow and I want to give him employment if I can. I wish he were a little stronger mentally. It is pretty hard for us to use an individual now here unless he has a pretty strong mental equipment." His assessment of Alexander's abilities seemed to improve after Alexander moved back to Boston. In 1904 Washington wrote to an

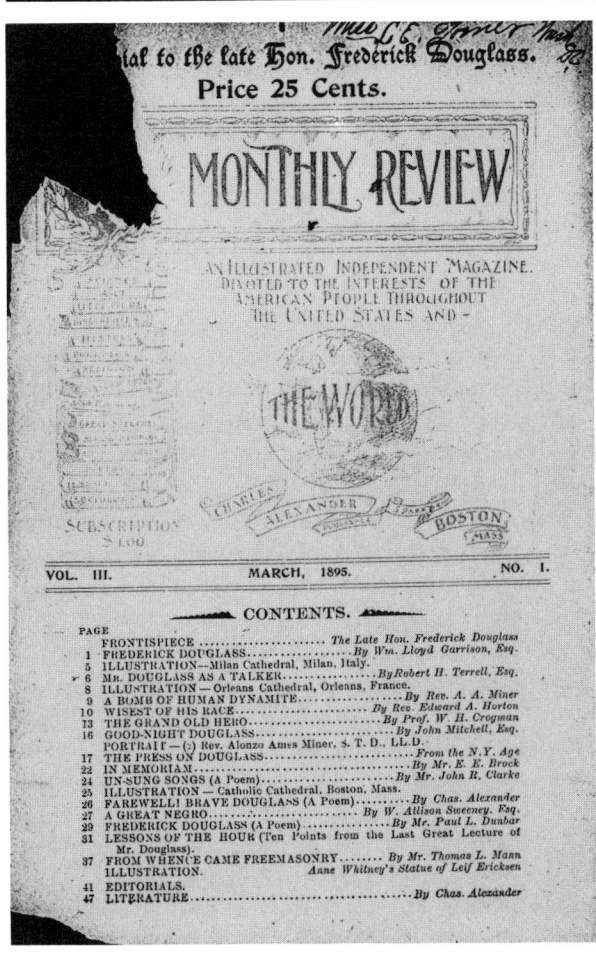

Cover for an issue of the magazine Alexander founded
in 1894

associate concerning Alexander's handling of the
Colored Citizen, "I cannot see how he could have
done better than he has." Then in 1905 he was
quoted in *Alexander's Magazine* as saying, "Alexander's Magazine is a gem; it will make a place for itself and will prove most helpful to the race."

Alexander considered the *Colored Citizen* a
sound business opportunity, but he arrived to
find the paper had no revenue from sales or subscriptions, little goodwill, a formidable competitor in the *Guardian,* and no office equipment,
which had been sold to pay old debts. Washington advanced Alexander $150 of a promised
total of $700 and provided him with the Tuskegee news service, letters of encouragement, introductions to prospective advertisers, and job printing. However, Alexander soon found it impossible to operate without a subsidy, so Washington provided $65 a week, just as he had for
Alexander's predecessor. Also, in 1904 Washington wrote to one of his political associates near

Boston concerning a job for Alexander's wife:
"Could you possibly find employment in one of
the headquarters for the wife of Charles Alexander, who is publishing a good Republican newspaper here? It would help forward the interest of
the paper very much if this could be done. For
the present perhaps she would not object to taking a rather menial position with the understanding that she could get something better later."

Washington tried to keep secret his involvement in this and other publications. Several times
Washington or his representatives wrote to Alexander advising him to take care not to let anyone
see their personal correspondence, not to use
Washington's name too often, and to take care
where he cashed his checks from Washington.
However, Trotter charged Washington with "virtual ownership" of the *Colored Citizen.* The *Guardian* also noted that Alexander had become secretary of the Boston branch of Washington's
National Negro Business League.

Despite Washington's help, Alexander was
forced to borrow heavily from local sources to
cover the paper's expenses. In fact, Washington's
efforts to help Alexander may have backfired. As
Betty Lou K. Rathbun observed in her study of
black periodicals, "One of Alexander's difficulties
was publishing a journal that would stimulate his
readership while at the same time give full space
to the many items sent his office from Tuskegee.
His newspaper appeared to be so blatantly
backed by Tuskegee that black advertisers, a
large number of whom were fierce anti-Bookerites, shunned it."

Alexander was able to keep the *Colored Citizen* alive for less than a year. However, he took
Washington's advice and launched the monthly *Alexander's Magazine* in its place, again with a subsidy from Washington. The first issue was published on 15 May 1905. The price was ten cents
per copy (which ranged from twenty-four to forty-eight pages) or one dollar a year, and circulation
was estimated at five thousand.

Alexander's Magazine heralded the accomplishments of the Negro race. The magazine contained news notes, long features on Negro colleges and their graduates, political endorsements,
and poetry. The masthead of the magazine said
the periodical was devoted to "the spreading of reliable information concerning the operation of educational institutions in the South; the moral, intellectual, commercial and industrial improvement of the Negro Race in the United States." In
one news story in his periodical, Alexander was

quoted as saying, "My magazine teaches optimism. It selects the best examples of race development as a means of inspiration to others." Also, in an editorial, Alexander boasted that his was the only magazine he knew of that was produced by Negro printers and that the cover of that particular issue was designed by a Negro "unaided by any suggestion from anyone."

The first issue contained a sketch of black English composer Samuel Coleridge-Taylor written by Booker T. Washington, reprints from other black periodicals, and a news story reporting on a speech by Alexander entitled "The Negro in the Professions in Boston." The first issue of 1906 was a special tribute to abolitionist William Lloyd Garrison. Later that year an entire issue celebrated the twenty-fifth anniversary of the Tuskegee Institute. In 1907 the magazine ran a regular column on Liberia and Africa to support the Liberian Development Association's plan for blacks to migrate to Africa and settle a colony in Liberia. Alexander was vice-president of that association. Also, for a time Fanny Alexander provided an advice column entitled "Heart-to-Heart Talk With Our Women." In one column she advised that a cup of coffee after dinner aids digestion if one is accustomed to it, but not if taken only occasionally and at late hours. However, Alexander was the magazine's most prolific writer. He wrote editorials, book reviews, poetry, and feature articles.

Alexander's most frequently quoted article is "Negro Journalism," which appeared in the March 1906 *Alexander's Magazine*. He wrote: "The man who attempts to publish a Newspaper or magazine in New England in the interests of the Colored people undertakes a task that offers little or no inspiration or emolument. He must be prepared to labor under great difficulties and embarrassments for fully 18 hours out of every 24, make great sacrifices, meet with all sort of discouragements, and sometimes suffer humiliation and deprivation in order to accomplish his purpose. Nothing but the strongest fascination for the work and the profoundest devotion to what he regards as a worthy cause can hold him to his task—for there is no radiant hope of large rewards before him."

Alexander frequently reprinted flattering reviews of his magazine. For example, an article from the *Norfolk News and Advertiser* was quoted thus: "Alexander's Magazine is the cleanest and best magazine printed by our race." A *Boston Evening Transcript* editorial stated that *Alexander's Mag-*

azine was "proving its value as a guide, philosopher and friend of the Negro race by an even handed and courageous independence and candor in criticism of current events and the actors in them."

However, Alexander had little success battling the anti-Bookerite influence of the *Guardian*, and only occasionally during his tenure as a Boston publisher could Alexander claim victory against Trotter and his publication. In early 1905, as the feud between the *Colored Citizen* and the *Guardian* raged, Alexander published articles written by Emmett Scott, Washington's secretary, that referred to Trotter as a pirate who begs for political cash and as a toady who would sell himself to Washington for recognition. Trotter sued Alexander for libel, and Alexander countersued. Alexander wrote to Scott, "If this fellow wins out in his case, he will of course kill the influence of the Boston Colored Citizen, but if he loses, the Boston Colored Citizen will be more firmly rooted in the confidence of the people and will really have a boom that will be worth while." The court awarded $500 in damages to Alexander and only $100 to Trotter.

Then in 1906 Alexander reported to Washington that he had finally broken the backbone of the *Guardian*. He said he had advised the printer of the *Guardian* of that newspaper's attacks on Washington. The printer then refused to do any more work for Trotter, who was forced to take his business to another printer who Alexander said was more expensive and less competent. In fact, however, the *Guardian* survived.

Alexander's Magazine struggled along financially. To promote circulation, Alexander sold subscriptions to his publication in combination with subscriptions to *Woman's Home Companion* and *Farm and Fireside*. In 1907 *Alexander's Magazine* absorbed the *National Domestic*, which had been published in Indianapolis since 1905, and for a few months *Alexander's Magazine* was titled *Alexander's Magazine and the National Domestic*. In her study of black magazines, Penelope L. Bullock observed that black magazines were plagued by poor distribution, delinquent and too few subscribers, and a shortage of national advertising. She said that only a few black periodicals of this period that were published without the support of established black institutions lasted ten years. She noted that *Alexander's Magazine*, which folded in 1909, did not survive that long.

Over the years *Alexander's Magazine* became increasingly independent of Washington editori-

Printing-press room at Tuskegee Institute. Alexander was an instructor of printing at Tuskegee from 1899 to 1901.

ally. For example, Theodore Roosevelt supported his secretary of war, William Howard Taft, for the Republican nomination in the 1908 presidential election. Despite Roosevelt's close ties with Washington, Alexander only reluctantly and unenthusiastically supported Taft. In the end Alexander offered his magazine to the newly formed, anti-Bookerite National Association for the Advancement of Colored People.

After *Alexander's Magazine* folded in 1909, Alexander attempted to launch his own political career. In 1908 and 1910 he was an unsuccessful candidate for the Massachusetts House of Representatives. He received about 850 votes in each election, never finishing higher than third and both times losing to Democrats.

Then Alexander moved to California. There he established the *Citizens Advocate* newspaper and operated it for several years before becoming editor of the *Los Angeles Post.* He covered the West for the *New Era Magazine,* which was launched in Boston in 1916 by Pauline E. Hopkins and Walter W. Wallace. He traveled throughout California giving speeches on black poet Paul Laurence Dunbar, whose poetry Alexander had published in *Alexander's Magazine,* and he wrote and published his own poetry. One of Alexander's contemporaries, Delilah L. Beasley, wrote that as a speaker "Professor Charles Alexander occupies a conspicuous place." She said Alexander's Dunbar lectures offered "a subtle analysis and sincere appreciation of the poet's genius. The

thought and feeling of the speaker find full expression in a voice of rare sweetness. Through his interpretation of the Negro dialect poems, the quaint picturesqueness of the Negro nature are vividly portrayed. . . . Professor Alexander is a fine writer, a poet of high ability and a platform orator of rare powers." Some of Alexander's own poetry was published in the *Los Angeles Times* and republished in Beasley's 1919 anthology entitled *The Negro Trail Blazers of California,* which identified Alexander as a participant in the fight for equal opportunities for blacks in California. One of Alexander's poems, entitled "My Mother's Custard Pie," begins thus:

> You may talk about the cooking
>   They do in Italy;
> And the kind the Frenchman
>   Sets before his company;
> Of the German's Toast and "weinies,"
>   Or the English mutton-chop.
> But there is one thing to remember
>   That will start you on the hop;
> It's delicious, it is luscious,
>   It will brighten up your eye;
> It is like a view of heaven—
>   That is mother's custard pie.

Alexander also continued to be active in politics, even in the last decade of his life, appearing before the Los Angeles County supervisors in 1918 to urge them not to rescind their vote to admit black girls to nurses' training school. Alexander died in September 1923 at his home in Los Angeles after a brief illness.

While Alexander's periodicals and his poetry received profuse praise during his lifetime, today he is primarily recognized as a chronicler of black achievement. Walter C. Daniel offers this assessment of *Alexander's Magazine* in his *Black Journals of the United States* (1982): "Because its variety of news was wide and its editorial policy not largely personal, *Alexander's Magazine* in many ways provides the best background history of the black experience in America of any national magazine published by blacks in the first two decades of the twentieth century." Daniel claims that Alexander's chief contribution to American culture was his recognition and labeling in 1908 of a black renaissance in America.

References:

Analytical Guide and Indexes to Alexander's Magazine, 1905-1909 (Westport, Conn.: Greenwood Press, 1974);

Delilah L. Beasley, *The Negro Trail Blazers of California* (Los Angeles, 1919);

Penelope L. Bullock, *The Afro-American Periodical Press, 1838-1909* (Baton Rouge: Louisiana State University Press, 1981);

Walter C. Daniel, *Black Journals of the United States: Historical Guides to the World's Periodicals and Newspapers* (Westport, Conn.: Greenwood Press, 1982);

Stephen R. Fox, *The Guardian of Boston: William Monroe Trotter* (New York: Atheneum, 1970);

Louis R. Harlan and Raymond W. Smock, eds., *The Booker T. Washington Papers*, 13 volumes (Urbana: University of Illinois Press, 1972-1984);

Betty Lou K. Rathbun, "The Rise of the Modern American Negro Press: 1880 to 1914," Ph.D. dissertation, State University of New York at Buffalo, 1979;

G. F. Richings, *Evidences of Progress Among Colored People* (Philadelphia: G. S. Ferguson, 1896).

Margaret Anderson

(24 November 1886-19 October 1973)

Kathleen Kearney Keeshen

See also the Anderson entry in *DLB 4: American Writers in Paris, 1920-1939.*

MAJOR POSITIONS HELD: Literary editor, *Continent* (1913-1914); publisher and editor, *Little Review* (1914-1929).

BOOKS: *My Thirty Years' War: An Autobiography* (New York: Covici Friede, 1930; London: Knopf, 1930);
The Fiery Fountains (New York: Hermitage House, 1951; London: Rider, 1953);
The Unknowable Gurdjieff (London: Routledge & Paul, 1962; New York: Samuel Weiser, 1973);
The Strange Necessity (New York: Horizon, 1970).

OTHER: *The "Little Review" Anthology,* edited by Anderson (New York: Hermitage House, 1953).

Margaret Caroline Anderson, born to prosperous midwestern parents, yearned from youth for a life "beautiful as no life had ever been." She pursued that beauty in her own life by seeking the highest forms of thought, conversation, and music. This lifelong passion enthralled her, guiding her friendships and working relationships with many of the leading artists, intellectuals, and literary figures of her time. More important, her pursuit of this passion bore fruit in the creation and fifteen-year life of the *Little Review,* an unprecedented avant-garde magazine of literature and the arts. As editor, she followed the trail of important early twentieth-century artistic and literary movements, beginning with the magazine's introduction in Renaissance Chicago in 1914, its subsequent move to New York's Greenwich Village in 1917, a pause for a brief spate in Muir Woods, California, and its final immigration to Paris in the 1920s. While she also wrote three volumes of fairly well-received autobiography and a book-length account of her life as a Georges Gurdjieff disciple, it was the creation of the *Little Review* and her contributions to the maga-

Margaret Anderson

zine that garnered a special place for her in American literary and artistic history. The *Little Review* is unparalleled, having made history with almost every issue, publishing the new, the provocative, the untried, including work by writers Sherwood Anderson, Ernest Hemingway, Emma Goldman, James Joyce, William Butler Yeats, Wallace Stevens, T. S. Eliot, Ezra Pound, William Carlos Williams, Ben Hecht, Edgar Lee Masters, Theodore Dreiser, Gertrude Stein, and Jean Cocteau. She founded the *Little Review,* as she described it, "the way one begins playing the piano or writing poetry: because of something one wants violently. The thing I wanted—would die without—

17

was conversation. The only way to get it was to reach people with ideas. Only artists had ideas . . . and of course only the good ones. So I made a magazine exclusively for the very good artists of the time."

Anderson, an ardent feminist, also used the pages of the *Little Review* to espouse the cause, which was one of many she embraced, by publishing or reviewing the works of Olive Shreiner, Emma Goldman, and other feminists of the early twentieth century. Lest there be any doubt of her position, she once said, "I am no man's wife, no man's delightful mistress and I will never, never, never be a mother."

The most widely familiar and noteworthy achievement and the one that most firmly establishes Anderson's place in literature was the serialization, beginning in 1918, of James Joyce's *Ulysses* (1922). The manuscript had been sent to her by Ezra Pound, who, by then, had become the magazine's foreign editor. Declared obscene, four issues of the *Little Review* in which it appeared were burned by the United States Post Office, and Anderson and her associate editor, Jane Heap, were convicted of obscenity charges. For Anderson the conviction meant less than the loss of the articles. From the outset she had loved Joyce's precedent-shattering manuscript and had been willing to stake all in printing it in the magazine. To have the issues destroyed was like "a burning at the stake. . . . The care we had taken to preserve Joyce's text intact; the worry over the bills that accumulated when we had no advance funds; the technique I used on printer, bookbinder, paper houses–tears, prayers, hysterics, or rages–to make them push ahead without a guarantee of money; the addressing, wrapping, stamping, mailing; the excitement of anticipating the world's response to the literary masterpiece of our generation . . . and then a notice from the Post Office: BURNED."

Anderson's forte essentially was her seemingly uncanny ability to recognize masterpieces and the application of her courageous and unswerving conviction that these works must be published, no matter what the consequences. Many of those whose works she published were not generally able to find publication elsewhere, but they would later prove to be among the most widely accepted writers and artists of merit of their time. She was committed to fostering the change their works represented, not so much because she felt change was necessary but because she believed their works deserved to be published. As R. N.

Linscott pointed out in the *Saturday Review of Literature* (14 June 1930), "She performed the miracle of publishing a magazine without resources, of getting the best writers without paying them, and of living, meanwhile, in a state of spiritual inebriation that would have left a lesser soul limp in a week." The story of the magazine, as another chronicler put it, "begins as, and in many ways remains, the story of Margaret Anderson."

From an early age Anderson sought freedom from the strictures of middle-class respectability, particularly those embraced by her prosperous family. Though her father, Arthur Aubrey Anderson, a successful railroad executive, was, in her view, fairly liberal, she found her mother, Jessie Shortridge Anderson, highly hypocritical and was not fond of her. She was born in Indianapolis on 24 November 1886 but spent her childhood in Columbus, Indiana. Early on, life in Columbus, for Anderson, was stultifying. At sixteen, she entered the Western College for Women in Oxford, Ohio, where she studied piano, but she left before graduating because, as she later explained, she was "bored." Here, however, she had been able to indulge in her fascination with the piano, an interest that would provide an important richness in her life, though she preferred the role of listener to that of performer. Journalist Janet Flanner described her in this period as "the born enemy of convention and discipline–a feministic romantic rebel with an appetite for Chopin and for indiscriminate reading," and all this while embracing her primary passion for conversation.

Conversation, particularly with artists, as the embodiment of all Anderson held beautiful, consistently attracted and held her fast, as did its variation, argument; both captivated her throughout her life. In pursuit of that elusive "conversation," and to contribute what she felt was worthwhile to a literate readership, she vowed that the *Little Magazine* would be filled "with the best conversation the world has to offer."

Anderson was a strikingly beautiful woman, exceedingly charming and a delightful conversationalist herself. Flanner reported that she "enveloped a will of tempered steel, specifically at its most resistant when she was involved in argument, which was her favorite form of intellectual exercise." Her charm and pulchritude on more than a few occasions were instrumental in securing contributions to sustain the magazine, which was always bordering on insolvency. She attracted financial resources or assistance from sup-

THE LITTLE REVIEW

THE MAGAZINE THAT IS READ BY THOSE
WHO WRITE THE OTHERS

MARCH, 1918

Ulysses, 1.	*James Joyce*
Imaginary Letters, VIII.	*Wyndham Lewis*
Matinee	*Jessie Dismorr*
The Classics "Escape"	*Ezra Pound*
Cantico del Sole	
Women and Men, II.	*Ford Madox Hueffer*
Bertha	*Arthur Symons*
A List of Books	*Ezra Pound*
Wyndham Lewis's "Tarr"	
Raymonde Collignon	
The Reader Critic	

Copyright, 1918, by Margaret Anderson
MARGARET ANDERSON, Editor
EZRA POUND, Foreign Editor

24 *West Sixteenth Street, New York*

Foreign office:
5 *Holland Place Chambers, London W. 8.*

25 cents a copy $2.50 a year

Entered as second-class matter at P. O., New York, N. Y.
Published monthly by Margaret Anderson

Contents page for the issue of the magazine founded by Anderson that included the first installment of James Joyce's Ulysses *(1922). The serialization of Joyce's novel ceased with the July-August 1920 issue because the work was declared obscene by a New York state court.*

porters, printers, suppliers, and other interested parties.

When Anderson arrived in Chicago in 1908, the city was a teeming intellectual and artistic center and, for her, an escape from boredom. Having convinced her family, notably her father, that she was capable of supporting herself, she moved to the city with her sister Lois. In her first job she reviewed books for the *Continent,* a religious weekly, and for the *Chicago Evening Post.* The work load was prodigious. At one point she reportedly reviewed as many as fifty books over a single weekend. Later, a job as a bookstore clerk in what she hailed as the "most beautiful bookshop in the world," a Frank Lloyd Wright design in the Fine Arts Building, led to a subsequent assignment on the staff of the literary re-

view, the *Dial,* and the unique opportunity to observe the makings of a magazine from the inside out, an invaluable primer for publishing and one she would find vital in producing the *Little Review.* Responsibilities with the *Dial* as its literary editor also provided her with the opportunity to travel to New York, visiting editors whose books she reviewed, and it was here that she made important contacts that would prove helpful later.

The Chicago Renaissance that Margaret Anderson found herself immersed in was fertile ground for unique growth of arts in a wide variety of forms. By 1912 the *Friday Literary Review* of the *Chicago Evening Post,* for example, had become a regular rallying point for discussion of the city's artists' and intellectuals' works. Of somewhat like mind, Harriet Monroe had introduced

Anderson (right) with actress Georgette Leblanc and composer George Antheil in Bernardsville, New Jersey, summer 1921 (Allen Tanner)

her own pioneering *Poetry: A Magazine of Verse*, promising "to refuse nothing because it is too good, whatever be the nature of its excellence." The following year the Armory Show of Post-Impressionist Art at the Chicago Art Institute drew great crowds and critical acclaim, and Chicago theatergoers were delighted and intrigued by an Irish Players visit in which J. M. Synge's and Lady Gregory's plays were presented, representative of the Irish turn-of-the-century literary Renaissance, a seeming follow-up to the establishment the year before of Malcolm Browne's Chicago Little Theatre. The Chicago Little Theatre was considered the prototype of the whole little-theater movement that followed. Presenting Sunday evening lectures were leading figures of the period, such as Theodore Dreiser, Emma Goldman, and John Cowper Powys. Anderson once attributed much of her inspiration for starting the *Little Magazine* to a Little Theatre lecture by

Powys. A coterie of writers, artists, and intellectuals grew up around these institutions, and Anderson found herself part of the group, relishing the fine conversation and stimulating company it provided.

That summer Anderson came to a startling and most significant self-assessment of a depression she had been suffering, perhaps aggravated by the coming prospect of reviewing the fall's books, which, for the *Continent*, could mean as many as one hundred described in a single issue. Awakening in the middle of the night, she reasoned: "First precise thought: I know why I'm depressed–nothing inspired is going on. Second: I demand that life be inspired every moment. Third: the only way to guarantee this is to have inspired conversation every moment. Fourth: Most people never get so far as conversation; they haven't the stamina, and there is no time. Fifth: if I had a magazine I could spend my time filling it up with the best conversation the world has to offer. Sixth: marvelous idea–salvation. Seventh: decision to do it. Deep sleep."

And do it she did. With next to no financial backing or the promise of much to come, save for advertising funds she had solicited from a few New York editors and a reported male admirer, Anderson launched the *Little Review* in 1914. Her intent was clear. Its purpose would be to present creative criticism that was "fresh and constructive and intelligent from the artist's point of view."

She had little patience with public opinion, believing implicitly in her own. Underscoring that, she printed her first issue under the motto "A Magazine of the Arts, Making No Compromise with the Public Taste." Her rationale for producing such a magazine was that "people who make art are more interesting than those who don't; that they have a special illumination about life; that this illumination is the subject matter of all inspired conversation; that one might as well be dead as to live outside this radiance."

In retrospect, her first issue provides but a hint of the influence the magazine would ultimately come to hold. Interspersed with articles on feminism, Nietzschism, and cubism was poetry by Vachel Lindsay and Arthur Davison Ficke. Anderson herself contributed book reviews, an article on Jan Paderewski's playing, and offered articles from colleagues such as Sherwood Anderson and his first wife, Cornelia. She included, as well, events considered of literary interest in Chicago. The first issue was distributed to positive press reports, thanks to an admiring review in the *Chicago Evening Post* by Floyd Dell, another of the Renaissance circle.

The first issue was especially important in setting the tone and in identifying areas that would be of future interest in the magazine. As Jackson R. Bryer has pointed out, "perhaps the single most characteristic aspect of the *Little Review* (an aspect announced in that first editorial and suggested in the course of that first issue) is an open mindedness towards all sides of a question and an interest in argument and discussion about it." This aspect of the magazine was seen by many as a breath of fresh air in the publishing of criticism.

Anderson described her standards for the magazine by responding to critics who attacked the publication as lacking in substance by saying, "my idea of a magazine which makes a claim to artistic value is that it should be conducted more or less on the lines of good drama or good fiction; that it should suggest, not conclude; that it should stimulate thinking, rather than dictate thought." But a lot of her essential passion for "inspiration" rather than knowledge was also expressed when she qualified that position by saying she would "rather see one side of a question violently than to see both sides calmly.... I should rather feel a great deal and know a little than feel a little and know a lot," a considerable departure from more commonly accepted critical objectives.

The second issue offered less variety, focusing in its entirety on an article by William Butler Yeats that consisted of advice for American poets; the third proved sensational in that it engendered a full-fledged scandal. At press time Anderson, an admirer of Emma Goldman, who was then in Chicago lecturing, added an article extolling the principles Goldman espoused, denouncing the ownership of private property and praising "the anarchist religion."

The slender tendrils of financial support were instantly severed, and Anderson's reputation for daring was firmly established. Even her previously admiring suitor withdrew financial assistance, lest his own employment be jeopardized by the association. The first of what would be perennial financial problems was at hand, forcing Anderson to return part-time to the drudgery of book reviewing to provide the needed funds to cover printing costs. Subscription campaigns were instituted and contributions accepted from concerned observers who viewed the plight of the fledgling magazine with alarm.

However dark the situation, Anderson plunged ahead, keeping tight control along the way. Harriet Monroe presented Amy Lowell to her as a potential solution to the financial quandary. Lowell, in exchange for a position as the magazine's poetry editor, would provide the needed financial support. That demand was too great for Anderson, who declined, saying it was not possible for her to function "in association."

When funds were diminished and the magazine's quarters became unaffordable, the indomitable Anderson, together with her divorced sister Lois and Lois's two boys, as well as a volunteer office assistant, moved into a tent on the shores of Lake Michigan, an action that attracted much notoriety. Here the group lived from mid May until the chilly middle of November, gathering interviews and press coverage sufficient to elicit sympathy and, most important, financial contributions.

Cover for the special issue of Anderson's magazine devoted to English naturalist and novelist W. H. Hudson

The notoriety unfortunately also brought the group's plight to the attention of the owner of a house previously promised them. That offer was immediately withdrawn, the owner distressed with the apparently irresponsible nature of his tenants-to-be. As winter approached, the group was rescued by a socialist friend of Goldman who offered them a vacant, dismal house as a respite, and the magazine continued.

True to her standards, Anderson left half of the pages of the September 1916 issue blank because she "found no suitable material." In the constant juxtaposition of her taste versus that of the public, the following year's October issue, running a Wyndham Lewis short story on a young girl's brutal seduction, was confiscated by censors, once more providing evidence of the maga-

zine's independent stance and unpredictability.

While Anderson insisted on controlling the magazine herself, great concessions were made to the only other individual who would be as instrumental as she, a newcomer to the magazine, Jane Heap. Heap, whose identification on the masthead was simply "jh," brought special gifts, training, and expertise to the publication as its associate editor. Best of all for Anderson was the fact that she found Heap "a great talker." Heap, a trained artist, had studied at the Chicago Art Institute, as well as abroad, and put these talents to work in improved design for the magazine, an important adjunct to her editing abilities. In addition, she brought consummate wit and a gift for repartee to the job. The magazine's letters-to-the-

Anderson at the grave of Georgette Leblanc, who died in October 1941 (courtesy of the Library of Congress)

editor column and Heap's editorial responses, which appeared under the byline "The Reader Critic," became one of its liveliest sections, an integral part of the *Little Review*. Heap would also be responsible for the magazine's ultimate shift in emphasis from literature to international art movements such as dadaism and surrealism, an adventurous direction.

In 1917 the magazine moved to Greenwich Village, continuing to publish new writers, among whom T. S. Eliot and James Joyce were included. In the magazine's New York years readers were introduced to a further variety of fiction, poetry, and criticism, including works by Wyndham Lewis, Richard Aldington, and Hart Crane, among others. In this period Ezra Pound expanded the magazine's base of contributors, drawing manuscripts from William Butler Yeats and Joyce, which led to the historical serialized publication of *Ulysses* and the problems its appearance would create for the magazine. The magazine became a quarterly in 1921, the year of the obscenity conviction, and appeared irregularly thereafter, with publication halting in 1927, to be revived only for the final issue in 1929. Anderson, in the final years of the magazine, had turned its editing over to Heap, remaining responsible only in a titular sense.

The *Little Review,* always faced with financial struggle, interested Anderson less after her move to Paris in the early 1920s. By 1929, bored with the magazine, she allowed its demise. In its final issue more than fifty artists and writers responded to a highly personal questionnaire seeking responses to queries about their philosophies of life, work, and art. The thoughts, values, and statements they provided Anderson remain of interest today. Anderson, however, concluded that, based on the responses, "even the artist doesn't know what he is talking about. And I can no longer go on publishing a magazine in which no one really knows what he is talking about. It doesn't interest me."

If the *Little Review* provided Anderson with the opportunity for artistic expression, meeting and living with Georgette Leblanc, a French singer and actress, allowed her to experience love, as her autobiographical *The Fiery Fountains* (1951) details. LeBlanc and Anderson for several years were disciples of Georges Gurdjieff, a Russo-Greek mystic who had attracted a following at his Institute for the Development of Man, which also included Katherine Mansfield. Out of these experiences came Anderson's biographical *The Unknowable Gurdjieff* (1962). The only other significant emotional attachment Anderson would have was in her thirty-year friendship with Dorothy Caruso, Enrico Caruso's widow, ending only with Dorothy Caruso's death, upon which Anderson returned to France, where she lived until her own death on 19 October 1973. She was eighty-six.

Extraordinarily complex, Anderson was responsible for what at least one critic has said was a magazine that may well be the most consistently excellent of its kind ever produced. Her good friend Janet Flanner once noted, "She was a peculiarly complicated and inflated personality. In the *Little Review*, she had been leading readers onto a superior plane of appreciation of the new, constructive, detonating and deflating twentieth cen-

tury art, but her psychic self was still housed in an elaborate old-fangled euphoria, embedded in her nature like a mild incurable malady. By her own statement, she 'lived her life on a cloud and was the happiest person she knew.' "

Letters:

Pound/The Little Review: The Letters of Ezra Pound to Margaret Anderson, edited by Thomas L. Scott, Melvin J. Friedman, and Jackson R. Bryer, volume 6 of *The Correspondence of Ezra Pound* (New York: New Directions, 1988).

References:

Jackson R. Bryer, " 'A Trial-Track for Racers': Margaret Anderson and the 'Little Review,' " Ph.D. dissertation, University of Wisconsin, 1965;

J. M. Edelstein, "Exuberance and Ecstasy," *New Republic,* 162 (13 June 1970): 19-22;

Janet Flanner, "Profiles: A Life on a Cloud," *New Yorker,* 50 (3 June 1974): 44-67;

Hugh Ford, *Four Lives in Paris* (San Francisco: North Point, 1987), pp. 227-286;

Abby Ann Arthur Johnson, "The Personal Magazine: Margaret C. Anderson and the Little Review," *South Atlantic Quarterly* (Summer 1976): 351-363.

Papers:

The Little Review Collection at the University of Wisconsin–Milwaukee includes the bulk of Anderson's papers. Others are held at Houghton Library, Harvard University.

William F. Bigelow

(14 August 1879-5 March 1966)

Maurine H. Beasley
University of Maryland

MAJOR POSITIONS HELD: Managing editor, *Cosmopolitan* (1909-1913); editor, *Good Housekeeping* (1913-1940).

SELECTED PUBLICATIONS: "Is Marriage on the Skids?" *Good Housekeeping,* 94 (June 1932): 8;
"Ones Who Pay," *Good Housekeeping,* 102 (April 1936): 4;
"A Peace Amendment," *Good Housekeeping,* 102 (May 1936): 4;
The Good Housekeeping Marriage Book: Twelve Ways to a Happy Marriage, edited, with an introduction, by Bigelow (New York: Prentice-Hall, 1938);
"Wintry Weather," *Good Housekeeping,* 114 (January 1942): 10.

William F. Bigelow, a demanding editor who held fast to the beliefs of his Methodist background, guided *Good Housekeeping* magazine through almost three decades of the early twentieth century. Under his direction the magazine attained phenomenal success, gaining the distinction of being what was probably the single most profitable monthly periodical published during the Depression. It offered an extensive variety of articles and service features, fiction, verse, and high-quality illustrations, achieving popularity with readers in both large cities and small towns.

As a youth Bigelow received a firm grounding in middle-class, Protestant values, which he later advocated in the pages of *Good Housekeeping.* Born 14 August 1879 on a farm near Milford Center, Ohio, Bigelow was the son of Alpheus Russell and Hattie Parthemore Bigelow. In 1905 he received a bachelor of literature degree from Ohio Wesleyan University, in Delaware, Ohio, a Methodist school to which he remained passionately attached throughout his life. He also took some classes at Columbia University in New York during the 1904-1905 school year.

Bigelow started his career as a copyboy on *Cosmopolitan* magazine in 1905, the same year it

William F. Bigelow (courtesy of Ohio Wesleyan University)

was bought by the William Randolph Hearst organization. He soon became an editor and in 1909 was named managing editor. During this period *Cosmopolitan* joined other popular magazines in crusades for political reform commonly referred to as muckraking. In 1913, two years after Hearst purchased *Good Housekeeping,* Bigelow took over as editor. He remained in this position until he retired in 1940.

Bigelow's long tenure with *Good Housekeeping* illustrated his enthusiasm for providing information that he deemed useful and important in the lives of American homemakers. He made no radical change in the direction of the magazine but instead expanded on a solid base built by the previous editor, James Eaton Tower. At the time Hearst purchased the magazine, which started publication in 1885, it enjoyed good advertising patronage and a circulation of more than 300,000 readers. The subscription rate was $1.50 a year and issues averaged 125 pages. Bigelow enlarged the fiction offerings, buying works by well-known authors.

Consumer service immediately drew his attention also. He gave prominent display to contributions by Dr. Harvey W. Wiley, the former chief chemist of the United States Department of Agriculture, who led the fight against food adulteration that spurred passage of the Food and Drug Act of 1906. Brought to *Good Housekeeping* in 1912 under Tower's editorship, Wiley conducted his own Bureau of Foods, Sanitation and Health as part of the Good Housekeeping Institute that tested products advertised in the magazine. Bigelow greatly broadened the scope of the institute, which offered the magazine's "seal of approval" to goods advertised in its pages.

While Bigelow geared the publication to traditional ideas about the role of women, he did respond to changing social currents that affected the lives of his readers. Prior to World War I fictional heroines, for example, were depicted as sweet models of propriety, but during the 1920s women characters displayed considerably more independence. In the 1930s, during the Depression, heroines bravely overcame hardships. At the same time they were shown as clinging to traditional, middle-class moral standards, although they often tolerated the use of cigarettes and alcohol by more worldly, aristocratic women.

In common with its two chief competitors, *Ladies' Home Journal* and *McCall's*, *Good Housekeeping* under Bigelow purchased fiction from writers such as Booth Tarkington, Somerset Maugham, John Galsworthy, Ellen Glasgow, Ring Lardner, Mary Roberts Rinehart, Kathleen Norris, and other popular figures, some of whom produced literary works of enduring value. Much of the fiction published in *Good Housekeeping*, however, falls into the escapist category, picturing a world of romance where the "good girl" triumphed. In a 1926 issue Edith Newell Blair explained to readers that happy endings did not necessarily denote works of literary merit, yet she went on to recommend uplifting novels.

Bigelow perfected a literary formula for each issue that spelled financial success. During the mid 1930s, for instance, issues typically contained three serials, five short stories, four articles, poems, children's stories, and advice on architecture, home furnishings, cooking, fashions, and

beauty. The work of talented illustrators such as Charles Dana Gibson and James Montgomery Flagg highlighted the fiction. Colorful drawings of stylish young women and attractive children appeared on the covers. During the 1920s *Good Housekeeping* offered full-color paintings of places of biblical interest and a colored page for children to brighten its black-and-white illustrations. Rose O'Neill's "Kewpies," drawings of cupid-like figures with bright pink cheeks, were also included for their interest to children. By the 1930s photographs accompanied poems and articles.

In political and legal areas affecting women, Bigelow steered *Good Housekeeping* on a quiet course. However, he did not avoid all controversial matters. During the suffrage campaign *Good Housekeeping* sided with the suffragists, contending women would use the ballot to elevate the level of politics. In a signed column in November 1913 Bigelow wrote, "the power of the vote puts in women's hands the possibility of enforcing a higher idealism than has ever yet been invoked in the conduct of affairs without the home." Voting, he continued, would allow women to "close many an avenue that leads enticingly to sin." Emphasizing the development of matrimony as a "new profession," a May 1913 *Good Housekeeping* article entitled "How Many Children?" provided support for family limitation so children could be adequately educated. Bigelow adamantly opposed child labor, which he saw as the result of large numbers of children born into poor families.

Nevertheless, the magazine under Bigelow reflected some of the national ambivalence toward the emancipation of women. Writing as a black servant, "Mirandy," Elizabeth Meriwether Gilmer, the well-known advice columnist who wrote under the byline Dorothy Dix, declared in the July 1916 issue that laws governing divorce should be the same throughout the nation and should prohibit second marriages for men, measures thought to elevate the status of women. An editorial in the same issue quoted a judge who stated, "Women should share in making the laws that regulate their life." Yet a later issue carried another opinion by "Mirandy," calling suffragists "millinery sufferinyets" and comparing women to hens, claiming that they would never stand together on political issues. Men, she said, would have to give the ballot to women.

Occasionally women wrote on political themes. Frances Parkinson Keyes, the wife of New Hampshire senator Henry Wilder Keyes

*Cover for a 1913 issue of the magazine with which Bigelow began his journalism career. In 1905 he was hired as
a copyboy; in 1909 he became managing editor.*

(and later a best-selling novelist), touched on topical issues in her monthly Washington article entitled "Letters From a Senator's Wife." For the most part, though, she chatted about leading personalities and their families. In 1923 she covered the International Women's Suffrage Alliance meeting in Rome for *Good Housekeeping*. Another woman's view of politics appeared in a 1935 serial entitled "The Real Calvin Coolidge," written by his widow, Grace Goodhue Coolidge, and others.

Reflecting Bigelow's interest in providing his readers with sentimental fare that satisfied curiosity about famous persons, Mrs. Coolidge published two poems in *Good Housekeeping*. In 1929 the former first lady sent an unsolicited poem to Bigelow in memory of her son, who had died five years earlier. It was accompanied by a note apologizing for the poem's lack of form and asking for the editor's "honest opinion." Bigelow replied that true emotion did not have to conform to any set standard and sent Mrs. Coolidge a check for $250. He assured her his readers would like it and they did. Displayed on a page by itself, the poem, "The Open Door," spoke of God and heaven. It drew a tremendous response and was often reprinted. *Good Housekeeping* also published the work of acclaimed poets such as Amy Lowell, Edna St. Vincent Millay, Alfred Noyes, and Ogden Nash.

Bigelow considered prohibition a major political topic of interest to his readers. The magazine backed passage of the Eighteenth Amendment, which outlawed the sale of alcoholic beverages in 1918, and refused to change its stand as opposition mounted during the 1920s. Bigelow pledged to fight the "liquor interests," arguing that "booze drinking is a waste of time, a waste of money–of everything that is worthwhile." He declined to accept the social behavior of the 1920s

27

Cover for an issue of the magazine that Bigelow edited from 1913 until 1940. During his tenure it became one of the most profitable monthlies published in the United States.

that negated the idea of prohibition and continued to support the law until 1933 when it was repealed.

Bigelow gave his personal views in signed editorials that usually ran on page four of the magazine. Many of these hailed the virtues of patriotism and piety and paid homage to American heroes such as George Washington. The editorials encouraged women to vote and urged interest in citizenship in general. Specific legislative measures were rarely mentioned, although in 1936 Bigelow urged that readers support the so-called peace amendment to the Constitution that called for a national referendum before war could be declared. But he called for military strength too–"a preparedness impressive enough to guarantee us against attack."

To Bigelow, a happy marriage represented the zenith of achievement for his readers. In an introduction to *The Good Housekeeping Marriage*

Book: *Twelve Ways to a Happy Marriage* (1938), a collection of articles on marriage from the magazine, Bigelow pronounced, "The articles that are printed in this book made what was in my opinion the most important, the most constructive, series on a single subject that *Good Housekeeping* has published in the quarter century and more that I have been its editor." He added, "If these articles make success in marriage seem something that must constantly be worked for, they at the same time show that success, plus the happiness that goes with it, can be achieved. Which is all, I think, that any man or woman has a right to ask for."

The articles presented a glowing picture of traditional marriage. Engaged couples were urged to avoid premarital sex, save money to pay for having at least two children, and promote religion in the home. Only one writer mentioned careers and that was Eleanor Roosevelt, whose article entitled "Should Wives Work?" began with the question, "Is it possible for a woman to marry and still have a career?" She answered it by declaring the question "foolishly worded for there are very few women who have careers," even though many women might work at least some time in their lives. Her conclusion echoed the sentiment of *Good Housekeeping* that "any young couple is fortunate when the woman has to do everything about the house and does it happily."

Bigelow himself was a happily married man who consulted his family on the contents of his magazine. Early in his career, on 24 December 1906, he married Mary R. Koch, also a graduate of Ohio Wesleyan University, and the couple had three daughters, Margaret, Miriam, and Elizabeth, all of whom also were graduated from Ohio Wesleyan. On the twenty-fifth anniversary of Bigelow's entrance into magazine journalism, he disclosed that he asked his wife and daughter Margaret about what to run in *Good Housekeeping* instead of simply guessing about the tastes of his readers.

"Women are not interested in the freakish," he maintained. "Their reading preference is for love stories, then stories of adventure and third, mystery stories." He thought that women were more interested in prohibition than men, increasingly eager to make their homes comfortable and beautiful and committed to higher moral standards than the women of a quarter of a century earlier, even if young people appeared "freer and franker" about moral questions.

Bigelow had little interest in running material about women who did not fit his ideas of proper behavior. In 1929 he balked at publishing an article by Sara Haardt about Zelda Fitzgerald, the wife of F. Scott Fitzgerald, the novelist who captured the spirit of the Roaring Twenties. At the time Haardt was engaged to H. L. Mencken, the iconoclastic journalist who debunked many of the American institutions that Bigelow held dear. In a letter to Haardt, whom he married the following year, Mencken referred to the rejection of her article and wrote, "Bigelow is a swine. Tell him that Zelda is a 100 percent Christian woman. I can find you 50 perjurers to substantiate it." Bigelow subsequently refused to print any of a series of interviews Haardt had done with the wives of famous men, although he paid her for them. According to Mencken, this was because of Haardt's relationship to him. "Bigelow was a poor fellow and regarded me as an anarchist," Mencken explained.

By the end of Bigelow's editorship, *Good Housekeeping* often had 250 pages per issue, glowing with color, picturing a life-style that symbolized American middle-class dreams. Bigelow often declared that it was not published exclusively for women. In Ohio State Penitentiary, he liked to point out, housekeeping was hardly a current concern of the inmates, but the publication was a favorite. By the mid 1920s, circulation had passed the million mark, and it doubled again in the next dozen years even in the midst of the Depression, when the magazine's annual subscription price was $2.50. In 1938 the magazine's operating profit stood at $2,583,202–more than triple the combined profit of Hearst's eight other magazines. This extraordinary success occurred during a year in which magazine advertising as a whole dropped twenty-two percent from the previous year, and many small periodicals perished.

Although he had stepped down as editor by the time the United States became involved in World War II, Bigelow wrote editorials for *Good Housekeeping* calling on American women to back the war effort. His writing displayed his customary emotional, florid style, as in this appeal from an editorial entitled "Wintry Weather" (January 1942): "Will the cold hearts of a sovereign race dictate the working hours, the playtime, of the world now opposing it? Oh, no, not that; not if the God it denies has any care for his children; not if we say not and are willing to put into willing hands a mightier might than can be marshaled against them."

Bigelow was awarded an honorary doctorate by Ohio Wesleyan University in 1927 and three years later an honorary doctorate by Kansas Wesleyan University. Beginning in 1929 he became a trustee of Ohio Wesleyan, a post he held for thirty-seven years, and in 1935, a trustee of American University in Washington, D. C. He held honorary membership in Phi Beta Kappa. He was a Mason and a Republican.

In 1952 he moved from his longtime home in Roselle Park, New Jersey, to Delaware, Ohio, where he visited the Ohio Wesleyan campus almost daily. A strong supporter of compulsory chapel attendance for students, Bigelow himself attended chapel programs three times a week. A major donor for a science building named in his honor, he also established a scholarship fund and aided needy members of his fraternity, Sigma Alpha Epsilon, which he served as chapter adviser.

However, he hid his generous nature under a gruff exterior. He confronted new secretaries in college offices and crisply lectured them on the virtues of thrift while he snapped off lights they had turned on. After each issue of the college alumni magazine was printed, staff members braced themselves for calls from Bigelow pointing out their mistakes.

In a convocation address at Ohio Wesleyan in 1963, Bigelow presented his philosophy of life: "belief in God, faith in God, loyalty to God constitutes an armor that every student should have put on, and securely buckled, before his Commencement Day. . . . College is not only a proving ground–It is a place where one should find, and cling to, belief, faith, loyalty." Of the three Bigelow defined loyalty as the most important–"a course of conduct, not merely a creed." In his own case loyalty to the values of his upbringing marked his career as an editor and accounted for his success in reaching a vast au-dience, since these values were those of mainstream middle-America. Bigelow died unexpectedly at the age of eighty-six while visiting at the home of his daughter, Miriam Bigelow Criss, in Newark, Ohio.

References:

Sarah Elizabeth McBride, "Woman in the Popular Magazines for Women in America: 1830-1956," Ph.D. dissertation, University of Minnesota, 1966;

Marion E. Rogers, ed., *Mencken & Sara* (New York: McGraw-Hill, 1987), pp. 408-9;

Ishbel Ross, *Grace Coolidge and Her Era* (New York: Dodd, Mead, 1962): p. 127.

Papers:

A few items pertaining to Bigelow's role as a trustee at Ohio Wesleyan University are in the university's archives.

Edward W. Bok

(9 October 1863-9 January 1930)

A. J. Kaul
University of Southern Mississippi

MAJOR POSITIONS HELD: Editor in chief, *Ladies' Home Journal* (1889-1919); vice-president, Curtis Publishing Company (1893-1919).

BOOKS: *The Young Man in Business* (Philadelphia: Curtis, 1894);
Successward (New York & Chicago: Revell, 1895);
A Story of Some Pictures (Philadelphia: Curtis, 1896);
The Young Man and the Church (Philadelphia: Altemus, 1896);
Explaining the Editor (Philadelphia?: 1901);
Why I Believe in Poverty as the Richest Experience That Can Come to a Boy (Boston & New York: Houghton Mifflin, 1915);
How the Y.M.C.A. Made Good: The Actual Facts Stated (Philadelphia?: 1919);
The Americanization of Edward Bok (New York: Scribners, 1920); adapted as *A Dutch Boy Fifty Years After*, edited by John Louis Haney (New York & Chicago: Scribners, 1921);
Two Persons (New York: Scribners, 1922);
A Man from Maine (New York: Scribners, 1923); adapted as *The Boy Who Followed Ben Franklin*, edited by Haney (New York & Chicago: Scribners, 1924);
Twice Thirty (New York & London: Scribners, 1925);
America, Give Me a Chance! (New York: Scribners, 1926);
Dollars Only (New York & London: Scribners, 1926);
You: A Personal Message (Boston & New York: Medici Society of America, 1926); republished as *You: A Thought for the Holidays and All Other Days* (Merion, Pa.: Swastika, 1928);
Mary's Son, A Christmas Brochure (Merion, Pa.: Swastika, 1927);
Perhaps I Am (New York & London: Scribners, 1928);
America's Taj Mahal, the Singing Tower of Florida (Tate, Ga. & New York: Georgia Marble Company, 1929?);

Edward W. Bok

The Man in the White House (Merion, Pa.: Swastika, 1929).

OTHER: *Beecher Memorial: Contemporaneous Tributes to the Memory of Henry Ward Beecher*, edited by Bok (Brooklyn, N. Y.: Privately printed, 1887);
"The Boy in the Office," in *Before He is Twenty* (New York & Chicago: Revell, 1894);
"Country Lad in the City," in *Practical Book for Practical People* (Springfield, 1896).

For three decades, Edward W. Bok filled the pages of the *Ladies' Home Journal* with sentimental verities–hard work, frugality, perseverance, honesty, common sense, service, and relentlessly congenial optimism–that helped forge an American middle-class ethos and built the *Journal* into the nation's first magazine to reach a circulation of one million subscribers. Bok used his editorship to educate his readers and to promote modest reform in the areas of advertising, patent medicine, and sex education. His immensely popular Pulitzer-prize winning autobiography, *The Americanization of Edward Bok* (1920), fused the self-help sensibilities of Benjamin Franklin with the pluck of Horatio Alger.

Born 9 October 1863 in the seaport town of Helder, The Netherlands, Edward William Bok was the second son of William John Hidde Bok and Sieke Gertrude Bok. The Bok family was descended from a line of distinguished Dutch burghers. Bok's great-grandfather was an admiral in the Dutch navy, his grandfather was chief justice of the supreme court of the Netherlands, and his father held diplomatic posts at the royal court. Bok's family was affluent–his earliest recollections are of his governess–but a series of bad investments swept away the family fortune.

William J. H. Bok took his wife and two young sons to America, where he hoped to start his life over. The Bok family arrived in New York City on 20 September 1870. Within a week of their arrival, Bok's father enrolled his two sons in a public school in Brooklyn. His parents could speak English, but for Edward and his brother "the English language was as a closed book." His public school classmates tormented him, making fun of his broken English and calling him "Dutchy." He often got into schoolyard fights. "I was in the full swing of my first real experiment in Americanization," he recalled in *America, Give Me a Chance!* (1926). "I now felt my Americanization had begun."

His "Americanization" also meant work: "I began to work, and to work hard, almost from the day I set foot on American soil." After school, he scavenged for kindling wood and coal to heat the modest family home. He was paid three cents for each label he collected from canned fruits and vegetables found in the refuse behind the homes of the well-to-do; the labels were put in scrapbooks and sold as picture books. His first job, cleaning a baker's shop window twice a week, paid fifty cents, and he earned one dollar a week delivering the *South Brooklyn Advocate*.

While still in grammar school Bok began writing a social column for the *Brooklyn Eagle*, reporting the names of those attending parties. As recounted in *The Americanization of Edward Bok*, he sold the idea to the newspaper's city editor with the rationale that "every name mentioned in that paragraph represented a buyer of the paper, who would like to see his or her name in print." He was paid three dollars for each column, and by recruiting the help of his classmates he was soon contributing two to three columns each week.

After six years of public-school education, Bok ended his formal schooling at the age of twelve when he became an office boy in the electrician's department of Western Union Telegraph Company at $6.25 a week. The first purchase from his earnings was a copy of *Appleton's Encyclopedia*. He was enthralled with accounts of "successful men" whose "beginnings had been as modest as my own, and their opportunities for education as limited."

Throughout his life, Bok was fascinated by successful men. He started an autograph letter collection after receiving a response to his query of James A. Garfield, asking if he had "once been a boy on the tow-path." He corresponded with Ulysses S. Grant, Jefferson Davis, William Wadsworth Longfellow, and Rutherford B. Hayes, among others, and called upon these dignitaries when they visited New York City. When he was eighteen years old Bok ventured to Boston, Cambridge, and Concord, where he visited Oliver Wendell Holmes, went to a play with Longfellow, and was introduced by Louisa May Alcott to Ralph Waldo Emerson.

Bok's fascination with celebrities also led to his "first adventure as an editor." He wrote 100-word biographies of famous Americans for ten dollars each for Joseph P. Knapp of American Lithograph Company, which produced cigarette advertisements redeemable for an album of famous actors and actresses. When Knapp asked for more biographies, Bok hired his brother and five others to produce the biographies for five dollars each. "I was speedily convinced," he wrote in the *Americanization of Edward Bok*, "that merely to edit biographies written by others, at one-half the price paid to me, was more profitable than to write myself." The editorial "adventure" was more than commercial: it "had a distinct educational value to a large public."

In 1882 Bok joined Henry Holt and Company, working as a stenographer. Two years later he began a long association with New York publisher Charles Scribner, first as a stenographer, later as *Scribner's Magazine* advertising director. While working for Scribner, Bok used his meager resources to found *Brooklyn Magazine*, a publication aimed at parishioners of Henry Ward Beecher's church. With regular contributions from Beecher, Bok formally established in 1886

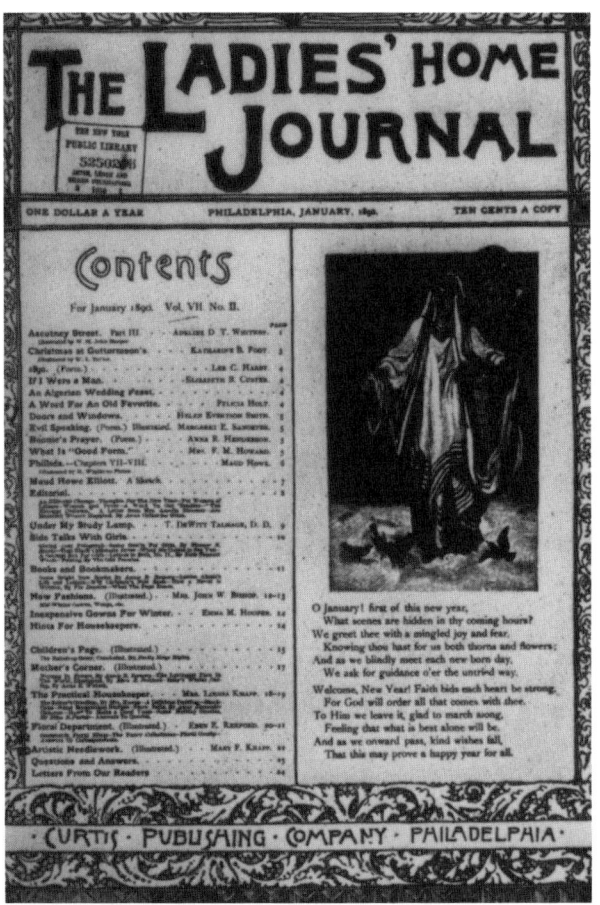 

Covers of the magazine Bok edited from 1889 to 1919. In February 1903 it reached a paid circulation of one million, becoming the first American magazine to obtain that goal.

the Bok Syndicate Press, the third American feature syndicate, which eventually attracted 137 subscriber newspapers.

The feature syndicate attracted the attention of Cyrus H. K. Curtis, publisher of the Philadelphia-based *Ladies' Home Journal,* then edited by the publisher's wife, Louisa Knapp Curtis. However, Mrs. Curtis was eager to relinquish her editorial duties to devote herself to rearing her daughter. The publisher offered the job to the twenty-six-year-old Bok, who became editor of the *Ladies' Home Journal* on 20 October 1889, at which time the magazine had a monthly circulation of 440,000.

The young bachelor joined the *Ladies' Home Journal* with the grand editorial aspiration (outlined in *America, Give Me a Chance!*) of making the magazine "a service which would visualize for womanhood its highest domestic estate." Bok wanted to edit a magazine "of higher standards, of larger initiative–a magazine that would be an

authoritative clearing-house for all the problems confronting women in the home, that brought itself closely into contact with those problems and tried to solve them in an entertaining and efficient way; and yet a magazine of uplift and inspiration: a magazine, in other words, that would give light and leading in the woman's world." And he wanted the magazine to have an intimate personal voice: "I felt the time had come . . . for the editor of some magazine to project his personality through the printed page and to convince the public that he was not an oracle removed from the people, but a real human being who could talk and not merely write on paper."

By his own account, one of Bok's first acts as editor was to ask *Journal* readers what they wanted to see in the magazine. He received thousands of replies, and he responded to readers' suggestions: "I gave them the subjects they asked for, but invariably on a slightly higher plane; and each year I raised the standard a notch. I always

Bok's wife, Mary Louise Curtis, whom he married on 22 October 1896. She was the daughter of C. H. K. Curtis, the publisher of the Ladies' Home Journal.

kept 'a huckleberry or two' ahead of my readers. My psychology was simple: come down to the level which the public sets and it will leave you at the moment you do it. It always expects of its leaders that they shall keep a notch above or a step ahead." His "editorial instinct" told him to aim for "a happy medium between shooting over the public's head and shooting too far under it." Bok confided to William Dean Howells, "We appeal to the intelligent American woman rather than to the intellectual type."

His personal editorial style was conversational. Bok started a regular column, "Side Talks with Girls," which appeared under the byline Ruth Ashmore. He received 700 letters after the first installment, and he was shocked by "how far the feminine nature would reveal itself on paper." Bok promptly turned the column over to Isabel A. Mallon, a contributor to his feature syndicate who continued the column for sixteen years. During her years as Ruth Ashmore the columnist received 158,000 letters and kept three stenographers busy "The number of girls who today bless the name of Ruth Ashmore is legion," Bok wrote in his autobiography. "Side Talks with Girls" proved so popular Bok started "Heart to Heart Talks" aimed at more mature women, and "Side Talks with Boys."

His counsel to boys covered a wide range, including a proper "attitude toward women" ("His mother should be the central figure of womanhood to him–his ideal, his standard"), rules for success in business ("Get into a business you like; Devote yourself to it; Be honest in everything; Be cautious; Don't worry; Avoid liquors of all kinds; Marry a good woman, and have your own home"), and marriage ("Wait until the right girl comes along and then marry her"). He even specified the appropriate age for marriage: "don't marry her this side of twenty years, and don't you marry this side of twenty-five." And he advised young men not to wait "too long"–"beyond the age of thirty"–to marry because by then their "bachelor habits" are "fixed." (Bok married Mary Louise Curtis, the daughter of *Journal* publisher Cyrus H. K. Curtis and Louisa Knapp Curtis, on 22 October 1896 when he was thirty-three years old; they had two sons, William Curtis Bok and Cary William Bok.)

Bok sentimentally idealized women for their civilizing influence. In *Successward* (1895), a book of advice for "young men," Bok commented: "There is no influence to be compared with that of a good woman over the life of a young man.... Men are by nature coarse and brutal; it is the influence of women that softens them. And we ought to be softened as much as we can. The good Lord knows we need it badly enough.... From the beginning of the world woman has been man's leader. She made him what he is today. All the qualities which we admire in men come from woman's influence."

A major influence in Bok's life was his mother. In a controversial April 1915 *Ladies' Home Journal* column later published as a book, *Why I Believe in Poverty as the Richest Experience That Can Come to a Boy* (1915), Bok argued that his own "untiring, ceaseless and unsparing" effort to break the shackles of poverty–"a condition to work out of: not stay in"–brought "the up-building: the development: the capacity to understand and sympathize; the greatest heritage that can come to a boy." Bok's mother, he acknowledged, was the wellspring of his determination: "I was determined to get out of poverty because my mother was not born in it, could not stand it, and did not belong in it. This gave me the first essential: a purpose."

A reviewer for the *New Republic* (4 December 1915), citing what he called Bok's "philistine nonsense" that made poverty "a moral gymnasium for boys," summed up Bok's experience

Bok in his office at the Curtis Publishing Company in Philadelphia

with poverty as "somewhat accidental and amateur. It was grim but it was not chronic. He did not inherit a tradition of helplessness, odium, and resignation. He was born of well-to-do parents who had happened to lose their place." The editor of the *Ladies' Home Journal,* he concluded, is bound to do "a great deal of harm if he veils in soft fog the hard realities of poverty."

Why I Believe in Poverty, among other essays, prompted critical misgivings of Bok and the *Ladies' Home Journal.* Bok felt, however, that the critical fusillade was aimed only at the "editorial Edward Bok." The "editorial Edward Bok" enjoyed pleasing readers' tastes, he wrote in his autobiography, the "real Edward Bok" did not. "The one was bottled up in the other. It was a case of absolute self-effacement. The man behind the editor knew that if he followed his own personal tastes and expressed them in his magazine, a limited audience would be his instead of the enormous clientele that he was now reaching." The "real Edward Bok" wrote his autobiography in the third person, he explained, "to separate the writer from his subject." They were two different people: "In fact, my chief difficulty during Edward Bok's directorship of *The Ladies' Home Journal* was to abstain from breaking through the

editor and revealing my real self. . . . Little by little I learned to subordinate myself and to let him have full rein."

The "editorial Edward Bok" held a tight rein on the *Ladies' Home Journal* and its staff. (Actually, Bok was more than an editor. By 1893, he was the second largest holder of Curtis Publishing Company stock and company vice-president.) His company policy of writing a personal response to every reader inquiry–ninety-seven thousand in the last four months of 1912–kept his carefully monitored staff busy. Periodically, Bok would write a fake query letter to each of his department editors to make sure their responses met his exacting standards. He praised good responses, criticized others. "Your letters to me have shown rather careless typewriting and two of them have gone unsigned," he informed one editor. "These are points I do not like."

Bok's editorial control of the *Ladies' Home Journal* was evident in the fiction that appeared in its pages. He solicited and published many first-rate writers: William Dean Howells, Rudyard Kipling, Sir Arthur Conan Doyle, Hamlin Garland, Joel Chandler Harris, Sarah Orne Jewett, and Mark Twain, among others. Amusement, entertainment, hope, and humor were standard ingredients for *Journal* fiction, and Bok scrupulously avoided authors with a realistic or naturalistic literary bent. To a short-story writer, Bok wrote: "Nothing could be more directly against our policy than a story the scenes of which are laid on the stage; and to make matters worse you give me a suicide at the end."

The paternalism of Bok's editorial policy meant that he had to "sugarcoat" the occasional bitter pill he asked readers to swallow. He told a Curtis Company Advertising Conference in 1913: "The policy of the *Ladies' Home Journal* has never been to publish anything unless there is an underlying reason. We will sugarcoat those pills so thick that you cannot see the pill, but the pill is there." Emboldened by wide popular acceptance–paid circulation reached one million in February 1903–the *Journal* defied a long-standing taboo and published a series of editorials advocating sex education for children, but without telling parents what their children needed to know. The magazine discussed venereal disease, rarely mentioning how it is transmitted.

Campaigns to clean up the patent medicine trade and to beautify America were more in keeping with the magazine's limited reform efforts. In 1892 the *Ladies' Home Journal* announced it would no longer accept patent medicine advertisements, a decision inspired in part by the desire to attract more reputable advertisers to its pages. A little more than a decade later, Bok opened fire against the patent medicine industry. He published an advertisement for Lydia Pinkham's patent medicine that stated: "Mrs. Pinkham, in her laboratory at Lynn, Massachusetts, is able to do more for the ailing women of America than the family physician. Any woman, therefore, is responsible for her own suffering who will not take the trouble to write to Mrs. Pinkham for advice." Next to the advertisement, Bok printed a photo of Mrs. Pinkham's tombstone in Lynn's Pine Grove Cemetery, showing that she had been dead for twenty-two years. "It was one of the most effective pieces of copy that the magazine used in the campaign," Bok recalled. "It told its story with absolute simplicity, but with deadly force." The *Journal* also listed the alcohol contents of specific patent medicines, drew attention to infant deaths from nostrums containing alcohol, morphine, and opium, and editorialized for legislation requiring content labeling of patent medicines.

The "Beautiful America" campaign, "Devoted to Beautifying Our Homes and Towns,"

began with an assault on the "atrocious" decor of Pullman railroad cars. Women of "the new money class" were using Pullman decor–"a veritable riot of the worst conceivable ideas"–for a standard of home furnishing. Bok was appalled, editorializing against "the wretched decoration of the cars." When Pullman cars were redesigned, Bok sought to eliminate "the hideous bill-board advertisements which defaced the landscape along the lines of the principal roads." Many municipalities passed ordinances regulating the size, character, and location of "the obnoxious bill-boards."

"Progressive women" were urged to form Beautiful America clubs to make their homes, streets, and towns pleasant places to live. Columnist J. Horace McFarland told the magazine's readers: "Together we will clean up our home grounds; we will move for sightly streets and towns; with one accord we will attack, and I hope demolish, unnecessary advertising signs, and reduce the number of hideous electric poles; we will raise our voices for grass and flowers, instead of ashes and garbage, and insist on play grounds and parks."

Bok and the *Ladies' Home Journal* projected a civic role for women exclusively in terms of domesticity. Politics was beyond the pale for the truly "progressive" woman, Bok argued, and woman suffrage was dangerous to the polity. He opposed woman suffrage, insisting in an 18 April 1909 *New York Times* report that the "personal equation" in the "constitutional" nature of women would lead to "a personal element in politics that would be disastrous to parties or policies." Woman suffrage would bring into existence a species of "hen politician as fully alive to political intrigues and tricks as the most out-and-out type of men politicians." The suffragist represented "a dangerous type of woman" who believed "her work in the world lay outside of the home" and who held an "aversion to motherhood." "The feeling of love in this type of woman seems to be stunted," Bok insisted; "in some cases, they ask for love but not for motherhood." The "unwillingness to be a woman in the highest sense" left the suffragist with "nervous energies unspent." "She must have an outlet–any outlet save the natural outlet. She hasn't enough to do; her hands are idle; her mind is not full–to be frank, her lap is not full." Again: "So, for what she cannot find a natural outlet in her home, she goes outside, looks around for what is going on, and plunges into the first excitement she meets. It may be

Bok in the garden at his home in Merion, Pennsylvania

bridge; it may be vivisection; it may be woman's clubs; it may be woman suffrage."

World War I postponed Bok's plans to retire from the editorship of the *Ladies' Home Journal* in 1914. He continued in editorial harness, offering "all the resources of his magazine to the government," serving the nation "by keeping up the morale at home and by helping to meet the problems that would confront the women." His task would be, as President Woodrow Wilson put it: "Give help in the second line of defense." The *Journal* provided comprehensive coverage of women's activities during World War I, which Bok thought was "one of the magazine's most noteworthy achievements. . . . "

On 23 September 1919, thirty years after becoming editor of the *Ladies' Home Journal,* Bok announced his resignation, effective 1 January 1920. One of the last acts of his editorship was the presentation of a series on "the problem of Americanization" that offered "a new conception of American ideals." Bok believed this "a fitting close to the career of a foreign-born Americanized editor." The October 1919 issue was the last under his full editorial control, and Bok could not disguise his pleasure that the issue was oversold with a printing of two million copies, "a re-

cord never before achieved by any magazine," and carried more than one million dollars in advertisements, "another record unattained in any single number of any periodical in the world."

In retirement, Bok devoted his energies to writing and philanthropy. He endowed an advertising award administered by Harvard University's Graduate School of Business, its aim to improve advertising quality through correct English usage and higher artistic and typographical standards; established the American Peace Award of one hundred thousand dollars for "the best practicable plan by which the United States may cooperate with other nations to achieve and preserve the peace of the world"; and built the nearly fifteen-acre Mountain Lake Sanctuary and Singing Tower, with its carillon of seventy-one bells, at Lake Wales, Florida. At the dedication on 1 February 1929, Bok called the tower, made of pink and white Georgia marble, "America's Taj Mahal." His "gift to the American people" was intended "to preach the gospel and influence of beauty reaching out to visitors through tree, shrub, flowers, birds, superb architecture, the music of bells, and the sylvan setting." Above the mantel in the room at the base of the tower are inscribed the words of his grandmother: "Make your world a bit better or more beautiful because you have lived in it."

Bok died of an acute heart attack on 9 January 1930 at his Mountain Lake estate near Lake Wales. His body was placed in a crypt at the base of the Singing Tower. He bequeathed two million dollars from his estate to charities. President Herbert Hoover issued a statement: "The nation has lost a most distinguished and useful citizen whose life must ever be an inspiration to its youth." Bok's longtime friend Calvin Coolidge commented: "His sense of public duty was high, his philanthropies were great, and his desire to improve the condition of the people economically, intellectually, and morally was shown in many ways." George Horace Lorimer, editor of the *Saturday Evening Post,* a Curtis publication, praised Bok as "the pioneer editor of the modern woman's magazine" who "strongly expressed his personality on that field. No man who has edited for women, either before or since, has so accurately gauged his audience."

During his thirty-year editorship, Bok ingratiated himself and the *Ladies' Home Journal* to an immense middle-class audience. His personal editorial style, with its preachy platitudes about civic responsibility, self-help, service, and uplift, deployed sentimentalism to sugarcoat harsh realities, nudging his audience toward modest reforms while projecting an idealized traditional image of the American woman. Often confused about women's role, he urged them to engage in community service but could not endorse their full political participation. Like his Singing Tower, Edward Bok's editorial legacy stands in shimmering contrast to the landscape of twentieth century America.

References:

Michael D. Hummel, "The Attitudes of Edward Bok and the *Ladies' Home Journal* Toward Woman's Role in Society, 1889-1919," Ph.D. dissertation, North Texas State University, 1982;

Salme Harju Steinberg, *Reformer in the Marketplace: Edward W. Bok and The Ladies' Home Journal* (Baton Rouge & London: Louisiana State University Press, 1979).

Papers:

Edward W. Bok's papers are held at the Historical Society of Pennsylvania, Philadelphia; the University of Pennsylvania Library, Philadelphia; the Library of Congress; and the National Archives.

Henry Seidel Canby
(6 September 1878-5 April 1961)

Ralph Engelman
Long Island University

MAJOR POSITIONS HELD: Assistant editor, *Yale Review* (1911-1920); editor in chief, *Literary Review* (1920-1924), *Saturday Review of Literature* (1924-1936).

BOOKS: *The Short Story* (New York: Holt, 1902; enlarged, 1913);
The Short Story in English (New York: Holt, 1909);
English Composition in Theory and Practice, by Canby, Frederick Erastus Pierce, Henry Noble MacCracken, Alfred Arundel May, and Thomas Goddard Wright (New York: Macmillan, 1909; revised, 1912); revised again, by Canby, Pierce, MacCracken, May, and Stith Thompson (New York: Macmillan, 1933);
A Study of the Short Story (New York: Holt, 1913); revised edition, by Canby and Alfred Dashiell (New York: Holt, 1935);
Elements of Composition for Secondary Schools, by Canby and John Baker Opdycke (New York: Macmillan, 1913); revised as *Good English, Book Two: Elements of Composition for Secondary Schools* (New York: Macmillan, 1925);
College Sons and College Fathers (New York & London: Harper, 1915);
Facts, Thought, and Imagination: A Book on Writing, by Canby, Pierce, and Willard Higley Durham (New York: Macmillan, 1917);
Good English, by Canby and Opdycke (New York: Macmillan, 1918); revised as *Good English, Book One: The Mechanics of Composition* (New York: Macmillan, 1925);
Our House (New York: Macmillan, 1919);
Education by Violence: Essays on the War and the Future (New York: Macmillan, 1919);
Everyday Americans (New York: Century, 1920);
Saturday Papers: Essays on Literature from the Literary Review, by Canby, William Rose Benét, and Amy Loveman (New York: Macmillan, 1921);
Definitions: Essays in Contemporary Criticism (New York: Harcourt, Brace, 1922; London: Cape, 1922);

Henry Seidel Canby

Definitions: Essays in Contemporary Criticism, Second Series (New York: Harcourt, Brace, 1924; London: Cape, 1925);
Better Writing (New York: Harcourt, Brace, 1926; London: Cape, 1927);
American Estimates (New York: Harcourt, Brace, 1929; London: Cape, 1929);
Classic Americans: A Study of Eminent American Writers from Irving to Whitman (New York: Harcourt, Brace, 1931);
High School English, 4 volumes, by Canby, Opdycke, and Margaret Gillum (New York: Macmillan, 1932-1935)–expanded edition of *Good English, Book One* and *Book Two;*

39

The Age of Confidence: Life in the Nineties (New York: Farrar & Rinehart, 1934; London: Constable, 1935);

Seven Years' Harvest: Notes on Contemporary Literature (New York: Farrar & Rinehart, 1936);

Alma Mater: The Gothic Age of the American College (New York: Farrar & Rinehart, 1936);

Thoreau: A Biography (Boston: Houghton Mifflin, 1939);

The Brandywine (New York & Toronto: Farrar & Rinehart, 1941);

Extending Good English, by Canby, Opdycke, and Gillum (New York: Macmillan, 1942);

Handbook of English Usage, by Canby and Opdycke (New York: Macmillan, 1942);

A Modern English Course, 3 volumes, by Canby, Opdycke, and Gillum (New York: Macmillan, 1942-1943);

Walt Whitman, An American: A Study in Biography (Boston: Houghton Mifflin, 1943);

The American Scholar and the War, An Address for the Modern Language Association of America (New York: Book-of-the-Month Club, 1943?);

Family History (Cambridge, Mass.: Riverside, 1945);

A New Land Speaking: An Essay on the Importance of a National Literature (Melbourne & London: Melbourne University Press, 1946);

American Memoir (Boston: Houghton Mifflin, 1947);

Turn West, Turn East: Mark Twain and Henry James (Boston: Houghton Mifflin, 1951).

OTHER: *The Book of the Short Story,* edited by Canby and Alexander Jessup (New York & London: Appleton, 1903); enlarged edition, edited by Canby, Jessup, and Robeson Baily (New York: Appleton-Century-Crofts, 1948);

Selections from Robert Louis Stevenson, edited by Canby and Frederick Erastus Pierce (New York: Scribners, 1911);

Poems of John Masefield, edited by Canby, Pierce, and Willard Higley Durham (New York: Macmillan, 1917);

War Aims and Peace Ideals: Selections in Prose and Verse, Illustrating the Aspirations of the Modern World, edited by Canby and Tucker Brooke (New Haven: Yale University Press, 1919);

James Fenimore Cooper, *The Spy: A Tale of the Neutral Ground,* introduction by Canby (New York: Bowling Green, 1929);

"The Best Bait for Mosquitoes," in Stewart Beach's *Short-Story Technique* (Boston: Houghton Mifflin, 1929), pp. 175-205;

Twentieth-Century Poetry, edited by Canby, John Drinkwater, and William Rose Benét (Boston: Houghton Mifflin, 1929);

Ernest Hemingway, *The Sun Also Rises,* introduction by Canby (New York: Modern Library, 1930);

Designed for Reading: An Anthology Drawn from the Saturday Review of Literature, 1924-1934, edited by Canby and others (New York: Macmillan, 1934);

The Works of Thoreau, edited by Canby (Boston: Houghton Mifflin, 1937);

Erskine Caldwell, *Stories by Erskine Caldwell: Twenty-four Representative Stories,* selected, with a foreword, by Canby (New York: Duell, Sloan & Pearce, 1944);

Henry Wadsworth Longfellow, *Favorite Poems,* introduction by Canby (Garden City, N.Y.: Doubleday, 1947);

Literary History of the United States, edited by Canby, Robert E. Spiller, Willard Thorp, and Thomas H. Johnson (New York: Macmillan, 1953).

SELECTED PERIODICAL PUBLICATIONS: "The Teaching of American English," *Education,* 29 (November 1908): 179-186;

"Égalité," *Atlantic Monthly,* 107 (March 1911): 331-338;

"Culture and Prejudice," *Harper's Magazine,* 130 (May 1915): 853-858;

"Radical America," *Century,* 98 (September 1919): 577-583;

"Henry Seidel Canby, By Himself," *Nation,* 119 (8 October 1924): 375-376;

"In Answer to 'Has America a Literary Dictatorship?,'" *Bookman,* 65 (June 1927): 444-445;

"The Magazine Industry," *Independent,* 117 (11 December 1936): 665-667;

"American Summer," *Harper's Magazine,* 181 (June 1940): 78-85;

"Diamond Age of Lecturing," *Atlantic Monthly,* 179 (April 1947): 99-101;

"How the Book-of-the-Month Club Began," *Atlantic Monthly,* 179 (May 1947): 131-135.

As founder of the *Saturday Review of Literature* and the first chairman of the editorial board of the Book-of-the-Month Club, Henry Seidel Canby played a critical role in expanding the appreciation and readership of American literature over a three-decade period during the early twentieth century. Canby, a Quaker, was known for his genteel manners, tolerance, and a wide

First page of an issue of the magazine Canby founded in 1924 (covers were added in 1935)

breadth of interests. As editor and literary critic he sought to strike a balance between academic criticism and popular taste, between tradition and innovation in American letters. Historian Allan Nevins, long associated with Canby, characterized him as "chief moderator over the literary energies of a whole generation."

Canby's ancestors came to America with William Penn. He grew up in an upper-middle-class milieu in Wilmington, Delaware, the son of Edward Tatnall Canby, a founder and president of the Delaware Trust Company, and Ella Augusta Seidel. Canby attended the Friends School in Wilmington and received a Ph.B. from the Sheffield Scientific School at Yale University in 1899. As a result of a growing interest in literature Canby did his graduate work at Yale in English, re-

ceiving a Ph.D. in 1905. Canby taught English at the Sheffield School from 1903 to 1908, inaugurating a lengthy tenure as a member of the Yale faculty.

Canby was the first professor at Yale who specialized in American literature and who sought to establish its legitimacy as a field distinct from English literature. He believed that writing in the United States should be studied in relation to American social history. Canby championed Willa Cather, E. A. Robinson, Robert Frost, and other American writers who in his view had received insufficient critical recognition. Canby criticized the college curriculum of the period for being unresponsive to many of the immediate concerns of American undergraduates and citizens. Canby's first publication, a pamphlet entitled *The*

Short Story (1902), and his book-length study, *The Short Story in English* (1909), became standard works on the subject. He later wrote a series of grammar texts that served a generation of high-school students. Canby's desire to promote American literature and educate beyond the confines of academia shaped his subsequent career as a magazine editor.

In 1911, when Prof. Wilbur L. Cross reconstituted the *Yale Review*, Canby was named assistant editor. Cross wanted the journal to be a national review with appeal to academics and nonacademics alike. Canby, who worked at the *Yale Review* until 1920, ascribed to this experience "my first peeps through the ivory wall, my first professional contacts with contemporary American literature."

In 1920 Canby left the *Yale Review* to become the first editor of the *Literary Review*, a weekly supplement to the *New York Evening Post*—an important development in Canby's career and in the history of American letters in the 1920s. Thomas W. Lamont purchased the *Evening Post*, the renowned newspaper founded by Alexander Hamilton, where William Cullen Bryant, Carl Schurz, and E. L. Godkin had once labored. After World War I it was known primarily for its financial reporting. In order to reassert its tradition of intellectual leadership, Canby was invited to launch the *Literary Review*. Canby's acceptance of this offer marked a shift in the focus of his career from academia to literary journalism.

Canby appointed to the editorial board of the *Literary Review* three persons with whom he would long remain associated: William Rose Benét, the poet and critic; Christopher Morley, a columnist for the *Evening Post*; and Amy Loveman, who managed the newspaper's library. Canby published both serious essays and lighter commentary on modern literature in the pages of the *Literary Review*. Thus a substantial lead review would be supplemented by poetry, cartoons, short causeries, and what Canby termed "enlightened gossip" about authors. Canby contributed to each issue of the supplement front-page editorials on contemporary letters and life. He later referred to these editorials as "experiments in the search for values," and as vehicles to make the *Literary Review* "a magazine devoted to liberal leadership."

During its four years of existence, from 1920 to 1924, the *Literary Review* acquired a national following and was considered by many the best weekly devoted to cultural affairs in the

Caricature of Canby by William Gropper that appeared in the September 1924 issue of the Bookman

United States. However, the financial difficulties of the *New York Evening Post* led to its sale in December 1923 to Cyrus H. K. Curtis, president of the Curtis Publishing Company. Curtis did not share Lamont's aspirations for the *Literary Review*, Canby's editorial team resigned, and the supplement ceased publication soon thereafter.

The demise of the *Literary Review* resulted in the establishment of the *Saturday Review of Literature* as an independent journal through which Canby would reach the pinnacle of his influence as a literary editor. Lamont provided capital for the new venture. Henry R. Luce and Briton Hadden, who had launched *Time* magazine in 1922, offered Canby office space for his new literary weekly. At Yale, Luce and Hadden had studied under Canby and solicited his advice for their planned newsweekly. Time Inc. bought substantial stock in the *Saturday Review of Literature*, and Roy E. Larsen, circulation manager of *Time*, served Canby's magazine in the same capacity.

Thus in 1924 Canby and his staff–Benét, Morley, and Loveman–moved from the *Evening Post* building on Vesey Street in Manhattan to *Time* offices on East thirty-ninth Street, where

Canby and contributing editor Christopher Morley, whose column, "The Bowling Green," was one of the most popular features of the Saturday Review of Literature

they would remain for two years. Canby also retained his old subscription list and magazine format. According to Canby, the *Saturday Review of Literature* "was *The Literary Review* come of age, more humorous, wiser, more literary, better printed, but with the same will to further the cause of good thinking, good feeling, good writing, and good books."

Under Canby's editorship (1924-1936) the *Saturday Review of Literature* became the leading literary weekly in America. It did so in a period of unparalleled ferment in American literature. In the credo which appeared on the front page of the first issue Canby wrote that "criticism, which is part of the living fabric of contemporary literature, must be keenly aware of past and present, and a partisan of both. It must be like a modern university where one seeks Principles, but also works in laboratories of immediate experience

amid the vivid confusion of experiment." Canby wished to avoid what he considered the dogmatism of the *Nation* and the *New Republic*. To underscore its neutrality, the magazine welcomed critiques and rebuttals in response to its articles. The *Saturday Review of Literature* regularly provoked heated contributions to the letters-to-the-editors section, which came to play a major role in the life of the publication. The scope of the magazine's contents was reflected in essays by James Harvey Robinson, Harold Ickes, H. G. Wells, and George Santayana, and open-minded treatment of the writings of John Dos Passos, James Branch Cabell, Robinson Jeffers, and William Faulkner. The magazine served Canby's quest to inform the American public about the leading literary and intellectual currents of the day.

Canby brought both a gentlemanly tolerance and a high level of energy to his editorial work. Norman Cousins, who would serve as editor of the magazine from 1940 to 1971, found Canby physically unprepossessing and diminutive: "But, like John Adams, he benefited from high compression and maximum energy utilization." A profile in the September 1924 issue of the *Bookman*, describing a day in Canby's life, suggested that his frenetic activity was fueled by a passion for American literature and a liberal philosophy, by a "spirit of open mindedness which recognizes divergent claims, combined with the will to achieve harmony between them. . . ."

Despite their common Yale ancestry, the *Saturday Review of Literature* and *Time* magazine soon ended their affiliation. Nonetheless the two magazines continued to share a paternalistic approach that they applied to literature and politics respectively: to raise the awareness of a busy, unschooled public about the unique character and destiny of American society. Canby advocated an authentically American literature rooted in native themes and idioms. Thus Canby's long association with the Book-of-the-Month Club represented an extension of the mission of the *Saturday Review of Literature* to build a broader constituency for American authors.

When Harry Scherman founded the Book-of-the-Month Club in 1926, he established an eminent editorial board to determine book offerings. Canby was named chairman of this editorial board, and Morley and Loveman subsequently joined the board as well. Heywood Broun, Dorothy Canfield, and William Allen White also served as judges. A new monthly magazine played a key role in the undertaking: reviews in *BOMC News* provided the basis for the book selections made by members. The Book-of-the-Month Club quickly became a financial success and an important mediator between publisher and reader in the United States. After two years, membership numbered one hundred thousand, and after twenty years more than nine hundred thousand. Canby seized the opportunity to support a broad spectrum of American authors–Pearl Buck, Arthur Miller, A. B. Guthrie, Sinclair Lewis, Eugene O'Neill, and William Faulkner, among others. By 1949 the club had sold more than one hundred million books.

Canby's authority as editorial director of both the *Saturday Review of Literature* and the Book-of-the-Month Club during the 1920s and 1930s did not go unchallenged. As Joseph Wood Krutch wrote in reference to Canby's approach to American letters, "It may fall between the two stools of mass popularity and cult support. It will certainly be accused of obtuseness or worse by every cult. By the esoteric it will be called philistine, timid, and safe. And, of course, it will be labeled by the superior as middlebrow." In 1927, a year after the establishment of the Book-of-the-Month Club, an article in the April issue of the *Bookman* asked, "Has America A Literary Dictatorship?" The anonymous author criticized the venture "as a literary Sears-Roebuck affair" that would foster standardization and mediocrity in American literature. The article suggested that Canby, by linking commerce and criticism, had forsaken the opportunity to become the nation's leading literary critic.

In response Canby asked, "Would you have all reading cease until the rare masterpiece is produced? Are men made for books, or books for men?" Reflecting on his career two decades later in *American Memoir* (1947), Canby wrote that he had gladly sacrificed a more prestigious academic career to make literature a more important part of mainstream American culture.

Others challenged Canby's commitment–both literary and political–to the *juste milieu*. Malcolm Cowley, a frequent contributor to the *Saturday Review of Literature*, once parodied Canby's quest for the golden mean in a mock news bulletin in the journal *Aesthete 1925*: "Editor Outlines Middle Course Between Heaven and Hell. Solution Deemed Acceptable to Both Modernists and Fundamentalists."

The civil tone of the *Saturday Review of Literature* was in marked contrast to the more raucous criticism of American life and letters contained in H. L. Mencken's *American Mercury*. "In Canby," Mencken remarked, "a trace of the schoolmaster sticks. He tries to give his customers their honest money's worth in light and leading." In the 1920s Canby felt himself increasingly estranged from a new generation of writers that included F. Scott Fitzgerald, E. E. Cummings, and Ernest Hemingway. Ezra Pound and Edmund Wilson, among others, considered Canby a well-entrenched foe of the literary avant-garde.

Moreover, Canby had little insight into the contending forces of communism and fascism in the 1930s. This epoch of ideological polarization would not be propitious for a person about whom it could be said: "No other man . . . was more at home with a qualifying clause." He turned his attention increasingly to the past, writing a cycle of memoirs as well as biographies of his two favorite authors: *Thoreau: A Biography*

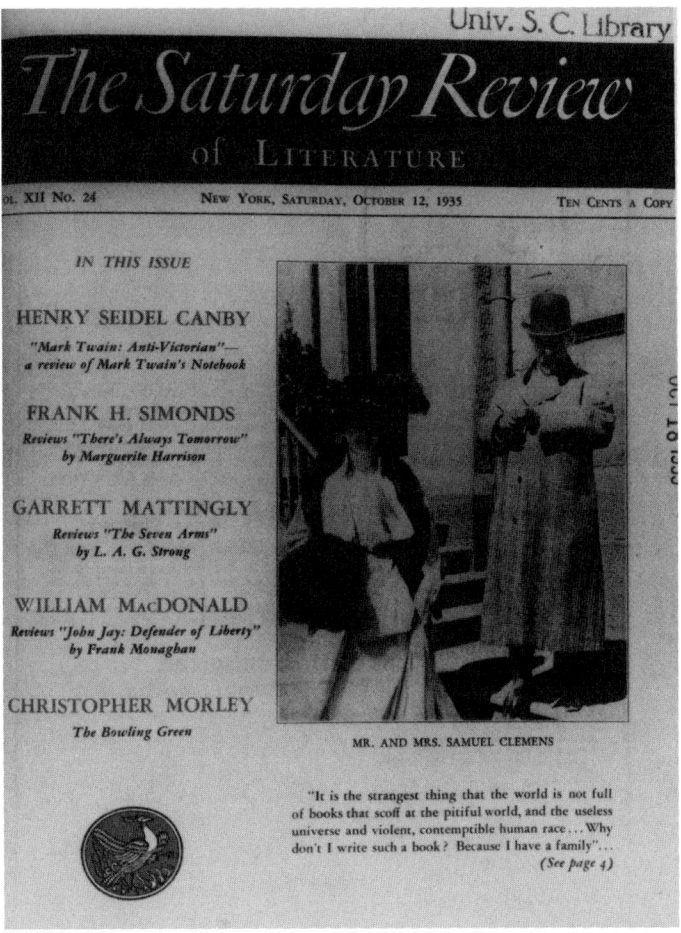

Cover for an issue of the magazine Canby created to "further the cause of good thinking, good feeling, good writing, and good books"

(1939) and *Walt Whitman, An American: A Study in Biography* (1943). Despite his moderate rebellion against the literary academic establishment as a young man, LeRoy Harvey's study of Canby's early years suggested that his sensibilities remained rooted in the liberalism of the nineteenth century: "He would insist that his life had been 'typically American,' but he had known only men and women of means, well-bred and educable, with deep roots in an older America–and he would write and speak for them." Literary historian Fred B. Millett placed Canby in "the genteel wing of the conservative sociological group" and added, "No ardent propagandist for his critical faith, he made the *Saturday Review of Literature* an organ for criticism . . . vague as to principles and tepid as to judgments. . . ."

Canby continued to play an important role in American letters until shortly before his death on 5 April 1961. He resigned as editor of the *Saturday Review of Literature* in 1936, at a time when

the magazine experienced a financial crisis. Canby described his successor, Bernard De Voto, as "a new helmsman more at home than I among the reefs of controversial public affairs." Canby remained a contributing editor and member of the editorial board for nearly two decades, during which time the magazine came under the stewardship of Norman Cousins and shortened its name to the *Saturday Review*. Canby retained his position as chairman of the editorial board of the Book-of-the-Month Club until 1954.

Through his career Canby remained a committed internationalist and foe of censorship. During World War I he did liaison work for the British Ministry of Information to promote understanding among the Allies. This experience inspired a collection of essays on the war and on British and American traditions entitled *Education by Violence: Essays on the War and the Future* (1919). During World War II Canby once again served the Allied cause as a liaison officer of the United

States Office of War Information in Australia and New Zealand.

In addition, Canby was an active participant in the efforts of the P.E.N. International Clubs to promote international understanding and freedom of expression. For example, it was Canby who introduced the resolution at the tumultuous P.E.N. congress in Dubrovnik, Yugoslavia, in 1933 condemning cultural repression in Fascist Italy and Nazi Germany. Canby served as president of the P.E.N. American Center in 1926-1928 and 1948-1949. Opposing censorship at home as well as abroad, Canby criticized the threat to freedom of expression posed by McCarthyism. Thus in 1948 he protested the banning of the *Nation* magazine from school libraries in New York City, and in 1955 he signed a petition calling upon the United States Supreme Court to declare the Internal Security Act unconstitutional.

Canby's career—as literary editor and foe of censorship—was grounded in a desire to extend the marketplace of books and ideas. In *American Memoir* he characterized his ethos as "the Jeffersonian belief in the necessity of education for a successful democracy. I wanted to go in for adult education in the value of books—all kinds of books, foreign as well as native, but particularly the current books of our own country. I wished to make criticism first of all a teaching job, backed up by explorations and estimates of new ideas."

Canby observed that he grew up in "the age of the magazine," a medium he considered destined to play a more important cultural role in America than in Europe. He fashioned the *Saturday Review of Literature* into an effective instrument to promote American authors. As the guiding force behind both the leading literary review and book club of his day, Canby presided over the transition to a predominantly middle-class literary culture in the United States. In a tribute to Canby in the 29 August 1961 issue of the *Satur-* *day Review* Malcolm Cowley wrote that "his essential purpose was to encourage the writing of good books by finding more readers for them." He added that never far from Canby's mind was Walt Whitman's maxim, "To have great poets there must be great audiences too."

References:

Sherilyn Cox Bennion, "*Saturday Review:* From Literature to Life," Ph.D. dissertation, Syracuse University, 1968;

Norman Cousins, *Present Tense: An American Editor's Odyssey* (New York: McGraw-Hill, 1967);

Norman Foerster, "The Literary Historians," *Bookman,* 71 (July 1930): 365-374;

LeRoy Harvey, "Days of Confidence: The Early Life of Henry Seidel Canby," Ph.D. dissertation, University of Michigan, 1984;

"Has America a Literary Dictatorship?," *Bookman,* 65 (April 1927): 191-199;

Joseph Wood Krutch, Introduction to The "*Saturday Review*" *Treasury,* edited by John Haverstick (New York: Simon & Schuster, 1957);

Charles Lee, *The Hidden Public: The Story of the Book-of-the-Month Club* (Garden City, N.Y.: Doubleday, 1958);

"The Literary Spotlight: Henry Seidel Canby," *Bookman,* 60 (September 1924): 66-70;

Fred B. Millett, *Contemporary American Authors* (New York: Harcourt, Brace, 1944).

Papers:

The Division of Manuscripts and Archives of Sterling Memorial Library and the American Literature Collection of the Beinecke Library at Yale University possess manuscripts and correspondence of Henry Seidel Canby spanning a fourteen-year period. Significant collections of Canby's correspondence are also housed at the Butler Library of Columbia University, the Van Pelt Library of the University of Pennsylvania, and the American Academy of Arts and Letters in New York.

Edna Woolman Chase

(14 March 1877-20 March 1957)

Janene Roberts
Virginia Polytechnic Institute and State University

MAJOR POSITION HELD: Editor, *Vogue* (1914-1952).

BOOK: *Always in Vogue,* by Chase and Ilka Chase (Garden City, N.Y.: Doubleday, 1954).

For nearly half a century, Edna Woolman Chase reigned as America's "high priestess of fashion" in her position as editor of *Vogue.* She virtually invented fashion journalism and set a high standard of excellence for her profession. Under her stewardship, *Vogue* grew from an amateur society gazette to the world's premier fashion magazine. For her contributions to the fashion industry, Chase received many accolades and awards, including the Legion of Honor from France.

Born to Franklyn Alloway and Laura Woolman in Asbury Park, New Jersey, on 14 March 1877, Chase was reared by her maternal Quaker grandparents after her parents divorced. She attended a country school and was tutored by her grandfather in the evenings. Her mother, who lived in New York City with her second husband, visited frequently. In her teens, Chase went to live with her mother in a small New York apartment. She followed newspaper accounts of society debutantes and avidly took in the details of their balls, dinners, escorts, and, of course, their gowns, jewels, furs, and feathers. Envying these wealthy girls her own age, Chase knew she had little prospect of emulating them. She would have to earn her own living.

In October 1895 Chase, eighteen, was looking for some way to earn money for Christmas presents. A friend who worked at *Vogue* helped her get a temporary job addressing envelopes for the three-year-old weekly. Willing to perform any task that came her way, she began to absorb editorial policies and angles on the publishing business. Chase soon attracted the notice of the magazine's founder and publisher, Arthur Baldwin Turnure. Finding her bright, hardworking, and conscientious, Turnure increasingly came to rely on her.

In its early years *Vogue* had not yet established its identity as a women's fashion magazine. It was a small, elegant society sheet, carrying fiction and poetry as well as articles on social affairs, fashions, interior decoration, etiquette, and the theater. Men's fashions and sports played a large role in the young *Vogue,* which was intended to please both ladies and gentlemen of distinction. The magazine's contributors were mostly personal friends of the publisher, who recruited them more for their social standing and knowledge of correct form than for their literary talents.

With its eclectic, well-bred, though decidedly amateur quality, *Vogue* was popular, though it attracted very little advertising. In the late 1890s Tom McCready was hired as advertising manager to turn this situation around. He instigated the development of *Vogue* primarily as a fashion magazine and shopping guide rather than a gazette of social activities. By concentrating on the New York fashion scene, *Vogue* began to garner advertisers of fashion-related merchandise, who expected the magazine's smart set of subscribers to pay as much attention to its big, well-illustrated advertisements as its text and editorial drawings. Thus evolved the symbiotic relationship between the magazine's journalism and its advertising which persists today.

On 5 January 1904 Chase married Francis Dane Chase, a banker's son who lacked the self-discipline to succeed in business. By the time she had her daughter, Ilka, in 1905, Chase realized she would have to bear the burden of supporting her alone. Chase separated from and eventually divorced Frank Chase. In 1921 she married Richard T. Newton, an English automotive engineer and inventor, with whom she remained until his death in 1950.

Turnure died in 1906, and three years later Condé Nast purchased *Vogue.* At first apprehensive about her new boss, Chase eventually developed a warm friendship and productive working relationship with him. Marie L. Harrison,

Edna Woolman Chase, circa 1898

tion about what would charm *Vogue* readers and enhance the magazine's prestige, influence, and circulation. The designs were immensely popular. One prizewinning dress was copied by Florenz Ziegfeld for his "Midnight Frolics."

In 1914, after Harrison retired, Chase became editor "by a process of osmosis" rather than competition for the post. In her nineteen years with the company, she had absorbed *Vogue*, and it had absorbed her. Magazine historian Frank Luther Mott describes her as "the ideal editor for the period of expansion on which the magazine was entering."

Nast was a dedicated expansionist. In 1913, while *Vogue* and its pattern business were thriving, he bought a magazine called *Dress and Vanity Fair*, which soon became *Vanity Fair*. In 1915 he acquired *House and Garden*. During this period he also added the French *Gazette du Bon Ton* to his collection. The British edition of *Vogue* was established during World War I and the French edition shortly after the war ended. Against Chase's advice, Nast took over a fashion supplement of the famous French magazine *L'Illustration* in 1921 and rechristened it *Jardin des Modes*. Chase did not share Nast's enthusiasm for rapid growth and particularly opposed the development, in 1927, of a German edition of *Vogue*, feeling that the German hausfrau lacked the requisite taste to ensure the magazine's success (the German edition was a failure).

Though lacking Nast's expansionist ambitions, Chase contributed to the growing affluence and influence of the magazine with her innovative ideas. Her first coup as editor, in 1914, was her idea to organize the first New York fashion show. At that time, Paris was the unrivaled center of the fashion world. When the outbreak of war in France interrupted business in the great Paris houses, the fashion press in America was left with nothing to cover. Chase conceived the idea of "The Fashion Fête," an exhibition of live models wearing original creations by the best New York designers. Proceeds from the admission charge would be donated to the Committee of Mercy to aid widows and orphans of the Allied countries. The leading New York fashion houses readily agreed to participate. But the success of the Fête depended on the patronage of the social elite, and Nast doubted that society women would work to advance the cause of commerce, even in the guise of charity. However, Chase managed to persuade the leading society matron of the period, Mrs. Stuyvesant Fish, to par-

Turnure's sister-in-law, remained as editor of *Vogue*, but when a financial disagreement chilled Harrison's relationship with Nast, Chase, as reported in her autobiography, *Always in Vogue* (1954), acted as a "human telephone system between publisher and editor." Harrison relegated more and more authority to Chase, who soon was performing the duties of managing editor.

During that time Chase came up with an idea that initially met with Nast's resistance but proved quite successful. Fancy-dress balls were very popular in 1911, and *Vogue* had published several pages of photographs of society women in their costumes, many of which had been borrowed from the Metropolitan Opera. Unimpressed by the opulent but conventional attire, Chase proposed to commission *Vogue* artists to design original costumes which would be published in the magazine. Nast liked the showy operatic garments and opposed the idea, but Chase chipped away at him until he relented. As on many future occasions, Chase demonstrated a fine intui-

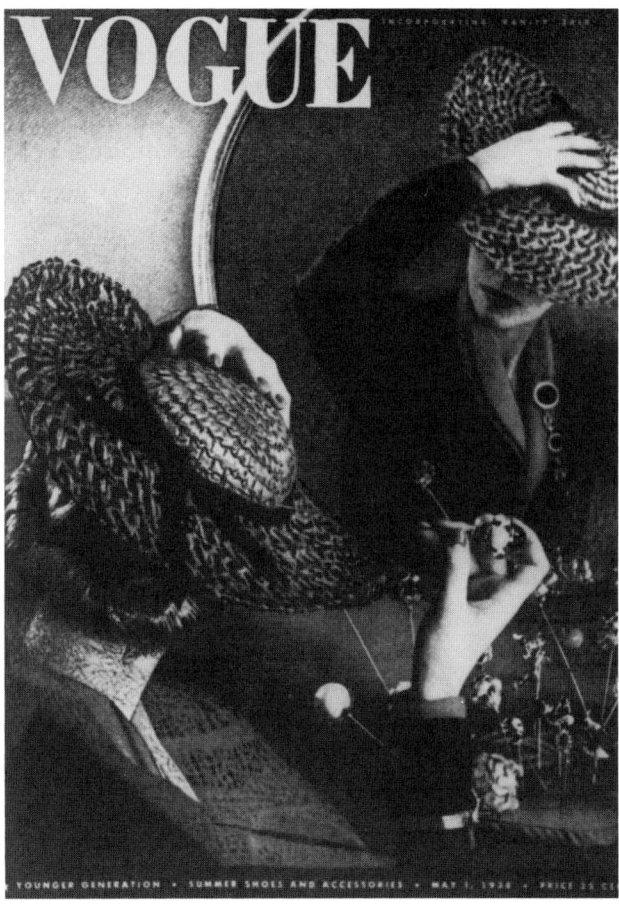

Cover for an issue of the magazine Chase edited from 1914 until 1952 (copyright 1938, Condé Nast, Inc.)

ticipate in the show by appealing to her patriotism and her vanity; the rest of the smart set fell in line. For the most part, the gowns displayed by the American couturiers were not strikingly original, but they upheld the tradition of style and elegance that was threatened by war abroad.

Encouraged by the enormous publicity it received for the Fête, *Vogue* sponsored many fashion shows thereafter. Despite the war, the Paris establishments were back in business within a short time; but they feared that *Vogue* would now back American fashion at their expense. To reassure them that *Vogue* still valued its special relationship with the French couture, Chase planned a New York show for them a year later. By organizing such events, *Vogue* dramatically increased its prestige and prosperity. No longer a mere reporter of fashion, *Vogue* was becoming a powerful force in the business and politics of fashion.

Though Nast's genius was for expansion and Chase's for innovation, both recognized the importance of advertising to the success of the magazine. Catering to a small but select audience—the wealthy and sophisticated—Nast concentrated on attracting advertisers of luxury goods. This strategy worked: by 1926 *Vogue* had the highest annual income of all American magazines, even though its circulation was only 150,000.

The unabashedly snobbish mission of *Vogue* was to set the standard of taste and elegance for people of wealth, culture, and social position. To achieve this goal in all four editions of *Vogue*, Chase tried to include on each staff one editor with a flair for clothes, one close to the artistic and literary community, and one who moved in high social circles. Presiding over her far-flung, international staff of talented but often temperamental artists and editors required just the right combination of diplomacy and firmness. Although she encouraged dissent among the staff, liking "nothing better than a sharp exchange of opposing views," her decisions were final. Known by all who worked with her to be difficult to please, she considered her perfectionism one of her greatest assets as an editor (in a 1947 *Time* magazine profile she stated: "my wastebasket is my strongest ally"). Her demands on her staff were formidable, but the excellence of the final product justified Chase's zeal. She was named editor in chief of all *Vogue* editions in 1929.

Chase dominated every aspect of the magazine's production. One of her greatest contributions to the magazine was in attracting talented artists to its staff. She hired Heyworth Campbell, who, as art director, designed an elegant new format. Chase expanded the use of photography and commissioned gifted artists to illustrate the magazine. The application of modern art to the magazine's fashion illustrations and advertisements gave *Vogue* particular distinction. At times, however, Chase had to resolve a conflict between business and art, and she usually resolved in favor of business. Knowing that subscribers would not purchase a dress unless they could see its design, Chase insisted on accurate illustrations. And when the magazine's avant-garde photographers swathed their subjects in dark shadows, Chase had this emphatic bulletin posted in the studio: "Concentrate completely on showing the *dress, light it for this purpose* and if that can't be done with art then art be damned. *Show the dress.*"

Another perennial conflict Chase faced throughout her career was the struggle between taste and money. As editor, it was her responsibility to maintain the high standards of taste for which *Vogue* was famous. At the same time, she was loath to offend advertisers by refusing to feature merchandise she considered unworthy. In these conflicts, Chase's strict judgment in matters of taste prevailed. Manufacturers advertised in *Vogue* because of its prestige, she reasoned, and to allow bad taste to creep into the editorial pages in order to win or keep advertisers would ultimately destroy that prestige and drive all the advertisers away.

Throughout its history, *Vogue* has shown a sporadic interest in literature, and several well-known writers have been published in its pages. In 1915 Dorothy Parker got her first break at *Vogue*, writing captions and special features, such as "Interior Desecration" and "Life on a Permanent Wave." However, Chase believed, with good reason, that the magazine's clear focus on fashion and beauty was responsible for its fabulous success. She did not want to blur this focus by running fiction, poetry, or other charming distractions. This editorial position was vindicated in

the 1920s. Dorothy Todd, then the editor of the British *Vogue*, was a passionate devotee of art and literature. She hobnobbed with the Bloomsbury Group of English artists and intellectuals who frequently contributed to the magazine. With an almost infallible eye for genius, Todd was the first in England to show Jean Cocteau's painting and the first to publish Gertrude Stein's verse and photographs of Le Corbusier's architecture. At the same time she gave short shrift to the service features, such as "Seen in the Shops" and "Smart Fashions for Limited Incomes," that were so popular in the American edition. As the artistic currency of the British *Vogue* soared, advertising revenues plummeted. With Nast seriously considering closing down the British edition, Chase hastened to London to put the magazine back on the right track.

When *Vanity Fair* fell victim to the Depression in 1936, it was merged with *Vogue*, bringing with it a distinguished stable of contributing writers, such as Thomas Wolfe and William Saroyan. Chase was not averse to having such literary luminaries grace the pages of *Vogue*, but she insisted that their features be relevant to the magazine's chosen themes. For example, in 1937, inspired by the majesty of the Triborough Bridge, Chase decided to devote an entire issue of *Vogue* to the wonders of America, and she was delighted to engage Wolfe to write the introductory article, "Prologue to America." By 1940 the magazine's editorial policy was fixed: the magazine would accept articles but no fiction. And Nast's successor, Iva Sergei Voidato ("Pat") Patcévitch, agreed with Chase that running fiction in a fashion magazine "shows a lack of sustained thinking . . . it is distracting."

For the most part, Chase tried to keep *Vogue* apolitical. In its early years, *Vogue* had spoken out, predictably, against woman suffrage, stressing "important public work" that women could "perform without the ballot." Then World War I forced *Vogue* to acknowledge the tragic situation abroad, if only because of its effect on the fashion business. A bitter joke of the time noted that the latest style in Paris was mourning. Finally, with the advent of World War II, Chase decided readers of *Vogue* must "see the world they lived in." The magazine's roving correspondent, Mary Jean Kemper, sent back reports from Asia and Europe that had nothing to do with hats and hemlines. And at the end of the war, *Vogue* printed pictures of the atrocities at Buchenwald. This sober-mindedness prevailed throughout the

Chase with Richardson Wright, editor of House & Garden, *and Frank Crowninshield, editor of* Vanity Fair *(Iva Patcévitch)*

1940s as *Vogue* ran several serious articles by well-known writers; in the July 1945 issue, for example, Owen Lattimore wrote "China is Changing," Jean-Paul Sartre contributed "New Writing in France," and Senator William Fulbright provided "The Price of Peace." Other contributors during the 1940s included Bertrand Russell, Jean Cocteau, and Margaret Mead. Whenever world events would permit it, however, Chase wanted *Vogue* to take a leading role in its chosen domain of fashion and stay out of politics.

Chase was unapologetic about the snobbish and, to some, trivial mission of *Vogue*. Her reply to an editorialist who, in 1940, predicted the extinction of *Vogue* in a world absorbed in more serious concerns, reveals her conviction that the magazine plays an important role in preserving the art of civilized living. To counter the assertion that *Vogue* was near death, she pointed out that fashion was one of the top grossing industries in America and that more copies of *Vogue* were sold during the war than during peacetime. And in answer to the charge that fashion is frivolous, she

states in *Always in Vogue*: "behind those shop windows are not only a vast army of garment workers, but millions of other people who design, manufacture, distribute, advertise, sell, alter, repair, clean and deliver fashion merchandise. Fashion, to them . . . is bread and meat and coal and comfort and security." Finally, with a touch of wit that relieves her earnestness, she concludes: "We shall not be unmindful of changing times, however. If the new order is to be one of sackcloth and ashes, we think some women will wear theirs with a difference! Perhaps *Vogue* will cut the pattern for them, for we still believe we shall survive."

Of all the outstanding personal characteristics that made Chase such a successful editor, loyalty may have been foremost. She was absolutely devoted to the company, which she regarded as her real home. From her first day on the job, she "felt a proprietary interest in the whole organization." And in her autobiography she rankles at the memory of William Randolph Hearst's frequent raids on the magazine's best talent and scorns the disloyalty of those who left *Vogue* after having been trained and cherished there. Especially galling was the defection of Carmel Snow, who was being groomed to succeed Chase. Lured by offers of more money and less work, Snow left in 1932 to become editor of William Randolph Hearst's rival fashion magazine, *Harper's Bazaar.*

Although Chase's pronouncements on fashion were generally taken to heart not only by thousands of readers, but also by manufacturers, merchants, and designers throughout the world, she was not always successful in dictating styles. For years she waged an unsuccessful campaign against open-toed, open-backed shoes for street wear. Her disapprobation was also powerless against the trend toward using gaunt fashion models who, in her opinion, did not look like ladies ("I've never seen so many slatterns in my life," she once remarked of the new wave of models).

At seventy-five Chase retired from active editing, becoming chairman of the editorial board of *Vogue* in 1952. Two years later she cowrote *Always in Vogue* with her daughter, Ilka Chase, an actress and author. In an era when women were not encouraged to pursue full-time careers, Chase regarded the fashion business as one of the few fields in which women could be extremely successful. She prided herself on having made *Vogue* a training school for hundreds of talented young women who went on to make their marks in every area of the fashion industry. Chase admitted she probably had missed a good deal in the "one-goal" life she had led but added, "I know too that everything else together could not have made up the sum of satisfaction I have derived from my job." In March 1957 she died of a heart attack while on vacation in Sarasota, Florida.

References:

"Fifty-nine Years in Fashion," *Life,* 37 (8 November 1954): 123-127;

Frank Luther Mott, *A History of American Magazine,* volume 4 (Cambridge, Mass.: Harvard University Press, 1938-1958), pp. 756-762.

Robert J. Collier

(17 June 1876-17 April 1918)

Donald R. Avery
University of Southern Mississippi

MAJOR POSITIONS HELD: Editor (1898-1902, 1912-1913) and publisher (1909-1918), *Collier's, the National Weekly*; president, P. F. Collier and Son (1909-1918).

SELECTED PERIODICAL PUBLICATIONS: "1879-1909," *Collier's*, 42 (2 January 1909): 13;
"Collier's and the Post-Office," *Collier's*, 44 (29 January 1910): 7;
"Lincoln Farm Becomes the Property of the Nation," *Collier's*, 57 (9 September 1916): 19.

If libel suits are a measure of a magazine publisher's success, then Robert J. Collier had more than his share. He was sued often, he liked to believe, because he championed the people's causes (primarily through muckraking). He and his magazine were sued by business tycoons that his publication had attacked; by other publishers, most notably William Randolph Hearst; and even by advertisers, because he did not permit all comers to advertise in his magazine.

Through his social, political, and business contacts, Collier had the attention, if not always the active support, of many leaders of the period. Certainly, the muckraking work done by *Collier's* while he was editor and publisher had enormous impact in the areas of policy development and the passage of statutory remedies for a number of societal ills in the early part of this century. After all, Pres. Theodore Roosevelt continued to praise the work of *Collier's* long after he began to attack other muckraking publications. Collier also provided the model for a publisher concerned with protecting consumers long before the term "consumer protection" entered the language. Unlike other publishers and editors of the day, Collier would often attack advertising, the very hand that fed his publication. Not only would Collier turn down advertising for questionable and dangerous medicines, his magazine would actually provide a warning for its readers by naming the individual products.

Robert J. Collier

Robert J. Collier was born in New York City on 17 June 1876 to Peter Fenelon and Katherine Louise Dunne Collier. He attended schools in New York and was graduated from Georgetown University in 1894. He also studied for a year each at Oxford and Harvard universities before giving up educational pursuits to join his father's publishing business, P. F. Collier and Son. While he worked most of his adult life for the publishing house, because of illness and outside activities he actually ran the business for only about five years following his father's death in 1909. However, it is his work with one division of the publishing company, *Collier's, the National Weekly*, for which Collier is best known.

To understand the message of the magazine it is necessary to understand its founder, Collier's father, Peter F. Collier. The elder Collier arrived from his native Ireland just after the American Civil War. As a lad he intended to enter the priesthood, and he actually attended St. Mary's Seminary in Cincinnati for a time. However, by the early 1870s he had abandoned study for the priesthood and become a salesman for a publisher of Catholic books in New York City. It was during this period that he developed the idea that would make a success of his own later publishing ventures: he would sell books on the installment plan.

P. F. Collier first published only Catholic books, which he sold on an installment basis. Following some marginal success in the field, he began to publish standard works as well. It was during this period, in 1876, that his only child, Robert Joseph Collier, was born. Because P. F. Collier was interested in books of lasting value, he began in 1877 to publish the works of William Shakespeare and Charles Dickens and sell them inexpensively and in small installments so that common people could read the classics. In fact, Collier pioneered the sale of books by subscription. Later with his son he published *The Harvard Classics,* the so-called "Five-Foot Shelf of Books." His early work was actually printed under contract with several New York printers and binders. However, by the early 1880s Collier began to develop one of the best-equipped printing plants in the country. P. F. Collier is said to have published some fifty million books during the remaining years of his life. His publishing empire included books, encyclopedias, and magazines.

In 1888 P. F. Collier founded a general weekly magazine named *Once a Week.* This popular family-oriented publication was established, his critics said, to promote the firm's book publishing. In 1896 the magazine's name was changed to *Collier's, the National Weekly,* and under a group of very capable editors, the most important of whom was Norman Hapgood, the magazine grew in circulation and stature. Toward the end of his life Collier publicly gave his son much of the credit for the success of *Collier's.* P. F. Collier died on 24 April 1909, and his son took over management of the firm.

While his father might give him much of the credit for the magazine's success, the younger Collier served only two stints as editor, 1898-1902 and 1912-1913. His second period as editor

occurred when Hapgood resigned (some say he was fired) in an editorial dispute over whether Woodrow Wilson or Theodore Roosevelt should get the magazine's endorsement for president. *Collier's* endorsed Roosevelt. Although Collier edited the magazine for only about five years, his influence at the publication was certainly much greater than his short tenure as editor suggests.

However, as a businessman, Collier left much to be desired. When he took over the business in 1909, the company began a skid that ended with its absorption by the Crowell Publishing Company in 1919. Collier was not very good at managing the firm's finances, and he began borrowing money immediately upon his father's death, a practice that continued until the company was sold. Despite his education, which served him well as editor, Collier was not prepared to run a major company.

In its early years *Collier's* produced a legacy of journalistic achievement. It was a muckraking magazine that stood with the best during the first decade of the twentieth century, the heyday of crusading magazines. The publications appeared at times single-minded in their crusades, which fits Roosevelt's characterization of the muckrakers. Roosevelt, who at first supported the muckrakers but later took umbrage at some of their attacks, likened the crusaders to the Man with the Muckrake in *Pilgrim's Progress,* a character so single-minded that he would not look up from his raking even when a crown was offered. Among the subjects for the muckrakers were exposés on patent medicines, city slums, monopolies, stock market fraud, and advertising.

Collier's was particularly concerned with the adulteration of medicines and foods and published extensively on the subjects. Fraud in the Department of the Interior and do-nothing politicians were subjects that received considerable attention. The magazine favored the income tax, child labor laws, and woman suffrage. It was particularly harsh in its attacks on questionable news and advertising practices of newspapers. It was this last concern that led to the magazine's most lasting contribution to journalism: Will Irwin's "The American Newspaper," which ran as a series of fifteen articles in *Collier's* from January to July 1911.

Despite the fact that the muckraking era had about run its course by 1911, not one of the muckraking journals had sought to find corruption and evil in newspapers themselves. Although writers had examined political and business scan-

Covers for the magazine that Collier published from 1909 until his death in 1918

dals involving newspapers, no one had undertaken a major investigation of the press itself. When *Collier's* assigned Irwin to undertake such an investigation, the editor, Hapgood, and publisher, Collier, expected that Irwin would return with his usual scathing muckraking piece. After all, his earlier work had included studies of fake spirit mediums and prohibition. What *Collier's* got was not so much a muckraking story as a carefully researched study of the origins, purposes, and principles of journalism. That Collier really wanted such a contemporary history seems clear from Irwin's introduction, in which he gives the publisher credit for the scope of the work.

While Collier may have hoped to receive from Irwin a significant history of journalism, it is Irwin's account of contemporary journalism that gives the series its importance. Irwin wrote of the era of Yellow Journalism, advertising influence, business alliances with newspapers, and societal influence over the press. His description of the rise of Yellow Journalism and the reasons it

flourished is particularly incisive. It was also a time of powerful advertising influence over news content. This part of the series led directly to a libel suit against *Collier's* by William Randolph Hearst. In fact, a Hearst attorney threatened *Collier's* with a libel suit before the series ever ran. *Collier's* won, as it did in the many other libel suits it faced. The series was also concerned with the power exerted over the newspaper industry by business and other interests.

Collier and his magazine found themselves in court numerous times in matters growing out of his personal and journalistic crusades. As the Hearst libel suit was concerned with a muckraking issue, so was a blackmailing case involving the Postum Cereal Company. A claim by the makers of a Post cereal that its products had medical value had been attacked vigorously by *Collier's*. Postum claimed in an advertising campaign that *Collier's* had attacked their product because Postum would not advertise in the magazine. Collier sued Postum for libel, citing the blackmail

Collier in 1909, seated next to a portrait of his father, P. F. Collier

charge. Collier won, though the case was later overturned on appeal. Another court case shows a dark side of Collier's character. *Town Topics*, a New York society journal, made disparaging remarks about Theodore Roosevelt's daughter Alice Roosevelt, a personal friend of Collier's. Collier used his magazine to liken the society sheet's editor to a forger and a horse thief. Because he was editor, Hapgood was named in an indictment for criminal libel. However, the attorneys for *Collier's* were able to obtain Hapgood's acquittal.

Collier's published the works of many of the best-known muckrakers of the day. These included Louise Eberle, Frank Norris, Louis R. Glavis, Finley Peter Dunne, and Mark Sullivan, among others. Dunne and Sullivan were both editors at *Collier's* in addition to appearing in its pages. Many other writers and illustrators, including Edith Wharton, P. G. Wodehouse, Frederic Remington, Howard Chandler Christy, and

James Montgomery Flagg, appeared in the magazine.

Throughout its early years *Collier's* was a fierce and independent voice that often seemed to be going against the current of other publications. It refused advertising for alcoholic beverages, patent medicines, medical apparatuses, and get-rich-quick schemes, all in keeping with Collier's publicly stated intention of truth-telling and serving the best interests of the public.

For all practical purposes, Collier began and ended his journalism career as a correspondent for *Collier's*. He left Harvard University in 1896 to become a correspondent in Cuba for the magazine, and the day he died he had just returned from Europe, where he supervised correspondents and contributed material on the conduct of World War I. Following a serious illness (press accounts mention both a stroke and uremic poisoning) in 1914, Collier turned over the operation of P. F. Collier and Son to three business associ-

The American Newspaper

A Study of Journalism in Its Relation to the Public

 ILL IRWIN has spent over a year and a half in the study and investigation of a subject which, strangely enough, never yet has been adequately treated by any writer or any magazine. He has written fourteen articles which are to appear approximately every other week, with supplementary articles by other writers in the issues between. This is not a muckraking series. It is historical, descriptive, and analytical—and, naturally, as such, is bound to disclose the evil as well as the good side of our press.

Everybody knows there is a good side as well as a bad side to our American journalistic system. But how many of us know how to define or explain either? Every one of us reads newspapers every day. Every day we take into our system their statements, their opinions, their pictures of life. Our opinions are largely formed by the newspapers we read. On the other hand, we, the public, help to create the newspapers. Our habits, our tastes, our wishes are the main factors in determining their course. Yet how much do we, how much do you, MR. READER, know about newspapers—about the newspaper that comes into your house every morning? Practically nothing.

COLLIER'S believes that the public ought to be in closer touch with these sources of opinion and power. We expect therefore to devote COLLIER'S in 1911 mainly to the purpose of presenting a series of articles on the newspaper as a force in society.

We shall give the history of the newspaper; show why free government could not exist without it; describe the value of yellow journalism, and its harm. We shall answer such questions as: What is News? We shall explain the forces which a newspaper is compelled to face, including the financier, the advertiser, and the general reader. Part of the series will be written by experts from the inside. Part will present the views of outsiders. We shall take up journalism in various specific places. Residents of Boston, San Francisco, Charleston, Chicago, and many other towns and cities will not only learn new things about their newspapers, but will tell us what they think about them.

It would be easy to muckrake American journalism—to take an instance here, a defect there, and by massing detrimental truths present a picture of a press untrue to its ancient tribunate of the people.

We have avoided that. We have tried to take the broad view of journalism, the virtues with the defects.

The series is alive with interest, for we are dealing with the most romantic calling of modern times. Stories of the crises in journalism; glimpses of great characters hidden from the public view in the anonymity which clouds the profession; intimate discussion of the failings and strengths of individual American newspapers—perhaps your own paper—make these articles as interesting as they are important.

We have taken such precautions to cover the ground fully that the American people at the end of 1911 will understand the press better than they understand it to-day. They will read it more intelligently. They will control it more effectually.

The articles of this series will appear in the following order:

"The Power of the Press" . . . . . . January 21

What a newspaper is, and what it is not. The dominance and use of the news-function in modern journalism. The mistakes of popular commentators on journalism, and the difficulty which confronts the students of the subject.

The Dim Beginnings . . . . February 4

A brief history of early English and American journalism. The dominance of the editorial page in the primitive newspaper. James Gordon Bennett's discovery of news. The passing of the old editorial journalism. Charles A. Dana's influence on the art of newspaper writing. The growth of mechanical devices and of circulations. The ethical and technical condition of journalism in the decade between 1870 and 1880.

The Fourth Current . . . . February 18

Joseph Pulitzer, with the St. Louis "Post-Dispatch," introduces a method new to journalism—fighting for popular causes as a means of getting circulation. William Randolph Hearst, with the San Francisco "Examiner," finds how to get journalism down to the language of the street. Pulitzer and Hearst invade New York. Morrill Goddard discovers, and Arthur Brisbane extends, the real principle of yellow journalism. The yellow madness; its humors and its extravagances.

The Spread and Decline of Yellow Journalism . March 4

Expensive machinery and processes had made newspaper publication a huge business proposition, and the court of last resort on a city newspaper had become not an editor but a business man. These people snatched at the method of extending circulation which Pulitzer and Hearst had shown. The yellow influence affected all newspapers, even the most conservative. The sudden decline of pure yellow journalism. The good and bad in it; and what it meant to the ultimate development of journalism.

What Is News? . . . . March 18

Since news is the really important function of a newspaper, since it is becoming more and more the tool of the editor in assisting popular causes, getting his opinions before the people, and spreading intelligence, an understanding of the nature of news is necessary to an understanding of journalism. This is

an analysis, with many illustrative examples, of news and news-interest in the reader.

The Editor and the News . . . . April 1

The ethics of the editorial art, and a special plea for the professional, rather than the business, attitude toward journalism. Illustrated by examples from the history of contemporary American newspapers. The importance of the point of view.

The Reporter and the News . . . . . . April 22

The art of reporting, as first worked out by Charles A. Dana. Where journalism blends with literature, and where it stands apart. The faculty of accurate and minute observation in artistic reporting. How the yellow reporter conceals his lack of art by melodrama and faking. Where technique joins hands with truth. Some great news stories.

"All the News That's Fit to Print" . . . . . May 6

The ethics of news and news-writing. The danger of too great delicacy in telling the scandalous truth, and the equal danger of too little delicacy. The question of private right as opposed to public curiosity. The formula—"a newspaper, like the man who owns it, should be a gentleman." The ethical code which governs all good reporters.

The Advertising Influence . . . . May 20

Beginning a study of the conflict between the business of newspaper-making and the interests of that public which the newspaper serves. In this, the infancy of modern journalism, a system has grown up whose inception was the fault of no one man, but which is nevertheless a serious handicap to American journalism. Nature and causes of this system as shown by the example of one great American city.

And then these five articles—on commercial journalism, on the relations between big business and newspaper capital, and on the future of newspaper publication:

The Unhealthy Alliance, June 3; Our Kind of People, June 17; The Foe from Within, July 1; The New Era, July 8; The Voice of a Generation, July 22 : : : :

Announcement for Collier's *most important muckraking series (14 January 1911)*

ates. This action was apparently intended to hold the publishing house, and particularly the magazine, together after Collier's death. The attempt failed. P. F. Collier and Son, along with *Collier's*, was sold to the Crowell Publishing Company. The magazine abandoned its serious journalism for light feature articles, fiction, and cartoons. It survived until 1956, when it suspended operations following several years of substantial losses.

Collier spent much of his later years in leisure and philanthrophic pursuits. He founded the Lincoln Farm Association, which bought Abraham Lincoln's log-cabin birthplace in Hodgenville, Kentucky, and erected a monument at the site, all paid for through public subscription. He was a member of many influential organizations, including the American Association for the Advancement of Science, the American Historical Association, the Civic Forum, the New York Academy of Sciences, the Municipal Art Society, the Metropolitan Museum of Art, the New York Botanical Society, the American Museum of Natural History, the Irish-American Historical Association, the American Geographical Society, the National Conservation Society, and the New York Horticultural Society.

Collier was, as had been his father, a leading American sportsman and was strongly interested in conservation and in the outdoors. He was one of the first aviators in the United States and served as president of the Aero Club of America. The Collier Trophy, created by Collier in 1912, is awarded each year to a person, organization, or group that does the most to improve the performance, safety, or efficiency of aircraft (in recent years spacecraft have been added) during the preceding year. He also was a member of the Automobile Club of America and the National Golf Links of America. He was for much of his life among the best American polo players and enjoyed all types of equestrian sports.

For much of his life Collier was an administrator as well as a writer and an editor. Without diminishing his importance as the guiding force behind one of the major muckraking publications of its day, in the final analysis he should probably be remembered for overseeing the accomplishments of others at *Collier's*, rather than for what he accomplished in the magazine or with the publishing house.

Herbert Croly

(23 January 1869-17 May 1930)

David L. Anderson
University of Northern Colorado

MAJOR POSITIONS HELD: Editor, *Record and Guide* (1889-1891), *Architectural Record* (1900-1906); editor in chief, *New Republic* (1914-1928).

BOOKS: *Stately Homes in America from Colonial Times to the Present Day,* by Croly and Harry William Desmond (New York: Appleton, 1903);
Houses for Town or Country, as William Herbert (New York: Duffield, 1907);
The Promise of American Life (New York: Macmillan, 1909);
Marcus Alonzo Hanna: His Life and Work (New York: Macmillan, 1912);
Progressive Democracy (New York: Macmillan, 1914);
Willard Straight (New York: Macmillan, 1924).

SELECTED PERIODICAL PUBLICATIONS
UNCOLLECTED: "Unregenerate Democracy," *New Republic,* 6 (5 February 1916): 17-19;
"The Two Parties in 1916," *New Republic,* 8 (21 October 1916): 286-291;
"The Counsel of Humility," *New Republic,* 13 (15 December 1917): 173-176;
"A School of Social Research," *New Republic,* 15 (8 June 1918): 167-171;
"The Paradox of Lincoln," *New Republic,* 21 (18 February 1920): 350-353;
"The Eclipse of Progressivism," *New Republic,* 24 (27 October 1920): 210-216;
"In Memoriam, Willard Straight," *New Republic,* 29 (21 December 1921): 94-96;
"The New Republic Idea," *New Republic,* 33 (6 December 1923): supplement, 1-16;
"What Ails American Youth," *New Republic,* 41 (11 February 1925): 301-303;
"Christians Beware!" *New Republic,* 45 (25 November 1925): 12-14;
"The Progressive Voter: He Wants to Know!" *New Republic,* 55 (25 July 1928): 242-247.

Herbert Croly, founder and editor of the *New Republic,* was a prophet of the liberal politi-

Herbert Croly

cal faith. He refined and crystallized much of the thinking behind the Progressive movement in *The Promise of American Life* (1909), an astute, timely book that was at once programmatic, philosophical, and critical. Consequently, he was able to make the *New Republic* a small but significant national forum for primarily urban, eastern perspectives on politics and letters.

Croly was the only son of parents who were prominent polemicists and journalists. His father, David Goodman Croly, worked as a *New York Evening Post* reporter in the 1850s before joining his wife in an ill-fated publishing venture with a Democratic newspaper in Rockford, Illinois. Returning to New York, he served as city editor and then as managing editor of the *World* during the Civil War. He edited and was a stockholder in the *Daily Graphic* from 1873 to 1878. In between he and a friend started the *Real Estate Record and Builders' Guide.* Jane Cunningham Croly, a Victorian feminist, was one of the best-known American women of her time and under the pseudonym "Jenny June" wrote for, and edited, several magazines. Her advice and opinions were found in a half-dozen weekly and daily newspapers and in nine books she wrote or compiled between 1868 (when she founded the first important American women's club) and 1898.

Herbert Croly appears to have been heavily influenced by his father, a disciple of Auguste Comte. Father and son were given to Sunday walks in Central Park during which conversation was devoted to positivism, altruism, and the "Religion of Humanity" espoused by Comte in his later years. The two men continued their philosophical discussions in remarkably heavy correspondence after the son entered Harvard in 1886. Herbert Croly's favorite professor was Josiah Royce, a theist and idealist who persuaded him, despite his father's strenuous protests, that theology and metaphysics were not obsolete modes of thought. But the father's teachings, based on the Comtean belief in the inevitability and desirability of concentrated wealth and power, withstood Croly's Harvard experience, which also exposed him to the influences of George Santayana and William James.

Croly's career as a college student was a lonely, asocial preoccupation with philosophy and its applications to politics. Fellow students who met him again in the years of his fame often could not recall knowing him, although they had sat together in the same classrooms. Croly throughout life was shy, his reticence reinforced by a speech impediment. At the time of his father's death in 1889 Croly dropped out of Harvard to edit and write for the *Record and Guide.* His editorials in the next two years show an early antipathy to laissez-faire policies. A sister publication, *Architectural Record,* was started in 1891, and Croly became a member of its staff. At about the same time he became engaged to Louise Emory, a Harvard Annex student whom he married in 1892, before returning to college. Croly was forced to withdraw again the following year as a result of a nervous breakdown of unknown cause. In 1895 he returned a final time, performing well in economics, literary criticism, the arts, and

philosophy but leaving in 1900 without a degree, to return to the *Architectural Record* as an editor.

In six years Croly wrote forty-six signed articles in the *Record* and also coauthored a book and compiled an anthology on home architecture. Although he developed no systematic architectural theory, his work led him to three topics that foreshadowed his later writing: the role of the artist in modern America, the "nationalization" of artistic life, and the millionaire as a social type. Early on he saw that the inheritance of Jacksonian suspiciousness of experts, including artists, meant a fate of lonely isolation for the architect who insisted upon standards of excellence rather than popularity. In 1900 Croly had been deeply impressed by the theme of a deservedly obscure novel by Robert Grant, *Unleavened Bread.* Its hero, an architect named Wilbur Littleton, becomes a victim of crassness and individualism when he tries to express in his work high ideals of design without the support of a cultural tradition. Croly's growing sense of disenchantment with American life soon attached itself to his understanding of the defects in American culture, which he began to trace to the triumph of Jeffersonian democracy over Hamiltonian nationalism, and to a rapacious frontier consciousness which found it convenient to ignore the claims of the community.

Croly labored for four hours each morning from 1905 to 1909, through three drafts, on *The Promise of American Life.* In spite of the book's turgidity and tendentiousness, its conception of a nationalist revival made it one of the most important political writings of the twentieth century. At its core was the argument that in the modern world, the prospect of prosperity, freedom, individual and social excellence, and human brotherhood, which together Croly took to be the promise of American life, could be redeemed only if Jeffersonian ends were deliberately and purposefully sought by Hamiltonian means. In so arguing, Croly was challenging what was then, and remains even now, the widely held and deeply cherished assumption that the promise would fulfill itself automatically.

In some ways the old struggle among Hamilton, Jefferson, and their respective intellectual heirs for the soul of America had been a standoff, Croly recognized. Whereas the Jeffersonians had avoided the question of nationalism, the Hamiltonians had avoided that of democracy. Each had thereby "perverted" his own idea, although Hamilton's failure to recognize the need for a

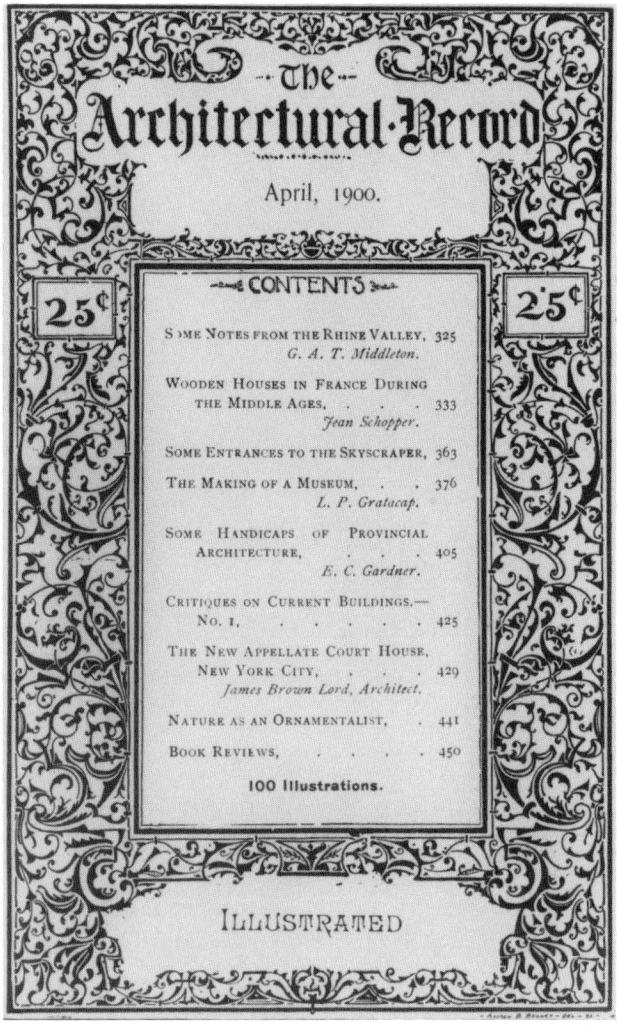

Cover for an issue of the journal Croly edited from 1900 to 1906

democratic element in nationalism had far less dreadful effects than Jefferson's rampant individualism, his superficial thought, and his tendency to recommend drift rather than mastery in both domestic and foreign affairs. Only Lincoln among presidents had struck the perfect chord of democratic nationalism, preserving the Union while ending slavery with justice and mercy.

The growth of big business after the Civil War should have laid bare the inadequacies of atomistic thinking, Croly asserted, but instead prompted reactionary reform programs aimed at breaking up trusts, unseating officeholders, weakening political bosses, and initiating populist legislation. None of these ideas was appropriate, because they failed to take account of dwindling natural resources, the harmful effects of competition, and the infirmities of governments.

Fundamentally, the Jeffersonian individualist's belief in equal rights was damaging insofar as it required a hands-off attitude even as life became more specialized, organized, and concentrated. The notion of impartial laws was a delusion. All laws discriminated in favor of some and against others. The Sherman Anti-Trust Act, for example, discriminated against large corporations, for small businesses, and, not incidentally, for inefficient resource allocation and against the public interest. The barons and the bosses filled a vacuum created by a small, weak public sector. Intervention by the federal government alone could master the power of irresponsible tycoons and conniving ward heelers. Workers who refused to join unions were "industrial derelicts." Small businessmen should not be sentimentalized, either.

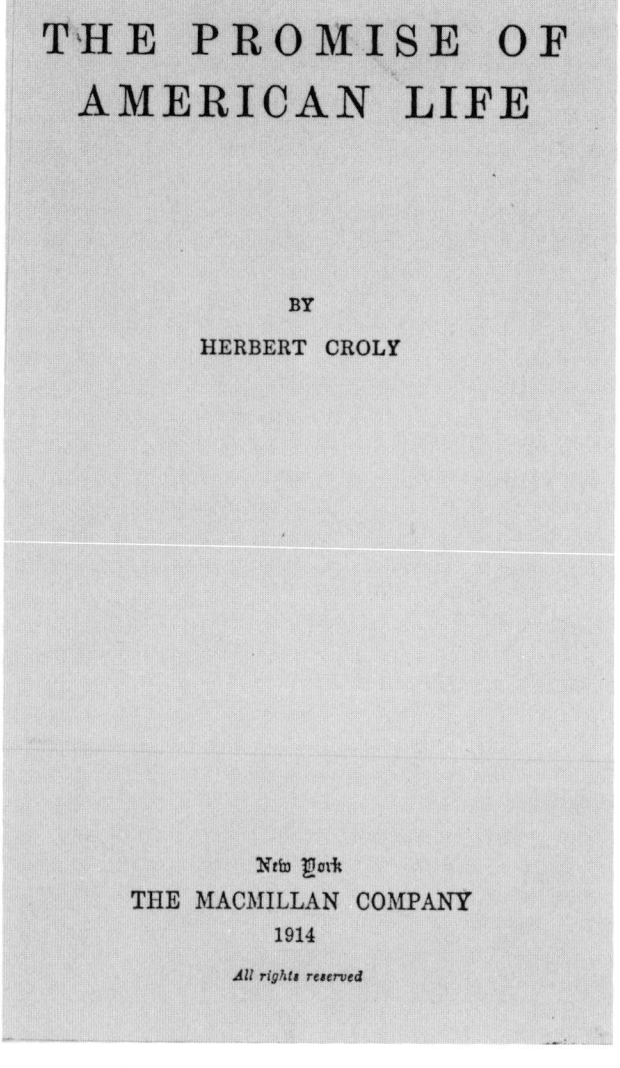

THE PROMISE OF
AMERICAN LIFE

BY

HERBERT CROLY

New York
THE MACMILLAN COMPANY
1914

Title page for a later edition of the 1909 political treatise in which Croly defines his concept of "the New Nationalism"

A strong foreign policy was needed to protect American interests in faraway places. Big government, big business, and big labor, under the guidance of a democratic elite, a strong executive, and the nationalist wing of the Republican party, would be required to assure opportunities for specialization, discriminate constructively on behalf of the weak, and keep the elements in society from flying apart.

Yet democracy and excellence, the ideals of Jefferson and Hamilton, could never be fully reconciled by political action alone. In social life, education must be reconstructed, freedom of thought guaranteed, and technical excellence and moral conversion achieved by individuals. "The common citizen can become something of a saint and something of a hero, not by growing to heroic proportions in his own person," Croly wrote, "but by sincere and enthusiastic imitation of heroes and saints, and whether or not he will ever come to such imitation will depend upon the ability of his exceptional fellow-countrymen to offer him acceptable examples of heroism and saintliness." This concluding sentence became the most frequently quoted from the book.

As Felix Frankfurter and others were to observe, and as Croly himself knew, his prose rarely lent itself to pithy quotation. However, by dubbing his program "the New Nationalism," he provided the public with a memorable slogan. It was hardly an original phrase, but former president Theodore Roosevelt appropriated it as the theme of his campaign to return to the White House in 1912.

Justice Frankfurter later estimated that seventy-five hundred copies of the book were sold during Croly's lifetime, and historians have not questioned what may seem a low sales figure for a volume to which so much influence has been ascribed. Croly "was never meant for mass readers," the jurist remarked. But one of those readers was Roosevelt, who may not have read the book extensively, but who found enough in it to be powerfully persuaded that it lent historical and sociological credence and provided an intellectual setting for points of view he had long held and forcefully propagated. It seems unlikely that either Roosevelt or the eventual winner of the 1912 election, Woodrow Wilson, changed any important positions because of Croly. The book's significance lies in two related areas: it may well have reinforced their predispositions, and it certainly created an impression among many thoughtful people that Croly had influence at the highest level of government.

The Promise of American Life was widely and favorably reviewed in scholarly circles and in opinion journals. It earned Croly access to Roosevelt and a belated degree from Harvard. More fatefully, it brought him to the attention of Willard Straight, an ex-Reuters correspondent who had become J. P. Morgan's man in Asia, and Straight's heiress wife Dorothy. In the summer of 1912 they left China and contacted Croly, proposing that he start a weekly journal of opinion with their help. Having considered something similar in the 1890s, Croly readily agreed.

On the heels of his first success Croly had written several articles on politics, including a ten-part series for the *Cleveland Leader,* seeking to update and popularize the book's themes. Two relatively minor books also appeared under Croly's authorship before he could found the *New Republic,* a biography of the Ohio political boss Mark Hanna and an anthology of the Godkin lectures Croly had been invited to give at Harvard in 1913 and 1914. The biography, *Marcus Alonzo Hanna: His Life and Work* (1912), received mixed reviews because it was perceived in some quarters as an apology for individualism written under the supervision of Hanna's family (whose members authorized and approved it), though others praised it for destroying the caricature of "Dollar Mark" that had dominated a popular impression of Hanna as a soulless manipulator. Croly's biographer, David W. Levy, concludes that in the book Croly had "been less than completely honest" in omitting an obvious conclusion about

Hanna's career, namely that it epitomized the very pioneer spirit Croly had condemned as outmoded in *The Promise of American Life.* In contrast, *Progressive Democracy* (1914), the Godkin lectures anthology, argued more boldly than ever for "intellectual and moral emancipation" through mass-democratic education. Moving beyond his earlier, more qualified optimism about human nature, Croly suggested that the will and intelligence of human beings could be counted on to justify the freedom to experiment in search of a nobler and more just society. Reflecting the points of agreement between positivism and newly arrived exponents of pragmatism such as John Dewey and William James, Croly rejected orthodox and conservative objections to innovations such as the mechanics of direct democracy. He even denounced social theories that purported to lay down inexorable laws and to prescribe "permanent rules" for any social behavior or process.

Close to euphoria, Croly looked forward to the possibility that, as an outcome of progressive democracy, mundane concerns might disappear, and that people could subordinate the economic fears of life to concentrate their energies on leisure and self-improvement: "it might make every woman into something of a novelist and every man into something of a playwright."

Most reviews of *Progressive Democracy* were favorable but not as enthusiastic as those of *The Promise of American Life.* It was attacked as too utopian and too reliant upon the state for the regeneration of society. One critic chastised Croly for overlooking the extent to which the Wilson administration had already carried out, through creation of the Federal Trade Commission, for example, some of Croly's dearest wishes. Most complained about his abstractness and dryness.

The *New Republic* opened its offices on the very day that war came to Europe in 1914. As Eric F. Goldman wryly notes, it began life in two adjoining brick houses at 419 and 421 West Twenty-first Street, in the fading Chelsea neighborhood, "on the edge of [Greenwich] Village, next door to a home for wayward girls and across the street from the General Theological Seminary." Willard Straight, a well-connected banker, had fashioned an imperialist brand of nationalism as an aide to Roosevelt. Dorothy Whitney Straight, the daughter of a Standard Oil heiress, possessed literary and philosophical erudition and a penchant for social causes. They told Croly they would subsidize "the paper" to whatever extent necessary. (By 1953, David Seideman

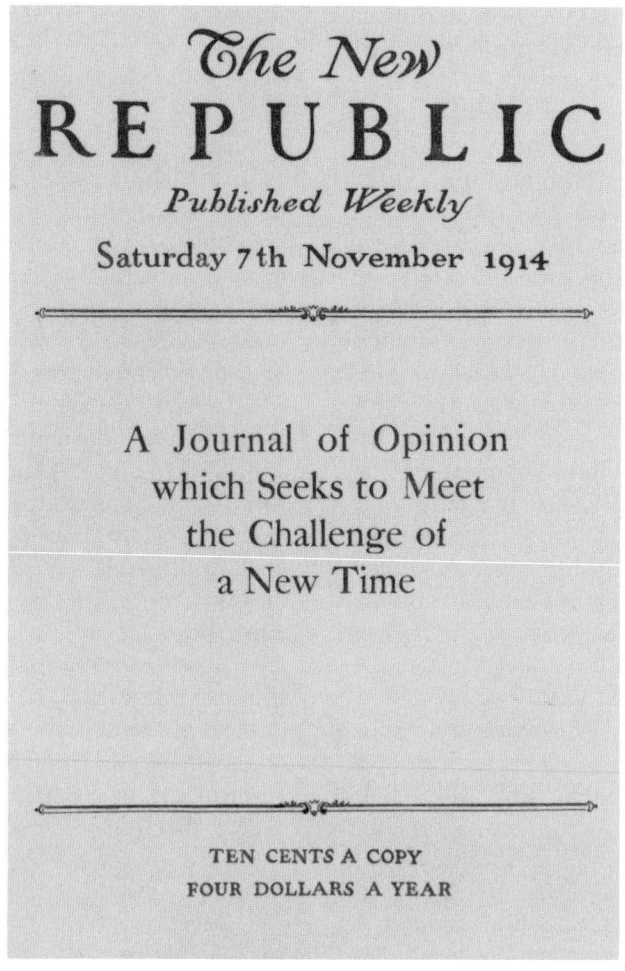

Cover for the first issue of the journal founded by Croly. The original staff included Walter Lippmann,
Walter Weyl, Francis Hackett, and Philip Littell.

has calculated, Dorothy had poured about $3,700,000 into the enterprise. Croly devoted much of late 1913 and early 1914 to recruiting a staff whose qualities would offset shortcomings he saw in himself as editor in chief. Young ex-socialist Walter Lippmann and muckraker-statistician Walter Weyl agreed to serve as editors; Irish immigrant Francis Hackett as literary editor; Harvard classmate Philip Littell as book columnist; and Robert Hallowell as business manager and unofficial art editor. Charlotte Rudyard, who had edited *The Promise of American Life*, edited copy, wrote headlines, and made up the pages. Of the editors, only Littell was personally known to Croly before 1913. Weyl and Hackett were committed Jeffersonians.

The plan was to publish the first issue after the congressional elections. Eight hundred seventy-five people paid four dollars in response to

a subscription flyer that promised "no taboos . . . no favorites . . . no set creed . . . a faith rather than dogma." By the next year circulation had climbed to ten thousand, and by the time of United States entry into World War I, to thirty thousand. The magazine was growing in part because of the misleading appearance of intimacy with President Wilson (Lippmann had become an adviser, and Croly had access to Wilson's closest confidant, Col. Edward House), and partly because of the regular appearance in its pages of such provocative contributors as John Reed, Charles A. Beard, John Dewey, Graham Wallas, H. G. Wells, Bernard Shaw, and George Santayana. The poetry of Carl Sandburg, Amy Lowell, and Robert Frost graced "the back of the book," as did criticism by Randolph Bourne. However, not everyone was pleased with Croly's magazine. William Allen White thought it "too deadly serious" and urged the editors to lighten up. Denunciatory letters in the *New Republic* said it was too radical, or too moderate; that it was pro-Allied, or pro-German. The phrase "Crolier than thou," ascribed to an unknown wag, referred to the editor in chief's "wooly" writing and "snarled syntax." Bourne complained of "priggishness" and of a "surrender to militarism" when Wilson's war policy gained the editors' endorsement. (The editors had experienced an abrupt falling-out with Roosevelt by 1915.)

To Levy, writing in the 1980s, it seemed that their pragmatism amounted to "the formula of superiority masked as humility"–that they saw too late the truth in Bourne's claim that by going along on the war, they had badly miscalculated the reactionary consequences of seeking to control such a cosmic event. After Versailles, Croly and the others tried to atone by bravely condemning the cynical compromises in the treaty, thereby cutting themselves off from any hope of influencing the Wilson administration. In any case the riptide of postwar reaction against moral exhortation and progressive reform must have astounded Croly. By 1923 readership had fallen to 19,384, and the operation had to declare bankruptcy and reorganize. By 1925 it was down to 14,000. The editor in chief paid a heavy price for the general public disillusionment with all three of his publication's major wartime beliefs: in a pragmatic, disinterested, dispassionate search for truth; in a nationalized society; and in a peace settlement that was just and durable.

The carefully assembled staff began to drift away. Bourne, as well as Willard Straight, had died in the influenza epidemic of 1919. Lippmann, after a doctrinal feud with Hackett, quit in 1921. Hackett resigned and joined expatriates in Denmark, while Hallowell headed for Paris. Croly's loyal friend Littell, whose diplomatic finesse had surmounted many a rift, fell ill and quit. By 1926 Croly was the only editorial survivor from the brave beginning. But he was able to replace his staff with some writers of comparable, if not always equal, renown: Bruce Bliven, Edmund Wilson, Malcolm Cowley, Stark Young, Lewis Mumford.

Together with Croly, they struggled to keep the liberal flame flickering. They fought hysteria, lynchings, bigotry, labor baiting, deportations, and decentralization. Croly scorned Calvin Coolidge as "ignorant" and "absurd" and supported Robert La Follette in 1924. The magazine condemned the Sacco-Vanzetti executions in forty edi-

torials and twenty-five articles. It emphasized more than before, however, topics such as religion and education.

Early in 1920 Croly had planned to publish a book called "The Breach in Civilization." At the urging of his friend Frankfurter he withdrew the manuscript at the last minute, perhaps because it seemed to represent too abject a renunciation of liberal hopes. Eleven years earlier Croly had warned that brotherhood, although essential, was no substitute for efficient organization. In the post-Versailles mood of outrage and bitterness, he identified spiritual regeneration as the solution to modern evils. These included moral anarchy, blind belief in science, and complacent reliance on the state, and he traced their cause to the sixteenth-century rise of Protestantism, with its emphasis on individualism, subjectivism, and materialism. The only answer, Croly now maintained, was a careful restoration of a unified moral and intellectual authority, "the social ideal of Catholicism," which had been destroyed in the emergence of secular life.

Historians disagree as to whether this represents a return to David Croly's injunction ("Cultivate all the religious emotions") to follow Comte's "Religion of Humanity" or a new discovery of the liberating possibilities of Christianity. In either case, and despite his flirtation after 1924 with the esoteric mysticism of A. R. Orage, a disciple of Georges Gurdjieff, two points remain clear: Croly's writings always reflected a concern for religious and spiritual fulfillment that was generally uncharacteristic of Progressives; and Croly's interest in politics, though subdued in his final decade, never disappeared. Croly did say in 1927 that he found "omissions and stupidities" in *The Promise of American Life* "depressing."

In the early autumn of 1928 Croly suffered the first of a series of strokes, which affected his speech and mobility. He died on 17 May 1930. The *New Republic* devoted a special supplement to its 16 July issue to tributes from his friends and associates. Dorothy Straight Elmhirst wrote that Croly had "suffered bitter disappointments and cruel personal hurts" but never became cynical. Edmund Wilson said Croly "seemed all his life to be seeking truth in collaboration with others," rather than trying to tell others what to think. Lippmann asserted that *The Promise of American Life* was "the political classic which announced the end of the Age of Innocence, with its romantic faith in American destiny, and inaugurated the process of self-examination." Frankfurter recalled that Croly had said the purpose of the *New Republic* was "to start little insurrections in the realm of ... convictions." Three years after Herbert Croly's death, New Deal historian Arthur M. Schlesinger, Jr., wrote: "in another America, another Roosevelt began to use Hamiltonian means to achieve Jeffersonian ends in still another attempt to fulfill the promise of American life."

Biography:

David W. Levy, *Herbert Croly of the New Republic: The Life and Thought of an American Progressive* (Princeton, N.J.: Princeton University Press, 1985).

References:

John Patrick Diggins, "The New Republic and Its Times," *New Republic,* 191 (10 December 1984): 23-73;

Charles Forcey, *The Crossroads of Liberalism: Croly, Weyl, Lippmann, and the Progressive Era 1900-1925* (New York: Oxford University Press, 1961);

Eric F. Goldman, *Rendezvous With Destiny: A History of Modern American Reform* (New York: Knopf, 1952), pp. 146-161;

Richard Hofstadter, *The Age of Reform* (New York: Random House, 1955), pp. 246-268;

William E. Leuchtenburg, ed., *The New Nationalism* (Englewood Cliffs, N.J.: Prentice-Hall, 1961);

Robert B. Luce, ed., *The Faces of Five Decades: Selections from Fifty Years of the New Republic* (New York: Simon & Schuster, 1964), pp. 11-225;

Arthur M. Schlesinger, Jr., "Croly and 'The Promise of American Life,'" *New Republic,* 152 (8 May 1965): 17-22;

David Seideman, *The New Republic: A Voice of Modern Liberalism* (New York: Praeger, 1986).

Frank Crowninshield
(24 June 1872-28 December 1947)

Ralph Frasca
University of Iowa

MAJOR POSITIONS HELD: Publisher, *Bookman* (1895-1900); assistant editor, *Metropolitan Magazine* (1900-1902); assistant editor (1903-1907), literary agent, *Munsey's Magazine* (1908-1909); art editor, *Century Magazine* (1910-1913); editor, *Vanity Fair* (1914-1936); consulting editor to Condé Nast Publications (1936-1947).

BOOKS: *Manners for the Metropolis* (New York: Appleton, 1908);
The Bridge-Fiend, as Arthur Loring Bruce (New York: Moffat, Yard, 1909);
Log of Cleopatra's Barge II, 1928-1942 (Boston: Privately printed, 1948).

OTHER: *Short Stories from Vanity Fair, 1926-1927,* foreword by Crowninshield (New York: Liveright, 1928).

Frank Crowninshield was one of New York's foremost dilettantes, toastmasters, and patrons of the arts during the first half of this century. These attributes served not to diminish, but to enhance, his prestige as the gifted editor of what was likely the most sophisticated and witty magazine of its era. From its birth in 1913 to its demise in 1936, *Vanity Fair* boasted much of the best American writing, as well as some stellar contributions from foreign writers. Crowninshield and his staff had an uncanny knack for discovering new talent. Many great literary careers were launched from the pages of *Vanity Fair*. Domestic and foreign luminaries who received their first big break in *Vanity Fair* included Dorothy Parker, Robert Benchley, Clare Boothe Luce, Thomas Wolfe, Aldous Huxley, Paul Gallico, P. G. Wodehouse, Gertrude Stein, E. E. Cummings, Noel Coward, and Ferenc Molnár.

Additionally, *Vanity Fair* reproduced in four colors the works of many of the era's most celebrated painters and sculptors, often before they rose to prominence. Artists whose work it reproduced for the first time in America included

Frank Crowninshield

Pablo Picasso, Vincent Van Gogh, Henri Matisse, Georges Rouault, and Paul Gauguin.

Crowninshield was born on 24 June 1872 in Paris to American parents, Frederic and Helen Suzette Fairbanks Crowninshield. Frederic Crowninshield was a Boston-born watercolorist, stained-glass designer, and mural painter who never had a substantial income yet who possessed an affinity for living abroad, studying, and teaching art, first in Paris, then in the museum school of the Museum of Fine Arts in the American Academy in Rome.

It was during the artist's tenure in Paris that his son Francis Welch Crowninshield was born. Crowninshield's birthplace was the Pavillon de Rohan, a small Paris hotel later torn down so that the Louvre department store could be built on the site. As with many other occurrences during his life, Crowninshield saw humor in this development. Whenever he was in Paris, he used to take his companions to the second floor of the department store, point to the corset department, and tell them that he was born there.

Crowninshield attended various European schools, several of which he was asked to leave because of his predilection for pranks. He was expelled from one such institution for burning a pair of rubber overshoes in the school furnace on the day of a school charity affair, causing a substantial odor.

After nearly two years at the University of Rome, Crowninshield journeyed to New York in search of employment. On the strength of a character reference from family friend William Dean Howells, editor of the *Atlantic Monthly,* Crowninshield landed a job with Major George Haven Putnam's publishing house and bookstore. In the initial interview Putnam asked Crowninshield what he would like to do for a job. Crowninshield replied that he would like to critique manuscripts, meet authors, and be involved in publishing. Putnam replied that he could not offer the eighteen-year-old Crowninshield such a position, for Crowninshield had requested the duties reserved for Putnam himself.

A week later Putnam wrote to Crowninshield, expressing his regret that he could not offer the young man a position as head of the company, but noting that there was an opening for a clerk in the bookstore, paying eight dollars per week. Crowninshield accepted the job.

He remained at Putnam's for four years, the last two of which he served as Putnam's personal assistant. In 1895 Crowninshield left to become the first publisher of the fledgling New York literary review the *Bookman,* a career move that Howells saluted: "I am heartily glad of what seems a step forward for you, and I know you will make it an advantage to others as well as yourself. It is always pleasant to think of you, because you have not only a good head, but what is much rarer, a good heart; and your life is the daily effect of right feeling and right thinking in a world where there is so much of neither."

The *Bookman,* a Dodd, Mead and Company publication, presented book reviews, literary gossip, and announcements from publishing houses. As publisher of the monthly, Crowninshield solicited subscriptions and advertising, supervised printing operations, read the proof copies, paid bills and salaries, and ordered supplies.

After five years with the *Bookman,* Crowninshield became an assistant editor of *Metropolitan Magazine* in 1900. For the next thirteen years Crowninshield held an assortment of jobs in the tinsel-and-glitter world of New York periodicals. He remained with *Metropolitan Magazine* until 1902. In 1903 he took a job as assistant editor of *Munsey's Magazine,* when that monthly was selling more than five hundred thousand copies per issue. In 1908 and 1909 Crowninshield served as a literary agent in London, buying magazine stories and romantic serials for Frank Munsey.

During his London stint and shortly after his return to New York, Crowninshield authored two books—*Manners for the Metropolis* (1908), a collection of witty and sardonic aphorisms on proper etiquette, and *The Bridge-Fiend* (1909), about one of Crowninshield's favorite pastimes. (The latter book was published under the pseudonym Arthur Loring Bruce.)

Manners for the Metropolis contains such gems of wisdom as "After dinner, over the cigars, it is bad form for men to discuss any subjects but stocks and motor cars," "Do not address your wife as 'mother,' " and "Always be half an hour late for everything. Nothing is so tedious as waiting."

In 1910 Crowninshield left the Munsey fold for *Century Magazine,* for which he served as art editor for more than three years. However, it was not until 1914 that Frank Crowninshield, then forty-one, landed the job that would ensure him a place in the sanctum of New York celebrities, establish his reputation as a bon vivant and raconteur, and certify his prominence in the history of American periodicals.

Condé Nast, who had been publishing *Vogue* for four years, purchased a fashion magazine titled *Dress* in 1913 from Doubleday, Page and Company because he regarded it as a potentially successful rival to *Vogue.* Nast scrapped the narrow fashion format of *Dress,* paid three thousand dollars for the rights to the name *Vanity Fair* (the title of William Makepeace Thackeray's novel [1847-1848], *Vanity Fair* was also the name of a magazine of political satire that ran from 31 December 1859 to 4 July 1863), and launched *Dress and Vanity Fair* as a monthly in September 1913 with Frank Harris as editor.

In the first issue it was announced as the goal of *Dress and Vanity Fair* to: "touch on all that is of interest in the Drama, the Opera, and Music, both at home and in Europe. We shall discuss all that is new and worthy in the Fine Arts and in Books. We shall picture and record the manifold activities of the Great Outdoors. We shall not lack authority in those things which go to make the smart world smart. If 'the apparel doth oft proclaim the man,'–and the woman too– our proclamation shall be a worthy forecast as well as an accurate reflection of the best that is favored by men and women of taste."

Nast was dissatisfied with the first few issues and sought the opinion of Crowninshield, still working at *Century Magazine*. Crowninshield informed him that the publication was too much like the fashion-conscious *Vogue*. "There is no magazine that is read by the people you meet at lunches and dinners," Crowninshield said. "Your magazine should cover the things people talk about–parties, the arts, sports, theatre, humor, and so forth."

Nast was so impressed with Crowninshield's suggestions that he asked Crowninshield to edit the magazine in the manner he had suggested. Crowninshield agreed, on the conditions that the word *Dress* be dropped from the title, that the emphasis on female fashions be dropped from the contents, and that he have autonomy in determining the editorial content. Nast agreed (although he did not always abide by the final stipulation), and *Vanity Fair* was born.

An editorial in the magazine's fifth issue (January 1914) proclaimed: "For a year, at least, "Dress" was expected to continue the dominant influence; but so quickly has the Vanity Fair idea gathered its own following that we are emboldened in this, the First Number of 1914, to announce ourselves simply as "Vanity Fair," and to proceed directly to the construction of the sort of publication we hold so broad and sprightly a Title to signify. . . . To pattern Vanity Fair, in a general way, after the great English pictorial weeklies has been our aim from the start . . . we feel we have gained an excellent idea of the kind of English magazine Americans want." A ten-year retrospective on the magazine, published in 1924 and doubtless written by Crowninshield, offers insight into the magazine's whimsical intentions: "The pageant of American life began to be subjected to attention which was often good for it–satirical joshing of its gaucheries, mixed with a fresh effort to make our daily existence render up the material for the lighter forms at least of artistic expression."

Crowninshield thrived at the helm of the freewheeling new magazine, for it afforded him the means by which to secure his place as the

locus around which many literary and entertainment figures orbited. Before long the *Vanity Fair* offices (first situated on 449 Fourth Avenue, removed in 1917 to 19 West Forty-fourth Street, and finally coming to rest in 1927 in the thirty-story Graybar Building, which *Vanity Fair* proudly proclaimed was "the largest office building in the world," at Forty-third Street and Lexington Avenue) were crowded with aspiring actresses, dancers, painters, photographers, and illustrators seeking a market for their talents. Crowninshield befriended a great many of them, although he confessed years later that during his tenure at *Vanity Fair* some of the relationships, particularly those with actresses, may not have been genuine. "For twenty-two years I never knew which actresses were my friends," he said. "They all had an axe to grind."

Crowninshield's suave demeanor, charm, and flattery were sufficient to convince many established talents to contribute to the pages of *Vanity Fair*. Condé Nast wrote: "A trait in F.C. which has alway interested me is his concern over the aged, the sick, the underprivileged, and forlorn. (His friendships with servants always seem as close as those he maintains with their employers.) He has a remarkable way of continuing an active contact with old friends. A happy result, for our publishing organization, of his wide acquaintanceship has been that if a friendly contact had to be established, he seemed certain either to know the men and women we were after or to sense exactly how to bring them into line. It was always, for example, easy for him to persuade Joseph H. Choate to write for us, or Irene Castle to pose for photographs, or John Sargent to permit our use of his sketches, or Aldous Huxley to work on our staff, or Joe Louis to pass an hour or two before the cameras in our studio, or persuade August Belmont and Harry Payne Whitney to cooperate in photographing their horses in their stables, or Isadora Duncan to help in a benefit dance recital, or Geraldine Farrar to do us any order of favor."

However, Crowninshield dealt a mortal blow to his relationship with poet Amy Lowell in 1919 when he changed some words in one of her poems. When she received the edited proof from Crowninshield, she responded: "I have naturally put the words back to what they were, and I shall be awfully obliged to you if you will suggest to the erudite persons who run these things that I have a predilection in favor of having my poems printed as I write them." There is every reason

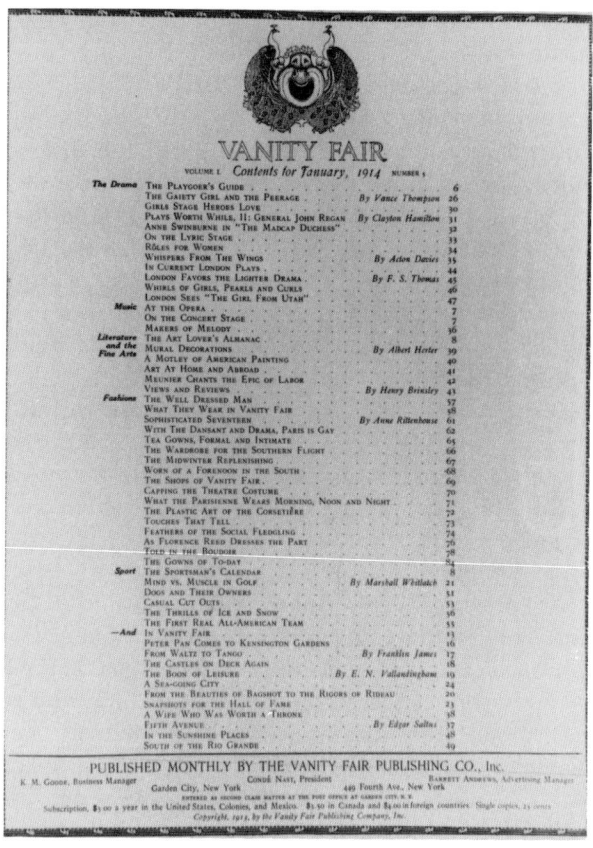

Contents page and cover for the revamped magazine originally published as Dress and Vanity Fair. *When he became editor in January 1914, Crowninshield changed the magazine's focus from fashion to "the things people talk about—parties, the arts, sports, theatre, humor, and so forth."*

to suspect that Lowell knew that Crowninshield was the culprit.

When not relying on the contributions of established names, Crowninshield encouraged and cultivated many young artists and writers, affording many their first exposure. His enthusiasm for their work extended to those occasions when he had to reject solicitations. In returning a manuscript to Paul Gallico, Crowninshield once raved, "My dear boy, this is superb! A little masterpiece! What color! What life! How beautifully you have phrased it all! A veritable gem!–Why don't you take it around to 'Harper's Bazaar?' " Gallico never did so but always cherished his rejection slip from Crowninshield.

However, Crowninshield did publish many of Gallico's sports stories. Gallico was one of many *Vanity Fair* contributors who went on to greater fame, but who never forgot Crowninshield's contribution in his rise to prominence. Noel Coward was like-minded. An unheralded English youth, he submitted a satirical piece to Crowninshield that was published in 1921. He later told Crowninshield's nephew Frederic Bradlee: "Your Uncle Frank paid me the first dollar I ever earned in America. As I was almost starving at the time, I was positively enchanted to get it."

Another unknown writer discovered by Crowninshield was Dorothy Rothschild, later Parker, whose first paid publication, a poem entitled "Any Porch," appeared in the September 1915 issue of *Vanity Fair* when she was twenty years old. She received five dollars for it. The following month's issue included her first prose publication, "Why I Haven't Married." Parker soon began attending parties at Condé Nast's home as Crowninshield's date, and when, in April 1918, Crowninshield noticed her profound interest in drama, the editor tapped her to replace P. G. Wodehouse as the magazine's drama critic. "Though she was full of prejudices, her perceptions were so sure, her judgment so unerring, that she always seemed to hit the centre of the mark," Crowninshield wrote years later.

Crowninshield gradually changed his mind about Parker's drama critiques, though. She was unabashedly critical of most of the plays she attended. Crowninshield and Nast often caught the backlash of Parker's barbs, as they were periodically harangued by offended dramaturgists at social functions.

The last straw came when Parker harpooned Florenz Ziegfeld's wife Billie Burke for her performance in *Caesar's Wife*. Ziegfeld was an important advertiser in *Vanity Fair*. Crowninshield took Parker to dinner on 12 January 1920, during which he told her that her days as a drama critic were over and assured her that her other writing would still be valued highly by *Vanity Fair*. However, the offended Parker left the magazine, and managing editor Robert Benchley resigned in sympathy.

Time healed the wounds, though. Parker later sent Crowninshield copies of her books of verse, one of which was inscribed, "To Frank Crowninshield–He accepted my first verse–Please, will he accept all these? With love and gratitude."

Although *Vanity Fair* chronically lost money for Nast, its early years were marked by popular and artistic triumphs. Artist Miguel Covarrubias drew an "Impossible Interviews" feature, lampooning conversations that might occur if, for example, John D. Rockefeller, Sr., met Josef Stalin or if Greta Garbo spent an afternoon with Calvin Coolidge. Crowninshield offered a whimsical "Hall of Fame" gallery annually, and many Picassos, Van Goghs, Gauguins, and Rouaults graced the pages of *Vanity Fair*.

Another feature that often found its way into the magazine was the "short short story," as Crowninshield called it, of two thousand words or less. Crowninshield wrote that due to the magazine's "single-page, quasi-patchwork policy, 'Vanity Fair' was forced, a good many years back, to send up an agonized prayer for stories . . . of a little under two thousand words, a length practically unknown in American literature."

Every few years Crowninshield found it necessary to print testimonials to the popularity of *Vanity Fair* among the elite. In a 1914 encomium commemorating the first birthday of the magazine, author Jack London wrote: "I find I really need Vanity Fair. It keeps me a little in touch with all the fripperies, insincerities, vanities, decadent arts and sinister pleasures of life." Joseph Choate wrote: "Vanity Fair is a wonderful baby. Its second summer, strange to say, finds it sound and lively, and free from the usual perils of intestine war."

Despite his promise to allow Crowninshield a free hand over the magazine's editorial content, Nast often balked at Crowninshield's predilection for modern art, much of it Postimpressionist and French, terming it decadent and offensive. Crowninshield usually overcame Nast's objections, though, smoothly but stubbornly selling the publisher on the then-obscure artists and

Crowninshield (right) with Vanity Fair *publisher Condé Nast at a racetrack (Rawlings)*

their works. On the subject of art, Nast wrote: "F.C.'s interest in the modern French art movement, at first, did us a certain amount of harm. We were ten years too early (1915) in talking about Van Gogh, Gauguin, Matisse, Picasso, etc. At first (1915 to 1925), people took the ground that we were (presumably) insane, and, even as late as 1929 and 1930, our readers were still confused by the paintings we reproduced. Our advertising department, too, was greatly concerned because our advertisers . . . thought the paintings distorted, and, as they said, decadent. In time, however, as the movement grew, we derived a very considerable benefit from having published such pictures."

Crowninshield was himself an art aficionado. One of the seven founders of the New

York Museum of Modern Art in 1929 and its first secretary, Crowninshield owned an impressive collection of paintings, sculptures, lithographs, bronzes, African masks, and French illustrated books. During Christmastime he usually sent reproductions of French paintings as cards to the seven or eight hundred people on his Christmas-card list.

He often brought his most recent acquisitions to the *Vanity Fair* offices to elicit comment from assorted staff members. A former *Vanity Fair* stenographer commented: "He'd bring ghastly African masks to the office, and the girls had to put them on. Oh, the things I had to admire there! He was always bringing in paintings and masks. He was sort of cold if you didn't react right."

Crowninshield sometimes used his art to tease people. When hiring stenographers, he often showed them a photograph of Isadora Duncan dancers in diaphanous costumes and said, "These are some of my stenographers, and this is what we do on Saturday afternoons." In the twilight of Crowninshield's life, a new secretary came to his apartment to take dictation. He pulled out a painting of a reclining nude and said, "My former secretary–she was awfully good at shorthand. I hope you'll do as well."

Remarking "It would make a frightful mess if I died and left all this stuff for other people to take care of," the seventy-one-year-old Crowninshield sold his art collection during a three-day auction at the Parke-Bernet Galleries starting on 19 October 1943. The sale netted $181,747.

His attitude toward art collecting may be discerned in this statement about his collection of African sculptures: "I have never collected an object or figure, from Africa or Oceania, because of anything curious about it, or because of its utility or historic interest. Everything has been chosen entirely because of its aesthetic significance; its form, feeling, structure, and plastic values."

Although art was not the only love in Crowninshield's life, he never married. Wedlock would have cluttered his life, inhibited his status as a social gadfly, and rendered impossible his sprightly "extra-man" quality. Former *Vanity Fair* staffer Edmund Wilson defined Crowninshield as "a born courtier" who lacked "an appropriate court."

For much of his adult life he lived with his brother Edward. From 1921 to 1927 he even shared an apartment with Nast. At age seventy Crowninshield reflected on his bachelorhood:

Crowninshield with Condé Nast's daughter Leslie (photograph by John Phillips, Life *magazine, copyright Time Inc.)*

"My sense of loneliness was not particularly great until I reached sixty. From that time on, I would have given an ex-king's ransom if I had been able, in my youth, to seduce a lady into thinking of me as a provider and handyman around the house."

Such an existence surely would have cramped his elegant style during the *Vanity Fair* years. Crowninshield has received much of the credit for establishing New York's "café society" during the 1920s and 1930s. During the years he lived with Nast, Crowninshield tried to help the publisher become comfortable and respected in high society. In doing so, he urged Nast to throw parties and invite both the social elite and the more malleable members of the arts. This was a startling practice in the days when social lines were firmly drawn.

During such soirees and at the hundreds of banquets Crowninshield attended, he raised his glass in toasts, proposing many himself. However, he claimed that he never swallowed a drop of alcohol. According to Crowninshield, his aver-

sion to liquor began at age ten, when, with his grandmother, he attended a Boston prohibition rally. When the chief speaker asked those in the audience who would promise to abstain permanently from alcohol to stand, his grandmother arose. Crowninshield, who had been taught never to remain seated in the presence of a standing lady, leaped to his feet. His parents later chided him about the incident, prompting Crowninshield to vow to keep his promise (however mistakenly given) of abstinence.

In discussing his forbearance years later, Crowninshield spoke of his "almost inhuman avoidance of alcohol," adding, "I am probably the only man . . . who has never so much as drunk a glass of wine, whiskey, beer, claret, white wine, cocktail, etc." In toasting cronies Crowninshield developed the technique of raising the glass to his lips yet never swallowing.

His avoidance of alcohol never served as an impediment to his literary treatment of the subject, however. In the 1926 *Vanity Fair* article "The Decay of Gastronomy in America," Crowninshield praises "old Madeira or a good burgundy." After the demise of *Vanity Fair,* Crowninshield reminisced in *Vogue* about nineteenth-century bicycle trips around Manhattan, during which times he used to stop for beer or champagne. "I am something of a fraud," Crowninshield confessed to an acquaintance who questioned him about this canard. "I really did have a bicycle, though."

Crowninshield disdained the radio, movies, and fountain pens, and enjoyed baseball, ice-cream sodas, chocolate, plaid cotton bow ties, and Rabelaisian wit. Once he nearly got in serious trouble because of his sense of humor. Under the heading "Not on Your Tintype–Five Highly Unlikely Historical Situations by One Who Is Sick of the Same Old Headlines," Crowninshield published five caricatures in the August 1935 issue of *Vanity Fair,* including one of Japanese Emperor Hirohito carrying the Nobel Peace Prize off on a gun carriage. The issue was quickly banned in Japan, and Crowninshield received a visit from a representative of the Japanese government who demanded an apology–not for lampooning the Emperor, but for portraying him engaging in a menial task. Crowninshield wrote a letter of apology to the Japanese ambassador.

However, Crowninshield's indiscretions were not always humorous or defensible. Wilson wrote that the "most shocking thing" he had ever seen Crowninshield do was mutilate a book. Wilson wrote that the editorial staff needed "for some reason to print the text of a letter of Voltaire's. He sent down to Putnam's bookstore below us and borrowed a volume of an expensive and splendidly printed edition of Voltaire, then simply cut out the pages with the letter and sent the volume back, knowing that this would not be detected."

Wilson claimed that he "never knew anyone who talked as much as Crowninshield about being and behaving like 'a gentleman' and . . . exemplified this less in his own relations. This has made me suspicious ever since of people who talk about 'gentlemen.' I think it ought to be a warning to be careful and hold on to one's wallet . . . there was the 'gentleman,' the personality to which he aspired and which he rather too ostentatiously acted, and the treacherous opportunist who so often destroyed these pretensions." Crowninshield himself confessed, "I am not as genial as I seem."

However, what geniality he did possess seemed to be quite satisfactory for his legions of friends, colleagues, and admirers. Crowninshield's charm and delicacy could not salvage the fortunes of *Vanity Fair,* though, which suffered a sharp decline in advertising following the 1929 stock-market crash. In an effort to boost readership and change the fortunes of the sagging magazine, Nast demanded that *Vanity Fair* carry major articles on politics and economics. These were edited by Clare Boothe, before her marriage to Henry Luce.

This formula change was not enough to save the magazine, which had a circulation of ninety thousand. On 26 December 1935 many of the key figures in the Condé Nast publishing empire met in Nast's office to discuss what could be done to cut the company's revenue losses. *Vogue* had a remarkably successful year in 1935, grossing $2,545,000, up fourteen percent from 1934. *American Golfer* had lost twenty-three percent, and *House and Garden* had dropped twenty-six percent, but the big liability was *Vanity Fair,* which was down thirty-nine percent in revenue, from about $480,000 to $292,895. The costly venture had to be discontinued.

The February 1936 issue of *Vanity Fair* carried a notice from Nast that the magazine would be merged with *Vogue* beginning the following month. Nast wrote: "I have decided on the amalgamation of VANITY FAIR with VOGUE–its sister periodical–for the reason that the lessening advertising patronage now accorded to periodicals like VANITY FAIR–magazines so largely devoted to the spread of the arts–books, music, criticism, sculpture, satire, essays, paintings, etc.–has made the publication of it, as a single publishing unit, unremunerative. It is for that reason that the magazine now closes its independent career."

The sixty-three-year-old Crowninshield remained as a consulting editor to the Nast publications, guiding the art policy of *Vogue,* primarily a fashion magazine, and helping launch *Glamour* magazine in April 1939. Crowninshield remained with the company after Nast's death in 1943 and until shortly before his own death from an undisclosed illness on 28 December 1947. He was seventy-five.

Even from his deathbed, Crowninshield displayed characteristic form. He supervised the sending of fifteen hundred Christmas cards and forty presents and played the courtier to his nurses. After he died a family member found a note from Crowninshield in the hospital room, instructing that a particular bottle of champagne be given to one of his doctors.

Raconteur Frank Crowninshield was the heart and soul of *Vanity Fair,* the literary voice of "cafe society" from the close of 1913 to 1936. A great patron of the arts and a pillar of high society, he edited what may be regarded as the most clever, satirical, sophisticated, and artistically daring magazine of its era.

Perhaps his most vital contribution to literature was also the most characteristic of his deferential and genteel nature. He discovered many of the greatest writers and artists of the twentieth century and offered a means by which they–and *Vanity Fair*–might achieve mutual prominence.

The *New York Times* (29 December 1947) saluted Crowninshield as "the undiminished and suave apostle of gracious living, elegant manner and true urbanity." However, perhaps former *Vanity Fair* associate editor Clare Boothe Luce defined Crowninshield best by saying, "He is the last and probably the greatest of a species which is rapidly disappearing all over the world known as 'the gentleman.' "

References:

Cleveland Amory and Frederic Bradlee, eds., *Vanity Fair: Selections from America's Most Memorable Magazine–A Cavalcade of the 1920s and 1930s* (New York: Viking, 1931);

David L. Ferguson, *Cleopatra's Barge* (Boston: Little, Brown, 1976), pp. 195-228;

Dickson Hartwell, "The Happy Gentleman," *Collier's,* 119 (12 April 1947): 38, 55;

Geoffrey T. Hellman, "Frank Crowninshield," in *The Saturday Review Gallery* (New York: Simon & Schuster, 1959);

Hellman, "Profiles: Last of the Species–I," *New Yorker,* 18 (19 September 1942): 22-27;

Hellman, "Profiles: Last of the Species–II," *New Yorker,* 18 (26 September 1942): 24-28, 30-31;

Hellman, "That Was New York," *New Yorker,* 23 (14 February 1948): 74, 76, 79-81.

Cyrus H. K. Curtis
(18 June 1850-7 June 1933)

W. Wat Hopkins
Virginia Polytechnic Institute and State University

MAJOR POSITION HELD: President, Curtis Publishing Company (1891-1932).

PRINCIPAL MAGAZINES OWNED OR CONTROLLED: *Ladies' Home Journal* (1883-1933), *Saturday Evening Post* (1897-1933), *Country Gentleman* (1911-1933).

As founder of the *Ladies' Home Journal* and publisher of the *Saturday Evening Post,* Cyrus H. K. Curtis did as much to build the magazine into a mass medium as any man in American journalism. Called the Henry Ford of the magazine business, Curtis made no pretense of being either a journalist or an editor. Instead, he was an innovator who brought new techniques and ideas to magazine journalism in order to sell a product. In the late nineteenth and early twentieth centuries he did more, according to Oswald Garrison Villard, "to mechanize and standardize the public mind of America than any other man." He did so by hiring good editors and letting them edit. Once asked what he did at Curtis Publishing Company if he did not edit his magazines, Curtis responded, "I edit the editors." However, Edward W. Bok, his biographer and son-in-law, who was editor of the *Ladies' Home Journal* for thirty years, reported that Curtis's idea of "editing the editors" stopped with hiring them. Bok wrote in 1923 that Curtis left his editors "severely alone." "Get the right editor," Bok quoted Curtis as saying, "and you'll have the right magazine. Then it's only a selling proposition."

Curtis was a master at selling. *Ladies' Home Journal* began as a column in Curtis's *Tribune and Farmer,* then became a supplement to that magazine. After the *Journal* became independent in 1883, its circulation increased eightfold in eighteen months, from 25,000 subscribers to 200,000. By 1900 the *Journal* was the first magazine ever to reach the 1,000,000-subscriber mark, and by 1919 it had 2,000,000 subscribers. It was the third-most-demanded periodical among servicemen overseas during World War I. Similarly, the *Satur-*

Cyrus H. K. Curtis

day Evening Post had 1,800 subscribers when Curtis bought the magazine in 1897. Within five years circulation had reached 315,000, and four years later circulation reached the 1,000,000 mark. At its peak the *Saturday Evening Post* had more than 3,000,000 subscribers and was the largest carrier of advertising of its day.

Curtis, who began his career in business journalism as a twelve-year-old newsboy with a capital base of three cents, controlled not only the Curtis Publishing Company, which also published the *Country Gentleman,* but was president of Curtis-

Martin Company, which published the *Philadelphia Inquirer,* the *Philadelphia Public Ledger,* the *Evening Public Ledger,* and the *New York Evening Post.* In 1930, three years before Curtis's death, the two publishing companies had combined capital of more than $40 million and did a gross annual business of more than $100 million. Curtis, a high-school dropout, had been listed as one of America's four wealthiest men and had received two honorary law degrees and a handful of other major citations, including one naming him the "Most Characteristic American."

Cyrus Hermann Kotzschmar Curtis was born in Portland, Maine, 18 June 1850, the son of Cyrus Libby Curtis, a manufacturer of home furnishings, and Salome Ann Cummings Curtis. He had a younger sister, Florence Gertrude. His two middle names were given him in honor of a musician and close friend of his father. Cyrus Libby Curtis induced Hermann Kotzschmar to move from Boston to play in the Portland orchestra. Kotzschmar also became organist in the First Parish Congregationalist Unitarian Church, where the Curtises attended services. From him young Cyrus learned a love for music that he would keep throughout his life.

Curtis's first experience selling periodicals came on 4 July 1862, when he was twelve and nearly without money to celebrate the holiday. His mother had no money to give the boy but suggested he earn some. With his last three cents Curtis bought the last three issues of the *Portland Courier* from a tired newsboy who wanted to unload his burden so he could be about the business of celebrating. It took Curtis hours, but he sold the three papers for their cover price–three cents each. The next day he reinvested his profits by showing up at the newspaper's circulation department and buying a bundle of papers to sell.

Buying the papers was easy–selling them was another matter. Newsboys in Portland were highly competitive, and sales territories were well defined. The established newsboys attempted to steal Curtis's papers. When that failed, they drove him off. Curtis was new at newspaper sales and was smaller than most of the other newsboys, so he had difficulty unloading his bundle. He succeeded, but the problems with his competitors continued. However, after slowly building his profits, Curtis bought the maximum number of papers allowable and, because of his large purchase, convinced the circulation department officials to allow him to slip out the office's back door, escaping attack by his competitors. He

made his way to nearby Fort Preble, where he quickly sold out his stock to news-hungry servicemen at the previously untapped market.

Curtis's success as a newsboy did not go unnoticed. He was soon hired by the *Portland Press* to handle two established routes for two dollars a week plus all the extra papers he could sell. Shortly thereafter, the *Portland Argus* hired Curtis away for more money.

In the spring of 1865, his career as a newsboy booming, Curtis decided to go into business for himself. With a friend he started the *Young America.* The first issue was published on 5 April with little fanfare and less interest. The entrepreneurs were five dollars in debt to their printer and had a stack of unsold newspapers. Bok wrote that the debt so distressed Curtis's partner that the boy's grades began to suffer, and his parents yanked him out of the partnership, leaving Curtis alone to pay the printer.

Curtis apparently recognized that his printing venture would not succeed unless he could cut expenses. He decided one way was to print his own papers. The decision required further investment. He took a train trip to Boston, where he bought an out-of-date press for $2.50 and type for fifteen cents. To pay off his $5 printing debt and fund the *Young America,* he began selling advertising. He soon had a successful enterprise, with a circulation of four hundred and a "plant" with $200 in printing equipment.

Curtis's first publishing enterprise lasted less than a year. A fire that destroyed much of Portland on 4 July 1866 not only left Curtis without a press, it left his family without a home. Curtis took a job delivering dry goods for three dollars a week to help support his family and never returned to school.

Over the next three years Curtis received regular raises, but in 1869, when offered a job as a dry-goods salesman in Boston for ten dollars a week, he decided to move. Within weeks of the move, at age nineteen, Curtis was reunited with the business side of journalism and would never leave it. He found a part-time position selling advertising for a publication called the *Traveller's Guide.* At a twenty-five percent commission, he quickly recognized that he could make much more money as an ad salesman than as a dry-goods salesman, so he announced his resignation. Curtis's employer, however, complained that Curtis owed him at least one year's service. Though no contract existed, Curtis agreed to stay on. At

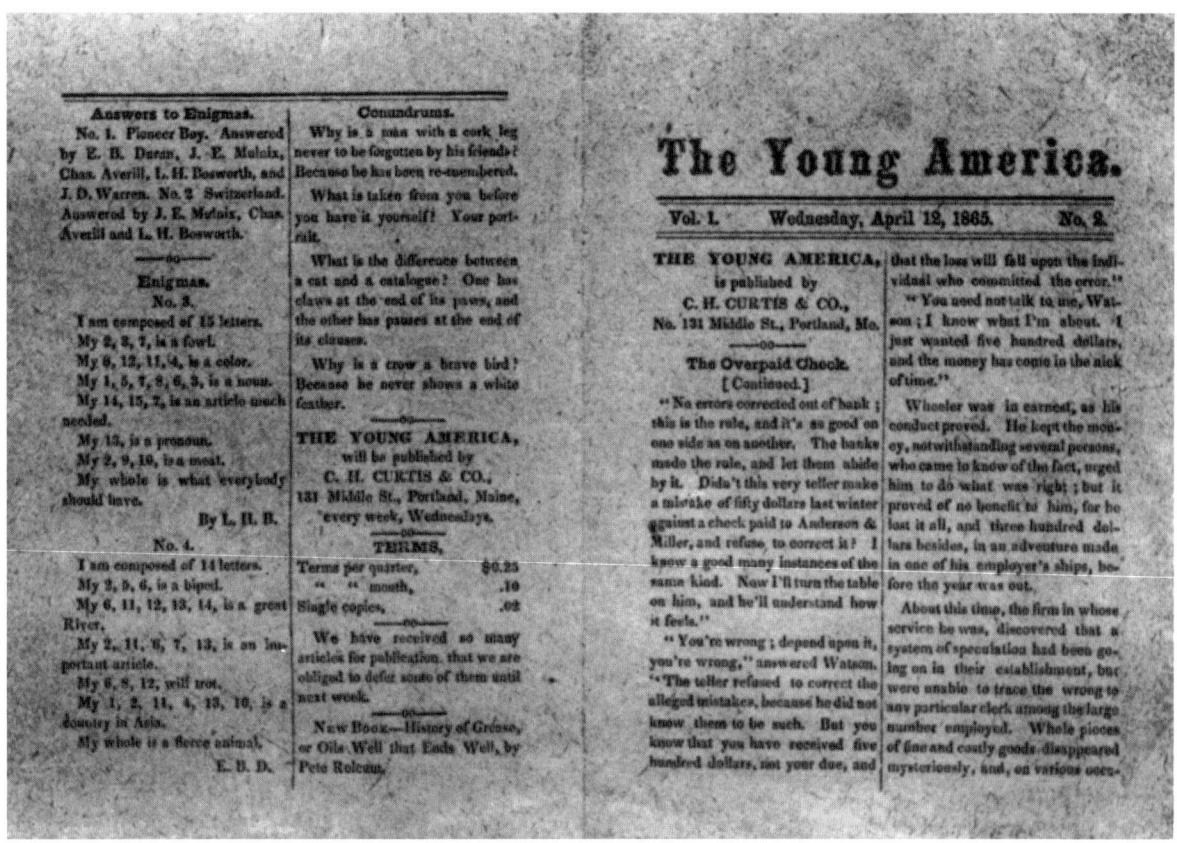

First and last pages of an issue of the Portland, Maine, newspaper Curtis founded at age fifteen
(Edward W. Bok, A Man From Maine, 1923)

the end of the year Curtis went to work full-time for the *Traveller's Guide*.

The move was the first in a series. Curtis went from the *Traveller's Guide* to the *Boston Times*, then to the *Boston Independent*, all in less than two years. Still dissatisfied, in 1872 he founded the *People's Ledger,* with a man named Thornton. Thornton promised to put up twenty thousand dollars to start the business if Curtis would run the publication. Thornton came through with neither the capital nor any labor, however, and he and Curtis soon parted company, leaving Curtis sole owner of a publication that rested on a shaky foundation.

During the next few years Curtis demonstrated some traits that would characterize his publishing career: a tenaciousness in building a sound financial investment in the face of hardships and doubts of those around him, a willingness to do what was necessary to succeed, a fierce loyalty to those who helped him, and a strict personal code that required him to repay his debts. "When I started in business," Curtis told an inter-

viewer years later, "I had no more idea than the man in the moon where I was going. But I knew I was going somewhere."

The *People's Ledger* was founded on a unique concept. Instead of running stories in serial form, each issue contained a complete story that had been published some thirty years previously in another publication. Curtis bought the stories for between five and ten dollars each. Despite this innovative approach the publication gained slowly in circulation and advertising, and Curtis found himself in debt to a printer once again. According to Bok, however, the printer, a Scotsman, told Curtis, "That's all right. . . . Do the best you can, pay me what you can, and pay the rest when you can."

Bok considered the incident a landmark in Curtis's career. "This evidence of confidence turned the tide in the career of Cyrus Curtis," Bok wrote. "The Scotchman's faith rallied the young publisher from his depression, and he worked harder than ever to make both ends of his venture meet." Though the circulation of the

Curtis's first wife, Louisa Knapp Curtis

People's Ledger began to climb, Curtis was unable to repay the debt before the printer's health failed, and the man returned to Scotland. It would be fifteen years before Curtis located the man in Minneapolis and repaid the debt, with interest.

Curtis slowly built the *People's Ledger* into a modestly successful publication. In 1872 he was making plans to move the publication to New York, where he could reduce printing costs, when fire once again destroyed his business. The day after the great Boston fire, Curtis located a new office and began to rebuild.

Four years later, during the centennial celebration, Curtis visited Philadelphia on business. He liked the city and, upon investigation, learned that he could cut the printing costs of the *People's Ledger* by about fifteen hundred dollars a year. "I figured that I could live on this saving," he said and moved his business and family. The move came as the Curtis family was growing. On 10 March 1875 he and Louisa Knapp of Boston had been married. The only child they were to have, Mary Louise, was born seventeen months later, 6 August 1876.

Two years after the move to Philadelphia, Curtis made another career change. He sold the *People's Ledger* and became advertising manager for the weekly edition of the *Philadelphia Press*. Curtis learned that the chief writer for the edition, Thomas Meehan, was an authority on agricultural and horticultural topics. Demonstrating his ability to create a successful advertising campaign by capitalizing on a publication's strong points, Curtis began to feature Meehan in his ad solicitations, encouraging agricultural and horticultural companies to advertise in the *Press*.

Advertising revenue, as well as circulation, began to grow. Curtis was justifiably proud of his campaign and took to a bit of boasting when his sister, Florence, and her new husband, banker Hamilton Mayo, came to Philadelphia from Massachusetts for a visit. Mayo was impressed and suggested Curtis begin his own paper, writing a two-thousand-dollar check to back up the suggestion. Curtis was soon a publisher again.

In 1879 he established the *Tribune and Farmer*, a journal, as its name indicates, devoted to agricultural topics. Curtis asked Meehan to be its editor. Meehan had been a relative unknown until Curtis began to feature him in advertising. He had enjoyed being in the limelight and welcomed the opportunity to continue working with Curtis.

The *Tribune and Farmer*, as did most of Curtis's publications, had a shaky start. Typically, Curtis attempted to boost circulation by advertising Meehan and his new publication in other periodicals. He quickly built a debt of eight hundred dollars with an ad agent who offered to eliminate the debt for part ownership in the paper. Curtis consulted with his silent partner, Mayo, who thought the idea wise, and settled the debt for a quarter ownership. It was a move that would eventually play a role in Curtis's decision to abandon the *Tribune and Farmer* to put all his energies behind the *Ladies' Home Journal*. The new partner was not nearly as silent as Mayo and regularly made suggestions to Curtis on methods of boosting circulation and other aspects of the business. Curtis often found the methods suggested by the partner to be improper, and their disagreements led to a parting of ways after Curtis began the *Ladies' Home Journal* as a supplement of the *Tribune and Farmer*.

The *Ladies' Home Journal* grew from a column in the *Tribune and Farmer*. The column, called "Women and Home," contained news clipped from other publications, ostensibly to help homemakers. Curtis's wife, however, took to ridiculing the contents of the column. Curtis responded to her criticism by telling her, "If you

Covers for the principal magazines published by Curtis

think you can do it any better, why don't you try it?" Louisa Curtis, using her maiden name, Knapp, thus began editing the column almost on a dare.

Curtis brought home some other periodicals–they were called "exchanges" because publishers exchanged them with other publishers for free–for his wife to clip. Louisa Knapp, though, rejected this method and began to write her own items and to encourage her friends to do likewise. The column became so popular that within two months it had grown to fill an entire page.

Curtis's partner, however, was not a fan of the page, so when Curtis proposed expanding "Women and Home" to a supplement for the *Tribune and Farmer*, edited by his wife, the partner balked. Curtis went ahead with the venture anyway, telling the partner that any expense would be borne entirely by Curtis and would not come from *Tribune and Farmer* profits. But since the partner would bear no expense, he would see no profits should the publication become profitable.

While the first issue was being put together, Mrs. Curtis asked her husband what the supplement should be called. Uninterested in such details, Curtis responded, "Call it anything you like. It's a sort of a ladies' journal."

The *Ladies' Journal*, then, was first published in December 1883. To demonstrate, in graphic form, the theme of the new publication, Mrs. Curtis had engraved in the banner, between the words "Ladies'" and "Journal," a picture of a house with the word "Home" in quotation marks underneath. The first person to request a subscription wrote for "The Ladies' Home Journal," as did the many subscribers who followed. The new name of the journal, therefore, was established.

Within a year the *Ladies' Home Journal* became a separate journal, no longer affiliated with the *Tribune and Farmer*. Curtis's partner continued to suggest a subscription scheme Curtis viewed as dishonest. When the partner suggested that Curtis was spending too much time with the *Ladies' Home Journal* to the detriment of the *Tribune and Farmer*, Curtis proposed a solution. He suggested a parting of ways–the partner could have the *Tribune and Farmer*, and Curtis would keep the *Ladies' Home Journal*. The deal was obviously attractive to the partner, whose quarter ownership was suddenly quadrupled in exchange for a woman's magazine he did not expect to survive anyway. The bargain was legalized, and the partner departed for New York City with the *Tribune and Farmer*, where it would soon die. Curtis, on the other hand, with ingenious marketing and dedication to editorial quality, turned the *Ladies' Home Journal* into a leading success story in American magazine journalism.

When the two men first split, however, Curtis found himself once again at the helm of a struggling publication. In 1884, when the *Ladies' Home Journal* became independent, it had a circulation of twenty-five thousand. Curtis initiated a two-pronged plan: he proposed to build his subscription list and to improve the quality of the magazine to keep its new subscribers.

To build circulation he initiated a revolutionary subscription scheme. *Journal* subscriptions were fifty cents a year. Curtis, however, offered four subscriptions–if they were ordered together–for one dollar. The "club" plan, as he called the scheme, required one new subscriber to become a salesperson, seeking out three more "club" members. During the next eighteen months ninety percent of all subscriptions came in under the club plan, and circulation doubled each six months. At the end of the eighteen months, then, there were two hundred thousand subscribers to the *Journal*.

Curtis recognized that the subscribers would not remain unless he published a magazine they wanted to read, and advertisers would not remain unless subscribers did. He began a campaign, therefore, to attract well-known writers to the *Journal*. His first target was popular woman's writer Marion Harland of Springfield, Massachusetts. She received Curtis graciously when he called but informed him that she was committed to other publishers. Undaunted, Curtis continued to press for at least one story and convinced her to sell him, for ninety dollars, a short story she had just written.

Curtis returned to Philadelphia jubilant, only to have his wife scold him for spending so much on a single story. He immediately called on an eggbeater manufacturer who had a record of advertising in magazines carrying Marion Harland stories and sold the man ninety dollars worth of advertising. Curtis bought his own advertisements in other publications to promote the story. He claimed that it would be the first in a series of stories by popular writers to be published in the *Journal*. By July 1888 the subscription list had doubled again, topping four hundred thousand.

Curtis was able to convince several well-known authors to write stories for the *Journal*, even though they first refused. When Louisa

The Curtis Publishing Company headquarters in Philadelphia. The building, which faces Independence Square and flanks Washington Square, was erected in 1911.

May Alcott declined Curtis's request, for example, he offered to donate one hundred dollars to her favorite charity. She agreed to write a one-column piece. When the piece was published, however, it ran to nearly two columns. Curtis sent Alcott a second one-hundred-dollar check, with a note explaining that, since she had agreed to write a column for one hundred dollars, Curtis owed her another hundred dollars for the second column. Alcott was so impressed with the action she told other authors, who became more willing to write for Curtis. Slowly he was building the list of writers he had promised his readers.

In the meantime Curtis's subscription campaign had become so successful that it was causing him problems. The circulation of the *Journal* was outrunning the advertising. In an attempt to slow new subscriptions, Curtis stopped the club subscription plan. The subscriptions continued to arrive, however. On 1 July 1889, with circulation at seven hundred thousand and continuing to climb, Curtis took drastic action. He doubled the subscription price to one dollar per year. He also doubled the size of his publication. At about the same time Mrs. Curtis resigned as the editor of

the *Journal* to spend more time with her thirteen-year-old daughter. To replace her, Curtis hired Edward W. Bok, a twenty-six-year-old Dutch immigrant who, by his own admission, knew nothing about women. Bok had edited *Brooklyn Magazine* briefly, but Curtis was attracted to him because of a syndicated column, "Bok's Literary Leaves," which Bok wrote while working for Charles Scribner's Sons.

The reaction to the appointment was anything but positive. John Tebbel reports that Bok's editorship was viewed as "a hilarious event," and that some of the lampooning was cruel and some "verged on the libelous." In 1896 Bok would marry Curtis's only daughter, "ending at least some of the gossip about his supposedly defective heterosexuality," the historian wrote.

Because of the increased price and the new editor, predictions for the future of the *Journal* were dire, even from within Curtis's own shop. Curtis's printer, for example, reportedly said that "Curtis's success had gone to his head. Now he's going to blow his whole outfit to pieces." The prognosticators were in error, as were the early critics of the Bok appointment.

The Curtis Publishing Company composing room

Curtis did not have an easy time, however. He turned once again to advertising the *Journal* in other publications. The N. W. Ayer and Son advertising firm granted him $200,000 in credit for advertising and helped him secure another $100,000 in credit with paper manufacturers to tide him through the rough times. As it turned out, Curtis would spend more than $310,000 with the Ayer company during this transition period.

The changes and the promotional advertising paid off. In 1890, when all the fifty-cent subscriptions had expired, Curtis found his company on a much better financial basis. The subscription list had been trimmed from 700,000 to 488,000, but the subscribers were paying one dollar per year rather than fifty cents.

Similarly, Bok's performance had been such that many of his critics had faded. Bok may have been "dame-shy" as one critic called him, but he seemed to know what his readers wanted. He began many features that became very popular. There were advice columns such as "Side Talks With Girls," which he initially wrote himself

under the byline Ruth Ashmore but turned over to Isabel A. Mallon, who used the same pseudonym. He also secured articles and stories from such writers as P. T. Barnum, Benjamin Harrison, Mark Twain, Rudyard Kipling, Jean Webster, Kate Douglas Wiggin, and Theodore Roosevelt. According to Tebbel, the appointment of Bok as editor was the move that "elevated the magazine to pre-eminence."

Bok, however, was not well loved by all his readers. When he editorially attacked "the intellectual woman" who was, among other things, seeking the right to vote, claiming such women were "donning masculinity" in their fight for additional rights, hundreds of women wrote Curtis demanding that Bok be fired. And when the editor discussed sex education in the *Journal*, using the word "syphilis" for the first time in a popular magazine, the reaction was similar. Both times, Bok later reported, Curtis "supported his editor's right to edit."

Once the *Journal* rebounded, it never again faltered. In 1903 its subscription list topped one million, making it the first magazine ever to

Curtis at his Etsey parlor organ with one of his grandsons

reach that figure. And circulation continued to climb so rapidly that once, at a luncheon, when Curtis was asked, "What is the circulation now of *The Journal?*" he responded, "Now? I really don't know. This morning it was two million."

The *Journal* was first in many other areas of magazine journalism as well. It was the first magazine to change its covers monthly, the first to refuse questionable advertisements, the first to use color illustrations, the first to have a garden department, and the first to have its own kitchen for testing recipes. In addition, because the *Journal* had so many subscribers, its oversized format was considered when the United States Post Office Department established the standard size for rural mailboxes.

As the *Journal* began to rebound, Curtis decided to establish a stock company for his publishing business. In June 1891 the Curtis Publishing Company was established. When the first board of directors met, the company had $49.35 cash on hand. A year later the company was still strapped for cash. In April 1892 the treasurer reported that liabilities exceeded assets by $162,000.

The figure is particularly remarkable in light of another drastic action Curtis took that year: he announced that the *Ladies' Home Journal* would no longer accept advertisements for patent medicines. The move meant a loss of thousands of dollars. Curtis, Bok wrote, "was the first publisher to realize the principle and sense the wisdom of having the advertisements in his magazine only of the most reliable nature, and to resolve that this should be." The treasurer, however, believed that Curtis could have found a more stable time to come to the realization. "He could not have chosen a more disastrous time than this to curtail our income," the treasurer complained, "when we need every penny we can scrape together."

His complaints were to no avail. Curtis never wavered in the policy. Bok reported that one Friday morning shortly after the announcement, Curtis received a check for eighteen thousand dollars from a major advertising agent and an order for six pages of patent medicine ads. Though the company had insufficient funds in the bank to make the weekly payroll, Curtis unhesitatingly returned the check to the envelope in which it had arrived and wrote "Return" across the front.

Curtis would eventually ban advertisements for cosmetics and for financial schemes he said were designed to bilk widows out of their inheritances. In the end the *Journal* did not need the advertising. During the first six months of 1892, when the company was in financial difficulty, its gross advertising income had been $119,613. During the first six months of 1893, however, gross advertising income had increased to $255,000, so other advertisements filled the space vacated by the patent medicines. Finally, in January 1895 the treasurer reported that company assets exceeded liabilities by about $100,000. The Curtis Publishing Company was on a sound footing.

From this point forward Curtis was looking to expand. His first acquisition was the *Saturday Evening Post*. The *Post* had been one of Curtis Publishing Company's exchanges, and Curtis apparently had had an interest in the publication for years. The interest was due to the heritage, rather than the quality, of the *Post*, which traced its lineage to 1728 and Benjamin Franklin. In the late nineteenth century the *Post* was a sixteen-page, unillustrated weekly of mostly clipped material and had been declining in quality since the Civil War.

In August 1897 Andrew E. Smythe, the owner of the *Post*, died. The only heir, a sister, would not put up the money to continue the publication. Representatives of the *Post* met with Curtis and offered him the struggling magazine. Curtis paid one hundred dollars down and bought the magazine for one thousand dollars.

Circulation–which was about eighteen hundred when Curtis bought the magazine–was steadily dropping, and many of the subscribers were in arrears. "Still," according to Walter D. Fuller, "it had a priceless heritage and a direct link to Benjamin Franklin, and both of these assets pleased Curtis tremendously."

The *Universal Instructor in All Arts and Sciences and Pennsylvania Gazette* was started by Franklin on 24 December 1728. The name was changed to the *Pennsylvania Gazette* in 1729, and to the *Saturday Evening Post* in 1821. There were variations on that name until 1839, when the *Satur-

day Evening Post went on the banner for good. In his research Curtis also learned that, except for a few issues, the *Post* had published continuously since its inception.

Curtis put William George Jordan in charge of the magazine, but Jordan would not last long. He was an admirer of Bok and apparently wanted to make over the *Post* in the image of the *Ladies' Home Journal*, which was not what Curtis wanted. Curtis fired Jordan and went off to Paris intending to hire Arthur Sherburn Hardy, former editor of *Cosmopolitan*, as editor for the *Post*.

Shortly after buying the *Post* Curtis had hired George Horace Lorimer, a former reporter, as literary editor, which was a title more than a job. There are contradictions on how Curtis and Lorimer first made contact. Bok reported that a mutual friend recommended Lorimer for a position on the *Post*, and that Curtis made first contact. A more likely account, however, is that Lorimer, a reporter at the *Boston Herald* when news of Curtis's purchase was received at the newspaper by wire services, wired Curtis within an hour asking for a job on the magazine. A mutual friend introduced the two the following week when Curtis was in Boston on business, and Lorimer was hired.

Two years later Curtis fired Jordan and, while making preparations to meet Hardy in Paris, made Lorimer temporary managing editor. The *New York Times* (7 June 1933) reported this story: "Three weeks before I sailed for Europe I put Lorimer temporarily in charge and those three weeks worked a lightning change in the sheet. I never saw such quick and brilliant action. . . . On the way to the boat I met the man who first had introduced me to Lorimer and I told him I should not think it a grievous loss if I did not get the man. When I came back from Europe and saw how things were going in Philadelphia I was certain that Lorimer was the right man and decided to hold on to him."

Indeed, Lorimer had recognized his opportunity. He made wholesale changes in the *Post*, first sweeping out material he believed to be dull. He killed, for example, "Report of Humane Lepidopterans," "Miss Imogene's Hints for Growing Girls," and "Facts About Holidays Here & Abroad." He also swept out dull, sappy fiction, replacing it with works by Joel Chandler Harris, Rudyard Kipling, Richard Harding Davis, Stephen Crane, Bret Harte, Rex Beach, and Owen Wister.

He secured stories from some of those writers by making policy changes at the magazine. First, he promised to pay writers on acceptance, rather than on publication. Second, he promised to give writers an answer within seventy-two hours. The changes drew writers who had grown accustomed to publishers who held stories for long periods and paid on publication.

In June 1899 Lorimer was officially named editor of the *Post,* a position he would hold until 1936. He immediately set about the business of building the magazine into a major publication. Curtis had originally seen the magazine as a counterpart to the *Ladies' Home Journal.* The *Journal* was for the woman at home; the *Post* would be for the man who came home from work. Scorning advice that businessmen did not want to read about business after the day was done, Curtis wanted to establish a journal about business for businessmen.

A group of employees at the Curtis Publishing Company, however, was opposed to the project almost from the outset. Led by Bok, who referred to the *Post* as *"The Ladies' Home Journal's* little brother," they urged Curtis to get rid of the magazine. They claimed it was draining revenue from the *Journal.* When Bok complained that the *Post* was $750,000 in the red, Curtis is said to have replied, "According to your figures, they leave Lorimer $250,000 to go. I like round figures."

Lorimer would spend even more–$1.25 million–before the *Post* showed a profit. According to Fuller, he began "interpreting business and romanticizing the careers of successful businessmen," as Curtis wanted. Lorimer succeeded in getting William Jennings Bryan, Sen. Albert J. Beferidge of Indiana, and former President Grover Cleveland to write for the *Post.* He was soon doing more, however. Lorimer wanted to make the *Post* a truly mass magazine–a magazine for each of the seventy-five million people in the United States. He published Frank Norris's *The Pit* (1903) in serial form. He hired Isaac Marcosson, whom Tebbel calls "the greatest interviewer of his time," to write about celebrities, and Sam Blythe to write about politics. He ran the life stories of Babe Ruth, Jack Dempsey, Bobby Jones, and other famous sports figures. And he brought the art of Norman Rockwell to the cover.

Lorimer's success became legendary. When he became editor of the *Post* in 1899, the magazine's circulation had increased to 250,000.

Within five years it was 700,000. In 1908 the circulation of the *Post* reached 1,000,000; five years later it reached 2,000,000; and in 1928 it topped 3,000,000, though it did not stabilize at that figure until 1937. The *Post* became the largest carrier of advertising of its day, grossing some $53 million a year. When Lorimer died of throat cancer, less than a year after retiring as editor of the *Post,* the *New York Times,* possibly recalling that Curtis had been called the Henry Ford of the magazine business, referred to Lorimer as "the Henry Ford of American Literature."

At the turn of the century, then, the Curtis Publishing Company was thriving. The *Ladies' Home Journal* was one of the most popular magazines in the country, and Lorimer was already making strides at the *Saturday Evening Post.* Cyrus Curtis was content with business but was not in good health. Bok reported that Curtis was shaken when he was denied additional life insurance by three different companies. As a businessman, Curtis was nervous, restless, and demanding. He required punctuality, had a short temper, and was always active. He made a concerted effort to improve his health. He bought a home in the country near Wyncote, Pennsylvania, built a golf course adjacent to the home, and became an avid golfer. He also began yachting, a hobby he would enjoy for the rest of his life.

Other major changes occurred in Curtis's life as well. On 25 February 1910 his wife of nearly thirty-five years died. Seven months later he married Mrs. Kate Stanwood Cutter Pillsbury of Milwaukee, a widow and his second cousin.

Early in the century, after establishing his new home in the country, Curtis began planning a new home for the Curtis Publishing Company. In 1910 the new building was nearly completed. Bok reported that Curtis recognized that there was room in the building to publish a third magazine and decided to publish an agricultural journal. Harry N. McKinney of N. W. Ayer and Son encouraged Curtis to go after the *Country Gentleman,* which was published in Albany, New York. The magazine had been in one family for eighty years, but publisher Gilbert Tucker was old and ailing.

Curtis and Tucker met, but a bargain could not be struck. Curtis had suspicions that another publisher of agricultural journals was interested in the *Country Gentleman,* however, and on the second meeting with Tucker, he made an offer of one hundred thousand dollars, which was accepted. The *Country Gentleman* was first published as part of Curtis Publishing Company on 6 July 1911. When Curtis bought the magazine, it had a subscription list of twenty-five thousand. When those subscribers with delinquent accounts were purged, however, only about two thousand remained. J. Clyde Marquis was named editor. The company invested $2 million in the magazine before it became profitable in 1917.

After buying the *Country Gentleman*, Curtis turned to daily journalism, but he had to be encouraged to enter the field. The primary encouragement came from Adolph S. Ochs, the publisher who had turned around the struggling *New York Times*. Ochs approached Curtis and, for more than a year, attempted to sell him part ownership in the *Philadelphia Public Ledger*. At first Curtis was not interested. After receiving additional encouragement from a friend, John Gribbel, who wanted part ownership of the paper, Curtis offered Ochs $2 million on the part of himself and Gribbel. They published their first issue 1 January 1913.

The move was the first in a series of expansions and purchases in daily newspaper journalism. Curtis founded an evening edition of the *Public Ledger* and then, so he could get a membership in the Associated Press for the evening paper, bought the *Philadelphia Evening Journal* in June 1913. Curtis bought the *Philadelphia Press* in 1920 and the *Philadelphia North American* in 1925 and merged the two papers with the *Philadelphia Public Ledger*. In 1924 Curtis bought the *New York Evening Post*, and in 1925 he incorporated all the newspapers as part of Curtis-Martin papers.

Curtis's newspapers were never as successful as his magazines. He announced that he hoped to make the *Public Ledger* a national newspaper. However, Oswald Garrison Villard, noting that the paper continued to drop in circulation after Curtis took over, said that the paper, "for all its excellent qualities and features, is without originality or distinction, and without a soul." That same critic would later call Curtis's "experiment in daily journalism . . . a disastrous failure" due to "faulty and inefficient management; reactionary, uninteresting, and visionless editorial direction." Eventually the *Public Ledger* would die, and the *Evening Public Ledger*, the *Evening Post*, and the *Inquirer* would be sold after losing enormous sums. Curtis's legacy was with the Curtis Publishing Company, not Curtis-Martin Newspapers.

Cyrus Curtis died at 2:10 A.M., Wednesday, 7 June 1933, eleven days before his eighty-third birthday, at his estate in Wyncote following a long illness. News of his death made the front page of the *New York Times* on the same day. A year earlier, while on his yacht, Curtis had a severe heart attack. While he was recuperating, his wife, Kate, died of a heart ailment.

Among those sending condolences to the Curtis family were Pres. Franklin Roosevelt, writers Sinclair Lewis and Dorothy Thompson, Associated Press president Frank B. Noyes, and *New York Times* publisher Adolph S. Ochs. Roosevelt, whose election was opposed by Lorimer in the *Post*, wrote to Curtis's daughter that "America has lost a great publisher, a noted leader in the field of journalism."

Curtis was remembered for many accomplishments, but primarily for his magazine empire and his uncanny knack for selecting superior editors. Curtis's particular genius, according to Tebbel, "lay in knowing how to create magazine properties, and in finding the men to edit them. After that, he had the good sense to leave them alone." Walter Davenport wrote that "No other publisher of magazines had such a record of perfect selections" of editors. Curtis, however, told an interviewer that his selection of editors was based simply on the ability of the men selected. He was impressed with Bok and Lorimer, he said, because they could "move fast and accurately, do things right and quickly."

The editors were also able to withstand pressure–from readers, from advertisers, and from Curtis, though Curtis generally made no comments on editorial decisions. Once Curtis casually mentioned to Lorimer that Mrs. Curtis did not like a story that had appeared in the *Post*. Lorimer's courteous reply was, "I'm not editing *The Saturday Evening Post* for your wife." The next day Curtis gave Lorimer a raise.

Curtis was also remembered for his philanthropy. He gave literally millions of dollars to colleges and universities, charities, hospitals, museums, and other institutions. He also chaired fund drives to raise money for such institutions.

In 1930 the Pennsylvania Society awarded Curtis its Gold Medal, bestowed annually to the "Most Characteristic American." The Harvard Graduate School of Business Administration that same year awarded him the Bok Annual Gold Medal for distinguished contemporary service to advertising. Indeed, a later president of Curtis Publishing Company, Walter D. Fuller, said one of Curtis's great contributions was that "He helped teach advertising to be truthful and reliable." To Curtis, Fuller said, "advertising was the generator to supply the power to operate the magazines. Advertising and nothing else, he felt, could produce high quality magazines at low cost." Curtis was also awarded two honorary law degrees, from the University of Pennsylvania in 1924 and from Ursinus College in 1913.

Upon his death the *New York Times* (8 June 1933) noted in an editorial: "Mr. Curtis was a great publisher and a great citizen. He contributed mightily and for the good to the life of America through the publications whose 'editors he edited,' and whose wholesome influence he carried into its homes, its offices, its schools, and even the streets of villages, towns and cities."

Interview:

John B. Kennedy, "Go Fast, Young Man, Go Fast; An Interview with Cyrus H. K. Curtis," *Collier's*, 76 (21 November 1925): 24.

Biography:

Edward W. Bok, *A Man From Maine* (New York: Scribners, 1923).

References:

Walter Davenport and James Derieux, "He Never Underestimated the Power of a Woman" and "The Henry Ford of American Literature," in their *Ladies, Gentlemen, and Editors* (Garden City, N.Y.: Doubleday, 1960), pp. 173-202, 328-353;

Walter D. Fuller, "The Life and Times of Cyrus H. K. Curtis (1850-1933)," *Newcomen Society of England in North America,* pamphlet no. 16 (1948);

"The Man From Maine," *Saturday Evening Post,* 249 (July 1977): 4, 114-115;

John Tebbel, "The Great Transformation: II," in his *The Media in America* (New York: Mentor, 1976), pp. 365-385;

Oswald Garrison Villard, "The Philadelphia *Public Ledger,* A Muffed Opportunity," in his *Some Newspapers and Newspapermen* (New York: Knopf, 1923), pp. 150-169.

Papers:

Some of Curtis's correspondence is held in the collections of the Historical Society of Pennsylvania.

George T. Delacorte, Jr.

(20 June 1894-   )

Peggy J. Kreshel
University of Georgia

MAJOR POSITION HELD: President, Dell Publishing Company (1921-1976).

PRINCIPAL MAGAZINES OWNED OR CONTROLLED: *Sweetheart Stories* (1925-1945); *Modern Romances* (1929-1976); *Modern Screen* (1930-1976); *Inside Detective* (1935-1975); *Front Page Detective* (1936-1976); *Western Romances* (1929-1942); *Ballyhoo* (1931-1939).

EDITED BOOKS: *The Famous Story Magazine: The World's Best Stories from Modern and Classic Literature*, 6 volumes (New York: Famous Story, 1925-1927);
The Book of Ballyhoo: A Selection of Famous Pictures From a Famous Magazine, edited by Delacorte and Norman H. Anthony (New York: Simon & Schuster, 1931).

George Thomas Delacorte, Jr.'s, fascination with magazines led him to found Dell Publishing Company in 1921. In a career which spanned more than fifty years, he built Dell into one of the largest and most diversified mass-market publishers in the world.

Success in the publishing business, he told reporter Ken McKenna in a 1 July 1962 *New York Herald Tribune* interview, is a matter of timing, of knowing what the public wants before the public becomes aware of it. This philosophy led McKenna to call Delacorte "the man who made money guessing what the low-brows wanted."

This philosophy also kept Dell competitive over the years in the face of persistent shifts in popular reading trends. Dell published pulps in the 1920s, launched movie and fan magazines in the 1930s, emerged as one of the largest comic-book publishers in the 1940s, and entrenched itself in the paperback-book industry in the 1950s. By 1954 Dell Publishing Company had become the largest publisher of magazines and comic books in the United States. At the time of Delacorte's retirement in 1976 (when Doubleday and Company purchased Dell for a rumored $35

George T. Delacorte (courtesy GTD Holdings)

million), Dell was credited with having created markets for some seven hundred periodicals.

Born in Brooklyn on 20 June 1894, Delacorte, the son of two attorneys, George T. and Cecila Koeing Delacorte, was educated in Brooklyn primary and secondary schools. He entered Harvard in 1910 but left after a year, purportedly because the school was "too sedate" for his liking. He then transferred to Columbia College of Columbia University. He "took the easiest courses," he admitted to Roberta Walton, a reporter for *Columbia* (Winter 1979), so he "wouldn't have to work so hard." He was graduated in 1913. He turned down a teaching post in English at Columbia to take a job with New Fiction Publishing Company.

One of Delacorte's jobs at New Fiction was circulation promotion. He spent time handing out cigars to newsstand owners in an effort to acquire more prominent displays of New Fiction titles. Within two years he had become business manager and then president. However, in 1921, when New Fiction was hit by an economic recession, Delacorte was fired for having failed to foresee the slump.

Delacorte used the money from the severed contract, fifteen thousand dollars, to begin Dell Publishing Company in 1921. William A. Johnston, former Sunday editor of the *New York World,* joined him in the venture. The business began with Delacorte and two employees in a one-room office in the Masonic Temple Building on West 23rd Street. Delacorte became the sole owner of the company upon Johnston's death the next year. In the years that followed Delacorte mastered every aspect of the publishing business, from editing to management.

At first, Dell only published ten-cent pamphlets on such topics as character analysis and horoscopes. Delacorte then started with a publication called *Sweetheart Stories,* which he edited himself. However, as confession magazines became increasingly important reading fare, Dell followed the cue of Bernarr Macfadden's *True Story* (begun in 1919) and published *I Confess* in 1921. This was followed by dozens of other titles for the pulp-hungry public, including the short-lived *My Story.*

In 1929 Dell introduced *Modern Romances.* In an imaginative marketing strategy modeled after Woolworth Tower Magazines, Delacorte agreed to publish *Modern Romances* and *Modern Screen* for sole distribution by S. S. Kresge and S. H. Kress variety chains. In cities where these chains did not have stores, the publications sold on newsstands. Despite the Depression, circulation for *Modern Romances* rose quickly to 660,118, putting it in fourth place in the competitive confession-magazine field in 1938.

Delacorte adopted an innovative management approach out of necessity. Talking to a *Tide* interviewer on the occasion of Dell's twenty-fifth anniversary, Delacorte commented on some of his early efforts to achieve economic stability. To pinch editorial dollars, he purchased inexpensive manuscripts from England. Ten thousand dollars bought enough manuscripts to fill a publication for two or three years. The manuscripts were then rewritten, with the characters and situations changed to American ones. Dukes became bank-

ers' sons, and the postmistress in the village became the stenographer in the city. Delacorte also created demand by passing out free copies of his publications.

He introduced pulp publications to retail outlets at the extremely low price of ten cents. At that price he could not risk having unsold copies. To eliminate that risk he developed an innovative marketing method whereby he numbered rather than dated issues. Copies were initially distributed east of the Rockies and south of Canada. When unsold copies of the publications were returned to him, he distributed the publications west of the Rockies and in Canada.

In *Magazines in the Twentieth Century* (1956), Theodore Peterson notes several other practices that contributed to Dell's early commercial success. First, Delacorte concentrated on newsstand sales. Approximately ninety-five percent of Dell's circulation in 1955 was derived from newsstand sales.

Second, Delacorte looked to circulation rather than advertising for its revenue. Advertising increased in importance following 1930, but, according to an interview in the October 1948 issue of *Advertising and Selling,* only five of Delacorte's more than fifty titles carried consumer advertising at that time. Those five publications were the Dell Modern Group consisting of *Modern Screen, Modern Romances,* and *Screen Stories,* and the Dell Men's Group, consisting of *Inside Detective* and *Front Page Detective.*

Additionally, Delacorte never based hopes on a single magazine. When he did sell advertising space, as noted above, he sold it in "Groups." Because he had few advertising commitments, Delacorte was not forced to subsidize publications that did not immediately find a market.

Dell introduced new publications as quickly as it eliminated those that did not show a profit, and it designed many publications as one-time shots. As a result, at the end of a decade of publishing, Delacorte had originated nearly three dozen publications and had abandoned half of them. By 1931 Dell was publishing fourteen magazines, primarily pulps, confession magazines, and movie-fan magazines. Titles included *War Stories, Western Romances, Cupid's Diary, I Confess, Modern Romances,* and *Modern Screen.*

In 1931 Delacorte and Norman H. Anthony, the past editor of *Life* (1929-1930) and of *Judge* (1922-1929), a satirical weekly, introduced one of Dell's most successful ventures, a satirical publication called *Ballyhoo.* Delacorte later

HAVE YOU THE RIGHT TO MARRY?

Modern Romances

JUNE
10 CENTS

EVERY
STORY
TRUE

LOVERS
AGAINST
THE WORLD

Cover for an issue of one of Dell Publishing Company's confession magazines. Delacorte founded the company in 1921.

claimed to have gone against his best judgment in agreeing to the magazine but allowed Anthony free editorial rein with *Ballyhoo*. The first issue came wrapped in a then-new product called cellophane, which Delacorte got free in exchange for promoting it. Readers were urged to "Read a fresh magazine." There was no question of the "freshness" of the publication. The magazine had a slapstick appeal. Peterson describes it by noting that "its humor, much of it deriving from the bathroom or sex, much of it in questionable taste, was broad and audacious." The publication carried no advertising. In fact, much of its humor burlesqued familiar advertising slogans. Although the advertising industry expressed concern at being the buffoon, some advertisers paid handsomely to have their ads lampooned.

The publication achieved incredible commercial success in the first few issues and begat imitations in games, songs, and greeting cards. At its peak *Ballyhoo* had newsstand sales of more than two million, a record unsurpassed until the 1940s. Its success, however, was short-lived. By its second anniversary, the magazine's circulation had dropped to only three hundred thousand. Originally a fortnightly, it became a quarterly and dropped to pocket size before it was discontinued in 1939.

Comic magazines, offshoots of newspaper comics, originated in the 1930s. In the 1940s the comic-magazine business boomed. Several publishers of successful pulp magazines adopted pulp themes in their comic books as well. These publications, anything but comic, met with considerable criticism from parents, educators, legislators, clergy, and the press. A Senate subcommittee on juvenile delinquency even quizzed the leading comic-book publishers.

Dell, the first large publisher of comic magazines, and the first to introduce four-color com-

*Cover for the October 1935 issue of one of Dell's most successful publications, a satirical magazine that,
at its peak, had newsstand sales of more than two million copies*

ics, steadfastly avoided crime themes and sex-filled drawings. The company thus avoided criticisms typically aimed at the comic book industry. Laurence Bell suggested that the chief reason for avoiding these themes was Delacorte's "own personal fondness for, and understanding of children." Dell's cast of comic-book characters included Gene Autry, Tom and Jerry, Little Lulu, Mickey Mouse, Donald Duck, the Lone Ranger, Roy Rogers, and Tarzan, all very respectable characters. Dell featured all of the Disney characters, and according to Delacorte, during hard times Dell kept Disney in business, paying as much as ten thousand dollars in royalties per month. Dell comics always received the highest approval from parent and educational organizations. In 1948, when comic-book publishers banded together in the Association of Comic Magazines Publishers to try to protect themselves from restrictive legislation, Dell, along with several other large comic-book publishers, refused to join. Dell argued that

they had no need to be regulated since their publications were not offensive, and they did not want to shelter those involved in comics of "questionable" character. In 1954, when the Comic Magazine Association of America was formed, Delacorte again refused to join.

During the 1940s Dell focused on comic books and crossword-puzzle magazines. It was estimated that by 1950 Dell comic-book sales had risen to more than thirty million each month. New titles were introduced at the rate of ten to twelve a month by 1955.

During that decade Dell embarked on yet another adventure, paperback books. A frequent visitor to Europe, Delacorte found himself fascinated by the paperbound books popular there. In the United States, booksellers did not want to deal with "bastardized" magazine books, so distribution remained a problem. However, because he was a successful magazine publisher, Delacorte was able to get wholesalers to carry the

*Mayor Robert Wagner (right) presenting Delacorte with the New York City Medallion in 1964
in recognition of his philanthropic work*

twenty-five-cent books, which soon appeared in supermarkets, drugstores, and train terminals. Dell entrenched itself in the paperback industry, acquiring the reprint rights to Grace Metalious's *Peyton Place* (1956), among other successful works. Delacorte told McKenna, "I'm more interested in books than I ever was in magazines." By 1963 Dell was one of the three leading publishers of paperback books. Dell then branched out into hardcover publications and signed several well-known authors, including Irwin Shaw, James Baldwin, and Kurt Vonnegut, Jr.

Delacorte retired in 1976 when Doubleday and Company purchased Dell. Commenting on the sale in the *Palm Beach Post-Times* (1 May 1977), Delacorte said he never really sat down and decided to sell but "just figured why should I take such big chances at this point in my life." Retrospectively, he felt that some mistakes had cost Dell millions. Dell had the paperback rights to Mario Puzo's *The Godfather* (1969) under consideration but backed out of the deal when the hardback publisher tried to make Dell take a second

book that Delacorte did not like. Similarly Delacorte had been offered *TV Guide* but turned it down. Today, weekly circulation of *TV Guide* is approximately seventeen million.

In 1979 Delacorte told Walton, "I spent much of my life accumulating money, so I decided I wanted to apply the rest of my years giving a good part of it away." To a *Time* (27 June 1969) writer he noted, "I was born and raised in New York, made my money in New York, and now I want to give my money back to New York." Toward that goal, Delacorte became one of New York's most imaginative philanthropists.

In 1952 he established the George and Margarita Delacorte Foundation (Delacorte had married Margarita von Doerhoff on 30 August 1912; the couple had six children: Albert, Margarita, Malcolm, Consuelo, Marianne, and Victoria). The foundation's first gift to the city was a grouping of bronze figures depicting the characters of Lewis Carroll's *Alice's Adventures in Wonderland* (1865). The statue, in Central Park, was dedicated in 1959 to the memory of Margarita

Delacorte, who had died in 1956. On 15 May 1959 Delacorte married Valerie Hoecker.

Delacorte also provided the funding for an outdoor amphitheater in Central Park, which was dedicated and named after him in 1962. The New York Shakespeare Festival gives free performances there each summer. Two years later the Delacorte Mobile Theatre, another gift from Delacorte, made it possible for the Shakespeare Festival to perform in parks throughout the city.

In 1964 Delacorte, with five other prominent New Yorkers, established Make New York Beautiful, Inc., a nonprofit philanthropic corporation which seeks to interest people in donating substantial funds for cultural improvements in the city. That year Delacorte received the New York City Medallion.

In 1966 he contributed a fully automated glockenspiel to the Central Park Zoo. It features a four-foot-high carousel of animals which rotates to nursery rhymes each half hour.

These contributions were followed by a series of fountains–the Columbus Circle Fountain (1966) at the entrance of Central Park, the Delacorte Geyser at the southern tip of Roosevelt Island opposite the United Nations building (1969), the Bowling Green Fountain in lower Manhattan (1976), and the City Hall Park Fountain (1979). It is no wonder that Delacorte was dubbed by one *New York Times* writer as "New York's own Santa Claus."

Delacorte's devotion to New York City is obvious, but his generosity has extended beyond the city's physical improvement. Delacorte, over the years, also has been a steadfast friend of his alma mater, Columbia University. His contributions total more than $6 million and include such landmarks as the Delacorte Gates at the main entrance to the Morningside Heights Campus (1971), a relandscaped campus, and the Delacorte Courtyard (1981). In 1976 the George T. Delacorte Professorship in the Humanities was created.

A large portion of Delacorte's contributions (approximately $4.25 million) directly benefited the development of magazine journalism at Columbia. In 1964 Delacorte pledged fifty thousand dollars from the Dell Publishing Company Foundation to the *Columbia Journalism Review* to undertake a three-year study of the role of public affairs columnists in the United States.

More recently, in 1985, a $1.25 million contribution established the Delacorte Center for Magazine Journalism in the Graduate School of Journalism. The center sponsors an annual lecture series by prominent magazine journalists; offers programs of instruction in writing, editing, publishing, and business management taught by visiting professors in the magazine field; sponsors research projects; and awards scholarships to outstanding students specializing in magazine journalism. In 1986 a $2 million gift established the George T. Delacorte Professorship in Journalism at Columbia.

Delacorte received the Columbia College Alumni Association's Alexander Hamilton Medal in 1978. In 1982 he received an honorary Doctor of Laws degree from the college.

George T. Delacorte, Jr., started Dell publishing "on a shoe string," built it into one of the largest publishing empires in the world, and never had a year when Dell failed to show a profit. A self-made millionaire, he has become a self-designated beautifier of his native city and benefactor of his alma mater. Although retired, Delacorte still walks to an office he keeps in midtown whenever he and his wife are in the city. And always, he tries to go through Central Park.

Interviews:

Laurence Bell, "Gallery: George Delacorte," *Advertising and Selling* (October 1948);

Ken McKenna, "He Captures the Trends for Readers' Flighty Taste," *New York Herald Tribune*, 1 July 1962, V: 6.

References:

Harland Manchester, "True Stories: The Confession Magazines," *Scribner's Magazine*, 104 (August 1938): 25-29;

Theodore Peterson, *Magazines in the Twentieth Century* (Urbana, Illinois: University of Illinois Press, 1956), pp. 290-293;

Roberta Walton, "Geysers, Gates and Glockenspiels," *Columbia* (Winter 1979): 23-25;

James Playsted Wood, *Magazines in the United States*, second edition (New York: Ronald Press, 1956): 342-344.

W. E. B. Du Bois

(23 February 1868-27 August 1963)

J. William Snorgrass
Florida A. & M. University

See also the Du Bois entries in *DLB 47: American Historians, 1866-1912* and *DLB 50: Afro-American Writers Before the Harlem Renaissance.*

MAJOR POSITIONS HELD: Publisher and editor, *Moon Illustrated Weekly* (1906-1907), *Horizon* (1907-1910); editor, *Crisis* (1910-1934), *Brownies' Book* (1920-1921); editor in chief, *Phylon* (1940-1944).

SELECTED BOOKS: *The Suppression of the African Slave-Trade to the United States of America, 1638-1870*, volume 1 of Harvard Historical Studies (New York & London: Longmans, Green, 1896);
The Philadelphia Negro: A Social Study (Philadelphia: University of Pennsylvania, 1899);
The Souls of Black Folk: Essays and Sketches (Chicago: McClurg, 1903; London: Constable, 1905);
The Negro in the South, His Economic Progress in Relation to His Moral and Religious Development; Being the William Levi Bull Lectures for the Year 1907, by Du Bois and Booker T. Washington (Philadelphia: Jacobs, 1907);
John Brown (Philadelphia: Jacobs, 1909);
The Quest of the Silver Fleece: A Novel (Chicago: McClurg, 1911);
The Negro (New York: Holt, 1915; London: Williams & Norgate, 1915);
Darkwater: Voices From Within the Veil (New York: Harcourt, Brace & Howe, 1920; London: Constable, 1920);
The Gift of Black Folk: The Negroes in the Making of America (Boston: Stratford, 1924);
Dark Princess: A Romance (New York: Harcourt, Brace, 1928);
Africa: Its Geography, People and Products (Girard, Kans.: Haldeman-Julius, 1930);
Africa: Its Place in Modern History (Girard, Kans.: Haldeman-Julius, 1930);
Black Reconstruction: An Essay Toward a History of the Part Which Black Folk Played in the Attempt to Reconstruct Democracy in America, 1860-

W. E. B. Du Bois (courtesy of the Library of Congress)

1880 (New York: Harcourt, Brace, 1935); republished as *Black Reconstruction in America* (Cleveland: World, 1964; London: Cass, 1966);
Black Folk, Then and Now: An Essay in the History and Sociology of the Negro Race (New York: Holt, 1939);
Dusk of Dawn: An Essay Toward an Autobiography of a Race Concept (New York: Harcourt, Brace, 1940);
Color and Democracy: Colonies and Peace (New York: Harcourt, Brace, 1945);
The World and Africa: An Inquiry into the Part Which Africa Has Played in World History (New York:

Viking, 1947; enlarged edition, New York: International, 1965);

In Battle for Peace: The Story of My 83rd Birthday (New York: Masses & Mainstream, 1952);

The Ordeal of Mansart (New York: Mainstream, 1957);

Mansart Builds a School (New York: Mainstream, 1959);

Worlds of Color (New York: Mainstream, 1961);

Selected Poems (Accra, Ghana: Government Printing Office, 1963?);

The Autobiography of W. E. B. Du Bois: A Soliloquy on Viewing My Life From the Last Decade of Its First Century, edited by Herbert Aptheker (New York: International, 1968);

An ABC of Color: Selections Chosen by the Author from Over a Half Century of His Writings (New York: International, 1969);

W. E. B. Du Bois Speaks: Speeches and Addresses, edited by Philip S. Foner (New York: Pathfinder, 1970);

W. E. B. Du Bois: The Crisis Writings, edited by Daniel Walden (Greenwich, Conn.: Fawcett, 1972);

The Education of Black People: Ten Critiques, 1906-1960, edited by Aptheker (Amherst: University of Massachusetts Press, 1973).

Collection: *The Complete Published Works of W. E. B. Du Bois*, edited by Aptheker (Millwood, N.Y.: Kraus International, 1973-1986)–comprises *Annotated Bibliography of the Published Writings of W. E. B. Du Bois; The Suppression of the African Slave-Trade to the United States of America, 1638-1870; The Philadelphia Negro: A Social Study; John Brown; The Quest of the Silver Fleece: A Novel; The Negro; Darkwater: Voices from Within the Veil; The Gift of Black Folk: The Negroes in the Making of America; Dark Princess: A Romance; Africa: Its Geography, People and Products; Africa: Its Place in Modern History; Black Reconstruction: An Essay Toward a History of the Part Which Black Folk Played in the Attempt to Reconstruct Democracy in America, 1860-1880; Black Folk, Then and Now: An Essay in the History and Sociology of the Negro Race; Dusk of Dawn: An Essay Toward an Autobiography of a Race Concept; Color and Democracy: Colonies and Peace; In Battle for Peace: The Story of My 83rd Birthday, with Comment by Shirley Graham; The Souls of Black Folk: Essays and Sketches; The Ordeal of Mansart; Mansart Builds a School; Worlds of Color; The World and Africa: An Inquiry into the Part*

Which Africa Has Played in World History; The Autobiography of W. E. B. Du Bois: A Soliloquy on Viewing My Life From the Last Decade of Its First Century; Book Reviews by W. E. B. Du Bois; Contributions by W. E. B. Du Bois in Government Publications; Creative Writings by W. E. B. Du Bois: A Pageant, Poems, Short Stories and Playlets; Newspaper Columns by W. E. B. Du Bois; Pamphlets and Leaflets by W. E. B. Du Bois; Writings by W. E. B. Du Bois in Non-Periodical Literature Edited by Others; Writings by W. E. B. Du Bois in Periodicals Edited by Others; Selections from the Brownies' Book; *Selections from the* Crisis; *Selections from the* Horizon; *and Selections from* Phylon.

OTHER: *Mortality Among Negroes in Cities*, edited by Du Bois (Atlanta, 1896);

Some Efforts of American Negroes for Their Own Social Betterment, edited by Du Bois (Atlanta: Atlanta University Press, 1898);

The Negro in Business, edited by Du Bois (Atlanta: Atlanta University Press, 1899);

The College-Bred Negro, edited by Du Bois (Atlanta: Atlanta University Press, 1900);

The Negro Common School, edited by Du Bois (Atlanta: Atlanta University Press, 1901);

The Negro Artisan, edited by Du Bois (Atlanta: Atlanta University Press, 1902);

The Negro Church, edited by Du Bois (Atlanta: Atlanta University Press, 1903);

Some Notes on Negroes in New York City (Atlanta: Atlanta University Press, 1903);

Some Notes on Negro Crime, Particularly in Georgia, edited by Du Bois (Atlanta: Atlanta University Press, 1904);

A Select Bibliography of the Negro American, edited by Du Bois (Atlanta: Atlanta University Press, 1905);

The Health and Physique of the Negro American, edited by Du Bois (Atlanta: Atlanta University Press, 1906);

Economic Co-operation among Negro Americans, edited by Du Bois (Atlanta: Atlanta University Press, 1907);

The Negro American Family, edited by Du Bois (Atlanta: Atlanta University Press, 1908);

The College-Bred Negro American, edited by Du Bois and Augustus G. Dill (Atlanta: Atlanta University Press, 1910);

The Common School and the Negro American, edited by Du Bois and Dill (Atlanta: Atlanta University Press, 1911);

Du Bois (seated left) and the other members of the 1888 graduating class of Fisk University (University Library, University of Massachusetts, Amherst)

Du Bois with his first wife, Nina Gomer, and their son Burghardt in 1905. Burghardt Du Bois died at age three (University Library, University of Massachusetts, Amherst).

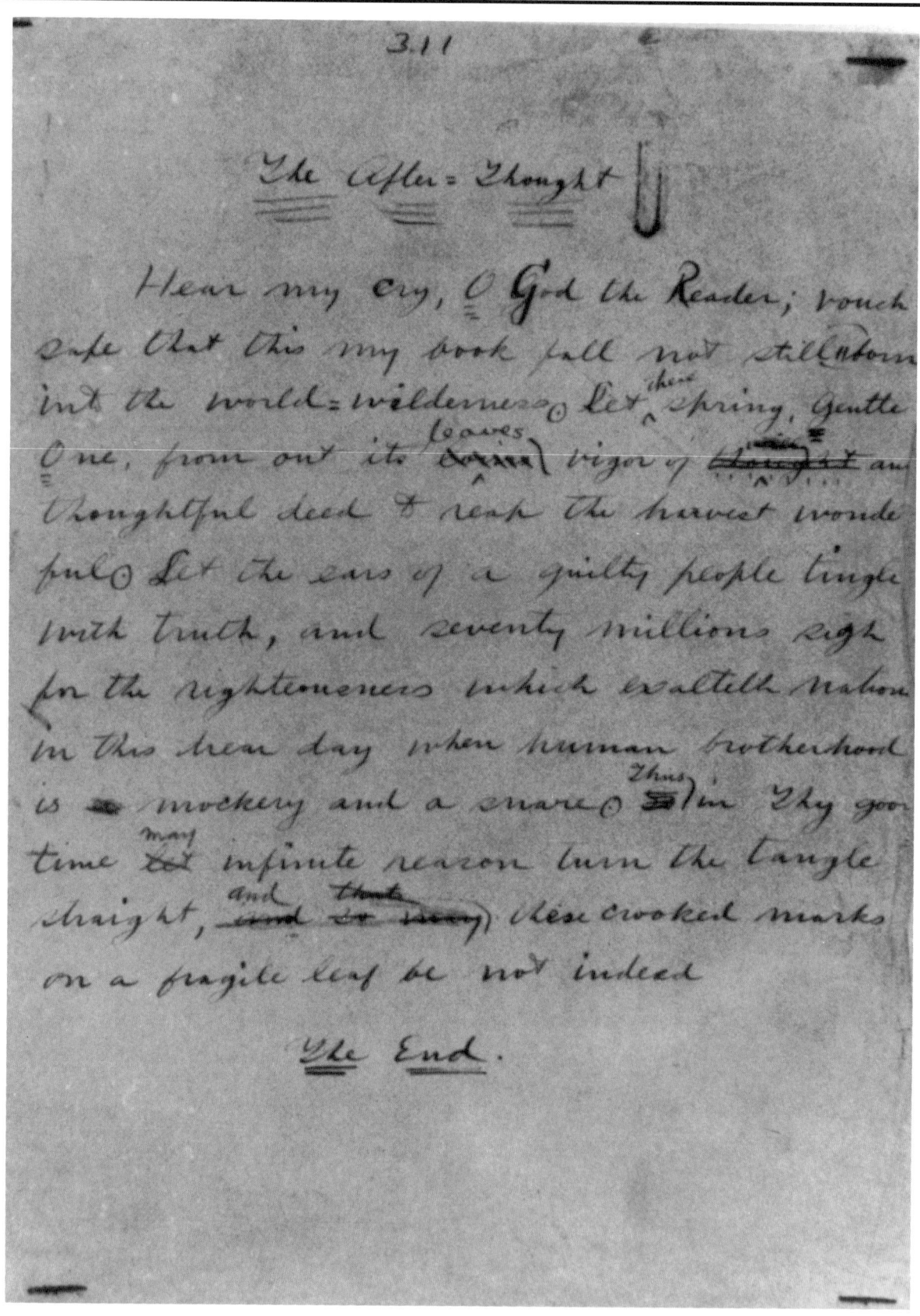

Concluding page of the manuscript for Du Bois's best-known work, The Souls of Black Folk: Essays and Sketches, *published in 1903 (University Library, University of Massachusetts, Amherst)*

The Negro American Artisan, edited by Du Bois
and Dill (Atlanta: Atlanta University Press,
1912);

Morals and Manners among Negro Americans, edited
by Du Bois and Dill (Atlanta: Atlanta University Press, 1914);

An Appeal to the World, edited by Du Bois (New
York: National Association for the Advancement of Colored People, 1947).

W. E. B. Du Bois, scholar, intellectual, historian, educator, author, and civil-rights activist,
was also an accomplished journalist who made expert use of the press to advance his philosophy
concerning race relations in the world as well as
the United States. Some of his most important
work in the field of journalism was done between
1910 and 1934 as editor of the *Crisis*, the official
publication of the National Association for the Advancement of Colored People (NAACP). Du
Bois's first journalistic efforts came as coeditor of
Howler, his high-school newspaper. He later became a correspondent for several notable black
and white newspapers in the East. At Fisk University he became editor of the school newspaper,
the *Fisk Herald*. Du Bois would go on to found
and hold the position of editor of five periodicals, contribute to several newspapers, and author numerous books and scholarly articles.

William Edward Burghardt Du Bois was
born on 23 February 1868 in the western Massachusetts town of Great Barrington, to a family
whose ancestry was made up of French Huguenot on the father's side and Dutch and Negro on
the mother's side. Du Bois's father, Alfred Du
Bois, left his family when his son was a young
boy. Aided by relatives and friends, Du Bois and
his mother, Mary Sylvina Burghardt Du Bois,
lived alone until her death in 1884. Penniless, Du
Bois moved in with an aunt and worked as a time-keeper at a local mill to support himself. The
same year he graduated from high school, the
only black student in his class.

An outstanding student, Du Bois was encouraged by his principal, Frank Hosmer, to attend college. With the aid of a scholarship he enrolled at
Fisk University in Nashville, Tennessee, in 1885.
Du Bois graduated with a B.A. degree in 1888
and entered Harvard University as a junior,
where he graduated, cum laude, with a second
B.A. degree in 1890. He stayed at Harvard and
earned an M.A. degree in 1891. Du Bois studied
at the University of Berlin in Germany for two
years before returning to Harvard, where he re-

ceived his Ph.D. in 1895. He was the first American black to receive this degree from Harvard.
From 1895 to 1897 Du Bois taught Latin, Greek,
German, and English at Wilberforce University
in Ohio. While Du Bois was at Wilberforce, his dissertation, *The Suppression of the African Slave-Trade
to the United States of America, 1638-1870*, was published in 1896 as the first installment in the Harvard Historical Studies series. Also in 1896 Du
Bois married Nina Gomer, a Wilberforce student. They had two children. In 1897 he moved
to Atlanta University, where he taught economics
and history until 1910. In 1903 Du Bois published his most widely acclaimed work, *The Souls
of Black Folk: Essays and Sketches*.

In 1905 Du Bois expressed the desire to publish a journal that would cater to intelligent Negroes. This was in concert with his belief that ten
percent of the most promising Negroes should
be educated in colleges and universities, and they
in turn would emerge to serve and lead the black
race. Since college-educated blacks would be depended on to carry out this mission, Du Bois
looked to books, magazines, and newspapers as vehicles to advance his philosophy. In 1906, with
the help of two Atlanta University graduates, he established a small printing shop in Memphis, Tennessee, and began the *Moon Illustrated Weekly*.

Du Bois's "Talented Tenth" theory put him
in direct conflict with the teachings of Booker T.
Washington, the most powerful black leader of
the period. Washington believed that blacks
should concentrate on becoming skilled workers,
craftsmen, and farmers. The *Moon* was discontinued after only a year in operation, probably because many blacks, some former slaves, were not
ready for the intellectual philosophy of Du Bois
and saw the ideas of Washington as being more
practical, especially in the South.

A year later Du Bois established the *Horizon*
in Washington, D.C. This publication was meant
to be the voice of the Niagara Movement, an organization of black intellectuals founded by Du
Bois in 1905. From the outset it was clear that
the publication would oppose the teachings of
Washington. (Du Bois still believed that Washington was behind the lack of support given the
Moon.) Among the purposes outlined were "to oppose firmly present methods of strangling honest
criticism; to organize intelligent and honest Negroes; and to support organs of news and public
opinion." The publication did not become the official voice for the Niagara Movement, but Du
Bois managed to keep the monthly publication

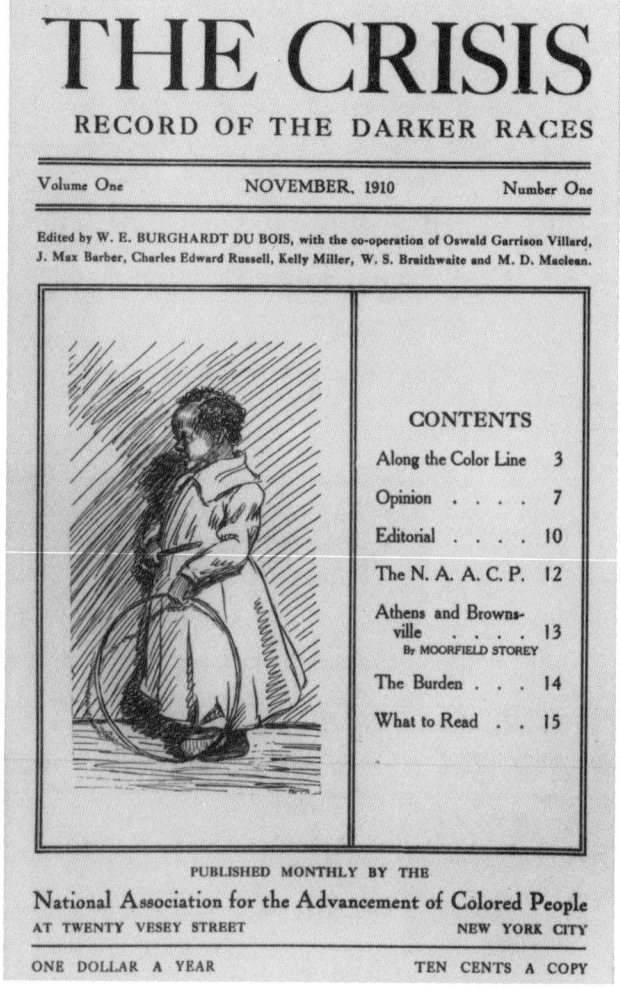

THE CRISIS

RECORD OF THE DARKER RACES

Volume One   NOVEMBER, 1910   Number One

Edited by W. E. BURGHARDT DU BOIS, with the co-operation of Oswald Garrison Villard, J. Max Barber, Charles Edward Russell, Kelly Miller, W. S. Braithwaite and M. D. Maclean.

CONTENTS

Along the Color Line   3

Opinion   7

Editorial   10

The N. A. A. C. P.   12

Athens and Browns-
ville   13
BY MOORFIELD STOREY

The Burden . . .   14

What to Read . .   15

PUBLISHED MONTHLY BY THE

National Association for the Advancement of Colored People

AT TWENTY VESEY STREET   NEW YORK CITY

ONE DOLLAR A YEAR   TEN CENTS A COPY

Cover for the first issue of the official organ of the NAACP. During Du Bois's twenty-four-year tenure as editor, the Crisis *became the leading black magazine in the United States.*

going until 1910, at which time he merged the Niagara Movement with the newly organized NAACP; resigned his faculty position at Atlanta University; became director of publications and research for the NAACP; and founded the *Crisis*, a magazine he would head for almost twenty-five years.

Du Bois started the *Crisis* in opposition to many of his associates. He saw the magazine as a vehicle to communicate to the world the problems faced by blacks in American society as well as those faced by other oppressed people, mainly Africans on the African continent. In the first issue of the *Crisis* (November 1910), Du Bois stated: "The object of this publication is to set forth those facts and arguments which show the danger of race prejudice, particularly as manifested today toward colored people." He went on

to explain, "It will record happenings and movements in the world which bear on the great problem of interracial relations, and especially those which affect the Negro-American." The circulation of the *Crisis* grew rapidly, from one thousand in 1911 to a peak of one hundred thousand in 1919. The magazine became a formidable foe of poll taxes, discrimination in transportation and public places, and any national policy that resulted in the unfair treatment of blacks.

The *Crisis* became well-known for its stand against lynching. The magazine carried an annual review of the lynchings that had taken place the previous year; and with information provided by NAACP investigators, the *Crisis* was able to report complete details, including numbers, ages, locations, causes, dates, and sex of the victims. This report became so accurate that it chal-

Du Bois (standing at right) in the Crisis *office, circa 1914 (Collection of Milton Meltzer)*

lenged those provided by the *Chicago Tribune* and the Tuskegee Institute.

Du Bois, whose career was marked by controversy, lost several of his closest supporters in 1918 because of an editorial entitled "Close Ranks," which appeared in the July issue of the *Crisis*. In regard to the participation of American blacks in World War I, the editorial urged: "Let us while this war lasts, forget our special grievances and close our ranks shoulder to shoulder with our white fellow citizens and the allied nations that are fighting for democracy." Some of his critics overlooked the phrase "while this war lasts" and claimed he had exchanged his support of the government for a commission in the army. He had been offered a commission, but the offer was withdrawn because of the loud protest raised about the editorial. Even two editorials, in the August and September issues of the magazine, advocating protest and demanding full citizenship rights did not change the minds of many of Du Bois's critics. In addition to criticism from his colleagues, Du Bois faced mounting political opposition. The *Crisis* was denounced in Congress, laws were passed in some southern states forbidding its circulation, and it was placed on a list of publications to be suppressed by the government during the war. However, Du Bois managed to hang on and to restore some of his lost credibility.

Following World War I Du Bois took an even greater interest in Africa, especially those colonies once held by the now-defeated Germans and Italians. With an agenda designed to place the problems of all blacks before the world, Du Bois helped organize the second Pan-African Congress in Paris in 1919. (A previous meeting of this body took place in London in 1900.) Du Bois argued for the seizure of German territories in Africa as the foundation for an international African state, and the *Crisis*, which had obtained an international circulation, became the platform from which Du Bois could argue for the concept of "Africa for the Africans." The 1919 congress and subsequent meetings in 1921, 1923, and 1927 were well chronicled in the magazine.

A children's issue of the *Crisis* had been published annually since 1911, and in 1920 Du Bois decided to publish a magazine for children. Du Bois was disturbed by a letter he had received from a twelve-year-old child that read in part: "I hate white people as much as I know they hate me. I want to know more about my own people." Du Bois responded on both issues in the *Crisis*: "We must not lose our children to hatred. To educate them in human hatred is more disastrous to them than to the hated, to seek to raise them in ignorance of their racial identity and peculiar situation is inadvisable, impossible. There seems to be one alternative. We shall publish hereafter not one children's number a year but twelve."

In January 1920 the first issue of the *Brownies' Book* appeared. Its purpose, according to Du Bois, was "to seek to teach universal love and brotherhood for all little folk, black and brown and yellow and white." The first issue proclaimed: "This is *The Brownies' Book*, a monthly magazine for the children of the sun–designed for all children, but especially for OURS. Its aim is to be a thing of joy and beauty, dealing in happiness, laughter and emulation, and designed especially for kiddies from six to sixteen."

The *Brownies' Book* followed the format of the *Crisis* with a wide variety of materials designed for pleasure as well as to build pride in the black race. Advertising was kept to a minimum, and that which did appear promoted books, schools, and self-improvement through education. The magazine was published until December 1921. In the last issue it was explained that "the fault has not been with our readers. We have had an unusually enthusiastic set of subscribers. But the magazine was begun just at the time of industrial depression following the war, and the fault of our suspension thereof is rather in the times which are so out of joint, than in our constituency."

Du Bois's interest in black children and their future in American society helped him gain back some of the support he lost with the "Close Ranks" editorial. However, controversy between Du Bois and fellow NAACP officials continued to escalate. The explosion came in 1934 over the issue of segregation. The policy of the NAACP was to be against any form of segregation practiced by blacks or whites. Du Bois, however, began to court the idea of "fighting segregation with segregation." In the April 1934 issue of the *Crisis* he told his readers: "The only thing that we not only can, but must do, is voluntarily and insistently organize our economic and social power, no matter how much segregation it involves. Learn to associate with ourselves and to train ourselves for effective association . . . run and support our own institutions." The NAACP board of directors issued the following statement: "*The Crisis* is the organ of the Association and no salaried officer of the Association shall criticize the policy, work or officers of the Association in the

pages of *The Crisis*." Du Bois resigned and returned to Atlanta University as chairman of its sociology department. In addition to building the *Crisis* into the leading black magazine in America between 1910 and 1934, Du Bois also wrote extensively during this period and produced his first novel, *The Quest of the Silver Fleece* (1911).

Now, without a publication of his own for the first time in nearly thirty years, Du Bois spent much of his time between 1934 and 1940 teaching, conducting research, and writing. Already a prolific and well-known author, during the next five years Du Bois published two of his most important historical works, *Black Reconstruction: An Essay Toward a History of the Part Which Black Folk Played in the Attempt to Reconstruct Democracy in America, 1860-1880* (1935) and *Black Folk, Then and Now: An Essay in the History and Sociology of the Negro Race* (1939). He also wrote articles for several of the leading periodicals of the time, including *Current History*, *Journal of Negro Education*, *Foreign Affairs*, and *American Scholar*.

However, Du Bois still desired the forum provided by a regular publication. He proposed a scholarly journal dedicated to research and the documentation of matters concerning race problems throughout the world. He believed this kind of research must include the study of all groups of men. He explained: "Naturally, we shall usually proceed from the point of view of black folk where we live and work to the wider world." Du Bois became editor in chief of such a publication in 1940 with the establishment of *Phylon* at Atlanta University. He stated in the first issue: "Here if anywhere the leadership of science is demanded not to obliterate all race and group distinctions, but to know and study them, to see and appreciate them at their true value, to emphasize the use and place of human differences as tool and method to progress; to make straight the path to a common world humanity through the development of cultural gifts to their highest possibilities."

Du Bois held the position of editor in chief of *Phylon* until he retired from the university in 1944. The same year he rejoined the staff of the NAACP as director of special research. However, in 1948 this association was again terminated as the result of a clash of ideologies. From this point on the influence and leadership of Du Bois began to decline steadily. The same year he was a candidate for U.S. senator from New York on the American Labor party ticket. By the 1950s Du Bois was shunned by most leading publishers

Cover, with illustration by Aaron Douglas, celebrating the twentieth anniversary of the NAACP

except those with leftist views (Du Bois had briefly been a member of the Socialist party). The *National Guardian* became a major outlet for his writings: from November 1948 through May 1961 Du Bois was published approximately 115 times in this radical newspaper.

For years Du Bois had made no attempt to conceal his approval of Soviet communism. After a trip to the Soviet Union in 1926, he wrote in the November issue of the *Crisis*: "I may be partially deceived and half-informed. But if what I have seen with my own eyes and heard with my own ears in Russia is Bolshevism, I am Bolshevik." In 1951 Du Bois married Shirley Lola Graham (his first wife died in 1950) and at age eighty-three was indicted by the U.S. Justice Department as an "agent for a foreign power." Although acquitted by a federal judge, he was not allowed to leave the country until 1958. This completely disillusioned Du Bois with American democracy, and in 1961 he officially joined the

Communist party. The same year he moved to Accra, Ghana. About a year later he renounced his American citizenship and became a citizen of Ghana. He began work on "The Encyclopedia Africana." However, this was a project he would not complete, nor would he see through to publication *The Autobiography of W. E. B. Du Bois: A Soliloquy on Viewing My Life From the Last Decade of Its First Century* (1968).

Du Bois was frequently referred to by his critics as arrogant, egotistical, proud, difficult, and stern. This is not to say he was shunned or was totally without friends. While Du Bois was at Harvard, William James became his favorite teacher as well as a close friend. Robert Morss Lovett was another friend at Harvard. In a chapter of his autobiography, Du Bois wrote: "Many men have judged me, favorably and harshly. But the verdicts of two I cherish." These men were Dr. John Hope, the first black president of Morehouse College and Atlanta University, and Dr. Joel

PHYLON

The Atlanta University Review of Race and Culture

Contents page for the first issue of the scholarly journal that Du Bois edited from its founding until 1944

Spingarn, chairman, NAACP board of directors. Du Bois was admittedly shy, and he turned down invitations to visit Henry James, H. G. Wells, Havelock Ellis, and Bernard Shaw. He passed up opportunities to meet presidents of the United States and other statesmen, as well as writers and artists, because he feared that "color cast would interfere with our meeting or understanding; if not with the persons themselves, certainly with their friends." He also admitted that he was not "what Americans called a 'good fellow.'" However, despite the controversial nature of Du Bois's career, he was by consensus a dedicated civil-rights leader and a pioneer in the use of media as a protest instrument. Lerone Bennett, Jr., claims in his book *Pioneers in Protest* (1968) that "As *Crisis* editor, Du Bois set the tone for the organization [NAACP] and educated a whole generation of black people in the art of protest." Roy Wilkins,

who succeeded Du Bois as editor of the *Crisis* and went on to become executive secretary of the NAACP, wrote in a winter 1965 issue of *Freedomways*: "A gifted writer, Du Bois articulated the aspirations and demands of Negroes as no other has done." Paul Robeson simply wrote, "Dr. Du Bois was, and is, in the truest sense an American leader, a Negro leader and a world leader." With some opposition Du Bois's homesite in Great Barrington was dedicated as a memorial park in 1976. The plaque reads in part: "William Edward Burghardt Du Bois was born here in Great Barrington on February 23, 1868. He is considered one of the most influential black intellectuals of the twentieth century."

Letters:

The Correspondence of W. E. B. Du Bois, 3 volumes,

Du Bois and Mao Tse-tung, April 1959. Touring several communist countries in 1958 and 1959, Du Bois celebrated his ninety-first birthday in Peking and received the Lenin Peace Prize in Moscow on May Day 1959.

edited by Herbert Aptheker (Amherst: University of Massachusetts Press, 1973-1978).

Bibliographies:

Herbert Aptheker, *Annotated Bibliography of the Published Writings of W. E. B. Du Bois* (Millwood, N.Y.: Kraus-Thomson, 1973);

Paul G. Partington, *W. E. B. Du Bois: A Bibliography of His Published Writings* (Whittier, Cal.: Privately printed, 1977; revised, 1979).

Biographies:

Francis L. Broderick, *W. E. B. Du Bois: Negro Leader in a Time of Crisis* (Stanford: Stanford University Press, 1959);

Elliott M. Rudwick, *W. E. B. Du Bois: Propagandist of the Negro Protest*, second edition (New York: Atheneum, 1968);

Leslie Alexander Lacy, *Cheer the Lonesome Traveler* (New York: Dial, 1970);

Shirley Graham Du Bois, *His Day is Marching On: A Memoir of W. E. B. Du Bois* (Philadelphia: Lippincott, 1971);

Virginia Hamilton, *W. E. B. Du Bois* (New York: Crowell, 1972).

References:

Lerone Bennett, Jr., *Pioneers in Protest* (Chicago: Johnson, 1968);

Thomas R. Brooks, *Walls Come Tumbling Down* (Englewood Cliffs, N.J.: Prentice-Hall, 1974);

Dorothy Davis, "*The Crisis* and W. E. B. Du Bois," *Encore American & World Wide News*, 6 (5 July 1977): 20-21;

Julius Lester, Introduction to *The Seventh Son: The Thought and Writings of W. E. B. Du Bois* (New York: Random House, 1971);

Rayford W. Logan, ed., *W. E. B. Du Bois: A Profile* (New York: Hill & Wang, 1971);

August Meier, Elliott Rudwick, and Francis L. Broderick, *Black Protest Thought in the Twentieth Century*, second edition (New York: Bobbs-Merrill, 1965);

"W. E. B. Du Bois Memorial Issue," *Freedomways*, 2 (Winter 1965);

Roland E. Wolseley, *The Black Press, U.S.A.* (Ames: Iowa State University Press, 1971).

Papers:

Du Bois's papers are at the University of Massachusetts, Amherst.

Max Eastman

(4 January 1883-25 March 1969)

Cynthia Goldstein

MAJOR POSITIONS HELD: Editor, *Masses* (1912-1917); editor and publisher, *Liberator* (1918-1922); contributing editor, *Reader's Digest* (1941-1969).

BOOKS: *Is Woman Suffrage Important?* (New York: Men's League for Woman Suffrage, 1911);

Values of the Vote: Address before the Men's League for Woman Suffrage of New York, March 21, 1912 ([New York:] Men's League for Woman Suffrage, 1912);

Enjoyment of Poetry (New York: Scribners, 1913; London: Mathews, 1913; revised edition, New York: Scribners, 1921); revised and enlarged as *Enjoyment of Poetry, with Other Essays in Aesthetics* (New York & London: Scribners, 1939); republished with *Anthology for Enjoyment of Poetry* as *Enjoyment of Poetry, with Anthology for Enjoyment of Poetry* (New York: Scribners, 1951);

Child of the Amazons, and Other Poems (New York & London: Kennerley, 1913);

Is the Truth Obscene? (New York: Free Speech League, 1915);

Journalism versus Art (New York: Knopf, 1916);

Understanding Germany: The Only Way to End War, and Other Essays (New York: Kennerley, 1916);

Address to the Jury in the Second Masses Trial in Defense of the Socialist Position and the Right of Free Speech (New York: Liberator, 1918);

Colors of Life: Poems and Songs and Sonnets (New York: Knopf, 1918);

The Trial of Eugene Debs, with Debs' Address to the Court on Receiving Sentence (New York: Liberator, 1918);

The Sense of Humor (New York: Scribners, 1921);

Leon Trotsky: The Portrait of A Youth (New York: Greenberg, 1925; London: Faber & Gwyer, 1926);

Since Lenin Died (London: Labour, 1925; New York: Boni & Liveright, 1925);

Marx, Lenin and the Science of Revolution (London: Allen & Unwin, 1926); republished as *Marx*

Max Eastman (New York Public Library Picture Collection)

and Lenin: The Science of Revolution (New York: Boni, 1927);

Venture (New York: Boni, 1927);

Kinds of Love, Poems (New York & London: Scribners, 1931);

The Literary Mind: Its Place in an Age of Science (New York & London: Scribners, 1931);

Artists in Uniform: A Study of Literature and Bureaucratism (New York: Knopf, 1934);

Art and the Life of Action, with Other Essays (New York: Knopf, 1934; London: Allen & Unwin, 1935);

The Last Stand of Dialectic Materialism: A Study of Sidney Hook's Marxism (New York: Polemic, 1934);

Enjoyment of Laughter (New York: Simon & Schuster, 1936);

The End of Socialism in Russia (Boston: Little, Brown, 1937);

Stalin's Russia and the Crisis in Socialism (New York: Norton, 1940; London: Allen & Unwin, 1940);

Marxism: Is It Science? (New York: Norton, 1940; London: Allen & Unwin, 1941);

A Letter to Americans (New York: Rand, 1941);

Heroes I Have Known: Twelve Who Lived Great Lives (New York: Simon & Schuster, 1942);

Lot's Wife (New York & London: Harper, 1942);

Enjoyment of Living (New York: Harper, 1948);

The Road to Abundance, by Eastman and Jacob Rosin (New York: McGraw-Hill, 1953);

Poems of Five Decades (New York: Harper, 1954);

Reflections on the Failure of Socialism (New York: Devin-Adair, 1955);

Great Companions: Critical Memoirs of Some Famous Friends (New York: Farrar, Straus & Cudahy, 1959; London: Museum, 1959); republished as *Einstein, Trotsky, Hemingway, Freud, and Other Great Companions: Critical Memoirs of Some Famous Friends* (New York: Collier, 1962);

Love and Revolution: My Journey Through An Epoch (New York: Random House, 1964);

Seven Kinds of Goodness (New York: Horizon, 1967);

Toward the Great Change: Crystal and Max Eastman on Feminism, Antimilitarism, and Revolution (New York: Garland, 1976).

MOTION PICTURE: *Tsar to Lenin, A Moving-Picture History of the Russian Revolution,* compiled and narrated by Eastman, written by Eastman and Herman Axelbank, Lenauer International, 1937.

OTHER: Claude McKay, *Harlem Shadows: The Poems of Claude McKay,* introduction by Eastman (New York: Harcourt, Brace, 1922);

Capital, the Communist Manifesto and Other Writings by Karl Marx, edited by Eastman (New York: Modern Library, 1932);

Anne Persov, *Whatever You Reap,* introduction by Eastman (Detroit: Shuman's, 1933);

Anthology for "The Enjoyment of Poetry," compiled by Eastman (New York & London: Scribners, 1939);

Echoes of Revolt: "The Masses" 1911-1917, edited

Eastman and his first wife, Ida Rauh, circa 1910

by William L. O'Neill, afterword by Eastman (Chicago: Quadrangle, 1966).

TRANSLATIONS: Leon Trotsky, *The Real Situation in Russia* (New York: Harcourt, Brace, 1928);

Alexandr Pushkin, *Gabriel: A Poem in One Song* (New York: Covici-Friede, 1929);

Trotsky, *The History of the Russian Revolution,* 3 volumes (New York: Simon & Schuster, 1932; London: Gollancz, 1932-1933);

Trotsky, *The Revolution Betrayed: What is the Soviet Union and Where is It Going?* (Garden City, N.Y.: Doubleday, Doran, 1937);

Trotsky, *In Defense of Marxism* (New York: Merit, 1965);

Trotsky, *The Young Lenin,* edited by Maurice Friedberg (Garden City, N.Y.: Doubleday, 1972).

SELECTED PERIODICAL PUBLICATIONS
UNCOLLECTED: "Poets Talking to Themselves," *Harper's Monthly,* 163 (October 1931): 563-574;

"Let's Face the Facts About Russia," *Reader's Digest,* 43 (July 1943): 1-4;

"Our Quarrel with Communism is Moral Rather than Political," *Saturday Evening Post*, 222 (5 November 1949): 12;

"I Acknowledge My Mistakes," *National Review* (22 February 1956): 11-14.

Those who knew Max Eastman when he edited and published the radical magazines the *Masses* and the *Liberator* in Greenwich Village remember him as a spellbinding speaker capable of charming an audience of skeptics. Whether he was soliciting funds for his magazines among wealthy radicals or persuading striking workers that socialism would solve their problems, Eastman was invariably articulate and effective. While his reputation today hinges on his magazines, Eastman was also a prolific poet, critic, political writer, translator, and scholar. Although he was often engaged in heated literary debate, it was his political writing, and the political content of his magazines, that made him the subject of much critical controversy.

Max Forrester Eastman was born in Canandaigua, New York, the fourth and last child of Samuel and Annis Ford Eastman, who had met as students at Oberlin College in Ohio. They both became ministers and, after Max's birth, were hired together by Park Church in Elmira, New York, made famous by its previous pastor, Thomas K. Beecher, and one of its congregants, Mark Twain. Annis Eastman, who was unquestionably more talented than her husband, soon assumed control of the church, while Samuel Eastman attempted first to establish himself as a farmer and later as a grocer. Samuel Eastman seems to have had little positive influence on his son's development, except that his interest in farming provided Max with an opportunity to acquire a lifelong love of nature. Eastman's closest family relationships were with his mother and his older sister Crystal. As a young man, he often described himself as a "mama's boy," and he felt that his inability to make male friends stemmed from the feminine influences of his childhood. As a child and for years as an adult, Eastman suffered debilitating psychosomatic illnesses, which he and his biographers relate to his complex family relationships.

Despite these problems, Max was an excellent student, as was Crystal and his older brother Anstice (the first Eastman child, Morgan, died of scarlet fever in 1884). Eastman attended Mercersburg Academy from 1898 to 1900 and received a B.A. degree from Williams College in 1905. He studied philosophy under John Dewey at Columbia University from 1907 to 1910 but did not receive his doctorate because he refused to submit his dissertation, which Dewey had read and accepted.

Eastman had no desire to be an academic. What he wanted to be was a poet, with the ancillary career of literary critic. His first important publication, *Enjoyment of Poetry* (1913), immediately became a successful textbook, but the cool reception given his first book of poetry, *Child of the Amazons, and Other Poems,* published the same year, dampened his enthusiasm considerably. Moreover, the quick reputation he had earned with *Enjoyment of Poetry* was not to last. In 1931 Eastman published *The Literary Mind,* an attack on modernism. At the time, Van Wyck Brooks said the book showed that Eastman wanted to "humiliate literature." In 1936 Charles I. Glicksberg found *The Literary Mind* to contain "inexcusable, glaring contradictions," although he said Eastman was "one of the few contemporary critics who have a comprehensive theory of esthetics combined with a splendid gift of literary appreciation and expression." In 1941 Edmund Wilson acknowledged that he had not appreciated, in *The Literary Mind,* "a deeper comprehension of the real issues raised by contemporary literature than almost anything that had been written during the twenties."

In the decade after Eastman's death in 1969, scholars could not agree on his place in American history. In 1970 Milton Cantor wrote, "Eastman is not a great literary figure nor one of the giants of American radicalism." Cantor limited himself to appreciation for Eastman's contribution to social history and to his "typicality." Four years later, however, John P. Diggins described Eastman as "the best-known literary radical of the Greenwich Village generation" and "one of the dominant figures in American cultural life" at that time. Despite Diggins's praise, in 1977 Frederick C. Giffin wrote that "few historians are likely to quarrel with" Cantor's modest judgment. Giffin, however, was willing to go farther than Cantor—in fact, as far as Diggins—and say that in 1917 Eastman was "probably the nation's best-known literary radical." Cantor praised Eastman as an "elegant stylist" but considered him neither "a finished craftsman" nor "a profound thinker," while Glicksberg perceived Eastman as "humorous, witty, eloquent, satiric and profound." Whatever the disagreement about Eastman's talents, no one has disputed his

*Cover for an issue of the radical magazine that Eastman edited from 1912 until it was discontinued in 1917
(Lilly Library, Indiana University)*

role in making the *Masses* the leading radical magazine of the period.

Piet Vlag, a socialist interested in cooperative living arrangements, had started the *Masses* in January 1911 as a vehicle for anticapitalist and literary writing. Thomas Seltzer became the first editor, but within eighteen months he and two others, Horatio Winslow and Vlag himself, had in turn served and quit. Rufus W. Weeks, vice-president of the New York Life Insurance Company, had agreed to finance the venture until it became self-sufficient. By fall 1912 it had not, and he withdrew his backing. The staff took over from Vlag, and all signed a letter to Eastman: "You are elected editor of the *Masses,* no pay."

He agreed to be editor, having been persuaded by the staff that a salary was imminent. Eastman, who had recently become a socialist, in part due to the influence of his wife Ida Rauh (the couple had married on 4 May 1911), envisioned an idyllic life: a paid writer for the socialist cause and an unpaid poet and literary critic.

In fact, two years passed before the editorship paid anything, and he lived off his lecturing and other writing, as well as his wife's private income, in the meantime. Ironically, Eastman, who had earlier established his reputation as a supporter of birth control, had just become a father, although he and his wife had not agreed to have children. Disinterested in fatherhood and frustrated with marriage, Eastman soon left his wife and abandoned his son, whom he avoided until the child reached adulthood. Eastman's wife later divorced him, but, even before that, the *Masses* provided him with an escape from family life.

With Eastman as editor, the *Masses* moved immediately from moderate socialism to revolutionary socialism. Eastman began his own column, "Knowledge and Revolution," explaining that revolution meant "a radical democratization of industry and society, . . . a sweeping change accomplished through the conquest of power by a subjected class." Correspondingly, the coverage of cooperatives gradually diminished, while news

Army Medical Examiner: "At last a perfect soldier!"

Lilly Library, Indiana University

Political cartoons published in the Masses: *top, by Robert Minor (July 1916); and bottom, "Freedom of the Press,"
by Art Young (December 1912)*

about labor strikes and radical speeches received more space. When Eastman took over, large political cartoons with brief captions appeared with increasing frequency. Although other magazines supported their cartoons with long, complex captions, the *Masses* artists held out for few words–or none. The influence of the format was later seen in *Harper's Weekly* and, most successfully, in the *New Yorker*.

Although Eastman had planned to remain as editor for only six months unless the magazine became self-sufficient, he decided to stay on, moved especially by a growing appreciation for the opportunity the *Masses* offered writers and artists, such as Sherwood Anderson, Carl Sandburg, Randolph Bourne, John Sloan, and Art Young, to break the stifling bonds of commercial journalism. Young, the most famous *Masses* cartoonist, remembered that the opportunity "loosened energies within me of which I had been unaware."

Eastman, in *Enjoyment of Living* (1948), saw the magazine as providing "for the first time in America, a meeting ground for revolutionary labor and the radical intelligentsia." He gave all the credit for the large size of the drawings, which he called "a notable innovation in American magazinedom," to the artists on the staff. Similarly, he credited the staff for the "dominantly realist note in text and pictures." And the idea of using one-line captions came from John Sloan, one of the artists. Eastman considered his own chief contribution to be the magazine's "freedom from the one-track mental habit of the rabid devotee of a cause," which he called the "central and spirit-giving trait of the whole enterprise." Critic Irving Howe wrote in 1966 that the *Masses* "became the rallying center . . . for almost everything that was then alive and irreverent in American culture."

William L. O'Neill, Eastman's biographer, who also edited an anthology of material from the *Masses,* praised the magazine's "great vigor and wit" and considered it "perhaps the best example in American history of a nearly successful synthesis of poetry and propaganda, politics and art." Eastman was able to provide "strong and sensitive editorial direction," O'Neill said, because of his "strength of character, tenacity, great charm, a gift of oratory, clarity and grace of literary style, intellectual flexibility and considerable organizational powers." Eastman himself, however, considered his own writing for the *Masses* generally inferior to his other work because the former was part of his "secular and moralistic" self,

while the latter was part of his "sacredly creative" self. He described his *Masses* writing in negatives: "ephemeral, unstudious, not highly wrought, not intense, not cut and chiseled to perfection."

When Eastman took over in December 1912, an editorial notice heralded changes in the *Masses,* although Eastman's name was not mentioned. The notice announced a "radical change of policy" to produce a *"popular* Socialist magazine." Cited by social critic Harvey Swados as "one of the best magazines ever published in the United States," the *Masses* was the product of a collective. The staff would meet to plan each issue, and Eastman would choose material from among whatever the staff had approved. Under Eastman, according to social historian Alex Baskin, the *Masses* was "more articulate, more creative and more attractive" than previously. Although he enjoyed laying out the pages, Eastman eventually hired Floyd Dell, a journalist recently arrived from Chicago, as managing editor, the first paid position on the magazine.

Among the political cartoons for which the *Masses* became known are many that would be timely today. One of Art Young's, which appeared in the October 1911 issue, shows two waifs outdoors at night, one saying, "Gee, Annie, look at the stars! They're as thick as bedbugs." Another, by Stuart Davis, in August 1914, shows two men leaning against a railing while a woman walks by. One of the men says, "Gee, but women are lucky–born with a job." An October 1914 cartoon by W. J. Enright shows a woman cowering with her children in a corner of the kitchen, while her husband wields an empty liquor bottle. The caption is "Incompatibility of Temperament." The cover of the November 1914 issue, drawn by Young, shows monkeys reading newspapers full of war news, with the caption, "Mother, never let me hear you tell the children that these humans are descendants of ours."

Three cartoons focused on birth control, which Eastman supported before he joined the *Masses.* In one, a May 1915 drawing by K. R. Chamberlain, a woman carries an infant along a dock out toward the water at night, and the caption reads, "Family Limitation–Old Style." In the second, a September 1915 drawing by Robert Minor, federal government censor Anthony Comstock stands before a judge. Comstock is exhibiting a bedraggled woman and complaining, "Your Honor, this woman gave birth to a naked child!" The third cartoon is a two-page spread by Young in December 1915. Theodore Roosevelt is point-

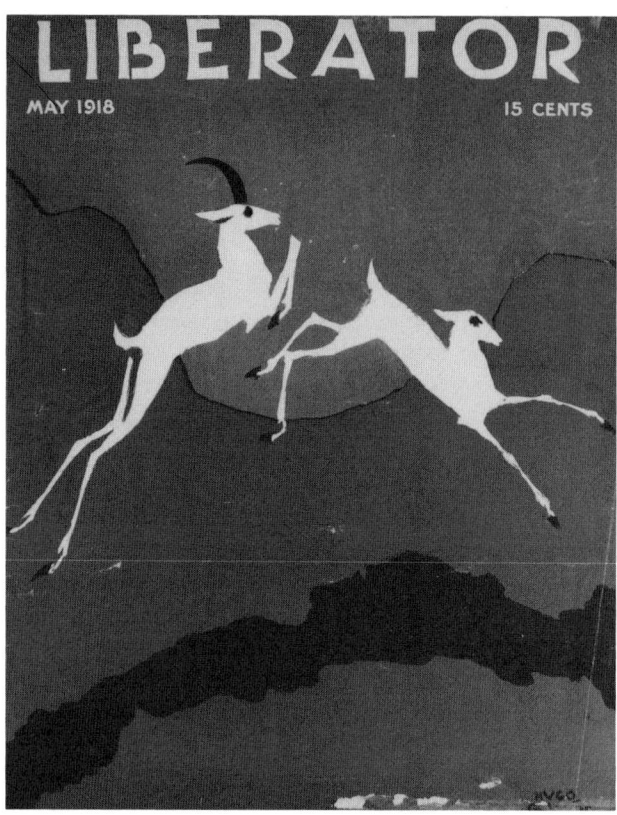

Cover for an issue of the magazine Eastman and his sister Crystal founded in 1918 (Lilly Library, Indiana University).

ing to an empty cradle and ordering a young woman standing nearby to "Breed!" In the background are dark clouds labeled "WAR."

While political cartoons made the *Masses* famous, they also contributed to two court battles. In 1913 the Associated Press sued the *Masses* for libel over a cartoon Young had drawn and an editorial Eastman had written. Appearing in the July 1913 issue, both concerned lack of Associated Press coverage of a miners' strike in West Virginia. The attendant violence had received no attention from newspapers that depended on the wire service. Eastman called the Associated Press a "Truth Trust" and said that "the substance of current history continues to be held in cold storage, adulterated, colored with poisonous intentions, and sold to the highest bidder to suit his private purposes." Young's cartoon depicted a man labeled "the Associated Press" secretively pouring bottles of liquid labeled "lies," "poison," "suppressed facts," "prejudice," "slander," and "hatred of labor organization" into a reservoir labeled "the news."

Six months later a grand jury twice indicted Eastman and Young for criminal libel, first for li-

beling the wire service and then for libeling its president, who claimed he was the model for the person in the cartoon. While the charges were eventually dropped when *Masses* attorney Samuel Untermeyer threatened to "subpoena the whole gang from J. P. Morgan down," the publicity boosted the morale of the *Masses* staff. New cartoons also resulted, including one by Young showing a wealthy fat woman labeled "the Associated Press" walking along carrying a large bag of money, a poodle labeled "aristocracy," and packages labeled "probity," "news," and "choice." Lying on the ground behind the woman is a scroll labeled "the *Masses* libel proceedings." The caption reads, "Madam, You Dropped Something."

Besides the lawsuit, the *Masses* experienced other rejections over the years because of its content. Eastman remembered distributors in Boston and Philadelphia refusing to carry it, the city of New York refusing it a place on the subway stands, the Columbia University library and bookstore refusing to subscribe to or sell it, and Canadian officials refusing to admit it into the country. The University of Wisconsin barred Eastman

Eastman (center) with Charlie Chaplin and Isaac McBride, 1919

from campus when he stopped there on a fund-raising tour.

Although Eastman felt that the *Masses* had achieved a triumph against the Associated Press, a second court case signaled the magazine's downfall. That story has since become an important part of journalism law. The *Masses* had always taken an antiwar stand, even in its early days, opposing the Boy Scouts for their paramilitary nature, but the magazine escalated its attack as the United States moved closer to participation in World War I. A cartoon by Robert Minor in the July 1916 issue shows an army physician examining a huge, muscular recruit without a head and declaring, "At last a perfect soldier!" The whole July 1916 issue was in fact devoted to the antiwar campaign, and in August 1917 Eastman made a cross-country speaking tour on behalf of peace.

However, this antiwar campaign would prove to be the undoing of the *Masses*. The Post Office Department declared the August 1917 issue unmailable under the recently passed Espionage Act. Seeking an injunction in federal district court against the postmaster, *Masses* attorney Gilbert Roe argued that the law did not apply to the articles, poems, and cartoons at issue because it concerned only agents of other countries. Judge Augustus Hand granted the temporary injunction and, on 26 July, ordered the August issue mailed. Meanwhile, however, the government had appealed the decision, and a circuit

court judge in Vermont stayed Hand's injunction and ordered a hearing on the appeal.

The September issue of the *Masses* was published nonetheless and included a chronology of the legal news, but the government had in the meantime rescinded the magazine's second-class mail permit, citing irregularity of publication as a result of the suspension of the August issue. Without its mail permit, and with its already limited distribution opportunities, the *Masses* had little chance of continuing. A combined November-December issue was the last one. It concluded with an appeal for subscriptions and a promise of a report on the Russian Revolution from John Reed in the Soviet Union.

In the meantime, the government indicted Eastman and several staff members for violating the Espionage Act by conspiring to cause people to oppose the draft. Four editors–Eastman, Young, Dell, and the business manager, Merrill Rogers–stood trial in April 1918. Eastman testified for the first three days of the nine-day trial, and his attorney remembered the editor as the "star witness" and "mastermind" of the trial, who personally convinced several of the jurors of the defendants' innocence. All the defendants denied a conspiracy, and after the jury deliberated for three days, the judge finally declared a hung jury. The government tried again in September, this time also indicting John Reed. Eastman's three-hour summation to the jury stood out in Reed's mind as the high point of the defense. Even the prosecutor congratulated Eastman on it. Again the deliberations resulted in a hung jury. This time, however, the government dismissed the indictments. Eastman's summation later circulated as a pamphlet.

Eager to influence American policy toward the Soviet Union, Eastman and his sister Crystal started a replacement for the *Masses* even before the second trial. The *Liberator* was similar in format and retained many of the contributors to the *Masses*, but the new magazine was not a collective. The Eastmans owned it, and Max Eastman controlled its editorial policy. Everyone received payment for contributions, but it had no second-class mail permit. In the first issue Eastman announced his "great magazine of liberty," whose mission would include advocacy of feminism, racial equality, peace, and workers taking over industry. At first Eastman also devoted dozens of pages to coverage of the *Masses* trials, complete with cartoons by Young and transcripts of

Eastman and his second wife, Eliena Vassilyenva Krylenko, on Martha's Vineyard

speeches given at a testimonial dinner after the first trial.

Then Eastman devoted the majority of the space in the *Liberator* to coverage of the Soviet Union, whose people, he said in the March 1918 issue, were leading the world in "the experiment of industrial and real democracy." He covered the war but much more gently than in the *Masses*— so gently that John Reed resigned from the editorial board. After the war most of the space went to coverage of revolutions in other countries and American labor strikes. The cartoons were more serious and more complex than those in the *Masses*. For example, one by Boardman Robinson in the January 1920 issue shows a scene accurately described in the caption: "Five minutes after prisoners of war are brought into a Bolshevik camp they are served with bread and tea, and five minutes later they are given propaganda literature in their own language." A headline for the caption reads, "A Typical Bolshevik Atrocity." Another cartoon on the Soviet Union, by Lydia Gibson in the November-December 1922 issue, shows a smiling family celebrating the birthday of a gleeful small child, with a huge birthday cake lighted by five large, glowing candles. The caption reads, "All Hail, Soviet Russia!"

Eastman also covered American labor news. In one cartoon by Young in the November 1918 issue, a man guarding the entrance to a room where a political rally is going on questions the first in a line of men waiting to enter. The caption is a dialogue: "Are you a Socialist?" "Certainly." "Show your indictment." Another Young cartoon, in the October 1922 issue, shows a rear view of an obese woman labeled "CAPITAL" holding the hand of a small child labeled "LABOR." The title of the caption is "PROGRESS," and the caption is a dialogue: "Where we going, Mama?" "Never you mind where we're going."

After nearly ten years of work on the *Masses* and the *Liberator*, in which he vigorously supported socialism, the Russian Revolution, Marxism, and Lenin, Eastman decided to resign his editorship in 1922 and go see for himself how the Soviet experiment was progressing. Because of his well-established radical reputation he received a warm welcome, especially from Leon Trotsky. Eastman studied Russian and began translating works by Trotsky, who was embroiled in a power struggle with Stalin. Taking Trotsky's side, Eastman brought out of the country documents supporting Trotsky's claim that Lenin had wanted him, not Stalin, as a successor. Before returning

Eastman in 1960 (New York Public Library Picture Collection)

to the United States in 1929, Eastman published the documents, translated more of Trotsky's work, wrote books about the political and philosophical changes in the Soviet Union, and married a Soviet woman, Eliena Vassilyenva Krylenko.

As a result of his examination of Stalin's leadership, however, Eastman withdrew his support of the Soviet Union. He was especially concerned about the disappearance in the Soviet Union of writers and artists. Stalin denounced Eastman by name after the publication of the documents disclosing Lenin's rejection of Stalin. Thus, Eastman became a traitor in Soviet eyes, and many of his radical fans in America abandoned him. For example, in *Partisan Review* (June-July 1934), Soviet writer Boris Pilnyak reminded Eastman that "the Soviet Union is showing humanity the road to a socialist world," and American writer Leon Dennen said that Eastman was "slandering the accomplish-

ments of the Soviet writers" with "brazen falsifications of Soviet history and Soviet literature." In *Pacific Weekly* (22 February 1935) French scholar Haakon Chevalier cited Eastman's bias, self-centeredness, contradictions, and irresponsibility.

Nevertheless, Eastman remained firmly anti-Soviet when the United States and the Soviet Union became allies in World War II, even writing cautionary articles for national audiences. During the cold war his opposition became government policy, and his articles appeared in such conservative magazines as *Reader's Digest* and *National Review*. He even called one article in the latter "I Acknowledge My Mistakes" (22 February 1956). While he eventually stopped writing for *National Review* because he disagreed with editor William Buckley about religion, he continued to publish in *Reader's Digest* as a "Roving Editor."

Many critics found his positions on the Soviet Union confusing and laughable, but in 1941 Edmund Wilson credited Eastman with "the most intelligent and searching as well as the best informed discussion of the implications of the Marxist movement and the development of the Revolution in Russia that has yet appeared in English." And thirty years later John P. Diggins considered Eastman "the first major American writer to subject Marxism to a penetrating philosophical and psychological critique by bringing Freud's insights to bear upon the Marxist concept of ideology . . . perhaps the first writer in the Western world to draw a critical distinction between the ideas of Marx and the actions of Lenin in order to make a case for the October Revolution that would infuriate both the Bolsheviks and Mensheviks . . . one of the first literary intellectuals to expose the suppression of cultural freedom under Stalin . . . and one of the first radical partisans of Lenin and Trotsky to renounce the whole Soviet experiment."

Eastman's second wife died in 1956, and on 22 March 1958 he married Yvette Szekely. He died on 25 March 1969 in Barbados after suffering a cerebral hemorrhage. He was at work on a translation of Trotsky's *The Young Lenin*, which was edited by Maurice Friedberg and published in 1972.

Biography:

William L. O'Neill, *The Last Romantic: A Life of Max Eastman* (New York: Oxford, 1978).

References:

Daniel Aaron, *Writers on the Left: Episodes in Ameri-

can Literary Communism (New York: Harcourt, Brace & World, 1961);

Van Wyck Brooks, *The Confident Years: 1885-1915* (New York: Dutton, 1952);

Brooks, *Sketches In Criticism* (New York: Dutton, 1932);

Milton Cantor, *Max Eastman* (New York: Twayne, 1970);

Haakon Chevalier, "Max Eastman: The White-Headed Boy," *Pacific Weekly* (22 February 1935): 88-89;

Leon Dennen, "Bunk By A Bohemian," in "Max Eastman: The Man Under the Table," *Partisan Review*, 1 (June-July 1934): 21-25;

John P. Diggins, "Getting Hegel out of History: Max Eastman's Quarrel with Marxism," *American Historical Review*, 79 (February 1974): 38-71;

Diggins, "Review of *The Last Romantic: A Life of Max Eastman*," *New Republic*, 29 (January 1979): 32-34;

James Feibleman, "Criticism of Modern Theories of Comedy," in *In Praise of Comedy: A Study in Its Theory and Practice* (London: Allen & Unwin, 1939; New York: Russell & Russell, 1962), pp. 123-167;

Richard Fitzgerald, *Art and Politics: Cartoonists of the "Masses" and "Liberator"* (Westport, Conn.: Greenwood, 1973);

Frederick C. Giffen, *Six Who Protested: Radical Opposition to the First World War* (Port Washington, N.Y.: Kennikat, 1977);

Charles I. Glicksberg, "Max Eastman: Literary Insurgent," *Sewanee Review*, 44 (July-September 1936): 324-337;

Max Lerner, *Public Journal: Marginal Notes on Wartime America* (New York: Viking, 1945);

Boris Pilnyak, "In Reference To Myself," in "Max Eastman: The Man Under the Table," *Partisan Review*, 1 (June-July 1934): 17-21;

Julien Steinberg, ed., *Verdict of Three Decades: From the Literature of Individual Revolt Against Soviet Communism: 1917-1950* (New York: Duell, Sloan & Pearce, 1950);

Harvey Swados, Review of *Echoes of Revolt*, *Massachusetts Review*, 7 (Spring 1967): 382-387;

Edmund Wilson, "Max Eastman in 1941," *New Republic*, 104 (10 February 1941): 173-176;

Art Young, *Art Young: His Life and Times* (New York: Sheridan, 1939).

Papers:
The main collection of Eastman's papers is at the Lilly Library, Indiana University.

Gilbert H. Grosvenor

(28 October 1875-4 February 1966)

Gary W. Selnow
Virginia Polytechnic Institute and State University

MAJOR POSITION HELD: Assistant editor (1899-1903), editor, *National Geographic Magazine* (1903-1954).

BOOKS: *Flags of the World*, with Byron McCandles (Washington, D. C.: National Geographic Society, 1917);
The National Geographic Society and Its Magazine (Washington, D. C.: National Geographic Society, 1936);
Insignia and Decorations of the U. S. Armed Forces, with J. R. Hildebrand, Arthur E. Du Bois, and others (Washington, D. C.: National Geographic Society, 1945).

OTHER: *Scenes from Every Land*, edited by Grosvenor (Washington, D.C.: National Geographic Society, 1907);
Scenes from Every Land, Second Series, edited by Grosvenor (Washington, D.C.: National Geographic Society, 1909);
Scenes from Every Land, Third Series, edited by Grosvenor (Washington, D.C.: National Geographic Society, 1912);
Scenes from Every Land, Fourth Series, edited by Grosvenor (Washington, D.C.: National Geographic Society, 1918);
E. W. Nelson, *Wild Animals of North America*, edited by Grosvenor (Washington, D.C.: National Geographic Society, 1918; revised edition, 1930);
The Book of Birds, edited by Grosvenor and Alexander Wetmore (Washington, D.C.: National Geographic Society, 1937).

SELECTED PERIODICAL PUBLICATIONS:
"The Tetrahedral Kites of Dr. Alexander Graham Bell," *Popular Science Monthly*, 64 (1903): 131-151;
"Our Heralds of Storm and Flood," *National Geographic Magazine*, 18 (1907): 586-601;
"Young Russia," *National Geographic Magazine*, 26 (1914): 423-520;

Gilbert H. Grosvenor, age ninety (National Geographic photograph by Thomas Nebbia, copyright National Geographic Society)

"The Land of the Best," *National Geographic Magazine*, 29 (1916): 327-430;
"Germany's Dream of World Domination," *National Geographic Magazine*, 33 (1918): 558-567;
"The Capitol, Wonder Building of the World," *National Geographic Magazine*, 43 (1923): 603-638;
"The Hawaiian Islands," *National Geographic Magazine*, 45 (1924): 115-238;

"A Maryland Pilgrimage," *National Geographic Magazine*, 51 (1927): 133-212;

"The Great Falls of the Potomac," *National Geographic Magazine*, 53 (1928): 385-400;

"Washington Through the Years," *National Geographic Magazine*, 60 (November 1931): 517-619;

"The National Geographic Society," *American Antiquarian Society, Worcester, Mass., Proceedings*, 52 (1943): 325-362.

Gilbert H. Grosvenor was the moving creative and administrative force behind the successful evolution of the *National Geographic Magazine*. As editor of the magazine from 1903 until 1954, when he turned the editorial post over to his son, Gilbert Grosvenor established standards for content and production that have yielded a magazine with such stature and audience appeal that many subscribers steadfastly refuse to discard their old copies. Early years of the magazine were beset by financial and philosophical problems fostered by a contentious board of trustees. It is widely accepted that the strong-willed Grosvenor, almost single-handedly, was responsible for shaping the image and style of this magazine, now recognized as an American institution.

Gilbert Grosvenor was born–along with a twin brother, Edwin–to Edwin Augustus Grosvenor, a professor of European history at the American-sponsored Robert College in Constantinople, Turkey, and Lillian Hovey Waters Grosvenor. With only a brief interruption during the Russo-Turkish War, the boys grew up in Turkey. They returned to the United States to attend prep school at the Worcester Academy, then studied at Amherst College, where both were graduated magna cum laude in 1897. Gilbert earned a master's degree in 1901. Although he was fond of the title "Dr. Grosvenor," using it on all his writings and insisting on its use by subordinates, his doctorates all were honorary. It was soon after he completed his undergraduate degree and began teaching prep school in New Jersey that Grosvenor became associated with Alexander Graham Bell, a founder of the National Geographic Society.

Circumstances surrounding Grosvenor's early involvement with the great scientist, best known as the inventor of the telephone, are not entirely clear. One plausible account suggests Bell saw in Grosvenor not only a promising editor and director of the floundering magazine, but also a most eligible suitor for his nineteen-year-

Grosvenor and Elsie Bell during their wedding at King's Weigh House Church, London, 23 October 1900 (copyright National Geographic Society)

old daughter, Elsie. Bell was a friend of Edwin Grosvenor, Sr., and became interested in the young Gilbert through press accounts of his and his brother's remarkable, well-publicized performances at Amherst. Nearly a year after the Grosvenor twins were invited to a house party at the Bells' summer home in Nova Scotia, where Gilbert was introduced to Elsie, Bell summoned him to Washington and proposed a position with the magazine. Grosvenor accepted and for the next several years received a salary paid directly out of Bell's pocket.

Up to this point the *National Geographic Magazine* had suffered serious problems. Its board of trustees was unable to decide on a direction for the publication, some believing (Bell among them) it should provide material for a general audience, others vigorously asserting the magazine should be pitched to the needs and interests of the professional scientific community. The first philosophy argued for a visually appealing, casually written publication that would attract large audiences, the second for a strictly scientific production that would appeal to a limited and esoteric audience. This internal battle had been ongoing since inception of the magazine in 1888, with several trustees advocating a scientific style, and the first president of the National Geographic Society, Gardiner Green Hubbard, and then Alexander Graham Bell, arguing for the open format.

Bell's interests in other areas, and particularly his affection for scientific experimentation, drew his attention from the magazine. He grew tired of the internal strife, and, it seems, eager to find a replacement who would hold the line against advocates of a technical publication and advance his objective of creating a magazine accessible to the general public. Bell saw Grosvenor as the ideal candidate.

Although Bell in no way could be considered a manipulative or power-seeking man–by this time he was world famous and quite wealthy from his invention of the telephone–he was interested in preserving his vision for the magazine and may have felt young Grosvenor presented the greatest opportunity for, and least risk to, accomplishing this goal. Grosvenor's age would ensure his continued deference to Bell, and his lack of publication experience would guarantee he arrived with few preconceived notions about how the magazine should develop. Grosvenor, therefore, would present no threat to Bell's objectives.

However, Grosvenor's academic achievements at Amherst were exemplary, and the scope of his interests and areas of expertise in language and the sciences were well recognized. As observers of the *National Geographic* would soon testify, Grosvenor also was a disciplined and pertinacious man, and one willing to take a chance to advance his purpose.

These features of his personality were perhaps best revealed in his early work with the National Geographic Society. Immediately after signing on, he was confronted with two related challenges. First, there was a need to increase membership in the National Geographic Society, which in turn would increase magazine circulation. The magazine always has been, and remains today, a benefit of society membership and cannot be purchased independently either through subscription or at a newsstand. The second challenge involved a renovation of the content and style of the magazine to render a publication more acceptable to the masses.

Grosvenor met the first challenge by instituting a policy of "unsolicited nominations of perspective members," whereby existing members were asked to nominate others for membership. Nominees then would receive a letter from the National Geographic Society telling them of their good fortune and asking them to respond with their dues. This successful policy was in force until the 1950s, when membership was granted to anyone requesting it. In practice, membership has almost never been denied to anyone throughout the history of the society. Despite the nonselective nature of the policy, the marketing technique was successful. Members felt a part of the prestigious organization and saw the magazine as an attractive bonus for their participation. Grosvenor's decision to employ this innovative marketing strategy initially met with considerable resistance by the obstinate board of trustees, and only with the substantial support of Bell was he able to get board approval.

For the first seven years of Grosvenor's tenure at the society, Bell's influence was crucial in persuading the board to grant the young editor license to carry out his plans for the magazine. This point is well made in a letter sent by Bell's personal secretary to Grosvenor in which, after writing about the need to increase membership and circulation, she writes, "remember, you have Mr. Bell behind you." Clearly, without Bell's interposition not only would Grosvenor have forfeited his programs, but his job as well. While Grosvenor rightfully receives credit for making the *National Geographic Magazine* what it is today, he might be unknown were it not for Alexander Graham Bell.

Grosvenor's second challenge, the overhaul of the magazine itself, was a most difficult task given the leanings of the board and the state of production technology. During his first five years Grosvenor attempted to include photographs in the magazine whenever possible, but photos were costly, and reliable sources were all but nonexistent. He did find, though, that various agencies of the federal government would lend him photoengravings after they had already been used for inhouse publications. He used these photos whenever possible to supplement stories. However, even this aroused the anger of the irascible board of trustees.

Supply and demand met as they sometimes do for the great fortune of a struggling soul. In December 1904 Grosvenor was deeply distressed in the waning moments of a production schedule

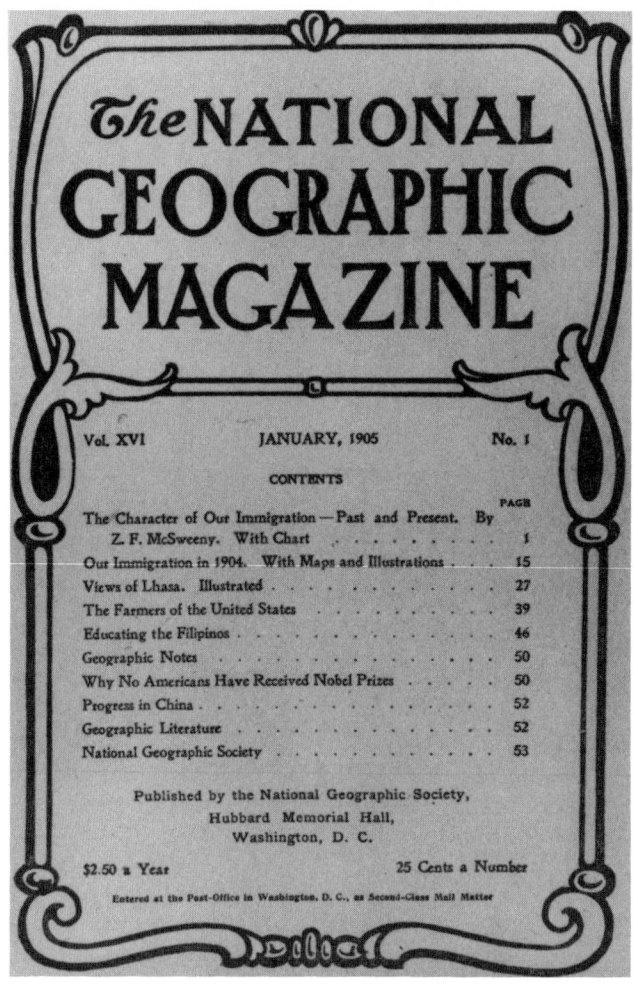

Cover for the issue that signaled the change of the National Geographic *from a scientific journal to a fully illustrated, popular monthly*

over an eleven-page hole in the layout for an upcoming edition. There just was not a good manuscript available to fill the space. As he tells the story (*The National Geographic Society and Its Magazine,* 1936), there was a large, bulky envelope lying on his desk that he had not yet had time to open. While struggling with his production problem, he unwrapped the package and discovered to his amazement a collection of "50 beautiful photographs of the mysterious city of Lhasa in Tibet, taken by a Russian explorer." The photographer asked only that he receive a byline for his efforts if the photos were used.

Despite the anticipated outrage by the board, Grosvenor proceeded on his own authority to fill the eleven pages with the photos of Lhasa. According to Grosvenor's accounts, in the days following publication of that edition readers stopped him on the street to offer congratula-

tions for the article. Apparently recognizing the wisdom of this decision, the board, within a short time after publication, unanimously elected Grosvenor to the board of managers and the executive and finance committees. Although it was uncharacteristic of the trustees to so congratulate Grosvenor, it is certain that publication of the Lhasa spread was a watershed event in the tempestuous relationship between the editor and the board. From this point on Grosvenor was in control; henceforth, he formed policy and offered direction that went without challenge.

In the midst of his work with the magazine and his hagglings with the board of trustees, Grosvenor found time to marry Elsie Bell. The two were wed on 23 October 1900, at the King's Weigh House Chapel in London. Their honeymoon was a storybook event that took them to Paris, Berlin, and other major cities throughout

Another View of the Palace of the Dalai Lama

The palace is about 1,400 feet long and about 70 feet high in front. In the construction of this palace the Tibetans displayed their highest architectural skill. Here are found the most precious treasures of Tibet, including the golden sepulchre of the fifth Dalai-Lama, which is about 28 feet high. The treasures and apartments of the Dalai-Lama are in the central portion of the temple palace. The remainder of the building serves as quarters for various attendants or followers of the Dalai-Lama, including a community of 500 monks, whose duty it is to pray for the welfare and long life of the Dalai-Lama.

One of the pictures of Lhasa, the capitol of Tibet, that was included in the first photographic spread published in the National Geographic *(January 1905)*

Europe, all under the patronage of local geographic societies that feted the young couple at every stop.

Following publication of the Lhasa photos, the philosophy and image for the *National Geographic Magazine* envisioned by Bell and Grosvenor were assured. Early in 1905 Grosvenor received another photographic windfall, this time from his cousin William Howard Taft, who at the time was governor general of the Philippines. Publication of 32 full-page plates (a total of 138 pictures) from the Taft Philippines collection brought such an overwhelming response from readers that Grosvenor ordered a second pressrun. Within a year of this edition membership in the society increased dramatically from 3,400 to more than 11,000 members.

Printing of the Taft photos was noteworthy for another reason. Among the collection of prints depicting the Philippine countryside and its wildlife were several conspicuously posed shots of bare-breasted native women. Despite the prevailing attitude in America toward nudity, Grosvenor, with Bell's blessing, decided to run the photos, even though his prudish personal philosophy would suggest otherwise. Grosvenor ab-

stained from alcohol and tobacco and avoided the use of even mild profanity. The selection of such photos did not appear congruous with his other behavior. If he gambled on the potential of these photographs to boost readership of the magazine, his instincts were well-founded. Expectations of outrage from the board or from readers never occurred; in fact, there was a run on membership. Although it would be unfair to ascribe this newfound popularity to the nude photos, one might reasonably argue they provided a feature to the magazine viewed by many as a dividend. Such photos have since become a trademark of the publication.

Grosvenor had firm ideas about directions for his publication, and as his control became ever greater, his policies became more entrenched within the organization. In 1915 he published a list of "seven principles" that essentially were canons of editorial policy:

> The first principle is absolute accuracy. Nothing must be printed which is not strictly according to fact. The magazine can point to many years in which not a single article has appeared which was not absolutely accurate.

Abundance of beautiful, instructive and artistic illustrations.

Everything printed . . . must have permanent value, and be so planned that each magazine will be as valuable and pertinent one year or five or ten years after publication as it is on the day of publication . . .

All personalities and notes of a trivial character are avoided.

Nothing of a partisan or controversial nature is printed.

Only what is of a kindly nature is printed about any country or people, everything unpleasant or unduly critical being avoided.

The content of each number is planned with a view of being timely. Whenever any part of the world becomes prominent in public interest, by reason of war, earthquake, volcanic eruption, etc., the members of the National Geographic Society have come to know that in the next issue of their magazine they will obtain the latest geographic, historical and economic information about that region, presented in an interesting and absolutely nonpartisan manner, and accompanied by photographs which in number and excellence can be equaled by no other publication.

While these principles evidently have prescribed a successful policy for the magazine, some argue they have rendered the publication little more than a forum for happy talk, ignoring unpleasant realities that often exist in the places and events covered. They often skirt over annoying features of travel such as passport problems, illness due to food and water changes, and conflicts with local officials.

Some critics see a greater danger in the potential to distort by omission. Author Howard S. Abramson proposes that the seven principles allowed Grosvenor to cover countries and regions he favored and ignore those he personally found undesirable. "Nations that Grosvenor and the Society approved of could be lavishly covered in pretty pictures and words; what was not so nice about those lands could be ignored. The Society could excuse its failure to carry articles about nations that weren't in its political favor by pointing to their instability or economic turmoil."

This happy-talk policy contributed also to one of the magazine's darkest episodes. In its February 1937 edition the *National Geographic* ran an article by Douglas Chandler that applauded Adolf Hitler's Germany for what he saw as its efficiency and enchanted life-styles. He touted Germany's four-a-day mail deliveries and its

Grosvenor with his daughter, Gertrude Hubbard, and son, Melville Bell, in 1906. The photograph was taken by Grosvenor's wife, Elsie, the daughter of Alexander Graham Bell (copyright National Geographic Society).

schools and universities. Accompanying photographs showed brightly colored buildings, bucolic countrysides, and the smiling faces of German youngsters. Swastikas were seen throughout the photo set. Missing from this story, of course, were references to Hitler's concentration camps, which were already in operation. Also missing, as Abramson notes, was mention of Germany's "Nuremberg decrees, which severely restricted the rights of Jews . . . or that Hitler had illegally reoccupied the Rhineland in March 1936; or even that Hitler had abrogated the Versailles Treaty in January 1937, clearly setting the stage for what would be called World War II."

During the war the National Geographic Society played a major role in supplying the United States military and its intelligence services with maps and photographs. Even before the Japanese attack on Pearl Harbor, the society made available its collection of more than fifty-three thousand maps of waterways and harbors, towns, roads, and topographical layouts. National Geographic maps often were more current, accurate, and detailed than those designed by federal cartographers.

At one point late in 1941 during a briefing on Japanese advances near Singapore, President Franklin Delano Roosevelt's advisers discovered they did not have a map on which to show the president the precise location of ongoing battles. In response to their requests Grosvenor sent not only an appropriate map of islands in the South China Sea, but an entire National Geographic collection of world maps on rollers housed in an impressive wooden cabinet. As Grosvenor tells the story, within an hour of its arrival, Roosevelt had the cabinet mounted directly behind his chair for easy use.

Throughout his reign at the National Geographic Society, Grosvenor ran a tight ship. He was known as "the Chief" among his employees but was nearly always addressed as Dr. Grosvenor. As a nonsmoker, for many years he forbade smoking among staff members, and it was not until one defiant soul named Frederick Simpich lit up a cigar at his own desk in 1925 that the rule was modified. No one smoked in the Chief's presence, however.

For years Grosvenor also maintained policies about dress and conduct for male and female staff members. For instance, in the presence of ladies, men were required to wear coats and ties. Women were compelled to wear stockings throughout the year, even through the hot and steamy Washington summers. Also, dining facilities were separate for male and female employees because Grosvenor believed that during lunchtime discussions men might become carried away with their language and utter a word or expression that would offend the women.

Although the National Geographic Society is a nonprofit organization for tax purposes, there is little evidence of austerity in its buildings or in its operation, particularly those serving the needs of the director and his executive staff. Once the magazine became successful Grosvenor felt quite comfortable spending money on lavish offices for the upper echelon of the organization. In a story on the society for the 25 September 1943 issue of the *New Yorker*, Geoffrey T. Hellman said, "These quarters reflect some of the rewards of the Grosvenor policy of freeing geography from its shackles. The Chief's two-room office is a good deal larger than, say, the ball-

room in the old Peter Cooper house on Lexington Avenue." Among the various dining rooms—for middle-level women, middle-level men, and upper-level men—there was a special dining room reserved exclusively for Grosvenor and his wife. It always was prepared with two place settings for the couple whether or not they even were in town that day.

Grosvenor's fondness for wealth and the good life was conspicuous. His relationship through marriage with the wealthy Alexander Graham Bell, and his own income, guaranteed him the resources to maintain a most opulent lifestyle. Several stories suggest this wealth may have cultivated an elitist attitude in the man. For instance, Abramson tells of a Miss Jane M. Smith of Pittsburgh, who, in 1911, willed the National Geographic Society five thousand dollars expressly for the purpose of providing lifetime memberships for worthy people who could not on their own afford them. Hellman, in the 27 September 1952 issue of the *New Yorker*, reported that Grosvenor's "disinclination to inquire into people's finances" led the society to give these memberships to people already of substantial means. One went to Hiram Bingham, an affluent explorer, another to King Leopold III of Belgium, and yet another to French automobile developer André Citroen.

Grosvenor retained control of the National Geographic Society for more than fifty years. It was not until May 1954 that the seventy-eight-year-old editor and director turned over the reins to younger hands. His son Melville Bell Grosvenor, who had been with National Geographic since 1924, was named vice-president of the society and associate editor of the magazine. John Oliver LaGorce, Gilbert Grosvenor's longtime friend and assistant in the society, was appointed to head the organization at the senior Grosvenor's direction. In this way Grosvenor was able to keep at least partial control through a trusted surrogate who would respect his wishes. Some three years later, in January 1957, satisfied that Melville could handle the job to his satisfaction, Grosvenor allowed his son to assume full control of the society and its magazine.

The Grosvenors spent their retirement years at their homes in Miami, Bethesda, and the family estate, "Beinn Bhreagh"—Gaelic for "beautiful mountain"—on Cape Breton Island in Nova Scotia, formerly owned by Alexander Graham Bell. On 26 December 1964 Elsie May Bell Grosvenor died. Two years later the ailing Grosvenor,

Grosvenor receiving the Grosvenor Medal Award from Charles Franklin Kettering at a ceremony held on 19 May 1949 to honor Grosvenor's fifty years of service with the National Geographic (Washington Post)

ninety years old, died quietly while taking an afternoon nap at Beinn Bhreagh.

There are few critical public statements regarding Grosvenor or the society he forged in his own image. He is generally seen as a man who through strong conviction brought the *National Geographic Magazine* from its sleepy state as a scientific journal with limited audience appeal to the lively, vastly popular publication it is today. Without question it was the power and prestige of Alexander Graham Bell that sustained Grosvenor during his early days as editor, but it is clearly Grosvenor's own tenacity and creativity during his fifty-one-year tenure that shaped the image and form of the magazine. Some writers have challenged Grosvenor's opulent life-style as ill befitting the director of a nonprofit organization. Contemporary critics continue to be distressed at the secrecy that surrounds (as it always has) the society's financial dealings.

Other contentions with Grosvenor and his conduct at the society concern his heavy-handed leadership style. Some believe there may have been too much control from the top and too little at mid-management levels. These criticisms

are muted, however, in light of the remarkable success of this singular publication. His contributions are, perhaps, best summarized in a tribute by LaGorce: "Behind the term geography is exploration. Behind that is adventure and just over the hill is romance. . . . Under Dr. Grosvenor, these three elements are stepped into closer focus. The Chief has removed the technical padlocks from the science of geography."

References:

Howard S. Abramson, *National Geographic: Behind America's Lens on the World* (New York: Crown, 1987);

Tom Buckley, "With the *National Geographic* on Its Endless, Cloudless Voyage," *New York Times Magazine* (6 September 1970): 10-23;

Geoffrey T. Hellman, "Geography Unshackled," *New Yorker*, 19 (25 September 1943): 26-34; (2 October 1943): 27-37; (9 October 1943): 27-36.

Papers:

Grosvenor's papers are held at the Library of Congress, Washington, D. C.

Briton Hadden

(18 February 1898-27 February 1929)

Carolyn Garrett Cline and Paula Cozort Renfro
Southwest Texas State University

MAJOR POSITIONS HELD: Publisher, editor, *Time* (1923-1929); *Tide* (1927-1929); business manager, Time Inc. (1926, 1928).

Briton Hadden, cofounder of *Time* magazine, was the genius behind the style of writing *Time* introduced in 1923. During the magazine's first three years of publication, Hadden edited every word of copy, and it was he who was responsible for the active verbs, the compound adjectives, the middle names, the inverted sentences, all designed to enliven the news that he and Henry R. Luce had culled from daily papers and repackaged into the first weekly newsmagazine. The slogan of *Time* for many years was "Curt, Concise, Complete," and it was Hadden's editing that accomplished the first two goals. He often pared news items to as few as three lines, seldom more than one hundred lines, and in doing so he created a distinctive style of writing others called "Timestyle." Unfortunately, Hadden did not live long enough to reap the benefits of his daring journalistic efforts. He died of a blood infection in 1929, at age thirty-one.

Hadden was born in Brooklyn, New York, on 18 February 1898, the son of Crowell and Elizabeth Busch Hadden. Both his father and paternal grandfather were bankers, and Hadden grew up in comfortable surroundings. At the age of twelve Hadden founded his own newspaper, the *Daily Glonk,* at Brooklyn Polytechnic Preparatory School. Several of the characteristics of the *Glonk* would later appear in *Time:* it was departmentalized, terse, and given to unusual phrasing. (Hadden also exhibited his penchant for including middle names of individuals mentioned in the paper, especially when he could thus achieve a comic effect.) Yet writing was not Hadden's chief interest. A lifelong baseball addict, he was continually frustrated by his ineptitude for the sport. When he was named editor of the school paper at Hotchkiss, a boarding school, he responded to his mother's note: "Thanks a lot for the congratulations, but I wish I was being congrat-ulated for making the ball team. I'd rather get one 'H' than be editor of all the papers in the world." Even after *Time* was established as a success, Hadden's dream remained to earn enough money to purchase a major league ball club.

At Hotchkiss, Hadden's interest in journalism led him into a competitive friendship that continued throughout his life. The well-to-do Episcopalian from New York found a natural journalistic rival in the son of Presbyterian missionaries to China, Henry R. Luce, a stammering scholarship student in ill-tailored clothes whose passions and abilities as an editor equaled those of Hadden. At Hotchkiss both won positions on the school paper. Hadden became editor in chief during his senior year, while Luce remained assistant editor of the newspaper and editor in chief of the literary magazine. Luce biographer W. A. Swanberg wrote: "Luce and Hadden measured each other in a singular relationship that always contained more rivalry than friendship, and would continue on that basis for fifteen years.... If Luce had a wide margin in scholarship, Hadden's bluff good humor surrounded him with friends."

In 1916 both Hadden and Luce entered Yale, where the rivalry continued. Hadden became chairman, and Luce managing editor, of the student paper, the *Yale Daily News,* during their sophomore year (under normal circumstances they would have assumed these positions their junior year, but with the entrance of the United States into World War I, the incumbent chairman resigned to join the army). Hadden was selected for Skull and Bones, as was Luce, although Luce was elected Phi Beta Kappa, thus surpassing Hadden academically.

Both Hadden and Luce were members of the Yale R.O.T.C., and in the summer of 1918, while stationed together at a training camp in Columbia, South Carolina (the signing of the armistice in November 1918 prevented them from seeing combat duty), they discussed for the first time the possibility of forming their own newspaper. However, the two went separate ways upon

Briton Hadden, shortly before his death in 1929

graduation in 1920–Luce to spend a year at Oxford, and Hadden to work as a reporter on the *New York World* under Herbert Bayard Swope. Swope never hired recent graduates as reporters, but Hadden burst into his office unannounced and declared he wanted a job. When Swope ordered him to leave, Hadden proclaimed: "Mr. Swope, you're interfering with my destiny." Swope later explained, "He told me that his destiny required him to work on the *World* for a year in order to get some experience to help him start a paper of his own."

In 1921 Hadden was reunited with Luce on the staff of Frank Munsey's *Baltimore News;* they had agreed that working on a small paper such as the *News* would give them the freedom to plan their own publication, then conceived of as a

newspaper to be called "Facts." In February 1922 Hadden and Luce took seven-week leaves from the *News* to return to New York and obtain financing and put together a staff for the newspaper, although Hadden's total capital at that time was one hundred dollars. In a shabby brownstone office they set about working on a prospectus for a revised publication: *Time: The Weekly News- magazine.* They identified a problem: "People in America are, for the most part, poorly informed . . . because no publication has adapted itself to the time which busy men are able to spend on simply keeping informed." Every Friday morning *Time* would deal "briefly with every happening of importance" and present these events as news rather than as comment. Their editorial purpose was simple: to keep men well-informed.

*Cover, featuring a sketch of retiring Speaker of the House Joe Cannon, for the first issue of the magazine
Hadden cofounded with Henry R. Luce (copyright Time, Inc., 1923)*

A network of friends and classmates offered the young men advice, but they soon discovered that enthusiasm and a prospectus were not enough to raise the $100,000 they felt necessary to begin the magazine; their original scheme had been to talk ten Yale classmates into putting up $10,000 each, but no member of the class of 1920 was willing to enter into such a scheme. By October they had squeezed every penny out of every possible prospect, but had only $86,000. At that point Hadden and Luce were earning only $30 a week each as editor-publisher, and they had lured Harvard graduate Roy E. Larsen as circulation manager for $40. They were willing to pay pubic-relations counsel Edward Bernays $125 each week to promote the venture, but Bernays turned down the offer and also passed on the chance to invest in the magazine.

Still hopeful, Hadden and Luce went ahead with the reduced capital, and the first issue of *Time* was published on 3 March 1923. Their edito-

rial scheme was simple and cost-effective: a small staff gleaned news from four hundred newspapers, although they chiefly relied upon the *New York Times* and the *New York World*. The news was rewritten in the magazine's distinct style and then sold for fifteen cents. They obtained subscribers through mail campaigns, although their eager but amateurish staff of postdebutantes botched the mailing of the first few issues so badly that some subscribers received three copies of one issue, but none of the other two.

Hadden and Luce had planned to alternate the positions of editor and business manager each year, but Hadden remained as editor for the first three years, giving each article in the magazine the style for which it would become famous. He refused to allow himself to write any copy, for he feared he would then be driven to write it all, but he carefully edited every word in the magazine, including the advertising, creating a style so striking that it appeared that the maga-

Hadden (top) in 1924 with the Time *editorial staff: (left to right) John Martin, T. J. C. Martyn, an assistant identified as "William, the Clipper," and Niven Busch. Martin and Busch were Hadden's cousins.*

The editorial staff of the Yale Daily News, *circa 1920. Hadden, chairman of the editorial board, is seated at center; Luce, managing editor, is seated at his right.*

zine was written by a single author–one with a penchant for compound adjectives, middle names, and strange syntax. A 1936 *New Yorker* parody written by Wolcott Gibbs would later observe of this peculiar style: "Backward ran sentences until reeled the mind."

In appearance *Time* was amateurish in its first few years. Eric Hodgins, a company executive, wrote in 1946, "Its printing standards were approximately those of a French provincial newspaper in 1910 and its pictures, in the words of the late Robert Benchley, looked as if they had been engraved on pieces of bread."

In 1925, despite the straitened finances at *Time*, Hadden and Larsen decided to vacation in Europe, a difficult goal for men still earning fifty dollars a week. The departure of two key staff members upset Luce, especially since Hadden had left another *Time* staff member, Manfred Gottfried, in charge with the instructions, "See that Luce doesn't meddle." Hadden and Larsen enjoyed the trip to Europe so much that they cabled from Paris for another fifteen hundred dollars to pay for entertainment. This action galvanized Luce, who had long been considering a move to the Midwest as a way of saving money on office expenses and expediting nationwide distribution. By the time Hadden and Larsen returned, Luce had arranged the move to Cleveland.

Hadden was enraged but moved to Ohio, where he allowed Luce to edit *Time* while he functioned as business manager and also developed *Tide*, a company house organ, into a trade journal. Under Hadden's editorship *Tide* was irreverent and controversial, and extremely critical of misleading advertisements and questionable sales angles. (After Hadden's death the magazine was sold in order to avoid a conflict of interest with the advertisers in *Time*.)

The editors soon discovered that while production and distribution of *Time* were improved by the relocation, the Cleveland papers could not provide the quality and quantity of news they needed to rewrite each week. Thus, while Luce was in Europe in 1927, Hadden arranged for the editorial offices to be moved back to New York.

With Luce as editor of *Time* and Hadden as business manager, it was clear business was not Hadden's strength. He seemed to do his best to hamper Larsen's attempts at improving circulation and appeared to go out of his way to offend advertisers and groups the subscription department had targeted. In 1925, for example, after the advertising manager had just landed the Fisher Body account, Hadden had included a story that so offended Fisher Body and Packard that they canceled fifty-two pages of advertising. Advertising growth came to a stop when he took over in 1928, though circulation still grew, from 9,000 in 1923 to 225,000 six years later.

The last vestiges of friendship were dissolving between Luce and Hadden, who had been wounded by Yale's awarding an honorary M.A. degree to Luce in 1926 for "distinguished accomplishments" in journalism, without even a mention of Hadden, whose editing had largely created this accomplishment. For his part, Luce felt stifled by Hadden, who never shared Luce's missionary passion to spread his own philosophy via his publications; Luce could expand only in those areas about which he and Hadden agreed.

Hadden's power came not only from his exceptional journalistic abilities but also from the personal charm he radiated in contrast to Luce's dour intensity. Swanberg quotes *Time* staffer Winsor French's portrait of Hadden: "His neckties were always askew, his trousers incredibly baggy.... He either ate voraciously or not at all, thought nothing of putting in 24-hour days when the pressure was intense and consequently saw no reason why anyone else, male or female, shouldn't and couldn't do the same. Hadden also had a quick, violent temper and his wild roaring, drifting down nine floors into the street, caused people . . . to come to an abrupt halt and wonder if someone wasn't being murdered.... Yet, for all his eccentricities, I don't think there was a single member of the staff who didn't love him."

After six years *Time* was an unqualified success, and Hadden had achieved his goal of becoming a millionaire, at least on paper. But in December 1928 the robustly healthy Hadden went home from work with a fever, caused, he supposed, by a cold. He moved in with his parents to recover from influenza but two weeks later was admitted to the Brooklyn Hospital with a streptococcus infection that had turned into septicemia and endocarditis. At first he barely slowed down, ordering his meals from Shrafft's and spending most of his time on the telephone to the office and his friends.

But by January he grew weaker; he was finally kept alive only by blood transfusions every forty-eight hours. Finally, at 4 A.M. on 27 February 1929, six years–almost to the hour–after he had sent the first issue of *Time* to press, Hadden died only days after his thirty-first birthday.

The 11 March 1929 issue of *Time* included a few of the hundreds of messages sent by those who had known Hadden. His friends and associates commented upon his character, his warm personality, his self-sacrifice, his kindness, and his great promise.

Earnest Elmo Calkins, author and president of the advertising firm Calkins & Holden, summed up his loss best: "*Time* Newsmagazine, original, individual, independent, sometimes cocky but never dull, copying no other pattern but creating its own form and a language to express its unhackneyed viewpoint will always remain a monument to Briton Hadden's uncompleted life no matter what heights it eventually attains, as he had the vision and courage to offer us a new attitude toward the day's news. We could better spare an older and less vivid editor."

Biography:

Noel F. Busch, *Briton Hadden: A Biography of the Founder of Time* (New York: Farrar, Straus, 1949).

References:

Eric Hodgins, *The Span of Time* (New York: Time Inc., 1946);

W. A. Swanberg, *Luce and His Empire* (New York: Scribners, 1972).

Papers:

Hadden's papers are in the Time Inc. archives.

Norman Hapgood

(28 March 1868-29 April 1937)

James Boylan
University of Massachusetts–Amherst

MAJOR POSITIONS HELD: Editor, *Collier's Weekly* (1902-1912), *Harper's Weekly* (1913-1916), *Hearst's International Magazine* (1923-1925).

BOOKS: *Literary Statesmen and Others: Essays on Men Seen from a Distance* (Chicago & New York: Herbert S. Stone, 1897; London: Duckworth/Chicago: Stone, 1898);
Abraham Lincoln: The Man of the People (New York & London: Macmillan, 1899);
Daniel Webster (Boston: Small, Maynard, 1899; London: Paul, Trench, Trübner, 1899);
George Washington (New York & London: Macmillan, 1901);
The Stage in America, 1897-1900 (New York & London: Macmillan, 1901);
Industry and Progress (New Haven: Yale University Press, 1911);
The Jewish Commonwealth (New York: Zionist Organization of America, 1919);
The Advancing Hour (New York: Boni & Liveright, 1920);
Up from the City Streets: Alfred E. Smith, a Biographical Study in Contemporary Politics, by Hapgood and Henry Moskowitz (New York: Harcourt, Brace, 1927);
Why Janet Should Read Shakspere (New York & London: Century, 1929);
The Changing Years: Reminiscences of Norman Hapgood (New York: Farrar & Rinehart, 1930);
The Columbia Conserve Company and the Committee of Four (Indianapolis: Columbia Conserve Company, 1934).

OTHER: "Journalism," in *Every-Day Ethics; Addresses Delivered in the Page Lecture Series, 1909, before the Senior Class of the Sheffield Scientific School, Yale University* (New Haven: Yale University Press, 1910);
Professional Patriots, edited by Hapgood (New York: Boni, 1927).

SELECTED PERIODICAL PUBLICATIONS: "Home Culture for Americans," *New En-*

Norman Hapgood

gland Monthly, new series 13 (February 1896): 721-726;
"The Reporter and Literature," *Bookman,* 5 (April 1897): 119-121;
"The Upbuilding of the Theatre," *Atlantic Monthly,* 83 (March 1899): 419-425;
"The Foreign Stage in New York," *Bookman,* 11 (July 1900): 452-458;
"Robert J. Collier," *American Magazine,* 69 (January 1910): 331;
"A Programme of Reconstruction," *New Republic,* 17 (16 November 1918): 70-73;
"Russia and the Nation's Business," *Asia,* 20 (April 1920): 289-294;
"Cowardice and Reaction," *Independent,* 103 (24 July 1920): 107-109;

"More Brains, Good Lord," *New Republic*, 24 (1 September 1920): 17-19;

"Liberal or Reactionary," *Yale Review*, new series 10 (October 1920): 26-42;

"Why I Shall Vote for La Follette," *New Republic*, 40 (15 October 1924): 168-169;

"Is Wilson's Dream Coming True?" *Annals of the American Academy of Political and Social Science*, 126 (July 1926): 151-153;

"Why I Am a Zionist," *Forum*, 78 (July 1927): 71-76;

"Should Government Ignore Superpower?" *Forum*, 79 (March 1928): 343-350;

"Foreign Issues in the Presidential Campaign," *American Scholar*, 1 (October 1932): 418-422;

"An Unbeliever Goes to Church," *Forum*, 90 (November 1933): 285-288.

Barring the ten years he spent as editor of *Collier's Weekly*, Norman Hapgood is scarcely distinguishable, historically, from a dozen other competent, well-regarded (and forgotten) early twentieth-century magazine editors. In those few years, 1902 to 1912, his editorials, although often criticized as hair-splitting, nonetheless helped set the pace of progressive reform, and his initiatives placed the magazine for a time in the mainstream of muckraking, the era's wide-ranging "literature of exposure." No radical, he was the exemplar of Justin Kaplan's characterization of muckraking as a "fundamentally loyalist, middle-class strategy" (*Lincoln Steffens: A Biography*, 1974) devoted to repairing the system, rather than altering it. After 1912 Hapgood spent much of the rest of his career trying to repeat the successes of the *Collier's* years, only to find that magazine audiences were no longer interested in what he had to offer, politically or editorially. He died in relative obscurity, alienated from what he considered the "banality" of the new entertainment-oriented, mass-circulation magazines.

As a youth Hapgood was given the upbringing and education of the well-off. He was born in Chicago, the oldest of three sons of Charles Hutchins Hapgood and Fanny Louise Powers. His brother Hutchins, a writer whose career ran parallel with Norman's, was a year younger; his other brother, William Powers, who became a businessman, was born in 1872. After their father lost his store in the great Chicago fire of 1871, he took the family to St. Louis, lost another business in a fire, and ultimately settled in Alton, Illinois, on the Mississippi River. Here he prospered as the owner of the Hapgood Plow Company and raised the three boys and a younger sister, Ruth, who died at the age of ten in 1890. The children learned from their father, the dominant influence in the household, standards of responsibility, thrift, and religious agnosticism.

Norman Hapgood was graduated from the Alton schools at fifteen and, after tutoring, entered Harvard in 1886. Both of his brothers later joined him there, and his parents also lived in Cambridge for a time after the death of their daughter. His contact on the campus with the great Harvard philosophy teachers of the era— William James, Josiah Royce, George Santayana— turned his interests toward the intellectual and aesthetic, and he became a founding editor and writer for a new literary magazine, the *Harvard Monthly*. He was graduated in 1890, having earned honors in French and philosophy as well as a Phi Beta Kappa key. After travel he returned to Harvard and received bachelor's and master's degrees in law in 1893.

Rather half-heartedly, Hapgood went to Chicago and practiced law, but it took only a year for him to decide that he preferred journalism. In 1894 he quit his legal position and picked up a five-dollar-a-week job on the *Chicago Evening Post*. After three months there as a cub reporter, he joined the *Milwaukee Sentinel* briefly as an editorial writer and drama critic. In mid 1895 he moved on to New York and soon had a novice reporter's job on the *Evening Post*, then edited by the formidable Edwin L. Godkin. At first Hapgood displayed few of the instincts of a big-city reporter. But within months he learned what he called in his autobiography, *The Changing Years: Reminiscences of Norman Hapgood* (1930), "a taste for blood, the competitive impulse, enjoyment of the fight." He earned the respect of senior colleague Lincoln Steffens, who praised him in an 11 November 1922 letter to his sister Laura as "liberal and clear-headed." Hapgood was less successful in impressing Godkin, who rejected his volunteered editorials and warned him against injecting opinion into his news stories.

Steffens thought Hapgood valuable enough to be recruited away from the *Post* in 1897 to join Steffens and others, including Hutchins Hapgood, on the *New York Commercial Advertiser*, which under new ownership was aimed at developing an original style of journalism, combining innovative news policies with literary quality. Hapgood thrived in his five years on the newspaper, rising to drama editor and enjoying increasing power as a critic of the New York stage. The

*Cover for an issue of the magazine Hapgood edited from 1902 until 1912. He was hired by publisher Robert J. Collier
primarily because of his skills as an editorial writer.*

most important of the five books he wrote in this period was *The Stage in America, 1897-1900* (1901), in which he deplored the mediocrity of Broadway. So persistently did he pursue these views in the *Commercial Advertiser* that in October 1901 the syndicate of New York theater owners boycotted the newspaper and demanded that he be fired; the *Commercial Advertiser* resisted the pressure, and the boycott collapsed. But Hapgood, possibly embarrassed by the advertising losses incurred by the newspaper, resigned from the paper and went to Italy to consider his future.

He was soon recalled with a new position—that of editor of *Collier's Weekly*. He had been recruited by Robert Collier, son of Peter Fenelon Collier; the father had founded the magazine in 1888 as a premium to be sold with his line of inexpensive books. Under the younger Collier, who

had been placed in charge in 1898, the magazine had enjoyed financial success and popularity but had gained little prestige. Hapgood remarked in his autobiography: "Nobody of my acquaintance read the magazine, or even knew its name." But for twenty-five thousand dollars a year he was willing to do what he could to remedy the situation.

Hapgood's skills—"a remarkable combination of scholar, journalist, and connoisseur of the arts," in the words of the magazine historian Frank Luther Mott—allowed him to adapt readily to his chief responsibility at *Collier's*, writing the editorials. His approach was to provide brief, critical essays, argumentative and discriminating rather than declamatory. Eventually they covered, repeatedly and in detail, all the major issues of progressive reform—the income tax, direct election of senators, railroad regulation, child labor laws, urban poverty and housing, woman suffrage, and more. Mott praised these essays as giving *Collier's* its distinctive character. Others held less favorable opinions: Hapgood's colleague Mark Sullivan, in *The Education of an American* (1938), complained of Hapgood's "love of refined disquisition and his what seemed to me almost perverse pleasure in arriving at hairline distinctions . . . ," and Hapgood's friend Finley Peter Dunne, in the guise of his fictional character "Mr. Dooley," dubbed him "Normal Slapgood," a master of "Yes——and No." Hapgood, reviewing his output in his autobiography, said that the editorials were "smart, bold, literary, and honest" but, on the other hand, too ephemeral to be worth anthologizing.

Probably more important was Hapgood's contribution to creating and capitalizing on editorial opportunities that enhanced the magazine's reputation. The first developed from his burst of anger over an item about the personal life of Alice Roosevelt, the president's daughter, in the 20 October 1904 issue of a New York gossip sheet, *Town Topics*. In *Collier's* for 5 November Hapgood assailed *Town Topics* as "the most degraded paper of any prominence in the United States." Several months later he resumed the attack so persistently that the paper's publisher, Col. William D'Alton Mann, filed a libel suit in August 1905. In addition, Hapgood was charged with criminal libel by Judge Joseph Deuel, whom Hapgood had accused of being associated with Colonel Mann.

The criminal libel trial, held in January 1906, was a sensation in the New York press. Hapgood, as it happened, was scarcely in danger of conviction because the district attorney, William Travers Jerome, and his assistant, Frank P. Garvan, prosecuted the case with a disguised levity that apparently eluded the sobersided defendant. The trial and acquittal served to make *Collier's* suddenly fashionable; Sullivan said that it had given the magazine "esteem, eclat, kudos" and had sent it on its way to becoming the country's most influential periodical.

In 1905 Hapgood led *Collier's* into the new wave of exposure journalism, initiated two years before by Steffens and his colleagues at *McClure's Magazine*. Hapgood's initial effort, against the patent medicine industry, began with criticism in an editorial of a product called Liquozone. A little later, in mid 1905, another opponent of patent medicines, Edward W. Bok of the *Ladies' Home Journal*, turned over to him an article by a young

lawyer, Mark Sullivan. Using the as-yet-unpublished article as a basis, Hapgood produced an editorial (8 July 1905), "Criminal Newspaper Alliances with Fraud and Poison," which laid bare the mutually protective relationship between newspaper publishers and the patent-medicine industry. The Hapgood brothers' biographer, Michael D. Marcaccio, praises the editorial as the acme of Hapgood's work–"a superb blend of fine purpose and shrewd showmanship."

The editorial campaign was followed by a memorable sequence of exposure articles written for *Collier's* by a young reporter, Samuel Hopkins Adams, and published starting in the 7 October 1905 issue under the heading "The Great American Fraud." Sullivan's article, "The Patent Medicine Conspiracy Against the Freedom of the Press," was published anonymously (because Sullivan was then on the staff of *McClure's*) in the issue of 4 November. In the same issue *Collier's* announced that it would accept no more patent medicine advertising. As soon as the new Congress met in December, a pure food and drug bill was introduced and, seven months later, adopted. The new federal law marked the beginning of regulation of patent medicines but did not solve the problem, and Hapgood was able over the years to return to the subject.

Although he was now himself a practitioner of the literature of exposure, Hapgood was impatient with exposures that he considered mere sensationalism. He assailed one of the most highly publicized series of the time–Thomas W. Lawson's "Frenzied Finance" in *Everybody's Magazine*–and declined the opportunity to publish another–Upton Sinclair's fictionalized exposé of the Chicago meat-packing industry, *The Jungle* (1906). By Hapgood's account, Robert Collier wanted to accept the novel for serialization, but Hapgood argued successfully that *The Jungle* would hurt the magazine's reputation for "telling the exact truth about important things." Sinclair felt so wounded by this rebuff and even more by the subsequent unsympathetic handling of a factual article based on the same material as *The Jungle* that fourteen years later he devoted a chapter of his exposé of the press, *The Brass Check: A Study in American Journalism* (1919), to belaboring Hapgood.

The vintage exposé of Hapgood's time at *Collier's*, a complex investigation that foreshadowed the journalistic roles in the Teapot Dome and Watergate controversies, was the scandal that has come down to posterity as the Ballinger-Pinchot

Hapgood in Petersham, Massachusetts, circa 1927

affair. *Collier's* had already tested its weight in the national political arena with campaigns against the Republican leadership of the houses of Congress, aiming especially at the speaker of the House of Representatives, Joseph G. Cannon. But a bigger opportunity presented itself when Gifford Pinchot, chief forester in the Department of the Interior, began to orchestrate a campaign by conservationists against Richard A. Ballinger, secretary of the interior, for allegedly plotting to turn over public coal lands in Alaska to a consortium of private investors. Pinchot's associate in the department, Louis R. Glavis, attempted to carry the charges against Ballinger to the White House, but Pres. William Howard Taft rebuked Glavis and dismissed him.

At this point, Glavis went public with his accusations. Through an intermediary he placed a manuscript in Hapgood's hands. Hapgood checked it thoroughly for accuracy and ran it in the 13 November 1909 issue under the heading "The Whitewashing of Ballinger." This article and the subsequent drumbeat of disclosures in *Collier's* and elsewhere led to an investigation by a reluctant Congress. Hapgood helped engage as Glavis's counsel in the hearings an activist Boston lawyer, Louis D. Brandeis, who was later named to the Supreme Court. It was Brandeis who found the "smoking gun" in the affair, the discovery that the facts on Glavis's charges prepared for the president by the attorney general had been assembled after, not before, Taft's decision to fire Glavis and backdated. Although this circumstance may have had little to do with the truth of the charges and although, after six months of hearings, the committee upheld the administration, Ballinger was discredited and quietly left office in 1911.

The Ballinger affair marked the high point both of Hapgood's editorial career and of the political influence of *Collier's Weekly*. There were other worthwhile campaigns, notably Will Irwin's series in 1911 exposing abuses and ethical lapses by newspapers, but an estrangement grew between Hapgood and Robert Collier. Largely unarticulated disagreements over the magazine's editorial objectives, expenditures, and relations with advertisers were all involved, but the precipitating issue was political: the question of whether *Collier's* would support Theodore Roosevelt or Woodrow Wilson in 1912.

Roosevelt and Hapgood had long had an uneasy political relationship. During his 1904 campaign for the presidency, Roosevelt had complained about Hapgood's editorials and later referred to the editor (in a 12 September 1906 letter to Henry Cabot Lodge) as "a conceited and insincere jack of the advanced mugwump type." Hapgood in turn resented Roosevelt's "man with the muckrake" speech in 1906 and the name it gave magazine journalists–"muckrakers." They were allies, however, in Hapgood's forays against the Taft administration. By 1912 Hapgood, strongly influenced by Brandeis, had become a Wilsonian. After Roosevelt was wounded by a would-be assassin in Milwaukee, Collier and Hapgood both wrote editorials for the magazine. Collier junked Hapgood's and ran his own, an effort that Hapgood said he would have thrown in the wastebasket. Days later Hapgood resigned, and he and Collier traded recriminations in print, making reconciliation impossible. Hapgood conceded in later years that he perhaps had been too rigid and too obstinate.

Given the course of his later career, Hapgood must often have felt reason to regret that he had left *Collier's*. In 1913 he found himself on his own for the first time in a decade. Seeking to reestablish his editorial reputation, he assembled one hundred thousand dollars from backers and took over the old and ailing *Harper's Weekly* and ran it as a frankly political magazine: progressive, Zionist, and, Hapgood claimed, feminist, although it did little on such issues as woman suffrage. Above all, it was a supporter of the Wilson administration. Hapgood recalled in his autobiography: "While I was free as editor of

Harper's Weekly to follow my own ideas, the new owners had put their money in the magazine partly to have an intelligent exposition of Wilson's politics and I stressed that duty as much as I legitimately could." For nearly three years, while relying on political commentary and on such warmed-over muckraking as another exposé of patent medicines, he tried to turn *Harper's Weekly* into a money-maker and a rival of *Collier's*. But early in 1916, with circulation falling and debts mounting, it was closed and merged with another weekly, the *Independent*.

In these post-*Collier's* years Hapgood's personal life underwent major alterations. In 1896 he had married Emilie Bigelow of Chicago. But Hapgood and his independent-minded wife often did not see eye to eye, notably on racial issues, on which Hapgood was an unbending conservative. The marriage ended in divorce in 1915, and Hapgood married Elizabeth Kempley Reynolds. In the early years of their marriage they lived in New Hampshire while she taught and founded a Russian department at Dartmouth College and he wrote free-lance articles. In February 1919 Hapgood, who had worked on a Wilson reelection committee in 1916, was nominated to be minister to Denmark. He was soon under attack in the Senate Foreign Relations Committee for remarks that were crudely interpreted as being too sympathetic with the Bolshevik revolution in Russia. He could gain only a recess appointment and was forced to resign and return to the United States before the end of 1919. For a year or more afterward, as if trying to recover his good name, he wrote prolifically on national and international issues, most notably in the *Independent*.

Next he swung into the orbit of William Randolph Hearst, whose newspapers *Collier's* had attacked with vigor a decade before. As a kind of liberal showpiece he wrote a short-lived column for Hearst's *New York American*. In 1923 Hearst named Hapgood editor of *Hearst's International Magazine*. He returned at once to tested formulas, underwriting a sequence of investigative campaigns, including exposés of the Ku Klux Klan and the anti-Semitic activities of Henry Ford. But Hearst kept him from using material Glavis had uncovered about still another corrupt secretary of the interior, Albert B. Fall, who was implicated in the Teapot Dome scandal. Even so, Hapgood claimed that the magazine was "as vigorous and intelligent as any American magazine I know anything about." Hearst decided after two years of fal-

Hapgood on a picnic in Germany in 1931 with his second wife, Elizabeth Reynolds, and their children:
Elizabeth, Norman, Jr., and Ten Eyck (or David)

tering circulation to merge the magazine with his *Cosmopolitan,* and Hapgood's career as an editor all but came to a close.

In the final dozen years of his life Hapgood continued to write and was active politically. He wrote for a year or two for Hearst newspapers, and in 1927, with Henry Moskowitz, he wrote a campaign biography of Alfred E. Smith. He completed an autobiography in 1930. In 1936 he was briefly editor of the *Christian Register,* a Unitarian weekly. On 29 April 1937 he died following a prostate operation, leaving his wife and four children—Ruth, by his first marriage; and Elizabeth, Norman, and Ten Eyck, or David, by his second.

Memorial commentary treated him as a figure from another time. The *Nation,* for example, noted his work during the progressive years and praised him as a "man of real ability and the finest character, without selfish ambitions." Memoirists and historians have similarly praised him, but almost always with qualification. Sullivan, who had played an ambiguously harmful role in Hap-

good's departure from *Collier's,* placed Robert Collier's abilities as a journalist above Hapgood's and dismissed Hapgood thus: "not a journalist at all, he was an essayist." Mott, in his brief history of *Collier's,* found this evaluation too severe, but wrote: "Hapgood, while he was extremely valuable to *Collier's,* was not a great editor.... Hapgood was a reformer, but he had a dislike for rant and fustian. He was not really a muckraker...." Marcaccio summed up Hapgood's career as follows: "Although he often wrote about trusts and labor, his thought on these topics was too derivative, too characteristic of other progressives, to be of much consequence. His experience as a critic during a significant period in the history of American journalistic drama criticism and his service as a progressive editor, especially his development as a political activist, were particularly important."

The impression left by Hapgood, both in third-person accounts and in his own autobiography, is that of an editor whose major achievements were dimmed by a professional personality that was pallid, distant, and finicky. His considerable editorial courage was tarnished by the manner of a compromiser. And his resistance to falling in with political and editorial fashions became, in its later forms, an inability to change with the times. Still, he was the creator of one of the most important institutions in a journalistic form that dominated the magazine field briefly at the start of the century: the politically involved mass magazine directed at a broad, middle-class national elite. *Collier's* lived on until 1957, but as an apolitical consumer periodical rather than the shaper and critic of issues that Hapgood developed; that *Collier's* died soon after he left in 1912.

Biography:

Michael D. Marcaccio, *The Hapgoods: Three Earnest Brothers* (Charlottesville: University Press of Virginia, 1977).

References:

Louis Filler, *Appointment at Armageddon: Muckrak-*

ing and Progressivism in American Life (Westport, Conn.: Greenwood Press, 1976);

Filler, *Crusaders for American Liberalism* (New York: Harcourt, Brace, 1939);

Arthur H. Gleason, "Norman Hapgood," *American Magazine,* 70 (August 1910): 460-462;

Judson Grenier, "Upton Sinclair and the Press: *The Brass Check* Reconsidered," *Journalism Quarterly,* 49 (Fall 1972): 427-436;

Hutchins Hapgood, *A Victorian in the Modern World* (New York: Harcourt, Brace, 1939);

Philip Littell, "Norman Hapgood as a Journalist," *New Republic,* 1 (12 December 1914): 13-15;

Andy Logan, *The Man Who Robbed the Robber Barons* (New York: Norton, 1965);

Frank Luther Mott, *A History of American Magazines,* volume 4 (Cambridge: Harvard University Press, 1957), pp. 453-479;

"Mr. Norman Hapgood and 'Collier's Weekly,'" *Collier's* (2 November 1912): 472-473;

Upton Sinclair, *The Brass Check: A Study in American Journalism* (Pasadena, Cal.: Published by the author, 1919), pp. 27-31;

Mark Sullivan, *The Education of an American* (New York: Doubleday, Doran, 1938).

Joel Chandler Harris

(9 December 1848-3 July 1908)

Robert L. Hoskins
Arkansas State University

See also the Harris entries in *DLB 11: American Humorists, 1800-1950; DLB 23: American Newspaper Journalists, 1873-1900; DLB 42: American Writers for Children Before 1900;* and *DLB 78: American Short-Story Writers Before 1880.*

MAJOR POSITION HELD: Editor, *Uncle Remus's Magazine* (1907-1908).

BOOKS: *Uncle Remus: His Songs and His Sayings* (New York: Appleton, 1881 [i.e., 1880]); republished in part as *Uncle Remus and His Legends of the Old Plantation* (London: Bogue, 1881); first edition republished as *Uncle Remus, or Mr. Fox, Mr. Rabbit, and Mr. Terrapin* (London & New York: Routledge, 1881); revised as *Uncle Remus: His Songs and His Sayings* (New York: Appleton, 1895; London: Osgood, 1895);

Nights with Uncle Remus: Myths and Legends of the Old Plantation (Boston: Osgood, 1883; London: Routledge, 1884);

Mingo and Other Sketches in Black and White (Boston: Osgood, 1884; Edinburgh: Douglas/ London: Hamilton Adams, 1884);

Free Joe and Other Georgian Sketches (New York: Scribners, 1887; London: Routledge, 1888);

Daddy Jake the Runaway and Short Stories Told after Dark (New York: Century, 1889; London: Unwin, 1889);

Balaam and His Master and Other Sketches and Stories (Boston & New York: Houghton, Mifflin, 1891; London: Osgood, McIlvaine, 1891);

A Plantation Printer: The Adventures of a Georgia Boy during the War (London: Osgood, McIlvaine, 1892); enlarged as *On the Plantation: A Story of a Georgia Boy's Adventures during the War* (New York: Appleton, 1892);

Uncle Remus and His Friends: Old Plantation Stories, Songs, and Ballads with Sketches of Negro Character (Boston & New York: Houghton, Mifflin, 1892; London: Osgood, McIlvaine, 1893);

Joel Chandler Harris (photograph by Frances B. Johnson)

Little Mr. Thimblefinger and His Queer Country: What the Children Saw and Heard There (Boston & New York: Houghton, Mifflin, 1894; London: Osgood, McIlvaine, 1894);

Mr. Rabbit at Home: A Sequel to Little Mr. Thimblefinger and His Queer Country (Boston & New York: Houghton, Mifflin, 1895; London: Osgood, 1895);

The Story of Aaron (So Named) the Son of Ben Ali (Boston & New York: Houghton, Mifflin, 1896; London: Osgood, 1896);

Stories of Georgia (New York, Cincinnati & Chicago: American Book Company, 1896);

Sister Jane: Her Friends and Acquaintances (Boston & New York: Houghton, Mifflin, 1896; London: Constable, 1897);

Aaron in the Wildwoods (Boston & New York: Houghton, Mifflin, 1897; London: Harper, 1897);

Tales of the Home Folks in Peace and War (Boston & New York: Houghton, Mifflin, 1898; London: Unwin, 1898);

Plantation Pageants (Boston & New York: Houghton, Mifflin, 1899; London: Constable, 1899);

The Chronicles of Aunt Minervy Ann (New York: Scribners, 1899; London: Dent, 1899);

On the Wing of Occasions (New York: Doubleday, Page, 1900; London: Murray, 1900);

The Making of a Statesman and Other Stories (New York: McClure, Phillips, 1902; London: Isbister, 1902);

Gabriel Tolliver: A Story of Reconstruction (New York: McClure, Phillips, 1902);

Wally Wanderoon and His Story-Telling Machine (New York: McClure, Phillips, 1903; London: Richards, 1904);

A Little Union Scout (New York: McClure, Phillips, 1904; London: Duckworth, 1905);

The Tar-Baby and Other Rhymes of Uncle Remus (New York: Appleton, 1904);

Told by Uncle Remus: New Stories of the Old Plantation (New York: McClure, Phillips, 1905; London: Hodder & Stoughton, 1906);

Uncle Remus and Brer Rabbit (New York: Stokes, 1907);

The Bishop and the Boogerman (New York: Doubleday, Page, 1909); republished as *The Bishop and the Bogie-Man* (London: Murray, 1909);

The Shadow Between His Shoulder-Blades (Boston: Small, Maynard, 1909);

Uncle Remus and the Little Boy (Boston: Small, Maynard, 1910; London: Richards, 1912);

Uncle Remus Returns (Boston & New York: Houghton, Mifflin, 1918);

The Witch Wolf: An Uncle Remus Story (Cambridge, Mass.: Bacon & Brown, 1921);

Joel Chandler Harris: Editor and Essayist, edited by Julia Collier Harris (Chapel Hill: University of North Carolina Press, 1931);

Qua: A Romance of the Revolution, edited by Thomas H. English (Atlanta: The Library, Emory University, 1946);

Seven Tales of Uncle Remus, edited by English (Atlanta: The Library, Emory University, 1948);

The Complete Tales of Uncle Remus, compiled by Richard Chase (Boston: Houghton, Mifflin, 1955).

OTHER: "Uncle Remus' Little Red Speckle Steer," in *The St. Jacobs Oil Family Calendar 1883-4 and Book of Health and Humor for the Million* (Baltimore: Vogeler, 1883?), pp. 29-30; republished in *Emory University Quarterly*, 10 (December 1954): 266-270;

"Biographical Sketch of Henry W. Grady," in *Joel Chandler Harris' Life of Henry W. Grady*, compiled by Grady's coworkers and edited by Harris (New York: Cassell, 1890), pp. 9-68;

Evening Tales; Done into English from the French of Frédéric Ortoli, translated by Harris (New York: Scribners, 1893; London: Low, 1894);

" 'Uncle Remus' Has a Word to Say of Putnam As It Was and Is," in *A Guide to Immigration: Putnam County, Georgia and Its Resources*, edited by D. T. Singleton (Atlanta: Methodist Book & Publishing Company, 1895), pp. 90-92; republished in *Emory University Quarterly*, 4 (December 1948): 229-231.

In his day Joel Chandler Harris was one of America's most popular authors, known throughout the world for his humorous Negro folktales told through the dialect of kindly old "Uncle Remus." Harris has also been recognized as a newspaper journalist (he served for twenty-four years as an associate editor of the *Atlanta Constitution*) but as a magazine editor he has been generally overlooked. Harris's importance in the development of magazine journalism is limited, but notable. He founded *Uncle Remus's Magazine* in 1907 and in one year managed it to a circulation of two hundred thousand; moreover, he provided the editorial impetus that carried the magazine for five years beyond his death in 1908.

Harris was born 9 December 1848 in the Putnam County, Georgia, community of Eatonton. His mother, Mary Harris, was from a respected family in nearby Newton County; his father was an Irish laborer. His parents were never married and his father deserted shortly after Harris's birth. According to his biographers, Harris's illegitimacy had a profound effect on his personality and also influenced recurrent themes in his work.

His mother never married but stayed in Eatonton and supported herself and her child by taking in sewing. Family friends helped with the expense of sending Harris to school. Nonetheless

Page from the 27 September 1864 issue of the weekly newspaper to which Harris was apprenticed as a printer's devil

The print shop at Turnwold, where the Countryman
was produced

he stopped his formal education at fourteen to take a full-time job at a weekly newspaper, the *Countryman*, published at nearby Turnwold Plantation by Joseph Addison Turner, an enterprising planter. Although the year was 1862 and the Civil War raged along the border of the new Confederacy, Turner's only involvement seems to have been the editorial support he voiced through the *Countryman* and the felt hats he manufactured on the plantation for the Southern army. For young Harris, life at Turnwold was almost idyllic.

When not working around the newspaper shop, where he was supervised by an Irish tramp printer with an appreciation for Shakespeare, Harris was encouraged by Turner to browse through the plantation's extensive library. It was at Turnwold, too, that Harris first met the slaves and

heard the folktales that became the seeds for his future Uncle Remus stories. Harris and Turner's own son and two daughters were frequent visitors to the plantation's slave quarters, where Old Harbert, Uncle George Terrell, and Aunt Crissy would entertain the children with Negro legends and fables.

While setting type for the *Countryman* Harris began to slip in his own paragraphs, setting "articles from the 'case' instead of committing them to paper," as he remembered in an autobiographical sketch in *Lippincott's Monthly Magazine* (April 1886), "thus leaving no evidence of authorship. I supposed that this was a huge joke; but as Mr. Turner read every line that went into his paper, it is probable that he understood the situation and abetted it." In fact, Turner actively encouraged his young employee's literary aspirations.

In April 1865 the Confederacy collapsed, and with it the plantation system of the Old South. Turner, ruined financially as William Tecumseh Sherman's Union army sliced through Georgia, hung on until May 1866 but finally had to suspend publication of the *Countryman*. Harris took a typesetting job with the *Macon Telegraph*, owned by a former resident of Eatonton. In spare moments he continued to write poetry, review books and journals, and compose humorous paragraphs.

Through such work he came to the attention of William Evelyn, editor of the *New Orleans Crescent Monthly*, a journal devoted to "literature, art, science and society." Still only eighteen, Harris accepted Evelyn's offer of a job as his private secretary and moved to Louisiana. Evidently he hoped to further his literary career, but, in fact, his time was used for Evelyn's own purposes and he had little opportunity to write. In May 1867 Harris returned to Georgia and accepted a job on the *Monroe Advertiser* in Forsyth County.

The weekly *Advertiser* was owned by James P. Harrison, another Eatontonian who also had worked for the *Countryman*. Harris, given the title of "editor," confessed later that he actually "set all the type, pulled the press, kept the books, swept the floor, and wrapped the papers for mailing. . . . " He continued, too, to provide anonymous humorous paragraphs that were picked up by other Georgia papers, the *Atlanta Constitution* initially attributing them to publisher Harrison.

By 1870 Harris's work had become well known throughout the state, and the *Savannah Morning News*, one of the better newspapers in Georgia, offered him the princely sum of forty dollars a week to join as an associate editor. The *Morning News*, under founder and current editor William Tappan Thompson, creator of the Major Jones sketches, had a well-deserved reputation for humor. Harris fit right in, the *Atlanta Constitution* shortly comparing him to Rabelais, Falstaff, and Mark Twain.

While in Savannah, Harris, of slight build with Irish-red hair, almost pathologically shy, with a tendency to stutter in the presence of strangers, met and fell in love with seventeen-year-old Esther LaRose, a convent-educated French Canadian whose father owned a steamship that plied the Georgia-North Florida coast. Essie, as she was called, returned to Quebec, but Harris overcame his timidity to court her with letters and poetry. They were married the next year on 20 April 1873. By 1876 they were the parents of

The house at Turnwold Plantation, where Harris lived from 1862 until 1866

two sons. Eventually, the Harrises had nine children, although three died in infancy.

Harris worked for the *Morning News* six years. He might have stayed with that paper indefinitely, publishing his daily column, "Affairs in Georgia," and solidifying his reputation as a humorist, had a yellow fever epidemic not driven him and his family to Atlanta. While waiting for the epidemic to subside, Harris accepted a temporary position with the *Atlanta Constitution*. About two months later the *Constitution* announced that Harris had joined the staff on a permanent basis as associate editor.

At the *Constitution* Harris wrote editorials and essays, penned book reviews, continued his column of humorous paragraphs, now called "Roundabout in Georgia," and began experimenting with a new form of humor, dialect sketches. Biographer Paul M. Cousins claims that Harris first tried his hand at dialect writing at the request of *Constitution* publisher Evan P. Howell. A former *Constitution* writer had gained some popularity with such material, and Howell was looking for something similar. Harris said he had "never done anything along that line," but that he would try. About a month later (November 1876), after three or four dialect columns, "Uncle Remus" appeared. (Harris included his second dialect sketch in his first collection of Uncle Remus stories, but its Remus character, as published originally in the *Constitution*, was unnamed.)

Harris created other characters in his early sketches, but Uncle Remus–sometimes a kindly old plantation hand, sometimes a more savvy city-dweller–became gradually the focus of his dialect material. Off and on over the next few years Harris provided *Constitution* readers with the increasingly popular sketches. And when he saw a folklore article on the familiar "brer rabbit and the tar-baby" theme, a fable he recalled from his Turnwold days, he experimented by having Uncle Remus recount "The Story of Mr. Rabbit and Mr. Fox." Response was favorable and a few months later he had Uncle Remus tell part of the tar-baby story.

Throughout his career Harris was painfully modest about his storytelling abilities. His success, he said, was an accident. He was not a real writer, he argued, only a chronicler of local color. But the growing audience who watched for his Remus tales and plantation proverbs felt otherwise. Letters from throughout the nation, where his material had been spread by the newspaper exchange tradition of the time, called for more. Finally D. Appleton and Company proposed that he issue his work in book form. Although Appleton's agent reported that Harris was "diffident in the extreme," he finally agreed, provided some new material, and published in November 1880 *Uncle Remus: His Songs and His Sayings.* (The book was dated 1881 but put on the market in late 1880 to catch the Christmas trade.)

The book was an immediate success; ten thousand copies were sold the first four months and critical reviews were overwhelmingly favorable. "Mr. Harris's book is altogether excellent of its kind," a *New York Times* (1 December 1880) reviewer wrote, "and in preserving certain quaint legends and giving us exactly the sounds of the negro dialect, he has established on a firm basis the first real book of American folk lore." An example from "How Mr. Rabbitt was too Sharp for Mr. Fox" confirms that early critic: "En who stuck you up dar whar you iz? Nobody in de roun' worril. You des tuck en jam yo'se'f on dat Tar-Baby widout waitin' fer enny invite', sez Brer Fox, sezee, 'en dar you is, en dar you'll stay twel I

fixes up a bresh-pile and fires her up, kaze I'm gwineter bobbycue you dis day, sho', sez Brer Fox, sezee."

The modern reader may have difficulty appreciating the Uncle Remus tales. The dialect requires concentration and the humor is less than obvious to residents of a different era. Harris himself is not much respected by many who see him as an active propagandist for racism and, as Robert Bone states, "a leading proponent of the plantation myth." At the turn of the century, however, as a nation only recently at war with itself tried to turn its back on sectional differences, Harris's romance of the old plantation, his fiction of kind masters and appreciative slaves, and his apparent affirmation of Negro simplicity and white superiority (which on a close second look was no affirmation at all) were all balms for still-ugly wounds.

With *Uncle Remus: His Songs and His Sayings*, Harris exhibited the narrative style that he would employ in nearly two hundred tales published over the next twenty-seven years. From memories of his days at Turnwold, when he and Addison Turner's children listened to Old Harbert recount the legends of his race, Harris created young Miss Sally and Master John, children of a large plantation in Middle Georgia, sitting at the knee of kindly, folk-wise old Uncle Remus as he spins tale after tale of Brer Rabbit and Mr. Fox and Old Man Terrapin and Brer B'ar.

It was as a journalist, however, not as an author of dialect and humor, that Harris continued to provide a steady living for himself and his growing family for the next twenty years. With Harris and young Henry W. Grady, the *Atlanta Constitution* had two of the most respected–and effective–journalists in the nation. Grady preached an industrialized "New South" and served as his region's personal missionary to capitalists of New England, while Harris wrote of the agrarian spirit of the "Old South." Especially, he championed a rebirth of southern literature. Grady, who became known as "the great pacificator," was acclaimed for his oratory as well as his journalism. Harris never made a speech. So fearful of public appearances was he that even Mark Twain could not prevail upon him to read one of his stories to a friend's children. For the ten years in which Harris and Grady shared editorial responsibilities at the *Constitution*, they provided an interesting study in balance between the progressive economic ideas of an expanding nation and nostalgia for the old order.

Cover for the July 1908 issue of the magazine named after Harris's popular fictional character.
Harris died soon after the issue was published.

Following his first book in 1880, Harris published four more in the next ten years, including his second collection of Remus stories: *Nights With Uncle Remus: Myths and Legends of the Old Plantation* (1883). By this time he had read deeply on the literature of folklore and introduced this volume with a thirty-one-page discussion of the origin of his stories. The other volumes were collections of regional sketches, rather than folklore–although thirteen Remus stories, first published in the *Constitution, Century Magazine, Scribner's Magazine,* and other periodicals, were included in *Daddy Jake the Runaway and Short Stories Told after Dark* (1889).

By 1890 Harris was acclaimed as America's most accomplished dialect writer, and his literary popularity was assured. Throughout the decade of the 1890s he maintained a prolific pace that resulted in twelve more volumes, including one Uncle Remus collection, *Uncle Remus and His*

Friends: Old Plantation Stories, Songs, and Ballads with Sketches of Negro Character (1892). During this period Harris also produced adult fiction, *Balaam and His Master and Other Sketches and Stories* (1891) and *Sister Jane: Her Friends and Acquaintances* (1896); an autobiography, *A Plantation Printer: The Adventures of a Georgia Boy during the War* (1892); juvenile fiction, *Little Mr. Thimblefinger and His Queer Country: What the Children Saw and Heard There* (1894), *Mr. Rabbit at Home: A Sequel to Little Mr. Thimblefinger and His Queer Country* (1895), *The Story of Aaron (So Named) the Son of Ben Ali* (1896), *Aaron in the Wildwoods* (1897), *Plantation Pageants* (1899); and regional tales, *Stories of Georgia* (1896) and *Tales of the Home Folks in Peace and War* (1898).

Also in this period Appleton published a new edition of *Uncle Remus: His Songs and His Sayings* (1895), attesting to Harris's ever-growing popularity. Near the end of the decade Harris intro-

The Harris family on the steps of their home at Snap Bean Farm, located on the outskirts of Atlanta (Emory University Library)

duced a female counterpart to Remus in *The Chronicles of Aunt Minervy Ann* (1899).

The year 1900 was a milestone in Harris's life. In that year he published *On the Wing of Occasions,* his first collection of "Billy Sanders" stories. Sanders, a young middle-class Georgian with a good deal of homespun philosophy, first appeared as a Confederate Army private in a *Saturday Evening Post* serial. Other Billy Sanders volumes are *The Making of a Statesman and Other Stories* (1902), *The Bishop and the Boogerman* (serialized in *Uncle Remus's Magazine* and published posthumously in 1909), and *The Shadow Between His Shoulder-Blades* (serialized in *Saturday Evening Post* in 1907 and published posthumously in 1909). In many of his articles for *Uncle Remus's Magazine* Harris employed the engaging youth to voice his views on contemporary issues and personalities, and though the Billy Sanders stories did not receive the acclaim the Remus yarns had achieved, they were generally popular with the broad magazine readership of the period and they kept Harris's name before the public.

The second event to mark 1900 was Harris's retirement from the *Atlanta Constitution.* After twenty-four years with the prestigious newspaper (and more than thirty-five years in newspaper journalism) and not quite fifty-two years of age, he signed a new contract with McClure, Phillips publishers that allowed him to leave the demanding grind of daily journalism and devote his full energies and talents to his stories and his large family. On the four-acre, West End Atlanta "Snap-Bean Farm" that surrounded his home, the "Wren's Nest," he tended his flower gardens, read extensively to keep up to date with current literary trends, entertained close friends, wrote his Billy Sanders articles, and experimented with other literary forms.

From as early as 1878, when he had serialized "The Romance of Rockville" in the weekly edition of the *Constitution,* Harris had been frustrated with his efforts to write a novel. In 1896 he produced *Sister Jane: Her Friends and Acquaintances* but recognized deficiencies in the book and wrote his publisher that "if I had the money to pay you for the trouble and expense it has already cost you, I'd recall the stuff and burn it." In fact, *Sister Jane* offered interesting and accurate glimpses of small-town life in Middle Georgia, but as a novel it was plodding and improbable, as critics were not hesitant to point out. Now, near the end of his career, he tried again with *Gabriel Tolliver: A Story of Reconstruction* (1902). Again he demonstrated difficulty with what he called "the knack of narration." Criticism was mixed, but the book does provide a balanced, honest characterization of life for both whites and blacks in the Reconstruction period.

The next year Harris published *Wally Wanderoon and His Story-Telling Machine,* the last of his non-Remus books for children. Though a child's tale, on another level *Wally Wanderoon* was the author's recognition that the Old South was, in 1903, only a wispy memory, and that the era when readers found great enjoyment in his simple plantation tales was drawing to a close.

A Little Union Scout was published in 1904, following serialization in the February and March issues of the *Saturday Evening Post.* Some critics considered the short novel chronicling the adventures of two young Confederates and a Negro slave as one of Harris's most imaginative works, and popular reaction was enthusiastic.

Then, after a hiatus of twelve years, there followed three new Uncle Remus volumes: *The Tar-Baby and Other Rhymes of Uncle Remus* (1904), *Told by Uncle Remus: New Stories of the Old Plantation* (1905), and *Uncle Remus and Brer Rabbit* (1907). The new stories suggest Harris was unhappy with the direction of the New South, and public reaction to these volumes was less than enthusiastic.

By 1905, however, Harris was at the height of his literary reputation. In May of that year he was named a charter member–one among twenty–of the American Academy of Arts and Letters, joining such luminaries as Mark Twain, Henry Adams, and Henry James. In October, President Theodore Roosevelt visited Atlanta and publicly acclaimed the author as one of Georgia's foremost citizens. At age fifty-seven, financially secure, nationally loved, but physically drained, Harris might have been expected to settle back and take his remaining years a little easier. In fact, he embarked on a new career.

Early in 1906 several Atlanta businessmen, including Roby Robinson, vice president and business manager of the *Constitution,* and Harris's son Julian, at thirty-two, a *Constitution* editor who was growing weary of duty on the night desk,

hatched a scheme to launch a new monthly magazine. The Constitution Publishing Company already published *Sunny South,* a weekly miscellany with a circulation of about 100,000. Young Harris and his partners secured $200,000 with which to gain control of *Sunny South* and to organize the Sunny South Publishing Company. They proposed to rename the original periodical, change it to a monthly, and issue it under the editorial direction of the senior Harris.

The famous author was enthusiastic about the plan until Julian and his partners revealed the name they had in mind: *Uncle Remus's Magazine.* Harris, who understood the commercial value of his name on the masthead, balked at including his most popular character in the title. He suggested the "Home Magazine," unaware that such a journal already existed, or the "Optimist." However, after securing a pledge that he would have "absolute control of the contents, including the advertisements," he finally agreed to the name, arguing even then that it would handicap their venture by causing prospective readers to think it contained principally dialect stories.

In spite of inexperience in the advertising office, serious problems with the press chosen to print the journal, and the fact that Harris had to supply six of the first issue's eight articles, *Uncle Remus's Magazine,* after more than a year of preparation, finally made its debut on 1 June 1907. The first number was almost a disaster. According to Julian, "typographical deficiencies" blamed on a new press resulted in a magazine of "miserable appearance." Advertisers grumbled. Not until December were printing problems finally resolved. Editorial content confirmed that the magazine was Harris's not only in name but spirit, too. It preached a cheerful philosophy and practiced tolerance in all matters. Its motto–"Typical of the South–National in Scope"–suggested it offered to the whole nation those southern qualities of sentiment and affection in which Harris took such pride. At the end of the magazine's first year Harris wrote that it "has had a success far beyond the hopes of those engaged in producing it."

Besides installments of new Harris fiction–*The Bishop and the Boogerman* was serialized beginning with the first number and a few Uncle Remus folktales were also offered–the editor included book reviews under the pseudonym Anne MacFarland, editorial comment on current issues, and articles and poems from literary friends. Don Marquis, a budding young humorist, served as an associate editor and was highly regarded by his boss, journeying with the Harris family in November 1907 to visit the Roosevelts at the White House.

In May 1908 *Uncle Remus's Magazine* absorbed the *Home Magazine*, published by Bobbs-Merrill in Indianapolis. The *Home Magazine* had been launched in 1888 and was edited in Washington, D.C., by Mrs. John A. Logan, who emphasized national affairs. Bobbs-Merrill purchased it in 1906, combined it with *Madame*, which Arthur S. Ford had begun in Springfield, Ohio, in 1903, and, according to magazine historian Frank Luther Mott, "published it on a higher plane than it had ever before known." Harris, then, could be excused a hint of pride when he announced the merger in an editorial. "To swallow, at one gulp, a popular Western magazine is a feat of considerable importance," he wrote. Combined circulation was said to be 200,000 and the name was changed to *Uncle Remus's–The Home Magazine*.

Harris was overtaxed by the responsibilities of editing the magazine, writing much of its content and receiving a never-ending flow of well-wishers, friends, and the curious, and his health began to fail early in 1908. Through April and May he persisted in his work, but his condition worsened and doctors described his illness as acute nephritis and cirrhosis of the liver. In June he was confined to his bed, where he died on 3 July 1908.

That *Uncle Remus's–The Home Magazine* could continue to publish for almost five more years attests to the depth of the public's esteem for its editor as well as its love for the magazine's fictional namesake. As biographer Cousins summed up, "Harris' name and fame gave *Uncle Remus's Magazine* a sufficient momentum for it to continue publication through the issue of February, 1913, but without his direct influence it simply became another periodical without any distinguishing features."

Today, Harris is recognized not so much for his humor or his journalism or his magazine as for his role in preserving Negro culture. As Robert Bone has written, "Out of simple justice, . . . let it be entered on the record that, whatever else he was, Joel Chandler Harris was a complicated man, full of neurotic conflicts and self-deceiving ways; a Southern maverick, capable of stubborn orthodoxies and equally tenacious heresies where black people were concerned; an admirer of

black folklore, and an ethnologist of strict integrity, to whom black Americans owe a considerable debt for the preservation of their folk heritage; and a catalytic agent of prime importance in the history of the Afro-American short story."

Letters:

Mark Twain to Uncle Remus: 1881-1885, edited by Thomas H. English, Emory University Sources and Reprints, series 7, no. 3 (Atlanta: Emory University Press, 1953).

Bibliography:

William Bradley Strickland, "A Check List of the Periodical Contributions of Joel Chandler Harris (1848-1908)," *American Literary Realism*, 9 (Summer 1976): 207-209.

Biographies:

Julia Collier Harris, *The Life and Letters of Joel Chandler Harris* (Boston & New York: Houghton, Mifflin, 1918);

Robert Lemuel Wiggins, *The Life of Joel Chandler Harris, from Obscurity in Boyhood to Fame in Early Manhood* (Nashville, Tenn.: Publishing House Methodist Episcopal Church, South, 1918);

Paul M. Cousins, *Joel Chandler Harris: A Biography* (Baton Rouge: Louisiana State University Press, 1968).

References:

R. Bruce Bickley, Jr., *Joel Chandler Harris* (Boston: Twayne, 1978);

Bickley, Jr., ed., *Critical Essays on Joel Chandler Harris* (Boston: G. K. Hall, 1981);

Robert Bone, *Down Home: A History of Afro-American Short Fiction from Its Beginnings to the End of the Harlem Renaissance* (New York: Putnam's, 1975), pp. 19-41;

Stella Brewer Brookes, *Joel Chandler Harris-Folklorist* (Athens: University of Georgia Press, 1950);

Alvin P. Harlow, *Joel Chandler Harris: Plantation Storyteller* (New York: Messner, 1941).

Papers:

Many of Harris's manuscripts and letters are in the Joel Chandler Harris Memorial Collection, Emory University, Atlanta, Georgia.

Elbert Hubbard

(19 June 1856-7 May 1915)

Hank Nuwer

MAJOR POSITIONS HELD: Publisher, *Philistine* (1895-1915), *Fra* (1908-1915).

SELECTED BOOKS: *The Man: A Story of Today,* as Aspasia Hobbs (New York: Ogilvie, 1891);

One Day: A Tale of the Prairies (Boston: Arena, 1893);

Forbes of Harvard (Boston: Arena, 1894);

No Enemy (But Himself) (New York: Putnam's, 1894);

Little Journeys, biographical booklets (New York: Putnam's, 1894-1900; East Aurora, N.Y.: Roycrofters, 1900-1908);

These Pages Recount Little Journeys Made to the Homes of Ruskin and Turner (East Aurora, N.Y.: Roycroft, 1896);

This Is the Story of the Legacy (East Aurora, N.Y.: Roycroft, 1896);

As It Seems to Me (East Aurora, N.Y.: Roycroft, 1898);

A Message to Garcia (East Aurora, N.Y.: Roycroft, 1899; Richmond, Surrey: Dimbleby, 1915);

So This Then Is The Appreciation of Ali Baba of East Aurora, as Fra Elbertus (East Aurora, N.Y.: Roycroft, 1899);

Time and Chance, 2 volumes (East Aurora, N.Y.: Roycrofters, 1899; revised edition, New York & London: Putnam's, 1901);

So Here Then Are the Preachments Entitled the City of Tagaste, and a Dream and a Prophecy, as Fra Elbertus (East Aurora, N.Y.: Roycroft, 1900);

Old John Burroughs, as Fra Elbertus (East Aurora, N.Y.: Roycroft, 1901);

Contemplations, selected by Heloise Hawthorne (East Aurora, N.Y.: Roycrofters, 1902);

This Then Is Consecrated Lives (East Aurora, N.Y.: Roycrofters, 1904);

The Man of Sorrows (East Aurora, N.Y.: Roycrofters, 1904); revised edition, edited by John T. Hoyle (East Aurora, N.Y.: Roycrofters, 1916);

Respectability: Its Rise and Remedy, as Fra Elbertus (East Aurora, N.Y.: Roycrofters, 1905);

Elbert Hubbard in 1904

Love, Life and Work (East Aurora, N.Y.: Roycrofters, 1906);

Justinian and Theodora, by Hubbard and Alice Hubbard (East Aurora, N.Y.: Roycrofters, 1906);

This Then Is a William Morris Book (East Aurora, N.Y.: Roycrofters, 1907);

So Here Cometh White Hyacinths (East Aurora, N.Y.: Roycrofters, 1907);

Health and Wealth (East Aurora, N.Y.: Roycrofters, 1908);

The Complete Writings of Elbert Hubbard, 20 volumes (East Aurora, N.Y.: Roycroft, 1908-1915);

Three Great Women (East Aurora, N.Y.: Roycroft, 1908);

The Cigarettist (East Aurora, N.Y.: Roycrofters, 1908);

The Doctors (East Aurora, N.Y.: Roycrofters, 1909);

The Motto Book, as Fra Elbertus (East Aurora, N.Y.: Roycrofters, 1909);

The Mintage (East Aurora, N.Y.: Roycrofters, 1910);

The Closed or Open Shop (East Aurora, N.Y.: Roycrofters, 1910);

A Thousand & One Epigrams (East Aurora, N.Y.: Roycrofters, 1911);

Hollyhocks and Goldenglow (East Aurora, N.Y.: Roycrofters, 1912);

The Book of Business (East Aurora, N.Y.: Roycrofters, 1913);

The Roycroft Dictionary Concocted by Ali Baba and the Bunch on Rainy Days (East Aurora, N.Y.: Roycrofters, 1914);

So Here Then Cometh Pig-Pen Pete; or, Some Chums of Mine (East Aurora, N.Y.: Roycrofters, 1914);

The Liberators, edited by Hoyle (East Aurora, N.Y.: Roycrofters, 1915);

In the Spotlight, selected by Hoyle (East Aurora, N.Y.: Roycrofters, 1917);

John Jay, the First Chief Justice of the United States (New York: Hartford Lunch Company, 1918);

Abe Lincoln and Nancy Hanks (East Aurora, N.Y.: Roycrofters, 1920);

Concerning Slang, and Other Droll Stories (East Aurora, N.Y.: Roycrofters, 1920);

Elbert Hubbard's Scrap Book (New York: William H. Wise, 1923);

Elbert Hubbard Speaks (East Aurora, N.Y.: Roycroft, 1933);

The Elbert Hubbard Book, edited by William Griffith (Racine, Wis.: Whitman, 1934).

OTHER: *Little Journeys to the Homes of American Authors*, edited by Hubbard (New York & London: Putnam's, 1896);

The Song of Songs, includes commentary by Hubbard (East Aurora, N.Y.: Roycrofters, 1896).

From the waning years of the nineteenth century until his death aboard the *Lusitania* in 1915, publisher Elbert Hubbard exerted a tremendous influence upon his contemporaries as a pundit, thinker, and lecturer. All but forgotten today ex-

Title page for Hubbard's epistolary novel about life at Harvard. He enrolled at the university in September 1893, at age thirty-seven, but withdrew the following December.

cept for a few epigrams rarely credited to him, Hubbard is one of those illustrious men of his times whose glory failed to extend beyond the grave. His greatest talent was his Barnum-like ability to fleece the unsophisticated American public. While he lived, his self-described "periodical of protest," the *Philistine*, helped him achieve the literary stature he lusted after, although few men attracted more vocal enemies.

Elbert Green Hubbard (at age thirty-seven he dropped his middle name) was born in Bloomington, Illinois, on 19 June 1856 to Silas Hubbard, an eccentric country doctor, and Juliana Frances Hubbard. A latecomer to the world of letters, the industrious Hubbard peddled soap door-to-door for a living until he was thirty-six years old, although later in life he concocted a false biography that had him spending part of his early adulthood in Chicago as a free-lance journalist. More than a little vain, he possessed offbeat taste in clothing and, after forsaking business for the life of a publisher and thinker, switched from the rakish clothes of a dandy to a costume made up of baggy corduroy pants, Buster Brown cravats, flannel shirts, thick brogans, and a western Stetson. Likewise, he eventually grew his hair long. His ostentatious but distinctive appearance helped him gain a healthy income as a traveling lecturer, prompting a fellow showman to quip, "Elbert is the only one of us who wears his makeup on the street."

A ladies' man during his drummer years, Hubbard wooed a customer named Bertha Crawford of Normal, Illinois, marrying her in 1881. She was a pretty woman but he found her otherwise unremarkable, tiring of her long before the two finally divorced in 1903. In 1884 the Hubbards purchased a Queen Anne style house in the quaint village of East Aurora, New York, located sixteen miles from Buffalo, soon after adding a farm on acreage close by. The junior partner of the soap firm J. D. Larkin & Company, which had begun dispensing with outside soap "slingers" in favor of mail-order sales tactics, Hubbard staved off boredom by trading trotting horses. He and Bertha had three children by 1888.

In 1889 Hubbard's life changed suddenly when he met an East Aurora high-school teacher named Alice Moore, who offered him the intellectual sounding board that his wife could not. A feminist and a free thinker, but no beauty, Moore inspired Hubbard to begin a writing career at age thirty-three. His first work was a novel written in 1890 under the pseudonym Aspasia Hobbs. A novel of ideas, *The Man: A Story of Today* is, and was, tedious reading. By the time the book was published in 1891, Moore had already departed western New York to attend the Emerson College of Oratory in Boston, but the literary bug had infected Hubbard, inspiring him in 1892 to sell his interest in the soap company for sixty-five thousand dollars. "Why have I gone and done this thing?" he told his mother in a letter. "Because, dear Mother, I have all the money I want and there is a better use I can make of my time."

Hubbard's first use of his free time was to complete a fictional sketch called *One Day: A Tale of the Prairies,* a sentimental tale about a bright girl doomed to an unhappy existence on a small farm. Arena Publishing Company of Boston, owned by Benjamin Orange Flower, a friend and admirer of Hubbard, published this short novel in 1893, and a more substantial work, *Forbes of Harvard,* in 1894. Hubbard also wrote essays on the

constitutional liberties of tramps and a defense of Catholics for Flower's magazine, *Arena,* and he put his mail-order experience with his old soap firm to use, working to increase the magazine's subscription list by five thousand names. No doubt Hubbard's excitement at appearing in the same magazine that published such well-known figures as Hamlin Garland, Clarence Darrow, and Stephen Crane excited in him the dream of someday publishing his own magazine.

In 1893 Hubbard left Bertha and his small children in East Aurora and entered Harvard to seek a formal college education. He took several classes with humbling results, failing to show the distinction necessary to gain formal entrance to the institution. Some measure of the humiliation he felt after this rejection may be seen in several diatribes he wrote at those in academia, including a May 1896 essay in the *Philistine* entitled "By Rule of Three," which attacked Harvard English professors Adams Sherman Hill and Barrett Wendell. Of course, besides Hubbard's loftily expressed reason for going to Boston to further his education, he went there to keep company with Moore until she found a teaching job at Potsdam State Normal in September 1893. According to biographer Freeman Champney, "in effect, Hubbard was a man with two wives at this time." In 1894 he fathered an illegitimate daughter, Miriam, with Moore (the child was left with Moore's relatives), and with Bertha he sired a daughter named Katherine.

During a trip to Europe in 1894 Hubbard briefly visited William Morris, the poet, utopian thinker, and furniture maker who believed that making quality goods by hand would counter the dehumanizing ill effects of the industrial revolution. In 1895, following his return to East Aurora, Hubbard established the Roycroft Shop, which he announced was dedicated to printing fine books, making handmade furniture, and crafting copper goods. In June 1895 the Roycrofters printed twenty-five hundred copies of a little magazine called the *Philistine* that included the work of Hubbard and a group of Buffalo journalists and would-be artists such as Harry P. Taber, Eugene White, David Gray, and William McIntosh. It was so popular that a second number came out in July. The idea, curiously, was not Hubbard's but that of McIntosh and White. However, the energetic, comparatively wealthy Hubbard soon became its most influential voice, and his name became synonymous with the *Philistine.* According to a notice carried in every issue,

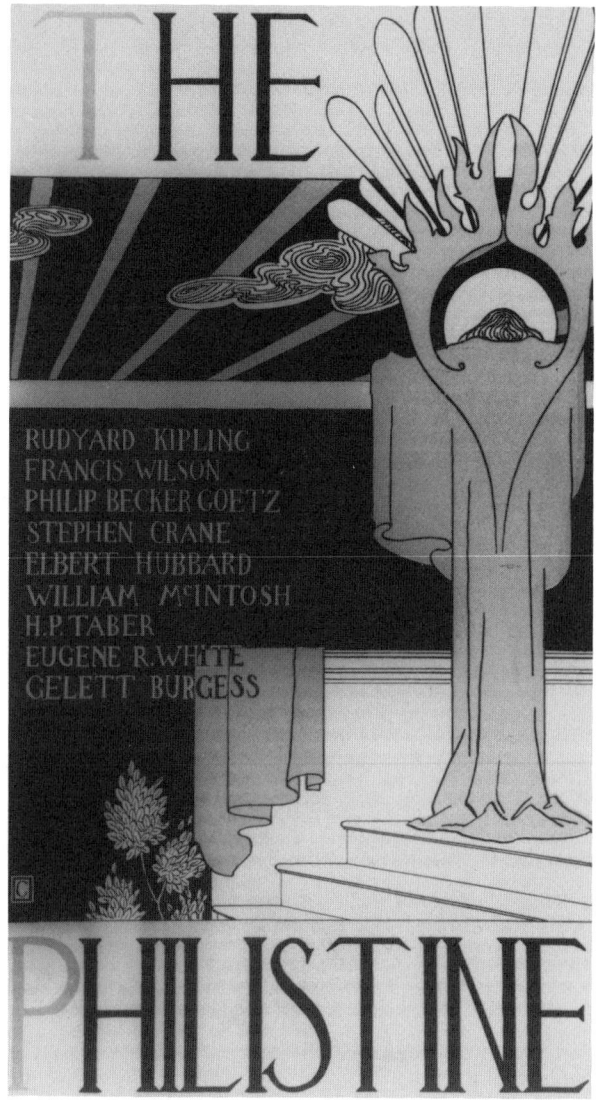

Poster for the December 1895 issue of the pocket-size magazine Hubbard described as a "periodical of protest" (Bruccoli Collection)

Cover for an issue of the magazine Hubbard founded in 1908. Though the editorial content was similar to that of the Philistine, the Fra was much larger and included more advertising.

Title page, designed by Bertha Crawford Hubbard, for the first book published by Elbert Hubbard's press. The Roycrofters device was adapted from that of fifteenth-century French typographer Nicolas Jenson.

the *Philistine* was "Printed Every Little While for the Society of the Philistines and Published by Them Monthly." Subscriptions were available for one dollar a year or ten cents a month, according to a February 1910 announcement. Hubbard believed in extending credit to subscribers, and other publishers soon adopted this practice. The magazine's eventual 5 1/2-by-7 1/2-inch size was intended to fit in the subscriber's pocket.

An article by Mark S. Hubbell that appeared in the inaugural issue of the magazine gives a clear indication as to the magazine's future content: "I doff me hat to The Philistine, and hail it brother, well met. In the name of all who have hated shams, in the name of all brave knights whose lances have shivered against the dead walls of human stupidity, ignorance, malice and convention; in the name of every pilloried hope and dead ambition killed in the long battle with the Mediocrities and the banalities, I greet thee, knight errant from Philistia and bid thee

God speed." Also, in that first issue Hubbard wrote: "It is because we cannot say what we would in the periodicals [that] we have made this book."

Hubbard and his cohorts deliberately attacked the literary establishment, the "Chosen People," in his vernacular, that he had once aspired to join, including such respected names as William Dean Howells (referred to snippily as W. Dean Howl) and Mark Twain. "Mark Twain says he is writing *Joan of Arc* anonymously in *Harper's* because he is convinced if he signed it the people would insist the stuff was funny," said a *Philistine* column. "Mr. Twain is worried unnecessarily. It has been a long time since any one insisted the matter he turns out so voluminously was or is funny." By the fifth issue Hubbard could boast that the *Philistine* would do reviews only of authors the publisher deemed worthy of pillory. The little magazine also poked fun at such leading periodicals of the day as *Century, McClure's, Ladies' Home Journal,* and *Cosmopolitan,* as well as at their respective editors. By and large, the leading literary figures of the age failed to contribute items to the *Philistine.* The major exception was Stephen Crane, who published four poems in the magazine in 1896. Hubbard held an elaborate banquet in Crane's honor in December 1895 and used the opportunity to distribute a forty-eight-page journal, the *Roycroft Quarterly: A Souvenir and a Medley,* which consisted of highly appreciative commentaries on Crane's work by Hubbard and others. Hubbard wanted to be thought of as Crane's patron, and, indeed, John Berryman credited Hubbard's championing of Crane in the *Philistine* as a major boost to the young author's reputation.

In January 1899 the forty-fifth issue of the *Philistine* announced an important change in policy. "Beginning with the next number of the magazine I propose to write every article and paragraph in it," wrote Hubbard. "If it were possible to secure any one to write so well as myself I would not do it." Champney notes that it was not true Hubbard wrote every word in the *Philistine* as claimed, but "the great bulk of it was his." Often Hubbard wrote epigrams attributed to the person of Ali Baba, who espoused convictions such as "Art is largely a matter of hair-cut."

Significantly, while Hubbard made many enemies in the literary community, he nonetheless found a niche for his magazine with readers who liked his sophomoric humor, gossipy tone, and iconoclasm. There were 20,000 copies of the *Philis-*

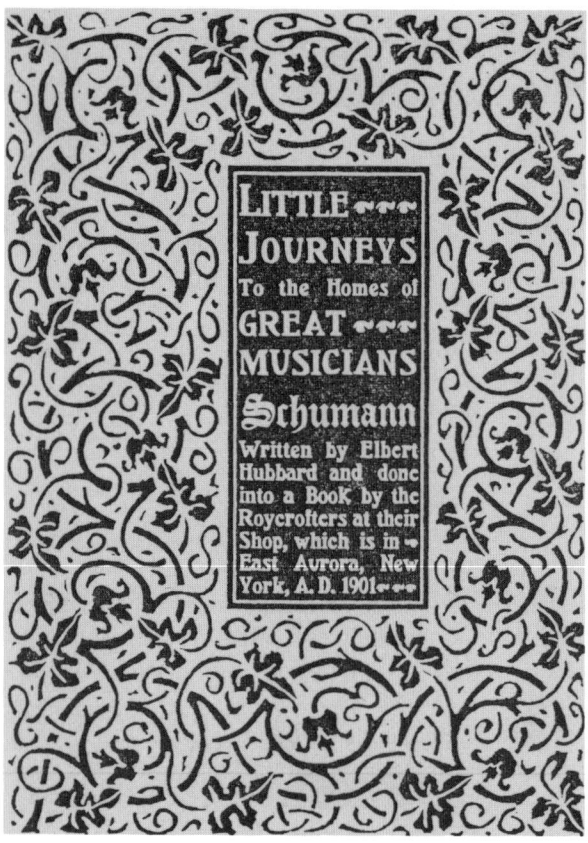

Title page for one of the monthly biographical booklets that Hubbard produced between 1894 and 1908

tine in circulation after three years, 52,000 after five years, and 225,000 at the time of Hubbard's death. Among the advertisers attracted to the magazine were a bicycle manufacturer, a typewriter company, the Emerson College of Oratory, and two railroad companies. Hubbard wrote the advertisements for the handmade books printed by the Roycrofters, including his own edition of *The Song of Songs* (1896), offered as a defense of free love, and for the furniture his people constructed upon the premises. The flyleaves of the books and the distinctive Roycroftian furniture all bore a Roycroft emblem. In fact, Hubbard even sponsored a baseball team that displayed the emblem prominently.

In 1897 Hubbard's periodical inspired a rival called the *Anti-Philistine,* which lasted but four issues. Other little magazines of the day also parodied and mocked Hubbard's style, but none approached his success with the general public.

Brom Weber, in his doctoral dissertation, convincingly demonstrated that Hubbard depended upon a gullible public to hawk his "handmade" magazines and books. Roycroft publications were

never fully made by hand since many, for example, were bound by a nearby Buffalo printer. In addition, Hubbard lacked the pride and knowledge a good printer must possess. Weber noted that Hubbard's red and black inks frequently were printed out of register, one color upon the other instead of aligned, and that the Roycrofters frequently reduced leading to make an article "fit" on a page. Moreover, according to biographer David Arnold Balch, even Hubbard's signed editions were often phonies. He ordered assistants to perfect his signature so that not even he could tell his from theirs. And Hubbard's so-called limited editions of three hundred copies—purchased by consumers who thought scarcity would add to their value—were seldom ever limited to the number he claimed. He also made slight changes in type or design to sell a brand new "limited edition" of a sold-out series.

The hundreds of Roycrofters who lived on the premises came to East Aurora in search of a utopian existence. Hubbard allowed anyone to stay on his premises in exchange for work. He was personally magnetic and a glutton for work, always conscious of his role as an American sage. His most famous surviving epigrams are those that deal with work: "If you want to get the work done, select the busy man—the other kind has no time," and, "Get your happiness out of your work—or you'll never know what happiness is." One of Hubbard's assistants, Michael Monahan, wrote that Hubbard's "smile was very beautiful in those days; both men and women readily yielded to its fascinating charm." Hubbard agreed, noting in the *Philistine* that "my smile was contagious, also infectious, as well as fetching."

Hubbard gained international fame with the publication of a *Philistine* essay in March 1899 that became known as *A Message to Garcia.* Written, claimed Hubbard, in a single evening hour, "when I had been endeavoring to train some rather delinquent villagers to adjure the comatose state and get radioactive," the essay is basically a defense of capitalists who too long have suffered at the hands of incompetent and lazy hired help. The author's point is that a hero is a man who does his job without questioning why, just as the messenger, Lt. Andrew Rowan, did when he overcame all adversity to deliver a note from Pres. William McKinley to Gen. Calixto Garcia, leader of Cuban insurrectionists, during the Spanish-American War. Hubbard wisely allowed the New York Central Railroad to reprint the essay several times, and this practice was imitated

Engraving of the Roycrofters community in East Aurora, New York. Hubbard's office was in the tower.

not only by businesses and industries of the day but also by the governments of Japan and Russia. Hubbard boasted that the essay had been reprinted forty million times in his lifetime, but this number, of course, cannot be verified.

In 1902 Hubbard's long-suffering wife filed for divorce, naming Moore as corespondent. The ultimate indignity for her had occurred when Moore's brother-in-law, a lawyer, had sued Hubbard for payment of child support and Hubbard had been exposed for his deeds in the national press. One year later the author announced his engagement to Moore, describing her in an article as his "affinity," and thereby opening himself up to ridicule for the term in both the local and national press. At the height of the scandal Hubbard married Alice Moore on 20 January 1904. Hubbard retained custody of his eldest sons from the first marriage, Bert and Sanford (the latter nationally known because a photograph of his muscular, bare-chested body appeared on boxes of Grape-Nuts, a breakfast cereal). Hubbard had, for some time, increased his fortune by writing ad copy for such national advertisers as Armour, Burroughs Adding Machines, Wrigley's Chewing Gum ("Box vobiscum," wrote Hubbard, "buy it by the box"), Heinz's Fifty-Seven Varieties, and the Gillette Safety Razor. (Many of these advertised in the *Philistine* by 1906.) His secret for writing ad copy was "to let a smile go into the ink bottle" and "to say it and stop." He had no patience with those who criticized him for writing drivel.

"The man who is afraid of advertising is either a nincompoop, or has something to hide," Hubbard declared, forgetting that he had called advertising "our daily rot" in a *Philistine* essay before he hired out to write copy.

Hubbard's writings and lectures (including many given on vaudeville stages) made him well-known across the nation. To be sure, he had his detractors. The *Indianapolis News* called him "the idol of silly sentimental women." The *Chicago Journal* said, "his egotism is insufferable." And the *New York Nation* wrote, "He says he's not a college graduate, a fact that need not have been stated." Hubbard himself published excerpts from derogatory reviews in the *Philistine*.

In the March 1908 issue of the *Philistine* Hubbard announced that he intended to publish a new magazine. This nine-by-five-inch magazine was called the *Fra*. (Hubbard's byline for the magazine was likewise "The Fra.") Although such famous names as Luther Burbank wrote essays for it, Champney argues that the venture was a failure artistically, charging that "There was too much material and too little focus," and claiming that the main reason for launching the publication was to accept advertising that could not fit in the pocket-sized *Philistine*.

Hubbard's untimely end came with wife Alice aboard the *Lusitania*, the British liner sunk off the coast of Ireland by a German submarine on 7 May 1915. Although the German Embassy had published warnings to United States citizens to stay out of German waters, Hubbard went abroad anyway, declaring that one of his purposes was to try securing an appointment with the kaiser. He and Alice were two of the 128 Americans lost on the *Lusitania,* and their deaths helped rally support of those who favored an end to American isolationism in World War I.

Hubbard's son Bert and the Roycrofters printed a final, "valedictory number" of the *Philistine* in July 1915. The magazine would appear no more, said Bert, since "No one else can now do it as he did." It was announced that the *Fra* would continue, but high costs and a diminished readership caused its demise in 1917. In 1938 the Roycroft Shops were officially declared bankrupt.

Biographies:
Felix Shay, *Elbert Hubbard of East Aurora* (New York: Wise, 1926);
Mary Hubbard Heath, *The Elbert Hubbard I Knew* (East Aurora, N.Y.: Roycrofters, 1929);

David Arnold Balch, *Elbert Hubbard: Genius of Roycroft* (New York: Stokes, 1940);
Freeman Champney, *Art & Glory: The Story of Elbert Hubbard* (New York: Crown, 1968).

References:
H. Kenneth Dirlam and Ernest E. Simmons, *Sinners, This Is East Aurora: The Story of Elbert Hubbard and The Roycroft Shops* (New York: Vantage, 1964);
Charles F. Hamilton, *As Bees in Honey Drown: Elbert Hubbard and the Roycrofters* (South Brunswick & New York: Barnes, 1973);
Bonnie Ruth Baker Thorne, "Elbert Hubbard and the Publications of the Roycroft Shop, 1893-1915," Ph.D. dissertation, Texas Woman's University, 1975;
Brom Weber, "Spurious Sage: A Study of the Conspiracy Between Elbert Hubbard and His Times," Ph.D. dissertation, University of Minnesota, 1957.

Charles S. Johnson

(24 July 1893-27 October 1956)

Carolyn A. Stroman
Howard University

See also the Johnson entry in *DLB 51: Afro-American Writers from the Harlem Renaissance to 1940.*

MAJOR POSITION HELD: Editor, *Opportunity: A Journal of Negro Life* (1923-1928).

BOOKS: *The Negro in Chicago: A Study of Race Relations and a Race Riot,* attributed to Johnson (Chicago: University of Chicago Press, 1922);

The Negro in American Civilization: A Study of Negro Life and Race Relations in the Light of Social Research (New York: Holt, 1930);

The Economic Status of Negroes (Nashville: Fisk University Press, 1933);

Shadow of the Plantation (Chicago: University of Chicago Press, 1934);

Race Relations: Adjustment of Whites and Negroes in the United States, by Johnson and Willis D. Weatherford (Boston & New York: Heath, 1934);

The Collapse of Cotton Tenancy: Summary of Field Studies & Statistical Surveys, 1933-35, by Johnson, Edwin R. Embree, and W. W. Alexander (Chapel Hill: University of North Carolina Press, 1935);

A Preface to Racial Understanding (New York: Friendship Press, 1936);

The Negro College Graduate (Chapel Hill: University of North Carolina Press, 1938);

Growing Up in the Black Belt: Negro Youth in the Rural South (Washington, D.C.: American Council on Education, 1941);

Statistical Atlas of Southern Counties: Listing and Analysis of Socio-economic Indices of 1104 Southern Counties, by Johnson, Lewis W. Jones, Buford H. Junker, and others (Chapel Hill: University of North Carolina Press, 1941);

Patterns of Negro Segregation (New York & London: Harper, 1943; London: Gollancz, 1944);

Charles S. Johnson (copyright Fabian Bachrach; courtesy of the Schomburg Center for Research in Black Culture, the New York Public Library, Astor, Lenox, and Tilden Foundations)

To Stem This Tide: A Survey of Racial Tension Areas in the United States, by Johnson and others (Boston & Chicago: Pilgrim Press, 1943);

Into the Main Stream: A Survey of Best Practices in Race Relations in the South, by Johnson, Elizabeth L. Allen, Horace M. Bond, Margaret McCulloch, and Alma Forrest Polk (Chapel Hill: University of North Carolina Press, 1947);

People Vs. Property: Race Restrictive Covenants in Housing, by Johnson and Herman H. Long (Nashville: Fisk University Press, 1947);

Education and the Cultural Crisis (New York: Macmillan, 1951).

OTHER: *Ebony and Topaz, A Collectanea,* edited by Johnson (New York: National Urban League, 1927);

Negro Housing: Report of the Committee on Negro Housing, prepared by Johnson, edited by John M. Gries and James Ford (Washington, D.C.: President's Conference on Home Building and Home Ownership, 1932).

SELECTED PERIODICAL PUBLICATIONS UNCOLLECTED: "The Negro Migration: An Economic Interpretation," *Modern Quarterly,* 2 (July 1925): 314-326;

"How the Negro Fits in Northern Industries," *Industrial Psychology,* 1 (June 1926): 399-412;

"The Rise of the Negro Magazine," *Journal of Negro History,* 13 (January 1928): 7-21;

"The Changing Economic Status of the Negro," *Annals of the American Academy of Political and Social Science,* 140 (November 1928): 128-137;

"The Conflict of Caste and Class in an American Industry," *American Journal of Sociology,* 42 (July 1936): 55-65;

"The Negro Minority," *Annals of the American Academy of Political and Social Science,* 223 (September 1942): 10-16;

"The Present Status of Race Relations in the South," *Social Forces,* 23 (October 1944): 27-32;

"Social Changes and Their Effects on Race Relations in the South," *Social Forces,* 23 (March 1945): 343-348;

"American Minorities and Civil Rights in 1950," *Journal of Negro Education,* 20 (Summer 1951): 484-493;

"Some Significant Social and Educational Implications of the U.S. Supreme Court's Decision," *Journal of Negro Education,* 23 (Summer 1954): 364-371;

"A Southern Negro's View of the South," *New York Times Magazine,* 23 September 1956, pp. 15, 64, 66, 67.

First and foremost a leading black sociologist, Charles S. Johnson's primary contribution to the literary arena was his editorship of one of black America's most important historical publica-

tions, *Opportunity: A Journal of Negro Life.* It was in this position that Johnson played a major role in the development of black writers, poets, and artists during the 1920s and had a substantial influence on the dissemination of information by and about black Americans.

A stern advocate of racial equality, Johnson advocated "the careful marshalling of scientific discussion of problems related to blacks and to race relations." In the course of his lifetime, which spanned sixty-three years, Johnson was sociologist, editor, writer, race-relations expert, research director, first black president of Fisk University, and a member of numerous committees, commissions, and foundation boards. In all of these positions he sought to use research and scholarship to upgrade the status of blacks in America and to effect social change in the area of race relations.

Born on 24 July 1893 in Bristol, Virginia, Charles Spurgeon Johnson was the eldest of five children born to Charles Henry and Winifred Branch Johnson. Johnson was reared in a solidly middle-class family. His father, who was an emancipated slave and a minister, had the good fortune of being well educated. Johnson was the recipient of his father's broad knowledge and enjoyed reading his father's classical and theological books.

After completing a preparatory school, Wayland Academy, Johnson matriculated at Virginia Union University, from which he was graduated cum laude in 1916. Afterward he moved to Chicago to attend graduate school at the University of Chicago, where he became associated with sociologist Robert E. Park, who was to become a friend and mentor and have a profound influence upon Johnson's development as a social scientist. It was also here that Johnson adopted the scientific objectivity and detached style of writing that characterized much of his work. While enrolled as a student at the university, Johnson was also employed at the Chicago Urban League as director of research and records.

Johnson served in Europe as a sergeant major in the army during World War I. Soon after his return in 1919 he reportedly came close to losing his life while observing the dynamics of the Chicago race riot. Later, when asked to provide testimony regarding the riot, Johnson presented a plan he had developed on how to study its causes. His testimony was so impressive that he was subsequently appointed associate director of the Chicago Commission on Race Relations,

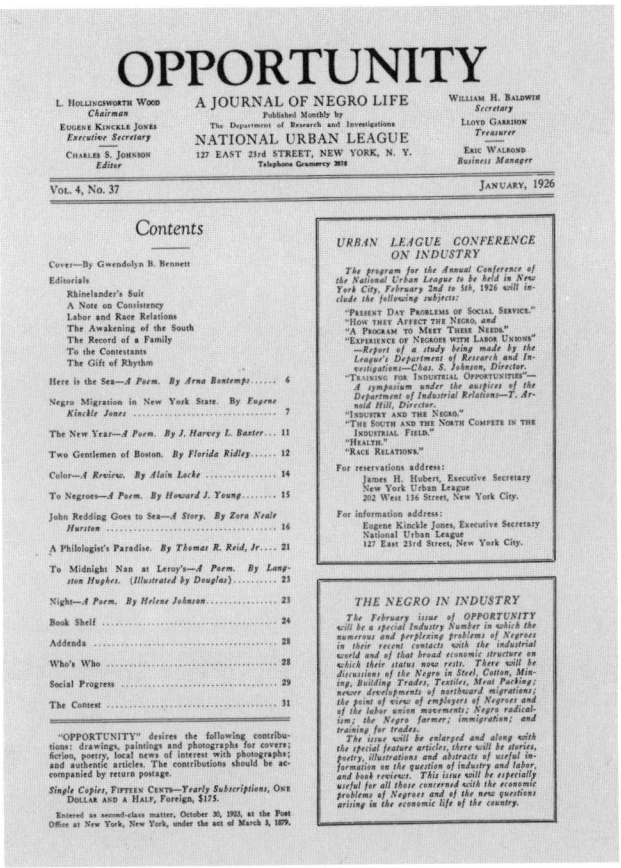

First page of an issue of the official organ of the National Urban League. During Johnson's tenure as editor (1923-1928), the journal became a leading forum for the artists of the Harlem Renaissance.

the body officially charged with investigating the causes of the race riot. The result of the commission's investigation was the landmark *The Negro in Chicago: A Study of Race Relations and a Race Riot* (1922). In addition to cataloging the events leading up to the riot, the book documents the living conditions of blacks in Chicago and the erroneous perceptions that contributed to the city's racial problems. Regarded as a classic among sociological literature, *The Negro in Chicago* is still recognized as one of the best analyses of the background of a race riot.

When the commission's work was completed in 1921, Johnson had gained a national reputation in the field of race relations, and as a result he received several job offers. He accepted a position in New York with the National Urban League, an organization whose priorities included research and education on race relations. Prior to this, on 6 November 1920, he married Marie Antoinette Burgette, with whom he had three sons (Charles, Jr., Robert, and Jeh Vincent)

and a daughter (Patricia Marie).

During Johnson's tenure at the Urban League, a portion of his duties as director of research and investigations involved serving as editor of *Opportunity: A Journal of Negro Life.* The official publication of the Urban League, *Opportunity* had considerable influence among blacks during the Harlem Renaissance, a period characterized by a marked increase in creative expression by and about blacks. In introducing the new magazine in January 1923, the executive secretary of the Urban League, E. K. Jones, noted that Johnson was eminently qualified by both training and experience to edit a journal that would "lay bare Negro life as it is."

Directed at an interracial readership, *Opportunity* had two distinct purposes: to be intellectual in nature, artistic in tone. "*Opportunity*," wrote Johnson in the February 1923 issue, "is a venture inspired by a long insistent demand, both general and specific, for a journal of Negro life that

OPPORTUNITY

JOURNAL OF NEGRO LIFE

PUBLISHED BY THE NATIONAL URBAN LEAGUE
127 EAST 23RD STREET, NEW YORK CITY

OFFICE OF
CHARLES S. JOHNSON
EDITOR

April 10th, 1925.

Mr. Arthur B. Spingarn,
19 West 44th St.,
New York City.

Dear Mr. Spingarn:

In anticipation of your interest, may I ask
that you reserve the evening of Friday, May 1st,
for OPPORTUNITY'S Dinner at which awards will be
made to young Negro writers in this magazine's
first literary Contest for stories, poetry, plays
and essays?

The occasion will be perhaps a bit more significant than the mere holding of a meeting and awarding of prizes. It will introduce that group of
Negro writers now dealing with the sparkling
materials of their own group life, about whose
work all of our judges have expressed a surprised
delight, one of them going so far as to say that
the "stories mark an epoch in the history of
American letters - the entrance into the domain
of art of a new race, differently dowered but
with something we cannot well do without. a revelation to the whites - through the intensified
vision of creative mind of the soul of the black
man.. giving to him the seal of a new equality.. "

An invitation enclosing a slip for reservation
will come to you later.

Sincerely,

Editor

OPPORTUNITY
JOURNAL OF NEGRO LIFE

INVITES YOU TO BE
PRESENT
AT THE
AWARD DINNER OF
ITS FIRST LITERARY
CONTEST
AT THE
FIFTH AVE. RESTAURANT
FIFTH AVE. BLDG. 24TH ST.
SIX THIRTY P.M. MAY 1ST 1925
2.75   A PLATE

Announcement letter and invitation to the 1925 awards banquet sponsored by Opportunity *(courtesy of the Arthur B. Spingarn Collection, Moorland-Spingarn Research Center, Howard University)*

would devote itself religiously to an interpretation of the social problems of the Negro population." Added to this was Johnson's goal of giving expression to the cultural side of black life by bringing black writers "into contact with the general world of letters to which they have been for the most part timid and inarticulate strangers."

In providing a view of life in black America through the use of objective facts, *Opportunity*, under Johnson's direction, examined a variety of topics of importance, including housing, health, migration, education, intelligence testing, and interracial matters. A sampling of titles conveys the flavor of the articles included in the magazine: "The Recent Northward Migration of the Negro" (April 1924), "Helping Negro Workers to Purchase Homes" (January 1924), "What the Army 'Intelligence' Tests Measure" (July 1924). Many of the articles were based on studies conducted by the Urban League's Department of Research and Investigations, which Johnson headed. A section variously entitled "Survey" or "Social Progress" displayed the achievements of individuals and organizations; a column entitled "Book Shelf" consisted of reviews of books pertaining to Negro life and culture.

Published monthly and generally carrying at least three editorials by Johnson, the magazine served as a forum for Johnson's racial philosophy and ideology. Johnson held a lifelong desire to improve the self-images of blacks and to change white perceptions of (and attitudes toward) blacks—actions that he perceived would lead to improved race relations. Publicizing the problems as well as the achievements of blacks in *Opportunity* was one way for Johnson to accomplish this goal.

Johnson, in his role as editor, attempted to use facts to educate and provide a basis for understanding between blacks and whites. In an editorial in the January 1925 issue of *Opportunity* assessing the educational effectiveness of the magazine, Johnson pointed out that *Opportunity* provided a framework for education by having a policy that was "one of intelligent discussion rather than fireworks, of calm analysis rather than tears."

Although Johnson placed great emphasis on providing social-service data, he realized also that poetry, fiction, and other forms of art were essential in the transmittal of a picture of black life in urban America and in bridging the gap separating the races. Indeed, he promulgated the notion that literature was "a great liaison between races." Thus, in his role as editor of *Opportunity*, he stimulated young blacks in particular to de-

velop a body of literature reflective of black life and culture.

In 1924, his second year as editor of *Opportunity*, Johnson began making substantial progress toward his goal of providing blacks in the creative arts an outlet for their creations. In March 1924 he helped arrange a dinner meeting in which young black writers, such as Countee Cullen, Jessie Fauset, and Alain Locke, met and conversed with editors and publishers of leading publications. The Civic Club dinner, as it came to be called, was significant in that it brought competent black writers to the attention of white publishers.

Johnson continued in his quest to provide publishing opportunities for blacks in the arts by having *Opportunity* sponsor three literary contests. In the September 1924 issue of *Opportunity*, Johnson announced the first contest, noting that it was expected "to stimulate and encourage literary effort among Negroes, to stimulate interest in work by Negro authors, and to develop a market for Negro writers."

The contest, which took place in 1925 and received more than 732 entries, was successful beyond expectations. The May 1925 issue of *Opportunity* lists a number of prizewinners who later gained significant literary reputations, including Zora Neale Hurston, Langston Hughes, Countee Cullen, Sterling Brown, and E. Franklin Frazier. Subsequent issues of the magazine carried many of the prizewinning poems, essays, and short stories, as well as reproductions of paintings and carvings submitted by young artists. Even those who were not prizewinners profited; Johnson and the well-known critics (including James Weldon Johnson, Alain Locke, Blanche Cotton Williams, and Clement Wood) who judged the contests provided entrants with critiques of their submissions.

Johnson arranged for the prizewinners to meet with the judges at gala dinners, and these meetings produced tangible benefits. As a direct result of the first dinner, Langston Hughes's *The Weary Blues* (1926) was published by a major publishing house, Alfred A. Knopf. The subsequent two contests inspired less impressive submissions, but even so, due to Johnson's efforts, the works of many outstanding black writers began to receive recognition and to appear in anthologies.

In 1927 Johnson collected and edited many outstanding works previously published in *Opportunity*. Published under the title *Ebony and Topaz, A Collectanea*, the book provides a glimpse of the variety of black talent existing in the 1920s. Includ-

Johnson and L. Hollingsworth Wood, vice-chairman of the Fisk University board of trustees, at Johnson's inauguration as the school's first black president in 1947 (courtesy of the Schomburg Center for Research in Black Culture, the New York Public Library, Astor, Lenox, and Tilden Foundations)

ing a blend of poetry, sociological essays, one-act plays, short stories, and paintings by several of the prizewinners of the *Opportunity* literary contests, *Ebony and Topaz* is an important contribution to the literary and cultural history of black Americans.

As he had done so deftly with objective facts, Johnson used the creative expression of blacks as a means of challenging among whites and blacks the myth of black inferiority. In providing "asylum and encouragement to aspiring Negro writers and poets for whom there was no place in the pattern of American culture," Johnson and *Opportunity* were able to demonstrate that blacks had a history and culture that was rich and full.

From all indications the magazine, particularly under Johnson's editorship, was well re-

ceived and well respected; it enjoyed a high reputation among both black and white subscribers. Johnson's contemporary Edwin R. Embree viewed Johnson and the magazine as "a lively leaven in creating the Negro Renaissance." Recent researchers and critics also applaud Johnson's use of the magazine to further the goals of the Harlem Renaissance and to promote a greater understanding of black life. Although its circulation never exceeded eleven thousand, *Opportunity* was clearly a forceful channel of communication for and about blacks during the 1920s.

After editing *Opportunity* for almost six years, in 1928 Johnson accepted the chairmanship of Fisk University's Department of Social Science. His relationship with *Opportunity* continued, however. He was listed as contributing editor through October 1931, and in 1943 he offered to edit the magazine in absentia. *Opportunity* eventually ended publication with the winter 1949 issue.

Johnson chaired the Department of Social Science for nearly two decades. In this position he continued conducting research on black communities and race relations; he also established a race relations department and founded the Institute of Race Relations. Utilizing his immense talents and connections, Johnson built a reputation for Fisk University as one of the leading centers for the study of race relations, southern sociology, and social research on blacks.

Johnson published widely during the years he was a professor of sociology. Characterized by scientific detachment, most of his writings attempt to provide an objective analysis of the social and economic status of blacks and the impact of racism on this status. Johnson's three best-known works deserve special attention: *Shadow of the Plantation* (1934), an important community study that describes the influence of a plantation economy on the lives of rural sharecroppers; *Growing Up in the Black Belt: Negro Youth in the Rural South* (1941), which details how being black affected the personality development of black youth living in the rural South; and *Patterns of Negro Segregation* (1943), a documentation of variations in the behavioral adjustment of blacks to segregation and discriminatory practices.

Johnson's other works, although less impressive than those mentioned above, have commanded the respect of other social scientists. Indeed, *The Negro in American Civilization: A Study of Negro Life and Race Relations in the Light of Social Research* (1930) and its sequel, *Race Relations: Adjustment of Whites and Negroes in the United States* (1934; cowritten with Willis D. Weatherford), were the basic texts for race relations courses for several years. Also, *The Negro College Graduate* received the Wolf-Anisfield Award as most distinguished work pertaining to race published in 1938.

Over the years, Johnson developed an enviable record of solid scholarship on blacks. Using a research technique in which empirical data were combined with personal profiles, Johnson objectively and dispassionately conveyed the effects of racism on the social, economic, and psychological development of blacks, particularly black Southerners.

From 1943 to 1948, amid his other duties, Johnson served as editor of *A Monthly Summary of Events and Trends in Race Relations*. Aimed at policymakers rather than the general public, the report provided analysis and interpretation of race-related events.

In 1947 Johnson was selected to be the first black president of Fisk University. Even then he still maintained his interest in scientific inquiry. In his inaugural address he stated: "There is only one way to understand the nature of the social processes and that is by intensive and dispassionate investigation."

His years as president of Fisk University were fruitful ones. Under his leadership the university made great strides: national and international scholars became associated with the school; more than $1 million was added to the university's endowment; innovative educational practices were introduced; and five major buildings were added to the university's physical plant.

Yet Johnson's tenure as a university president was not a particularly gratifying period for him. In the view of Patrick G. Gilpin, Johnson's years as Fisk's president were filled with frustrations and disappointments.

Throughout his career in academia Johnson readily utilized his race-relations expertise to provide technical assistance to various committees and commissions. As examples, he was appointed to two presidential committees: Pres. Herbert Hoover's Commission on Negro Housing and Home Building and Pres. Franklin D. Roosevelt's Committee on Farm Tenancy; and he was one of twenty educators appointed by Pres. Harry S. Truman to provide advice on the reorganization of the Japanese educational system. As a result of his international reputation Johnson was appointed a member of the League of Nations Commission to Study Forced Labor in Liberia and served as a member of the first delegation to UNESCO in Paris. He also served as one of the social-science consultants to the legal staff of the NAACP when the Supreme Court rendered its historic 1954 decision (*Brown* v. *Board of Education of Topeka*) on school desegregation. In short, Johnson's public service activities were as exceptional as his scholarship.

Johnson's efforts on behalf of his race, his country, and the sociology profession were recognized and applauded. He received honorary doctorates from his alma mater, Virginia Union University (1928), Howard University (1941), Columbia University (1947), Harvard University (1948), the University of Glasgow (1952), Lincoln University (1955), and Central State University (1956). In addition, he was elected president of the Southern Sociological Society and vice-president of the American Sociological Society in 1936, at that time the highest office attained by a black person in the field of sociology.

On 27 October 1956, while en route to a meeting with the Fisk University board of trustees, Johnson died of a heart attack in the Louisville, Kentucky, train station. Johnson enjoyed an exceptionally productive career, and though his achievements as a sociologist and race-relations expert may overshadow his accomplishments as a magazine journalist, he was also an ingenious, influential editor. With *Opportunity* as his vehicle, Johnson astutely used black arts and letters as another tool in the struggle for racial equality; Ralph L. Pearson considers Johnson's editorship of *Opportunity* one of his most important contributions. Johnson's role in the Harlem Renaissance was perhaps best characterized by Langston Hughes, who concluded that Johnson "did more to encourage and develop Negro writers during the 1920's, than anyone else in America."

Bibliography:

George L. Gardiner, *A Bibliography of Charles Spurgeon Johnson's Published Writings* (Nashville: Fisk University, 1970).

Biography:

Patrick J. Gilpin, "Charles S. Johnson: An Intellectual Biography," Ph.D. dissertation, Vanderbilt University Press, 1973.

References:

John H. Bracey, Jr., August Meier, and Elliott Rudwick, *The Black Sociologists: The First Half Century* (Belmont, Cal.: Wadsworth, 1971);

Edwin R. Embree, "A Scholar and a Gentleman," in *13 Against the Odds*, edited by Embree (New York: Viking, 1944), pp. 47-70;

Patrick J. Gilpin, "Charles S. Johnson: Entrepreneur of the Harlem Renaissance," in *The Harlem Renaissance Remembered*, edited by Arna Bontemps (New York: Dodd, Mead, 1972);

Ralph L. Pearson, "Charles S. Johnson: The Urban League Years: A Study of Race Leadership," Ph.D. dissertation, Johns Hopkins University, 1970;

Richard Robbins, "Charles S. Johnson," in *Black Sociologists: Historical and Contemporary Perspectives*, edited by James E. Blackwell and Morris Janowitz (Chicago: University of Chicago Press, 1974), pp. 56-84;

Nancy Weiss, *The National Urban League, 1910-1940* (New York: Oxford University Press, 1974).

Papers:

Collections of Johnson's papers are located in the Special Collections Department of Fisk University Library, the Armistead Research Center at Dillard University, and the Schomburg Center for Research in Black Culture, New York Public Library. The papers of the National Urban League, which include material related to Johnson, are on deposit at the Library of Congress.

Joseph Palmer Knapp

(14 May 1864-30 January 1951)

Robert E. Alber
Dakota State University

MAJOR POSITIONS HELD: Chairman, principal owner, Crowell Publishing Company, became Crowell-Collier Publishing Company in 1919 (1906-1946); chairman, principal stockholder, Publications Corporation (1911-1946).

PRINCIPAL MAGAZINES OWNED OR CONTROLLED: *Farm and Fireside,* retitled *Country Home* in 1930 (1906-1939), *Woman's Home Companion* (1906-1946), *American Magazine* (1911-1946), *Collier's Weekly* (1919-1946), *Mentor* (1920-1930).

Among publishers, Joseph Palmer Knapp was the master of the low profile. During his life he owned and directed five magazines, three newspaper supplements, one New York City daily newspaper, and a book-publishing house. These publications were printed at a Knapp-owned plant that at one time held some of the most sophisticated presses and produced half the newspaper rotogravure sections in the United States.

When he died, however, on 30 January 1951, at the age of eighty-six, Knapp received only a short, one-column obituary in the *New York Times.* And the publisher whose magazines had a combined total circulation of more than fifteen million was not mentioned in *Who's Who in America* and was given but a one-paragraph obituary in both *Time* and *Newsweek,* the latter listing him as a "leader in lithography." Knapp, however, was one of the country's major publishers, and while he did pioneer the multicolor printing process, his contributions to magazine publishing were equally important. Yet he remains largely unknown and is mentioned in only a handful of references. Although the obituaries in the weekly newsmagazines were incomplete, they were, in a sense, accurate. Knapp did have a strong reputation in lithography, and it was through that interest that he gained entry into publishing.

Knapp completed high school at Brooklyn Polytechnic Institute and after an academically unsuccessful year at Columbia University joined his father's business in 1881. Joseph Fairchild

Knapp, a partner in the successful New York City lithographic firm of Major & Knapp and founder of the Metropolitan Life Insurance Company, did not look kindly on his son's failure at the university. He agreed to hire Knapp, but only as a printing apprentice at five dollars a week. In addition, Knapp's mother, Phoebe Palmer Knapp, the daughter of a Methodist evangelist, and a composer of Methodist hymns, demanded that Knapp contribute three dollars a week of his already meager salary to the Methodist church.

Undaunted, Knapp, at seventeen, began his apprenticeship. It was the beginning of a lifelong interest in printing, and although he would make his mark in several areas, he would always return to lithography. During his lifetime he would set industry standards in printing quality and press speed. Knapp would also be instrumental in developing a relatively new four-color printing process that would establish a benchmark for quality. His process depended on using excellent but extremely volatile inks, run at high press speeds. This was accomplished through the use of specially designed airtight ink containers. But that was later, and young Knapp knew that to fulfill his ambitions he would have to take home more than his current two-dollars-a-week pay. He began to use his lunch hours and spare time to sell printing contracts, realizing that salesmen, at least, had some control over their earnings. Knapp married the former Sylvia Kepner in 1886 and needed to increase his income. He took to sales easily, but more significantly, a strong, innate sense of business began to emerge in him.

One of Knapp's early business acquaintances was James B. Duke, founder of the American Tobacco Company and later the namesake of Duke University. Duke, impressed by Knapp's enthusiasm and industry, became an important customer, friend, and business partner. One of Knapp's sales ideas showed his keen eye for editorial talent as well as his ability to recognize a profitable sales angle, in this case for Duke's tobacco company. Knapp hired a young man to write and edit short biographies of famous Americans that would be included in cigarette packages. The young writer was Edward Bok, who would later become, for thirty years, the crusading editor of the *Ladies' Home Journal*.

It was not long before Knapp's success and sales commissions drew his father's attention. Concerned that his son's increasingly large income would lead to problems, Joseph Fairchild Knapp offered him company stock and a reduced amount of cash instead of full commissions. The idea appealed to Knapp, possibly because he now had two children, Joseph Fairchild and Claire Antoinette, increasing his family responsibility. The agreement allowed the father the opportunity to buy back the stock if he desired. But the contract also permitted Knapp to purchase additional shares, and a few years later, after an argument with his father, Knapp, borrowing on his stock

holdings, had enough leverage to buy his father's business.

In ten years, at the age of twenty-seven, Joseph Palmer Knapp held the controlling interest in one of the country's most successful lithographic firms. The businessman had fully emerged. He changed the name of the firm to Knapp & Company and during the next year, 1892, used his newly learned merger technique to accumulate more than a dozen competitors. While his initiative made him successful, it came at a personal price. One of his most distinguished employees, *Collier's* editor William L. Chenery, would later write that Knapp's father never forgave him, and when the elder Knapp died he left his stock in the Metropolitan Life Insurance Company to his only other child. In an effort to reunite the family, Knapp's sister divided her inheritance with her brother.

For the next few years Knapp continued to develop the business and work heavily with his four-color printing process. He did, during this time, join friend James Duke for a brief publishing venture. For five years, 1891 to 1896, the two published the *Recorder*, a New York City daily newspaper. There is no clear indication as to why the publication died, but there is evidence to suggest that it bowed to heavy competition. Knapp, however, was not one to allow setbacks the upper hand. Although he might have had trouble in the newspaper business (Knapp never owned another one), he quickly took another, innovative tack into print journalism. He established, in 1903, the first newspaper supplement, the *Associated Sunday Magazine*. The *Sunday Magazine*, the forerunner to similar current-day publications, achieved a circulation exceeding 1,500,000. It became the first of its type to be syndicated, and much of its popularity was attributed to the color reproductions on its pages.

Knapp, now thirty-nine, was enjoying the rewards of business, but again at personal expense. In the same year that he began the *Associated Sunday Magazine*, his marriage of seventeen years ended in divorce. Knapp would be married two more times, first to Elizabeth Laing McIlwaine and, after her death, to Margaret E. Rutledge of Currituck County, North Carolina. Rutledge was thirty-seven at the time of the marriage and lived to the age of seventy-four, dying in 1960, nine years after Knapp. This last marriage, in 1923, came on the heels of Knapp's greatest strides in publishing.

Covers for several of the principal magazines Knapp owned or controlled

In 1906 Knapp, with Samuel Untermeyer and Thomas W. Lamont, purchased the controlling interests in the Crowell Publishing Company for $750,000. This purchase included two leading magazines, *Farm and Fireside* (later renamed *Country Home*) and *Woman's Home Companion*. Five years later the Knapp group, operating under the generic title of a holding company, Publications Corporation, purchased *American Magazine*, and in 1919 the group acquired the business of P. F. Collier and Son for a reported sum of $1.75 million. The Collier holdings included *Collier's Weekly* and a large subscription book business. *Mentor*, which, unlike the other magazines controlled by Knapp, was not designed for mass circulation, was added to the Knapp holdings in 1920.

It was also during this time that Knapp began to divest his, and his sister's, controlling interests in the life insurance company. Knapp's father started the company originally as a method of providing insurance and benefits for his printing employees. In 1914 Knapp began to sell the controlling stock, at greatly reduced prices, back to policyholders in an effort to mutualize the corporation. Chenery points out in his book, *So It Seemed* (1952), that Knapp was one of those responsible for the development of programs in public health and in the building of public housing through Metropolitan Life.

Knapp's support of worthy causes, many of them located in his wife Margaret's home state of North Carolina, exhibited itself in other ways as well. He donated nearly $1 million toward the construction of a model school system in Currituck County. He also donated heavily to support public-school music, to train adult bus drivers, and to provide instructional equipment for public health work in both New York and North Carolina. Knapp also founded and endowed a conservation group named More Game Birds for America in 1930. The organization became the present-day Ducks Unlimited, one of the largest conservation organizations in the world.

Chenery, attempting to describe a bit of his publisher's personality, wrote that Knapp was a man with passionate wants. Knapp and his wife Margaret, both devoted fly casters, owned several miles of a trout river in the Catskill mountains. Knapp also once leased a Canadian estate in order to control a stretch of river where the salmon fishing was extraordinary. Chenery wrote that another of Knapp's great desires was to make *Collier's*, which had been a leading publica-

Joseph Palmer Knapp (North Carolina Collection, UNC Library at Chapel Hill)

tion during the muckraking era of American magazine journalism, once again a powerful and respected magazine, a project that both Chenery, as editor, and Knapp, as publisher, would come to grips with on several occasions.

With the addition of *Collier's*, Knapp's magazine holdings were complete, though he appears to have been somewhat aloof from the actual management of the publications. The *New York Times* noted that Knapp's office was located in a separate building, away from the offices of his publications. However, the sign on the door to Knapp's office still read "Publications Corporation," and Chenery and others attest to his involvement with the magazines.

From 1919 until 1930 Knapp struggled with the financial problems of his publishing business. During this time Knapp would dispose of the *Mentor*, never a commercial success, and reposition *Farm and Fireside*. Although its circulation had grown from 600,000 in 1915 to 1,237,000 in 1927, the production costs of *Farm and Fireside* were cutting profits severely. Knapp and his associates decided to rename the magazine *Country Home*, changing its editorial policy from a farm magazine to a publication that covered home, garden, and farm. They also brightened the look with four-color covers and coated paper. In the next few years *Country Home* profits were up and circulation came close to 3,000,000. But *Collier's* still struggled, and by 1927 Knapp had spent $10 million on the magazine. Despite stockholders' reservations Knapp predicted a turnaround in three years and offered to buy out any stockholder who wished to divest his holdings. Knapp had to invest another $5 million in the magazine, but at the end of the three years it began to break even. Over the next two decades its advertising revenues exceeded those of all the other Crowell-Collier magazines combined.

Many observers attribute the success of *Collier's* to the selection of William L. Chenery as editor. Chenery, a former Chicago newspaperman and editor of the *Rocky Mountain News,* joined *Collier's* in January 1925 and provided the editorial stability that the magazine had not enjoyed in over a decade.

About Knapp, Chenery reported that his publisher certainly evinced no early ambitions for journalism of any sort, and to his knowledge Knapp never wrote a line that appeared in print. But it was his ownership of printing businesses that led him into the ownership of great publications, a marriage of convenience and possible profit. Chenery described Knapp's editorial policies as "having the ambition to develop a better America." However, while Knapp wanted to return *Collier's* to its earlier muckraking reputation, Chenery wrote that Knapp was "much too rich to be carelessly radical, but he wanted a publication that would be unconventionally daring and at the same time prosperous–not a bad journalistic goal!"

Other Knapp observers agreed with Chenery's assessment. Knapp rarely encouraged crusading journalism, but his periodicals were success-oriented and celebrated opportunities available to individuals within a competitive capitalistic society. But the politically Republican businessman did have a sense of public necessity and possessed some of the characteristics of a crusader. Most of Knapp's strong editorial concerns, however, centered around his interests in conservation and in telling uplifting stories of American life rather than in the journalism of social reform.

This editorial movement away from crusading journalism and toward an inspirational editorial line was typical, according to magazine historian James Playsted Wood, for publishers with

Knapp in a hunting blind. He endowed the conservation group More Game Birds for America, *now Ducks Unlimited, in 1930 (North Carolina Collection, UNC Library at Chapel Hill).*

Knapp's background. Wood's research turned up several examples of publishers whose childhoods, like that of Knapp's, were influenced by a strongly religious relative. In Knapp's case it was his mother and grandfather. But Wood noted that DeWitt Wallace, the founder of *Reader's Digest,* was the son of a minister; Henry Luce, the son of Presbyterian missionaries, founded Time, Inc.; and George Horace Lorimer, of the *Saturday Evening Post,* was the son of a Baptist evangelist. All of these men were American success stories and, reasoned Wood, used that as a common editorial theme in their publications. But if that was the case, Knapp, at least, would ask for the opinions of his editors and defer, although at times painfully, to their judgment.

Chenery reports several heated arguments with Knapp and relates one instance when he had been at *Collier's* only a few weeks and received a Knapp memorandum proposing an article:

> I wrote in the journalese of the newspaper shop, "Is this a must or am I to use my judgment?" . . . a few days later Mr. Knapp came to my office in a mood of imperfectly restrained fury. He opened up directly: "Chenery, how often do I have to tell you that there are no Musts in this office?" I said: "Mr. Knapp, you are the principal stockholder in the company that owns this magazine. I respect the rights that go with ownership. If you want to have that editorial line taken, that is your privilege. If, however, you want me to use my judgment, then I am going to use it and do what I think is best for the magazine." Mr. Knapp said grimly: "You have got to use your judgment." I said: "All right, I will." Then he followed: "Are you going to publish that article?" I said "I am not." For a long and angry hour we discussed the question of the article. He insisted on my making the decision, but he fought to bend my judgment to his will. I did not yield.

> That insistence on the part of Joseph Palmer Knapp that the editor use whatever judgment he had regardless of the inclination of the owner explained the success that came to *Collier's* in the succeeding years. . . . never once was I compelled to adopt a policy I did not approve.

During the magazine's successful years Knapp divested himself of the American Lithographic Company but retained ownership of Alco Gravure, which had grown to be the largest rotogravure business in the world. He then held the reins of the Crowell-Collier Publishing Company until his retirement in 1946 at the age of eighty-one. Five years later Knapp died in his sleep at his Park Avenue home in New York City. The death of *Collier's* followed five years later.

References:

William L. Chenery, *So It Seemed* (New York: Harcourt, Brace, 1952), pp. 161-169;

Theodore Bernard Peterson, *Magazines in the Twentieth Century*, second edition (Urbana: University of Illinois Press, 1964), pp. 130-138;

James Playsted Wood, *Magazines in the United States*, second edition (New York: Ronald Press, 1956), p. 222.

Papers:

The Dudley Warren Bagley Papers in the Southern Historical Collection at the University of North Carolina, Chapel Hill, contain an unpublished biography of Knapp by Dudley W. and Charles R. Bagley, along with several of Knapp's letters.

Laurence W. Lane

(5 March 1890-20 February 1967)

John C. Bromley and Bruce W. McKinzie
University of Northern Colorado

MAJOR POSITION HELD: President, Lane Publishing Company (1928-1959).

MAGAZINE OWNED: *Sunset* (1928-1959).

PERIODICAL PUBLICATIONS: "We will edit *Sunset* for Westerners ... and for Westerners only," *Sunset,* 112 (February 1954): 14-15;
"The articles we don't print in *Sunset* ...," *Sunset,* 112 (April 1954): 26;
"For 25 years *Sunset* has been a how-to-do-it magazine," *Sunset,* 112 (May 1954): 16;
"Which *Sunset* do you read?" *Sunset,* 112 (June 1954): 16;
"Why is *Sunset* staff-written?" *Sunset,* 113 (July 1954): 16;
"Who reads *Sunset?*" *Sunset,* 113 (August 1954): 16;
"The advertising in *Sunset,*" *Sunset,* 113 (September 1954): 16;
"An unseen but vital influence on publishing integrity," *Sunset,* 113 (October 1954): 16;
"Why is *Sunset*'s subscription price higher outside the West?" *Sunset,* 113 (November 1954): 16;
"To improve *Sunset*'s service to Westerners," *Sunset,* 113 (December 1954): 12;
"Who is reading *Sunset* with you?" *Sunset,* 115 (October 1955): 13.

It is impossible to consider either the few successes or the many failures of the regional magazine in America apart from the career of Laurence W. Lane of *Sunset,* the transplanted Kansan who studied the American West with a scholar's eye and then grafted *Sunset* to the contours of the western topography and life-style. Lane was the founder of Lane Publishing Company, which is still the publisher of *Sunset* magazine, the Sunset Book series, and, more recently, *Sunset* films. He was remarkable, not only for the prosperity of his publishing ventures, but also for the stern integrity of his vision of the regional maga-

Laurence W. Lane (photograph by Jon Brenneis; courtesy of the Lane Publishing Company)

zine as the faithful servant both of readers and advertisers.

Born in Horton, Kansas, on 5 March 1890, Lane was raised first in Illinois and then in Iowa by his mother, Estella Louise Lane. His father, William Earl Lane, died when Lane was two. Lane redeemed his 1906 decision to drop out of high school by later finishing his remaining two years' work in a single year. Following his belated 1913 high-school graduation, Lane enrolled as a college student, first, but only briefly, at the University of Chicago, and then at Drake University. It was from Drake that he was graduated in 1917, capping a whirlwind year in which he also married Ruth Bell, the daughter of Drake University president Hill M. Bell, began work for the Meredith Publishing Company, and received his World War I commission as a lieutenant.

After the war Lane returned to Meredith, where he served first as personnel manager for *Successful Farming,* then as assistant advertising manager for *Better Homes and Gardens,* and finally as advertising manager for all the Meredith publications, including *Dairy Farmer.* It was in the early 1920s, and from the vantage point of a young publishing executive, that Lane began the journeys through the western United States that were to figure so prominently in the course of his later career.

It was in California, his son Laurence W. Lane, Jr., recalled in 1969, on a trip taken both by private railroad car and by stagecoach, that the elder Lane first captured his vivid sense of the extraordinary variety of the West, and of its sharp differences from the rest of the country. "The dramatic transition," said L. W. Lane, Jr., "from sea coast to broad valley to high mountains in only a few hours' time made a lasting impression on Dad, and convinced him that travel and recreation would increasingly play a significant role in the lives of Western families as one of the viable differences from the rest of the country."

Laurence Lane's extraordinary sense of the West–of western opportunities, and of western differences–was never to leave him, and in 1928 Lane resigned from Meredith to go to California and to *Sunset,* which, with the help of a Des Moines investors' group, he had bought for sixty-five thousand dollars.

Lane's new magazine had already been a considerable part of the history of California. Begun in 1898 by the Southern Pacific Railroad and named for its crack train, *Sunset Limited,* the magazine was developed as a method of publicizing the advantages of California life and travel, especially in the eastern United States. The Southern Pacific's urgent need for publicity about California passed, at least momentarily, and *Sunset* was sold in 1914 to its employees, who hoped to make it a literary magazine of national importance. The publication of work by Jack London, Ambrose Bierce, Erle Stanley Gardner, Vachel Lindsay, and Kathleen Norris established *Sunset* as a showcase for the era's writers. The high regard felt by the literary community for the pre-Lane *Sunset* was not, however, registered in sales or profit, for Lane was able to negotiate not only a low purchase price with his financially desperate predecessors but also a delay in assuming own-

ership until the former owners had helped raise circulation.

In February of 1929 Lane put out his first issue of *Sunset*–only eight months before the stock market crash engulfed the business community. But Lane brought to *Sunset* sufficient financial acumen to survive the Depression, although three reincorporations were required between 1928 and late 1933, and generous credit from both the magazine's printer and its paper supplier, to rescue *Sunset* from the edge of disaster. And he had brought with him, from his years at Meredith, many of the ideas with which he was to remake *Sunset*–and to make *Sunset* preeminent among regional magazines.

Lane was a meticulous planner, and he saw for the new *Sunset* a future based upon the divergence of the western United States from the rest of the country. In his travels through the broad expanse of America west of the Continental Divide, Lane saw an area made distinct by its climate, its patterns of marketing and distribution, its sparse settlement, and its magnificent travel opportunities. It became, in Lane's mind, the function of *Sunset* to serve readers and advertisers west of the Continental Divide with a zeal unmatched by any national or other regional magazines.

If *Sunset* was to be built upon regional differences, Lane had already had, in Meredith's *Successful Farming,* a model rooted in the distinct agricultural richness of his native Midwest. With this sense of geographical uniqueness Lane combined the practicality of the editorial content he had known in Meredith's *Better Homes and Gardens*–and *Sunset* was reborn as a western "how to" magazine.

In the *Sunset* formula Lane began to institute in his own first issues, and which he refined through the Depression years, lie the seeds of the primacy of *Sunset* among regional magazines. To Lane the West was a place apart, a place of year-round gardens, fresh local foods, year-round travel and vacations, and the land of the home patio. To this new life-style, prevalent only west of the Continental Divide, Lane brought his own intense sensitivity to the unique features of western life, and he restricted *Sunset* to an exploration of the American West in four areas only: food, travel, gardening, and home styles and modification.

The pages of *Sunset,* Lane hoped and believed through the early financial crises of his tenure, would appeal to the relatively affluent, the new class of single-family homeowners who

Lane (right) with his sons, Laurence William, Jr., and Melvin Bell

cooked in the western style, enjoyed holidays by automobile largely in their own western region, and undertook at least some of their own gardening and home renovation. And Lane was a prophet, for in the 1930s *Sunset* began to grow, not just in size (in 1932 several issues were no more than thirty-four pages long) but in circulation as well. By late 1932 the magazine's paid circulation was stabilized at a robust 203,059.

Lane did not tire of modifications. Impatient with wordiness, he asked one of his editors to condense information contained in past *Sunset* articles, and when the job was successfully done, it became the genesis of the magazine's staff-writing formula. Without bylines, Lane felt, readers would hold *Sunset* responsible for accuracy, rather than the writers. A survey in 1935 had shown him that readers remembered the content of relatively short articles best, and in consequence *Sunset* editors were made to require the short, fact-filled articles Lane felt his readers preferred. By February of 1936, with several *Sunset* branch offices in place, the magazine became the only completely staff-written magazine outside the news-weekly field. Lane wanted each *Sunset* story to teach readers, in the most practical terms, how to do something that they had not

been able to do before–a function he felt was left unfilled by the journals of byline and fiction so popular in the 1930s.

Even earlier, in 1932, Lane's concern with regionalism expressed itself further in his subdivision of the *Sunset* area into three separate zones divided by climate. This division, begun experimentally for a garden section as early as 1929, permitted the expression of divergences even within the *Sunset* region–just as *Sunset* itself had become the expression of the divergence of the West from national norms and trends. This process of subdivision represented what *Sunset* editor Ken Cooperider once referred to as "the first known example of a consumer magazine's 'zoning'–changing article content–to give different regions localized editorial service." Incentives to local advertisers were given as well, for an advertiser could come into one of the three new *Sunset* zones at a reduced rate.

Pressed by the Depression, Lane developed for *Sunset* in the 1930s a subscription strategy that was the envy of his competitors. Department-store charge-account lists became the basis of circulation promotionals, which provided *Sunset* with an automatic credit check and provided the charge-account customer, who could charge his

The Lane Publishing Company offices, erected in 1951, in Menlo Park, California (courtesy of the Lane Publishing Company)

Sunset subscription to his department-store account, with an easy way of paying for a new magazine in the cash-short Depression years. There were no door-to-door *Sunset* subscription salespeople, and no hucksterism. *Sunset* came to the potential subscriber as both a part and a reflection of the prestige of some of the best retailers in the *Sunset* area.

In 1938 *Sunset* turned its first profit, an event that became, like the color cover photographs that replaced the standard drawings in 1936, a *Sunset* tradition. And to the *Sunset* subscriber came another of Lane's innovations, the premium pamphlets that were the basis for the later Sunset Books. Arising essentially from *Sunset* magazine copy, the pamphlets were at first given away to the department-store charge-account customers who bought new *Sunset* subscriptions. But the department stores often asked for more of the *Sunset* pamphlets and wanted to

sell them separately. Just after World War II Lane created a separate division for books, and in 1946 the first hardcover, large-format Sunset Book was published.

In 1940, as *Sunset* circulation passed 250,000, Lane added the last of the prewar elements of his new magazine: a ban on beer and tobacco ads, which fortified an earlier prohibition against liquor advertisements. During World War II *Sunset* was restricted by the rationing of paper, but the magazine's growth at war's end was explosive. In 1947 circulation passed 300,000; a year later circulation had increased to 400,000. It was by then apparent that the Lane formula–the staff-written, western, "how-to," strongly family oriented magazine appealing chiefly to the crafts-minded owner of a detached home–had found a secure place.

Lane was to preside over the continued growth of his *Sunset* magazine and book empire until his retirement in 1959, relying increasingly on his two sons after their first appearance on the *Sunset* masthead in 1952. Hawaii was added to the *Sunset* territory in 1952, and in that year also the magazine crusaded for the preservation of California redwoods from logging. In 1954 Lane, his elder son, L. W. Lane, Jr., and his senior *Sunset* editor wrote a series of publishers' letters, signed by Laurence W. Lane, Sr., explaining the changes, essentially all completed by the beginning of World War II, that the senior Lane had made in *Sunset* magazine.

Only once more after World War II was the magazine stirred by Lane's restless innovation, in his 1951 corporate relocation to suburban Menlo Park. There, on seven acres of tree-studded land, Lane built his "laboratory of Western living," a low, spacious California mission-style office complex that now attracts more than fifty thousand visitors a year. Both *Time* and *Business Week* recorded the *Sunset* relocation to Menlo Park from San Francisco as a news event, the fulfillment of Lane's vision both of the West he described and the western life-style he came to share and symbolize.

Laurence Lane's contributions to American publishing stem, in large part, from the singular intensity of his vision. From the magazines he had known at Meredith he took both format and regional character, and from his distaste for verbosity he drew the compact, wholly staff-written style that was to satisfy the *Sunset* reader's need for practical advice. The synthesis among these elements became Lane's *Sunset*, and he defended the integrity of his conception from both the Depression and prosperity.

He refused on numerous occasions to modify his standards for potential advertisers, even in the days when he needed the money desperately, and he refused as well to open the columns of *Sunset* to subjects other than the four–gardens, travel, food, the home–he had preselected as right for the West.

By 1967 *Sunset* magazine had passed the three-quarter-million mark in circulation. That year the *Sunset* enterprise became international, as coverage was extended to the nations of the Pacific. Also in 1967 one-and-a-half million Sunset Books were sold.

Lane's activities with *Sunset* and the Lane Publishing Company earned him many professional and civic awards. In addition to his publishing duties he was a successful rancher and dedicated horseman, and a member of Kiwanis and the Bohemian Club of San Francisco. He died on 20 February 1967, at the age of seventy-six, in Portola Valley, California.

References:

"Glowing *Sunset*," *Newsweek*, 42 (2 November 1953): 56;

"Glowing *Sunset*," *Time*, 58 (15 October 1951): 84;

Proctor Mellquist, "*Sunset* is Unique as a Magazine," *Quill* (February 1954): 12-14;

Theodore Peterson, "The Golden Glow of *Sunset*," *Saturday Review*, 48 (13 March 1965): 146-147;

"*Sunset* Gold," *Time*, 32 (5 December 1938): 34;

"*Sunset* Proves a Regional Magazine Can Succeed," *Business Week* (13 October 1951): 62-69;

The Sunset Story (Menlo Park, Cal.: Lane, 1951);

"The *Sunset* Way," *Time*, 82 (1 November 1963): 73;

"*Sunset*'s Lawrence [*sic*] Lane: He found the rich western grazing lands," *Printer's Ink*, 268 (11 September 1959): 60-67;

"Welcome to *Sunset* and our 'Laboratory of Western Living,'" *Sunset*, 174 (March 1985): 143-146.

George Horace Lorimer

(6 October 1867-22 October 1937)

Terry Hynes
California State University, Fullerton

MAJOR POSITIONS HELD: Literary editor (1898-1899), managing editor (1899), editor in chief (1899-1936), *Saturday Evening Post;* member, board of directors (1903-1936), vice-president (1927-1932), president (1933-1934), chairman (1934-1936), Curtis Publishing Company.

BOOKS: *Letters from a Self-Made Merchant to His Son* (Boston: Small, Maynard, 1902; London: Methuen, 1912);
Old Gorgon Graham: More Letters from a Self-Made Merchant to His Son (New York: Doubleday, Page, 1904; London: Methuen, 1905);
The False Gods (New York: D. Appleton, 1906);
Jack Spurlock–Prodigal (New York: Doubleday, Page, 1908; London: J. Murray, 1908).

As editor of the *Saturday Evening Post* from 1899 to 1936 George Horace Lorimer built that publication into the most widely read magazine of the period. He infused the *Post* with the Puritan ethic of hard work and a sense of the American Dream, and under his leadership it became an icon of American middle-class values and thus earned a broad base of readership loyalty and advertising support.

Lorimer was born 6 October 1867 in Louisville, Kentucky. He was the fourth and youngest child as well as the only son of George Claude and Arabella Burford Lorimer. His father, then twenty-nine, was an evangelical Baptist minister who had come to the United States from his native Scotland in 1856. The elder Lorimer was a successful minister who devoted his energies to increasing church membership and eliminating his church's debts. As a result of his father's growing prominence, Lorimer lived in four cities before he was ready for college in the mid 1880s. The family moved to Albany, New York, in 1868, where they stayed for two years; then to Boston from 1870 until 1879, during which time Lorimer attended the Dwight School; and finally to Chicago, where he attended Mosely High School.

In one of his rare interviews, published in the 27 November 1926 issue of *Collier's*, Lorimer reported that during his early years his parents permitted him to read chiefly in history and religion. Not until he was almost sixteen was he allowed to read fiction; then he explored the writings of Sir Walter Scott, Charles Dickens, and William Makepeace Thackeray. Throughout his life he read voraciously. As editor of the *Post* he usually brought home manuscripts every evening and read them after dinner, until he went to bed at midnight. There, to relax, he read books on economics, biographies, and an occasional novel until one or two in the morning. He read and re-read masterpieces, as well as relatively trivial matter. He particularly liked Thomas Henry Huxley and Arthur Schopenhauer and said they would have been ideal writers of special articles for the *Post* because they wrote so clearly.

At his father's suggestion Lorimer entered Yale as a member of the class of 1888, but he stayed only through his freshman year. A chance encounter in Chicago with Philip D. Armour, the wealthy meat packer and one of his father's parishioners, led to a job with Armour's company. Lorimer's chief expectation of his job seems to have been that it would make him, as his boss had promised in that chance meeting, a millionaire. He started at the mail desk, working fourteen hours a day for ten dollars a week. After two years he was made assistant manager of the canning department, causing him to travel six months each year to Armour branches all over the country. Lorimer's biographer, John Tebbel, notes that this was invaluable experience for the man who was to become editor of one of the most popular magazines in United States history because it gave him "a sense of the whole living, breathing nation." It was from these travels, also, that Lorimer developed his deep, enduring love for the West and his zeal for conservation.

In 1892 Lorimer married Alma Viola Ennis, seventeen, the youngest daughter of a prominent Chicago judge and former lawyer for the Pullman Palace Car Company. For the next three years Lorimer remained at Armour's. During this period he was made head of the canning department and earned an annual salary of five thousand dollars, a substantial figure at that time. Ambitious, and apparently still eager to become a millionaire, Lorimer left Armour's for what turned out to be a disastrous venture into the wholesale grocery business. In the midst of this troubled time, Alma almost died of typhoid fever.

This business failure marked the major shift of Lorimer's career: he turned to writing. Many years later, in 1924, he wrote of this career change to a *Post* reader: "I went into newspaper work . . . for practical experience and training. I hoped to be both an editor and a writer. . . ." After a brief stint as a reporter for the *Boston Standard*, again at his father's urging he returned to college, this time to Colby College in Waterville, Maine, where he spent a year taking courses in En-

glish and history. Although information is sketchy, Lorimer appears to have spent part of his time during this year working as a correspondent for Boston and Maine newspapers. In addition, he wrote a novel, "The Search for Simpkins," which was never published in its original form but which provided material for other writings. According to Tebbel, Lorimer once said of this novel, "You see, it was a first novel, so I put everything that I knew in it. Whenever I wanted a story or an article or an editorial, I went to it and sawed out the proper lengths."

After a year at Colby, Lorimer returned to Boston and, through his father's influence (George Claude Lorimer, whom parishioners called "The Little Giant," had returned to Boston as pastor of Tremont Temple in 1891), got a job as a night reporter on the *Boston Post,* the local newspaper which appealed mainly to upper-class Democrats. His salary was eighteen dollars a week. When his boss refused his request for a two-dollar raise, Lorimer quit and went over to the *Boston Herald.*

Increasingly restless, when he saw a wire story reporting that Cyrus H. K. Curtis, publisher of the successful *Ladies' Home Journal,* had recently purchased the name and goodwill of the *Saturday Evening Post,* Lorimer asked Curtis for a job. Curtis, in Boston a week later on business, met with Lorimer in a local hotel and, after a two-minute (or one-half hour, or two-hour—depending on the source) interview, hired Lorimer to be the *Post*'s first (and last) literary editor.

The *Post* had been published almost continuously since its first issue appeared in 1821. The myth that the magazine was originated by Benjamin Franklin is rooted in the fact that its early issues were published in the same Philadelphia printing plant that had housed Franklin's *Pennsylvania Gazette.* This fact became muddled in the 1880s in some historical writings about Pennsylvania and, by the early 1890s, the owner of the *Post* was claiming Franklin as its founder. The Franklin connection was exaggerated further when, in its 29 January 1898 issue, three months after Curtis purchased the magazine, the line under the *Post*'s nameplate was changed to read "Founded A.D. 1728." In 1899 "by Benj. Franklin" was added after the year. Many connected with the magazine continued to claim this lineage even decades after Curtis and Lorimer were both gone.

In its first quarter-century the quality of the content of the *Post* was uneven both because of fre-

Lorimer in his office

quent changes in owners and editors and because, as one of the "weekly miscellanies" that were published for weekend reading, it was in a highly competitive field, especially before Sunday editions of newspapers became common.

Under the editorship of Henry Peterson, from the late 1840s through the Civil War, the *Post* was at the height of its early quality and popularity. It carried fiction by some of the most sought-after writers of the day, including E.D.E.N. Southworth, Fanny Fern (Sara Payson Willis Parton), and Charles Dickens; and it boasted, by the mid 1850s, a circulation of eighty to ninety thousand, the highest it achieved prior to Curtis's purchase. After Peterson sold it in 1873, however, the *Post* began to decline. By 1897, when Curtis purchased the magazine for one thousand dollars, its quality had deteriorated seriously; it published little editorial matter of any distinction in its unillustrated sixteen pages, and what paid advertising it had consisted mostly of patent medicine testimonials.

Its circulation, too, had withered. Sources differ, but Lorimer claimed the weekly circulation was 1,800; Frank Luther Mott claimed the subscription list had about 2,000 names in 1897; Tebbel said the paid circulation was 10,473; the

company itself, in a 1913 report on advertising, claimed the circulation was 3,000. "The *Post* was proud of its age," Mott said of the 1890s stage of the magazine. "Its age was about all it had left to be proud of."

Edward W. Bok, editor of the *Ladies' Home Journal* and Curtis's enthusiastic biographer, claimed that Curtis bought the *Post* with the clear intention of making it a male counterpart to his women's magazine. Mott disputes this and argues from evidence in the magazine itself that, in the early months under Curtis's ownership, the *Post* imitated the *Journal*, in content and style, perhaps a reflection of the fact that the first editor of the *Post* under Curtis, William George Jordan, had been part of the *Journal* staff. Unlike the monthly *Journal*, which sold for ten cents per copy, the *Post*, which had been bought by Curtis as a weekly newspaper, became under Lorimer a five-cent, weekly magazine. Its price was one half that of other major weeklies of the 1890s, such as *Harper's* and *Collier's*. The five-cent price became such a hallmark of the *Post* that Lorimer insisted on holding to it even during and after World War I when the cost of paper alone in some issues was as high as twenty-eight cents.

In February 1898 the annual subscription rate of the *Post* was raised from two dollars to two and one half; the single-copy price remained the same. According to Mott, by June of that year only 1,200 of the 2,000 subscribers remained. But in the same month a circulation drive was begun, and by December 1898 the *Post* claimed a subscription list of 250,000. (It is worth noting, of course, that prior to 1912 there was no legal sanction for misreporting circulation figures. Although, beginning in 1869, the annual Rowell—subsequently Ayer—and other similar directories were more credible than the self-reports by editors of newspapers and magazines, even these directories were not wholly accurate.)

Exactly when in 1898 Lorimer began working at the *Post* is not clear, but he appears to have served as literary editor for several months until, early in 1899, Curtis fired Jordan as editor and left for Europe to find a successor. Lorimer, at his own request, according to most accounts, was left in charge as managing editor of the magazine.

When Curtis returned from Europe he was sufficiently impressed with Lorimer's accomplishments that he made Lorimer editor in chief, effective 17 March 1899. Lorimer's name appeared as editor for the first time in the magazine in the 10

June 1899 issue (he developed a habit of saying he had been born in 1868 so that he could claim to have become editor of the magazine by the time he was thirty. During Lorimer's lifetime very few people knew the real year of his birth). Although his salary of forty dollars a week was relatively high, he still had to live frugally in order to save money to bring his wife and their baby daughter to Philadelphia from Boston. By Christmas they had arrived. Lorimer and his wife subsequently had three more children: another daughter and two sons, Graeme (who was born in 1903 and who, like his father, became a writer and editor at the *Post*) and George Burford, who was born in 1908. Both daughters died in childhood, the second, Belle, of spinal meningitis in 1908, four days before Burford's birth.

After he was made editor Lorimer proceeded to refashion the editorial and advertising content of the *Post* and to transform it from a weekly newspaper into a magazine. As managing editor he oversaw the inclusion of the first full-page advertisement to appear in the *Post* (for a Philadelphia seed company) in the 4 March 1899 issue. By 10 June 1899 the *Post* carried twenty-two ads on the last two pages of its sixteen-page edition. By the end of 1899 the pages were larger and the number of pages per issue had increased to twenty-four regularly and thirty-two occasionally. The first cover of the *Post* (2 September 1899), first color cover (30 September 1899), and first full-page color ad (for the Quaker Oats Company, also 30 September) had appeared. And Lorimer had attracted major writing talent, including Stephen Crane and Bret Harte, whose stories had appeared in the fall. Also by this time illustrations appeared frequently with fiction and nonfiction articles. Among the early illustrators for the *Post* were Harrison Fisher, Howard Chandler Christy, Francis Xavier and Joseph Christian Leyendecker, and George Gibbs. Thus, Lorimer had begun to achieve the goal he set for his magazine in a 30 September 1899 *Post* editorial: that it should "be the best and largest weekly magazine in the world."

Some of the early successes of the *Post* deserve to be credited directly to Curtis. His forte was advertising and promotion, and it was apparently he who, in the face of much skepticism about his ability to make a success of a nickel weekly, mounted an extensive campaign during 1899 to increase circulation and attract major, especially national, advertising. The campaign, which continued into the following year, included testimonial ads in publications such as *Printer's Ink,* in which advertisers themselves would extol the weekly, even daily, increases in the circulation of the *Post.* According to Bok, Curtis lost about eight hundred thousand dollars in the early years of trying to turn the *Post* into a financial success. For a time, circulation seemed to have reached a plateau. Then, in the fall of 1900 the annual subscription rate was lowered to one dollar. Before the year was over circulation had passed the 250,000 mark, where it had been stuck since late 1898, and advertising, which had earlier peaked at eight pages out of thirty-two (twenty-five percent), reached fourteen pages out of thirty-six (thirty-nine percent) in the pre-Christmas issue of 1900. (A 1926 study of advertising content in the *Post* showed a significantly steady increase from 1900 in the use of full-page ads as well as a corresponding decrease in smaller ads. The study also noted a similarly significant rise in the average annual proportion of advertising space to that of editorial content: the advertising space ratios rose from approximately thirteen percent in 1900 to almost fifty percent by 1910, and to almost sixty percent by 1920.)

By the end of 1901 the magazine's circulation had risen to approximately three hundred thousand and by early 1903 it was reported at five hundred thousand. Before 1903 ended, the covers of the *Post* indicated its circulation was at six hundred thousand and by March 1904 at seven hundred thousand. By the end of 1908 the *Post* boasted a circulation of more than 1 million. The *Post* reported its circulation at "more than two million" on its cover for 20 December 1913. Circulation slipped somewhat during World War I, but in 1919 the phrase "more than two million" was returned to the magazine's covers. By the late 1920s circulation had reached almost 3 million on an annual basis, and occasionally exceeded 3 million for single issues, giving it the largest circulation of any magazine in the world.

In 1909 the advertising rate was raised to three thousand dollars per page. By 1913 the cost of a full-page ad was forty-five hundred dollars. (By 1930 a full-page, black-and-white ad cost eight thousand dollars.) By 1910 total annual advertising revenue passed $5 million; by 1914 the total was more than $10 million. These increases occurred despite the fact that the *Post* did not accept ads for liquor, cigarettes, or patent medicines. Lorimer felt cigarette advertising should not be carried because young boys were selling the *Post.* He also banned liquor advertising, say-

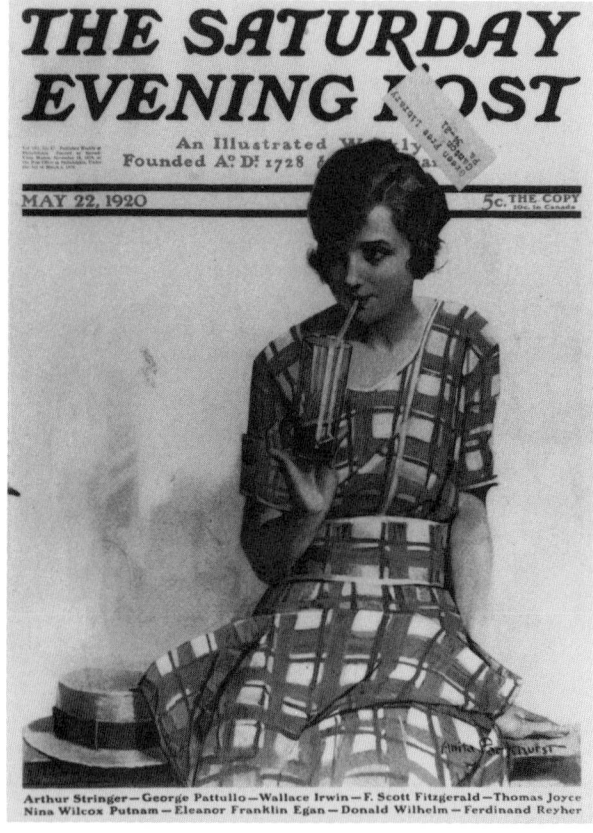

Covers for the magazine Lorimer edited from 1899 until 1936. During his tenure it obtained the largest circulation in the United States.

ing he did not want to encourage people to drink more than they already did. (Lorimer himself drank and smoked heavily–pipes, cigars, and more than two packages of cigarettes per day.) Nor did the *Post* carry any real estate or financial advertising because Lorimer wanted writers to feel free to write critically about those fields, and because he did not want to assume responsibility for any losses readers incurred as a result of investing in financial deals advertised in the magazine. In the Easter 1915 issue the *Post* reached 100 pages for the first time, with an unparalleled 229 columns of advertising. By the mid 1920s weekly issues of more than 250 pages became commonplace.

Lorimer's contribution on the editorial side was a determination to make the *Post* unlike the *Ladies' Home Journal*. His aim was to make the magazine appeal primarily to young, ambitious businessmen, men like himself, who believed in the middle-class American Dream and their ability to achieve it. But the content was also designed, especially after the early years of struggle to establish the magazine's new identity, to appeal to women or, more particularly, businessmen's wives. One reflection of the complexities of American culture during the progressive era is that the first decade of the twentieth century marked the growth of both a probusiness magazine like the *Post* and the muckraking phenomenon exhibited in magazines like *McClure's*, *Collier's*, and *Cosmopolitan*.

Lorimer established two policies to attract writers: prompt reading of manuscripts (a decision within seventy-two hours, when possible) and prompt payment for articles and stories accepted. Payment upon acceptance, in contrast to the common practice of payment on publication, provided writers with greater financial stability. Furthermore, Lorimer traveled frequently to New York in search of writers. These three elements figured strongly in the success of the magazine in its early years under his editorship. Another bonus for the writers whose works were published in the *Post* was that they were required to sell to the magazine only the North American periodical rights for their works, rather than all rights, and they could have the copyright on other aspects upon request. Other magazines soon had to follow Lorimer's lead, especially with respect to payment and copyright.

From the beginning Lorimer retained some of the romance content that had been the hallmark of the *Post* and added proportionately more material on business and public affairs. To Lori-

mer these were not necessarily mutually exclusive areas: for example, an article emphasizing business prospects in an exotic foreign country viewed as important to the United States would include all three. This new diversity in the magazine's content is reflected in titles and contributors that appeared during Lorimer's first year as editor: public affairs articles by former president Grover Cleveland, Speaker of the House Thomas B. Reed, and United States Senator Albert J. Beveridge; fiction by Hamlin Garland and Robert W. Chambers, among others; and business articles such as "Our New Prosperity," "Getting and Keeping a Business Position," and "Why Young Men Fail."

Lorimer's perception of business-related subjects was far from narrow. Anything that might affect business, from sports to science, literature to foreign affairs, photography to theater–and the humor that permitted one to maintain a sense of balance about the whole–could be cut and polished for the *Post* setting. By 1901 the business emphasis dominated the editorial policy of the *Post*: Brooklyn Mayor Charles Schieren wrote an article entitled "Why Young Men Should Begin at the Bottom," University of Chicago President William Harper provided "The Business Side of a University," and several financial leaders contributed to "Why Millionaires Can't Stop Making Money."

In Lorimer's hands, the fiction, too, would reflect American business themes. Lorimer told the *Collier's* interviewer in 1926 that when he became editor of the *Post* in 1899 he regarded fiction in American magazines as too imitative of British models, which, in his view, were based on a caste system and portrayed a life of leisure as an ideal goal. Lorimer believed such a view of the world could "have no wide appeal in a working democracy that measured human values by achievement, not inheritance." Some early titles illustrate how the business theme was incorporated into the fiction published in the *Post*: Henry K. Webster and Samuel Merwin's business romance about a grain elevator, "Calumet K: A Romance of the Great Wheat Corner," Frank Norris's *The Pit*, and Lorimer's own *Letters from a Self-Made Merchant to His Son*, a series of witty, pragmatic, fictional essays about business and life that appeared in the *Post* in 1901 and 1902. Norris's and Lorimer's works were subsequently published in book form and were listed by the *Bookman* as bestsellers for 1903. Lorimer's book was also published in England, Germany, and several other countries, remaining in print for many years. He wrote a sequel, *Old Gorgon Graham: More Letters from a Self-Made Merchant to His Son* (1904), which was serialized in the *Post* in 1904.

When he was asked why he did not write his autobiography, Lorimer reportedly always answered that it was being written every week in the pages of the *Post*. In its delineation of American business morals and manners, *Letters from a Self-Made Merchant to His Son* provides a vivid instance of Lorimer's own life, at least his views about how business dominates the lives of Americans. When the original, anonymous series of twenty "letters" ran in the magazine, it was believed that they were the main reason for the surge in the circulation of the *Post*. Reader response was startling: the magazine received about five thousand letters in reaction to the series before the end of 1901. Other publications mimicked and mocked the series with such titles as "Letters from a Son to His Self-Made Father," "Letters from a Self-Made Chorus Girl to her Hand-Made Mother," and "Letters from a Custom-Made Son to His Ready-Made Father." More than two decades later Will Rogers wrote a series for the *Post*, "Letters of a Self-Made Diplomat to His President," which echoed Lorimer's original work.

John Graham, the hero, was modeled loosely on Lorimer's former boss, P. D. Armour. The fictional Graham, known to his colleagues as "Old Gorgon Graham" (hence, the title of Lorimer's second series and book), was a Missourian who had been educated in the "School of Experience of the Great Southwest" and had become head of a pork-packing house in Chicago; his son, Pierrepont, was known to his friends facetiously as "Piggy." Graham's letters to his son at college were filled with advice about how to build a business and explicitly cautioned him that his father's wealth did not exempt him from the responsibility of making a man of himself, by himself. As Tebbel reports, when William Allen White was asked to write about *Letters from a Self-Made Merchant to His Son* for advertising purposes, he stated, "it reproduces and reflects Chicago. In no other book is the dirt and riches and unformed mass of the town more vividly yet unconsciously set down than in these 'Letters.' The book is Chicago boiled to an essence."

In the next few years Lorimer wrote two other books, *The False Gods* (1906), and *Jack Spurlock–Prodigal* (1908). Both reiterate the themes of the previous works, but neither was as commercially successful as his two earlier books, and Lorimer did not write any others after this period. *Jack Spurlock*, cast in novel form, reflects Lorimer's belief that one of the great defects of a university education was its failure to concern itself with what a person must do with his life after graduation.

Lorimer's recruiting efforts paid off in sustained loyalty by writers, many of whom referred to him affectionately as "the Boss" and, if they knew him well enough, addressed their letters "Dear Boss." By the end of Lorimer's first decade as editor, writers could earn as much as five hundred dollars for a top short story. By the end of the 1920s top writers could earn six thousand dollars for a short story and sixty thousand dollars for a serial. Mott notes, however, that it would be unfair to say Lorimer simply sought well-known writers without concern for the quality of their work. As Lorimer said to a *Post* writer, Isaac F. Marcosson, "One of the great fallacies in making magazines is the 'big name' fallacy. When you get a good story under a big name you have the ideal combination. But when you have the big name and a bad story, you simply disappoint the high expectations of your readers. I should always prefer a good story by an unknown man to a moderately good story by Kipling."

Lorimer was likewise loyal to his writers, but his allegiance did not extend to hiring them as regular staff members; it was his policy that each piece should be submitted on a free-lance basis. Lorimer expressed the rationale for this policy in a 1926 letter to the editor of a Kansas City newspaper: "We do not make contracts with writers as we believe their work deteriorates under the contract system." But the policy did not deter writers. By 1910 regular contributors included Mary Roberts Rinehart, who brought her "Tish" stories; and Montague Glass, whose long series of humorous stories about Potash & Perlmutter, partners in the New York cloak-and-suit trade, began the same year. Others who became well-known contributors in the early years of Lorimer's tenure include Irvin S. Cobb, George Randolph Chester, Jack London (whose *The Call of the Wild* was serialized in 1903), O. Henry, David Graham Phillips (whose *The Grain of Dust* was being serialized in the *Post* when Phillips was murdered in 1911), Booth Tarkington, Arthur Train, Samuel G. Blythe, Isaac F. Marcosson, Will Payne, and William Allen White.

Not everyone appreciated Lorimer's ambitions for, or accomplishments with, the *Post*.

Lorimer with his wife, Alma Viola Ennis, and their sons, Graeme (right), who was an associate editor at the Saturday Evening
Post *from 1932 until 1938, and George Burford (Historical Society of Pennsylvania, Philadelphia Record Collection)*

From his early years with the company, one of Lorimer's chief opponents was Curtis's son-in-law and editor of the *Ladies' Home Journal*, Edward Bok. Initially, Bok seems to have feared that the losses incurred by the *Post* would jeopardize the financial stability of the *Journal;* as Lorimer's success grew, Bok appears to have seen the *Post* editor as a rival for power within the company. Lorimer's position was secured, however, because of Curtis's support. The only time Curtis seems to have questioned Lorimer's judgment occurred at an early stage, when Curtis complained that his wife did not think that a recently published short story was suitable for the magazine. Lorimer supposedly responded, "I'm not editing the *Saturday Evening Post* for your wife." Curtis, apparently reassured that editorial decisions were in the hands of a man with clear vision for how to

make the *Post* a success, let the matter rest. Lorimer's salary was subsequently raised to $250 per week. Whenever he was asked, Curtis denied that he made any attempts to influence the contents or general running of the *Post* and often repeated what became his famous description of Lorimer's importance to the magazine: "Lorimer is the *Post* and the *Post* is Lorimer."

Bok's jealousy was primarily that of a professional colleague who shared his rival's values and goals. Others, less sympathetic to Lorimer's worldview, saw him as simplistic and even insolent. For example, in a biting critique published in *Outlook and Independent* in 1930, Benjamin Stolberg described Lorimer as one of those who suffer "a good deal from the parochialism of all the adjusted apologists for an arrogant culture." Stolberg castigated Lorimer for his complacency

The Saturday Evening Post *masthead, which appeared in the back of the magazine. The small number of associate editors is noteworthy.*

about the dominant standards of his era, for "flattening his whole outlook on life" in his dismissal of dissent about fundamental values and for an anti-intellectualism which prevented him from making the *Post* a genuine forum for public debate about major social concerns. For Lorimer, Stolberg claimed, "common sense," rather than a freshly reasoned consideration of evidence, was the court of last appeal in any dilemma. "He is irrationally contemptuous of everything 'intellectual' and insolently irritated with all dissent from the dominant standards. He protests his common sense too much. He defends not merely those truisms which are true enough, but all the flummeries of Rotary. . . . He betrays the stunted intellectual within him by his hatred of all free intellectual expression." Lorimer, according to Stolberg, had "a sure mastery of his opinions, especially when they matter to him, and then they grow muscular with ruthless prejudice."

This was not the first such criticism of Lorimer. Another commentator, Leon Whipple, had written in an earlier and generally balanced *Survey* article about Lorimer's "skilled direction of popular thought": "It replaces debate with a kind of Machiavellian paternalism; it molds popular thinking without popular knowledge; it blurs the picture by calculated emphasis and unsuspected omissions." In *Money Writes!* (1927), Upton Sinclair, one of the magazine's most caustic critics, wrote of the *Post:* its "stuff is as standardized as soda crackers; originality is taboo, new ideas are treason, social sympathy is a crime, and the one virtue of man is to produce larger and larger quantities of material things." As Mott notes, however, although the *Post* was generally conservative and became increasingly so after it grew successful, it was never wholly inhospitable to new ideas. Lorimer did give space to writers such as Leon Trotsky and Gertrude Stein, whose ideas he opposed. And, although Lorimer did not try to create a "literary" magazine, he managed to include in the pages of the *Post* representative examples of some of the best American and British fiction of the early twentieth century.

By the end of his first decade as editor in chief, Lorimer had established a pattern for the *Post* that remained essentially unchanged during the rest of his tenure. The modifications made during the next quarter century intensified the direction begun in the early years but did not alter that foundation in significant ways. (Lorimer once told a British writer that he believed great men are most interesting in the years before their greatness is recognized. To some extent, that may be said of his own work with the *Post.*) As Whipple noted in 1928, "The formula it [the *Post*] started with has simply been adapted to changing conditions. . . . What he started to do in the first years he is still doing, only bigger and better."

Unwritten policies required that the *Post* cover middle-class American manners and mores; so as manners and mores changed, the magazine's contents captured the shifts. As Americans developed a love for the automobile, for example, the pages of the *Post* mirrored the affair: the first automobile ad in the *Post* was a twenty-one-line entry by W. E. Roach in 1900. By 1914 more than forty manufacturers of automobiles and accessories advertised in the *Post*. By 1915, according to Mott, about one-fourth of the magazine's advertising was for automobiles and their accessories.

In the 1920s Anne Cameron's stories of the indigent, ever-cheerful Mrs. O'Malley, her family, and her car, captured one dimension of American life lived on the highway. By the mid 1930s Cameron's focus shifted slightly to reflect a growing trailer boom. (One critic has noted that Millie O'Malley is one of the few lower-class white heroines to appear in a *Post* story or series. The portrayal is not a positive one: Mrs. O'Malley is deceitful, neglects her children, and takes advantage of relief efforts. From a middle-class perspective, she may well have been a negative symbol of those on the dole. As a character she was an object of contempt and, thus, may have fed the myth that those on welfare were there because of their own failings.)

Another indicator of the magazine's sensitivity to social trends is F. Scott Fitzgerald's stories, which began appearing in 1920, of "flappers," the short-skirted, bobbed-haired younger female generation of the "Roaring Twenties." In another realm, when many critics in the late 1920s were dismissing "talkies" as a passing fad, Lorimer sent Wesley Stout to Hollywood to investigate the potential of the new kind of movies. "Beautiful, But No Longer Dumb" and "Lend Me Your Ears" were the resulting articles that reported the death of the silent picture.

Yet, Lorimer never forgot his audience. "He is never too far ahead of his day, never beyond the day after tomorrow," Stolberg wrote in describing what he saw as the editor's narrow vision. "But, above all, the essential shortness of his point of view has robbed him of the imagination beyond his immediate period. He is the child of a limited age. . . . He trimmed his philosophy to the pragmatism of one brief generation, and he identified it with the long destiny of a great people."

Lorimer was stunned by the outbreak of World War I, but he recovered quickly. When the war broke out, regular *Post* writers, including Irvin S. Cobb, Mary Roberts Rinehart, Isaac Marcosson, and Corra Harris, headed a group of *Post* correspondents in Europe. By the time the United States entered the war in 1917 Lorimer had attracted to the *Post* Ring Lardner, whose stories of the illiterate athlete Jack O'Keefe began in 1914; Harry Leon Wilson, whose Ma Pettingill character first appeared in the same year; Joseph Hergesheimer and P. G. Wodehouse, both of whose work first appeared in 1915 (although Wodehouse's first Jeeves stories did not appear until the following year); Sinclair Lewis; and Norman Rockwell, a twenty-two-year-old artist whose first cover appeared 20 May 1916 and whose work (324 covers and numerous illustrations for stories and ads) came to signify the essence of the *Post* and to embody its homey spirit of the American Dream. By 1919 Rockwell averaged a *Post* cover almost every six weeks, and Lorimer se-

lected Rockwell to paint the first four-color cover for the 6 February 1926 issue.

As a result of Lorimer's early efforts to attract writers, the *Post* developed a reputation of being especially hospitable to unknown writers and their work. In 1926 Lorimer's *Collier's* interviewer expressed this notion in glowing terms: "When something good from a new author reaches his desk he springs from his chair to spread the tidings to his subordinates and usually sends an assistant to see the new writer, wherever he or she may be, to give first-hand encouragement. He has been the literary name maker of a generation, and he is always on the hunt for new names." Lorimer had precise views about the role of an editor in the publishing process. As Frederick S. Bigelow said in 1936, "in general Mr. Lorimer operates on the rule that stories should be written by authors, not by editors. He is reluctant as a rule to offer plots, slow to suggest the revision of [an] unsatisfactory manuscript. The primary objection to both practices is that they tend to commit the editor to enterprises which may never work out properly." But Lorimer also was willing to trust his own judgment about the worth of a manuscript, even when all of his associate editors ruled against him. His acceptances of the first Ring Lardner "Busher" stories and John P. Marquand's "The Late George Apley," for example, were made over the dissents of his editors.

Lorimer's "favorite intellectual hobby," according to the *Collier's* interview, was biography. He viewed that genre as "a power for self-improvement, an inexhaustible fount of human interest." The *Post* reflected his belief by carrying many biographies and autobiographies during his tenure. Among those profiled were 1928 Democratic presidential candidate Al Smith, Benito Mussolini, film star Harold Lloyd, Jack Dempsey, Babe Ruth, and Sen. Huey Long, whose three-part biography began appearing in the *Post* only hours before he was assassinated in September 1935.

Not everyone saw a positive outcome to Lorimer's search for writing talent. Some critics argued that characters in *Post* fiction were often contrivances rather than rounded individuals and that the fiction had to fit Lorimer's outlook. "The *Saturday Evening Post* has done more to develop the technique of the short story as good composition and second-rate literature than any other periodical I know" was Stolberg's blistering critique. "It is the only magazine where one may

Table of Contents
May 29, 1920

SHORT STORIES

	PAGE
The Offshore Pirate—*F. Scott Fitzgerald*	10
Way I See It—*Sinclair Lewis*	14
Derelict Isle—*Elizabeth Frazer*	18
The House of Fuller—*Maryse Rutledge*	30

SERIALS

Gwen's Tongue—*Charles Brackett*	5
It's a Long Worm That Has No Turning—*Ferdinand Reyher*	24
The Man From Ashaluna—*Henry Payson Dowst*	26

ARTICLES

The Wonders of Washington—*George Kibbe Turner*	3
Handing it Back—*Kenneth L. Roberts*	8
Chasing the Rainbow—*George Pattullo*	12
White Lights and a Lean Larder—*Forrest Crissey*	16
The Leaven of the Pharisees—*William Allen White*	20
Sweden's Position in the New World of To-Day—*Ira N. Morris*	22
The Eternal Warfare—*Stanley M. Rinehart, M. D.*	40
School-Teachers	109

DEPARTMENTS

Editorial—*By the Editor*	28
Everybody's Business—*Floyd W. Parsons*	34
Sense and Nonsense	44
Small-Town Stuff—*Robert Quillen*	70

A Request for Change of Address must reach us at least thirty days before the date of the issue with which it is to take effect. Duplicate copies cannot be sent to replace those undelivered through failure to send such advance notice. Be sure to give your old address as well as the new one.

Table of contents showing a typical editorial mix

find a surprising amount of excellent writing which is not worth reading, except as an index of what the popular mind is allowed for its taste in the best of our mass periodicals. . . . Some of the most competent craftsmen have been among [Lorimer's] contributors. But not very often have even the gifted among them written also creatively. . . . But on the whole, fiction in the *Post* is clever, craftsmanlike and deftly commonplace when the writer is a good workman. When he is not, when his material is too flimsy for skilful construction then we get merely neat trash, carefully piled into the requisite number of columns. . . . The stories in the *Post* are at bottom really grown-up bedtime stories, putting to sleep the critical faculties." It was Stolberg, too, among others, who criticized the inherent racism in *Post* stories by Octavus Roy Cohen, whose work projected a broad and crude humor. Stolberg saw Cohen's

black characters as caricatures and his work as "obtuse and offensive travesties of the American race problem." Nevertheless, the popular stories ran for years in the *Post* because Lorimer judged their humor to be in good taste.

It is true that Lorimer insisted that stories and articles in the *Post* be free of any off-color situations or any suggestive elements that might be viewed as offensive in a publication read by every member of the family. One lapse in this requirement occurred in 1931. At the end of the first installment of Katharine Brush's "Red-Headed Woman," the secretary-heroine was having a late-night drink with her boss at his home while his wife was away. The second installment began with the secretary and boss having breakfast, the wife still away, and no clear explanation of what had transpired between the nightcap and breakfast. With characteristic sardonic humor Lorimer prepared a form letter to be used in responding to indignant readers. *"The Post,"* Lorimer wrote, "cannot be responsible for what the characters in its serials do between installments."

Although *Post* stories had their shortcomings, the positive assessment was aptly summed up by Bernard De Voto in his essay "Writing for Money" (*Saturday Review of Literature*, 9 October 1937) when he asserted that only two kinds of writers did not write for the *Post:* "Those who have independent means or make satisfactory incomes from their other writing and those who can't make the grade. Many of the former and practically all of the latter try to write for the *Post*." Lorimer also noted, in defense of the magazine, "In our experience, our severest critics are usually men who have been only superficial readers of the weekly and those who have been unsuccessful in their efforts to contribute to it."

Generally, Lorimer's political views reflected his perception that, as he said in 1919, "business is or should be the specialty of government." For a time during the progressive era Lorimer's friendship with Sen. Albert J. Beveridge led him to support reform efforts in the *Post* and even firmly to endorse the Progressive party in 1912, while strongly chastising the Republican party, which he later championed. But his vision and style were not even distant relations to those of the "muckrakers." As he reportedly said when muckraking was at its peak, "What this country needs are a lot of professional Pollyannas on the job. Norm is King!" Lorimer retained some progressive ideas throughout his career, however; for example, he clearly and consistently supported conservation efforts, including campaigns for national parks and forests, and for irrigation and reclamation. He supported Woodrow Wilson in 1916 in the hope that the president, seeking a second term, would fulfill the promise of his campaign slogan to "keep us out of war," but when Wilson abandoned that policy in 1917, Lorimer abandoned Wilson. Although he remained supportive of the administration out of a sense of patriotism while the United States was involved in the war, Lorimer never got over Wilson's policy reversal. It turned him against the Democrats permanently. From that time, although he did not belong to any political party, he actively supported the Republican party and its positions in the magazine.

In the postwar years Lorimer supported isolationism and crusaded in the pages of the *Post* to keep the United States out of what he saw as entangling alliances with Europe. His position on isolation seems puzzlingly naive because he sought at the same time world markets for the goods being produced by businesses in the United States. He opposed the League of Nations, as he said in his *Collier's* interview, "not because of its promises but because of its failures to perform. European nations play international poker for blood, while we play it for beans. We simply don't know enough about their game to sit in." During the 1920s Lorimer fought to keep Europe out of the United States by arguing for restricted immigration and against cancellation of war debts. His editorials on the subject of immigration were both eloquent and, if not racist, at least chauvinistic. In the May 1922 issue of the *Post* he wrote, "The trouble with our Americanization program is that a large part of our recent immigrants can never become Americans. They will always be Americanski—near-Americans with un-American ideas and ideals." Regarding the war debts, year after year he fought against anyone who proposed canceling any part of Europe's obligations. Lorimer seems to have had no perception of the growing interdependence of nations in the postwar era; he still thought of the United States in its pre-World War I status.

For Lorimer, the model of progress and source of solutions lay in American business. He believed that improvements in the conduct of business during his professional lifetime were the major cause of increased distribution of wealth and "vast material and moral progress." Furthermore, Lorimer declared in the *Collier's* interview, "Business ethics shows a striking improvement over the rough-and-tumble tactics of the '90s. . . . Industrial disputes are more rare and more readily settled because labor and capital have both learned from the foolish past. The old-time hard-boiled employer is passing, because it is an axiom of industry that no business can be in a truly sound and flourishing condition if disharmony and suspicion prevail in it. . . . There is no finer product of modern civilization than the American business man. Because he is largely inarticulate . . . he is portrayed as a money-grubbing ignoramus, when in fact he is often more clear-headed, more clear-thinking and better educated than his critics. For every money grubber we have a constructive business genius who works on for the love of the work, because he is actually making the world a better place to live in, while his critics are only talking about making it a better place to live in."

Lorimer viewed American business as one happy family; he refused to see any antagonistic relationship between labor and management. Whipple quotes Lorimer as saying, "The editor of *The Post* has never visualized industrial America as the home of two opposing parties . . . and it has therefore never occurred to him to present the news of industrial developments as if it were the news of two opposing armies. We are all Americans together and all trying to get a living. . . . For the past generation *The Post* has been preaching high wages and low costs. During that period unprecedented progress has been made in attaining these ideals until today the American workingman is the happiest, healthiest, and best paid in the world."

Some of Lorimer's critics objected to what they saw as his naive view of the positive values of the business ethic. They argued that the veil of romantic adventure which surrounded Lorimer's portrayal of American business applied only to those with power, the captains of industry and business managers. Such critics said that Lorimer failed to acknowledge the spirit-depleting experience that constituted the jobs of ordinary workers. As Whipple noted in 1928, "If work is the soul of America, then it must feed the souls of all of us. *The Post* does not live up to its own doctrine; and the reason it is so bitterly reviled by radicals is that it does not hasten, but retards the seeking of labor to have a creative and democratic control over its own destiny." Two years later Stolberg wrote of Lorimer, "Probably more than any one else he trained the American people to see high adventure in the business game and to believe in the ethics of its sociology. He helped to fashion a public mind which wanted national prosperity, with merely nominal reference to distributive justice, for the scaffolding of the national attitudes. He has been editing a national outlook for a business society."

One of the challenges Lorimer faced in the immediate postwar years was a succession of raids on his most frequent and popular contributors, by Ray Long of William Randolph Hearst's *Cosmopolitan*. Among those Long succeeded in luring away were Ring Lardner, Peter B. Kyne, and P. G. Wodehouse. But the defection of Irvin S. Cobb, one of Lorimer's close friends, was perhaps the most painful. The *Post* also lost some writers as a result of both the postwar boom in the magazine market and the lure of Hollywood, where increasing numbers of writers went to make their fortunes writing scripts for motion pic-

Lorimer, circa 1936, when he retired as editor of the Saturday Evening Post *(UPI/Bettmann Newsphotos)*

tures. And, as a different style of realistic writing became popular, the magazine lost its way for a time. Lorimer recovered by hiring new associate editors and buying the work of new writers such as John P. Marquand, Kenneth Roberts, Sophie Kerr, William Faulkner, and Thomas Wolfe, although, of course, the work of some of the old favorites, such as Mary Roberts Rinehart, continued to appear.

Thomas B. Costain, who was hired in 1920 and was, perhaps, the most ambitious of the new editors, persuaded several of the "defectors" to return, including Ben Ames Williams, Clarence Budington Kelland, P. G. Wodehouse, and Booth Tarkington. Costain was less successful, however, in persuading Lorimer about the value of photography. Lorimer trusted Costain, and although their relationship over the years was somewhat rocky, when Costain resigned in 1934 and went to Hollywood their parting was amicable. Another of the new editors, Wesley Stout, came to the *Post* in 1922. Stout recognized that Lorimer had become too complacent about the success of the *Post*. Of all the new editors he was the most like Lorimer and ultimately succeeded "the Boss" as the magazine's editor when Lorimer retired in 1936. The rejuvenation of the staff in the 1920s helped the magazine recover its leadership role, although Lorimer, as always, had a hard time delegating authority. The magazine's resurgence reached its peak in 1929 and its largest issue appeared more than a month after the stock-market crash.

Among Lorimer's long-time, trusted staffers was one of the few women who worked as an associate editor on the *Post*, Adelaide Neall. It was a general rule at the magazine that no married woman could be on the staff because Lorimer believed no woman could do two jobs well. Lorimer met Miss Neall in 1908 on one of his almost-annual trips with his family to the western United States. She had been graduated from Bryn Mawr the previous year. In August 1909 she began work at the *Post* as Lorimer's chief editorial aide and remained in that position until he retired. Often, when he was finished with a day's work, he would sit down with her or another trusted editor and talk shop. Whenever he was away, he relied on her to write him daily and keep him abreast of what was happening at the magazine.

In 1931 Lorimer changed the publication day of the *Post* from the traditional Thursday to Tuesday of each week. By summer of that year advertising revenues had fallen substantially and some issues of the *Post* had fewer than one hundred pages–about one-third to one-half the pre-1930 size. Also in 1931 the *Post* lifted its traditional taboo against cigarette advertising, but that was not enough to stop the financial erosion. By the end of 1932, as the result of a continuing decline, some issues had only sixty pages, including twelve to fifteen pages of advertising. In 1933 ad-

vertising revenues were below $18 million, slightly more than one-third of the magazine's 1929 revenues of $50 million. Circulation, on the other hand, after a slight decline from 1933 to 1935, was relatively stable and in 1937, after Lorimer had retired, again reached–and maintained–three million copies per issue. Maximizing the timeliness of the magazine's contents was no small feat under any circumstances since, by this stage of its development, issues of the *Post* were made up five weeks in advance of reaching its readers.

Although in his early years as editor Lorimer reportedly read every manuscript that was submitted to the magazine, after the *Post* became successful that would have been an impossible feat by virtue of the sheer volume of material. By the mid 1930s the *Post* received approximately seventy thousand manuscripts per year. Still, however, Lorimer continued to read everything that appeared in the magazine, advertising as well as editorial content, even when its pages exceeded 250 per week.

Lorimer's involvement with the advertising aspects of the *Post* is somewhat paradoxical because, on the one hand, he had a strict policy keeping the advertising and editorial departments separate in order to prevent advertisers from pressuring the magazine to alter any editorial content. The long-term absence of liquor, cigarette, and financial advertising reflects his resistance to advertiser pressures. Lorimer also refused (and insisted his editors refuse) junkets and "freebies" offered by advertisers. And only in extremely rare instances did Lorimer permit his name to be used in support of a cause. He even pulled stories from the magazine right up to a deadline if he discovered that the advertising department had sold space as a tie-in to the editorial content. In some instances, when advertisers tried to pressure him personally, he would simply ban the relevant topic from the editorial section for as long as a year.

On the other hand, Lorimer was involved with the advertising department of the *Post* almost from his earliest days with the magazine, first because Cyrus Curtis believed that the editors knew his magazines better than anyone else and, therefore, were the best people to sell them. Thus, Lorimer wrote many of the newspaper and trade publication ads for the *Post* in the early years. Moreover, after becoming a director of the company in 1903, Lorimer was naturally more deeply involved in the business affairs of the company than is normally the case for an editor. Over the years, his business-related responsibilities grew.

Lorimer, who had been a member of the board of directors of Curtis Publishing Company since 1903, became vice-president of the company in 1927. In the same year he was given one of the highest honors the Italian government could confer upon a foreigner, when he was made a Commander of the Crown of Italy. He had long since achieved the financial goal he had set when he went to work for Armour, namely, to become a millionaire. His personal fortune reached a peak of $10 million in 1923. When he died it was still intact.

When they were still good friends, Irvin S. Cobb called Lorimer "the original easy boss." In 1918 Cobb described the editor as "a compactly built, rather sinewy looking man with a long, strong, angular jaw, a small, keen, blue eye and a squarish think-box of a head thatched with brown hair which is beginning to turn gray above the lean temples." Ten years later Whipple's physical description of "the Boss" was similar, but he also saw character traits in the physical ones: "He seems designed for hard work and high tensions without frictions or torsions. His eyes give you a jolt of power and his voice has the resonant burn of success and high energy. He looks healthy and happy. . . .He is arrogant . . . but passionately sincere."

Lorimer disliked almost all sports, although he would play golf with Curtis if he were drafted. He had little appreciation for classical music or the theater, although he would attend the opera or similar functions if his wife insisted. Away from the magazine, he loved most having a good time with his family and friends. Almost penurious with expense accounts for the *Post,* he spent lavishly when entertaining.

Lorimer had two leisure-time passions: the outdoors and collecting antiques. His deep love for the outdoors manifested itself not only in his lifelong support for conservation but in a zeal for tree planting (Lorimer supervised the planting of nearly a million trees in and around Philadelphia). He owned an eleven-hundred-acre farm about six miles from his home at Wyncote and visited it whenever possible. At Wyncote he planted oaks, azaleas, and masses of rhododendrons. One of the only two public offices Lorimer ever accepted was an appointment by Pres. Herbert Hoover to the Commission on Conservation and Administration of the Public Domain. (The other

Lorimer at the Grand Canyon

was an earlier appointment by Pres. Woodrow Wilson as chairman of a committee for Chinese relief.) He had an interest in the national parks that amounted almost to a pride of ownership, and he was recognized and given special hospitality when he visited them on his trips west. His most frequent trips were to the Rocky Mountain region and the Grand Canyon, one of the few things that awed him. He was enamored of the beauty of the West generally, but of the Grand Canyon most particularly and, after his wife Alma introduced him to it, he almost never went West without stopping to see it. He would sometimes stand silent at the canyon's edge for an hour at a time, oblivious even to his family and friends.

Collecting antiques, including tapestries and British porcelain but especially antique glass, was another source of endless pleasure for Lorimer. He permitted himself frequent forays in pursuit of a rare piece, often in the company of one or more of his collector-friends, who were also *Post* contributors. These antique hunters included

Kenneth Roberts, Joseph Hergesheimer, Edwin Lefevre, and Hugh Kahler, and their camaraderie was of the special kind shared by devotees. Lefevre, the *Post* financial writer who reported on Wall Street, was the most serious of the group besides Lorimer about antiquing and shared "the Boss's" bottle mania. Lefevre's single-minded pursuit of a rare bottle was a constant source of fun for his friends. Roberts's 1928 book, *Antiquamania,* captured the essence of the antique-hunting trips with some of the quiet humor that pervades Lorimer's own letters on the subject. Lorimer was a shrewd buyer and was respected by other collectors. After his death in 1937 the best of his early American glass and furniture was placed in the Philadelphia Museum of Art. The remainder, after his family had selected other choice pieces, brought more than $1 million at a series of public auctions in New York.

In October 1932 Lorimer became president of the company after Curtis resigned following a heart attack he had experienced during the summer. By this time Lorimer's annual income was more than one hundred thousand dollars. He served as both president of the company and editor of the *Post* until, just over two years later, he gave up the presidency and became chairman of the board. While he was president, however, he managed to salvage the *Ladies' Home Journal* from the continuing decline it had suffered since Bok's departure in 1919; he persuaded Bruce and Beatrice Blackman Gould to join the *Journal* as co-editors. Beatrice Gould worked only three days a week, the first woman executive the company accommodated with a part-time schedule.

By the early 1930s the nation had changed in ways that Lorimer could neither foresee nor accept. A close friend of Herbert Hoover and an active Hoover supporter in the presidential elections of 1928 and 1932, Lorimer strenuously opposed Franklin Delano Roosevelt and continued the battle in an almost relentless fashion after the campaign was over. He firmly believed that the New Deal "would retard or prevent genuine recovery rather than produce it." He worked vigorously during his last years as editor of the *Post* to expose in the pages of his magazine any shortcomings he could uncover in Roosevelt's plans for renewal.

After Roosevelt's reelection in 1936 Lorimer retired, aware that the mood of the country escaped him but still unable to accept either intellectually or emotionally what had happened. Hundreds of thousands of readers wrote to the magazine to express their disappointment at his retirement. Before the next year was over, on 22 October 1937, after a bout with pneumonia, but primarily as a result of throat cancer, Lorimer died at his home just outside Philadelphia. With him when he died were his wife and two sons. Alma Lorimer, who had many accomplishments in her own right, particularly through her leadership in the Republican Women of Pennsylvania, died in 1941.

Lorimer was a generous philanthropist. He gave hundreds of thousands of dollars to the Benjamin Franklin Memorial Fund; the Franklin Art Museum (for a "museum of electricity"); the Philadelphia Museum of Art, Colby College (for a chapel in memory of his father); and Abington Memorial Hospital. He rarely referred to his charity or to the honors he received, including honorary doctoral degrees from Colby, McGill, and Colgate universities.

Although Lorimer had his critics, partly because of his overly optimistic faith in what he called "the good sense, good judgment, and good taste of our popular audience," he also, as many commentators have said, interpreted America to Americans during nearly forty years as editor of one of the most successful and significant American magazines. Some said his success stemmed from the fact that he edited the *Post* to please himself as a typical American and thus pleased other typical Americans. The sources of his success were more complex, however. For decades he had a superb sense of timing, a feeling for the flow of events that was sometimes referred to as "Post luck" because of the frequent coincidence between articles in the magazine and current news events. It sometimes seemed that Lorimer had an uncanny ability to anticipate public events. He had the good fortune to be a firm believer in business when business and its values were on the ascendancy in the United States. For most of his professional career he "had a sense of the wind, knowing always where it was and when it changed and what was likely to be riding it," as Garet Garrett, a *Post* political writer who began contributing to the magazine after World War I, said in the obituary of Lorimer, published in the 27 November 1937 issue. By whatever name, that sense helped Lorimer produce a magazine that served for many years as a mirror of a broad spectrum of American culture.

Interviews:

John B. Kennedy, "Nothing Succeeds Like Common Sense: Interview With George Horace Lorimer," *Collier's,* 78 (27 November 1926): 8, 47-48;

Milton Glaser, "The Importance of Being Rockwell," *Columbia Journalism Review,* 184 (November/December 1979): 40-42.

Biography:

John Tebbel, *George Horace Lorimer and The Saturday Evening Post* (Garden City, N.Y.: Doubleday, 1948).

References:

Frederick S. Bigelow, *A Short History of The Saturday Evening Post* (Philadelphia: Curtis, 1936);

Edward W. Bok, *A Man From Maine* (New York: Scribners, 1923);

Irvin S. Cobb, "George Horace Lorimer, Original Easy Boss," *Bookman,* 48 (December 1918): 389-394;

Jan Cohn, *Creating America: George Horace Lorimer and the Saturday Evening Post* (Pittsburgh: University of Pittsburgh Press, 1989);

Charles Hall Garrett, "The Arrival of George Horace Lorimer," *Reader,* 4 (October 1903): 497-502;

Maureen Honey, "Images of Women in the *Saturday Evening Post,* 1931-1936," *Journal of Popular Culture,* 10 (Fall 1976): 353-358;

Frank Luther Mott, *A History of American Magazines,* volume 4 (Cambridge: Harvard University Press, 1957), pp. 671-716;

Benjamin Stolberg, "Merchant in Letters: Portrait of George Horace Lorimer," *Outlook and Independent,* 155 (21 May 1930): 82-86, 115-117;

C. J. Warden, Earl Yahn, Gordon Lewis, and Thora Eigenmann, "A Study of Certain Aspects of Advertising in *The Saturday Evening Post,*" *Journal of Applied Psychology,* 10 (March 1926): 63-66;

Leon Whipple, "SatEvePost: Mirror of These States," *Survey,* 59 (1 March 1928): 699-703.

Papers:

Lorimer's office correspondence and personal letters (about five thousand items) and four unsigned biographical sketches probably written by him are in the Historical Society of Pennsylvania, Philadelphia.

Henry R. Luce

(3 April 1898-28 February 1967)

C. Zoe Smith
Marquette University

MAJOR POSITIONS HELD: Editor in chief, Time Inc. publications (1923-1964); editorial chairman, Time Inc. (1904-1907).

PRINCIPAL MAGAZINES OWNED OR CONTROLLED: *Time* (1923-1964), *Fortune* (1930-1964), *Architectural Forum* (1932-1964), *Life* (1936-1964), *Sports Illustrated* (1954-1964).

BOOKS: *The American Century, by Henry R. Luce; With Comments by Dorothy Thompson, John Chamberlain, Quincy Howe, Robert G. Spivack, and Robert E. Sherwood* (New York & Toronto: Farrar & Rinehart, 1941);
Towards Freedom: India and the World, by Luce, Wendell Willkie, Jawaharlal Nehru, Lin Yutang, and others (Bombay: International Book House, 1943);
The Dangerous Age of Abundance (New York: Newcomen Society in North America, 1959);
The Ideas of Henry Luce, edited by John K. Jessup (New York: Atheneum, 1969).

SELECTED PERIODICAL PUBLICATIONS
UNCOLLECTED: "Let It Die!," *Saturday Review of Literature*, 5 (27 October 1928): 296-297;
"The Press is Peculiar," *Saturday Review of Literature*, 7 (7 March 1931): 646-647;
"America and Armageddon," *Life*, 9 (3 June 1940): 40, 100;
"National Unity: We Must Not Falter Now," *Vital Speeches of the Day*, 6 (15 June 1940): 523-524;
"This Great Moment," *Life*, 9 (21 October 1940): 29-30;
"China to the Mountains," *Life*, 10 (30 June 1941): 82-86, 88, 90-91, 93-94, 96;
"The Day of Wrath," *Life*, 11 (22 December 1941): 11-12;
"America's War and America's Peace," *Life*, 12 (16 February 1942): 82-86, 88-91;
"The New Age of the Church," *Christian Century*, 64 (19 March 1947): 362-365;

Henry R. Luce (Gale International Portrait Gallery)

"The Reformation of the World's Economies," *Fortune*, 41 (February 1950): 58-63;
"Moral Law in a Reeling World," *Christian Century*, 67 (May 1950): 553-554;
"Holmes Was Wrong," *Fortune*, 43 (June 1951): 85-86;
"Reverse Mr. Justice Holmes," *Vital Speeches of the Day*, 17 (15 July 1951): 596-599;
"America and Asia," *Life*, 34 (23 February 1953): 120-122, 125-126, 128, 131-132, 134;
"Responsibility of the Press in the Cold War," *Vital Speeches of the Day*, 19 (1 April 1953): 368-372;
"The Promised Land," *New Republic*, 131 (6 December 1954): 19-21;

"A Speculation about A.D. 1980," *Fortune*, 52 (December 1955): 104-105, 214, 217-218, 220, 222, 224;

"The Character of the Businessman," *Fortune*, 56 (August 1957): 108-109;

"To Ike, the Wall Rises Between Opposing Ideas of Man," *Life*, 51 (8 September 1961): 46-49;

"Letter to the Publisher," *Sports Illustrated*, 21 (17 August 1964): 4;

"A Great Thinker's Joyful Vision: the Spiritual Perfection of Mankind," *Life*, 57 (16 October 1964): 12;

"The First Thirty-Five Years of *Fortune*," *Fortune*, 71 (February 1965): 136-137, 184, 189-190;

"To See Life in Its Full Dimensions," *Fortune*, 75 (January 1967): 88.

OTHER: Clare Boothe Luce, *Margin for Error: A Satirical Melodrama*, introduction by Henry R. Luce (New York: Random House, 1940).

Few American publishers in the twentieth century achieved the success or international reputation Henry R. Luce did during his sixty-eight years. A controversial yet influential figure, Luce is best remembered as founder of *Time, Fortune, Life, Sports Illustrated*, and Time-Life Books. Herbert R. Mayes, editor at large of *Saturday Review*, said of his contemporary: "No man in our time made as forceful an impact on magazine journalism as he did."

Henry Robinson Luce was born on 3 April 1898 in Tengchow, China, where his parents, Henry Winters and Elizabeth Root Luce, were American Presbyterian missionaries and educators. His extraordinary background helped shape his lifelong interest in theology, Christianity, and Far Eastern affairs. These concerns often made their way into the content of his magazines. Luce was an avid reader all his life, and by the time he went at the age of fifteen to the Hotchkiss School in Lakeville, Connecticut, he was a world traveler as well. He had visited the United States with his parents at the age of seven, studied in northern China at the British Chefoo School, and journeyed alone to England to study briefly at St. Albans.

At the Hotchkiss School, where he worked to help pay his way, Luce met Briton Hadden, a fiercely competitive Brooklyn boy from a well-to-do family. Both young men went to Yale in 1916, where Luce became managing editor and Hadden chairman of the student newspaper, the *Yale*

Daily News. Luce and Hadden interrupted their studies during World War I to enlist in the Student Army Training Corps. They were stationed at Camp Jackson, near Columbia, South Carolina. Both became second lieutenants and student officer instructors, but they did not see active service overseas. According to Luce, the idea for *Time* was first discussed with Hadden at Camp Jackson.

After returning to Yale, Luce and Hadden graduated in 1920, and Luce then went back to England for a year to study history at Oxford. While on a European tour he met Lila Ross Hotz, a sophisticated young woman from a wealthy Chicago family. Luce went to Chicago in 1921 to work at the *Daily News* for sixteen dollars a week as an assistant to columnist Ben Hecht. However, he soon moved on to the *Baltimore News* with Hadden, who had been working at the *New York World*. During their brief time together in Baltimore Luce and Hadden decided to bring to fruition their idea of starting a weekly newsmagazine. Early in 1922 they left the *News* with the understanding that they could return to their jobs if the project was a failure.

To raise the capital needed to fund their new venture Luce and Hadden sold stock. Working out of an old remodeled house on East Seventeenth Street, they wrote a prospectus that said, in part, "People are uninformed because no publication has adapted itself to the time which busy men are able to spend on simply keeping informed. TIME is interested not in how much it includes between its covers but in how much it gets off its pages into the minds of its readers. To keep men well-informed—that, first and last, is the only ax this magazine has to grind . . . the editors recognize that complete neutrality on public questions and important news is probably as undesirable as it is impossible, and are therefore ready to acknowledge certain prejudices."

With the help of this twelve-page-prospectus they gathered eighty-six thousand dollars (short of their one-hundred-thousand-dollar goal) in a little more than a year from seventy-two investors, including relatives, friends, and an elderly, philanthropic woman, Mrs. William L. Harkness, who pledged twenty thousand dollars. Although they considered calling the magazine "Facts," they settled on the name *Time* before publishing the first issue on 3 March 1923 with an initial circulation of nine thousand.

The two men formed an effective team in spite of the fact that they had very different per-

Briton Hadden, Luce, and city manager William R. Hopkins, who is holding the first issue of Time *that was printed in Cleveland. Time Inc. moved from New York to Cleveland in 1925 in order to cut production costs. The organization moved back to New York in 1927.*

sonalities. Hadden, considered the more creative of the two, had the charm and social graces Luce seemed to lack. In comparison to the flamboyant Hadden, Luce, at twenty-five, seemed prematurely middle-aged and settled. On 22 December 1923 Luce married Lila Hotz (they had two sons, Henry Robinson III and Peter Paul). Because of Luce's small salary Lila's mother subsidized his thirty- to forty-dollar-a-week salary and retained a day maid to clean their four-room apartment on Fifth Avenue. This parental assistance was not needed for long; the Luces were living in a fashionable townhouse on East Forty-ninth Street by their fifth wedding anniversary.

Luce and Hadden had planned to alternate annually their jobs as editor and business manager, but Hadden ended up spending the first three years at *Time* as managing editor, while Luce wrote for the religion department and served as business manager. Listed on the first masthead were eighteen people, including eleven Yale alumni, most quite inexperienced. Early issues of the magazine looked rather crude; budget-

ing concerns prohibited the use of many photographs, and it was nearly a year before *Time* was printed on slick paper stock. The now-famous red border on the cover was not used until nearly the end of the third year, when the first color advertising also appeared.

For the first four years Hadden and Luce did what they could to get the magazine established, which included the cost-cutting measure of moving the headquarters in September 1925 to Cleveland, where the magazine's printer was located and rents and salaries were cheaper. The operation moved back to New York City after nearly two years in Ohio. In 1925 Time Inc. also began sponsoring the "March of Time" radio series as a promotional device for the magazine. Although circulation more than doubled within the first year, it took until 1927 for *Time* to be securely in the black. Nevertheless, by the time they were thirty years old Luce and Hadden were millionaires.

In April 1927 the two men expanded their holdings by purchasing *Tide,* an advertising trade

Covers for the first issues of two of the magazines Luce founded after Time *(copyright Time Inc.)*

Luce in 1941

magazine similar to *Time* in format and the summary-style presentation of news. The death of Hadden on 27 February 1929, of a streptococcus infection, along with plans to begin another magazine, prompted Luce to sell *Tide* in late 1930 to Raymond Rubicam, cofounder of the Young & Rubicam advertising agency.

Despite his untimely death Hadden left his mark on Luce and *Time*. The two young men, without any professional magazine experience, had developed a new type of publication–the newsmagazine–though it was Hadden, according to journalist Joseph Epstein, who "invented the notorious *Timestyle*, with its double barreled adjectives and inverted syntax."

Luce and Hadden had talked about starting a high-priced magazine for businessmen, initially called "Power" but later changed to *Fortune*. The business-section writers of *Time* routinely had

many more stories than could be used each week, so Luce thought this material could be the basis for a limited-circulation publication. This new magazine was to concentrate on business affairs because, as outlined in the prospectus, "Business is the greatest single denominator of interest among the active leading citizens of the U.S. . . . *Fortune*'s purpose is to reflect Industrial Life in ink and paper and word and picture as the finest skyscraper reflects it in steel and architecture."

Just as the first issue of *Fortune* was about to be published (at an unheard-of cost of one dollar a copy), the stock market collapsed and the Great Depression began. In spite of this seemingly unfortunate timing, the first issue, dated February 1930, was mailed to 30,000 subscribers; by 1936 the subscriptions had increased to 139,000 and gross advertising revenue had tripled.

Unlike *Time*, from the outset *Fortune* benefited from costly production expenditures, including the use of slick paper stock, fine printing, well-reproduced photographs and illustrations, and carefully researched articles. In-depth profiles of corporations were pioneered in the pages of *Fortune* during the Depression. No other magazine before it had analyzed so thoroughly the internal structure, finances, policies, and problems of corporations. Also of interest to its readers were more general pieces on social questions, government, politics, foreign countries, and powerful families. Photography played an important role in *Fortune* and included the work of Walker Evans and Margaret Bourke-White, who later became one of the four original staff photographers at *Life*.

In April 1932 Luce purchased *Architectural Forum*, a professional journal first published in 1892 as the *Bricklayer*. According to the Time Inc. prospectus, this magazine was "to bring together, around the central art and science of architecture, all the influences which will build the new America." Even though the editorial scope of this newest venture was broadened to include all branches of the construction industry, Luce's ambitions for *Architectural Forum* were never fully realized.

Luce then established an experimental department in December 1933 to determine what project Time Inc. should undertake next. For the next seven months three of his staff members considered various proposals, including a British edition of *Time*, a woman's magazine, a children's magazine, a daily newspaper, a sports magazine, and a picture magazine, but the picture magazine received the greatest attention. However, Luce had strict requirements for this type of publication. He insisted it be large format so the photographs would be well displayed, printed by letterpress rather than rotogravure, and sell for a dime. The project had to be temporarily abandoned, since Luce's demands could not be met at that point.

Time Inc.'s next undertaking involved a pictorial treatment of current events, but it was through newsreels rather than print. The "March of Time" series, which originated in 1931 as radio broadcasts, was expanded in 1935 to newsreels, which appeared in movie theaters across the country. The popular movie shorts often presented (as did the radio version) reenactments of the news of the day. These dramatizations, considered by some to be outside the boundaries of acceptable journalism, continued until 1951.

In the meantime Luce specifically set out in the spring of 1935 to introduce more photographs into the pages of *Time* and to locate photographers who could make significant contributions to Time Inc. in general. Daniel Longwell, who had been involved with the "March of Time" series and *Architectural Forum,* was assigned this task by Luce. A challenge in 1933 by a new magazine called *Newsweek,* which advertised itself as the "illustrated news magazine," had prompted Longwell, Luce, and his editors to increase their use of visual material at *Time* and *Fortune.* Portraits by German photographer Dr. Erich Salomon appeared in the pages of *Fortune,* and work by Peter Stackpole, who became another of the original four staff photographers at *Life,* was published there as well.

Several other factors seem to have simultaneously prompted Luce's interest in photography. During the time of the first experimental department he met a young woman who had been an editor at Condé Nast's *Vanity Fair* and *Vogue.* As early as 1931 Clare Boothe Brokaw had suggested that Nast start a picture magazine; she even prepared a dummy to show how the new magazine should look. Unable to convince him to take on this new publication, Brokaw held on to this idea and discussed it with Luce when they met for the third time at a dinner party in December 1934.

Luce found Brokaw captivating and went against his strict religious upbringing when he decided to pursue the young divorcée. Despite much personal anguish, and his parents' firm disapproval, Luce asked his wife for a divorce. She re-

luctantly agreed, and the Luces' Reno divorce became final on 4 October 1935, with Lila retaining custody of their two sons. Luce then married Brokaw about six weeks later on 23 November. (Although they had no children of their own, Brokaw had a daughter, Ann, from her first marriage. While a student at Stanford University, she was killed in an automobile accident in 1944.)

Brokaw's hopes for a picture magazine, and Longwell's interest in the same, were not the only reasons Luce was interested in pursuing this new project: picture magazines had been popular in Europe, especially Germany, since the mid 1920s. Numerous photographers, picture agents, and editors from these European magazines fled to the United States in the early to mid 1930s to escape the rise of Nazism. Luce took advantage of this influx of immigrants by hiring Kurt Korff as a consultant.

Korff, the former editor of Germany's largest-circulation picture magazine (the *Berliner Illustrirte Zeitung*), worked secretly for a year (1935-1936) with several members of Luce's staff as part of a reformulated experimental department. The time was ripe during the mid 1930s for a picture magazine, and Luce was determined to be the first American publisher to establish one, which is why the second experimental department kept their plans strictly confidential. Only a few Time Inc. staffers even knew Korff was acting as a consultant. Although Korff was no longer employed by Time Inc. when the first issue of *Life* came off the press late in 1936, many of his suggestions were incorporated into the venture.

After considering several names for the new magazine, including "Show-Book of the World," Luce paid ninety-two thousand dollars in October 1936 for rights to the name of a failing fifty-four-year-old humor magazine, *Life.* The prospectus for the new version of *Life* outlined the grandest of all Time Inc.'s projects: "To see life; to see the world; to witness great events; to watch the faces of the poor and the gestures of the proud; to see strange things—machines, armies, multitudes, shadows in the jungle and on the moon; to see man's work—his paintings, towers and discoveries; to see thousands of miles away, things hidden behind walls and within rooms, things dangerous to come to; the women that men love and many children; to see and take pleasure in seeing, to see and be amazed; to see and be instructed."

*Luce and Roy E. Larson, who served as president of Time
Inc. from 1939 to 1960*

Luce (right) and John Shaw Billings, the first managing editor of Life *and editorial director of Time Inc. from
1944 until 1955 (John Shaw Billings Collection, South Caroliniana Library, University of South Carolina)*

In spite of Luce's previous triumphs, advertising agencies were skeptical, doubting that this kind of magazine would be of interest to the public. Many predicted it would fail. Luce had earmarked $1 million "to see *Life* to success or into an honorable grave." Other Time Inc. executives also were not predicting the level of success *Life* would achieve; the circulation department anticipated approximately 200,000 copies by subscription and approximately half of that for newsstand sales. Initially, advertisers paid rates based on a guaranteed circulation of just 250,000.

These low projections nearly forced the picture magazine to go under because the guaranteed advertising rates were set much too low for the great demand for copies of the magazine. Prior to the first issue, 235,000 charter subscriptions were obtained through a mailing to 755,000 *Time* and *Fortune* subscribers. Dated 23 November 1936, the first issue of *Life* sold out at newsstands within a day or two (within hours in some locations) in spite of a record 466,000 pressrun, the largest first-issue printing in magazine-publishing history at the time. Within the first year Time Inc. lost $3 million on *Life* because most of its revenue was going to cover just the paper and ink. Luce ended up spending a total of $5 million to save the magazine from dying of too much success. After a year the advertising contracts were adjusted to the higher circulation rates, allowing *Life* to begin recovering financially. In 1939 the magazine finally turned a profit when the circulation reached more than 2 million.

Although Clare Luce is thought to have had an influence over the content of *Life*, she never became an editor there because of the objections raised by several members of Luce's staff. Nevertheless, she continued her career as a playwright and was active in Republican politics, including two terms (1943-1947) in the House of Representatives. In addition, she was appointed U.S. ambassador to Italy in 1953 by Pres. Dwight D. Eisenhower. Six years later she was nominated as U.S. ambassador to Brazil, but resigned before having a chance to take the post because of a public quarrel with Democratic senator Wayne Morse.

Luce was a strong advocate for United States participation in World War II. In the 17 February 1941 issue of *Life* he published an essay entitled "The American Century," which declared that the United States should come to the defense of those nations beleaguered by the Axis powers in order to establish its own position as a leader of world affairs. The essay was much discussed, often reprinted, and published in book form later in the year.

During World War II Time Inc. expanded its coverage in Europe, ultimately resulting in the establishment in 1945 of Time-Life International to distribute *Life* and *Time* outside the United States and administer the magazines' foreign news coverage. Eventually there were five international weekly editions of *Time* and a fortnightly international edition of *Life*. In 1953 a fortnightly edition of *Life en Español* was established. It was suspended seventeen years later. (Life International was suspended in 1970 because it was not producing enough income in spite of its more than six hundred thousand worldwide circulation figure.) Luce's global operation expanded even further in 1962 when he launched *Panorama*, an Italian monthly magazine, and then established an Argentine version of the same publication. In May 1963 Luce joined with a Japanese publisher in starting *President*, which was similar in content to *Fortune*.

After World War II Luce considered starting a publication similar in content to the *Partisan Review*, *Harper's*, *Atlantic Monthly*, or the old *Dial*. However, Luce was not satisfied with the plans for his new "think magazine," so the project was abandoned. The 1940s turned out to be a relatively quiet period for Time Inc.

Conversely, the 1950s were a busy time for Luce. During the economic prosperity of the Korean War period Luce began an expansion and diversification plan. Time Inc. entered the book-publishing business in 1950, promoting new titles through mass mailings to *Time* and *Life* subscribers. A separate division, called Time-Life Books, was created in 1961, and within three years about nine million volumes were sold in the United States and Canada, plus another two million in eleven foreign languages.

In light of the great housing expansion that was going on in the United States in the early 1950s, Luce decided to try appealing to two different audiences by splitting *Architectural Forum* into *The Magazine of Building: Architectural Forum* and *The Magazine of Building: House & Home*. The former was aimed at the heavy-building industry while the latter was for architects, mortgage lenders, and builders of residential homes. (After six months the titles were changed to simply *Architectural Forum* and *House & Home*.) The two magazines lost $1.1 million by the end of 1953 and con-

Luce at the 1964 Republican convention (Burt Glinn)

Luce with Chiang Kai-shek

tinued to be financial drains on Time Inc. through the early 1960s. In 1964 Luce sold *House & Home* to McGraw-Hill and then suspended publication of *Architectural Forum* after a special August/September 1964 issue. A well-established nonprofit organization, American Planning and Civic Association (later Urban America, Inc.), took over *Architectural Forum* and began publishing it again in April 1965.

Luce began to pursue journalistic ventures outside of publishing with the acquisition in 1952 of fifty percent interest in KOB and KOB-TV in Albuquerque, New Mexico. Time-Life Broadcast Inc., a subsidiary, bought and sold during the next seven years a variety of other radio and television operations in Salt Lake City, Denver, Grand Rapids, Indianapolis, Minneapolis, San Diego, and Bakersfield. The East Texas Pulp and Paper Company, which Time Inc. owned jointly with the Houston Oil Company, was established in December 1952.

During this period of expansion and diversification Luce established an experimental department to plan a weekly sports magazine. Because of the increased leisure time Americans had after the war, a magazine aimed at well-educated, higher-income readers seemed like a good proposition to Luce, even though he was not much of a sportsman himself–golf, swimming, and tennis were the only sports in which he participated. (Hadden had been an enthusiastic baseball fan and had hoped to start a sports magazine once *Time* was a success.) To prepare himself for this new undertaking, Luce had his more knowledgeable staffers take him to sporting events, and he learned what he could in a short time about horse racing, baseball, boxing, and the other areas *Sports Illustrated* was to cover. However, many of Luce's staff did not share his interest in a sports magazine, feeling it was not a "dignified" undertaking for Time Inc. Some staffers disparagingly referred to the latest magazine idea as "Muscle," while others called it "Harry's Yacht."

Some of the work Luce did during the planning of this newest magazine was carried out long-distance. Luce had moved with his wife, the new U.S. ambassador to Italy, to Rome early in 1953. He remained actively involved in Time Inc. but did not have the daily contact with the staff to which he had been accustomed. Although he made frequent trips back to New York City, Luce stayed in Italy until Clare resigned her post in November 1956.

Luce and his second wife Clare Boothe Luce

Luce wrote in the advertisement announcing the first issue of the new *Sports Illustrated*: "There has never been a National Sports Weekly. Furthermore, it has been brilliantly proved that there never can be. People's interests are too varied. The fisherman cares nothing for baseball. The skier couldn't care less about the Kentucky Derby. Maybe. Maybe that's the way it was. Maybe that's still the way it partly is. But one thing is sure: the world of Sport is a wonderful world and everyone enters it with Joy. And so we enter it–as journalists, editors, writers, photographers, resolved to put something of the joy and awareness of Sport into the form of a magazine.... You may find that it makes more enjoyable what you already enjoy. And *that* could have consequences. One consequence could be that, at last, America will have a great National Sports Weekly." In 1954 Luce spent more than $6 million, including start-up costs, to bring his latest idea to fruition.

Apparently the public was ready for *Sports Illustrated*. Even before the magazine had a name, nearly 350,000 subscriptions were obtained. Advertising was sold based on a circulation of 450,000. The initial pressrun established a new first-issue publishing record–550,000 copies of *Sports Illustrated* were printed for the 9 August 1954 issues. All but ten percent of the magazines disappeared from the newsstands on the first day. By the end of six months sales were up to nearly 575,000 per issue, and in less than ten years the figure exceeded 1,000,000. In 1964 the magazine began to turn a profit, and it has remained a money-maker ever since.

Readers seem to have been attracted to the wide-ranging content of the magazine. Not only did *Sports Illustrated* cover the usual spectator sports of football, basketball, baseball, and boxing, but it also included fox hunts, field trials, and mountain-climbing expeditions. Articles and photographs on golfing, skiing, swimming, boating, snorkeling, and riding were published as well. While other publishers had concentrated on a single sport, once again Luce had found the magic formula.

Although he did not begin any additional projects prior to his retirement in 1964, Luce did concern himself with locating larger quarters for his corporation, which had outgrown its space in Rockefeller Center. After considering sites in other parts of Manhattan and in suburban Westchester County, he agreed in 1956 to move into a new building that would go up between Fiftieth and Fifty-first streets on the Avenue of the Americas. Luce convinced the owners of Rockefeller Center, Inc., to organize a corporation, Rock-Time, Inc., which meant Time Inc. would have forty-five percent ownership. By June 1959 the cornerstone on the skyscraper Time-Life Building was in place.

Just as one of his magazines was experiencing some difficult times, Luce became ill. Two months before he was to turn sixty Luce was stricken with a coronary occlusion while at his vacation home in Phoenix, Arizona. Because the attack was fairly mild, this illness in February 1958 was not even disclosed to his colleagues, and the Phoenix newspapers' reports said he had pneumonia. His recovery was swift, but he remained in Phoenix for two more months. After this incident the Luces began spending more time at their vacation home, especially during the winter months. Luce had learned while living in Rome that he could remain in touch with his staff in New York City, so he employed these same tactics while spending time in Phoenix.

At this time the circulation of *Life* was slipping, and much of Luce's energy was spent trying to solve this problem. Television seemed to

be taking its toll on the picture magazine, but Luce was not satisfied with blaming the new medium. He felt the key to recovery was in general promotion of the special qualities of greatness he felt *Life* possessed. But nothing seemed to help; in the late 1950s the magazine lost newsstand sales and some of its advertising revenue while production and circulation costs continued to increase. A new publishing strategy was formulated in 1959 to increase circulation from six million to seven million by the early 1960s by lowering its price. The magazine's newsstand price was dropped from twenty-five cents to nineteen cents an issue, and a period of recovery began. (However, in the late 1960s the magazine began to falter; the December 1972 issue of *Life* was its last due to losses of more than $30 million since 1969.) *Time,* on the other hand, was increasing its readership by approximately 100,000 a year and in the late 1950s was consistently profitable, with an overall circulation of 2,350,000.

In 1959 Luce began what was to be the transfer of his long-held title editor in chief, to Hedley Donovan, then managing editor of *Fortune.* Although the staff was surprised that he was thinking of passing the title on to such a young man (Donovan was just forty-five years old), Luce had long admired Donovan because of the way he handled *Fortune.* Donovan began the transition period by first apprenticing himself to *Sports Illustrated,* then took over the managing editorship of *Time,* then *Life.* A major reorganization of Time Inc. came in April 1960, a point at which the total assets of the corporation were more than $230 million. By 1963 Time Inc. was the largest publisher of magazines in the United States.

That same year the fortieth anniversary of *Time* was celebrated with a dinner where nearly three hundred people who had appeared on its covers were honored. It was a grand finale for Luce, who retired eleven months later from his position as editor in chief. While taking on the title of editorial chairman of Time Inc., he recommended the board of directors appoint Donovan as his successor. Because of the corporate reorganization in 1960, Donovan joined Andrew Heiskel, chairman of the board of directors, and James Linen, president of Time Inc., in a triumvirate that was in charge after Luce left.

During his three-year retirement Luce kept busy by working with the Presbyterian church on several projects, writing his memoirs, and making speeches. Just a few days before his death he gave a speech in San Francisco, and he had been to New York City to consult with his staff the week before. Upon returning to Phoenix he was taken to St. Joseph's Hospital for tests. Around 3 A.M. on 28 February 1967 he suffered a fatal heart attack while alone in his hospital room.

Luce's presence could be felt in all of his magazines. He was a businessman who never apologized for making millions, but he had a larger purpose than simply becoming wealthy. Time Inc. reflected his missionary zeal in its support of Christianity, the Republican party, the free-enterprise system, big business, Chiang Kai-shek, the cold war, as well as his disdain for most Democrats (Lyndon Johnson being an exception), big labor, and communism. This acknowledged slant resulted in frequent criticisms of the journalistic integrity of the Time Inc. publications. However, Luce never intended his magazines to be "objective"; instead, he intended to use them to reflect his vision of America's role in the world, his faith in the "American Century."

Biographies:

John Kobler, *Luce: His Time, Life and Fortune* (Garden City, N.Y.: Doubleday, 1968);

W. A. Swanberg, *Luce and His Empire* (New York: Scribners, 1972).

References:

James L. Baughman, *Henry R. Luce and the Rise of the American News Media* (Boston: Twayne, 1987);

William F. Buckley, Jr., "The Life and Time of Henry Luce," *Esquire*, 100 (December 1983): 251-258;

David Cort, "Once Upon a Time Inc.: Mr. Luce's Fact Machine," *Nation*, 182 (18 February 1956): 134-137;

Cort, *The Sin of Henry R. Luce: An Anatomy of Journalism* (Secaucus, N.J.: Lyle Stuart, 1974);

Robert Elson, *The World of Time, Inc.: The Intimate History of Publishing Enterprise*, 2 volumes (New York: Atheneum, 1968, 1973);

Joseph Epstein, "Henry Luce and His Time," *Commentary*, 44 (November 1967): 35-47;

John M. Harrison, "The Hearst-Luce-Hill Stereotype," *Saturday Review*, 42 (11 July 1959): 9-11, 34;

"Henry R. Luce: End of a Pilgrimage," *Time*, 90 (10 March 1967): 26-33;

John K. Jessup, "Henry R. Luce: The Values that Shaped His Work," *Life*, 62 (10 March 1967): 30-38;

John Kobler, "The First Tycoon and the Power of His Press," *Saturday Evening Post*, 238 (16 January 1965): 28-45;

John P. Mallan, "Luce's Hot-and-Cold War," *New Republic*, 129 (28 September 1953): 12-15;

T. S. Matthews, " . . . tall, balding, dead Henry R. Luce. . . ," *Esquire*, 68 (September 1967): 131-132, 183;

Herbert R. Mayes, "Henry R. Luce: 1898-1967," *Saturday Review*, 50 (18 March 1967): 16-17;

Curtis Prendergast and Geoffrey Coluin, *The World of Time Inc.: The Intimate History of a Changing Enterprize* (New York: Atheneum, 1986).

Papers:

The Time Inc. archives and the Library of Congress hold Luce's papers.

Bernarr Macfadden

(16 August 1868-12 October 1955)

Bruce M. Swain
Ithaca College

See also the Macfadden entry in *DLB 25: American Newspaper Journalists, 1901-1925.*

MAJOR POSITIONS HELD: President, chairman of the board, Macfadden Publications, Inc. (1924-1941).

PRINCIPAL MAGAZINES OWNED: *Physical Culture,* (1899-1941, 1943-1955); *True Story* (1919-1941); *True Romances* (1923-1941); *Dance Lovers Magazine* (1923-1931); *True Detective Mysteries* (1924-1940); *True Experiences* (1925-1941); *Own Your Own Home* (1925-1931); *Model Airplane News* (1929-1932); *Liberty* (1931-1941); *Photoplay* (1931-1941).

BOOKS: *The Athlete's Conquest: A Novel,* as B. A. McFadden (New York & St. Louis: Brown, 1892; revised edition, as Macfadden, New York: Physical Culture, 1901);
McFadden's System of Physical Training, as McFadden (New York: Hulbert, 1895); republished as *Macfadden's Physical Training* (New York: Macfadden, 1900);
Fasting–Hydropathy–Exercise, by Macfadden and Felix L. Oswald (New York: Physical Culture, 1900); republished as *Macfadden's Fasting, Hydropathy, and Exercise* (London & New York: Macfadden, 1903);
The Virile Powers of Superb Manhood: How Developed, How Lost, How Regained (New York: Physical Culture, 1900);
Macfadden's New Hair Culture, third edition, enlarged (New York: Physical Culture, 1901);
Physical Culture Cook Book, by Macfadden, Mary Richardson, and George Propheter (New York: Physical Culture, 1901); republished as *Macfadden's New Cookery Book* (London & New York: Macfadden, 1903);
The Power and Beauty of Superb Womanhood (New York: Physical Culture, 1901);
Strength from Eating (New York: Physical Culture, 1901);
Strong Eyes (New York: Physical Culture, 1901);

Bernarr Macfadden

Natural Cure for Rupture (New York & London: Physical Culture, 1902);
Marriage a Lifelong Honeymoon: Life's Greatest Pleasures Secured by Observing the Highest Human Instincts (New York & London: Physical Culture, 1903);
Building of Vital Power (New York & London: Physical Culture, 1904);
Diseases of Men (New York & London: Physical Culture, 1904);

*Health–Beauty–Sexuality, from Girlhood to Woman-
hood,* by Macfadden and Marion Malcolm
(New York & London: Physical Culture,
1904);

How Success Is Won (New York & London: Physical Culture, 1904);

Physical Culture for Babies, by Macfadden and Marguerite Macfadden (New York & London:
Physical Culture, 1904);

*A Strenuous Lover: A Romance of a Natural Love's
Vast Power,* by Macfadden and John R.
Coryell (New York: Physical Culture, 1904);

Muscular Power and Beauty (Spotswood, N.J.: Physical Culture, 1906);

*The Macfadden Prosecution–A Curious Story of
Wrong and Oppression under the Postal Laws*
(Battle Creek, Mich., 1908);

Lecture on Exercise for Strength (Battle Creek,
Mich.: United Schools of Physical Culture,
1909);

Sweethearts for Life (New York: Physical Culture,
190?);

Macfadden's Encyclopedia of Physical Culture, 5 volumes, by Macfadden and others (New York:
Physical Culture, 1911-1912; revised edition, New York: Macfadden, 1926);

Vitality Supreme (New York: Physical Culture,
1915);

Brain Energy Building and Nerve-Vitalizing Course
(New York: Physical Culture, 1916);

Manhood and Marriage (New York: Physical Culture, 1916);

Womanhood and Marriage (New York: Macfadden,
1918; revised, 1923);

Strengthening the Eyes (New York: Physical Culture, 1918);

Making Old Bodies Young (New York: Physical Culture, 1919);

*The Olympian System of Physical and Mental Develop-
ment,* by Macfadden, Carl E. Williams,
Hereward Carrington, and others (Chicago:
Olympian System, 1919);

Eating for Health and Strength (New York: Physical
Culture, 1921);

Hair Culture (New York: Physical Culture, 1921);

The Truth about Tobacco (New York: Physical Culture, 1921);

The Miracle of Milk (New York: Macfadden,
1923);

Fasting for Health (New York: Macfadden, 1923);

How to Keep Fit (New York: Macfadden, 1923);

Keeping Fit (New York: Macfadden, 1923);

Preparing for Motherhood (New York: Macfadden,
1923);

Constipation, Its Cause, Effect and Treatment (New
York: Macfadden, 1924);

Physical Culture for Baby (New York: Macfadden,
1924);

Physical Culture Cook Book, by Macfadden and
Milo Hastings (New York: Macfadden,
1924);

*The Walking Cure, Pep and Power from Walking–How
to Cure Disease from Walking* (New York:
Macfadden, 1924);

Diabetes, Its Cause, Nature and Treatment (New
York: Macfadden, 1925);

Headaches, How Caused and How Cured (New York:
Macfadden, 1925);

Strengthening the Nerves (New York: Macfadden,
1925);

Strengthening the Spine (New York: Macfadden,
1925);

Tooth Troubles: Their Prevention, Cause and Cure
(New York: Macfadden, 1925);

Asthma and Hay-Fever (New York: Macfadden,
1926);

The Book of Health (New York: Macfadden, 1926);

Colds, Coughs, and Catarrh (New York: Macfadden, 1926);

Foot Troubles (New York: Macfadden, 1926);

How to Raise the Baby (New York: Macfadden,
1926);

*Plain Speech on a Public Insult: Bernarr Macfadden
Replies to the Atlantic Monthly* (New York:
Macfadden, 1926);

Predetermine Your Baby's Sex (New York: Macfadden, 1926);

Rheumatism, Its Cause, Nature and Treatment (New
York: Macfadden, 1926);

Skin Troubles: Their Causes, Nature, and Treatment
(New York: Macfadden, 1927);

Digestive Troubles, How Caused and Cured (New
York: Macfadden, 1928);

Exercising for Health (New York: Macfadden,
1929);

Health for the Family (New York: Macfadden,
1929);

Tuberculosis (New York: Macfadden, 1929);

Home Health Manual (New York: Macfadden,
1930);

Home Health Library, 5 volumes, by Macfadden
and others (New York: Macfadden, 1933);

10 Minutes a Day for Health (New York: Macfadden, 1933);

After 40–What?, by Macfadden and Charles A.
Clinton (New York: Macfadden, 1935);

Man's Sex Life (New York: Macfadden, 1935);

Cover for an early issue of the first magazine founded by Macfadden

Practical Birth Control and Sex Predetermination, by Macfadden and Clinton (New York: Macfadden, 1935);

Woman's Sex Life (New York: Macfadden, 1935);

How to Gain Weight (New York: Macfadden, 1936);

How to Reduce Weight (New York: Macfadden, 1936);

Be Married and Like It (New York: Macfadden, 1937);

Exercise and Like It (New York: Macfadden, 1937);

Bernarr Macfadden's Handbook of Health (New York: Macfadden, 1938); revised as *New Handbook of Health with First Aid* (New York: Macfadden, 1940);

More Power to Your Nerves (New York: Macfadden, 1938);

Science of Divine Healing, with Key to Health and Happiness: The Cosmotarian Gospel (New York: Cosmotarian Library Service, 1945);

Confessions of an Amateur Politician (New York: Macfadden, 1948).

OTHER: *The Encyclopedia of Health and Physical Culture*, 8 volumes, edited by Macfadden (New York: Macfadden, 1931; revised, 1937; revised again, 1940; revised again, 1942).

Bernarr Macfadden, with his maniacal dedication to diet and exercise, was perceived during his lifetime as either a clownish eccentric, a true visionary, or a social menace. All these perceptions helped give *Physical Culture, True Story*, and the many other magazines he published a combined circulation of over seven million by 1935. He is re-

207

*Photograph of Macfadden published in the April 1899 issue
of* Physical Culture

membered, as well, for founding a sensational tabloid, the *New York Evening Graphic*, in 1924.

Macfadden, whose fortune was estimated at
thirty million dollars in 1930, was born to a life
of abject poverty on a farm near Mill Spring, Missouri, on 16 August 1868. He was named Bernard Adolphus McFadden. His alcoholic father,
John R. McFadden, an unsuccessful farmer and
breeder of racehorses, died when his son was
four. His mother, Elizabeth Miller McFadden,
died of tuberculosis when Bernard was ten, and
the sickly youth was presumed headed for an
early grave with the same disease. But, bound
over by relatives to a farmer near Macomb, Illinois, he found that he thrived on chopping
wood, tending stock, and other farm chores. It
was a discovery that was to shape his life.

As a teenager he experienced a relapse
while living with relatives in St. Louis. Inspired
by a Ringling Bros. & Barnum and Bailey Circus
trapeze performance and remembering the ro-

bust health of his farm days, he dedicated himself to weight lifting, gymnastics, and wrestling at
a gymnasium—an institution of questionable re-
pute in the 1880s. His renewed strength was important to a subsequent job with a dentist in
McCune, Kansas, where Macfadden's role was to
hold sufferers' heads motionless. In 1886 the dentist became a weekly newspaper publisher, and
on the *McCune Brick* the young Macfadden got
his first taste of publishing, in the time-honored
position of printer's devil. The paper's motto was
"To hurl advice at the community." The community's receptivity to this advice was such that
the enterprise soon collapsed.

As a young man Macfadden had brief stints
in a number of other occupations: hotel attendant, bookkeeper, dry cleaner, coal miner, hobo,
and beer-wagon driver. Eventually he hung out
his shingle in St. Louis as a kinistherapist, a title
he interpreted to mean "a healer of disease, by
use of movements."

Initially it was through his wrestling skills
that Macfadden attracted followers. His prowess
allowed him to best any challenger, then lecture
the crowd on the benefits of what he termed physical culture. Even after he ceased taking on chal-
lengers, his lectures were often preceded by a display of rippling muscle. At age forty-five, for
instance, he toured Britain with his third bride,
the English swimming champion Mary Williamson, whom he met when she won a contest
he sponsored to identify the perfect specimen of
British womanhood. By way of an opener, Macfadden would lie on the stage and have his
stocky wife leap feet-first onto his stomach from
a high table. Then he would spring to his feet,
take a few bows, and proselytize for his No Breakfast clubs or other activities.

The young "Professor," as Macfadden
called himself, quickly defeated a succession of
local wrestling champions of various weight
classes. Even sportswriters began to take him seriously when, at 137 pounds, he emerged victori-
ous in a bout with the reigning heavyweight champion of Chicago. A lecture tour to that city
allowed the new champion an opportunity to deliver to a publisher his manuscript for *The Athlete's Conquest*, a novel dedicated to abolishing
what he saw as a dire threat to women's health: cor-
sets. The rejection slip called the work "the crud-
est piece of junk" the publisher had ever read—
hardly surprising since Macfadden's schooling to
that point had been sporadic. Macfadden reacted
by taking coaching jobs at two private academies

in Missouri and Illinois, where he exchanged his athletic know-how for instruction in literature and rhetoric. The novel was published in 1892.

In 1894 Macfadden moved to New York, where he turned two rented rooms on Broadway into a gym. Soon overweight businessmen were paying him well for instruction in bodybuilding. However, newspaper editors he approached with articles on physical culture pronounced the public uninterested in the topic, a frustration that set the kinistherapist to manufacturing and marketing an exercise machine in order to bankroll a publication of his own.

Physical Culture actually began during a lecture tour of England as a four-page leaflet advertising the exercise machine and Macfadden's exhibitions. Shortly thereafter Macfadden abandoned interest in the device and concentrated exclusively on diet and exercise. *Physical Culture* appeared first in the United States in March 1899, about the time its publisher decided to enhance his public image by expunging any hint of weakness from his name. Bernard became Bernarr, and Adolphus disappeared. Several historians suggest he was taken with the new, powerful Mack truck. Thus, Macfadden instead of McFadden. The cover of the first issue of *Physical Culture* was illustrated with photographs of the publisher in classical poses that left no doubt as to his desire to avoid the appearance of weakness. In fact, for years the *Physical Culture* cover carried the slogan, "Weakness is a crime; don't be a criminal." Macfadden wrote, under various masculine and feminine pen names, the entire first issue–a practice he continued long after the magazine's enormous financial success allowed him to hire an editorial staff. He enjoyed arguing, via pseudonyms, both sides of a question such as "Is Meat Necessary to the Human Diet?" In a double-page layout he would provide competitive answers: "Absolutely," by J. Walter Smithson, and "Certainly Not," by Harold DeHavilland–or Alexander Marshall, or Vincent Perry.

Never one to discourage controversy, Macfadden made the columns of *Physical Culture* available to the purveyors of alternative health doctrines, some wildly original. These included a Persian physician who cured patients by walking barefoot on their backs, and Eusebio Santos, who advocated eating grass regularly. With his characteristic flair for showmanship Macfadden illustrated that article with a photograph of Santos, dressed in opera cape and top hat, grazing with a herd of cattle. He even published an article by

Macfadden in 1928. He walked barefoot daily from his home in Nyack, New York, to his office in Manhattan, a distance of eighteen miles (Wide World Photos).

an Apache, Chief One-Eye, who argued that most Indians grew strong by avoiding exercise. Macfadden declared the "greatest leader and most remarkable reformer in a century" to be one John Alexander Dowie, founder of Zion City, Illinois, where doctors and druggists were banned.

Macfadden's war against organized medicine, which he viewed as a formidable commercial trust with almost despotic control over individual physicians, was a lifelong commitment. In essence, he believed that natural therapy was always superior to drugs. And he used *Physical Culture* to parade a legion of his therapeutic notions: fasting and a milk diet to cure syphilis and cancer, fighting baldness by tugging at one's hair and standing on one's head, the avoidance of "eye crutches" (glasses) through a system of optic exercises, and the advantages of long hikes and deep-breathing exercises. He especially enjoyed calling attention to such dubious highlights of the history of orthodox medicine as the application of leeches to terminally ill patients.

Macfadden outraged physicians with his stand against compulsory vaccination, and at one point during the 1930s hardly a national convention of the American Medical Association passed without consideration of resolutions viewing his ideas with alarm or calling for his books on health to be banned from the mails. In 1924 *Hygeia*, an A.M.A. magazine, declared *Physical Culture* to be "an outstanding example of the money that is to be made from catering to ignorance." But many of what *Hygeia* called Macfadden's "fantastic and bizarre fads" have since become wholly acceptable to orthodox doctors–especially his ideas concerning the negative effects of alcohol, coffee, red meat, and white flour.

Certainly Macfadden could not be accused of failing to practice what he preached. Admiring biographers report that he slept, with windows open, on the floor, and that he often walked to his Manhattan office from his home in Nyack, some twenty-seven miles away. Barefoot walking was best, he believed, in order to put the body in touch with magnetic currents of the earth. When Mary Macfadden once suggested a vacation, he is reported to have responded, "I think a good long hike would do me good–say a walk from here to Chicago. We could go by way of Pittsburgh, over the mountains." Doctors were never allowed into his home, even to attend the births of his children. It should also be noted that he took the lead in barring lucrative advertising for patent medicines, some of them endorsed by physicians, when he refused to run them in his magazines.

The utter seriousness with which Macfadden took his philosophies–which he later identified as the religion of Cosmotarian Science, emphasizing the body as the temple of the soul–and the degree to which his own personality pervaded *Physical Culture* help account, no doubt, for the response it sparked. Soon devoted readers were writing to him about both health and personal problems, and Macfadden responded with an advice column.

Mary Macfadden claims credit for suggesting that such confessional correspondence could inspire a new magazine, and in May 1919 Macfadden established *True Story*. The cover portrayed a man and woman gazing lovingly at each other, but the caption read: "And Their Love Turned to Hatred." Inside were a series of first-person stories, including "A Wife Who Awoke in Time," "My Battle with John Barleycorn," "An Ex-Convict's Climb to Millions," "How I Learned to Hate my Parents," and "How a Man Won Out Against Prejudice." Despite a price of twenty cents a copy, the magazine soon achieved the largest newsstand sales of any monthly in the world. Its circulation reached more than two million at one point, with Macfadden realizing ten thousand dollars a day from the magazine at its peak.

The *True Story* formula, which was to defy imitators for decades, was shockingly innovative–and flatly unbelievable to many. When he hired John Brennan, a former *Physical Culture* editor then editing *Success*, to head up *True Story*, Macfadden stipulated that the editor's duties would not include selecting its content. Those decisions would be made by Macfadden after the rulings of a panel of young, part-time manuscript readers whose only qualifications were that they were devoted magazine readers who keenly enjoyed a good story. Of them, Macfadden asked only one question: Does this story hold your interest? Fulton Oursler, a Macfadden executive and biographer, reports: "What he wanted was stories from people who were not story writers, but who had suffered so smartly from experience that they could tell it with conviction and with fire. He did not care how crudely they might be expressed. . . . He felt that sincerity could not be imitated, and that only the people who believed in what they were writing could give him the stories he desired." Macfadden offered a monthly prize of one thousand dollars for the most compelling first-person account, and *True Story* was soon receiving seventy thousand to one hundred thousand submissions a year. In order to preserve the sincerity of the submissions, his editors were only allowed to make grammatical changes.

To combat rumors of fabrication, Macfadden required that all stories be accompanied by an affidavit that the incidents had actually occurred to the contributor or to someone he or she knew personally. An essential requirement of all *True Story* first-person accounts was that they teach a strong moral lesson. To offset the criticism that the magazine's moral instruction often involved titillating details of sin, Macfadden convened a five-man ministerial advisory board consisting of three prominent Protestant clergymen, a Catholic priest, and a rabbi. Macfadden promised not to publish any story of which the clergymen disapproved. "Our stories have only the normal amount of sex that you'll find in anyone's life," argued a subsequent *True Story* editor, William Jordan Rapp. "They're written in the common idiom, that is all." It was Rapp who later al-

Cover for an issue of Macfadden's first, and most popular, confession magazine, founded in 1919

tered the content of *True Story*, diluting the attention to sex and choosing stories about marital discord and even current social problems.

Ingredients of a typical early issue of *True Story* included installments of serials, some by well-known writers; puzzles and contests for children; an editorial by Macfadden; and advice from Prof. Bristow Adams of Cornell University on cooking, fashion, beauty, or needlework.

Competitors were quick to appear. George T. Delacorte of Dell Publishing brought out *I Confess* in 1921, followed by *Modern Romances* in 1929, and Fawcett launched *True Confessions* in 1922. Macfadden, blithely going into competition with himself, in short order began *True Romances* (1923), *Dream World: Into the Land of Love and Romance* (1924), and *True Experiences* (1925). Foreign editions of *True Story* circulated in England, France, Germany, and Scandinavia. A genre of "purge literature" was born.

Life at the headquarters of Macfadden Publications, Inc., established in 1924, was, by all accounts, hectic. As more magazines were launched, Macfadden doubled office space by installing loft cubicles. Editorial conferences would come to a halt when Macfadden's personal trainer announced it was time for a wrestling bout in the office gymnasium—a practice Macfadden said gave him needed "brain power" for decision making. One of his editors, asked at a dinner party how many magazines Macfadden published, replied: "Eight. At least it was eight when I left the office tonight." Macfadden could decide overnight to kill an unpromising magazine and discharge its entire staff. Editorial employees often had reason to check the roof to see if their magazine's flag was still there.

Macfadden Publications at one time or another was the home of twenty-seven magazines. Macfadden arranged the finances of each separately so that one failure would not damage the remainder of his publishing empire. Among those magazines whose flag remained aloft for some time were *True Ghost Stories* (1925), *True Lovers* (1925), *True Detective Mysteries* (1924), *Master Detective* (1929), *Dance Lovers Magazine* (1923), *Own Your Own Home* (1925), *Model Airplane News* (1929), and *Photoplay* (1931). Others failed quickly, some virtually in their infancy: *Beautiful Womanhood* (1922), *National Pictorial Brain Power Monthly* (1921), *Movie Weekly* (1921), *Midnight* (1922), *Your Car* (1925), *Sport Life* (1924), *Muscle Builder* (1924), *Modern Marriage Problems* (1925), *True Proposals* (1925), *True Strange Stories* (1929), *Radio Stories* (1924), and *Flying Stories* (1928). *Metropolitan* was purchased by Macfadden in 1923, folded, and was then retitled *Fiction Lovers Magazine*. In 1931 Macfadden purchased prestigious *Liberty* magazine, which he published for a decade.

In 1941 he withdrew from his company, which had begun to operate at a loss in 1938, and agreed not to compete directly with it for five years. When his successors transformed his cherished *Physical Culture* into a woman's magazine named *Beauty and Health* and dropped its hostility to organized medicine, Macfadden purchased it and reissued *Physical Culture* in pocket size in 1943. In 1950 he titled it *Bernarr Macfadden's Health Review*. As of 1954 it was still reaching twenty thousand readers.

Reorganized by Irving S. Manheimer in 1951, the firm Macfadden left behind was soon profitable again. Today the Macfadden Women's Media in New York City publishes–in addition to the stalwart *True Story*–*Modern Romances*, *Secrets*, *True Confessions*, *True Experience*, *True Love*, and *True Romance*.

The parting of ways in 1941 came after minority stockholders filed a suit charging that company funds were financing Macfadden's other wide-ranging interests, including a sanitarium in Battle Creek, Michigan, his Penny Restaurants for vegetarian cuisine in various cities, Strenthro breakfast cereal, and the Physical Culture Training School in Chicago, where in one year's time one could become a doctor of physcultopathy. Macfadden even tried his hand at movie producing, although he bowed out of that enterprise quickly. However, several movies starring Rudolph Valentino were based on *True Story* narratives. Valentino announced in a book published by Macfadden that he maintained his sex appeal by adhering to physical culture doctrines. Mac-

fadden later purchased Castle Heights Military Academy in Lebanon, Tennessee, and reorganized it along physical culture lines. After his death the Bernarr Macfadden Foundation, which he had founded with a grant of five million dollars, also bought the Sanford Naval Academy in Sanford, Florida.

Macfadden's fondness for displaying photos of himself and other minimally clad athletes in the pages of *Physical Culture* brought him into conflict with Anthony Comstock and the New York Society for the Suppression of Vice. A Madison Square Garden exhibition featuring female athletes in tights led to a 1905 Comstock-instigated raid on Macfadden's office, where police seized posters and even photos of the Venus de Milo as evidence. In that instance Macfadden received a suspended sentence, but he never relented in his attacks on would-be censors, Comstock in particular. A 1907 case was more serious. Alarmed by the prevalence of venereal disease, Macfadden commissioned a *Physical Culture* serial by John R. Coryell, later to become well known for his "Nick Carter" stories, to warn against the dangers of promiscuity. So explicit were the details in "Wild Oats, or Growing to Manhood in Civilized (?) Society" that Macfadden was convicted of sending lewd and obscene matter through the mails, fined two thousand dollars, and sentenced to two years in prison. Loyal readers deluged the White House with appeals for clemency, and President William Howard Taft issued a pardon on the recommendation of Attorney General George Wickersham.

It was not to be Macfadden's last clash with the Society for the Suppression of Vice. Coverage of sensational trials in his newspaper, the *Graphic*–especially its use of composite photos–led John S. Sumner, who had assumed control of the society after Comstock's death in 1915, to sue in 1927, charging that the newspaper's stories had a "strain of dangerous filth running through them harmful to all society." The case was thrown out of court, but the tabloid was actually banned in White Plains, New York, and Princeton, New Jersey.

The 1907 conviction, however, did help spell doom for perhaps Macfadden's most ambitious project. After health homes he operated in New York State proved popular, Macfadden established Physical Culture City near Helmetta, New York, as a Mecca where treatment and instruction based on his health philosophies would be available. He sued the *New York World* for fifty thou-

Macfadden in his office at the Macfadden Building, located on Broadway (Culver Pictures)

sand dollars for an article suggesting extensive sexual relations among the students and impossibly high graduation standards. He lost when a jury concluded that the reporter had simply reported what he had seen. Nonetheless, Upton Sinclair, who was later to expose the unsanitary practices of the meat industry in *The Jungle* (1906), emerged from a stint there convinced that fasting and a milk diet had restored his health.

Another of Macfadden's controversial doctrines was his advocacy of the importance of a vigorous sex life to health, which culminated in 1922 when he announced in *Physical Culture* that he had discovered a means of determining the sex of children and that he and wife Mary, having produced four daughters, would now produce only males. They proceeded to have three sons in rapid succession. The experiment did much to heighten Macfadden's profile, even if it later was revealed that he had failed to give proper credit to Dr. David H. Reeder, an Indiana physician whose research on the timing of con-

ception he had utilized.

For an author quick to provide marital advice for readers, Macfadden was not thoroughly successful in his own experiments with wedded bliss. His first marriage, to Tillie Fontaine, lasted a very short time and was never mentioned by Macfadden in his extensive writings. His marriage in 1901 to Marguerite Kelly, a nurse and *Physical Culture* writer, ended in divorce in 1911. They had one child, a daughter. His third marriage, to Mary Williamson, lasted from 1913 to 1946. In 1948, at the age of eighty, Macfadden married Johnnie McKinney Lee, a promoter and lecturer who was thirty-eight years his junior. They divorced in 1954.

Like many other prominent figures with ample personal fortunes, Macfadden found the lure of public office irresistible. First he flung his *New York Evening Graphic* into vigorous support of Mayor Jimmy Walker, who nonetheless failed to appoint him city health commissioner, saying:

A sampling of periodicals published by Macfadden

"Everyone knows you can live to be a hundred by following Macfadden's ideas. But New York wants to live the way I do." When he sent *Graphic* editor Emile H. Gauvreau to sound out Tammany Hall about a Macfadden candidacy for the New York governorship, the editor was told by Judge George W. Olvany: "He doesn't realize that practical politicians who drink and smoke and eat what they please look upon his health ideas as some kind of megalomania." Macfadden used the pages of *Liberty* to point out the benefits the nation might enjoy by electing him president, and three book-length biographies of Macfadden published in 1929 feature the worshipful praise characteristic of campaign biographies.

Macfadden declared himself a Republican candidate for the presidency in the 1936 election, when he was nearing seventy, and at least

one Macfadden for President club was organized in Illinois. His *Health Review* carried an article entitled "The Man Who Should Have Been Elected President in 1932 Instead of Franklin D. Roosevelt." Earlier, however, Macfadden had supported Roosevelt. He even employed Eleanor Roosevelt and her daughter to edit, from the White House, a short-lived magazine called *Babies, Just Babies*—a step his wife Mary attributed to his hope that Mrs. Roosevelt would help establish a department of health and support Macfadden's appointment to be its secretary. Ironically, Mrs. Roosevelt used the magazine to praise physicians. H. L. Mencken put Macfadden's presidential aspirations into perspective in the *American Mercury* in May 1930: "His central doctrine is to the effect that bodily vigor is the foundation of all virtue. John L. Sullivan could floor an ox at a blow;

Franz Schubert was floored by a few miserable bacilli; ergo, John was a better man than Franz. . . ." However, Macfadden's political ambitions were not furthered by his infatuation with Benito Mussolini, whom he declared to be the strongest man in power in Europe, or from his employing on the *Liberty* staff George Sylvester Viereck, who was imprisoned during World War II as a Nazi agent. Yet, for all his liabilities as a politician, Macfadden ran a close race in Florida for the United States Senate in 1940 as a Republican. Eight years later he entered the gubernatorial race there as a Democrat.

As controversial as many of his ideas were, Macfadden counted–in addition to the millions of readers of his magazines–some prominent men of his day among his friends and supporters: fellow vegetarian George Bernard Shaw, auto mogul Henry Ford, promoter Florenz Ziegfeld, boxer Jack Dempsey, and several congressmen and presidents. In 1930 a peak in northern California was named for him. Some of his employees, such as Gauvreau, Walter Winchell, and Ed Sullivan, were first-rate journalists who distinguished themselves in other ventures.

It can safely be said that Macfadden resisted mellowing with age. In his eighties, existing on a meager annuity that an auditor had set up against his wishes, he maintained that a diet of grapes and water could cure cancer and offered a reward of ten thousand dollars to anyone who could prove the remedy worthless. He publicized his eighty-first, eighty-third, and eighty-fourth birthdays by parachuting from a plane near a hotel he owned in Dansville, New York. At eighty-six he landed in jail in New Jersey for refusing to pay alimony after the failure of his marriage to Johnnie Lee. Believing that his health regimens would allow him to live to at least 125, he was hard at work in his final year on plans to launch a string of hotels in California.

Macfadden died on 12 October 1955 in the Jersey City Medical Center when his standard reaction to illness, a three-day fast, failed to restore him to health after a case of jaundice. It was, at eighty-seven, his first visit to a hospital.

Biographies:

Fulton Oursler, *The True Story of Bernarr Macfadden* (New York: Copeland, 1929);

Grace Perkins Oursler, *Chats With the Macfadden Family* (New York: Copeland, 1929);

Clement Wood, *Bernarr Macfadden: A Study in Success* (New York: Copeland, 1929);

Mary Macfadden and Emile H. Gauvreau, *Dumbbells and Carrot Strips: The Story of Bernarr Macfadden* (New York: Holt, 1953).

References:

Frederick Lewis Allen, *Only Yesterday* (New York: Bantam, 1931);

Oliver H. P. Garrett, "Another True Story," *New Yorker* (19 September 1925): 9-10;

Alva Johnston, "The Great Macfadden," *Saturday Evening Post*, 213 (21 June 1941): 9-11, 97-100; (28 June 1941): 9, 21, 90-93;

Frank Mallen, *Sauce for the Gander* (West Plains, N.Y.: Baldwin, 1954);

Harland Manchester, "True Stories: The Confession Magazines," *Scribner's*, 104 (August 1938): 25-29;

H. L. Mencken, "An American Idealist," *American Mercury*, 20 (May 1930): 124-125;

Fulton Oursler, "The Most Unforgettable Character I've Met," *Reader's Digest*, 65 (July 1951): 78-82;

Henry F. Pringle, "Another American Phenomenon, Bernarr Macfadden–Publisher and Physical Culturist," *World's Work*, 56 (October 1928): 659-666;

William H. Taft, "Bernarr Macfadden," *Missouri Historical Review*, 63 (October 1968): 71-89;

Taft, "Bernarr Macfadden: One of a Kind," *Journalism Quarterly*, 45 (Winter 1968): 627-633;

Allene Talmey, "Millions From Dumb-bells," *Outlook and Independent*, 155 (3 June 1930): 164-168;

Robert Lewis Taylor, "Profiles," *New Yorker*, 26 (14 October 1950): 39-40, 42, 44-45; (21 October 1950): 39-51; (28 October 1950): 37-50;

Oswald G. Villard, "Sex, Art, Truth, and Magazines," *Atlantic*, 137 (March 1926): 388-398.

S. S. McClure

(17 February 1857-21 March 1949)

James Glen Stovall
University of Alabama

MAJOR POSITIONS HELD: Editor, business manager, *Wheelman* (1882-1883); principal owner, editor in chief, McClure Syndicate (1884-1912), *McClure's Magazine* (1893-1912); editor, *New York Evening Mail* (1915-1917).

BOOKS: *My Autobiography,* ghostwritten by Willa Cather (New York: Stokes, 1914; London: Murray, 1914);
Obstacles to Peace (Boston & New York: Houghton Mifflin, 1917; London: Paul, 1917).

The January 1903 issue of *McClure's Magazine* stunned its readers with its extraordinary content and came to be regarded by many historians as the most important single issue of a magazine in its era, if not in the history of American journalism. It stands as the supreme example of the journalism that characterized the time: investigative reporting that Theodore Roosevelt later called "muckraking."

That issue included Ida Tarbell's third installment of a devastating history of the Standard Oil Company ("The Oil War of 1872"), as well as an article by Ray Stannard Baker on the lawlessness of members of the United Mineworkers ("The Right to Work: The Story of Non-Striking Miners"). The lead article, however, came to be the most noted work of muckraking journalism; it was Lincoln Steffens's "The Shame of Minneapolis," an article that detailed widespread municipal corruption with shocking frankness and accuracy. This article was part of a series that eventually came to be known as "The Shame of the Cities," which established Steffens's enduring reputation as a writer and reporter.

The man behind that famous issue of *McClure's Magazine* was the editor who had founded and given his name to the publication, Samuel Sidney McClure. He never received proper credit for putting together that landmark January 1903 issue, and the fault lies partially with his own description of how it came to be. In an editorial he wrote for that issue he dismissed

S. S. McClure (photograph by Arnold Genthe)

as "coincidence" the fact that the three articles appeared together, saying, "We did not plan it so." That statement has been interpreted to mean that McClure was simply lucky or that he had no clear idea of where he was taking his publication. An examination of his life and his work, however, reveals McClure to be an editor with a clear sense of direction and an unusually perceptive vision of the magazine journalism of his day and of its readership.

Samuel McClure (the middle name of Sidney was his own invention later in life) was born in Frocess, County Antrim, Ireland, in 1857. He was the oldest of four sons of Thomas McClure and Elizabeth Gaston McClure and was descended from a line of Scottish Lowlanders and French Huguenots. When McClure was eight his father was killed in an accident at a Clydesdale shipyard, and a year later his mother–fearing that the family would be separated–brought her children to America, where two of her brothers and two sisters had already immigrated. They settled near Valparaiso, Indiana, and battled continually with poverty.

In 1867 McClure's mother married Thomas Simpson, also an Irish immigrant, and they had four more children. The burden of poverty had been lifted somewhat with this marriage, and young Samuel was able to attend the local high school in Valparaiso. He was of slight stature, but he exhibited an impatience and an energy that in adulthood amazed and confounded his colleagues. He read voraciously, but he had to return to the farm in 1873 when his stepfather died of typhoid. He and his brothers thereupon accomplished what his late stepfather had been unable to do–run the farm well enough to pay off their debts and make a profit. By 1874 McClure accepted the urgings of an uncle who was studying for the ministry at Knox College in Galesburg, Illinois, and joined him there as a freshman. The people that McClure met during his eight-year college career at Knox were to have a continuing effect on his career for the rest of his life.

McClure proved himself to be an outstanding student. In addition, he was editor of the *Knox Student*, issued an intercollegiate news bulletin, and formed the Western College Associated Press. He also worked as a farmhand to pay his expenses. Academic pursuits were of primary importance at Knox College, with no athletics, fraternities, or other extracurricular distractions. The institution was so single-minded that McClure later wrote that during his years there he scarcely even read an outside newspaper.

The one distraction that McClure did find turned out to be a confounding one. Invited to a luncheon by the wife of the local Congregational minister, McClure met Harriet Hurd, the daughter of one of his professors, Albert Hurd. The couple fell in love immediately, but the road to their eventual marriage was long and rocky. Both families believed that a marriage between the gently reared daughter of a college professor and the son of an Irish immigrant was unthinkable.

McClure's mother asked her son to accompany her to Ireland as a way of separating him from Hurd, and he could resist neither a chance

to travel nor a request from his mother. His mother's plan was to leave him in Ireland and force him to find work there or in England. Instead, McClure worked his way back to America on a tramp steamer and resumed his education and his romance. Hurd's parents tried with only partial success to keep the couple apart. With her graduation the next year, her father sent her to Andover, Massachusetts, where she taught at Abbott Academy. In June 1882, after McClure's graduation, he went to see her at Marcy, New York, where she was visiting friends. There, she told him with all finality that she did not love him and that he was to return all of her letters and never see him again. McClure was stunned. He began walking along the train tracks, he wrote later, and when he heard a train coming up behind him, he thought "for a moment . . . that it was not worth while to get out the way."

He wound up in Boston and got a job with a bicycle manufacturer, Col. Albert Pope, who soon had the idea of starting a monthly magazine devoted to bicycling. Pope named him editor of the *Wheelman,* and McClure received some valuable on-the-job training on how to start a publication. McClure persuaded Pope to hire a college friend, John Phillips, and McClure's brother John to help launch the magazine, and in August 1882 the first number of the *Wheelman* appeared. McClure described his editorship as an "accident," but he came to a characteristic conclusion about it: "I had never expected to be an editor or planned to be one; but now that I found myself one, I was not surprised." The magazine appeared at just the right time. Bicycling was becoming a popular outdoor sport, and the magazine helped fire public enthusiasm for this activity. The *Wheelman* also gained support within the magazine industry. The *Nation* commented that it was "among the most attractive of the monthly magazines."

In mid September McClure received what he had been hoping for all summer, a letter from Hurd. She was returning some books, but something in her letter prompted him to respond, and in return he received another letter telling him that her dismissal of him was done at the instance of her father and did not reflect her feelings. "I loved you then," she wrote, "and I love you still." That was all the impetuous McClure needed. He rushed to Andover, and their courtship resumed.

During the next few months McClure divided his energies between marriage plans and

The founders of McClure's Magazine, *S. S. McClure and John Phillips, in 1895*

his work for the *Wheelman*. He managed to get a small raise from Pope, something that would provide a livable wage for him and his bride. Hurd's family reluctantly consented to their marriage, even though her father made it clear that McClure would never be welcome in his house. They were married on 4 September 1883; during their long married life they had three daughters, Eleanor, Elizabeth, and Mary, and a son, Robert Louis Stevenson. They also adopted a son, Enrico, whom they called Henry.

The next year Pope merged the *Wheelman* with *Outing*, owned and edited by William Howland. The conditions of the merger provided that McClure and Howland share equally the editorial and business duties of the revamped magazine. In anticipation of these events, McClure had already put out feelers to publishing firms in New York, and he had little trouble getting offers for his services. The De Vinne printing house offered him a job paying twenty-five dollars a week. In addition, Harriet McClure obtained a job with the Century Company paying fifteen dollars a week. However, at De Vinne McClure once again demonstrated his unwillingness, or inability, to function in a business environment that did not place him in charge of the operation. At his employer's urging, he accepted a position as

junior editor for the *Century* magazine. Harriet soon became pregnant with their first child, and when the baby was due, the company gave McClure two weeks off to be with her when the child was born. McClure used the time to draw up ten different plans that the company could use to make more money. For McClure, who was constantly bursting with ideas, it was a natural activity. Within two hours of his presenting these ideas to his superiors, however, he found himself without a job. His boss, Roswell Smith, perceptively noted that he was not suited to employment in a large operation, and that he should consider starting his own small business. (Generously, Smith said McClure would be paid his salary for two months, and if he did not find any work, he could come back and work during the winter.)

McClure took the ideas that he had offered to the *Century* and set them in motion for himself. The most potent of these ideas was to buy material from the most popular writers of the day and then sell it to newspapers around the nation. The idea of a literary syndicate was not a new one (despite the claim made by McClure that he had invented it), but McClure was the first to mold it into a fully profitable venture. In doing so, according to McClure's biographer Peter

Cover for the issue of McClure's Magazine *that included the third installment of Ida Tarbell's history of the Standard Oil Company, "The Oil War of 1872," Ray Stannard Baker's "The Right to Work: The Story of Non-Striking Miners," and Lincoln Steffens's "The Shame of Minneapolis"*

Lyon, he changed the nature of American newspapers and the character of American fiction. McClure had two traits that made his idea work–an innate sense of what Americans wanted to read and what editors would buy, and an inexhaustible supply of energy.

He traveled through New England visiting writers, some of whom he knew and others he did not. He also visited newspapers trying to line up clients. On 4 October 1884, with less than twenty-five dollars in the bank, he sent out an announcement of his syndicate, saying that he had commitments from such writers as William Dean Howells, Helen Hunt Jackson, and Harriet Prescott Spofford. The response from newspaper editors to this announcement was not overwhelming, but McClure charged ahead. He sent out another announcement later that month with more authors on his list and the news that fifty

newspapers had signed up for the service. (Actually, although fifty newspapers had responded to his announcement, only about thirty had agreed to terms.) The syndicate's first offering was to be H. H. Boyesen's "A Daring Fiction," and McClure still had little capital to cover the business expenses.

In desperation, McClure took to the road again, this time to use his considerable talents for sales on the editors themselves. He visited Philadelphia, Baltimore, Washington, and Boston, paying for his trip with the money he received from editors for the syndicate's first offerings. When he returned he found that newspapers in St. Paul and San Francisco had signed on. His business had gained some room to maneuver, but not much. Editors had signed on for different amounts and on different schedules. Keeping them straight and delivering the copy was a daunting task.

McClure's debts mounted, and he warded off bankruptcy by asking his authors to wait on their payments. Most of them did, accepting only his promise that their patience would eventually be rewarded.

McClure's venture faced a danger in addition to debt: competition. Shortly after McClure had announced the beginning of his syndicate, Allen Thorndike Rice, editor of the *North American Review,* returned from a European trip to begin plans to syndicate four or five articles a week from "the most famous writers in the world." These would be nonfiction pieces, so they constituted no immediate threat to what McClure was doing, but friends worried that their markets would begin to overlap. If McClure were drawn into a direct fight with Rice, he would not have the resources to sustain himself that Rice would have. McClure was urged to seek a merger with Rice.

McClure's response to his debts and his competition was typical. He decided to expand. He decided that the nonfiction market was one that he, too, could enter. He engaged Kate Field, a well-known Washington journalist, to write a series on Mormonism, and the series sold well. In January he announced his intention to furnish articles by "the most noted writers" to newspapers on a daily basis. Still the debts mounted. In April 1885, seven months after he began his syndicate, McClure totaled his income and his bills for the first time and found that though his newspapers owed him $1,000, he owed his authors $1,500. Just at that point Harriet Prescott Spofford sent him a two-part short story that, she told him, was a belated New Year's gift. He sold it for $275, and by June he was finally showing a profit and making about $100 a month. By the end of the year McClure had charged ahead of all his competitors, and the syndicate begun by Rice had played out completely.

McClure owed the life of his syndicate to the goodwill of his writers, but they had reason to be patient. McClure was offering them a new outlet, one they desperately needed. No longer would they be encumbered by either book publishers or a small number of elite, narrowly focused national magazines. They found that their fiction had to fit into the parameters drawn by the editors of the *Century, Harper's,* or the *Atlantic.* Many writers found these editors too delicate in their tastes and too ready to give space and money to English writers, and they were eager to have a less critical market for their work. The realistic fiction that American writers were producing was less than satisfying to the denizens of New York and Boston, but it was more to the tastes of provincial journals that were springing up all over the country. McClure provided a conduit for the writers to these journals, and his early authors' forbearance allowed his idea to work.

McClure was fortunate to find himself in an expanding market. In 1884, when he began his syndicate, there were fewer than twelve hundred dailies in the country; ten years later there were more than two thousand. The editors he served were by no means uncritical of his offerings, but as long as the syndicate expanded the venture remained profitable. He was always on the lookout for new authors, and he was constantly attempting to sell his wares to editors.

In 1887 McClure pursuaded his old Knox College friend John Phillips to join him in running the syndicate. Phillips, unlike McClure, showed a penchant for organization. He brought his orderly frame of mind into the central office, and that freed McClure to roam around looking for material and clients. In February he sailed to Europe, the first of six trips in eight years. He also traveled in the opposite direction, crossing the continent a half-dozen times, and the list of authors he was able to sign on would make an impressive anthology. Among them were Robert Louis Stevenson, Rudyard Kipling, Arthur Conan Doyle, John Ruskin, Charles Swinburne, Emile Zola, Willa Cather, Bret Harte, Henry James, Walt Whitman, Julia Ward Howe, Stephen Crane, Joel Chandler Harris, O. Henry, Jack London, and Booth Tarkington.

He traveled and worked at a breakneck pace. He talked to everyone. He was constantly selling and asking to buy. He read incessantly. He made deals instantly, often on impulse with no apparent prospect of payoff. Yet he was often right in his perceptions of authors, and the payoffs were handsome. In his autobiography (which was ghostwritten by Cather), he tells how he judged fiction: "I had but one test for a story, and that was a wholly personal one–simply how much the story interested me. I always felt that I judged a story with my solar plexus rather than my brain; my only measure of it was the pull it exerted upon something inside me."

The idea of starting a magazine was another one of McClure's ambitions that emerged at the right time. Magazines were becoming cheaper to illustrate and produce; manufacturers were seeking national markets for their products

The McClure family, circa 1905: S. S. and Robert (back); Eleanor, Harriet,
and Elizabeth (middle); and Mary and Enrico (front)

and more ways to advertise them; and the public was becoming more attuned to magazine reading. The most successful magazines of the period, such as *Harper's,* the *Century,* and the *Atlantic,* were high-priced and limited in their appeal. McClure was convinced that a larger audience existed, one that would accept a broader vision of literature and one that needed a cheaper price tag on the product. That product he produced in *McClure's Magazine,* which sold at first for fifteen, and later ten cents a copy. (*Harper's,* the *Century,* and the *Atlantic* sold for thirty-five cents.) McClure also realized that while his syndicate had been successful, it had not obliterated his rivals; he felt that there was little room for growth in that business. He had some two thousand unsold manuscripts in his safe, and he needed a means for making something out of them.

Consequently, early in 1892 he and John Phillips began planning for an inexpensive publication. Phillips put up forty-five hundred dollars, and McClure contributed twenty-eight hundred

dollars from syndicate profits (just about all there was). Besides the unsold manuscripts, they planned to reprint some of the syndicate's most successful offerings. McClure made yet another transatlantic voyage attempting to gather material for the book. It was nearly a year and a half before the magazine was set to appear, and when it did, it looked as if McClure's timing had gone terribly awry. The panic of 1893, a run on almost all of the nation's banks, had frozen the currency system, and there was little cash available. Newspapers that owed the syndicate could not pay, and worse, many newspapers began dropping their syndicated services. As the first issue of *McClure's Magazine* rolled off the presses in May 1893, the publication and the syndicate itself faced a very uncertain future.

The first issue was not a success. About twenty thousand copies were printed, and twelve thousand were returned. Shortly before the first number was published, McClure went to see Henry Drummond, a Scottish theologian and au-

McClure as a correspondent in China, 1917

thor of a scientific article for the magazine. Drummond offered McClure $3,000 for stock in the magazine, and that enabled McClure to publish the next two issues. A novel by Stanley Weyman, *A Gentleman from France* (1894), which McClure had bought for $250, sold well and brought in about $2,000. McClure obtained $6,000 from his old employer, Colonel Pope in Boston, that was to be repaid by advertising space. McClure continued to put together financing for the magazine on an ad hoc basis. After a year the magazine was losing about $1,000 a month, and the debts–particularly those to authors–were mounting. McClure had seemingly exhausted every resource and knew of no one to consult. At the time Arthur Conan Doyle was lecturing in the United States, and McClure paid a courtesy call because of their prior association. Doyle expressed an interest in investing in the magazine, and he wrote a check for $5,000 to McClure. That sum was the exact amount McClure needed to cover some of his immediate debts, and the magazine continued. By the end of the year *McClure's* had a subscription list of sixty thousand and was carrying sixty pages of advertising. The future was still uncertain, however, because other magazines were cutting their prices to match *McClure's*.

Once the magazine had begun to function, McClure formed a partnership with Frank Doubleday to publish books. They began with Ida Tarbell's biography of Abraham Lincoln, which brought a profit of eighty thousand dollars, but they were both too strong-willed to work together very well. Doubleday finally split with McClure and formed a publishing house that long outlived the McClure organization. McClure had also undertaken to purchase Harper and Brothers, one of the nation's oldest and largest publishing houses, but the deal fell through.

Beset by financial worries, McClure was also unable to take much comfort in the magazine's editorial content. Neither McClure nor his staff was producing the kind of product that he had envisioned. He had the idea that he should bring out a magazine in which everything was of interest to every reader. "Things must be written so as to be made attractive to people not ordinarily interested in those subjects," he said. Like his financing of the magazine, McClure's recruitment of staff was done by instinct and impulse, and it often produced the best that was available. The jewel in this crown was Ida Tarbell, daughter of an oil-producing family from Titusville, Pennsylvania. Her family was also involved in the feminist and temperance movements, and her abilities with the written word were soon recognized. She was in Paris, making a precarious living as a writer, when McClure spotted her on one of his European trips. When he began the magazine, he invited her to come back to America to be an editor. At first she resisted, but when he offered to let her write a series about Napoléon Bonaparte, she accepted. McClure found an excellent collection of portraits of Napoléon in the possession of G. G. Hubbard of Washington, D.C. (the father-in-law of Alexander Graham Bell), and he persuaded Hubbard to allow some to be used as illustrations.

The series on Napoléon was a modest success, but it led to other triumphs. Tarbell's next assignment was a series on Abraham Lincoln, and she applied instinctive and thorough research techniques to her work, eventually producing a series that paid off immediately in thousands of new subscribers to the magazine. (Later, when someone asked Richard Watson Gilder, editor of the *Century,* what he thought of *McClure's Magazine,* he replied curtly, "They got a girl to write a Life of Lincoln.")

Along with Tarbell, McClure added an odd mixture of talent to the magazine's staff. Viola Roseboro, a hard-smoking ex-actress from Tennessee, was one of the main fiction editors. She had worked for McClure's syndicate and transferred to the magazine when it began. There she read unsolicited manuscripts, and McClure came to respect her strong and original mind. One of her finds was William Sidney Porter, who wrote under the pen name of O. Henry. She should also be given credit for recognizing the talents of Booth Tarkington, Edith Wyatt, Jack London, and Willa Cather. Much of the poetry the magazine published was under the direction of Witter Bynner, a poet who was first discovered by Roseboro and who later persuaded the magazine to grant the first American publication to the poems of A. E. Housman.

Despite McClure's belief in a strong, unified editorial staff, the magazine developed a justifiable reputation as a forum for reporters and writers. The star of this group was Lincoln Steffens, although William Allen White and Ray Stannard Baker also were to achieve prominence in their days with the publication. Steffens was a San Franciscan who graduated from the University of Cali-

fornia. He wandered Europe for a while and returned to New York in 1891 in search of practical employment. He landed a job with the *New York Evening Post,* published a short story in *Harper's,* became friends with Theodore Roosevelt, and moved to the *New York Commercial Advertiser.* In 1901 Steffens was finally persuaded by John Phillips to leave the newspaper staff and come to work for *McClure's Magazine.* Steffens's title was managing editor, but he discovered that he was not comfortable behind a desk. McClure also recognized this, and he urged Steffens to travel around the country and to "meet people and find out what's on." Steffens did just that, traveling through the East and Midwest, developing the idea for a series on municipal misgovernment. He told Tarbell, "If I should be entrusted with the work, I think I could make my name."

Steffens was not so much the investigative reporter as the recorder of what people commonly knew and freely told him. Steffens's preference in writing was for the generalized statement, the sweeping indictment. McClure, however, demanded facts. Tarbell's methods and products were more to his liking, but he recognized Steffens's ability. McClure's instincts were justified by the January 1903 issue of *McClure's Magazine.* Steffens's article on Minneapolis, along with Tarbell's painstaking history of the Standard Oil Company and Baker's chronicling of union abuses, led McClure to describe that issue as the magazine's "greatest success." Subsequent issues continued to expose the wrongs of society to public view, and *McClure's* led the way for other publications and writers to do the same. In 1906 this journalistic movement was given the name of "muckraking" by President Roosevelt, who had grown weary of it along with much of the reading public.

The environment of *McClure's Magazine* reflected the temperament of its principal owner, and it was not one conducive to long-term harmony. The magazine's circulation had reached four hundred thousand by 1906, and the readership had come to expect much of the magazine. It continued to deliver, but the pressures were taking their toll. McClure, characteristically, had plans for expansion, but his staff—particularly those who owned stock in the company—saw this scheme only as a means of dwindling their profits and adding to the magazine's debts. Finally, a confrontation occurred, and it ended with the resignations of Tarbell, Phillips, Baker, and Stef-

McClure in 1944, when he received the Order of Merit from the National Institute of Arts and Letters

fens, all of whom joined together to purchase the *American Magazine.*

The revolt had been a long and drawn-out affair, but for those staff members left behind, and for those whom McClure hired to replace them, it was ultimately invigorating. The magazine gained new life and continued to produce perceptive articles. Reporters continued to investigate municipal and industrial wrongdoing; they wrote engaging profiles on well-known people of the day; and they examined political and social issues. On the financial side, however, *McClure's* continued a downward slide into debt. In 1911 the company reorganized, and the next year McClure was forced out as editor. McClure had little in the way of personal assets. He had never amassed a personal fortune, even during the magazine's thriving years. His annual stipend after his removal as editor was ten thousand dollars.

Although McClure remained active for the next twenty years, his actions did little to enhance his reputation or fortune. Soon after leaving the magazine, he became involved with the *New York Evening Mail,* a newspaper that had a pro-German reputation. McClure was tarred with the same brush, and he was never able to clear his name completely. He joined an ill-advised Peace Ship–a group of idealists organized by Henry Ford in 1915–that sailed to several European capitals, though McClure cut short his participation. After World War I he returned briefly to *McClure's,* but the magazine never regained its reputation or financial stability. It was finally sold to Hearst's International Publications in 1925; the name lingered on, eventually to disappear in 1930.

McClure had a brief romance with fascism, met Benito Mussolini, and defended much of what he had done in Italy. On the whole, however, McClure's active life was ended. His wife died in 1930, and he continued to live and write occasionally in New York. He kept in touch with his colleagues and publicly disagreed with the conclusions of those who had begun to write the history of the muckraking era. He considered much of what Steffens's autobiography had said about him and his magazine to be Steffens's inventions.

McClure died on 21 March 1949; he was ninety-two years old. His body was taken to Galesburg, Illinois, and buried next to that of his wife. His last years were especially sad considering the frenzied life that he had led when his magazine was the central discussion point of the reading nation, though he was extremely gratified to be awarded the Order of Merit gold medal by the National Institute of Arts and Letters in 1944. In an era of magazines, McClure exploited the medium's full potential. His lasting contribution was in his vision of the effect an editor could have, not only on a publication but on the reading public. "My definition of an editor is this," he wrote late in life, "one who, by the use of other minds, makes a transcript of our civilization. If he does this successfully and with true art and sanity, the result of his work will be to aid good causes and to hinder evil causes. . . . It is for the editor to translate this upward march of humanity into the printed word."

Biography:
Peter Lyon, *Success Story: The Life and Times of S. S. McClure* (De Land, Fla.: Everett/Edwards, 1967).

References:
Justin Kaplan, *Lincoln Steffens* (New York: Simon & Schuster, 1970);
Harold S. Wilson, *McClure's Magazine and the Muckrakers* (Princeton: Princeton University Press, 1970).

Papers:
The McClure papers are located in the Lilly Library at Indiana University.

Harriet Monroe

(23 December 1860-26 September 1936)

Judith Paterson
University of Maryland

See also the Monroe entry in *DLB 54: American Poets, 1880-1945.*

MAJOR POSITIONS HELD: Editor and publisher, *Poetry: A Magazine of Verse* (1912-1936).

BOOKS: *Valeria and Other Poems* (Chicago: Printed for the author, 1891);
Commemoration Ode (Chicago: Printed for the author by Rand McNally, 1892); republished as *The Columbian Ode* (Chicago: W. I. Way, 1893);
John Wellborn Root: A Study of His Life and Work (Boston & New York: Houghton, Mifflin, 1896);
The Passing Show: Five Modern Plays in Verse (Boston & New York: Houghton, Mifflin, 1903);
The Dance of Seasons (Chicago: Seymour, 1911);
You and I (New York: Macmillan, 1914);
The Difference and Other Poems (Chicago: Covici-McGee, 1924);
Poets and Their Art (New York: Macmillan, 1926; revised and enlarged, 1932);
Chosen Poems: A Selection from My Books of Verse (New York: Macmillan, 1935);
A Poet's Life: Seventy Years in a Changing World (New York: Macmillan, 1938).

OTHER: *The New Poetry: An Anthology*, edited by Monroe and Alice Corbin Henderson, with an introduction by Monroe (New York: Macmillan, 1917); revised and enlarged as *The New Poetry: An Anthology of Twentieth-Century Verse in English* (New York: Macmillan, 1923; revised and enlarged again, 1932).

SELECTED PERIODICAL PUBLICATIONS
UNCOLLECTED: "Grand Cañon of the Colorado," *Atlantic*, 84 (December 1899): 816-821;
"Literary Women and the Higher Education," *Critic*, 46 (April 1905): 313-318;
"To the Snake-dance," *Fortnightly*, new series 78 (October 1905): 665-677;

Harriet Monroe

"Poetry, a Zest for Life," *Poetry*, 2 (July 1913): 140-142;
"The Enemies We Have Made," *Poetry*, 4 (May 1914): 61-64;
"The Poet's Bread and Butter," *Poetry*, 4 (August 1914): 195-198;
"The Audience, II," *Poetry*, 5 (October 1914): 31-32;
"The Question of Prizes," *Poetry*, 7 (February 1916): 246-249;
"The New Era," *Poetry*, 9 (January 1917): 195-197;
"These Five Years," *Poetry*, 11 (October 1917): 33-41;
"The Great Renewal," *Poetry*, 12 (September 1918): 320-325;

"Those We Refuse," *Poetry,* 15 (March 1920): 321-325;

"Poets the Self-Revealers," *Poetry,* 23 (January 1924): 206-210;

"Ezra Pound," *Poetry,* 26 (May 1925): 90-97;

"Looking Backward," *Poetry,* 33 (October 1928): 32-38;

"Twenty-One," *Poetry,* 43 (October 1933): 32-37;

"Poets as Leaders," *Poetry,* 48 (September 1936): 330-334.

Monroe in 1892 (photograph by Loomis & Powes)

A poet of substance in her own right, Harriet Monroe is best known as the founder of *Poetry: A Magazine of Verse.* Monroe's twenty-four-year editorship of the magazine earned her a prominent place among those who shaped twentieth-century poetry and literary taste. Her leadership and the role the magazine played in nurturing and focusing the modern movement in poetry can hardly be overestimated. The magazine provided early and continued recognition for a rising generation of poets that included Carl Sandburg, Ezra Pound, D. H. Lawrence, T. S. Eliot, Rabindranath Tagore, Amy Lowell, and Robert Frost. Its pages became a forum for the development of poetic theory and the airing of controversies that arose as modern poetry moved away from romanticism and toward realism, free verse, and precise imagery.

Monroe was born in Chicago on 23 December 1860. In childhood, she saw herself as a loner in a family kept off balance by the tension between her intellectual lawyer father, Henry Stanton Monroe, and her gregarious but poorly educated mother, Martha Mitchell Monroe. A frail, bookish girl dominated by her older sister Dora Louise, Monroe turned for solace to the art histories, classics, and poetry volumes that she found in her father's library. As she explained in her autobiography, *A Poet's Life: Seventy Years in a Changing World* (1938), "I started in early with Shakespeare, Byron, Shelley, with Dickens and Thackeray; and always the book-lined library gave me a friendly assurance of companionship with lively and interesting people, gave me friends of the spirit to ease my loneliness."

She received her schooling ·at Moseley School in Chicago and later at Visitation Convent in Georgetown, Washington, D.C., where the nuns in charge of her education encouraged her to read and write poetry. Inspired by her education, she returned to Chicago to fulfill her ambition to become "great and famous" as a poet or playwright. "I cannot remember," she said,

"when to die without leaving some memorable record did not seem to me a calamity too terrible to be borne." For the rest of her life, she would move slowly–and with little apparent anxiety–toward her destiny.

In an era when careers for women were not common, Monroe set about making one for herself. First by gathering friends in the newspaper and art worlds and then by writing poetry, drama, and essays for publication, she carved out a place for herself in cultural circles in Chicago. Inspired by correspondence with Robert Louis Stevenson, she began writing verse based on the works of William Shakespeare and John Milton.

Her first acceptance came from *Century* magazine in 1889 for a conventional poem entitled "With a Copy of Shelley." Exhilarated by her success, she imagined a life of acclaim and affluence as a professional poet. Gradually, she realized how poorly poets were rewarded and, many years later, remembered her disillusionment: "The minor painter or sculptor was honored with large annual awards in our greatest cities, while the minor poet was a joke of the paragraphers, subject to the popular prejudice that his art thrived best on starvation in a garret." Her awareness over poor remuneration and the low regard in which poets were held paved the way for her later decision to create a magazine that would accord status and decent pay to talented poets.

While making a slender living as a woman of letters and free-lance cultural correspondent for the *Chicago Tribune* and living at home with her parents, Monroe cultivated a widening circle of prominent literary acquaintances and friends, including the influential New Yorker Edmund Clarence Stedman. Encouraged by Stedman and his wife, she spent a year in New York as art, drama, and music critic for the *Tribune*, always adding to the circle of friends and acquaintances who would help her launch her magazine. When she returned to Chicago, she found Carl Sandburg's "hog butcher" city awash in youthful enthusiasm for the arts.

Monroe continued to be involved in the city's expanding cultural scene. She wrote the official poem for the World's Columbian Exposition held in Chicago in 1893. She worked on *The Columbian Ode* (1893; first published as *Commemoration Ode*, 1892) for three years. Although it is essentially a patriotic, occasional piece, she was always proud of the poem and enjoyed the fame that followed when it was read by a chorus of five thousand voices in 1892 at a ceremony to dedicate a new auditorium built on the Exposition grounds. When a pirated version of the poem appeared without her permission in the *New York World*, her father sued the paper. Eventually she was awarded a five-thousand-dollar settlement that established a legal precedent granting authors the right to control their own unpublished works.

During the 1890s Monroe undertook two trips to Europe. With travel, her poetry took on a new dimension, celebrating new cultures as she absorbed them: the architecture of Greece, the art in Cairo, Rubens's nudes in the Louvre. Travel in the southwestern part of the United States produced a new spirit of realism in her nature poetry as she began to let go of the romanticism and "poetic diction" characteristic of American poetry of the period. In a cautious way her own poetry was beginning to move in the direction of the new mode of poetic expression that would burst onto the scene with her help a few years later.

Her first collection, *Valeria and Other Poems*, was privately published in 1891. A few poems appeared in the *Atlantic* and in *Fortnightly Review*, a British publication. Otherwise, publication of her conventional, well-made poetry continued to be sparse. Most magazines at the turn of the century were seeking romantic verse written to appeal to the casual reader, and poems were often used merely as filler.

Although Monroe had a profound talent for attracting people who shared her literary interests, she was not a socialite, as were her sister and mother, and none of her brief amorous encounters resulted in marriage. Daniel J. Cahill states that "Perhaps she was too independent of mind or could not imagine herself bound to a life condition which imposed so many restrictions upon her personal freedom. For a woman of her intellectual aspirations, she simply preferred the single life."

Monroe's own comments suggest a level of independence not common in women of her day. She knew of few flawless marriages, she said, and nothing short of perfection would do for her. Admitting a degree of ambivalence and envy of more conventional women, she added, "I gave up the problem and retired from the great game," accepting the "spinster's comparatively narrow lot [without] severe agony, either physical or mental."

In 1896, still deeply involved in Chicago's cultural renaissance, Monroe published *John Wellborn Root: A Study of His Life and Work*, a memorial to her deceased brother-in-law whose architectural innovations and taste had helped mold the Exposition. Though her reputation continued to grow between 1900 and 1910, deaths in her family and disappointment in her career as a poet brought sorrow. "These were dark days," she wrote in her autobiography. "Professionally also I had need of consolations against continual disappointment and the distracting effort to earn a living in various small ways."

By the time she returned from a trip around the world in 1911, Monroe had become convinced of the need for a magazine that would encourage serious poets by publishing their work and paying them decently for it. She had often spoken of her concern over the plight of poets and poetry with an enthusiastic group of Chicago writers and prominent arts boosters known as "The Little Room." Hobart Chatfield-Taylor, publisher of the local literary magazine *America* and a highly regarded member of the group, had be-

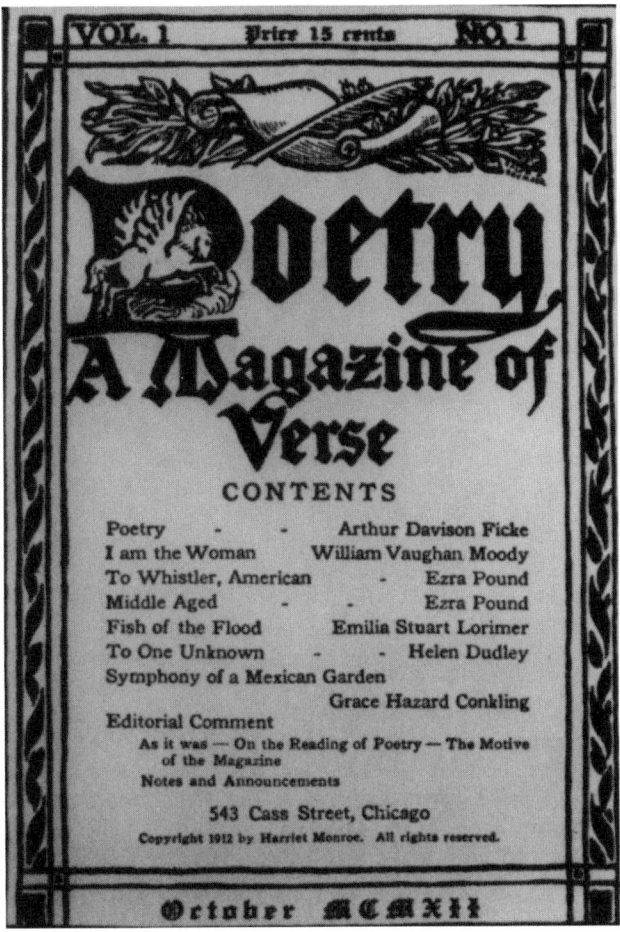

Cover for the first issue of the magazine Monroe founded with the "desire to print the best English verse which is being written today, regardless of . . . under what theory of art it is written"

come Monroe's close friend. With his encouragement she set out to establish her poetry magazine.

First she had to solve the problems of obtaining financing and finding her audience. Following Chatfield-Taylor's suggestion, she decided to get one hundred prominent Chicago business people to sponsor the magazine with subscriptions of fifty dollars a year for five years. For a year she called on her contacts in the literary and business worlds of Chicago and finally raised fifty-two hundred dollars with which to launch the magazine.

When she was not soliciting sponsors or sending out a "poets' circular" to explain the proposed magazine and her philosophy, she was studying English and American poetry, especially as it appeared in magazines. She promised to pay poets as much as the magazine could afford, hoping to set a new standard on the monetary value of poetry in the literary marketplace. Through

lean financial times she kept her promise and refused to accept a salary for herself until 1914, when she resigned her duties as art critic for the *Tribune* in order to devote all her energies to the magazine. To make ends meet she began taking a salary of fifty dollars a month, which she raised to one hundred dollars in 1925.

As might be expected, poets responded to the idea of *Poetry* with enthusiasm, and Monroe's call for quality verse and criticism brought immediate submissions from established poets as well as unknowns. Her first issue, which appeared on 23 September 1912, included poems by Emilia Stuart Lorimer, Helen Dudley, Arthur Davison Ficke, Grace Hazard Conkling, William Vaughn Moody, and Ezra Pound.

Pound, a twenty-seven-year-old American poet living in London, had responded optimistically to her poets' circular, writing "I *am* interested, and your scheme, as far as I understand it,

Pages from the first draft for Monroe's posthumously published autobiography, A Poet's Life: Seventy Years in a Changing World *(by permission of Dr. and Mrs. Edwin S. Fetcher, the Estate of Harriet Monroe; courtesy of University of Chicago Library, Department of Special Collections, Box 8, Folder 1)*

By the time *Poetry* was four years old I was beginning to feel like that goblin in the quaint old myth who, blowing the fog out of his face, started a tornado which went careering around the world. A great wind was blowing Cinderella's ashes away, and on the horizon were rolling clouds of words. There was.

It was inevitable, perhaps, that as the cause became more conspicuous, Ezra Pound, instinctive rebel, should begin to lose interest in our campaign. His letters, which had regaled and inspired us so often during the first year or two, gradually faded out, and when he surprised me by taking on a connection with the *Little Review* during the summer of 1917, at the very time we were serializing the early version of his first three *Cantos*, I felt that a new understanding was necessary, and sent him a long letter rehearsing our differences and mutual interests. His answer was amiably explanatory, but we had drifted apart, and soon he resigned informally as *Poetry's* Foreign Correspondent. However, through all these years he has sent us poems at intervals, and prodded us now and then in different moods of humor or impatience or violence. And if his stings and stabs should cease, it would mean for me the loss of life's most deliciously acrid flavor.

The cause was becoming more conspicuous, in spite of the world's major preoccupation with war. Indeed, there was danger that poetry might become

seems not only sound, but the only possible method. There is no other magazine in America which is not an insult to the serious artist and to the dignity of his art."

Pound became the magazine's foreign correspondent, combing Great Britain and Europe for poets worthy of publication and sending his own poems in the new style of the Imagists. He defended that style in essays published in *Poetry* and called for a new realism and concreteness in verse. On technique he became the radical voice on the magazine, urging Monroe to condone experimentation and move rapidly away from the traditional European influence that encouraged elevated language and abstract ideas.

Monroe was fifty-two years old when the first issue of *Poetry* was published. Her talents as an organizer and administrator and her ambitions for "greatness" had finally found expression. They were soon to be matched, if not surpassed, by an almost uncanny ability to recognize and nurture greatness in other poets.

The establishment of the magazine's annual award for poetry reflected Monroe's determination to gain recognition for poets. The first annual *Poetry* award, which went to William Butler Yeats for the poem "The Grey Rock," set a high standard for the prize. Other early winners included Carl Sandburg, Edgar Lee Masters, Wallace Stevens, Hart Crane, Amy Lowell, Marianne Moore, Robert Frost, Vachel Lindsay, Dylan Thomas, and others whose potential was yet to be recognized by the poetry-reading public.

In 1913 another *Poetry* contributor, Rabindranath Tagore, won the Nobel Prize for Literature. "I drew a long breath of renewed power," Monroe wrote, "and felt that my little magazine was fulfilling some of our seemingly extravagant hopes."

With the second issue of *Poetry*, Monroe began an editorial policy that carried the magazine into the modern literary era. "Open Door will be the policy of this magazine–may the great poet we are looking for never find it shut, or half-shut, against his ample genius! To this end the editors ... desire to print the best English verse which is being written today, regardless of where, by whom, or under what theory of art it is written."

Monroe's high-minded statement of editorial purpose also promised to keep the magazine free of "entangling alliances with any single class or school." Although she was influenced by Pound's enthusiasm for the new poetry of the Im-

agists, she stuck to her position and put the survival and integrity of the magazine ahead of factionalism. Guided by her steady hand, *Poetry* was distinguished by both the quality and the diversity of the works it published.

As historian Horace Gregory has said, "Read swiftly and without discrimination it would seem that the secret of *Poetry*'s editorial selection of verse was to have no policy at all." Ultimately, the selection process was governed by Monroe's personal taste and her willingness to publish writers with whom she did not agree, so long as the quality of the work met her standards.

Jessica North Nelson, one of the magazine's early manuscript readers and editor of the publication in 1942 and 1943, recalls that Monroe's standards were clear and pragmatic. Poems were unacceptable if they were imitative, unnecessarily lengthy, padded, stilted, or too personal. According to Cahill the procedure worked well. He concludes that "By rejecting poetry that failed to come to terms with modern life, she imposed an editorial value that helped determine the shape of modern poetry in America."

The lines Monroe drew were fine ones, however, and she was often criticized by both conservatives and progressives. Those with conservative literary taste thought her acceptance of new forms and free verse too radical. Others, including Pound, wanted her to move ahead more rapidly than she was willing.

When the *Dial*, a conservative literary magazine, held that Monroe was destroying quality poetry by publishing free verse and the Imagists, Monroe defined her position on the editorial page of *Poetry*: "Imagism is by no means the last word, as Mr. Pound, or Mr. [F. S.] Flint, or Miss [Amy] Lowell, would be the first to acknowledge. But in so far as it is a protest against narrow-mindedness and provincialism–against myopia, in short–it is a good word, and a word that needs to be uttered."

In 1917 the Macmillan Company published *The New Poetry: An Anthology*, a ground-breaking collection of modern poetry edited by Monroe and her assistant, Alice Corbin Henderson. Monroe's introduction to the book clarifies her strongest beliefs about poetry. The best poetry, she insists, always harks back to ancient traditions, regardless of how new it might seem. Nevertheless, her definition of the best in modern poetry obviously approves of certain developing trends: good poetry represents life in a concrete and realistic fashion; it avoids the abstraction and remoteness of the second-rate literature of the past by being "less vague, less verbose, less eloquent"; its ideal is "absolute simplicity and sincerity"; it is concrete rather than diffuse; it looks more to the external world in which the poet lives than to the poet's inner life. Finally, poetry should reflect and serve the needs of its times; and, she concludes, "Many critics feel that poetry is coming nearer than either the novel or the drama to the actual life of our time."

The coming of World War I provided Monroe with an all too vivid opportunity to print poetry that conveyed reality. Beginning in 1914 she urged her contributors to avoid glamorizing the war. A special issue included war poetry by Maxwell Bodenheim, Carl Sandburg, Amy Lowell, and Wallace Stevens. *Poetry* continued to publish protest poems throughout the war, and Monroe learned firsthand of the difficulties of writing and publishing poetry during wartime. As she wrote in her June 1917 editorial, "Every artist, striving to reveal truth and beauty, finds his vision veiled by the smoke of battle and violated by the scent of blood. And the world seems mad, lost for its sins, bent upon extinction, upon suicide. And yet war is a builder. Out of the ruins of eras it tumbles together foundation-stones for new ones."

Meanwhile, skirmishes to determine the leadership and guiding philosophy of the magazine continued. As the magazine's stimulating but contentious foreign correspondent, Pound had recruited major new voices in America and Europe—including H. D. (Hilda Doolittle), Richard Aldington, Yeats, Lawrence, Frost, Ford Madox Ford, Eliot ("The Love Song of J. Alfred Prufrock" was published in the June 1915 issue), and James Joyce. Despite her appreciation for Pound's efforts and talents, Monroe was determined that her "open door" approach prevail over Pound's pugnacious advocacy of his own perspective. Pound finally resigned his post on the magazine in 1917 but remained on the roster of editors until 1919. According to Monroe, the two parted without bitterness to follow separate paths toward their mutual goal of perpetuating the best in modern poetry.

Despite the amount of time and energy she devoted to putting out the monthly magazine, Monroe continued to write increasingly sophisticated poetry of her own. In the collection *You and I* (1914), poems such as "The Turbine" and "A Power-Plant" demonstrate her growth as a poet learning the lessons of modernity. Her im-

ages had become more concrete and precise, the language simpler, but the poems remained personal and lyrical, based on her own experiences.

Although *The Difference and Other Poems* (1924) shows further development in poetic technique and subject matter, it marks the end of Monroe's abiding optimism over the state of American culture and the promise of a future bright with technological and artistic progress. This disillusionment surfaced again in Monroe's final collection, *Chosen Poems: A Selection from My Books of Verse* (1935).

Yet nothing indicates that the pessimism reflected in Monroe's postwar verse extended to her editorship of *Poetry*, which she headed until her death in 1936. The magazine's last fifteen years were as brilliant as its start had promised, as new poets, including Yvor Winters, Hart Crane, Archibald MacLeish, Robert Penn Warren, W. H. Auden, Louise Bogan, Stephen Spender, Allen Tate, Countee Cullen, William Empson, Paul Engle, and R. P. Blackmur, continued to be discovered, nurtured, and published.

Cahill summarizes Monroe's contribution as a poet by saying, "Perhaps her vision as a poet was limited and her range of human experience too confined for modern taste, but much of what she produced as a poet still remains as a quiet testimony to excellence in modern poetry." However, it was as editor and founder of *Poetry* magazine, rather than as a poet, that she realized her youthful ambition to achieve greatness in the arts. As she recalled in her autobiography: "Indeed that public was growing under our eyes even though *Poetry*'s subscription list increased with disappointing slowness. Less than four years after our crusade began, the situation had changed—it was as though some magician had waved his wand—presto, the beggar is robed in scarlet!"

Harriet Monroe died on 26 September 1936 after attending the International Association of Poets, Playwrights, Editors, Essayists, and Novelists (P.E.N.) Conference in Buenos Aires. Intending to hike through the Andes and the Inca ruins in Peru, she suffered a cerebral hemorrhage, perhaps brought on by the altitude.

A Poet's Life: Seventy Years in a Changing World was almost finished when she left Chicago for the last time. The manuscript for the final chapter, written on the ship to Buenos Aires, was found in her baggage after her death. The book, which is an exuberant account of her life and the establishment of *Poetry*, draws heavily on her voluminous correspondence with the generation of poets that set the standard for modern poetry after World War I. The final chapter explains her almost religious devotion to creativity and beauty.

In their book, *The Little Magazine: A History and Bibliography* (1946), Frederick J. Hoffman, Charles Allen, and Carolyn F. Ulrich summarize the significance of *Poetry* and Harriet Monroe's leadership. "The first issue of *Poetry* marks the turning point in American poetry of the twentieth century. . . . [Monroe's] intelligent judgment, and that of her first assistant editor, Alice Corbin Henderson, gave it a consistently high rate of creditable performance. . . . one is surprised to find that any single magazine could so consistently uncover and recognize the talent of its age. Its alertness to new writers, to new trends, has been little short of phenomenal."

References:

Daniel J. Cahill, *Harriet Monroe* (New York: Twayne, 1973);

Stanley K. Coffman, *Imagism: A Chapter for the History of Modern Poetry* (Norman: University of Oklahoma Press, 1951);

Mary Colum, *Life and the Dream* (Garden City, N.Y.: Doubleday, 1947);

Malcolm Cowley, ed., *After the Genteel Tradition: American Writers 1910-1930* (Carbondale: Southern Illinois University Press, 1964);

Bernard Duffey, *The Chicago Renaissance in American Letters: A Critical History* (Ann Arbor: Michigan State University Press, 1956);

John Gould Fletcher, *Life Is My Song* (New York: Farrar & Rinehart, 1937);

Horace Gregory, "The Unheard of Adventure– Harriet Monroe and Poetry," *American Scholar*, 6 (Spring 1937): 195-200;

Gregory and Marya Zaturenska, *A History of American Poetry: 1900-1940* (New York: Harcourt, Brace, 1942);

Harry Hansen, *Midwest Portraits: A book of Memories and Friendships* (New York: Harcourt, Brace, 1923);

Frederick J. Hoffman, Charles Allen, and Carolyn F. Ulrich, *The Little Magazine: A History and Bibliography* (Princeton, N.J.: Princeton University Press, 1946);

E. L. Masters, "The Poetry Revival in the United States," *American Mercury*, 26 (July 1932): 272-280;

Whittemore Reed, *Little Magazines* (Minneapolis: University of Minnesota Press, 1963);

Ralph F. Seymour, *Some Went This Way* (Chicago: Seymour, 1945);

Alson Smith, *Chicago's Left Bank* (Chicago: Regnery, 1953);

Ellen Williams, *Harriet Monroe and the Poetry Renaissance: The First Ten Years of Poetry, 1912-22* (Urbana, Chicago & London: University of Illinois Press, 1977);

Morton Dauwen Zabel, ed., *Literary Opinion in America*, revised edition (New York: Harper, 1951).

Papers:

Monroe's papers are held in the Harriet Monroe Collection in the Joseph Regenstein Library at the University of Chicago.

Charles Clayton Morrison

(4 December 1874-2 March 1966)

Mark Fackler
Wheaton College

MAJOR POSITIONS HELD: Editor and publisher, *Christian Century* (1908-1947); editor, *Pulpit* (1929-1947), *Christendom* (1935-1938).

BOOKS: *The Meaning of Baptism* (Chicago: Disciples Publication Society, 1914);
The Outlawry of War (Chicago: Willett, Clark & Colby, 1927);
The Social Gospel and the Christian Cultus (New York & London: Harper, 1933);
What is Christianity? (Chicago: Willett, Clark, 1940);
The Christian and the War (Chicago & New York: Willett, Clark, 1942);
Can Protestantism Win America? (New York: Harper, 1948);
The Unfinished Reformation (New York: Harper, 1953).

OTHER: *Hymns of the United Church*, edited by Morrison and Herbert L. Willett (Chicago: Christian Century Press, 1916);
The American Pulpit: A Volume of Sermons by Twenty-Five of the Foremost Living American Preachers, edited by Morrison (New York: Macmillan, 1925).

Charles Clayton Morrison edited the *Christian Century* for most of the first half of the twentieth century, as the American nation grew from progressivism through the chaos of the Depression and two world wars into the atomic era. Morrison likewise moved through the era of the Social Gospel, grappled with John Dewey's pragmatism and Reinhold Niebuhr's realism, and emerged with a principled call to social democracy and ecclesiastical union. Morrison developed the *Christian Century* into the nation's most influential religious journal of opinion, believing, despite all the momentous personal and cultural changes that had occurred, that his magazine accurately reflected the nation's chief strength and source of hope.

Morrison was born the second of four children to Hugh Tucker Morrison, a carpenter turned itinerant preacher, and Anna MacDonald Morrison, a musically gifted woman. (Morrison was also inclined toward music, and he compiled a hymnbook of modern songs for use in the churches of the Disciples of Christ, his spiritual home.) Morrison's father was reared on a farm in Nova Scotia. When the Campbellite revivals reached his area in the early 1870s he was converted and thereafter devoted himself to the ministry. He moved to the United States first to attend

Bethany College in West Virginia, then to preach throughout the Ohio Valley. On a visit to Nova Scotia he married McDonald. The couple then settled in Harrison, Ohio, where Morrison was born. For the next four decades Hugh Morrison conducted frontier revivals and pastored churches in the Campbellite movement, an appeal to simple theology and church unity fostered by the Scottish father-son preaching team of Thomas and Alexander Campbell. Alexander Campbell, a prolific author and founder of Bethany College, had died just a few years before Hugh Morrison entered the school, but the themes of the Scotsman's frontier theology were to become Charles Morrison's guiding tenets during his nearly forty-year publishing career.

Around 1890 Hugh Morrison settled down to a pastorate in Red Oak, Iowa. One Sunday morning, when Hugh Morrison's voice was victim to a cold, Charles Morrison, age sixteen, preached for twenty-two minutes, thereafter deciding to follow his father into the ministry. Not a gifted child (he would need remedial schooling to qualify for admission to Drake College in Des Moines), Morrison was nonetheless named class valedictorian in high school, speaking on the theme "The Progress of Civilization." (In his unpublished autobiography he later mused at his optimism: "I surely had civilization going onward and upward forever.")

After graduation from high school in 1892 Morrison took a vacant pulpit in Woodbine, Iowa, and after a year there reluctantly agreed to comply with his father's desire that he attend college. "I had no insatiable desire for knowledge," Morrison later wrote, and his first year at Drake was so unsuccessful that he gladly dropped out at the offer to conduct evangelistic services three nights a week and twice on Sunday at a new Disciples of Christ church in Osceola, where he attracted large crowds and the notice of the Des Moines newspapers. When asked to serve the largest Disciples church in Des Moines as soloist and reader, Morrison took the opportunity to return to Drake, taking his degree in 1898.

During most of his college years Morrison was the weekend pastor at the Disciples of Christ church in Perry, Iowa, forty miles from Des Moines. At this time he began to articulate a liberal, progressive theology that was greatly influenced by discussions with H. O. Breeden, a distinguished Disciples pastor who was also a believer in evolution and higher biblical criticism. Of these talks with the esteemed church leader Morri-

son wrote: "I was too naive to ask good questions, but a seed had taken root, and it would be a source of troubled awareness for me from that point on."

Now fired with a zeal for learning, Morrison accepted the pastorate of the First Church in Springfield, Illinois, and enrolled for graduate studies in the department of philosophy at the University of Chicago, at the time chaired and guided by John Dewey. Morrison chose philosophy over the Divinity School because he felt that theology rested on the rational sciences and needed their critique. Morrison also needed intellectual moorings, for by now he had abandoned the revivalist faith and sought new substance for his preaching. He drew close to Dewey, who wrote the afterword to Morrison's 1927 book *The Outlawry of War*. Morrison finished course work for the doctorate but declined to complete his degree, believing that a minister did not need such academic credentials.

At the Springfield church he met a member of the choir, Laurel Scott, to whom he was married in October 1906. They were to enjoy nearly fifty years together and had two daughters, Helen and Jane. Because the attractive and single minister had now chosen the affections of only one of several candidates (brother Hugh, who was Morrison's associate at the church, later married the woman most thought would surely be Morrison's wife), Morrison found it judicious to accept a call to the Monroe Street Church on Chicago's west side, thus setting the stage for his departure from preaching and entry into publishing. (Morrison, however, never surrendered his clergyman status.)

The Monroe Street Church was much smaller than the prestigious church Morrison had led in Springfield. Moreover, his immediate neighborhood in Chicago was rapidly filling with East European immigrants uninterested in Protestant worship. Morrison could plainly see that the future of that work was not promising.

While a student at Drake, Morrison had met and grown to admire Herbert L. Willett, a champion of the new higher biblical criticism who had since moved to Chicago with William Rainey Harper from Yale to help launch the University of Chicago. Morrison had fostered the friendship again during his graduate studies and in 1908 learned through Willett that an old Disciples magazine was soon to be sold at a sheriff's auction. Willett was an editor of this struggling journal and hoped to keep it alive.

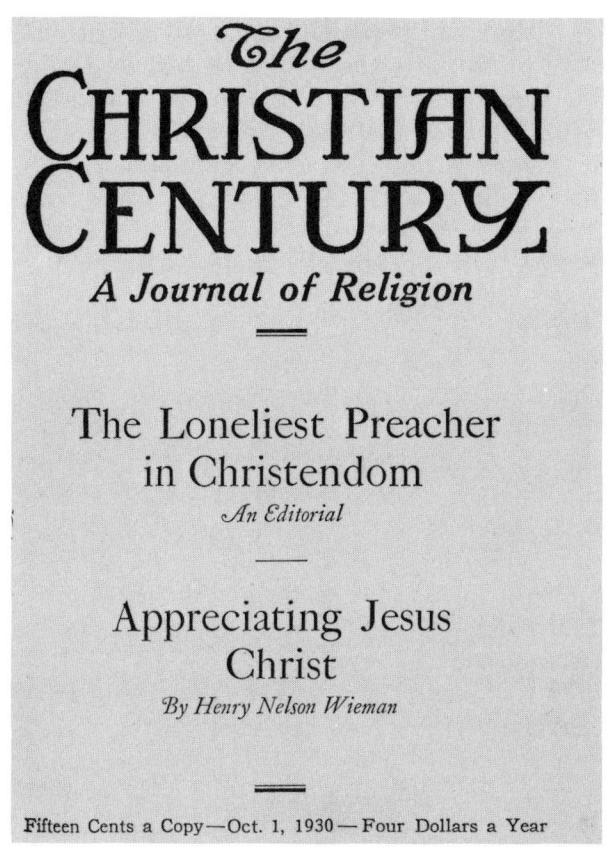

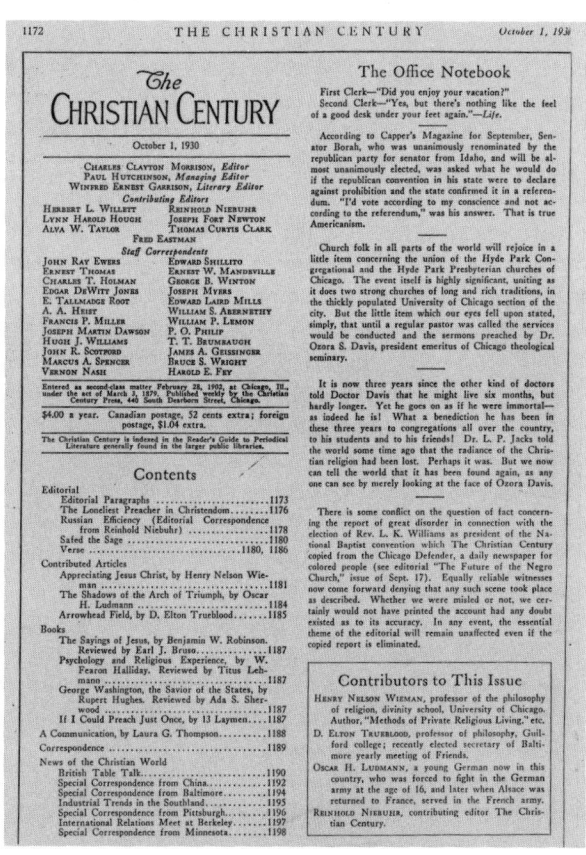

*Cover and contents page for an issue of the magazine Morrison published and edited from 1908 until 1947
(courtesy of the* Christian Century *Archives, Southern Illinois University at Carbondale)*

The Oracle was first published on 12 July 1884 in Des Moines. It was one of several independent magazines serving the largely autonomous congregations and ministers of the Disciples of Christ churches. In 1891, with Willett's strong encouragement, the magazine moved to Chicago, and in 1900 its name was changed to the *Christian Century*, an idea inspired by its pastor-editor, George A. Campbell, to symbolize the optimism of century's turn. But optimism could not pay printing bills. A mortgage of fifteen hundred dollars was owed to a worker in the shop where the *Christian Century* was printed. Probably through Willett's intervention, Morrison was asked to edit the magazine, temporarily at least, during the summer of 1908. Morrison reports that "by September I had become fully intrigued, and when the sheriff's deputy arrived to sell the property on the block I bid $1500 and became the owner."

Morrison was joined in funding the venture by Willett, O. S. Bowman, J. C. Kilmer (owner of the *Advance*, a magazine of conservative Congregationalism), and the Campbell Institute (a think

tank of Disciples churchmen educated at Yale and Chicago who wanted to heighten the intellect among Disciples ministers). Morrison himself borrowed on life insurance and probably had help from brother Hugh, who by marriage had become an heir to the estate of Judge Stephen Logan, Abraham Lincoln's second law partner. So in 1908 Morrison took over a list of three hundred paying subscribers (at two dollars a year), resigned the Monroe Street Church, and became a publisher.

Morrison considered changing the name of the *Christian Century* but decided instead to keep it as a link to the 1884 *Oracle*. He immediately turned his magazine into a voice for the Social Gospel movement, securing articles from Washington Gladden, Walter Rauschenbusch, and Jane Addams. An early column entitled "The World is Growing Better" reflected that movement's progressive optimism. Morrison could see winds of change in child labor, urban housing, church and community relations, and commercial films. In 1910 he adopted a subtitle for the journal: "A Constructive Weekly." The subtitle was again changed in 1917, after Morrison observed to his surprise that several subscription renewals were coming from prominent people outside the Disciples of Christ church. "An Undenominational Journal of Religion" was to be the new motto of the *Century*, reflecting the traditional disdain of the Disciples of Christ for denominationalism and Morrison's intention to position his journal at the center of American Protestantism.

As finances stabilized for the *Christian Century*, the nation faced the end of the progressive era. Morrison spoke out boldly on suffrage, prohibition, and pacifism. He opened a regular column entitled "Poems of the Social Awakening" and secured works from Edwin Markham and Vachel Lindsay. He fully supported the passage of the Nineteenth Amendment and argued that churches, too, must correct "an ancient wrong" and give women "full opportunity . . . in organized religion." In order to address the situation he hired Ida Withers Harrison to write a column called "Modern Womanhood."

On liquor Morrison was unequivocal. The alcohol business was corrupt and powerful, and the worker was its exploited victim. Since 1908 Morrison had campaigned for prohibition, and he fully supported the Volstead Act. Even after repeal of prohibition in 1933 the abstinence theme was a frequent *Christian Century* topic.

Although he supported the entrance of the United States into World War I, declaring in a *Christian Century* editorial that "war brings men duties," Morrison turned hard toward pacifism soon after the armistice. He called the terms of Versailles "unjust and vicious." He told *Christian Century* readers that the treaty "looked to the past and sought punishment when it should have looked to the future and sought reconciliation." Morrison felt personally betrayed by Woodrow Wilson, whom he had called "the most peace-loving president in America's history." A long series of *Christian Century* articles entitled "What the War Did to My Mind" gave liberal Protestant leaders a forum for their critique of war. Henry Emerson Fosdick wrote in the 5 January 1928 issue: "I do not propose to bless war again, or support it, or expect from it any valuable thing. It is an unmitigated curse." Morrison's own sentiments were identical. He had seen the war, toured the battlefields, and talked with Europeans struggling to rebuild. In one of his memos he wrote simply, "I shall not try to describe the desolation."

Morrison dwelled on the issue of Christian pacifism in years ahead, and he had to endure the painful loss of friendships when he opposed United States intervention in World War II. Chief among those lost alliances was to be contributing editor Reinhold Niebuhr, whose career Morrison advanced by arranging, with Herbert Willett, for the publication of Niebuhr's first book. He was surely critical of war but did not share Morrison's campaign for church union and was increasingly less sanguine than Morrison about the possibilities for outlawing war. The rift was still friendly when Morrison's *The Outlawry of War* was published in 1927. Morrison argued that war should be handled like piracy and the slave trade, by declaring it a crime, but acknowledged the "naive confession that a new motive force" is needed to sustain the campaign. Throughout the 1920s and early 1930s, as Niebuhr was moving closer to the Democratic platform, Morrison was breaking away. The *Christian Century* supported Franklin Delano Roosevelt in 1936 but only a year later called him "the Fuhrer of an inchoate fascism" for falling prey to pressure from industrialists eager for war profits. Morrison praised Mahatma Gandhi's nonviolence campaign while Niebuhr launched a new magazine, *Christianity and Crisis*, in which to expound his "Christian realism," a pragmatic mix of faith and politics. When their break finally came in the early 1940s Morrison was deeply hurt. Their families had been close, but now Niebuhr, clearly the more politically ambitious, was stringently critical of the *Christian Century* and of Morrison himself.

The *Christian Century*, for all of its injection of moral principle into political movements and war, was reluctant to align itself with those who sought to become the moral guardians of culture. While Catholics were organizing the Legion of Decency to protest the content of Hollywood films, the *Christian Century* remained skeptical. At pronouncements of reform from Hollywood moguls, the *Christian Century* (3 April 1930) editorialized: "if pious resolutions and vows of chastity could have saved the motion picture industry, it would have been saved long ago. The big producers . . . get converted too often." In a seven-part series the magazine accused Hollywood of "vicious falsification of human values" and called for an end to the block-booking system and for government screening of films released to foreign markets, lest the nation be misunderstood abroad as a gang of moonshiners and hooligans.

Reinhold Niebuhr, who served as a contributing editor to the Christian Century *(Religious News Photo Service)*

Equally abhorrent was the specter of federal censorship of the airwaves. When the Federal Radio Commission revoked the broadcast license of radio preacher Robert Schuler in 1932, the *Christian Century*, no friend of religious bigotry, came to Schuler's defense. "A more vicious and danger-fraught basis for censorship could not be set up," argued a *Christian Century* editorial that year. In response to Father Charles E. Coughlin's controversial radio preachments, Morrison declared, "Let the minister have absolute freedom of speech." What the *Christian Century* feared most was the possibility that Catholics were behind the Schuler license denial, and that Protestants would gather political muscle against Coughlin, who was accused of fostering anti-Semitic sentiment. Such bickering was a denial of the faith, to Morrison's mind, and surely a denial of the promise of radio. (In the 22 March 1923 issue of the *Christian Century* Morrison had hailed the advent of radio as the coming of "what sectari-

anism has always forbidden . . . people of various denominations all repeating the Lord's Prayer together.") Even in matters of communication technology Morrison's chief concerns were peace between nations and unity among Christians. Yet as the airwaves became more vitriolic in the 1930s, the position of the *Christian Century* moved more toward federal control of outspoken religious bigots. Of the twin evils of censorship and religious hatred, Morrison's mind recoiled at the former while his soul burned against the latter.

On the Depression, the *Christian Century* would argue that unrestrained capitalism was reaping its whirlwind. The crash of 1929, painful as it was in some quarters, offered Americans "the privilege of sobering up" after a two-year "speculative debauch." The church was complicit in the unfair distribution of wealth that lay behind market woes. Needed was a "new economic man" who would voluntarily surrender maximized profits for the general good. Here was "the movement for which the social gospel has been waiting," proclaimed the magazine in its 11 October 1933 issue. The church's "new evangelism" was a call to the "voluntary liquidation of the competitive system" in favor of a planned economy to insure "to every person in the nation an adequate supply of the goods of life."

While the appeal for voluntary measures was Morrison's strongest call, the need to advocate for politicians and political movements did not escape his pages. Morrison endorsed Herbert Hoover in 1932, believing he would be a more liberal leader than Roosevelt, his Democratic challenger, who was, in Morrison's view, beholden to "the most sinister figure in American life, William Randolph Hearst." Moreover, while Hoover was equivocal on prohibition, Roosevelt was firmly opposed to it.

Morrison's trusted managing editor, Paul Hutchinson, chose to support Norman Thomas in the 1932 election, but outright support of the Socialist party was too extreme for Morrison, who never questioned the necessity of the two-party system. (Again the rub with Niebuhr, an occasional candidate for office on third-party tickets.) Yet the *Christian Century* did go so far, in the early 1930s, to propose the establishment of the "Disinterested party," which would stand for political principles rather than special interests, patronage, and office-seeking. Only such a party, as stated in a series of unsigned editorials, could serve "the whole body politic" by drafting "progressive policies" that might save the nation from

Hundreds Have Signed This; Will You?

To the President and Congress of the United States:

The recent decision of the Supreme Court, which denies the right of citizenship to persons who refuse to abdicate their conscience on the question of participation in armed conflict, forces us, the undersigned citizens, to notify the constituted authorities of our nation that we share the convictions of those who have been denied citizenship.

Some of the undersigned find it impossible, because of religious and moral scruples, to render any kind of combatant service in time of war. Others share the conviction of one of the persons denied citizenship in the recent Supreme Court decision and cannot promise support to the government until they have had the opportunity of weighing the moral issues involved in an international struggle.

We concur in the minority opinion of the Supreme Court that "in the forum of conscience, duty to a moral power higher than the state has always been maintained. The reservation of that supreme obligation, as a matter of principle, would undoubtedly be made by many of our conscientious citizens. The essence of religion is belief in a relation to God involving duties superior to those arising from any human relation."

....

Finding myself in agreement with the foregoing statement concerning a decision of the Supreme Court with regard to conscientious objectors to war, I desire to have my name added as a signatory.

Name..

Position...

Street Address..

City and State..

A petition published in the 7 October 1931 issue of the Christian Century. *Throughout the 1920s and 1930s Morrison used the magazine to advance his belief in Christian pacifism.*

"its present moral chaos, from the tyranny of entrenched interest . . . and a communist dictatorship." The planks of this Deweyan ideal political party included United States adherence to World Court protocol, recognition of the Soviet Union, support for rights of conscientious objectors, steeply progressive income-tax rates, national ownership of utilities and basic industries (including banks), and enforcement of the constitutional rights of minorities. His proposal for this new party represented Morrison's last flickering hope for the instrumental progressivism he learned at Chicago. Soon after 1932 Morrison rallied behind Roosevelt, displaying the NRA eagle on page 2 of the *Christian Century* and devoting a three-part series to the virtues of the Tennessee Valley Authority, which heralded, he wrote, "a new order of life for this country."

In the early 1940s Morrison opposed the Zionist movement. In a series of *Christian Century* editorials he disputed the statistics and reports of Zionist leader Rabbi Stephen Wise in 1942. Morrison's circle of friends included many in Reform Judaism who opposed the establishment of a Jewish state, and Morrison had received a letter

(now lost) from the State Department suggesting that Wise was exaggerating the Nazi terror for political reasons. Some historians have claimed that Morrison thus abetted the Holocaust. On Morrison's behalf, it should be reported that he noted the reign of terror against Jews as early as April 1933. When Morrison visited the death camps in 1945 he called for a worldwide spiritual awakening and moral reconstruction by a guilty humanity. Between those years the *Christian Century* often criticized Hitler and supported the boycott of the Berlin Olympics.

The stature of the *Christian Century* earned for Morrison a platform far larger than the pulpits that inspired him to undertake a public life. In 1932 he delivered the Walter Rauschenbusch lectures at Colgate-Rochester Divinity School, and in 1939 the Lyman Beecher lectures at Yale. He was a frequent overseas traveler and conference organizer whose vision for peace, if not church unity, was only intensified by exposure to Latin and European cultures.

After nearly forty years at the editor's desk, Morrison stepped down in 1947. The *Christian Century* had approximately forty thousand subscribers and a strong base of support. Paul Hutchinson, so long an understudy, became editor of the magazine. (Hutchinson died six years later, to Morrison's grief.) Ownership of the magazine passed into the hands of a foundation.

As blindness overtook him, Morrison praised Dwight D. Eisenhower's peace efforts and later Martin Luther King, Jr.'s, leadership of the Civil Rights Movement. (The *Christian Century* was the first national magazine to publish King's "Letter from Birmingham Jail.") He argued with the World Council of Churches, claiming that they spent too much time in theological disputes, and took exception to the National Council of Churches' decision to locate offices in New York City, where the large non-Protestant population would "blight the realization of the Protestant mission in the land." Morrison was one of the founders in 1949 of Protestants and Other Americans United for Separation of Church and State, a veiled effort (at that time) to retard Catholic influence in national affairs. In later years he turned toward the Episcopal church.

Morrison died in Chicago in the spring of 1966, only six weeks before his wife, who burned the personal chapters of his unpublished autobiog-

raphy. At death an inauspicious bronze marker also muted the legacy of a colorful page in the story of America's struggle to mid century, but his real monument is the *Christian Century*. Upon his retirement in 1947, *Newsweek* referred to his magazine as "the most important organ of Protestant opinion in the world today."

References:

Linda-Marie Delloff, Martin E. Marty, Dean Peerman, and James M. Wall, *A Century of the Century* (Grand Rapids, Mich.: Eerdmans, 1987);

J. Theodore Hefley, "Freedom Upheld: The Civil Liberties Stance of The Christian Century," *Church History*, 48 (1968): 174-194;

Hefley, "War Outlawed: 'The Christian Century' and the Kellogg Peace Pact," *Journalism Quarterly*, 37 (1971): 26-32.

Papers:

Morrison's unpublished autobiography is part of the Christian Century Archives, Special Collections, Morris Library, Southern Illinois University.

Frank A. Munsey

(21 August 1854-22 December 1925)

Jack H. Colldeweih
Fairleigh Dickinson University

See also the Munsey entry in *DLB 25: American Newspaper Journalists, 1901-1925.*

MAJOR POSITION HELD: President, Frank A. Munsey and Company (1888-1925).

PRINCIPAL MAGAZINES OWNED: *Golden Argosy*, retitled *Argosy* (1883-1925); *Munsey's Weekly*, retitled *Munsey's Magazine* (1889-1925); *All-Story Magazine* (1905-1925); *Scrap Book* (1906-1912); *Railroad Man's Magazine*, retitled *Railroad Magazine* (1906-1925); *Live Wire* (1908-1912); *Cavalier* (1908-1914).

BOOKS: *Afloat in a Great City: A Story of Strange Incidents* (New York: Cassell, 1887);
The Boy Broker; or, Among the Kings of Wall Street (New York: Munsey, 1888);
A Tragedy of Errors (New York: Munsey, 1889);
Under Fire; or, Fred Worthington's Campaign (New York: Munsey, 1890); republished as *Under Fire: A Tale of New England Village Life* (New York: Munsey, 1897);
Derringforth (New York: Munsey, 1894);
Advertising in Some of Its Phases (New York, 1898);
Getting On in Journalism (Ottawa, 1898);
Journalism; An Address Delivered by Frank A. Munsey at Yale University, January 12, 1903 (New Haven: Yale University Press, 1903);
The Founding of the Munsey Publishing House, Quarter of a Century Old: The Story of the Argosy, Our First Publication, and Incidentally the Story of Munsey's Magazine (New York: De Vinne, 1907);
What Colonel Roosevelt's Election Will Mean to the Business World (New York: Munsey, 1912);
Starve the Railroads and We Starve Ourselves (New York, 1914);
An Address Before the American Banker's Association at the Hotel Commodore, New York, October 4, 1922 (New York, 1922);
Militant American Journalism (New York: Munsey, 1922).

Frank A. Munsey in 1887

As a publisher of magazines and newspapers, Frank A. Munsey was a man ahead of his time. His methods of applying the principles of industrialism to publishing are echoed throughout the publishing business today, and although he never succeeded in realizing his dream of operating a chain of newspapers across the United States, others have validated the concept. Some of the most prestigious newspapers and magazines of his day passed through his control and were modified, merged, and, often enough, eliminated. Sadly neglected now, when the name

Munsey does come up among newsmen, it is usually accompanied by the dimly remembered cry, "Let Munsey kill it!"

The fourth of six children, Frank Andrew Munsey was born on 21 August 1854 on a farm near Mercer, Maine, to Andrew Chauncey Munsey, a carpenter and farmer, and Mary Jane Merritt Hopkins Munsey. Although his father was from Quebec, Canada, a genealogy Munsey commissioned in 1920 authenticated his solid American credentials with the claim that his mother's ancestors included twelve Mayflower passengers, John Alden and Priscilla Mullens among them.

Other than a few months at Poughkeepsie Business College in 1881, Munsey's business education was largely self-taught. He began working in a grocery in Lisbon Falls, Maine. After teaching himself telegraphy, he left the grocery before he was seventeen and became telegraph operator in several New England hotels. His appointment as local manager of the Western Union Telegraph Company office in Augusta, the state capital, was decisive to his career.

Here he was exposed to politics on both state and national levels through his position in the telegraph office and his residence in Augusta House, where he met many of the state's leading politicians, including Sen. James G. Blaine, Augusta's own presidential hopeful. Munsey acquired a taste for politics that he would indulge throughout his life.

In Augusta, Munsey was also able to observe the town's other significant activity, magazine publishing. The magazines published in Augusta were cheap tabloids that served primarily as an extremely lucrative mail-order advertising medium. The originator of this particular format was Edward C. Allen, the owner of the *People's Literary Companion*, who had amassed the largest fortune in town. He served as a mentor to Munsey, carefully explaining the problems and prospects of the magazine industry. Munsey soon lost interest in any other career, becoming obsessed with the idea of going to New York and becoming a publisher.

Eventually saving five hundred dollars of his own, he was able to convince two others to invest a total of thirty-five hundred dollars in his scheme. He began acquiring manuscripts, including a long serial by Horatio Alger, Jr., "Do and Dare, or a Brave Boy's Fight for Fortune." His publication model was a Philadelphia juvenile magazine, *Golden Days*. Munsey's was to be called *Golden Argosy*.

Munsey arrived in New York in September 1882 with forty dollars, a bagful of manuscripts, and high expectations. He was soon disappointed when his major backer withdrew from the project; he then felt honor bound to release the other backer and proceed on his own. He ultimately found the help he needed in a printer, E. G. Rideout, who became his publisher and employer in the print shop.

The first issue of *Golden Argosy*, dated 9 December 1882, was actually published on 2 December 1882, ten weeks after Munsey's arrival. The magazine never missed a weekly publication day thereafter. But after five months of struggle, Rideout went bankrupt; Munsey took the title, subscription list, and good will in lieu of wages and became a publisher. With the aid of a three-hundred-dollar loan from an Augusta banker and an enormous amount of work, Munsey forced the magazine to succeed. Unable to pay for new manuscripts, or to find suitable rewrite material, he began to write his own, beginning in 1885 with the serialized novel *Under Fire; or, Fred Worthington's Campaign* (1890). He continued later with *Afloat in a Great City: A Story of Strange Incidents* (1887), *The Boy Broker; or, Among the Kings of Wall Street* (1888), *A Tragedy of Errors* (1889), and *Derringforth* (1894).

When Senator Blaine received the Republican presidential nomination in 1884, he set up campaign headquarters in New York City. Munsey renewed his acquaintance and joined the campaign by getting the party's endorsement for a new magazine, *Munsey's Illustrated Weekly*. Although it was never an official party organ and received no party funding, the weekly ran through the election campaign, from 6 September to 8 November. Munsey gained time, experience, and a subscription list, as well as a sufficient debt, so that his creditors could not afford to let him go under.

By May 1887 Munsey had pushed *Golden Argosy* to a circulation of 150,000 and a weekly profit of fifteen hundred dollars. Trying to push these figures higher, he began his lifelong habit of redesigning his publications, altering the title (to *Argosy*), format, page size, price, and content.

He began a new comic magazine, *Munsey's Weekly*, similar to the popular weekly *Life*, in 1889. It was a failure, and he converted it to a monthly, *Munsey's Magazine*, in 1891. He also bought his first newspaper, on option, the *New York Star*. He changed the name to the *Continent*

First page of the inaugural issue of the magazine with which Munsey began his publishing career

and converted it into a tabloid, but he had to surrender his option four months later.

In 1893, trying to interest the large mass of nonmagazine readers, Munsey dropped the price of *Munsey's Magazine* from a quarter to a dime, formed his own distributing company, Red Star News, and began to advertise the magazine heavily. Munsey realized that if he achieved a true mass circulation, advertisers could not afford to pass him by. By 1898 *Munsey's* claimed the largest circulation of any magazine in the world (Munsey did not believe the *Ladies' Home Journal,* which had a higher circulation, to be a true magazine), and the advertising profits mounted. In an address to the Sphinx Club in that year he stated, "There was never anything deader in this world than the old idea of big profits and small volume."

The content of *Munsey's* nonfiction articles was fairly pedestrian in quality, providing primar-

ily social uplift. Its response to the muckraking era was only to drop liquor and patent medicine advertising. Its most noteworthy content initially was frequently a pretty (but unsmiling) girl on the cover and articles about artists and their models, as well as sculpture and dance, that permitted a variety of discreet but well-done seminude pictures.

Although never lavish with pay, *Munsey's* did publish poetry by Edgar Lee Masters and fiction by writers such as P. G. Wodehouse, Zane Grey, and O. Henry. In 1895 Munsey wrote his prescription for the type of short stories he would publish: "We want stories. That is what we mean—stories, not dialect sketches, not washed out studies of effete human nature, not weak tales of sickly sentimentality, not 'pretty' writing. This sort of thing in all its varieties comes by the carload every mail. It is not what we want, but we do want fiction in which there is a story,

Covers for the most successful magazines published by Munsey

force, a tale that means something–in short a story. Good writing is as common as clam shells, while good stories are as rare as statesmanship."

As his profits rose Munsey began construction of a large building for a printing plant in New London, Connecticut, in 1895, later converting it into the Mohican Hotel, then a department store, and finally the basis for his highly profitable interstate chain of Mohican grocery stores. Here, too, he was following his method for magazines: "I keep on experimenting, creating and killing, till I happen to hit the public's taste."

Munsey expanded and contracted his magazine empire in several ways. He bought *Peterson's Magazine* in 1895 and merged it with *Argosy*. He founded *Quaker* and *Puritan* in 1897. He changed the title of the former to *Junior Munsey* in 1900, purchased *Godey's Ladies Book* and merged it with the latter in 1898, merged *Puritan* into *Junior Munsey* in 1901, then merged *Junior Munsey* into *Argosy* in 1902.

Similar fates befell his other magazines.

Woman lasted but a year beyond its founding in 1906. *Scrap Book,* purchased the same year, was later split into all-picture and all-fiction editions; the picture edition was merged with *Ocean,* begun in 1907; *Ocean* was retitled *Live Wire* in 1908; and *Live Wire* was merged into *Cavalier* in 1912. The fiction edition of *Scrap Book* was also merged into *Cavalier* in 1912. *Cavalier* was published from 1908 to 1914, *Railroad Man's Magazine* from 1906 to 1919, when it was changed to *Railroad Magazine.*

Often Munsey purchased an established magazine (such as *Peterson's* or *Godey's Ladies Book*) and merged it into one of his other holdings. He was thus able to neutralize competitors while simultaneously retaining the best features of these acquisitions for his own publications. He constantly adjusted his publications to appeal to changing public tastes. His success with this process is attested by his claim in 1907 of total earnings, after twenty-five years, of nearly $9 million.

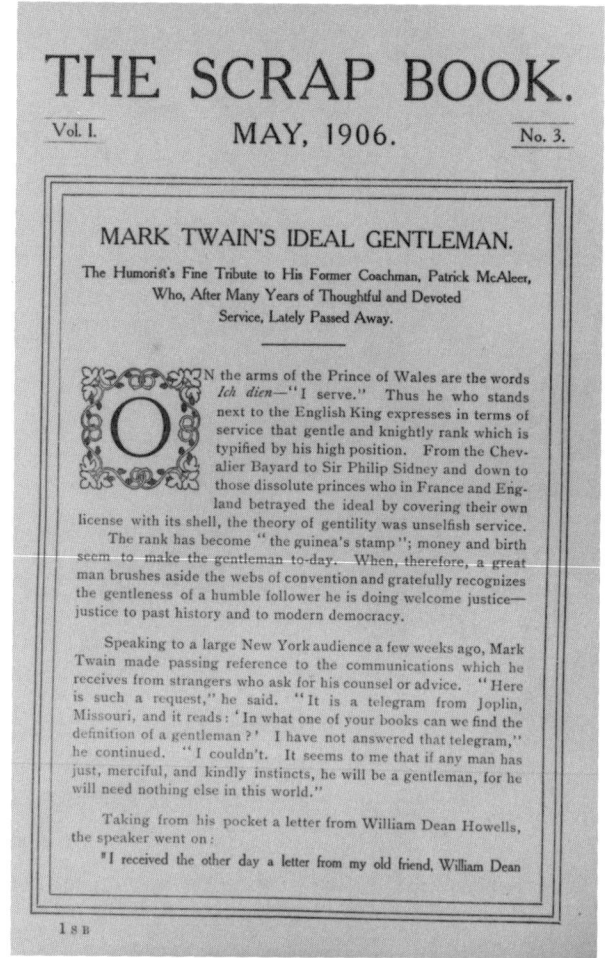

Covers for a ladies' magazine and a literary digest published by Munsey

In 1901 he claimed to have twice the combined circulation of *Harper's, Scribner's,* and *Century.*

Flush with triumph, Munsey began dabbling in newspapers again, following the same model he was using with his magazines, though with less success. The *New York Daily News* and the *Washington Times* were purchased in 1901, the former killed three years later, the *Times* sold to Arthur Brisbane in 1917. He purchased the *Boston Journal* in 1902, killing the evening edition a year later, then starting the *Evening News* in the same shop, only to kill it in 1904. The rest of the *Journal* was sold in 1913. Although the visual appeal of his papers was noteworthy, especially in the quantity and quality of photographs used, Munsey rarely gave his changes enough time to have a good effect on circulation before he called for further restructuring.

Munsey at this time had a grandiose dream

of a gigantic, all-encompassing trust. Speaking before the Merchants' Club of Boston in 1902, he said: "I think I shall be able to make good by the power of organization and by applying the methods that are now employed by our great business combinations, popularly known as trusts. In my judgment it will not be many years–five or ten, perhaps–before the publishing business in this country will be done by a few concerns, three or four at the most. There will be a line of newspapers representing each of the two great political parties, and another chain independent of politics. . . . This is an age of organization and of consolidation, and the man who opposes that tendency of modern life might as well oppose his puny strength to the torrent of Niagara." Included in this plan were businesses outside of publishing, including farms, stores, shops, factories, banks, and real estate, all working efficiently and profitably together.

Backed by the immense profits of his magazines, grocery chain, banking interests, and stock market speculations, Munsey tried to realize his dream. In 1908 he founded the *Philadelphia Evening Times* and bought the *Baltimore Evening News;* he killed the former in 1914 and sold the latter twice, first to Stuart Olivier in 1915, then, after retrieving it in 1917, to William Randolph Hearst in 1922. Munsey acquired the *New York Press* in 1912 and merged it with the *New York Sun,* which he purchased in 1916. The morning edition of the *Sun* was merged with the *New York Herald* when it was purchased in 1918. That year he also bought the *New York Evening Telegram* and in 1921 the *Baltimore American, Baltimore News,* and *Baltimore Star* (which was promptly merged into the *News*). The Baltimore papers were sold to Hearst in 1922 and 1923. The *New York Globe* was purchased in 1923 and immediately merged into the *New York Evening Sun.* A similar fate occurred to the *New York Evening Mail* when it was purchased and merged with the *Evening Telegram* in 1924. Finally, unable to buy or compete with the *New York Tribune,* he sold his last major paper, the *Herald,* to Mrs. Ogden Reid in 1924.

Munsey suffered other disappointments as well. A staunch Republican, he rarely strayed from mainstream politics, although he did support Theodore Roosevelt in the "Bull Moose" campaign of 1912. He aspired to political appointment, and when Warren G. Harding was elected (with the endorsements of Munsey's publications) in 1920, Munsey hoped to be named ambassador to the Court of Saint James. However, Harding ignored him, and Munsey withdrew from active participation in politics.

Munsey died, after two operations for appendicitis, on 22 December 1925, attended by a few acquaintances and upper-level employees. Neither his surviving family members nor other newspapermen were present.

Munsey never married, and he spent his last years worrying about the disposal of his estate. He was a great admirer of J. P. Morgan, and he saw himself as a member of the elite stratum of the wealthy to which Morgan belonged. To everyone's surprise, he left the bulk of his estate to the Metropolitan Museum, an institution that he apparently knew little about, except that it was approved of by the Morgans, the Astors, the Vanderbilts, and the Reids.

As Munsey's biographer, George Britt, points out, it was a perfect gesture. Given his philosophy, journalistic practices, and lack of outside interests, it would have made little sense to endow a literary prize or a scientific institute (as had Joseph Pulitzer and Edward W. Scripps). The Metropolitan was most respectable, socially useful, and totally alien to anything else in his life.

Biography:

George Britt, *Forty Years–Forty Millions: The Career of Frank A. Munsey* (New York: Farrar & Rinehart, 1935).

References:

Allen Churchill, *Park Row* (New York: Rinehart, 1958), pp. 290-295, 312-315;

Robert L. Duffus, "Mr. Munsey," *American Mercury,* 2 (July 1924): 297-304;

D. O. S. Lowell, *A Munsey-Hopkins Genealogy, Being the Ancestry of Andrew Chauncey Munsey and Mary Jane Merritt Hopkins* (Boston: Privately printed, 1920);

E. J. Ridgeway, *Frank A. Munsey: An Appreciation* (Chula Vista, Cal.: Privately printed, 1926);

Oswald Garrison Villard, *Some Newspapers and Newspaper-Men* (New York: Knopf, 1923).

Condé Nast
(26 March 1873-19 September 1942)

Carolyn Garrett Cline
Southwest Texas State University

MAJOR POSITIONS HELD: Advertising manager (1900-1905), business manager (1905-1907), *Collier's Weekly*; publisher, *Vogue* (1909-1942), *House and Garden* (1911-1942), *Vanity Fair* (1914-1936), *Glamour* (1939-1942).

Condé Nast became the supreme chronicler of society from 1909 until 1942 through three major publications: *Vogue, Vanity Fair,* and *House and Garden.* As a publisher, his name came to represent sophistication, quality, and style, a reputation his company has maintained for nearly eight decades, but his life was one of quiet irony. He pioneered the concept of limited-circulation magazines targeted to an affluent audience but never began a new publication until three years before he died. His parties were legendary, yet he attended them as a detached observer, quietly watching from a corner. His magazines helped legitimatize avant-garde movements in art, photography, fashion, and literature, but Nast's taste remained conservative. His genius lay in the business side of publishing, and he turned editorial control over to an innovative, loyal triumvirate.

Condé Montrose Nast was born on 26 March 1873 in New York City, the son of William Frederick Nast, an unsuccessful speculator-inventor, and Esther Ariadne Benoist Nast, who came from a St. Louis family rich in tradition and culture. Nast's Benoist ancestors included a chamberlain to King Louis XI of France and a court painter to Louis XIV. Nast's mother was determined to raise her children in her own traditions of an economic, rigidly Catholic, middle-western family. His father was often absent and his family's finances limited, so Nast, his brother, and two sisters were reared in St. Louis by his mother. Nast's paternal grandfather, Wilhelm Nast, was a leading founder of German Methodism in America and edited its leading newspaper, *Der Christliche Apologete,* for more than fifty years. It was perhaps from this stern ancestor that Nast inherited his love of publishing as well as his solemn and methodical nature.

Nast was never the creative one, his mother remarked to *Vogue* editor Edna Chase. Rather, his notable skills were thoroughness, neatness, and completeness. "He's always been like that, even as a child," she said. "When they were boys, he and [his brother] Louis used to cut the lawn in front of our house in St. Louis. . . . There was a path down the middle of the plot and Condé's side was always very neat, each blade of grass in scrupulous order, but Louis's was more laissez faire, uneven spots and artistic outcroppings."

Nast's devotion to order impressed a wealthy aunt, who agreed to finance his education at Georgetown. He became the first student president of the athletic association his freshman year, garnering impressive publicity and raising money for the teams. His success brought him to the attention of Robert Collier, whose father, P. F. Collier, owned a thriving publishing business in New York. They became close friends, but after graduation Collier returned to work for his father and Nast stayed to work on a master's degree.

Nast returned to St. Louis to earn an LL.B. in 1898 from Washington University but showed little eagerness in setting up a law practice. Rather, he turned to a small printing plant in which his family had invested two thousand dollars. The plant was doing badly until Nast used the St. Louis Exposition as a way of attracting new business. Collier visited his friend in St. Louis and was impressed with Nast's success. Robert Collier had, upon his father's death, taken control of *Collier's Weekly,* a slim, unimpressive premium offered for ten cents to purchasers of Collier's books, and in 1900 he offered Nast a job as advertising manager at twelve dollars a week.

Nast's aggressive work in advertising sales, along with Collier's changes in the magazine's format, soon attracted top-level talent and with it subscribers and advertisers. Nast carried *Collier's* to first place in magazine advertising revenue and in 1905 was promoted to business manager. Besides such innovations as color illustrations and special issues, Nast's strategy included segmentation of the audience into marketing areas, and promotions aimed at a select, affluent audience, not necessarily a mass circulation.

In less than a decade advertising revenue had increased from fifty-five hundred dollars a year to one million dollars, and the thirty-five-year-old Nast was earning forty thousand dollars a year. Although his salary was outrageous, according to Collier, Nast quit the magazine in 1907 to devote his efforts to a small business, the Home Pattern Company, he had organized in 1904 with Theron McCampbell. They had a franchise for the manufacture and sale of *Ladies' Home Journal* patterns in a series of pattern books and fashion sheets. Although the sheets were considered throwaways, he convinced advertisers to purchase space in them, and this success convinced Nast that there was a market for fashion news. He worked for four years to acquire what he saw as the ideal vehicle for his marketing strategies, a foundering weekly called *Vogue.*

Vogue had been founded by Harry McVicar and Arthur Baldwin Turnure in December 1892 as "a dignified, authentic journal of society, fashion and the ceremonial side of life." The 250 stockholders had such names as Fish, Vanderbilt, and Morgan. Turnure left the actual running of the magazine to his sister-in-law, Marie L. Harrison, who kept it functioning after Turnure's premature death. While the magazine survived, it had not shared in the general growth in advertising revenue after the turn of the century; rather, its revenues dwindled, reflecting the stockholders' feelings that advertising was somehow too "commercial" a concern.

Nast saw in *Vogue* the potential to reach the elite, a group he had joined with his 1902 marriage to Clarisse Coudert and his subsequent listing in the *Social Register.* Nast had met Clarisse while riding in New Jersey with Collier and was taken with the suave socialite, but their marriage was not a success. Their son, Charles Coudert, was born on 23 July 1903, and a daughter, Natica, on 5 January 1905. Clarisse showed signs of increased restlessness and some degree of instability, and in 1906 she took the children to France, where she joined the social circle of her sister, an intimate friend of and model for Auguste Rodin. Although their marriage was a failure, Condé and Clarisse remained friends, and her contacts from this period later served *Vogue* well. The couple divorced in 1925.

After four years of negotiation, Nast acquired *Vogue.* His name appeared on the masthead as president of the Vogue Company for the first time on 24 June 1909. He took over with little fanfare, and Harrison stayed on as editor. According to Chase, only an "occasional rumble from Olympus and a head rolling" reminded the editorial staff that they had a new owner, for Nast's immediate concern was the business side of the operation. Chase wrote that he was "merely dedicating himself to that pursuit for which all his life he had a passion as cold and burning as dry ice, the perusal of figures. He lusted after mathematics."

He clearly set forth his philosophy in mathematical terms: "If you had a tray with two million needles on it and only one hundred and fifty thousand of these had gold tips, which you wanted, it would be an endless and costly process to weed them out. Moreover the one million, eight hundred and fifty thousand which were not gold-tipped would be of no use to you, they couldn't help you; but if you could get a magnet that

Nast (center) with Vanity Fair *editor Frank Crowninshield and* Vogue *editor Edna Chase, circa 1915*

would draw out only the gold ones, what a saving!" *Vogue*, with its established tie to high society, would be that magnet, and advertisers would pay nearly five times the rate of other women's magazines of the era to reach that audience.

After establishing a base with *Vogue*, Nast continued to expand. By 1911 he had acquired part of *House and Garden, Travel*, and the *Housekeeper*. He had purchased the *Housekeeper* with Collier, though it appears that he was mainly interested in obtaining its circulation list for *House and Garden*, for the magazine was shut down the next year. In 1915 *Travel* reverted to Nast's copublisher, Robert McBridge. In 1913 Nast bought a fashion magazine named *Dress*, and, for three thousand dollars, *Vanity Fair*, which he combined into *Dress and Vanity Fair* in September 1913.

During this era Nast also made his most successful acquisition: a trio of vastly different, immensely talented editors who stamped upon his three major publications their unique character and style–Chase at *Vogue*, Frank Crowninshield at *Vanity Fair* (he insisted that "Dress" be dropped from the title), and Richardson Wright at *House and Garden*.

Vogue had continued under the editorship of Harrison until Nast's legal battles with Turnure's heirs made her position awkward and she retired. Chase became editor of *Vogue* in 1914. From a Quaker family in New Jersey, Chase had joined *Vogue* as a clerk in the circulation department, but her obsession with the publication matched Nast's; for fifty years it was, she said, "their child," their accomplishment in turning the failing little journal into the ultimate arbiter of fashion and taste.

At the same time Nast hired Crowninshield as editor of *Vanity Fair*, which would become a journal of art, literature, and world events. Crowninshield was a true cosmopolite, a descendant of Boston Brahmins born and educated in Europe, devoted to avant-garde art and writing. He was determined to publish not only the established artists but also innovators, and this devotion led to confrontations with Nast, who never quite understood why an article by Eric Satie had to be run entirely in French, or what Crowninshield saw in the paintings of Henri Matisse. For Nast, it was more a matter of economics than aesthetics. Such

Nast (center) in 1937 with Michel de Brunhoff, editor of the French edition of Vogue, *and Iva Patcévitch, who became president of Condé Nast Inc. in 1942 (Iva Patcévitch)*

creative bursts as running a drawing of J. P. Morgan in his underwear were controversial enough, but even the less offensive art was a problem for Nast. He later complained to Chase that *Vanity Fair* had published the avant-garde art ten years too early; advertisers complained to him that they thought the paintings were "distorted and . . . decadent."

Crowninshield's willingness to take risks may have made *Vanity Fair* a trendsetter, but not even Nast could make it profitable. Despite its high advertising revenue, production costs kept the magazine in the red for most of its life.

The third member of the editorial triumvirate was Richardson Wright, who joined *House and Garden* before Nast acquired it and stayed on as editor for thirty-six years after the magazine had changed from a male-oriented architectural journal to an authority on interior design. Of the three editors, Wright's taste and style were closest to Nast's, with a loyalty to traditional design influence. During the first decade of Nast's ownership the journal more than doubled its circulation.

Constant growth was a passion for Nast, and he began distributing *Vogue* in Britain as

early as 1912 and in 1916 established a British edition of the magazine, edited by William Wood. Nast also purchased control of a French journal, *La Gazette du Bon Ton,* in 1915. Although he claimed he intended to publish it in New York, he was apparently less interested in putting out another magazine than in beating rival William Randolph Hearst to ownership. After abandoning the idea of importing a French publication, Nast returned to exporting, with the establishment of a French *Vogue* in June 1920 edited by Phillipe Ortiz. In 1921 Nast purchased *L'Illustration des Modes* and renamed it *Jardin des Modes,* launching it as a fashion magazine for women of more limited means. He began a short-lived Spanish-language *Vogue* for South America; a 1927 attempt at a German version also failed because of a lack of advertisers as well as readers. In 1925 Nast began the semimonthly *Vogue Pattern Book.*

During the 1920s Nast established a spectacular life-style in his thirty-room penthouse at 1040 Park Avenue. At work he maintained an open-door policy, roaming the office and lunching cafeteria style at Horn and Hardart. His personal life was far more opulent; while he lacked imagination, he hired expert designers for his home and parties.

Crowninshield masterminded many of the parties, even moving into the penthouse with Nast, but the publisher kept a precise account not only of expenses but of attendance and possible reasons for low turnouts. Nast's attention to detail, his orchestration, his lavishness, made the parties, according to F. Scott Fitzgerald, comparable to the "fabled balls of the Nineties." Caroline Seebohm relates a typical anecdote: "Going up in the private elevator . . . jammed together with Astors, Vanderbilts, and other persons of consequence, Groucho Marx was overheard . . . to remark to his brother Harpo: 'This is a classy joint.'" It was indeed. Nast and Crowninshield created café society, that blend of Morgan and Gershwin, Astor and Marx.

Nast also spent lavishly on his printing plant, built in 1921 in Greenwich, Connecticut, paying $350,000 for landscaping alone. He rewarded employees with outrageous bonuses, such as the $100,000 he gave Chase in 1928 to use in decorating her planned home on Long Island.

In the mid 1920s Nast succumbed to the stock-market craze, and though his initial investments were successful beyond expectations, the market would prove to be his downfall. Nast was warned to get out of the market in early 1929, but he refused, for he trusted financial experts in the same way he trusted editors and designers.

During this period Nast remarried. He had met Leslie Foster, of Lake Forest, Illinois, when she was eight; she was the same age as his daughter and his son's fiancée. Shortly after her arrival in New York, Leslie began seeing Nast discreetly. When she was offered a job by *Vogue* editor Carmel Snow, Nast begged her not to take the position, but she worked there for eight months while the rumors circulated and Nast worried over their age difference. After months of on-and-off engagements, they finally married on 28 December 1928, shortly after son Coudert's wedding, and the couples honeymooned together, even cabling daughter Natica, who joined them in Nassau. After the marriage Leslie quit her job, and in early 1930 Nast's third child, Leslie, was born.

His marriage, however, was a casualty of the Depression, which saw Condé Nast stock drop from a high of $93 down to $4.50. Nast at first refused to accept the Depression; in personal financial ruin, he convinced his bankers to

sell him a three-year, $2-million note, explaining that "I decided upon this financing because I was, naturally, uncertain as to what might be the length and seriousness of the oncoming depression, and wanted to be in a position not only to liquidate the remaining capital expenditures for the printing press equipment, but I wanted also to be in a financial position to continue to manage these publications in accordance with their tradition, in a manner that would give full value to our readers and advertisers." He refused to abandon his plans to enlarge and modernize his printing plants, and in 1931 introduced color photographs into *Vogue, Vanity Fair,* and *House and Garden.* Whatever else he may have lost, Nast maintained faith in his own ability to succeed.

Yet the power was no longer in his hands; control of the Condé Nast empire passed into the hands of his bankers in 1930, beginning a confusing series of ownership changes. In February 1931 he underwent a prostate operation. In 1932, suffering serious financial reversals and still uneasy about the age difference, he insisted Leslie divorce him. She reluctantly complied.

Nast's fortunes improved somewhat in 1934 when British press baron Lord Camrose bailed him out with a loan enabling Nast to regain control of his magazines. With his financial situation somewhat settled, Nast turned back to his publications. *Vogue* had fared well, but *Vanity Fair* was a drain on the company. Even with a circulation of ninety thousand, the magazine was losing money, for Crowninshield had little interest in courting advertisers. The Depression made the arch elegance of the magazine seem dated, and even adding new staff members, such as managing editors Donald Freeman and Clare Boothe Brokaw, who attempted to bring a stronger political slant to the journal, could not save it. Nast finally killed it in 1936, incorporating certain of its features, mostly art pages, into *Vogue.* Crowninshield joined *Vogue* as an adviser and special writer, and for a few years the merger did broaden the editorial base of the magazine, but by 1940 it was back to its traditional fashion emphasis. Nast also closed *American Golfer,* which he had purchased in 1928. He did resist advice to shut down *House and Garden,* believing that it would again prosper "on the recovery of the building and decoration industry." His instinct was correct, and by the late 1930s it was again a viable member of his publication group.

Nast also resumed his parties, despite his financial problems, and expanded on his 1932 experiment, Hollywood Patterns, turning the less expensive fashion line into a new magazine, *Glamour of Hollywood,* aimed at working women. *Glamour,* the first magazine Nast ever created, was introduced in 1939 and was a success from the beginning.

But Nast was changing, and after 1941 the staff noticed his increasing compulsion with work. His memos became irascible, almost haughty, and he refused to consider anyone's opinion but his own. He became so difficult to deal with that Chase considered resigning. Nast refused to be consoled by increasing circulation and advertising figures and began to speak of his own death.

His preoccupation with his own mortality was more than intuition, for in late 1941 he learned he had a serious heart condition. Nast concealed his deteriorating health from everyone except his secretary, for she needed to know about the oxygen tank he had hidden behind a filing cabinet. Even when his ill health became obvious to everyone at the office, he kept up the pretense that his second severe heart attack was pneumonia, and he refused to slow down. He wrote a sixty-seven-page memo to the *Vogue* staff detailing mistakes in the recent issues; his assistant and successor, Iva Sergei Voidato-Patcévitch, recalled that Nast "was in a terrible state of mind in the last months before he died. He did nothing but dictate memos. He was attempting to write an appraisal of every member of the staff before he died." To the end Nast would not relinquish control.

He did, however, find time for his other great passion, parties, and continued to play host at dinners and cocktail and birthday parties. He also continued his pursuit of younger women, despite increased worries over new financial difficulties.

In September 1942 he visited his twelve-year-old daughter Leslie at a camp in Vermont and apparently suffered his most severe attack while climbing a hill with her. From that point on he was confined to his bed. Ill as he was, he apologized to Chase for his compulsive criticisms of the past year and explained that "I am carrying a very heavy burden. I seem to have no interest in life but seeing these properties through. Whether I am to break under this ordeal I do not know."

A few days later, two weeks after the attack in Vermont, Nast was dead at the age of sixty-nine.

The *New York Times* eulogized Nast as the creator of "class" publications which were the embodiment of his purpose to "publish magazines which are authoritative in their fields." *Time* reported that "for a generation he was the man from whom millions of American women got most of their ideas, directly or indirectly, about the desirable standard of living." After a funeral in the Roman Catholic Church of St. Ignatius Loyola, Nast was buried next to his mother in the Gate of Heaven Cemetery in Pleasantville, New York.

Before his death he had appointed forty-year-old Patcévitch his successor, and the company continued under his direction until S. I. Newhouse purchased controlling interest in 1959. Nast died burdened by crushing personal and business debts, and his estate was forced to sell the contents of his magnificent penthouse at depressed wartime prices.

Nast wrote his own epitaph only months before he died when he told Rosamond Riley, a young woman he was courting who would later became an editor at *Vogue,* "Think of it. Here I was, just a boy from St. Louis, and Edna Chase a Quaker from New Jersey. Between us, we set the standards of the time. We showed America the meaning of style."

Biography:
Caroline Seebohm, *The Man Who Was Vogue: The Life and Times of Condé Nast* (New York: Viking, 1982).

References:
Edna Woolman Chase, "Fifty Years of *Vogue,*" *Vogue* (15 November 1943): 33;

Chase and Ilka Chase, *Always in Vogue* (Garden City, N.Y.: Doubleday, 1954);

Henry Pringle, "High Hat," *Scribner's Magazine* (July 1938): 19;

Walter G. Robinson, "With the Makers of *Vogue,*" *Vogue* (1 January 1923): 74.

Papers:
Nast's papers are gathered at the Condé Nast Archives, Condé Nast Publications, Inc., 350 Madison Avenue, New York, N.Y.

Walter Hines Page

(15 August 1855-21 December 1918)

Bert Hitchcock
Auburn University

See also the Page entry in *DLB 71: American Literary Critics and Scholars, 1880-1900*.

MAJOR POSITIONS HELD: Editor, *Forum* (1891-1895), *Atlantic Monthly* (1898-1899); vice-president, Doubleday, Page and Company (1899-1913); editor, *World's Work* (1900-1913).

BOOKS: *The Rebuilding of Old Commonwealths: Being Essays towards the Training of the Forgotten Man in the Southern States* (New York: Doubleday, Page, 1902); republished as *The School That Built a Town* (New York: Harper, 1952);

A Publisher's Confession, anonymous (New York: Doubleday, Page, 1905; London: Gay & Bird, 1905); enlarged edition, credited to Page (Garden City, N.Y.: Doubleday, Page, 1923; London: Heinemann, 1924);

The Southerner: A Novel, as Nicholas Worth (New York: Doubleday, Page, 1909; London: Heinemann, 1910).

SELECTED PERIODICAL PUBLICATIONS:
"The Last Hold of the Southern Bully," *Forum*, 16 (November 1893): 303-314;

"The War with Spain and After," *Atlantic Monthly*, 81 (June 1898): 721-727;

"The End of the War, and After," *Atlantic Monthly*, 82 (September 1898): 430-432;

"An Intimate View of Publishing," *World's Work*, 4 (September 1902): 2561-2565;

"The Cultivated Man in an Industrial Era," *World's Work*, 8 (July 1904): 4980-4984;

"The People as an Exhibit," *World's Work*, 8 (August 1904): 5110-5113;

"A Glance at the Ending Year," *World's Work*, 11 (December 1905): 7003-7008;

"A Journey through the Southern States," *World's Work*, 14 (June 1907): 9003-9042;

"Teaching Morals by Photographs," *World's Work*, 19 (March 1910): 12715-12725;

"On a Tenth Birthday," *World's Work*, 21 (January 1911): 13903-13917;

"The Hookworm and Civilization," *World's Work*, 24 (September 1912): 504-518;

"What *The World's Work* Is Trying to Do," *World's Work*, 25 (January 1913): 265-268.

A genteel, liberal southerner and an ardent nationalist, Walter Hines Page helped to transform American monthly magazine journalism during two decades on either side of the time line that marked the beginning of the twentieth century. To those southerners desiring proof, Page's editorship of the *Atlantic Monthly* and his founding partnership in a major national publishing house provided firm evidence of what an intelligent, articulate man from the defeated Confederacy could achieve in the mainstream of the nation's cultural and business life. After serving as ambassador to the Court of St. James's and becoming the subject of a Pulitzer Prize winning biography in the 1920s, Page was made into an inspiring national symbol, a patriotic legend just after his own time. Although today he seems less an epic hero than an illuminating "representative" man, his representativeness includes innovation that was important for American literature and American journalism.

Page was born in a small village not far from Raleigh, North Carolina. Established by his father, Allison Francis Page, and originally known as "Page's" or "Page's Station," the settlement was incorporated as Cary, North Carolina, when Walter Page was a teenager. Although owning slaves and materially supporting the Confederacy, Page's father was more a nationalist than a sectional secessionist, and he passed along to his son deep democratic convictions. From his mother, Catherine Frances Raboteau Page, Walter Page gained a love of literature and language. His boyhood knowledge of the Civil War came in striking, experiential stages: seeing coffins come in at the depot, having the enemy housed in his own home, viewing the decomposing bodies of soldiers of both armies along the North Carolina roadside.

254

Walter Hines Page

His earliest formal education he received at home, in local private academies, and at Bingham, a military school, forty miles away in Meban, North Carolina. In 1871, apparently planning on becoming a Methodist minister, he entered Trinity College (now Duke University) in his home state, but he transferred after a year and a half to Randolph-Macon College in Ashland, Virginia. After his graduation, having been highly recommended by his Greek and English professor, Page was named among the first group of fellowship recipients for graduate study at the new Johns Hopkins University in the fall of 1876. By 1878, however, he had decided that classical philology was not his calling.

After leaving Johns Hopkins, Page took employment as a teacher before becoming a journalist and finding his life's work: not the cloistered study of classical language but the active, public,

assertive, educational (always educational) use of his native language. He taught English literature in summer school at the University of North Carolina in 1878 and was "professor of English" at Boys' High School in Louisville, Kentucky, during the following academic year. The "literary" career he desired, however, was one that would have *him* writing, that would be "higher scholarly work" than teaching. Having contributed a series of European travel letters to the *Raleigh Observer* in 1877 and an article about the poet Henry Timrod to the *South-Atlantic* review in 1878, Page knew what it was like to see one's work in print, and he liked what he knew. In 1879 he prophetically declared to a cousin, "I am going to write–I am going to edit a magazine. And I am going to own the magazine that I edit."

Page achieved his goal in sixteen major steps over a period of twenty years. First, he

A photograph of Page taken in 1878, while he was teaching English at Boys' High School in Louisville, Kentucky

wrote for and indeed became part owner of the *Age*, a Louisville journal that proved short-lived. Moving to the newspaper world he accepted the offer of a trial position as editor of the *St. Joseph* [Missouri] *Gazette*. Encouraged by the appearance of his essay "Study of an Old Southern Borough" in the *Atlantic Monthly* in 1881, he took a leave of absence from the *Gazette* to travel in the South and published his observations in letters to the *New York World* and *Boston Post*. A second article in a national magazine, the *International Review*, soon followed, and before the end of 1881 Page accepted a staff position on the *World*, one of the country's top big-city newspapers.

During the less than two years he was with the *World*, Page was often given assignments that took him away from New York. It was on one such trip, to Atlanta in 1882, that he met Woodrow Wilson, then a young attorney. He also

continued to think about, and to write and lecture from a reformer's viewpoint on, distinctively "Southern" problems. When Joseph Pulitzer bought the *World* in 1883, Page returned to North Carolina to found a weekly newspaper in Raleigh, the *State Chronicle*.

He worked with the *State Chronicle* for about the same period of time, a year and a half, that he had worked for the *World*. The *State Chronicle* was practically a one-person operation. While he engaged in enthusiastic boosterism of North Carolina, Page did not hesitate to offer critically and freely what he believed were constructive suggestions to remedy the social and political ills of his state and region. The *State Chronicle*, he said, would deliver "plain speaking editorials about living subjects, advocating honest democratic politics, industrial education, material development, money making and hearty living." In format and editorial practices Page combined the old and the new of contemporary newspapering, but there was even at this time clear evidence of a periodical pioneer at work. With the *Chronicle*, Page did not realize his ambitions either for the region or for himself, professionally or financially, and early in 1885 he left once more for New York. He would not reside in the South again until the last few days of his life.

Contributing to such newspapers as the *Boston Post* and *Brooklyn Union* and magazines such as the *Independent*, Page earned a living as a freelance writer until he became a salaried editorial writer for the *New York Union*. For more than a year he also sent back regular letters to the *State Chronicle*, the more candid and caustic of which made his name anathema to many North Carolinians. The most notorious of these communiqués, in February 1886, labeled as "mummies" the powerful reactionaries who choked intellectual life and stood in the way of progress in the South. Page joined the staff of the *New York Evening Post* in 1887 but left before the year was out in order to become business manager of the *Forum*. He was finally, as he had desired, entering the world of the major national magazine, a world he would help transform.

Page functioned effectively enough but found managing only the business affairs of the *Forum* increasingly unfulfilling. He was quick to accept the editorship of the magazine when it was offered to him in 1891. Making the *Forum* "a great periodical" would have been impossible without his having financial control, Page believed, and when he lost a stock battle in 1895 he was hurt but consented willingly to being replaced as editor. In less than three months he was in Boston in an even more prestigious post: chief assistant to the editor of the *Atlantic Monthly* and literary adviser for Houghton Mifflin and Company. For all practical purposes he ascended to the editorial chair of the *Atlantic* in mid 1896, although Horace Scudder titularly retained the editorship for two more years. Page was named the sixth editor of the renowned monthly in 1898, but he kept the post only into the following year. Still feeling that he was more a hired employee than his own man, he responded to the appeals of S. S. McClure to return to New York, where McClure was attempting a takeover of Harper and Brothers publishers. The attempt failed, but Page formed a friendship with another McClure associate, Frank Doubleday. In December of 1899 Doubleday, Page and Company was established, and

Page in 1899, the year in which he left the editorship of the Atlantic Monthly *to join publisher Frank Nelson Doubleday in forming Doubleday, Page and Company*

the next November, with Page as editor, the new publishing house brought out the first number of the *World's Work*. Page at last had a magazine that was truly his.

For this literary newspaperman-turned-magazine-editor, the *World's Work*, subtitled *A History of Our Time*, was a final evolutionary step. To the already innovative *Forum*, Page, with his fresh editorial style, had supplied new gusto for additional journalistic and commercial experimentation. A "bluff, hearty, unconventional type," he made an indelible impression on one *Forum* staff member who remembered his coming into the editorial offices, sitting on a flattop desk, and gaily kicking his heels as he talked. Those who initially thought he "couldn't edit the label on a tomato can" were forced to recant. *Forum* contributor Henry Holt, who said he did not recognize Page's greatness at first because he was so kind with manuscripts and got along so well with everyone, did realize early, he said, that Page was the best periodical-literature editor America had had up to that time.

Eschewing the obsessive, meticulous, repeated reworking of manuscripts that characterized his predecessor's editing, Page as *Forum* editor devoted his energies rather to seeking out and developing new talent. He did not do so, however, at the expense of the distinctive *Forum* practice of securing well-known authors for articles on certain topics; in fact, according to one colleague, he considerably strengthened the practice by not only getting well-known contributors but also ensuring that the topics were up-to-date and the persons well-informed about their subjects. Among frequent contributors during Page's tenure were Theodore Roosevelt, Woodrow Wilson, Sen. George F. Hoar, and professors William P. Trent and Brander Matthews. For Page, solicitation of a manuscript did not mean automatic acceptance; he was fully capable of refusing any submission.

The profit that the *Forum* finally started to show in 1893 was the direct result of its editor's daring, democratic move to halve the price, and an enlarged readership increased the already high prestige of the magazine. Page promoted investigative reporting and ran series of articles that provided both depth of treatment and balanced debate of important contemporary issues. The range of subjects treated was wide–political, social, religious, economic, scientific, industrial, educational, artistic. While no primary imaginative literature was included, there was ample critical discussion of belles lettres. "It would be difficult," concludes Frank Luther Mott, "to find a better exposition of the more serious interests of the American mind in the decade 1886 to 1896 than is afforded by the first twenty volumes of the *Forum*," volumes which, moreover, "contain much that is of comparatively permanent value." The *Forum*, says Mott, made an "admirable contribution to the free and open discussion of great public questions," and its second editor, Walter Hines Page, was a major reason for that contribution.

Page's predecessors at the *Atlantic Monthly*, founded in 1857, were James Russell Lowell, James T. Fields, William Dean Howells, Thomas Bailey Aldrich, and Horace Scudder. Subtitled *A Magazine of Literature, Science, Art, and Politics*, the *Atlantic* was in the late 1880s and 1890s the kind of staid, elite literary periodical, identified with old New England, to which such magazines as *Forum* and *Munsey's* were direct reactions. A semiofficial history of the *Atlantic* uses Page's editorship as evidence of "the identification of the *Atlantic* with America rather than with any section of it" and claims that Page "gave a stronger color to the political aspect of the *Atlantic* than any previous editor had imparted to it" because his "powerful personality . . . had for its chief concern the problems of our national life." Page had in fact been brought to Boston to provide some new and different blood for Houghton, Mifflin and its well-known magazine, and he delivered.

Confident, affectionate, enterprising, a man of tremendous energy and enthusiasm, Page worked ceaselessly amid what seemed acres of paper clutter in his office. But, setting another new direction, he was not always in his office; he did not hesitate to go anywhere to court a new contributor or to capture a subject for a timely article. He sought ideas and subjects for *Atlantic* pieces constantly and could find inspirations or suggestions almost anywhere.

The "real thing," Page believed, was life and action, not theory; his interest was in the here and not the elsewhere, in the concrete not the abstract, in the present (as present and as determiner of the future) rather than the past. Under his direction, contemporary American life became the premier subject, and timeliness became the compelling publication principle for *Atlantic* pieces. Not that traditional "departments" were ignored: Page took perhaps special pains to cultivate belletristic contributors, as his relations with Ellen Glasgow, Charles Waddell Chesnutt, and Mary Johnston–and the enthusiastic reception accorded their *Atlantic* stories–indicate. Even here, though, contemporaneity and the new and timely were watchwords. Not simply because they were established writers but because their manuscripts did not meet his criteria, Page rejected submissions by writers such as Henry James and William Dean Howells. Page's editorial correspondence was always personal and comparatively informal, his letters always handwritten. Among American writers, both major and minor, the *Atlantic* editor's gentle generosity became legendary. To receive a letter of rejection from Page was more satisfying than to get a letter of acceptance from other editors. According to his fellow North Carolinian William Sydney Porter (O. Henry), "Page could reject a story with a letter that was so complimentary and make everybody feel so happy that you could take it to a bank and borrow money on it."

Page had definite ideas about what was good and effective English prose. Ellery Sedgwick, who became editor of the *Atlantic* in 1909,

Cover and table of contents for an issue of the magazine that Page founded in November 1900. Throughout his editorship, which lasted until 1913, Page's magazine displayed his "joyful confidence in the soundness of American life."

claimed that he and many others learned more about their profession from Page than from anyone else. Better than anyone he had known, said Sedgwick, Page could articulate as well as illustrate the secrets of successful editing. Do not produce a magazine for only your office colleagues, he would say; write for the outside. Forget all others, and work for only the upcoming issue; save no article for some vague future number. Insist on solid, thoughtful, interesting, terse writing; always reject the ignorant, the slipshod, and the pretentious. "He understood instinctively," said Sedgwick, "that to write well a man must not only have something to say, but must long to say it."

Page's boldest individual act with the *Atlantic* was the result of something that evidently he longed to say. It was deeply revelatory of the man, and of the extensive system of values that would underlie the *World's Work* later. Put simply, he embraced imperialism, urging overseas territorial expansion. An American flag on the cover of

the June 1898 *Atlantic* advertised Page's stance. Unambiguously and repeatedly Page posited America as the great modern representative of white English-speaking peoples, the supreme if not sole hope for civilization and the future of the world. The United States must do whatever was necessary, in order to save the holy, the good, and the healthy.

Page had long been possessed of confident answers and forward-looking vision. These he brought with renewed vigor into a new century and to new responsibilities as vice-president of Doubleday, Page and Company and as editor of the *World's Work*. John Tebbel's claim in *A History of Book Publishing in the United States* that Page saw this editorship, as well as his others, as "an instrument for promoting the social democracy, for advancing primary education, technical training, scientific agriculture, the improvement of country life, sanitation, and for emphasizing in the growing mind the dignity of American citizen-

*Frank Nelson Doubleday, Theodore Roosevelt, and Walter Hines Page in September 1910 at Country Life Press,
the new Garden City, Long Island, printing plant built by Doubleday, Page and Company*

ship" is notably more accurate for his *World's Work* tenure than for the others. The underpinnings of the Page editorial platform were the democratic ideal, defined in terms of the United States, and modernism, progress, and social advancement, also nationalistically conceived. Faithful optimism was the energy source of this new magazine, reformistic education and inspiration the desired result. The appeal was to be popular rather than elitist, but more intellectual than emotional. Imaginative literature could claim no place in realizing a new American periodical literature whose obligations were to the present and the future; poetry and fiction did not appear in the *World's Work*.

Page assured William Roscoe Thayer that he was "not going to make the new magazine my own megaphone," but he proceeded immediately to confess that it would "nevertheless contain my general interpretation of things, in which I swear I do believe!" He went on to say that once the *World's Work* was established, "then it can be shaped more nearly into what I wish it to become. If it seems unmannerly, aggressive, I know

no other way to make it heard." The secret that Page said he would "bawl out" for all to hear was the singular new subject for American magazines: "the new impulse in American life, the new feeling of nationality, our coming to realize ourselves" through "aggressive democracy" and "growth by action."

"It is with the activities of the newly organized world, its problems, and even its romance that this magazine will chiefly concern itself," the editor wrote in the first number of the *World's Work*. A year later he claimed that in featuring what he called the "literature of achievement" and "the literature of action" his enterprise had succeeded in adding "to the cheerful earnestness of American life." He pronounced that the purpose of the *World's Work* "to interpret the important things that are done" was being fulfilled, defining those things as "whatever men do better than men have done before" in the present "most active era." The task undertaken, he said, was "as definite as it was serious, and a somewhat new one–to make an interesting magazine that should have a higher aim than to fill an idle

Walter Hines Page, United States ambassador to the Court of St. James's, 1917; portrait by P. A. Lazlo
(by permission of the Division of Archives and History, Raleigh, North Carolina)

hour, and a more original aim than to thresh over old straw and call the chaff 'Literature,' or to publish the commonplace that men in official positions dictate in their decline for cash." On the magazine's tenth anniversary, and again just before he left the editorship in 1913, Page declared that the aims of the *World's Work* were being effectively met. As Page saw it, the *World's Work* had become a leader in a revolution that had made the magazine in America a positive force in public affairs after decades of its being limited to literature and art, of its dealing "remotely and harmlessly and in great generalities with large subjects." Now it could be said, he asserted, that "the magazines have told the American people more about themselves these ten years than all periodical literature told during the preceding century."

Having sometimes to tell himself what he did not want to hear, such as conditions in the Chi-

cago stockyards or ruthless immorality among some of the nation's businessmen, did not finally deter Page from speaking with "a joyful confidence in the soundness of American life." Studying it "in the large," the well-balanced man, while promoting certain needful reforms, could report the activities of many-sided life in the United States with a "hopeful and helpful spirit," he concluded. He took pride and found hope in the pioneering work of the *World's Work* and the many imitators it engendered, in both its editorial and its technical innovations. Nothing represents both these dimensions so well and vividly as the use of photographs. In 1907 the *World's Work* began including in each issue a dozen or more high-quality, full-page portraits grouped together as a "portrait gallery." Photographs appeared throughout each issue as well, and for definite educational purposes, not as haphazard ornamentation. In simply appearance Page's own magazine seems centuries away from the all-print *Forum* or the print-dominated *Atlantic*. While it has been disparagingly described as "a glorified monthly newspaper" and condemned as being "in the main an apologist for the trusts and current trends of big business," Mott concludes that the *World's Work* was, in content and form, a "quality magazine" that "made, for a third of a century, a notable contribution to the intelligent discussion of public affairs in America."

Busy as publisher and editor, and active in many social-cause organizations such as the Southern Education Board, the General Education Board, the Commission for the Extermination of the Hookworm Disease, and Theodore Roosevelt's Commission on Country Life, Page nevertheless found more time in the first decade of the century for his own writing than he had been able to find previously. From these years date his only three books, only the first of them bearing his name, and all published by Doubleday, Page. Two emerge directly from his southern heritage and his continuing concern for the region. All may be valued for other than literary reasons.

The Rebuilding of Old Commonwealths (1902) collected three essays that are typical but especially memorable renditions of Page's southern message to the South and to the nation. "The Forgotten Man" and "The School That Built a Town" were first delivered as addresses at state normal schools in North Carolina and Georgia in 1897 and 1901; the title piece appeared in the *Atlantic* in 1902. According to Page, the three influences that had held southern society stationary were slavery during its past (slavery "pickled all Southern life and left it just as it found it") and the region's politicians and preachers since. In the South, he claimed, were America's richest undeveloped human and natural resources, but it was "a realm . . . ruled by the dead."

The contents of Page's second book, *A Publisher's Confession* (1905), appeared originally as ten letters in the *Boston Transcript*. The title is ironic, for Page was presenting, with positive self-portraiture, a spirited defense of his profession. "A book," he wrote, "is a commodity. Yet the moment it is treated as a mere commodity it takes severe revenge on its author and on its publisher." He deals with both writers and academic critics summarily and caustically: What some might call a story, he said, might also be called "a mild mush of mustard, warranted to redden the faded cheeks of sickly sentimentality." Knowing literature's "royal qualities at once under strange and

new garments" is evidence of a great publisher, but "the critical crew and the academic faculty are sure not to recognize it at first sight."

Page's one completed attempt at long fiction was *The Southerner* (1909), a slightly reworked version of "The Autobiography of a Southerner since the Civil War," which ran serially in the *Atlantic* in 1906. Subtitled *The Autobiography of Nicholas Worth*, the book is clearly based on Page's own experiences, and it sets forth familiar Page conclusions. Nicholas plaintively reports, for example, how he learned at an early age that "nobody tells the whole truth about institutions. They prefer to accept traditions and to repeat respectful formulas." Here, Page named the destructive "ghosts" haunting the South: the fear of blacks, religious orthodoxy, and the old Confederacy. Nothing is dramatized nearly so well and so variously in *The Southerner* as is this third ghost.

Page disliked "professional Southerners," and yet some of the qualities that allowed him to be seen as self-appointed southern ambassador to the North made him the natural choice of President Wilson as the nation's ambassador to Great Britain in 1913. Although his relationship with Wilson became increasingly strained, he served with his usual forcefulness and flair. At the end of World War I, he returned to the United States from a grateful and admiring England. Only three Americans are honored in Westminster Abbey: James Russell Lowell, Henry Wadsworth Longfellow, and Walter Hines Page.

His being a member of this particular trio represents, for all its glory, a kind of sad final irony. Page's major contribution to American letters comes, it has been claimed, in his letters–in the correspondence of the years of his diplomatic career. That was not as he would have wished. Despite what he said, and the principles on which he operated as editor of the *World's Work*, he longed to write "literature," to be at least a candidate for the Poet's Corner of Westminster Abbey. From his early attempts at poetry to intense interest in dramatizing a Mary Johnston novel to a flurry of jottings for prospective fiction and personal essays in the years just prior to his ambassadorial appointment, Page was an aspiring writer in the most traditional sense of the word, but he was a man who never found the time, or had the talent, so to devote himself. For what he did with much of his life–as southerner and as ambassador, for example–he received both approbation and censure. His contribution to American periodicals through his major editorships was and remains, however, an unquestionable, enduring gift to the country he loved.

Biographies:
Burton J. Hendrick, *The Life and Letters of Walter H. Page*, 3 volumes (Garden City, N.Y.: Doubleday, Page, 1922-1925);

Hendrick, *The Training of an American: The Earlier Life and Letters of Walter H. Page, 1855-1913* (Boston & New York: Houghton Mifflin, 1928);

Ross Gregory, *Walter Hines Page, Ambassador to the Court of St. James's* (Lexington: University Press of Kentucky, 1970);

John Milton Cooper, Jr., *Walter Hines Page: The Southerner as American, 1855-1918* (Chapel Hill: University of North Carolina Press, 1977).

References:
Arthur E. Bostwick, *A Life with Men and Books* (New York: H. W. Wilson, 1939);

Robert D. W. Connor, "Walter Hines Page, A Southern Nationalist," in *Southern Pioneers in Social Interpretation*, edited by Howard W. Odum (Chapel Hill: University of North Carolina Press, 1925), pp. 51-67;

C. Hartley Grattan, "The Walter Hines Page Legend," *American Mercury*, 6 (September 1925): 39-51;

Fred Hobson, "A Page of Virginia and a Page from Lubberland," in his *Tell About the South: The Southern Rage to Explain* (Baton Rouge: Louisiana State University Press, 1983), pp. 129-179;

Henry Holt, *Garrulities of an Octogenarian Editor* (Boston: Houghton Mifflin, 1923);

M. A. De Wolfe Howe, *"The Atlantic Monthly" and Its Makers* (Boston: Atlantic Monthly Press, 1919);

Isaac F. Marcossom, *Adventures in Interviewing* (New York: John Lane, 1920);

Edwin Mims, "Walter Hines Page: Friend of the South," *South Atlantic Quarterly*, 18 (April 1919): 97-115;

Frank Luther Mott, *A History of American Magazines*, volume 4 (Cambridge, Mass.: Harvard University Press, 1957), pp. 773-788;

Edd Winfield Parks, "Walter Hines Page and the South," in his *Segments of Southern Thought* (Athens: University of Georgia Press, 1938), pp. 273-289;

Robert J. Rusnak, *Walter Hines Page and "The World's Work," 1900-1913* (Washington, D.C.: University Press of America, 1982);

Richard M. Weaver, *The Southern Tradition at Bay: A History of Postbellum Thought*, edited by George Core and M. E. Bradford (New Rochelle, N.Y.: Arlington House, 1968).

Papers:
The major collection is the Walter Hines Page Papers at the Houghton Library, Harvard University. Other repositories include the libraries of Duke University and the University of Virginia, and the Walter Hines Page Library of Randolph-Macon College. For the years of Page's government service, the Edward M. House Papers at the Yale University Library is an important collection.

Harry Thurston Peck

(24 November 1856-23 March 1914)

Hilbert H. Campbell
Virginia Polytechnic Institute and State University

See also the Peck entry in *DLB 71: American Literary Critics and Scholars, 1880-1900.*

MAJOR POSITION HELD: Editor, *Bookman* (1895-1907).

BOOKS: *The Semitic Theory of Creation: A Study of Language* (Chicago: Barclay, White, 1886);
Latin Pronunciation (New York: Holt, 1890; augmented, 1894);
The Adventures of Mabel, as Rafford Pyke (New York: Dodd, Mead, 1897);
The Personal Equation (New York & London: Harper, 1898);
Greystone and Porphyry (New York: Dodd, Mead, 1899);
What Is Good English? and Other Essays (New York: Dodd, Mead, 1899);
William Hickling Prescott (New York: Macmillan, 1905);
Twenty Years of the Republic, 1885-1905 (New York: Dodd, Mead, 1906; London: Hodder & Stoughton, 1906);
Hilda and the Wishes (New York: Dodd, Mead, 1907);
Literature (New York: Columbia University Press, 1908);
Studies in Several Literatures (New York: Dodd, Mead, 1909);
The New Baedeker; Being Casual Notes of An Irresponsible Traveler (New York: Dodd, Mead, 1910);
A History of Classical Philology from the Seventh Century, B.C., to the Twentieth Century, A.D. (New York: Macmillan, 1911).

OTHER: *The International Cyclopedia,* edited by Peck (New York: Dodd, Mead, 1892);
Roman Life in Latin Prose and Verse, edited by Peck and Robert Arrowsmith (New York: American Book Company, 1894);
Harper's Dictionary of Classical Literature and Antiquities, compiled and edited by Peck (New York: Harper, 1897);

Harry Thurston Peck

Petronius Arbiter, *Trimalchio's Dinner,* translated by Peck (New York: Dodd, Mead, 1898);
Masterpieces of the World's Literature, Ancient and Modern, 20 volumes, edited by Peck, Frank R. Stockton, and Julian Hawthorne (New York: American Literary Society, 1898-1899); revised and enlarged as *The World's Great Masterpieces; History, Biography, Science, Philosophy, Poetry, the Drama, Travel, Adventure, Fiction, etc.,* 30 volumes, edited by Peck, Stockton, Nathan Haskell Dole, Hawthorne, and Caro-

line Ticknor (New York: American Literary Society, 1901);

The New International Encyclopedia, 17 volumes, edited by Peck, Daniel Coit Gilman, and Frank Moore Colby (New York: Dodd, Mead, 1902-1904);

The Standard Illustrated Book of Facts, edited by Peck and Robert Campbell Auld (New York: Syndicate Publishing Company, 1912).

SELECTED PERIODICAL PUBLICATIONS
UNCOLLECTED: "A Novel of Lubricity," review of Thomas Hardy's *Jude the Obscure*, *Bookman*, 2 (January 1896): 427-429;

Review of *George's Mother*, by Stephen Crane, *Bookman*, 3 (July 1896): 446-447;

Review of *The Touchstone*, by Edith Wharton, *Bookman*, 11 (June 1899): 319-323;

"An Authoritative Dream Book," *Bookman*, 10 (December 1899): 346-347;

"American Opinion of the South African War," *Bookman*, 10 (February 1900): 527-532;

"Unleavened Bread," *Bookman*, 11 (July 1900): 463-467;

"A Note on Charles Dudley Warner," *Bookman*, 12 (December 1900): 369-371;

"President McKinley," *Bookman*, 14 (November 1901): 275-280;

"Mrs. Trollope's Book on the Americans," *Bookman*, 14 (January 1902): 486-495;

"Émile Zola," *Bookman*, 16 (November 1902): 233-240;

"Rudyard Kipling, Poet," *Bookman*, 18 (November 1903): 307-309;

"The Auto-Car," *Bookman*, 23 (July 1906): 544-548;

"Fonetik Refawrm By Edict," *Bookman*, 24 (October 1906): 171-172;

"Edmund Clarence Stedman," *Bookman*, 27 (March 1908): 31-34;

"Napoleon the Less," *Bookman*, 28 (December 1908): 368-377;

"One of the Parnassiens [Catulle Mendès]," *Bookman*, 29 (April 1909): 174-178;

"The Human Side of Tennyson," *Bookman*, 29 (August 1909): 600-609.

Today relatively few people would recognize an allusion to Harry Thurston Peck, but in the two decades between 1890 and 1910 he was a widely recognized, influential, and controversial figure. He held the respected Anthon Professorship of Latin Language and Literature at Columbia University, authored and edited many books in classical studies, history, travel, children's literature, and literary criticism, and delighted and shocked the public with light, witty essays on a variety of topics ranging from literature and language to popular songs and perfumes. He was associated prominently as staff member or frequent contributor with several journals, including the *Commercial Advertiser*, *Ainslee's Magazine*, *Cosmopolitan*, and *Munsey's Magazine*. He gained his widest reputation as editor of a new literary monthly, the *Bookman*, between 1895 and 1907.

Despite his accomplishments as editor of the *Bookman* and of the *Harper's Dictionary of Classical Literature and Antiquities* (1897), which still stands on the shelves of many scholars, much of his prolific output has not stood the test of time. He allowed the very range and catholicity of his knowledge and his interests to stand in the way of completing a contemplated definitive history of Latin literature, a work which many of his most distinguished contemporaries believed him uniquely qualified to produce. In 1910 a breach-of-promise suit brought against Peck by a stenographer was widely and gleefully detailed in the New York daily tabloids. This scandal led to his summary dismissal from Columbia University, where he had taught Latin literature and language since 1886, to the refusal of publishers and journals to accept his work, to mental decline and breakdown, and finally to his suicide on 23 March 1914. The disgrace of his last years led to a refusal, at Columbia and elsewhere, to honor his memory by calling attention to his earlier accomplishments. His reputation and even his name passed rapidly into obscurity.

Harry Thurston Peck was born in Stamford, Connecticut, on 24 November 1856, the son of Harry and Harriet Elizabeth Thurston Peck. His paternal ancestors had lived in Connecticut since the 1640s. He began his education at Peck's Military Academy, in Greenwich, Connecticut, where his lawyer-father was headmaster. His youth was a time of wide reading and hard study, and he early determined that he would learn something about every field of human thought. After a brief period of teaching at his father's school, Peck entered Columbia College with the class of 1881. He impressed his professors as brilliant, especially in Latin, and began his literary career by editing the college newspaper, the *Acta Columbiana*, which became under his editorship the best-known college paper in the United States.

After graduation he studied classical philology for a time in Berlin, Paris, and Rome. On 26

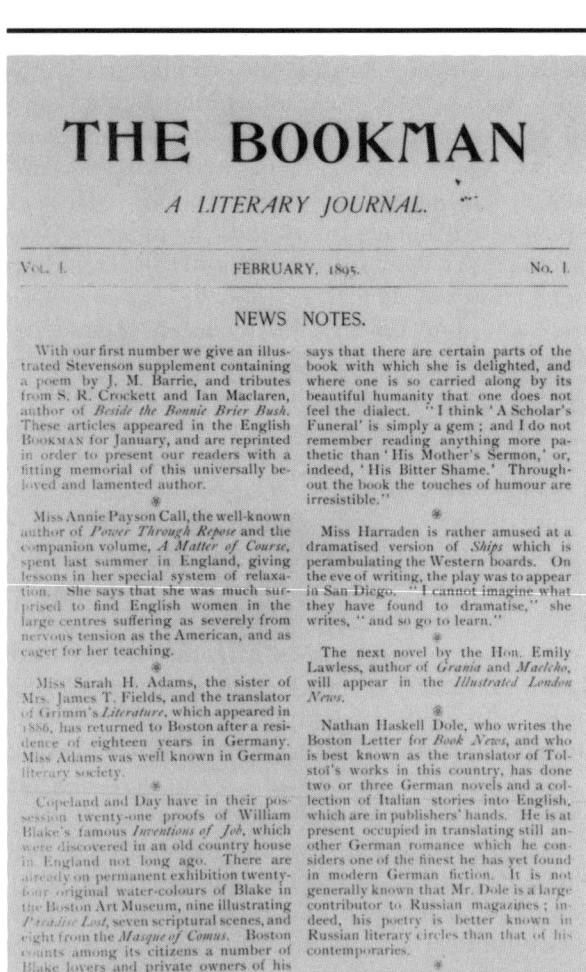

First page of the inaugural issue and cover for the April 1896 issue of the journal Peck edited from its founding until 1907

April 1882 he married Cornelia M. Dawbarn, with whom he had two daughters (the couple divorced in 1908). Peck returned to Columbia in the fall of 1882 as fellow and tutor in Latin. After receiving his doctorate from Cumberland University and an L.H.D. degree from Columbia, he was successively named acting professor of Latin and Semitic languages in 1886, professor of Latin in 1888, and Anthon Professor of Latin in 1904. Although he was said to know more about Latin literature than anyone else in America, he was impatient with the usual pedantic approaches to the subject. His own approach was to interpret the classical authors as a part of world literature and as a storehouse of interesting parallels to modern life and thought. His favorites were writers such as Petronius, Catullus, and Alciphron, in whose work he could find realistic portrayals of common life. Such inclinations may explain in part his fondness for contributing essays to popular magazines on what some of his more staid colleagues considered very unacademic subjects, such as "What Women Like in Men."

In 1895 Peck began editing the *Bookman*, a new literary monthly published in New York by Dodd, Mead and Company. The infant publication was modeled in part on the British *Bookman*, published in London since 1891 by Hodder and Stoughton and edited by W. Robertson Nicoll. However, the American *Bookman* borrowed little from its parent save the name and some similar organizational features. Frank Howard Dodd, who had employed Peck for editing projects as early as 1890 and who knew him to be a versatile contributor to journals around New York, chose

Peck (right) with associate editor James MacArthur and an unidentified stenographer

Peck as the first editor of the *Bookman*, a position he held until 1907. His greatest impact on the journal came in the years before 1902, during which he wrote a large part of the contents himself. During Peck's editorship his interest in history, his wit, his interest in non-English writers, his frankness, his discriminating taste, his lightness of touch, and his encyclopedic knowledge determined the nature and tone of the journal.

The miscellaneous nature of the material in the very early *Bookman* makes it seem almost fragmentary, but it was soon departmentalized, and within four to five years the *Bookman* was publishing about thirty-five signed articles each year in addition to its regular departments and serialized features. One of the most prominent and interesting departments during Peck's editorship was "Chronicle and Comment," which featured literary gossip about authors, poets, and critics of the day. It was later expanded from the original sixteen pages it occupied in each issue to include notes on interesting new books, rising young writers, and the accomplishments of persons in other fields. Characteristic of Peck's *Bookman*, and especially of "Chronicle and Comment," are copious illustrations, including striking photographs of literary figures. This attractive feature of the journal was gradually increased; no fewer than

350 illustrations appear in volume fourteen for 1901-1902. Although none of the "Chronicle and Comment" contributions are signed, most published during the first eight to ten years of the existence of the *Bookman* bear the indelible stamp of Peck's interests, wit, and style.

Peck's versatility and personality emerge most clearly in his many signed contributions to the *Bookman* between 1895 and 1910. From these writings he gained most of the recognition and influence he enjoyed at the time. Witty, learned, and frequently controversial in his opinions, Peck informed, amused, shocked, and sometimes infuriated his readers. He contributed book reviews, translations, essays, long articles, fiction, and poetry; he conducted a department on current affairs; he carried on a vigorous correspondence with his readers. Several of his own books, including *Twenty Years of the Republic, 1885-1905* (which was for a time one of the most popular histories of the period), were published serially in the *Bookman* before appearing in book form.

Peck skirmished with his readers in the famous "*Bookman's* Letter-Box," pointedly and wittily answering questions about literature and language, manners and morals, and other subjects. Although his responses were unfailingly interesting and informative, he also irritated many people with his authoritative pronouncements and his sarcastic dismissal of questions or opinions that he considered foolish. Especially during the first three years of his tenure as editor of the *Bookman*, Peck's unchastened egotism and dogmatic manner brought considerable protest. He wrote of one critic, "Another gentleman . . . used up all his writing paper before he had finished what he wanted to say; so that he had to cross his lines and write in the margin and around the corners. . . . We don't know exactly what it all means, but it is really rather impressive and confusing." Of another, who had criticized his preference for British spellings, he pronounced, "We have never had the pleasure of spending any time in the interesting town of Libertyville, Indiana, but we entertain a well-defined suspicion that it is just the sort of place to harbour the sort of person who would write this sort of letter. If we are wrong in this, we apologise most abjectly to Libertyville, Indiana."

Peck remained undaunted, and he dutifully printed such readers' opinions as "Will you please go to the devil and take your everlasting self-conceit and infamous injustice to women with you"; "Haven't you a pretty good opinion of yourself anyway? Why does everything that you write irritate me beyond endurance?"; and "You are a cursed, presumptuous magazine–you *Bookman!*" After 1898 there is a noticeable lessening of the hurling of insults in the "Letter-Box," but Peck's sarcasm never disappeared altogether.

A tireless reviewer, Peck frequently discussed as many as five or six books in a single review. Here, as elsewhere, all subjects–history, poetry, classical subjects, biography, humor, philosophy, fiction, and others–provided grist for his frank opinions. Of particular interest are his reviews of authors who were, or who have since become, well-known. He called Edith Wharton "a new writer who counts"; he dismissed Thomas Hardy's *Jude the Obscure* (1895) as a "mere speculation in smut"; and he judged Stephen Crane's *George's Mother* (1896) a poor work, while acknowledging that Crane had done good work elsewhere. His greatest admiration was reserved for Rudyard Kipling, who is featured far more than any other writer in the early *Bookman* and whom Peck called "a poet of the poets, a poet of life and action and daring and achievement, one who has no rival, and who stands alone in that supremacy which he has so superbly conquered for himself." Peck's interests, however, went beyond the English tradition, and one of his most important

Peck, circa 1896

contributions in the early *Bookman* was the attention paid to important European authors whose names were unfamiliar to most of his audience: Joris-Karl Huysmans, Stéphane Mallarmé, Gerhart Hauptmann, Emile Zola, and others. In 1902 the death of Zola provoked an article of high praise from Peck, in which he maintained that nothing in English literature since Shakespeare could compare with the genius of the nineteenth-century French masters.

The range of Peck's interests continued to be displayed year after year in the pages of the *Bookman*. He exercised his pen–and sometimes his contempt–on William Dean Howells, Theodore Roosevelt, Robert Ingersoll, and numerous other contemporaries. He wrote knowledgeably on the morality of the stage, the horse and the automobile, the scriptures, the psychological significance of names, and dozens of other miscellaneous topics. From 1900 to 1907 he contributed a department called "Here and There," in which he set forth his views and interpretations of national and world affairs. Here he expressed himself with equal confidence and flair on conditions in Italy and Russia, Queen Victoria, anarchism, and the mayor of New York. In a series of articles appearing over several years (1897-1907), Peck attacked vigorously the "simplified spelling" movement prominent at the time. In 1906 he severely criticized President Roosevelt for decreeing that the simplified spelling should be used in official documents. Peck became so insulting to what he called the "frantic faddists" of "fonetik refawrm" that Arthur Bartlett Maurice, who succeeded Peck as editor in 1907, announced that nothing more relating to the controversy would be published in the *Bookman.*

After 1902 Peck did not exercise as much control over the contents of the *Bookman* as he had earlier. Contributing in spurts, with noticeable lulls in activity, he increasingly let more of the actual work rest on the shoulders of his able assistant Maurice, who had been with the *Bookman* since 1899. Ever more controversial and eccentric, Peck gave up the editorship in 1907 amid the flurry of controversy over phonetic reform. After a period in 1907 and 1908 when he contributed little, he contributed prominently once more for a short period in 1909 and 1910.

In late 1910 the scandal which caused his dismissal from Columbia also undermined his prestige as journalist and author. Although the *Bookman* survived until 1933 (with Maurice as editor until 1917), it rarely mentioned Peck or his contributions to the publication. In 1914 the *Bookman* reprinted an obituary which had been published elsewhere; it briefly mentioned that Peck had once edited the journal. In September 1927 Maurice contributed an article entitled "Old Bookman Days," which was only partly about Peck.

Peck's long association with Dodd, Mead and Company began several years before he was chosen to be the first editor of the *Bookman.* As early as 1890 he began editing work for the firm on *The International Cyclopedia* (1892), and most of Peck's own books were published by Dodd, Mead. He also served in some capacity as a literary adviser to the firm. Dodd, Mead published the most complete set of the works of Anthony Trollope available at the time in England or America; and the division of Trollope's novels into three series–Parliamentary, Manor House, and Barsetshire–was Peck's idea. After his disgrace in 1910, Dodd, Mead gave him employment in revising articles for *The New International Encyclopedia* (1902-1904), which he had once edited. Sadly,

however, even this mainstay of his professional existence for nearly twenty-five years was closed to him in the months before his death because of his "marked mental decline"; and the once-bright relationship with Dodd, Mead ended in a petty squabble over a small amount of money that Peck maintained was owed him.

In addition to his *Harper's Dictionary of Classical Literature and Antiquities,* Peck's most notable books are *Twenty Years of the Republic, 1885-1905;* a children's book, *The Adventures of Mabel* (1897); his translation of Petronius's *Trimalchio's Dinner* (1898); and three books of his collected essays: *The Personal Equation* (1898), *What Is Good English? and Other Essays* (1899), and *Studies in Several Literatures* (1909). *The Adventures of Mabel* and the three essay collections are still available, along with two other books which have retained some significance: a short biography, *William Hickling Prescott* (1905); and *A History of Classical Philology from the Seventh Century, B.C., to the Twentieth Century, A.D.* (1911).

Twenty Years of the Republic, 1885-1905 was accorded the stature of a standard work for perhaps twenty-five years after its publication in 1906. Several of Peck's contemporaries and students considered it his most remarkable performance and predicted lasting status for it. But it would have surprised Peck and his contemporaries to know that the book that really endured was *The Adventures of Mabel,* a book of children's stories which Peck first wrote for the entertainment of his daughter Constance and published under the pseudonym Rafford Pyke. Although the book is now available only in a reprint edition, Dodd, Mead kept it in print for some seventy years, and as late as 1960 was still selling a few hundred copies annually.

Peck's translation of *Trimalchio's Dinner* was once considered another candidate for lasting importance. Filled with words and phrases which have no parallel to other extant Latin literature, and colored with slang, Petronius's work resists translation. Peck succeeded where others had failed because he was saturated not only with all phases of the language but also with details of the life and customs of the Roman lower and middle classes. (He described Trimalchio as "a bald, red-faced old fellow . . . , forever bragging of his money, and anxious to seem a man of literary attainments, though his ignorance of everything is unbounded.") Peck's collections of essays, gathered almost entirely from material that he had published in the *Bookman* and other magazines, were once popular reading but now seem interesting largely only as testimony to the catholicity and idiosyncrasy of his interests and tastes, and as examples of the facile brilliance of his wit and style.

On 2 June 1910 a stenographer brought suit against Peck for breach of promise of marriage and handed over to her lawyer more than one hundred letters which Peck had written her. Silly, and hurriedly composed, these letters soon began to appear in newspapers, to the huge delight of those whose tastes, language, and intelligence had been ridiculed at one time or another by the great Professor Peck. His very prominence became his downfall. Columbia University in 1910 could not tolerate the public stain; and the university's imperious president, Nicholas Murray Butler, demanded Peck's resignation. Refusing to resign, Peck was soon dismissed with only the barest ripple of protest. Dismissal from Columbia was followed by refusal by magazines to accept any more of his work; separation from his second wife, Elizabeth Hickman Du Bois, whom he had married on 26 August 1909; expulsion from the clubs and societies to which he had belonged; and desertion by many of his friends. His mental breakdown and eventual suicide seem unsurprising as aftermaths.

There is testimony that questions about Peck by later generations of junior faculty and students of Columbia University were met by a resolute refusal, even by those who had known him well, to speak of Peck. This wall of silence at Columbia and elsewhere hastened the decline of his name into obscurity. Peck once wrote in the *Bookman* of Catulle Mendès, "He touched almost every phase of life, [but] he merely touched it and passed on. He amused, he charmed, he shocked and he outraged those who lived in his own time, but he created nothing." It is tempting to apply Peck's words to his own career and accomplishments. However, it should be noted that H. L. Mencken wrote in *Newspaper Days, 1899-1906* (1941) that "The *Bookman* under Peck was the best literary monthly the United States has ever seen."

References:

Thomas Beer, *The Mauve Decade, American Life at the End of the Nineteenth Century* (New York: Knopf, 1926), pp. 185-189;

Walter G. Kellogg, "Harry Thurston Peck," *American Mercury*, 30 (September 1933): 83-88;

Arthur B. Maurice, "Old Bookman Days," *Bookman*, 66 (September 1927): 20-26;

H. L. Mencken, *Newspaper Days, 1899-1906* (New York: Knopf, 1941), p. 67.

Papers:
The relatively small amount of surviving material on Peck is in the Columbiana Collection of the Columbia University Library. Holdings include one of his scrapbooks; a portion of his published writings, including his undergraduate publications; college records; personal letters; and numerous newspaper clippings.

A. Philip Randolph

(15 April 1889-16 May 1979)

Harry Amana
Clark Atlanta University

MAJOR POSITIONS HELD: Coeditor and co-publisher, *Hotel Messenger* (January 1917-August 1917), *Messenger* (1917-1923); editor and publisher, *Messenger* (1923-1928), *Black Worker* (1929-1968), *March* (17 October 1942-20 December 1942).

SELECTED BOOKS: *Terms of Peace and the Darker Races*, by Randolph and Chandler Owen (New York: Poole Press, 1917);
The Truth About Lynching, by Randolph and Owen (New York: Cosmo Advocate, 1917?).

SELECTED PERIODICAL PUBLICATIONS:
"Pullman Porters Have Grievances," *Nation,* 121 (September 1925): 357;
"The Negro and Economic Radicalism," *Opportunity,* 4 (February 1926): 62-64;
"Porters Fight Paternalism," *American Federationist,* 37 (June 1930): 666-673;
"Why A Trade Union?," *American Federationist,* 37 (December 1930): 1470-1482;
"The Economic Crisis Of The Negro," *Opportunity,* 9 (May 1931): 145-149;
"Porters Seek Injunction," *American Federationist,* 38 (June 1931): 681-692;
"Sixth Annual Statement of Achievements and Hopes of the Porters Union," *American Federationist,* 39 (March 1932): 300-303;
"The Case of the Pullman Porter," *American Federationist,* 33 (November 1932): 1334-1339;
"An Open Letter to Mr. J. P. Morgan," *American Federationist,* 40 (July 1933): 704-710;
"Pullman Porters Vote for Organization They Want," *American Federationist,* 42 (July 1935): 727-729;
"The Trade Union Movement and the Negro," *Journal of Negro Education,* 5 (January 1936): 54-58;
"Pullman Porters Win," *Opportunity,* 10 (October 1937): 299-301ff.;
"The Case for Socialized Medicine," *Opportunity,* 13 (July 1940): 196-200;

A. Philip Randolph (Gale International Portait Gallery)

"Why Should We March?," *Survey Graphic,* 31 (November 1942): 488-489;
"The Menace of Communism," *American Federationist,* 56 (March 1949): 19-20;
"One Union's Story," *American Federationist,* 60 (November 1953): 20-23;
"U.N. and Labor," *American Federationist,* 62 (November 1955): 21;
"I Saw Ghana Born," *American Federationist,* 64 (May 1957): 10-11;
"Labor's Stake In An Emerging New Africa," *American Federationist,* 64 (October 1957): 20-21ff.;
"Don't The Railroads Want To Stay In Business?," *American Federationist,* 65 (July 1958): 18-20;

"If I Were Young Today," *Ebony,* 18 (July 1963): 82;

"The 'March'–What Negroes Expected . . . What They Want Next," full text of address at the National Press Club on 26 August 1963, *U.S. News & World Report,* 55 (9 September 1963): 82-85;

"The Moral Basis of Civil Rights," *American Federationist,* 73 (November 1966): 2-3;

"The Negro's Stake In The Elections," *American Federationist,* 75 (October 1968): 24-25.

Any serious discussion on blacks in the United States labor movement always includes some prominent mention of A. Philip Randolph for his role as organizer and leader of the Brotherhood of Sleeping Car Porters for forty-three years. Randolph is generally depicted as the single most important figure to sustain the initial twelve-year struggle of the nation's first black union to gain a negotiated contract from one of the country's wealthiest and most powerful companies. Many historians also call Randolph the father of the modern Civil Rights Movement. He organized the first planned nonviolent march on Washington in 1941–called off at the eleventh hour only when President Franklin Delano Roosevelt signed Executive Order 8802 eliminating employment discrimination in government and the defense industries. Randolph also is credited as a major force in influencing President Dwight D. Eisenhower to outlaw segregation in the military, as well as with organizing the August 1963 march on Washington in which Dr. Martin Luther King, Jr., delivered his "I Have a Dream" speech. In his sixty-year career as a labor leader and political activist Randolph led four delegations and was a member of a fifth that held face-to-face negotiations with five United States presidents on the issue of civil rights for black Americans. As a young Socialist radical in 1918 he was labeled by a New York newspaper "the most dangerous Negro in America," but by the mid 1940s, at the height of his popularity, he was courted by both Republicans and Democrats to run for public office. He always refused and maintained his commitment to democratic socialism. He served as vice-president of the AFL-CIO and retired from active public life in 1968 at the age of seventy-nine.

In literary history most accounts of the black cultural movement in the 1920s known as the Harlem Renaissance mention Randolph as the cofounder and coeditor of the *Messenger,* a forty-five-thousand-circulation, radical monthly magazine published from 1917 to 1928. In 1918 the *Messenger* lost its second-class mailing privilege for three years for publishing articles considered treasonable by the United States government. In 1919 the magazine was cited in a Justice Department investigation as "the most able and the most dangerous of all the Negro publications."

Asa Philip Randolph was born 15 April 1889 in Crescent City, Florida, to the Reverend James William and Elizabeth Robinson Randolph. He was the second of two boys. James William, Jr., two years older than Asa, was born in Baldwin, Florida, shortly before the Randolphs moved to Crescent City, where the Reverend Mr. Randolph, an ordained African Methodist Episcopal minister, had been transferred by the church. When Asa was two, the family moved to Jacksonville, where his father had been invited to take over a small AME congregation.

Randolph grew up in Jacksonville in a poor family that emphasized reading, high moral standards, and race consciousness. In 1907 he was graduated as class valedictorian from the Cookman Institute, the first high school for blacks in Florida, which was founded by Methodists. For four years after graduation he worked for an insurance company, a drug company, a lumberyard, a fertilizer factory, and a company that laid railroad crossties. In 1911 he left Jacksonville for New York City, where he would live and work for the rest of his life.

In New York the young Randolph worked as an elevator operator, pursued a career as an amateur thespian (memorizing "every line from Othello, Hamlet, and the Merchant of Venice"), and attended public-speaking classes at City College's evening school. Later he took courses in history, political science, philosophy, and economics, and became a member of the school's debating society and a founding member of a current-affairs discussion group called the Independent Political Council. This combination of courses, friendships, and experiences at City College would lead him to join the Socialist party and help to shape him for the rest of his public life as organizer, public speaker, and political activist.

In November 1914 another watershed event in his life occurred when he married Lucille Green, a beautiful and fashionable widow, Howard University graduate, and former teacher who operated her own beauty salon patronized by both blacks and "downtown" whites. She shared

Randolph, circa 1933 (Chicago Historical Society)

with him an interest in socialism—she later ran unsuccessfully for an aldermanic seat on the Socialist ticket—and for many years provided the moral support and financial foundation for Randolph and his various projects, including the *Messenger*. The couple had no children but maintained a deep, loving relationship as spouses and comrades until her death on 12 April 1963.

It was through Lucille in 1915 that Randolph met the other person who greatly influenced his development as a radical, Chandler Owen. The two young men liked each other immediately and became fast political comrades. Owen, a graduate of Virginia Union, stopped taking courses at Columbia, and Randolph stopped going to City College as they reorganized the Independent Political Council. Now the group had a distinctly radical slant, and its members met regularly at the Randolphs' apartment. It was Lucille's hairdressing business that provided not only the means to keep the apartment and council going, but also the means to establish what would be Randolph's lifelong reputation as a well-dressed man. Biographer Jervis Anderson quotes a former member of the council who "never knew him to do any work for a salary, but . . . never saw him without a starched collar, a carefully knotted tie, a white handkerchief in his

breast pocket, and a blue serge suit that looked like he had just bought it from Brooks Brothers. . . . He was lucky to have had a wife like that. Only she could have put up with all those people he used to bring home from political meetings two, three times a week to talk 'till one, two, three o'clock in the mornings."

Randolph, a tall, thin, dignified man who always sat and walked erect, would also establish a reputation as a dramatic and inspiring orator. The training had come from his activity in the theater, but the real practice would come from the street corners of Harlem where he and Owen gained reputations as soapbox orators who lambasted the political establishment and praised the socialist revolution. By 1919 they would become known as the "Lenin and Trotsky" of Harlem.

In January 1917 Randolph and Owen were approached by the president of the Headwaiters and Sidewaiters Society of Greater New York to edit a monthly magazine for the organization. They agreed and started the *Hotel Messenger*. The magazine folded in August after a disagreement between the editors and the president over an article that exposed a kickback operation the headwaiters worked on the sidewaiters. The two editors were fired, but, inspired by the editing and publishing venture, and backed by Lucille's financial assistance, they launched the *Messenger* in November 1917 (although it was listed as volume 1, "No. II"). Originally billed as "The Only Magazine of Scientific Radicalism in the World Published by Negroes," later the editors would call it "The Only Radical Negro Magazine in America." Still later, in 1923, it would become the "New Opinion of the New Negro," and in 1924, the "World's Greatest Negro Monthly."

The new magazine sold for fifteen cents a copy and was clearly a different organ than its predecessor, but an editor's statement conveyed the impression that some continuity had taken place. "We are no longer the 'Hotel' Messenger," the statement read, "the name was too narrow . . . the radical tone of the editors' writings did not set well with the 'thought-controller' in the hotel field. We did not always say 'nice' things about the head-waiters' attitude toward the side waiters and the inadequate wages paid them." The goals of the magazine, the statement continued, were to be "forward, aggressive, militant, revolutionary." Moreover: "The messenger shall ever fight for the economic and intellectual emancipation of the workingman. It shall ever fight the hydra-headed monster—race prejudice. It shall ever champion the cause of free speech, free press and free assemblage." Not only was this the creed that would guide the magazine for a decade, it was the creed that would guide Randolph through controversial and trying times until his death. The magazine and the struggle to keep it afloat would consume much of his life until 1925, when he would assume leadership of the porters union. More important, the magazine would serve as an outward expression of Randolph's political development for the next ten years and the sounding board for every major political activity in which he would become involved. Randolph's advanced political thinking was evident in the magazine's inaugural issue in that it included articles on the need to organize black actors, support the Irish revolt against England, and endorse woman suffrage. This thirty-six-page "Election Issue" also included an advertisement supporting Socialist party candidate Morris Hillquit for mayor of New York City.

The magazine was published irregularly during 1918 while the editors traveled the country on antiwar speaking engagements. On 4 August 1918 the two were arrested by Justice Department officials in Cleveland for advocating draft resistance and selling copies of the *Messenger* that contained the article "Pro-Germanism Among Negroes." Charged with violation of the Espionage Act of 1917, they were jailed and taken before a judge who thought they were dupes of the Socialists. "He couldn't believe we were old enough, or, being black, smart enough, to write that red-hot stuff in the *Messenger*," Randolph told biographer Jervis Anderson. "There was no doubt, [the judge] said, that the white Socialists were using us, that they had written the stuff for us." After scolding the pair, the judge released them. But by the end of August the postmaster general had denied second-class mailing privileges to the magazine (a ban that would remain for three years), and Owen was drafted and sent to an army camp. In September the *New York Age* labeled Randolph the "most dangerous Negro in America," and in October he was notified that his pacifism would not keep him out of military service and he soon received a draft notice. Two days later, however, armistice was declared. Undoubtedly he would have gone to jail; he had "no intention of serving," he said later.

Randolph's rifts with the Justice Department continued throughout the year not only for his Socialist activities as editor, speaker, and now part-time teacher at the Rand School of Social

Randolph in New York, circa 1912

Science, but also because of at least one of his early nonsocialistic political friendships–one that would, years later, turn to venom. He had befriended the young Jamaican Marcus Garvey in 1916 and introduced him to his first soapbox meeting on the corner of 135th Street and Lenox Avenue. By late 1918 the two men were working together in a group called the International League of Darker Peoples, whose list of demands on behalf of colonized peoples was to be presented at the Versailles conference after the war.

Randolph was to represent Garvey's Universal Negro Improvement Association in France but was denied a passport by the State Department.

With the rise of the "Red Scare" era under the guidance of Attorney General A. Mitchell Palmer, the *Messenger* continued to have trouble with the postmaster. In the August 1919 issue the *Messenger* editors stated that "His Honor, Postmaster Burleson, finally consented to allow the July MESSENGER to go through the mails.... The real cause of the release ... was the violent avalanche of protest which swept down upon the Post Office.... The people have not protested against the editorial and article entitled the "Hun in America" and "German Propaganda Among Negro Soldiers" and the cartoon portraying the American sport–lynching.... Burleson or no Burleson, the MESSENGER will continue to carry its message of economic, political and social justice to the Negro in particular and America in general."

By the end of the year the *Messenger,* along with a number of other black publications, had been investigated by Palmer's Justice Department. In a 17 November 1919 Justice Department report to the Senate of the 66th Congress– "Radicalism and Sedition Among the Negroes as Reflected in Their Publications"–the *Messenger* was described as "the most dangerous of all the Negro publications." The report continued: "It is representative of the most educated thought among the Negroes.... There was no April issue, and the May-June issue is one. Since then the *Messenger* has come out regularly and with an increasing crystallization of radical purposes. It is in the May-June issue that the *Messenger* strikes its gait with a short editorial on the progress of sovietism entitled–'THE MARCH OF THE SOVIET GOVERNMENT.' " Indeed, the magazine had come out for four consecutive months from July through October, each with thirty-six pages of text and three or four pages of advertising, but the "Thanksgiving Number" would be dated December, and the next issue would not appear until February. The magazine and its editors were beset with financial difficulties. Randolph, as president of the Messenger Publishing Company, was in charge of finances, and he had a good grasp of economics as it pertained to the geopolitical world–indeed, he also was known as a fair fund-raiser–but he had no head for business in the capitalistic sense and would gain a reputation for being a man who cared not in the least for money in any personal way. Even later, when

business managers were added to the staff, the magazine would always remain in or close to the red. Still the editors would not back down; they continued to criticize the government and its officials. Their response to Palmer's report, for example, was a press statement later published in the August 1920 *Messenger* in which they claimed that Palmer's "public career is all but ended. The shades of private life are awaiting him, and even there, he will ever remain a hated and detested memory." In 1920 eight issues of the magazine were published; in 1921 only seven appeared. Most had only sixteen pages.

Then in 1922, for the first time since its inception, the *Messenger* was published each month for the entire year. Most issues had twenty pages or more, and it had begun to solicit advertisements from black businesses. It continued publication on consecutive months through its demise in June 1928 with the exception of the double issues of October-November 1925 and May-June 1928. A total of 101 issues was published over a period of ten and a half years.

In late 1923 Owen left New York and the *Messenger* to live in Chicago. He contributed occasional articles, and his name was left on the masthead as editor, but the magazine would be run beginning in mid 1923 by George S. Schuyler, a sometimes bitter satirist who wrote the "Shafts and Darts" column in the magazine. Schuyler's name first appeared in 1923 as a contributing editor. Wallace Thurman would be listed as managing editor beginning in July 1926, and Schuyler would not appear as managing editor until March 1927, but historians say he probably managed the magazine for the last five years of its existence, especially when Randolph became involved with the porters union in 1925.

Meanwhile, Randolph would gain in stature and reputation among black Americans as a writer, orator, and political philosopher. He led the editorial assassination of Marcus Garvey by black publishers after it was revealed that Garvey had spoken favorably of white supremacists, and Randolph was included in a 1924 National Association for the Advancement of Colored People (NAACP) delegation of black leaders who petitioned President Calvin Coolidge to pardon blacks imprisoned after the Houston riots of 1917. But by 1925 Randolph's career seemed to have hit bottom. Nothing remained of the numerous organizations he had helped found; Lucille's beauty salon was in decline; the radical-left movement had been all but eliminated by the heavy

Randolph's wife, Lucille Green Randolph, circa 1928

sleep, paid for their own uniforms, meals, shoe polish, and brushes, and had to pay for articles that passengers took as souvenirs. They had no real pension plan and no outlet for grievances. If they complained about working conditions they could be fired on the spot with no hearing or appeal process. Passengers called all porters "George" after George Pullman, who, presumably, owned them. Randolph, always a union man, delivered a well-received speech and shortly thereafter was asked by Totten and others to take leadership in organizing the porters into a union. He refused but wrote pro-porters union articles and editorials in the July and August issues of the *Messenger.* The articles were so well received by the porters that Totten pressured Randolph again to assume the porters' leadership, and this time, in August, he accepted. Historian Harris notes that the porters, in choosing Randolph, "did not select a man of proven leadership skill, or one with practical experience in . . . union matters. Indeed, he had had few successes in life. . . ." But Randolph had a clear understanding of economic radicalism, was an indefatigable fighter for blacks and the working class, a "skilled polemicist," an editor of an established magazine, and, most important, he was not a porter and thus "was immune from Pullman vengeance." So beginning with the October-November 1925 issue through its demise, the *Messenger* became the official voice of the Brotherhood of Sleeping Car Porters (BSCP), the new porters union. Randolph was listed officially as the union's president and general organizer.

The BSCP immediately began operations in secret, with members paying their dues in various clandestine ways for fear of being reported to the company by the numerous snitches among the porters–"Too many [Uncle] Toms," Randolph would say in a *Time* magazine news brief. Other operating funds were raised with a drive publicized in the *Messenger* to raise fifty thousand dollars. Start-up funds were donated by the American Fund for Public Service, a philanthropic foundation that supported liberal and radical causes, also known as the Garland Fund. With five hundred dollars from a twelve-hundred-dollar Garland Fund grant, Randolph began "rejuvenating and rebuilding the magazine." He would also meet and become lifelong friends with Chicago organizer Milton P. Webster, the BSCP vice-president and chairman. The two would remain in almost constant contact throughout the ensuing twelve-year struggle.

hand of Palmer's Justice Department; and the *Messenger,* always in the red, had declined in circulation from a high of about forty-five thousand to a low in September 1925 of about five thousand. And even that issue, according to porters union historian William H. Harris, had been delayed in publishing because of a lack of funds. Also, the magazine had experienced such a change in content and perspective that Langston Hughes called it a "Negro society magazine and a plugger for Negro business with photographs of prominent colored ladies and their nice homes." Moreover, Randolph at thirty-six had no viable mainstream career and no prospects for one. Put simply by Harris, "Randolph needed a job."

Thus it was that Randolph was approached in June 1925 by Ashley L. Totten to speak to a group of railroad porters who were thinking about starting their own union. Many of the porters were educated men who had attended or graduated from college. They worked three to four hundred hours a month for $67.50, got little

The Messenger

Published monthly by The Messenger Publishing Co.,
513 Lenox Ave., New York City

A. PHILIP RANDOLPH,   CHANDLER OWEN,
President.   Secretary-Treasurer.

—:o:—

CONTENTS

Entered as second class mail matter at New York Post Office, N. Y., March, 1917,
under the act of March 3, 1879.

Contents page for the first issue (November 1917) of the socialist magazine founded by Randolph and Chandler Owen (Schomburg Research Center for Black Culture, the New York Public Library, Astor, Lenox, and Tilden Foundations)

Another of Randolph's tasks with the BSCP was the uphill battle to raise the consciousness of those black leaders who had given the union little support. Kelly Miller, dean of Howard University, was against unions, and most black church leaders were opposed to blacks unionizing. Exceptions included a few ministers in New York, chief among them the Reverend Adam Clayton Powell, Sr. Most of the black press was also in opposition. Notable exceptions were the *New York Amsterdam News* and the *Pittsburgh Courier*. The *Courier* had been a frequent advertiser in the *Messenger*. But by early 1928 the *Courier*, too, changed its tune and demanded that Randolph resign as president and that the porters negotiate directly with the Pullman Company. Some historians cite accusations that Robert L. Vann, the *Courier* editor,

was bought off–put on Pullman's "gravy train"– as a reason for his turnaround.

Meanwhile, Randolph waged another battle with the *Chicago Defender*, a paper that was pro-BSCP initially, then turned against it. Robert S. Abbott, publisher and editor of the *Defender*, had been one of Randolph's regular advertisers. In the July 1922 *Messenger* in a lengthy "Who's Who" article, Randolph wrote, "It is extremely fortunate that so powerful an organ as the *Chicago Defender* should be in the hands of a social equality advocate, a man of vision and character like Robert S. Abbott." But after Abbott's editorials took an anti-BSCP position, Randolph, in an October 1927 *Messenger* article, referred to Abbott's paper as the Chicago "Surrender, Misnamed Defender," the world's greatest "Weakly." Randolph also reminded Abbott of the role the porters played in distributing the paper across the country, and he urged porters and their supporters to boycott the *Defender* and not to distribute it. Moreover, as historian Brailsford R. Brazeal has noted, in mass meetings editors of black publications were verbally abused for their failure to support the union. These tactics apparently affected Abbott, who, according to Roi Ottley, his biographer, "watched the circulation figures decline, but he felt more keenly the antagonism of the porters and was exceedingly distressed by Randolph's charge that Negro editors who supported the Pullman Company were traitors to their race." Whatever the reason, the *Defender* soon reversed itself again and supported the BSCP.

In the final issue of the *Messenger* one witnesses a continuation of the upstream struggle to gain union support. In an article headlined "Randolph Replies to Vann," Randolph accuses Robert L. Vann of "being guilty of either bad judgment or insincerity, either one of which renders him untrustworthy." The debate and BSCP's twelve-year struggle for recognition by the Pullman Company would outlive the *Messenger* and be supported thereafter–beginning in November 1929–by the *Black Worker,* an irregularly published weekly tabloid newspaper edited by Randolph that never gained the popularity of the *Messenger.* It was a BSCP organ not intended for mass distribution.

In general, the existence of the *Messenger* can be divided into three periods, two of which run almost concurrently: the radical socialist period from 1917 through 1923, the Harlem Renaissance period from 1924 through May-June 1928, and the Pullman porters period from late 1925 through the magazine's demise in May-June 1928. With this evolution came an accompanying decline in left radicalism to a more liberal-left position that at times–in its strident anti-Communist positions, for example–leaned significantly to the political right. Although Randolph always considered himself a socialist, he was more a democratic socialist than a radical socialist–the conditions in the United States were not ripe, he thought, for a true revolutionary overthrow of the established government to be accomplished. Moreover, he was convinced that the United States Communist party was ideologically and uncritically tied to the Soviet Union and had no real understanding of the objective conditions that influenced American politics in general and black

politics in particular. Long after the demise of the *Messenger*–into the McCarthy period of the 1950s–many of his anti-Communist articles could not be distinguished from the red-baiting and anticommunism typical of the far right at that time. Much of this is seen in articles he published and commentary he made in the "What They Say" section in the AFL-CIO magazine *American Federationist* from 1926 through 1968, and in editorials and comment in the *Black Worker.*

The other important factor in the life span of the magazine is Randolph's ideological battles and discussions with other black activists, ideologues, and "race men" of the period who also had newspapers or magazines to express their positions. Newspaper publishers already noted included Abbott and Vann of the *Defender* and *Courier* respectively. An earlier opponent included T. Thomas Fortune of the *Amsterdam News* in New York. For example, in a July 1919 attack on the "Old Crowd" Negroes, a *Messenger* editorial said that Fortune was dead: "He is still walking around to save the undertaker's expenses, but his brain has ceased to operate. . . . Nearly all the old crowd leaders are ignorant, incompetent, controlled and corrupt. . . . They have truly been weighed in the balance by the New Crowd leaders and found sadly wanting."

Chief among the magazine editors were W. E. B. Du Bois of the *Crisis* (the organ of the NAACP); back-to-Africa advocate Marcus Garvey of *Negro World* (the Universal Negro Improvement Association); Cyril V. Briggs of the *Crusader* (the African Blood Brotherhood); Charles S. Johnson of *Opportunity* (the National Urban League). The *Crusader* and the *Messenger* exchanged advertisements and "lists of agents with mutual profit and fraternity" and agreed on some ideals; in addition Randolph respected Johnson and published articles in *Opportunity,* but his debates with, and criticism of, Garvey and Du Bois were mainstays in the pages of the *Messenger.* It should be noted, however, that Randolph's criticisms of Du Bois, while frequently sarcastic and biting, were in no way as personal and vitriolic as were those directed at Garvey. Anderson notes that Randolph always held some respect for Du Bois, but for Garvey there was enmity. It is certain that Randolph held hatred for the narrow black nationalism that did not pose integration as its ultimate goal. Years later, in 1966 as a guest on a "Face the Nation" program on Black Power, he would note with some pride that "Dr. Du Bois and myself led the fight against the Garvey movement, be-

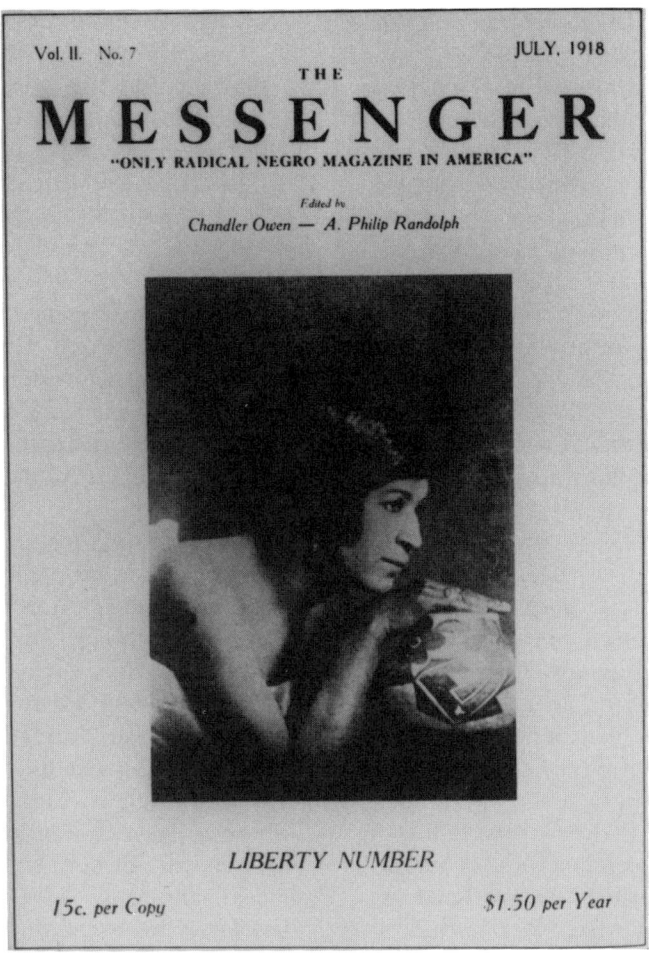

Vol. II. No. 7   JULY, 1918

T H E

MESSENGER

"ONLY RADICAL NEGRO MAGAZINE IN AMERICA"

Edited by
Chandler Owen — A. Philip Randolph

LIBERTY NUMBER

15c. per Copy   *$1.50 per Year*

Cover for an issue of the magazine created to "fight the hydra-headed monster–race prejudice" (Schomburg Research Center for Black Culture, the New York Public Library, Astor, Lenox, and Tilden Foundations)

cause Garvey was opposed to integration. He was opposed to civil rights."

Another difference in the criticism the *Messenger* leveled against Du Bois and Garvey is that the Du Bois criticism usually included some acknowledgment that Du Bois was literate and scholarly. The major criticisms, however, were of Du Bois's "Talented Tenth" theory, which proposed that the best tenth of blacks and whites would solve the race problem, and the fact that he was not a socialist and did not use the scientific (Marxist) method of analysis. Typical is the *Messenger* commentary of July 1918: "It needs to be said in extenuation of his scientific shortcomings that Dr. Du Bois was educated at a time and place where political science was not in great favor and where political science was little taught. . . . None of the older Negro leaders have had the modern education"; or the July 1919 issue's commentary that "The MESSENGER has frequently pointed

out that the editor of the Crisis . . . while possessing more intelligence than most Negro editors, is nevertheless comparatively ignorant of the world problems of sociological and economic significance." (Ironically, shortly before his death in 1963, Du Bois would completely embrace the scientific method when he joined the Communist party at a time when Randolph had slipped into what was basically liberal reformism.)

Du Bois was also criticized by the *Messenger*– and most of the major black newspapers of the time–for his infamous World War I "close ranks" editorial in the July 1918 *Crisis*, in which he urged blacks to "forget our grievances and close our ranks . . . with our own white fellow citizens . . . ." A year later the *Messenger* still blasted Du Bois on this issue. Its editorial of May-June 1919 began: "The Negro needs new leadership. The old leadership has failed miserably. . . . In the midst of the war when black men were giving their lives by the minute, Du Bois wrote his infamous 'Close Ranks' editorial . . . which will rank in shame and reeking disgrace with the 'Atlanta Compromise' speech of Booker Washington."

With Garvey, Randolph had always disagreed politically and had articulated that disagreement in the *Messenger* in numerous articles as early as October 1920. But in mid 1922 the magazine officially declared war on Garvey, and for the first time since the magazine's creation, the editors seemed to move in an unprincipled direction as they began a relentless attack not only on Garvey's movement, organization, and philosophy, but also on his nationality as well. "Here's notice," a July 1922 editorial concluded, "that THE MESSENGER is firing the opening gun in a campaign to drive Garvey and Garveyism in all its sinister viciousness from the American soil." In almost every issue thereafter until Garvey was deported, at least one editorial, news item, or feature article was published against Garveyism. In August 1922 Randolph wrote an article entitled "Reply to Marcus Garvey"; in September Owen wrote the first article pushing for Garvey's deportation. This was followed in October with an article stating that "the bulk of the Garvey following are foreigners"; and in December with "A Symposium on Garvey" with a byline, "Negro Leaders," in which fourteen of twenty-five black leaders responded to a *Messenger* letter and questionnaire in which it was asked whether Garvey should be deported. Ironically, while most agreed that Garvey's movement was not in the best interest of blacks, only three of the fourteen agreed that he should be deported, and some even noted that in the United States freedom of speech was no crime. But this did not deter Randolph and Owen. From November 1922 through February 1923, Randolph wrote four lengthy articles entitled "The Only Way to Redeem Africa." In the final article Randolph dwelled on Garvey's West Indian background, and while acknowledging that "The most prominent, intelligent West Indians are opposing Garvey," he added that "Garvey's non-citizenship policy is unsound."

Finally, in January and March 1923 two articles appeared that caused a permanent rift between the *Messenger* editors and one of its contributing editors, W. A. Domingo, who left the magazine. The January anti-Garveyism editorial ended: "Such logic could emanate only from the diseased brain of his Supreme Negro Jackass from Jamaica." The March article by Robert W. Bagnall of the NAACP was entitled "The Mad-

ness of Marcus Garvey" and described Garvey as "A Jamaican Negro of unmixed stock, squat, stocky, fat and sleek, with protruding jaws, and heavy jowls, small bright pig-like eyes and rather bull-dog-like face. . . ." He concluded that a mental health professional would probably pronounce Garvey "insane—a paranoiac."

Domingo, like Garvey, was a West Indian, and before he left the magazine he expressed in an open letter his concern that the *Messenger* editors overemphasized Garvey's nationality. Also, he said, it was inconsistent with their Socialist philosophy to "initiate an agitation for deportation or to emphasize the nationality of anyone as a subtle means of generating opposition against him. . . ." Domingo was correct, but the campaign would continue through 1924 when, strangely, the June *Messenger* included an article by Randolph in which Du Bois is held up as a hero over Garvey even though Du Bois was still being criticized by the *Messenger* as an "Old Crowd" Negro. The article was a poor attempt by Randolph to write a satirical dramatization of a "fight" between "Battling Du Bois" and "Kid Garvey" for the "Heavyweight Championship Bout for Afro-American-West Indian Belt." The article includes the "records" of both fighters against noted black leaders and ends in the "Sixth round" when "Garvey is too weak and badly beaten to return to fray."

The Harlem Renaissance influences on the *Messenger* are mainly expressed through the publication of poems, short stories, theater and book reviews, and the satirical columns of Schuyler. The *Crisis* was the first monthly to publish on a consistent basis the works of young artists of the time, and when *Opportunity* began publishing in January 1923, it, too, carried the works of the young artists. Indeed, the *Messenger* had included poetry in its pages even in its early issues—both Claude McKay's "If We Must Die" sonnet, which appeared in the September 1919 issue, and Archibald H. Grimke's "Thirteen Black Soldiers," in the October 1919 issue, were mentioned with concern in Palmer's Justice Department report to Congress—but these were largely poems with significant political content, valued more for their political statements than their artistry. It was not until 1923 that the *Messenger* began to notice the young artists, many of whom were those who would later become well-known contributors to black American literature and the arts. But the artistic publications of the *Messenger* were not as prestigious as those that appeared in either the *Crisis*

Randolph (fourth from right) and the other members of the Brotherhood of Sleeping Car Porters negotiating team: L. O. Manson, Bennie Smith, A. L. Totten, T. T. Patterson, Milton P. Webster, C. L. Dellums, and E. J. Bradley (Chicago Historical Society)

or *Opportunity. Messenger* scholar Theodore Kornweibel, Jr., contends, however, that the "most thought-out and consistent commentary on black theater to be produced during the Harlem Renaissance was the drama criticism of Theophilus Lewis [of the *Messenger*]." This could be attributed to Randolph's special interest in the theater. Moreover, Randolph had gradually affected an Oxford accent and had acquired a preference for European classical music. This served to push him and the magazine in the direction of a more classical criticism of the arts, a form with which Lewis seemed especially comfortable. However, this would lead the magazine away from the popular analysis of the times that praised black music—spirituals, gospel, and jazz. Lewis's criticism, though largely on the theater, also extended to poetry and fiction.

Another influence on the critical slant of the magazine was Randolph's Marxist training. Therefore he favored the writing of a critic such as Lewis who was less apt than others to praise art for art's sake. Both Randolph and Lewis saw the merits, for example, in actors organizing, creating an independent black theater company, and becoming involved in the business side of theater. Indeed, "Organizing the Negro Actor" was an article that appeared in the first issue of the

Messenger. Kornweibel's content analysis of the three magazines between January 1923 and June 1928 shows that each published about the same number of poems and short fiction, while there were five published plays in the *Crisis*, four in *Opportunity*, and one in the *Messenger*. He says that in general, "the most extensive cultural critique in the mid-1920s among the black magazines was to be found in *Opportunity*, with the exception of theater commentary, which was strongest in the *Messenger*. The two brightest lights among the young poets, Langston Hughes and Countee Cullen, published much more in the *Crisis* and *Opportunity* than in the *Messenger*. The same was true of Claude McKay, Arna Bontemps, and Lewis Alexander. But for other poets this was not the pattern." Two major factors for this pattern, Kornweibel contends, are that the meager finances of the *Messenger* did not allow it to have a full-time literary editor, and that the other two magazines had larger circulations and a "more national readership because they were the organs of integrated racial-uplift groups." Moreover, according to biographer Anderson, the *Messenger* readership was two-thirds liberal and radical whites, and the blacks who read it were largely the socially conscious middle class. It is likely that the shift away from politics to black culture was

Randolph (center) leading pickets during the 1948 Democratic National Convention in Philadelphia (UPI photo)

not particularly appealing to the majority of this readership group.

When Randolph became involved with the porters union, the magazine became more political, but much of its political content was oriented specifically toward the BSCP. Had the porters union opportunity not occurred, it is likely that Randolph would have poured much more of his energy into the magazine; it was the only thing he had left. As Anderson points out, "By 1925, not one of the political or trade union organizations that Randolph and Owen had founded remained." These included the Independent Political Council, the 21st A.D. Socialist Club, the United Brotherhood of Elevator and Switchboard Operators, the National Association for the Promotion of Labor Unionism, the National Brotherhood Workers of America, a Tenants and Consumers League, the Friends of Negro Freedom, and an attempt to organize a Harlem branch of the Journeyman Bakers and Confectioners Union.

It was during this Renaissance period also that the magazine began to lose its radical flavor and opt for a more mainstream, family-oriented format. In November 1923 the *Messenger* began to turn toward the business community in a major way when it published its largest issue–a sixty-four-page "Negro Business Achievement" issue that included approximately twenty-six pages of advertising. This would mark the beginning of business boosterism, which featured regular two-page, centerfold-illustrated histories on famous black business people as well as feature articles on the black well-to-do, with articles such as "The Society Leaders of Richmond Virginia" in the May 1924 issue and a report on two fraternity conventions in the February 1925 issue. The covers in 1924 turned nonpolitical and featured stylized drawings of pretty women. A sports section was added in 1925, and even in 1927 when, as the official organ of the BSCP its covers turned to social-realism drawings of workers, at least two nonpolitical themes were reflected– "Winter Sports" in February and "April Showers" in April. Langston Hughes described the *Messenger* of this period as a magazine of "God Knows What" that "reflected the policy of whoever paid best at the time."

Perhaps the most telling change in format occurred in 1924 when the editorial section gradually was placed lower and lower in the magazine– about a third of the way into the magazine by August. This might not seem significant until one reads Randolph's July 1918 criticism of Du Bois and the *Crisis* for the way in which its contents were arranged: "The leading column of the 'Horizon' is always 'Music and Art.' Then 'Meetings,' which signify the gathering of literteurs. Next 'The War,' . . . 'Industry' and 'Politics' sections follow. This is no coincidence, but a logical product of Du Bois's celebration. THE MESSENGER carried as its first column after editorials, 'Economics and Politics.'" Extrapolating Randolph's logic and applying it to his magazine after August 1924, one might conclude that political editorials were less important than Schuyler's "Shafts and Darts" column, a story on white labor in Africa, and the sixteenth story in a series about United States cities.

The porters-union phase of the magazine began in 1925 when Randolph published prominent pro-porter articles in three consecutive issues, beginning in July with "The Case of the Pullman Porter," followed in August by "Pullman Porters Need Own Union," and in September

Randolph with Whitney Young and President Lyndon Johnson at the White House, August 1965 (UPI photo)

with "The Pullman Company and the Pullman Porter." Consecutive issues from October-November 1925 through May 1926 would carry several articles, open letters, and replies written by Randolph and other BSCP members. A special issue, "The Brotherhood's Anniversary," was published in September 1926, and in October "Three Hours With a Porter" was written under the byline "A. Sagittarius"–a pseudonym that later would appear regularly in the *Black Worker*.

After the *Messenger* folded, the remainder of Randolph's life evolved around the BSCP. Eventually he led it into the American Federation of Labor, an organization he fiercely condemned in earlier days, and into full recognition by the Pullman Company. He continued to agitate within the AFL–and later within the AFL-CIO–for full union commitment to desegregation, and he agitated outside the union structure for civil rights legislation for black people. He remained a Socialist and headed the BSCP for its entire lifetime from a 1941 peak of fifteen thousand members to a 1968 low of two thousand members when, with the decline of the rail travel industry, the union was abolished. In 1941 he led a delegation that persuaded President Franklin Delano Roose-

velt to sign Executive Order 8802, and in later years he would lead similar civil rights delegations to Presidents Harry S. Truman, Dwight D. Eisenhower, and John F. Kennedy.

In 1944 he turned down both Republicans and Democrats in New York who tried to persuade him to run for Congress in the Twenty-second Congressional District, even though Adam Clayton Powell, Jr., already had announced his intention to run for that office. He was one of the most popular black figures in the mid 1940s, but twenty years later he would fail to be listed on a *Newsweek* magazine black leadership popularity poll either by the rank and file or by black leaders themselves.

In 1963, however, after he and his protégé Bayard Rustin helped to organize the march on Washington, his popularity rose again, and in a 1968 *Newsweek* black leadership survey he was eleventh on a rank-and-file list and second on a black leaders' list behind Martin Luther King, Jr. But it was also at this time that he apparently had relinquished his fervent commitment to pacifism and nonmilitarism. He advised young black men in an *Ebony* article to seek opportunities in the armed forces, where "without money or family in-

Randolph with Bayard Rustin, 1971 (photo by Irene B. Bayer, A. Philip Randolph Institute)

fluence, Negro young men may reach the higher echelon. Also, the Armed Forces offer college and technical training."

Randolph also established links with some of the firebrand leaders of this period and sponsored forums for militants such as Malcolm X. But the majority of the young black militants of the 1960s and 1970s saw him at best as a moderate spokesman whose hour of significance had passed—a person he might have described in his early *Messenger* days as an "Old Crowd" leader. He, in turn, saw them as politically immature and excessive and narrow in their perspective. He told a journalist in 1966 that "this cry for Black Power is an outcome of frustration, disillusionment, disenchantment, because the civil rights revolution had about run its course. . . ." However, Randolph concluded, "Black Power cannot achieve the objectives that the Negroes now need."

But Randolph must have seen something of himself and his *Messenger* comrades in the faces of the young militants, for he told another journalist in 1969 that he was "greatly concerned about the lack of historical knowledge on the part of some of the black militants, many of whom are brilliant young men. If I were physically stronger, I would like to be able to get groups of them

together for the study and analysis of history in relation to the struggle of the Negro today, to probe the economic, political and social forces that are playing an inevitable role in the development of world civilization today."

The "Chief," as he was called by his BSCP associates, is remembered as a man of tremendous dignity, pride, integrity, and commitment to principle. One story has it that he was offered a blank check for six or seven figures from the Pullman Company if he would step down as the porters union president (the figure varies depending on who is telling the story), but he refused. Many friends verify that he never made a decent salary, never owned an automobile or a piece of real estate, and never sought any sort of public recognition for himself. In the early 1930s, during one of the lowest periods of his life, Randolph, earning a BSCP salary of ten dollars a week, refused an offer from New York Mayor Fiorello La Guardia, a former Socialist, for a seven-thousand-dollar-a-year city job. Indeed, as late as 1963, Randolph wrote that "a leader of labor like the leaders of the church should be relatively poor." He lived his last thirty-five years in modest circumstances in a rented third-floor walk-up apartment at 150th Street and Seventh Avenue in Harlem.

Interview:

Face The Nation, collected transcripts from the CBS radio and television broadcasts, vol. 9, 4 September 1966 (New York: Holt Information Systems, 1972), pp. 236-240.

Biographies:

Jervis Anderson, *A. Philip Randolph: A Biographical Portrait* (New York: Harcourt Brace Jovanovich, 1972);

Daniel S. Davis, *Mr. Black Labor: The Story of A. Philip Randolph, Father of the Civil Rights Movement* (New York: Dutton, 1972).

References:

Richard Bransten, *Men Who Lead Labor* (New York: Modern Age, 1937);

Brailsford R. Brazeal, *The Brotherhood of Sleeping Car Porters: Its Origin and Development* (New York: Harper, 1946);

John Henrik Clark, "A. Philip Randolph: Portrait of an Afro-American Radical," *Negro Digest,* 16 (March 1967): 16-23;

Edwin Rogers Embree, *13 Against the Odds* (New York: Viking, 1944);

Philip S. Foner, "The IWW and the Black Worker," *Journal of Negro History,* 55 (January 1970): 45-64;

Herbert Garfinkel, *When Negroes March* (Glencoe, Ill.: Free Press, 1959);

William H. Harris, "A. Philip Randolph as a Charismatic Leader," *Journal of Negro History,* 64 (Fall 1979): 301-315;

Harris, *Keeping the Faith: A. Philip Randolph, Mil-* ton *P. Webster, and the Brotherhood of Sleeping Car Porters, 1925-37* (Chicago: University of Illinois Press, 1977);

Langston Hughes, *Famous American Negroes* (New York: Dodd, Mead, 1954);

Theodore Kornweibel, Jr., *No Crystal Stair: Black Life and the Messenger, 1917-1928* (Westport, Conn.: Greenwood Press, 1975);

Miles of Smiles, Years of Struggle: The Untold Story of the Black Pullman Porter, film documentary by Columbia Historical Society in cooperation with the Smithsonian Institute's Office of Folklife Programs, 1981;

Sally M. Miller, "The Socialist Party and the Negro 1901-1920," *Journal of Negro History,* 56 (July 1971): 220-229;

L. D. Reddick, "The Negro Policy of the American Army Since World War II," *Journal of Negro History,* 38 (April 1953): 194-215;

Victor Weybright, "Pullman Porters on Parade," *Survey Graphic,* 24 (November 1935): 540-544, 571-574.

Papers:

Papers of the Brotherhood of Sleeping Car Porters are located in the Library of Congress and at the Chicago Historical Society. Randolph's papers are located in the Tamiment Institute and the A. Philip Randolph Institute in New York City. Complete microfilm copy of the *Messenger* and original copies of the *March* are located in the Schomburg Center for Research in Black Culture, Lenox Avenue Branch, New York City Public Library. Complete microfilm copy of the *Black Worker* is located in the Library of Congress.

William Marion Reedy

(11 December 1862-28 July 1920)

Michael D. Murray
University of Missouri at St. Louis

MAJOR POSITIONS HELD: Editor and publisher, *Mirror*, retitled *Reedy's Mirror* in 1913 (1893-1920).

BOOKS: *A Message to Hubbard* (St. Louis, 1899);
Friendship's Garland (East Aurora, N.Y.: Roycroft, 1899?);
The Story of the Strike (St. Louis, 1900);
The Eugene Field Myth (St. Louis: Reedy, 1901);
The Imitator: A Novel (St. Louis, 1901);
The President of the United States (St. Louis, 1902);
The Law of Love (East Aurora, N.Y.: Roycrofters, 1905);
The Myth of a Free Press (St. Louis: Mirror, 1908);
A Golden Book and the Literature of Childhood (Cedar Rapids, Iowa: Torch, 1910);
The Feather Duster; Or, Is He Sincere? (East Aurora, N.Y.: Roycrofters, 1912);
'Frisco the Fallen (San Francisco: Robinson, 1916); republished as *The City That Has Fallen* (San Francisco: Book Club of California, 1933).

OTHER: J. S. Snoddy, ed., *A Little Book of Missouri Verse*, includes three poems by Reedy (Kansas City: Hudson-Kimberly, 1897);
"St. Louis, 'The Future Great,'" in *Historical Towns of the Western States*, edited by Lyman P. Powell (New York: Putnam's, 1901);
The Makers of St. Louis, edited by Reedy (St. Louis: Mirror, 1906).

William Marion Reedy (Mitchell Kennerley Collection, New York Public Library)

William Marion Reedy was among an elite group of American literary figures who became well-known not only as writers and editors but as catalysts and crusaders for others in the early years of the twentieth century. Many of those he assisted were authors who would become widely recognized and published. Zoe Akins, Kate Chopin, Alice French, Fannie Hurst, John Galsworthy, Orrick Johns, Vachel Lindsay, Sara Teasdale, and John Hall Wheelock were all encouraged by Reedy, and their work was found in the pages of the *Mirror*, Reedy's popular St. Louis-based weekly with an international following.

Reedy was born and reared in Kerry Patch, a north-side section of St. Louis, Missouri, populated mostly with Irish immigrants. His father, Patrick Reedy, a native of Clonmel, County Tipperary, Ireland, became a St. Louis police captain, and some of Reedy's earliest reporting assignments revolved around police work, his father's beat in Kerry Patch, the courts, and his childhood friends.

His mother, Anne Marion Reedy, was born in Dublin and encouraged her eldest son to excel in his studies. She was intent on sending him to St. Louis University, where he could study with Jesuit priests. Reedy attended the public schools along with his two younger brothers but then took an advanced course of study at a leading prep school in the area, Christian Brothers College. He was admitted to St. Louis University at the age of fourteen, thus fulfilling his mother's dream of a Jesuit education. Years after Reedy had fallen away from his Catholic faith he continued to credit the Jesuits with laying the foundation for his literary calling and work as an editor. He said that his religious mentors taught him Latin and Greek and thus introduced him to the ancient classics.

Because of encouragement from his father to pursue business interests, Reedy dropped his arts concentration in school and was graduated from St. Louis University with an accounting degree. Shortly after graduation, in 1880, he joined the staff of the *Missouri Republican*. He then worked as a court reporter for the *St. Louis Globe-Democrat* until he discovered the joys of feature writing.

Reedy was a voracious reader as a young man, and he is often credited with the ability to retain a tremendous amount of information from his studies. He was invited to do public readings at the St. Louis Library, and his acceptance of and dedication to the task endeared him to many patrons. His familiarity with the holdings of the library was said to be second only to that of the head librarian.

Reedy worked sporadically as a special writer at the *St. Louis Globe-Democrat* for nearly twenty years under Joseph B. McCullough, the hard-driving editor viewed as the chief St. Louis competitor of Joseph Pulitzer. During this period Reedy was also publishing free-lance work in *Brann's Iconoclast* of Waco, Texas, and the *Mirror* of St. Louis, the publication that would eventually bear his name and spread his thoughts worldwide.

While establishing a reputation as a writer, Reedy was also gaining some attention as a notoriously heavy drinker and womanizer. During a drinking spree in 1893 Reedy married the hostess of a well-known St. Louis brothel and shocked all of local society who had become accustomed to seeing his byline in the St. Louis press. He suffered the further indignity of having his bride insist that he seek a cure for his addiction to alcohol. Given the choice, Reedy sought a divorce, which was granted three years later. Unfortunately, Reedy's unlucky pairing overshadowed his relations with polite St. Louis society for the rest of his life.

Because of his association with the St. Louis underclass, Reedy's local standing was on the decline even as his national literary reputation was growing along with the readership of the *Mirror*. But Reedy lived as he pleased and cared little about what polite society thought. According to Orrick Johns's *Time of Our Lives* (1937), Reedy was once invited to stop publication of a biography containing some rather sordid details of his personal life by paying a small sum of money. Reedy not only rejected the offer but was prepared to turn over some additional details to spice it up even further.

Even though his marriage had created a local scandal of monumental proportions and one that was not forgotten, the literary world continued to credit him for his thoughtful insight on literature and his cynicism regarding world affairs. The attention Reedy paid to certain topics created a natural stir in the minds of local readers for additional information. In her book *Reflections of Reedy* (1961), Ethel M. King notes that the venerable Mercantile Library of St. Louis received scores of requests for books reviewed in the *Mirror*.

At times Reedy fell out of favor with even his most ardent supporters. One such crisis of confidence occurred when he took a strong stand against a popular Democratic platform. This resulted in a loss of sorely needed support for his publication, which, on occasion, courted bankruptcy. At one point the *Mirror* was put up for auction but was purchased by James Campbell, a close friend to Reedy. Campbell turned the magazine over to Reedy and continued to contribute to the financial well-being of the *Mirror*, which was renamed *Reedy's Mirror*.

Largely because of this financial support, *Reedy's Mirror*, with a national circulation of 32,250, was able to surpass both the *Nation* and *Atlantic* in readership. The stability the publication enjoyed during this period allowed Reedy to expand his efforts to help others, and he began to attract and encourage young writers of promise from the United States and Great Britain.

In addition, Reedy published interpretive essays along with editorials on the social, political, and civic controversies of the day. He always employed simple language, and biographer King notes claims that he wrote close to five thousand words each day. Many of his articles and essays from *Reedy's Mirror* were distributed worldwide and often reprinted.

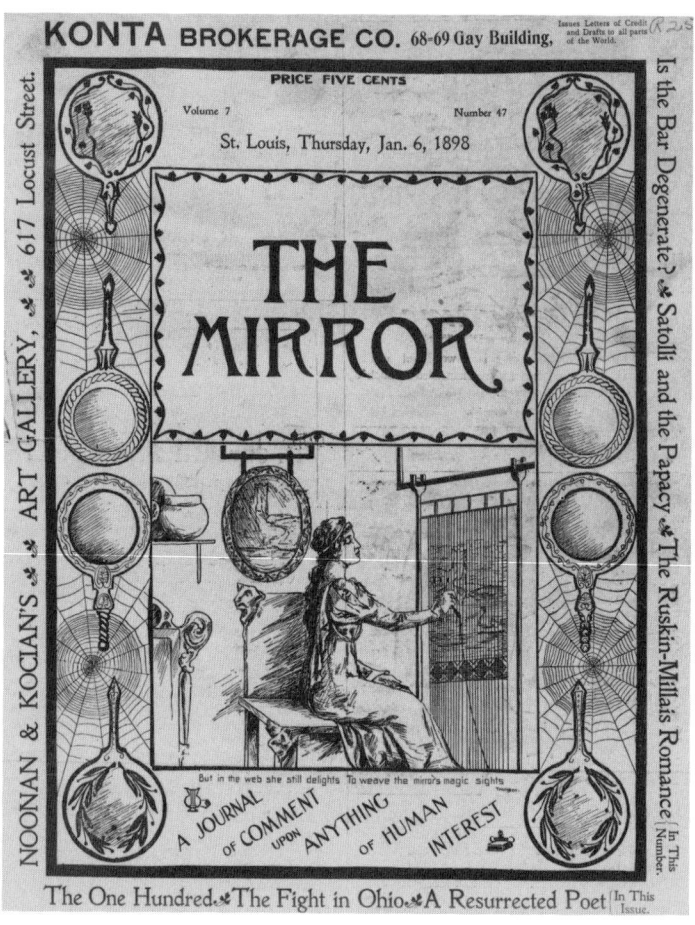

Cover for an issue of the magazine that historian Frank Luther Mott called "one of the most remarkable . . . periodicals of the urban weekly class" (Missouri Historical Society Collection)

Unfortunately, little of Reedy's work survives beyond issues of the *Mirror*. The exceptions are collections such as *The Law of Love* (1905) and *A Golden Book and the Literature of Childhood* (1910). A few published pamphlets and short speeches also survive. He was constantly in demand as a speaker, and some of his speeches created great interest. These include *'Frisco the Fallen*, published in 1916 as a pamphlet reviewing the financial status of San Francisco, and *The Myth of a Free Press* (1908), delivered before the Missouri Press Association and highly critical of the independent claims of editors of his day.

Reedy frequently expressed an admiration for the innocence of children and their experiences and wrote about the wisdom of simplicity that characterized youth. He praised many children's authors and wrote essays and even one short book on young love and the qualities of youthful intelligence.

Reedy's reputation grew as a result of this wide range of work, and because of the national and international exposure it brought with it, he became a welcome member of many literary circles. On the other hand, he continued to spend most of his time with struggling authors, providing them encouragement and a place to exhibit their work. For example, *Reedy's Mirror* first published the work of free-verse poet and attorney Edgar Lee Masters, whose *Spoon River Anthology* created a tremendous critical stir when it was published in 1915. The nine poems that comprise the first part of this work were said to have been the direct result of Reedy's prodding and his insistence that Masters apply himself to serious work worthy of his talents.

When Masters's work was published in *Reedy's Mirror* in 1914 under the pen name Webster Ford, it was immediately attacked and condemned as an indictment on midwestern character. Reedy, however, stood behind the work; and

288

Reedy in 1904 (Missouri Historical Society Collection)

other prominent figures, including H. L. Mencken, Sinclair Lewis, and Theodore Dreiser, each of whom had published in the *Mirror,* also came to Masters's defense.

Once the author of the work was made known, Masters's struggling Chicago legal practice suffered, although this was something he had anticipated. Reedy meanwhile continued to build a reputation for himself as a "writer's writer" while serving as impresario and host to British as well as American poets. Reedy's home in St. Louis became an intermediate stopover for visiting dignitaries, artists, and authors from around the world. He assisted Cunninghame Graham, John Galsworthy, and Thomas Hardy. Many of these individuals, as well as Reedy himself, engaged in extended debates on English style.

Reedy's use of humor enhanced his natural literary flair, and many of his most pointed barbs against pretense were directed at colleagues in

the publishing field. Even as a youngster still learning his trade, Reedy would castigate his employers, taking them to task for formality and convention he thought a waste of time. After a lapse in judgment caused him to lose his job at the *St. Louis Globe-Democrat,* he was rehired with a thorough understanding that he would reform. Encountering a *Globe* editor at a public outing, he related that he had already grown tired of the paper and would have no further use for it. He was, needless to say, a constant irritation to his employers but nonetheless entertaining to be around and a favorite of his coworkers. His subsequent writing and behavior frequently reflected this comic irreverence, which also carried over to his management of the *Mirror.*

Since Reedy was always willing to share his views with the press, he was in demand as commentator, political satirist, and literary humorist. Interviews with the celebrated editor would frequently appear in the New York press. He would hold forth in a Manhattan hotel, usually the Broadway, and a line of reporters would pass through his door in search of controversy, levity, or perhaps just good story ideas, as Reedy was always on the cutting edge of current events. Counted among the ardent and acknowledged admirers of Reedy were Carl Sandburg, H. L. Mencken, and most of the newspaper and magazine editors of the day. *Reedy's Mirror* was well-known as a magazine popular with journalists, and Reedy basked in the glow of that fact. While widely criticized and ostracized in his own hometown, he was welcomed by his peers in international literary quarters as enlightened and ahead of his time on many issues. He was, for example, one of the first to serve as judge for the Pulitzer Poetry Awards on the occasion of their introduction.

In economic matters, Reedy was an advocate of Henry George and the single-tax theory, which focused on land as the source of all material prosperity. George's book *Progress and Poverty*, first published in 1880, was widely accepted by idealists with roots in the middle class, such as Reedy. Eventually, Reedy's allegiance to the single-tax theory altered somewhat, but he and many of his *Mirror* readers accepted its tenets.

Reedy traveled far and wide and spoke out on many topics, some of which were of the most extreme and reactionary nature. After one of Reedy's campaigns against a particular cause or widely debated issue, the *Mirror* relayed the reaction to, as well as the cause of, the furor at hand. This gave the reader the idea that he was getting the inside story. Reedy addressed the international scene on many of these occasions but also focused on St. Louis, as in his discussion of the World's Fair of 1904 and its prospects for success in boosting the area into the national spotlight. He continued to comment on the light and dark sides of politics even after he began to experience serious health problems.

He was severely overweight and drank to excess just as he had done in his early days. He had high blood pressure, and his eyes began to fail

him during his final days. He suffered a retinal hemorrhage just before his death in San Francisco while attending the Democratic National Convention. His associates at *Reedy's Mirror* made a valiant struggle to keep the magazine going after his death in 1920, but the effort was unsuccessful. The publication folded in a little over a month. Reedy had used the meager earnings of his *Mirror* to bolster the fortunes of many struggling writers, and this obviously contributed to the publication's poor financial health. Reedy's passing hastened its demise.

Biographies:
Ethel M. King, *Reflections of Reedy: A Biography of William Marion Reedy of Reedy's Mirror* (Brooklyn: Rickard, 1961);
Max Putzel, *The Man In the Mirror: William Marion Reedy and His Magazine* (Cambridge, Mass.: Harvard University Press, 1963).

References:
Fannie Hurst, *Anatomy of Me* (Garden City, N.Y.: Doubleday, 1958);
Orrick Johns, *Time of Our Lives: The Story of My Father and Myself* (New York: Stackpole, 1937);
John Lindenbusch, "The Literary Boss of the Middle West," *St. Louis* (April 1981): 22-23;
Edgar Lee Masters, *Across Spoon River: An Autobiography* (New York: Farrar & Rinehart, 1936);
Clarence E. Miller, "William Marion Reedy: A Patchwork Portrait," *Missouri Historical Society Bulletin*, 17 (October 1960): 45-56;
J. B. Sheridan, "Reedy's Works Were Esteemed Most by Writing Men," *St. Louis Globe-Democrat*, 29 July 1920, p. 6;
Vincent Starrett, "Great Heart is Dead," *Reedy's Mirror*, 29 (5 August 1920): 605;
A. M. Sullivan, "The Kerry Patch Catalyst," *St. Louis Post-Dispatch*, 17 March 1963, p. B2.

Papers:
Reedy's papers are in the Reedy Collection at the St. Louis Public Library.

Ellery Sedgwick

(27 February 1872-21 April 1960)

Nancy L. Roberts
University of Minnesota

MAJOR POSITIONS HELD: Assistant editor, *Youth's Companion* (1896-1900); editor, *Frank Leslie's Popular Monthly Magazine*, retitled *Leslie's Monthly* in 1904, the *American Illustrated Magazine* in 1905, the *American* in 1906 (1900-1906); editor and publisher, *Atlantic Monthly* (1909-1938).

BOOKS: *Thomas Paine* (Boston: Small, Maynard, 1899; London: K. Paul, Trench, Trübner, 1899);
The Happy Profession (Boston: Little, Brown, 1946).

TRANSLATIONS: George Sand, *The Devil's Pool*, translated by Sedgwick and Jane Minot Sedgwick (New York: Richmond, 1894);
Honoré de Balzac, *Honoré de Balzac, Now for the First Time Completely Translated into English*, 53 volumes, volumes 1 and 2 translated by Sedgwick (Philadelphia: G. Barrie, 1895-1900);

OTHER: *Novel and Story, a Book of Modern Readings*, edited by Sedgwick and Harry A. Domincovich (Boston: Little, Brown, 1939);
Atlantic Harvest: Memoirs of the Atlantic, compiled by Sedgwick (Boston: Little, Brown, 1947).

SELECTED PERIODICAL PUBLICATIONS: "Dispatches on Rebel Spain," *New York Times*, 13 February 1938, p. 19; 15 February 1938, p. 12;
"Sedgwick Replies to Critics," *New York Times*, 13 March 1938, IV: 8.

Ellery Sedgwick, the eighth editor of the *Atlantic Monthly*, built that magazine into a social and political force. During his twenty-nine-year editorship the magazine's circulation increased from 10,000 to 125,000; it published works by such writers as Ernest Hemingway and Robert Frost; it championed many liberal causes, among them the League of Nations; it questioned the justice of the Sacco and Vanzetti case; and, in its coverage of the controversy over the presidential candidacy of Alfred E. Smith, it challenged religious bigotry.

Sedgwick was born in New York City on 27 February 1872 to Henrietta Ellery and Henry Dwight Sedgwick, an attorney. His family roots were in Stockbridge, Massachusetts. As a boy he attended a private boarding school, then the Groton School, from which he graduated in 1890. After obtaining his A.B. at Harvard in 1894, Sedgwick returned to Groton to teach Latin and English from 1894 to 1896. After a brief stint as a reporter for the *Worcester Gazette*, in 1896 he became assistant editor of the *Youth's Companion* in Boston. Three years later he wrote a popular biography of Thomas Paine for the Beacon Biographies of Eminent Americans series, edited by Mark A. De Wolfe Howe. In 1900 Sedgwick became editor of *Frank Leslie's Popular Monthly*, a post he held for six years. He emphasized wit and humor, publishing such writers as Marietta Holley, Sewell Ford, and Ellis Parker Butler, whose "Pigs Is Pigs" (the title was suggested by Sedgwick) was one of the magazine's most popular stories. Other contributors included Stephen Crane, Frank R. Stockton, Samuel Merwin, and Emerson Hough.

According to magazine historian Frank Luther Mott, under Sedgwick the magazine (which was retitled *Leslie's Monthly* in 1904, the *American Illustrated Magazine* in the fall of 1905, and, a few months later, simply the *American*) added more public events coverage. It was not a muckraker, as were many of its competitors, though in 1903 Sedgwick did conduct an editorial campaign against safety violations in the railroad industry. Citing the high injury and death rate among rail passengers, Sedgwick claimed that poor management of the rail systems had made America "The Land of Disasters." Readers were urged to write members of Congress, and the magazine provided free copies of legislative bills outlining new safety provisions. According to historian Louis Filler, Sedgwick's editorial leadership did much to spur government regulation of the railroads.

While editor of *Leslie's Monthly*, Sedgwick published several short stories by H. L. Mencken, initiating a lifelong friendship (Sedgwick once offered Mencken a job as associate editor, but Mencken declined). However, the correspondence between the two men suggests Sedgwick's influence in directing Mencken away from fiction and toward the essay as the best vehicle for his literary talents. When, in 1923, Mencken began to edit the *American Mercury*, he sought Sedgwick's advice. The veteran editor cautioned him not to "over-edit," for "by so doing you will estrange your writers and rob the magazine of its indispensable variety."

On 23 September 1904 Sedgwick married Mabel Cabot, with whom he had four children. In 1905, in addition to his duties with *Leslie's Monthly*, Sedgwick also served as editor of *Appleton's Booklovers Magazine*, a compendium of copious illustrations, miscellany, and short editorials by celebrities such as Amelia E. Barr, Henry

Cabot Lodge, and Theodore Dreiser. In 1906, following the string of reorganizations at *Leslie's*, Sedgwick resigned his editorship. He worked for a year at *McClure's Magazine*, and then briefly for D. Appleton and Company as a book editor. Later his editing career would include brief stints at *Living Age* (1919) and *House Beautiful* (1922), but his primary interest after 1909 was the *Atlantic Monthly*.

In 1908 Sedgwick bought the august but ailing *Atlantic* for fifty thousand dollars and became its editor and publisher. The magazine's circulation had dropped to nearly ten thousand a month and was running with an annual deficit of five thousand dollars. Sedgwick's leadership inaugurated a new era. From his earlier magazine experiences he had acquired an astute grasp of readers' interests, and he had learned, as well, to trust his own taste and judgment. Sedgwick added more political, social, and economic content to the *Atlantic* in an effort to modernize the magazine. In 1921 its circulation topped one hundred thousand, and the following year the *New York Times Book Review* (15 January) announced, "There is no use arguing the question–the *Atlantic Monthly* is not the staid magazine that refreshed our grandfathers. It has grown lively during recent years; it has moved with the times and, finely enough, yet retained that dignified composure that is associated with it. In other words, the editors have brought it up to date, but have done it in such a skillful manner that old readers will hardly guess that the magazine is moving on from their conservative views."

Sedgwick's catholicity of interests was impressive. His daily custom was to give the *New York Times* and the *London Times* thorough readings, he listened attentively to conversations among friends and colleagues about current affairs, and he corresponded heavily with writers, journalists, and public officials. By such strategies he identified the important issues of the day.

A former editorial associate, Frederick Lewis Allen, observed that Sedgwick "resolved that the *Atlantic* should face the whole of life, its riddles, its adventures; the critical questions of the day, the problems of the human heart; and that no subject should be taboo if only it were discussed with urbanity." Sedgwick especially favored what he called "human documents," which included personal confessions and firsthand stories of adventure, and he often commissioned such pieces.

THE ATLANTIC MONTHLY

JULY, 1927

FIFTY GRAND

BY ERNEST HEMINGWAY

I

'How are you going yourself, Jack?' I asked him.

'You seen this Walcott?' he says.

'Just in the gym.'

'Well,' Jack says, 'I'm going to need a lot of luck with that boy.'

'He can't hit you, Jack,' Soldier said.

'I wish to hell he could n't.'

'He could n't hit you with a handful of birdshot.'

'Birdshot'd be all right,' Jack says. 'I would n't mind birdshot any.'

'He looks easy to hit,' I said.

'Sure,' Jack says, 'he ain't going to last long. He ain't going to last like you and me, Jerry. But right now he's got everything.'

'You'll left-hand him to death.'

'Maybe,' Jack says. 'Sure. I got a chance to.'

'Handle him like you handled Kid Lewis.'

'Kid Lewis,' Jack said. 'That kike!'

The three of us, Jack Brennan, Soldier Bartlett, and I, were in Handley's. There were a couple of broads sitting at the next table to us. They had been drinking.

'What do you mean, kike?' one of the broads says. 'What do you mean, kike, you big Irish bum!'

'Sure,' Jack says. 'That's it.'

'Kikes,' this broad goes on. 'They're always talking about kikes, these big Irishmen. What do you mean, kikes?'

'Come on. Let's get out of here.'

'Kikes,' this broad goes on. 'Whoever saw you ever buy a drink? Your wife sews your pockets up every morning. These Irishmen and their kikes. Ted Lewis could lick you, too.'

'Sure,' Jack says. 'And you give away a lot of things free, too, don't you?'

We went out. That was Jack. He could say what he wanted to when he wanted to say it.

Jack started training out at Danny Hogan's health farm over in Jersey. It was nice out there, but Jack did n't like it much. He did n't like being away from his wife and the kids, and he was sore and grouchy most of the time. He liked me and we got along fine together; and he liked Hogan, but after a while Soldier Bartlett commenced to get on his nerves. A kidder gets to be an awful thing around a camp if his stuff goes sort of sour. Soldier was always kidding Jack, just sort of kidding him all the time. It was n't very funny and it was n't very good, and it began to get to Jack.

It was sort of stuff like this. Jack

VOL. 140 — NO. 1
A

Opening page of the first short story by Hemingway published in an American magazine (by permission of the Atlantic Monthly)

Moreover, Sedgwick did not shy from controversy. For example, he published an "open letter" from Charles C. Marshall to Alfred E. Smith in the April 1927 issue of the *Atlantic*, which candidly explored the American public's aversion to Smith's Catholicism and the role this prejudice would play in his campaign to become the Democratic nominee for the presidency. Smith wrote a ringing reply, "Catholic and Patriot," that was published in the next issue. According to magazine historian Theodore Peterson, "so newsworthy" was Smith's letter that "two newspapers published a copy of it, stolen from the plant where the *Atlantic* was printed." This forced the *Atlantic* to rush copies of the May issue to the stands, and to release the letter to the rest of the press. During Sedgwick's editorship the *Atlantic* published several noteworthy essays on social and political issues, including future Supreme Court Justice

Felix Frankfurter's penetrating discussion of the Sacco and Vanzetti case (March 1927); William Z. Ripley's "From Main Street to Wall Street" (January 1926), which led to a critical examination and subsequent reform of the New York Stock Exchange; and Rear Admiral William S. Sims's criticism of the system of naval promotions (September 1935).

In addition, under Sedgwick the magazine continued its tradition of publishing high-quality fiction and verse. Sedgwick was the first American editor to publish a short story by Ernest Hemingway ("Fifty Grand," July 1927). Edward Weeks, who succeeded Sedgwick as editor of the *Atlantic*, described Sedgwick's reaction to Hemingway's manuscript. Although Weeks's office was two doors away from Sedgwick's, he could hear the senior editor's characteristically forceful reaction: "he let out a crescendo of short explosions,

THE ATLANTIC MONTHLY

has the great honor to announce the publication of the

Original Love Letters

which passed between

Abraham Lincoln and Ann Rutledge

AT last, after nearly a century during which their existence was always suspected and hoped for, appear the priceless documents which lift the veil shrouding the love affair between Abraham Lincoln and young Ann Rutledge.

No longer need the biographer spend years of research, or the romancer dream of the idyll as it might have been. Here, for the first time, is revealed in Lincoln's own words, the tender love he bore for his "Dearly Valued Ann."

To the *Atlantic's* care has been confided the invaluable package inherited by Miss Wilma Frances Minor. Here are Lincoln's letters to Ann, and Ann's to Lincoln; letters from Lincoln to his friend and benefactor, John Calhoun; letters from the twenty-year old Ann to her cousin Mathilda Cameron, describing Lincoln's wooing ("he talks to me just like poetry," wrote the gentle, untutored girl); Mathilda's simply written revealing diary; the Bible Ann gave to Abraham; the little book of rhetoric with characteristic marginalia, which was the young Abe's daily companion through the days when he lived out the idyll of New Salem.

To those already privileged to see this collection, these documents seem the most moving personal mementoes in our history. Their deposit in the Treasure Room of the Congressional Library in Washington has been invited by the librarian.

Our first question, like the reader's, was,

of course, But, can this be *true?* Where have these letters been hidden all these years? When Lincoln scholars, students, lovers of his name, have eagerly searched for the proofs of this romance just hinted at in a few casual references and meager records of a scattered group of places and people, why have they not been discovered and given to the world before?

If there is one life of which the American people wish to know everything, it is Lincoln's, and his is the one life about which it long ago seemed impossible to unearth any new material.

And what have Lincoln scholars to say about this find? The leading Lincoln biographers and the country's most distinguished chemist who scrutinized the paper to determine if it were authentically of the period,— do they all accept these documents as the living record of the fragrant romance?

The answer to every question will be published in detail in the *Atlantic Monthly* beginning in December.

Miss Minor's story, with all its wealth of original, invaluable and long-sought Lincoln material, will begin in that issue. This feature alone, the first printing of these documents, will make an *Atlantic* subscription for the coming year a life-long keepsake—and incidentally a most appropriate Christmas remembrance.

The Lincoln story will be surrounded by an editorial program of true *Atlantic Monthly* standard.

The Lincoln serial will begin in the December Atlantic Monthly

Announcement for the series of letters that were later proven to be forgeries

'oh-oh-Oh-Oh. . . ,' – and whenever he did this it was a sure indication that he had found something exciting." On the other hand, when "some long-promised beauty turned out to be a lemon," Weeks could hear Sedgwick "moaning, beginning on a low note and swelling in volume, 'Ohoooo Oh,'" which confirmed that Sedgwick "had a dud."

Sedgwick also published work by H. G. Wells, Gertrude Stein, and Robert Frost, but he once sent Frost a rejection note that read, in part, "We are sorry but at the moment the *Atlantic* has no place for vigorous verse." Several of Amy Lowell's poems made their debut in the *Atlantic* during Sedgwick's editorship, although the correspondence between editor and poet (1912-

1925) reveals that Sedgwick did not always understand or appreciate the aims of Lowell's poetry. As Ellery Sedgwick III has pointed out, his forebear was an "aesthetic conservative," while Lowell wished to undermine that very orthodoxy in poetry that Sedgwick and his readers favored. Thus, in 1925 the editor accepted but delayed publishing Lowell's passionate poem "Fool o' the Moon" because he sensed it might shock *Atlantic* readers, particularly its last line, "I have lain with Lady Moon." So Sedgwick waited until July to publish the poem, when the schools and colleges whose English classes might have studied the *Atlantic* were recessed. Nevertheless, the publication of "Fool o' the Moon" sparked an immediate and angry outcry.

Ellery Sedgwick (Atlantic Monthly Company)

Although Sedgwick was sometimes cautious in literary matters, he was often overly enthusiastic in his efforts to bring historical accounts to his readers. He published "The Diary of Opal Whitely," the work of a young woman who claimed to be the daughter of Prince Henry of Orleans, as authentic, despite later claims to the contrary. Sedgwick also accepted the authenticity of a cache of love letters said to be written by Abraham Lincoln and Ann Rutledge, "discovered" in 1928 and brought to the offices of the *Atlantic* by Wilma Frances Minor. The magazine published the forgeries in the December 1928 and January 1929 issues. Although several authorities, including Lincoln biographers William E. Barton, Ida N. Tarbell, and Carl Sandburg, had vouched for the authenticity of the letters, evidence soon accumulated to the contrary. Minor later claimed that "the spirits of Ann and Abe were speaking through my Mother to me, so that my gifts as a writer combined with her gifts as a medium could hand in something worthwhile to the world." Choosing to cut the magazine's losses,

Sedgwick let the matter drop, and no explanation was ever published.

A canny manager, Sedgwick paid comparatively small salaries and limited manuscript fees. According to Allen, when writers discovered by Sedgwick found they could command higher rates elsewhere, the editor was "quite content" to let them go. Sedgwick valued not only the savings so generated but also the variety and spice lent to the magazine by a fairly regular turnover of contributors. In attracting the next group of authors to the *Atlantic*, he always emphasized the prestige of writing for such a hallowed cultural institution as compensation for low manuscript rates.

The forceful and occasionally irascible Sedgwick did not easily delegate editorial responsibilities. However, he relied on a cabinet of friends for advice on important matters. They included Thomas S. Lamont, Newton D. Baker, Walter Lippmann, Judge Joseph M. Proskauer, Justice Frankfurter, and Lewis W. Douglas. The only extended disagreement between Sedgwick and his staff was during the Spanish civil war, when the editor enthusiastically supported General Francisco Franco. In February 1938, after a tour in Spain, he published two articles for the *New York Times* in which he described life under Franco's rule as normal. Controversy erupted, and the *New York Times* subsequently printed two protest letters, one signed by sixty-three members of the League of American writers and another by more than one hundred educators. That same year Sedgwick resigned his editorship, although he insisted that his decision was in no way related to criticisms of his stand on Spain.

In 1939 Sedgwick sold the *Atlantic* for an undisclosed sum (said to be the largest in magazine history at that time) and devoted himself to writing book reviews and reminiscences. His autobiography, *The Happy Profession*, was published in 1946. It provides many interesting and generous-spirited glimpses of the many illustrious contributors to the *Atlantic* and gives a candid, witty, and urbane revelation of Sedgwick's philosophy as well. He admits, for instance, that "It has never occurred to me to change the colophon of the Atlantic to a distaff, and I have taken conscious pains that a preponderance of its contributors should be masculine." He went on:

My friend [Edward] Bok pointed out that I was sinning against the light of the cashbox, but I took comfort in the monthly comment of the historian, William Roscoe Thayer, who invariably commented: "I see the men are still ahead in this month's *Atlantic*."

Thus it happened that while it was to women I was forever writing letters of affectionate solicitude, my familiar company has been with men. With a single exception they have never betrayed me, and my heart goes out to them. It is amusing to think what the *Atlantic* would be like had it been turned into a salon, but I prefer the idea of a club.

The Happy Profession is also noteworthy for the overall view it presents of the magazine industry in the late-nineteenth and early-twentieth centuries. For instance, Sedgwick paints a richly detailed, humorous portrait of Samuel McClure, for a year his supervisor at *McClure's Magazine*. Sedgwick also notes that he never knew what his own job was at that magazine: "When I began one task I was sure to be switched to another. I began to think myself a problem child." Working for McClure was a challenge, for "never, . . . in American business, was there a brighter talent than McClure's for disorganization. If the chief did not originate a design, he could at least obfuscate it." But ultimately, Sedgwick admired the man's intensity, his ability to "bring any project to a white heat." No doubt this apprenticeship served Sedgwick well in his career at the *Atlantic*.

Mabel Cabot Sedgwick died in 1937. On 1 May 1939 Sedgwick married Isabel Marjorie Russell. In his later years he lived at a large estate in Beverly, Massachusetts, and often spent winters in Washington, D.C., where he died of a heart attack on 21 April 1960.

References:

Frederick Lewis Allen, "Sedgwick and the *Atlantic*," *Outlook and Independent*, 150 (26 December 1928): 1406-1408, 1417;

Don E. Fehrenbacher, "Lincoln's Lost Love Letters," *American Heritage*, 32 (1981): 70-80;

Louis Filler, *Crusaders for American Liberalism* (New York: Harcourt, Brace, 1939);

Isaac Goldberg, *The Man Mencken: A Biographical and Critical Survey* (New York: Simon & Schuster, 1925);

Gerald Gross, ed., *Editors on Editing* (New York: Grosset & Dunlap, 1962);

H. L. Mencken, *Letters of H. L. Mencken*, edited by Guy J. Forgue (Boston: Northeastern University Press, 1981);

Ellery Sedgwick, III, " 'Fireworks': Amy Lowell and the Atlantic Monthly," *New England Quarterly*, 51 (December 1978): 489-508;

Sedgwick, "HLM, Ellery Sedgwick, and the First World War," *Menckeniana: A Quarterly Review*, 68 (Winter 1978): 1-4;

Henry L. Shattuck, "Ellery Sedgwick," *Massachusetts Historical Society Proceedings 1957-60*, 72, 395-396.

Papers:

Sedgwick's papers, including business correspondence and personal letters, are at the Massachusetts Historical Society in Boston.

Albert Shaw

(23 July 1857-25 June 1947)

Lloyd J. Graybar
Eastern Kentucky University

MAJOR POSITIONS HELD: Editor and junior partner, *Grinnell Herald* (1879-1883); chief editorial writer, *Minneapolis Tribune* (1884-1890); editor and publisher, *Review of Reviews* (1891-1937).

BOOKS: *Icaria: A Chapter in the History of Communism* (New York & London: Putnam's, 1884);

Coöperation in a Western City (Baltimore: American Economic Association, 1886);

Municipal Government in Continental Europe (New York: Century, 1895);

Municipal Government in Great Britain (New York: Century, 1895; London: Unwin, 1895);

Life of Col. Geo. E. Waring, Jr., The Greatest Apostle of Cleanliness, as Told by Dr. Albert Shaw . . . and A. D., 1997–a Prophecy, by Colonel George E. Waring, Jr. (New York: Patriotic League, 1899);

Political Problems of American Development (New York: Columbia University Press, 1907);

The Outlook for the Average Man (New York: Macmillan, 1907);

A Cartoon History of Roosevelt's Career (New York: Review of Reviews, 1910);

Abraham Lincoln, 2 volumes (New York: Review of Reviews, 1929);

International Bearings of American Policy (Baltimore: Johns Hopkins Press, 1943).

OTHER: *The National Revenues: A Collection of Papers by American Economists*, edited by Shaw (Chicago: McClurg, 1888);

President Wilson's State Papers and Addresses, edited by Shaw (New York: Review of Reviews, 1917);

The Messages and Papers of Woodrow Wilson, 2 volumes, edited by Shaw (New York: Review of Reviews, 1924).

SELECTED PERIODICAL PUBLICATIONS
UNCOLLECTED: "Local Government in America," *Fortnightly Review*, new series 32 (October 1882): 485-495;

"The Growth of Internationalism," *International Review*, 14 (April 1883): 267-283;

"The American State and the American Man," *Contemporary Review*, 51 (May 1887): 695-712;

"The American Tariff," *Contemporary Review*, 54 (November 1888): 683-694;

"The American State Legislatures," *Contemporary Review*, 56 (October 1889): 555-573;

"Belgium and the Belgians," *Atlantic Monthly*, 65 (April 1890): 481-496;

"Hamburg's New Sanitary Impulse," *Atlantic Monthly,* 73 (June 1894): 787-796;

"Notes on City Government in St. Louis," *Century Magazine,* new series 30 (June 1896): 253-264;

"The Municipal Problem and Greater New York," *Atlantic Monthly,* 79 (June 1897): 733-748;

"The Trans-Mississippians and Their Fair at Omaha," *Century Magazine,* new series 34 (October 1898): 836-852;

"The American Presidential Election," *Contemporary Review,* 78 (November 1900): 609-632;

"The New President of the United States," *Contemporary Review,* 80 (November 1901): 609-633;

"The President and the Trusts," *Century Magazine,* new series 43 (January 1903): 381-387;

"The American Presidential Election," *Contemporary Review,* 86 (August 1904): 264-280;

"Walter Hines Page–Memorial Address," *North Carolina Historical Review,* 1 (January 1924): 3-25.

Albert Shaw's career has been unparalleled among editors and publishers. For more than forty years he put a strong personal stamp upon his widely circulated monthly magazine, *Review of Reviews,* bringing together popular, serious, and even scholarly articles in an appealing blend with other features and his own wide-ranging and thoughtful analysis of the news. A member of America's first generation of trained social scientists, he was a friend to both Theodore Roosevelt and Woodrow Wilson and was a well-known and respected public figure.

Albert Shaw was born near Cincinnati, Ohio, the son of Griffin Shaw, a physician and merchant, and Susan Fisher Shaw. After the sudden death of Dr. Shaw in 1863 Albert was influenced toward newspaper work by the example of his much older cousin, Murat Halstead, who would achieve national recognition as the editor of the *Cincinnati Commercial,* and through a father surrogate, Roger Williams, publisher of the weekly *Citizen* of Oxford, Ohio. The Shaw family had been comfortably provided for by Albert's father, and in 1875 Albert entered Iowa College (now Grinnell College). He enjoyed his years there, concentrating on English, logic, rhetoric, history, and political economy, subjects he thought suitable for an aspiring journalist. After graduating with a B.A. in 1879 he acquired a half-interest in the biweekly *Grinnell Herald.* His pur-

pose was to learn all aspects of the newspaper business, for the examples of Halstead and especially Williams had taught him that a sound education and working for a country newspaper provided the best schooling in journalism. (Academic training for that profession did not yet exist.)

Shaw, who had a keen and inquiring intellect, came to feel the need of further education beyond the master's degree he had acquired at Iowa College while working on the *Herald.* After two years with the paper he took a leave of absence in 1882 in order to start doctoral studies in history and political economy at Johns Hopkins University in Baltimore, where the rigorous scholarship and practices of the German universities were being pioneered in this country. Here he was much influenced by the thought of Herbert Baxter Adams and Richard T. Ely, who were to become two of the most eminent scholars of their generation. Under their guidance Shaw came into his own. He was admired by his teachers and fellow students for his informed comments and for his lucid and succinct prose style. His good friend from the Johns Hopkins glee club, Woodrow Wilson, sought Shaw's advice on the writing of his dissertation.

Shaw dropped out of school to go back briefly to the *Grinnell Herald* but continued to pursue some scholarly research on behalf of Ely. Shaw later took elements of this work and expanded it into his dissertation and then his first book, *Icaria: A Chapter in the History of Communism* (1884). Shaw's study examined a branch of the utopian-socialist movement that owed its existence to the theories of the Frenchman Etienne Cabet, author of *Voyage en Icarie* (1840). Followers of Cabet had founded a communal settlement in Texas in 1848. Shaw's research into this and other Icarian communities that had subsequently been established in the United States–including one that he visited at Corning, Iowa–convinced him that poor planning and factionalism had led to the decline of the movement.

Shaw severed his connection with the *Grinnell Herald* to return to Johns Hopkins to complete his doctoral studies. He also took on part-time work as an editorial writer for the *Minneapolis Tribune,* a Republican morning daily, and was promised a full-time job after graduation. Awarded the Ph.D. in 1884, Shaw then took up residence in Minneapolis. His work for the *Tribune* was outstanding, but being the chief editorial writer for a daily paper did not allow him adequate space to develop ideas as he would have

The Johns Hopkins University Glee Club in 1884. Woodrow Wilson and Albert Shaw are standing, second and third from the left

wanted. His inclinations and talents made him yearn for some other outlet, but he could not decide whether to leave journalism altogether to take an academic post.

After four somewhat frustrating years on the *Tribune,* the disillusioned Shaw took a leave of absence in 1888 and traveled for several months in Europe, combining research and relaxation. In London he met William T. Stead, editor of the *Pall Mall Gazette,* and dined at James Bryce's home with William Gladstone, Lord Acton, and other prominent Liberals. The articles on European urban government which Shaw wrote for the prestigious *Century Illustrated Monthly Magazine* following his return in 1889 did much to elevate his reputation as a journalist and scholar. Over the next few years he reworked his materials and did further research which enabled him to complete two substantial and much-praised volumes which appeared in 1895: *Municipal Government in Continental Europe* and *Municipal Government in Great Britain.* Shaw's reputation in the scholarly community was al-

ready such that he could have begun an academic career on any of several occasions. He had, in fact, just about decided to accept a professorship at Cornell when Stead offered him in November 1890 the editorship of the American edition of the *Review of Reviews.* Shaw promptly left for London to discuss details of the proposal and accepted the post.

As established by Stead in London earlier in 1890, the *Review of Reviews* was to be a venue for opinion and analysis of public affairs while also providing summaries and excerpts of the most interesting and worthwhile articles from a wide variety of periodicals. One of Stead's avowed goals was to foster greater unity among English-speaking peoples. (An Australian edition was also to be published.) Stead's British version of the *Review of Reviews* consisted of eighty-four, small-quarto pages. It featured his analysis of current events, "The Progress of the World," along with a character sketch of a prominent person. A selection of editorial cartoons was presented every month. The core of Stead's periodical was in two

Announcement by W. T. Stead, founder of the Review of Reviews, *of Shaw's appointment as editor of the new American edition of the London-based magazine*

sections of about twenty pages each: "Leading Articles in the Reviews" provided thorough summaries of the best of periodical journalism over the preceding month, while "The Reviews Reviewed" surveyed a wide range of English and American magazines and touched upon Western European and Russian publications, as well as some specialized journals. A major book review, a short listing of other new books, plus an index to current periodical literature rounded out Stead's efforts.

For a time Stead had arranged to have the British edition reprinted in the United States, but the results had not been satisfactory. Stead decided to publish a separate American edition and approached Shaw about the editorship. The first number of the American *Review of Reviews* appeared in April 1891. The American *Review of Reviews* was essentially the same as the English prototype in format, but from the outset Shaw enjoyed much autonomy and proceeded to institute

changes designed to make the magazine more appealing to the American middle class, whose patronage would determine the success or failure of the publication.

Under Shaw's editorship the American *Review of Reviews* contracted with a printing firm that used better paper and employed superior printing technology, considerably enhancing the periodical's appearance. Shaw added more illustrations and political cartoons, raised the number of contributed articles, and expanded "The Progress of the World," which, of course, he began writing. Stead's sometimes strident, soapbox manner was not Shaw's, a difference that was seen in their prose styles and, more important, in their attitudes. Over time these and other differences would widen into a gulf. Indeed, an undiluted dose of material from London which Shaw, under deadline pressure, unwisely printed in an early number probably cost Shaw his best chance at combining editorship with an academic post. He had unrealistically thought he could attempt both. At Woodrow Wilson's urging, Princeton had seriously considered offering Shaw a chair in political economy, but the alarmed trustees rejected his candidacy. Thereafter, the press of business made Shaw realize he could not possibly combine the two careers.

Stead's erratic financial management and inattention to the long-term development of the magazines soon caused increasing friction between the editors. Much to Shaw's horror, both magazines had to be mortgaged. Shaw sailed for England late in 1891 to try to clear the air with Stead and get things on a firm financial footing. Even after the lifting of the mortgage, problems between Stead and Shaw continued to flare up. Finally, at the end of 1892, the American *Review of Reviews* was incorporated as a separate legal entity with a board of Shaw's choosing. Over the preceding year Shaw had felt obliged to put his own resources into the periodical and wisely insisted on a dominant voice in its management as well as in its editorial affairs.

Shaw was supported as editor and publisher by a very able staff. The position of business manager initially went to William C. Gates, formerly of the *Milwaukee Sentinel*, but after two years Gates was released and ultimately replaced by Charles Lanier (son of the poet Sidney Lanier), who was to serve the magazine for more than thirty years. Those in subordinate editorial positions over the years included Robert Finley, William B. Shaw (no relation), Howard Florance, William Menkel, and George Pettengill.

The year 1893 was one of great significance for both Shaw and his *Review of Reviews*. A slender six-footer, Shaw had never been robust and frequently suffered from digestive and nervous ailments. The management conflict with Stead had told upon him, forcing Shaw to take most of the year to travel and recuperate. While visiting his sister in Noblesville, Indiana, in June, he met his future wife, Elizabeth Bacon, and married her on 5 September. They were to have two sons, Albert, Jr., and Roger, both of whom made careers on the *Review of Reviews* staff.

The takeoff of circulation figures for the *Review of Reviews* began in this year as well, but Shaw returned to the office after his leave to find even more contentiousness. Stead was just about to bring out his highly controversial book, *If Christ Came to Chicago,* a specific and graphic look at sin and corruption in the Windy City. In

his characteristic way, Stead intended the book to be shocking, but many were alarmed by its approach and doubtful whether it could succeed in Stead's declared purpose of causing reform in Chicago. Shaw, fearful that the hard work he was putting into establishing the reputation of the *Review of Reviews* would be undone, detached himself even further from Stead and would not market the book through the American magazine.

Stead's influence over the American edition reached its lowest point in 1897, when it was proposed that Charles Lanier also be brought into part ownership. A heated exchange followed, and although outwardly correct relations between Stead and Shaw were resumed, it was clearer than ever that Stead would have no meaningful say in the magazine's policies. Ironically enough, the American *Review of Reviews* was for the last years of Stead's life a principal source of his income. His own British edition had slumped after the Boer War. Stead died on the *Titanic* in 1912.

Under the leadership of the gifted Shaw, the *Review of Reviews* was unique in its time, although *World's Work,* founded by Walter Hines Page in 1900, had a few somewhat similar features. The *Review of Reviews* ran neither fiction nor muckraking articles but did incorporate economic, political, social, and scientific topics of current interest. It accepted few articles on speculation and insisted on timely, balanced commentary. The *Review of Reviews* was able to pay enough to compete for feature articles by some of the best writers in academia and American journalism. In its prime, from about 1893 to 1910, it was widely read and admired, circulation climbing to just over 205,000 monthly and advertising growing apace. Each issue had 128 pages of text and in some months even more pages of advertising. Estimates were that six people read each copy of the *Review of Reviews,* and Shaw was proud of the fact that his magazine's readership was comprised largely of students, teachers, clerics, and businessmen.

Albert Shaw's reputation as an intellectual in American journalism made him a public figure, much sought as a speaker, and Shaw somehow found time to lecture before civic groups and at universities. Selected lectures were compiled and published in two thick volumes: *Political Problems of American Development* (1907) and *The Outlook for the Average Man* (1907). Neither volume required substantial research of the sort Shaw had undertaken for his studies in municipal government, but like his earlier works they rep-

Cover for the second issue of the American edition of the British magazine W. T. Stead had founded in January 1890. Under Shaw's editorship, the American Review of Reviews *became far more successful than its British parent.*

resented an effort to further understanding of contemporary problems. In addition to his lecturing, Shaw participated in New York's civic affairs, served as a director of the Southern Education Board and the Rockefeller General Education Board, and periodically saw his name mentioned in connection with various university presidencies. Most of the talk was speculative, but he did feel obliged to tell Theodore Roosevelt he would accept no position in government. He had no intention of leaving the *Review of Reviews.*

Shaw wrote each paragraph of "The Progress of the World" himself. This section ran about twenty pages and was the thematic heart of the magazine. He often wrote in a detached, thoughtful manner; on issues where he believed that morality and integrity were at stake he took what others readily perceived as a partisan stance yet persuaded himself his analysis was the only honest one. A progessive Republican in politics,

he stood for efficient, nonpartisan government on the local level, regulation of the trusts, conservation, and America's destiny as a world power. A friend and supporter of Theodore Roosevelt in the early years of the century, he later became an admirer of Herbert Hoover and, in his last years as an editor, a biting opponent of the New Deal.

Shaw controlled the other editorial affairs of the *Review of Reviews* just as closely as he attended to the writing of "The Progress of the World." His was very much a one-man show, and criticism of his judgment by the magazine staff was unacceptable. As business manager and a major stockholder, Lanier could make recommendations but could not make substantive changes without Shaw's approval. Shaw's attitude stifled the continuous creativity necessary to keep a magazine in tune with the wants of its readers.

*Mr. and Mrs. W. T. Stead (at left) with Shaw and his wife, Elizabeth Bacon Shaw. When Stead died in
1912, Shaw wrote: "Although wholly independent of each other in editorship and control,
and quite different in method and appearance, there has been a close and unbroken
coöperation between Mr. Stead's English* Review *and its American namesake."*

Advertisements had remained abundant, but the *Review of Reviews* began to suffer a small circulation decline about 1908 and four years later a more substantial drop. The slump should have served as a warning to Shaw that troubles were facing his magazine. However, the events in Europe surrounding World War I revived the circulation of the *Review of Reviews* while at the same time further masking its fundamental deficiencies.

Perhaps Shaw's unflagging editorial commitment to Theodore Roosevelt at a time when the former Rough Rider was becoming a controversial figure within the Republican party had something to do with the prewar decline of the *Review*

of Reviews. In the long run, however, the trouble was with Shaw's increasingly outdated concept of what a magazine should be. After the war the magazine resumed its gentle but steady decline. In the early 1920s Albert Shaw, Jr., who by this time had a substantial input into business affairs (and eventually replaced Lanier, who sold out to the Shaws in 1928), brought a new energy that briefly halted the slide in circulation and in advertising revenue.

However, the nature of American journalism had changed. Small-circulation opinion magazines and weekly mass-circulation newsmagazines were to be the print media of the future, and the *Review of Reviews* was neither. A monthly review

Shaw (right) with Albert Shaw, Jr., who joined the Review of Reviews *staff in 1919*

of news events was no longer adequate, thanks in good measure to Henry Luce's *Time,* which from its founding in the 1920s enjoyed an enormous advantage in immediacy and had a zest that the *Review of Reviews* lacked. Nor were summaries of articles from other magazines equivalent to the deft condensations that *Reader's Digest* was to popularize in this same decade. Circulation fell to where it had been at the turn of the century, and with advertising falling off alarmingly Shaw belatedly began to acquiesce to changes. For the most part these were either cosmetic or tinkering with such matters as page size and the length and number of features. The *Review* began to shrink in length as more and more economies were imposed. In its last efforts to survive, the *Review of Reviews* in 1932 assumed the mailing list of the also-failing *World's Work,* which had been its chief rival, and in 1937 acquired the *Literary Digest,* under which the *Review of Reviews* was to be subsumed. This publication continued only briefly thereafter.

Henry Luce ultimately bought the rights to the *Literary Digest* title.

Shaw, in declining health, regretted the demise of the *Review of Reviews* but at eighty had no choice but to step aside. His wife had died in 1931, and on 4 May 1933 he married Virginia McCall, a former private secretary. He spent his remaining years in comfortable retirement, profits from the bountiful years of the *Review of Reviews* and shrewd investments having made him a millionaire. He worked on various projects but published only the dated *International Bearings of American Policy* (1943), a plea for a return to Wilsonian principles. He died on 25 June 1947.

Albert Shaw had a major place in American journalism for nearly a half century. After almost a decade of learning his craft on newspapers, he built the *Review of Reviews* into one of the most respected magazines of the early twentieth century. He adapted Stead's concept to an American audience but also possessed the sound business and editorial judgment Stead sometimes lacked, and was able to establish the *Review of Reviews* as a major voice in national opinion. Its appeal was predominantly to the members of the expanding white-collar class of the late nineteenth and early twentieth centuries who once a month could not only enjoy informative articles on a variety of topics but also ascertain what other magazines were saying and have the major events of the preceding month interpreted in twenty or so pages. Shaw's biases were those of an educated, Anglo-Saxon, male Protestant. The *Review of Reviews* enjoyed its major success at a time when a significant share of the reading public had these same biases and when a monthly analysis of world affairs was sufficient. Albert Shaw's editorial eye encompassed the entire world, and he did a remarkably sound job of presenting and explaining the highlights of an increasingly turbulent era. No one in the print media is likely to attempt such again.

Biography:

Lloyd J. Graybar, *Albert Shaw of the Review of Reviews: An Intellectual Biography* (Lexington: University Press of Kentucky, 1974).

References:

Lloyd J. Graybar, "Albert Shaw and the Founding of the *Review of Reviews*, 1891-97," *Journalism Quarterly*, 49 (Winter 1972): 692-697, 716;

Graybar, "Albert Shaw's Ohio Youth," *Ohio History*, 74 (Winter 1965): 29-34;

Graybar, "Albert Shaw's Search for the Ideal City," *Historian*, 34 (May 1972): 421-435;

Graybar, ed., "The Whisky War at Paddy's Run: Excerpts from a Diary of Albert Shaw," *Ohio History*, 75 (Winter 1966): 48-54.

Papers:

The papers of Albert Shaw are held by the New York Public Library.

Oswald Garrison Villard

(13 March 1872-1 October 1949)

Achal Mehra

Asian Mass Communication Research and Information Centre, Singapore

See also the Villard entry in *DLB 25: American Newspaper Journalists, 1901-1925.*

MAJOR POSITIONS HELD: Editor, *New York Evening Post* (1897-1918), *Nation* (1918-1932).

BOOKS: *The Early History of Wall Street* (New York: Putnam's, 1897);

William Henry Baldwin: A Life of Civic Endeavor, National Municipal League Leaflets, new series no. 1 (Philadelphia, 1905);

Self-Criticism North and South (Lexington, Va.: Washington and Lee University, 1906);

John Brown, 1800-1859: A Biography Fifty Years After (Boston & New York: Houghton Mifflin, 1910; London: Constable, 1910);

The Objects of the National Association for the Advancement of Colored People (Chicago: National Association for the Advancement of Colored People, 1912);

Some Weaknesses of Modern Journalism (Lawrence: University of Kansas, 1914);

Germany Embattled: An American Interpretation (New York: Scribners, 1915; London: Low, 1915);

Preparedness (New York: New York Evening Post, 1915);

The United States and Its Foreign Born Citizens (New York: Nation, 1915);

The Duty of the Press in War Time (Columbia: University of Missouri, 1917);

Universal Military Service (Boston: Massachusetts Branch of the Women's Peace Army, 1917);

Will the Real Germany Awake? (New York: Nation, 1917);

Universal Military Training Our Latest Cure-All (Washington, D.C.: American Union Against Militarism, 1918);

William Lloyd Garrison (New York: Fellowship Press, 1918);

Some Newspapers and Newspaper-Men (New York: Knopf, 1923; revised, 1926);

Prophets True and False (New York & London: Knopf, 1928);

Russia From A Car Window (New York: Nation, 1929);

The Press Today (New York: Nation, 1930);

The Tariff Scandal (New York: League for Independent Political Action, 1930);

Henry Villard: A True Fairy Tale (New York: Holt, 1931);

The German Phoenix: The Story of the Republic (New York: Smith & Haas, 1933);

Our Military Chaos: The Truth About Defense (New York & London: Knopf, 1939);

Fighting Years: Memoirs of a Liberal Editor (New York: Harcourt, Brace, 1939);

Inside Germany; With An Epilogue, England at War (London: Constable, 1939); republished as *Within Germany* (New York & London: Appleton-Century, 1940);

Disarmament in the Post War World (New York: Post War World Council, 1942);

Shall We Rule Germany? (New York: Post War World Council, 1943);

The Disappearing Daily: Chapters in American Newspaper Evolution (New York: Knopf, 1944);

Free Trade, Free World (New York: R. Schalkenbach Foundation, 1947);

How America is Being Militarized (New York: Post War World Council, 1947);

How Stands Our Press? (Chicago: Human Events, 1947).

OTHER: Henry Villard, *Lincoln on the Eve of '61: A Journalist's Story,* edited by Oswald Garrison Villard and Harold G. Villard (New York: Knopf, 1941);

Henry Villard, *The Early History of Transportation in Oregon,* edited by Oswald Garrison Villard (Eugene: University of Oregon, 1944).

SELECTED PERIODICAL PUBLICATIONS: "Preparedness is Militarism," *Annals of the American Academy of Political and Social Science,* 66 (July 1916): 217-224;

Oswald Garrison Villard (Kaiden Studios)

"Rights of Small Nations in America," *Annals of the American Academy of Political and Social Science,* 72 (July 1917): 165-171;

"Secrecy at Versailles," *Nation,* 108 (25 January 1919): 122-123;

"Wilson and the World," *Nation,* 108 (15 February 1919): 252;

"Conference at Berne," *Nation,* 108 (15 March 1919): 395;

"Germany Today," *Nation,* 108 (29 March 1919): 464-466;

"Truth About the Peace Conference," *Nation,* 108 (26 April 1919): 646-647;

"World's Greatest Newspaper," *Nation,* 114 (1 February 1922): 116-118;

"William Randolph Hearst and his Moral Press," *Nation,* 116 (28 March 1923): 357-360;

"New Fight for Old Liberties," *Harper's Magazine,* 151 (September 1925): 440-447;

"Sex, Art, Truth, and Magazines," *Atlantic Monthly,* 98 (March 1926): 388-398;

"True Woodrow Wilson," *Nation,* 122 (9 June 1926): 639-641;

"Tabloid Offences," *Forum,* 77 (April 1927): 485-491;

"Loyalty and the Editor," *Forum,* 80 (August 1928): 278-285;

"Crumbling Color Line," *Harper's Magazine,* 159 (July 1929): 156-167;

"Red Menace and Yellow Journalism," *Nation,* 132 (3 June 1931): 602-603;

"Waning Power of the Press," *Forum,* 86 (September 1931): 141-145;

"If I Were a Dictator," *Nation,* 134 (20 January 1932): 67-70;

"The Pot and the Kettle," *Nation,* 136 (7 September-9 November 1932): 206, 229-230, 247, 274, 299, 324-325, 345, 390, 418, 446;

"Issues and Men" [weekly column], *Nation* (11 January 1933-29 June 1940);

"Hitler and England," *Nation,* 136 (28 June 1933): 718-719;

"True Story of the Lusitania," *American Mercury,* 35 (May 1935): 41-51;

"We Militarize," *Atlantic Monthly,* 157 (February 1936): 138-149;

"Editor Balances the Accounts," *Atlantic Monthly,* 163 (April 1939): 452-460;

"Godkin's Nation," *Nation,* 150 (10 February 1940): 152-154;

"Investigate the Army!" *American Mercury,* 49 (April 1940): 427-434;

"Are We to Rule the World?" *Christian Century,* 58 (26 March 1941): 421-422;

"Press and the War," *Christian Century,* 59 (18 February 1942): 214-216;

"Credo of an Old-Fashioned Liberal," *American Mercury,* 55 (October 1942): 464-470;

"Head on for Imperialism," *Christian Century,* 60 (10 November 1943): 1300-1302;

"Press and the War News," *Christian Century,* 61 (1 March 1944): 267-268;

"Collapse of the War Liberals," *Christian Century,* 61 (25 October 1944): 1227-1228;

"Universal Military Training and Military Preparedness," *Annals of the American Academy of Political and Social Science,* 241 (September 1945): 35-45;

"Responsible Press?" *Forum,* 105 (April 1946): 706-709;

"Why Should Russia Fear Us?" *Christian Century,* 64 (25 June 1947): 793-794.

Oswald Garrison Villard was unquestionably the most energetic, outspoken, and courageous liberal editor in America during the first half of the twentieth century. During his thirty-five-year-long stewardship of the *New York Evening Post* and the *Nation,* Villard often defined the national liberal agenda and eagerly embraced every national controversy of any significance, with a genius, one social commentator remarked, for selecting the unpopular side of every issue. He campaigned tirelessly for the emancipation of minorities, blacks, and women; energetically resisted United States entry into the Spanish-American War and the two world wars; defiantly defended dissidents and conscientious objectors against political persecution during the xenophobia and nationalism of the war years; railed ceaselessly against conscription, political corruption, tariffs, and monopolies; and valiantly championed paci-

fism, civil liberties, prison reforms, and the right of self-determination for colonized peoples–indeed his activities covered the full spectrum of the most liberal reform movements of his era.

Villard, the third of four children, was born on 13 March 1872 to Henry Villard and Helen Frances (Fanny) Garrison Villard in Wiesbaden, Germany, during one of his parents' periodic sojourns abroad. His father had been a penniless German immigrant and had built a fortune in the railroad business, eventually becoming president of the Northern Pacific Railroad, and in 1881 he was to become owner of the *New York Evening Post* and the *Nation.* From his father, Villard acquired his wealth and his nineteenth-century laissez-faire liberalism. In *Fighting Years* (1939) he said of his inherited wealth, "The ability to roam the world in order to see for myself the kinship of all peoples; the power to aid in some slight degree the suffering, the oppressed, the victims of prejudice, of injustice, and of cruelty everywhere; above all, the freedom to say one's soul is one's own: these are the sole justifications of wealth that I have been able to discover."

His mother, the daughter of the famed abolitionist William Lloyd Garrison, imbued in Villard a puritanical and absolutist moralism. In his 1939 memoir he admitted, "It is one of my failings, I know, but I have never been able to work happily with men or women who were incapable of hot indignation at something or other–whether small or big, whether it stirred me personally or not, if only it was *something.* To minimize every evil is to my mind to condone it and in time to destroy one's influence." An unbending zealot, he was harsh with what he termed the "moral cowardice" of turncoats and those too timid to fight for their causes, as is reflected in this vituperative attack in *Fighting Years* on Newell Dwight Hillis, who abandoned pacifism during World War I: "Were there a Devil he must have reveled in every utterance of that noted divine who could not even remember the injunction not to bear false witness, to say nothing of some of the other Commandments." Fanny Garrison's own involvement in the women's and black movements was also the impetus for her son's active advocacy on behalf of these causes.

After private education in New York's Morse School, Villard entered Harvard in 1889 and was graduated with an undistinguished record in 1893. He returned to Harvard for an M.A. in 1894 and remained there for two years, during which time he also worked as a graduate as-

Villard (in pony cart) at Thorwood, his family's summer estate in Dobbs Ferry, New York, with his elder brother, Harold (at left) and sister, Helen (far right)

sistant in the department of history. Although he claimed to have been profoundly influenced by the teachers there, in his autobiography he commented about only "the polish, a courtliness, almost an old-worldliness" and the leisurely scholarship of these savants. Villard showed no inklings at Harvard of the reformist zeal that preoccupied his later life. As campus correspondent for his father's *New York Evening Post,* the future pacifist even denounced labor unrest and supported the use of troops to quell disturbances. His earliest writings for the *Evening Post* dealt with army administration, and his first contribution, on 11 January 1894, to the *Nation,* then an *Evening Post* supplement, reported on Spanish military forces in Melilla, Africa.

Despite his father's reservations he left teaching for journalism, dissatisfied with the Harvard life of "sitting in a club window and watching the world go by on the pavement outside." By contrast, he was drawn to journalism, with its "thrill of getting the news, of being in touch with and recording the daily kaleidoscope of public life at home and abroad as well as the opportunity to champion reforms."

He decided not to get his start on the *Evening Post,* however, to avoid the onus associated

with being the boss's son. With his father's assistance he landed a ten-dollar-a-week job at the *Philadelphia Press,* which he later scorned as "exactly what a newspaper office ought not to be," a "journalistic harlot. . . . absolutely subservient to its advertisers . . . a partisan Republican organ [with] a tremendously long list of sacred cows and a corresponding black list." He claimed in his autobiography, *Fighting Years,* that when he took over the *Evening Post* he strove to make it the "exact antithesis of the *Press.*"

In May 1897, after only six months at the *Press,* Villard joined the *Evening Post* in the wake of a mass·defection of several of its younger journalists to the *New York Commercial Advertiser.* Although the editors urged him to assume control of the *Evening Post,* Villard opted to begin as editor of the Saturday feature section in an effort to learn the ropes. But in less than a year he became the dominant force on the *Evening Post* following the illness of the newspaper's editorial stalwart Edwin L. Godkin, whom Villard called "the greatest editorial writer the American press has ever produced."

Villard soon found himself caught up in the newspaper's crusade against American intervention in Cuba and in the Philippines. He wrote

The Nation

FOUNDED 1865

Published Thursdays. Owned by THE NATION PRESS, INC.,
OSWALD GARRISON VILLARD, President.
EMIL M. SCHOLZ, Publisher, Secy. and Treas.

Entered at the New York City Post Office as second class mail matter.

OSWALD GARRISON VILLARD, EDITOR
HENRY RAYMOND MUSSEY, MANAGING EDITOR
R. B. McCLEAN, BUSINESS MANAGER
WILLIAM G. PRESTON, ADVERTISING MANAGER
ROBERT R. CLELAND, CIRCULATION MANAGER

SUBSCRIPTION RATES.—Four dollars per
annum, postpaid, in United States and Mexico;
to Canada, $4.50, and to foreign countries com-
prised in the Postal Union, $5.00.
Address, THE NATION, 20 Vesey Street.
P. O. Box 794, New York.

LONDON OFFICE: 16 Regent St., S. W.; WASHINGTON OFFICE:
Home Life Building; CHICAGO OFFICE: People's Gas Building.

Masthead from the 7 February 1918 issue of the Nation, *the first edited by Villard*

trenchant commentaries against the Spanish-American War and Pres. William McKinley, whom he later denounced as "one of the greatest murderers in American history." He also joined some of New England's most eminent citizens to found the Anti-Imperialist League, with the aim of opposing the war and U.S. imperialist designs.

Meanwhile the newspaper became embroiled in an advertising boycott because of its campaign against limits on duty-free imports on returning American travelers. Villard estimated the brief boycott cost the newspaper nearly one million dollars. In an exclusive scoop in 1910, Villard exposed in the *Evening Post* New York State Legislature Pres. Jotham P. Allds's involvement in a graft scandal, which led to the institution of impeachment proceedings and ultimately the resignation of that politician. It also increased Villard's clout as well as that of the *Evening Post*.

Villard married Julia Breckenridge Sandford of Covington, Kentucky, on 18 February 1903 in Athens, Georgia, during an educational

excursion to the South. They had three children: a daughter, Dorothea Marshall, and two sons, Oswald Garrison, Jr., and Henry Hilgard. The southern excursion sensitized him to the plight of blacks and intensified his involvement in their cause–a cause he aggressively championed for the remainder of his life.

In 1909 he was asked to prepare an address for a national interracial conference held to observe the centennial of Abraham Lincoln's birth. The conference led to the founding of the National Association for the Advancement of Colored People with the objective of abolishing racial and color-based distinctions in American society. Villard, who was among the association's five founding members, served it in several official capacities, including vice-president and chairman of the board of directors.

Soon after Woodrow Wilson's inauguration in 1913, Villard urged him to appoint a national race commission to investigate the problems of blacks, but Wilson balked at the idea because of po-

Villard at about the time he became editor of the Nation

litical opposition. Disappointed at Wilson's rejection of his proposal and disturbed also by reports of segregation within the Treasury Department, Villard began stumping the nation, accusing Wilson of hypocrisy in his commitment to democracy. Sen. Carter Glass of Virginia dubbed Villard the "rankest negrophile in America," a "distinction" Villard modestly declined because of the others "whose services on behalf of freedom and democracy for the American Negro are so superior to mine."

A confirmed suffragist, Villard was one of eighty-four men to join the first joint suffrage parade in New York City in 1911, braving boos, hisses, catcalls, and insults from members of the University Club. He helped form the Men's League for Woman Suffrage and served on its

board of directors. Even after women won suffrage Villard continued to fight for their legal, political, and professional advancement. He also lobbied for the American Indian cause and served on two government committees assigned to examine Indian problems.

In 1912 the *Evening Post* backed the candidacy of Woodrow Wilson. Villard was considered to be among Wilson's closest advisers in the early years of his presidency; there were even press reports of the influence he exercised in the White House. In 1915, when he became Washington correspondent for the newspaper, which he later said was "indubitably the most interesting experience" of his career, his easy White House access enabled him to "scoop" several stories, winning him widespread respect and envy among the press corps.

Following the sinking of the *Lusitania* in 1915, Villard resisted the war psychosis that gripped the nation. He marshaled the *Evening Post* to keep America out of World War I. To Theodore Roosevelt, who denounced the sinking as an act of piracy, Villard retorted that he did not doubt Roosevelt's qualifications as an authority on piracy. The bristling Roosevelt wrote a friend, "It is sometimes necessary to skin skunks; but it is necessary to choose the skunk! ... Really I do not think Oswald Villard ought to be honored with an attack.... he is the kind of crawling thing we step on, provided the resulting crunch won't leave too large a stain on the floor...."

Villard backed President Wilson, who, warding off the jingoists with his immortal phrase "too proud to fight" (a phrase Villard claimed to have coined), attempted a diplomatic resolution to the harassment of American naval ships by Germany. When Wilson won a diplomatic victory by getting a German assurance that United States vessels would not be harassed, Villard raved in the *Evening Post* that the president had forced Germany to capitulate "by sheer force of moral indignation nobly expressed in the name of the greatest Republic in history." He even broke a 114-year-old *Evening Post* tradition, over violent newsroom objections, by printing Wilson's picture on the front page with an exulting caption: "This is the man who, without rattling a sword, without mobilizing a corporal's guard of soldiers, or lifting the anchor of a warship won for civilization the greatest diplomatic victory in generations."

As Wilson edged toward increasing defense expenditures, however, the avowedly pacifist Villard began to drift away from him, accused him of capitulating to political expediency, and decided not to support his presidential candidacy in 1916. While other liberals wavered in their opposition to United States involvement in World War I, Villard with his unbending zeal and uncompromising pacifism stood his ground and berated them all. He broke irreconcilably with Wilson in 1917 when Wilson asked Congress for a declaration of war. Villard rued that the "blow" came "nearer to unmanning" him than anything in his life. "For I knew, as I knew that I lived, that this ended the republic as we had known it; that henceforth we Americans were to be part and parcel of world politics, rivalries, jealousies, and militarism; that hate, prejudice, and passion were now enthroned in the United States."

He defiantly wrote to Wilson's private secretary, Joseph Tumulty, "Believe me, I am ready for any concentration camp, or prison, but I am *not* at war and no one can *put me into war*—not the President of the United States with all his power; my loyalty to American traditions and ideals renders that impossible."

Years later, in an article that appeared in the August 1928 issue of *Forum*, he justified his break with Wilson, the man he had helped elect in 1912: "But there was a choice between loyalty to a principle and loyalty to—or rather, silence in regard to the act of a friend—which was exactly the same act as we had reprobated a hundred times in professional politicians. To have kept silent would have been disloyalty to the friend; it would also have in honor debarred us from criticizing any similar act by anybody else."

He advocated peaceful alternatives to international conflicts and urged the creation of a new seat in the president's cabinet for the secretary of peace. He founded the League to Limit Armaments and castigated Wilson for dragging the United States into war and for becoming a wartime "dictator." He sought the abolition of compulsory military service and when that failed proposed a generous administrative policy toward conscientious objectors. He called for universal and total disarmament.

Villard's outspoken opposition to military preparedness, universal military training, and the war, and his defiant championship of dissenters brought down public wrath upon him and his family. His children were taunted at school and his German dachshund stoned. As for Villard, "I soon discovered that half of [my friends] were afraid that I would land in prison and that the other half was afraid that I would not. It was amusing to see how many men got up and left the room if I went into a club and how many others had become too shortsighted to recognize me." He was accused of being a German sympathizer because of his own German heritage, and his public pronouncements to the contrary did little to dispel the misgivings.

He braved the xenophobia, writing stirring defenses on behalf of civil liberties and against suppressions under the Espionage Act of 1917, taunting detractors, "It is pleasant to serve one's country even when one's country temporarily doesn't appreciate it."

Determined to ward off the country's militarization, he claimed that he did his "uttermost to keep the *Evening Post* and *The Nation* free to print

Villard (in dark suit) with Ramsay MacDonald, leader of the British Labour party, and his daughter, Ishbel, in Concord, Massachusetts, 1927

as judicially as possible all news of significance, and even to report the undercurrent abroad." His pacifism estranged him from his intensely prowar staff, and in late 1917 he stopped writing for the paper. He rejected a staff proposal to withdraw from the paper and turn it over to them, however, saying he refused to "run under fire." He later boasted that he had kept his paper "from becoming, like all the others, a Hun-hater and suppressor of news. . . ."

Despite his proud and defiant resistance, he was forced to sell the deficit-ridden paper in August 1918 to Thomas A. Lamont. He later lamented, "I had given to *The Evening Post* the best of my younger years, all the idealism, the goodwill, and the devotion of which I was capable, never drawing a salary of more than $3,600 in order that others might have more, striving in every way to make the office a happy one and the conditions of labor the very best. . . . But I had failed in my task. . . ." Villard retained the *Nation*, of which he had been president and edito-

rial writer since 1900. He had assumed editorship of the *Nation* in February 1918, and one month before the newspaper's sale he separated the journal from the newspaper.

Lewis Gannett, a staffer at the *Nation* during Villard's editorship of the magazine, later wrote: "In the history of American journalism Villard will be remembered less for his twenty years' ownership and editorship of a 'good' newspaper than for his fifteen years at the helm of the rambunctious little weekly which challenged a hundred-million country with a circulation of 30,000."

Villard poured $150,000 into the *Nation* in his first year and transformed it from a staid literary magazine, which it had become during its thirty-seven-year association with the newspaper, into a crusading and influential political journal in the character of the *New Republic*. He restored news features, expanded foreign coverage, and introduced a fortnightly sixteen-page international-relations section. He recruited a staff of energetic young editors and reporters sympathetic to his political views, including Freda Kirchwey, with whom Villard later broke; Norman Thomas, who later became a perennial Socialist party candidate for president; Ernest H. Gruening, who became governor of Alaska; the Van Doren clan–Carl, Mark, Irita, and Dorothy; Lewis S. Gannett; Joseph Wood Krutch; and Arthur H. Warner.

As "captain and supercargo, pusher and recruiting officer," he said, "I had the complete satisfaction of molding my historic journal according to my exact wishes and beliefs." He gloated in his autobiography, "The general belief, however, among the war-mad, the reactionaries, the war profiteers, and the general public which did not read *The Nation*, was that we had suddenly gone violently 'red,' crazily pacifist, and openly pro-German, while the new adjective 'bolshevik' seemed expressly invented for the purpose of tagging the editors of this wicked sheet." Indeed, Villard was among sixty-two persons named as engaging in subversive activities before Sen. Lee Overman's subcommittee investigating German and Bolshevik propaganda.

The *Nation* became Villard's vehicle for espousing liberal causes and pacifism and soon acquired the reputation of being America's preeminent liberal journal. Villard wrote, "To many [readers] who had been utterly isolated in their communities, even in their families, who had suffered to their souls because of their conscientious opposition to the war folly and the madness of the peace, the weekly visit of *The Nation* was like a draught from a life-giving spring."

The postal service's seizure of the 13 September 1918 issue because of criticisms of a labor leader gave the *Nation* added notoriety. Although the seizure order was later rescinded, Villard crowed, "As is always the case, this bout with the censorship boosted our circulation greatly and got us a lot of publicity. . . ." Circulation of that issue topped 11,000, the highest since 1877. By 1920, circulation rose fivefold, from 7,200 in 1918 to 38,087–surpassing its main rival the *New Republic*. These circulation figures do not reflect the immense political power the journal exercised during the 1920s and the 1930s. Frank P. Walsh said that after he published an article on railroads in the *Nation*, his phone rang off the hook with calls from editors, senators, lobbyists, and reformers seeking additional information on his article; yet he never met anyone who recalled reading a series on the same subject that he had syndicated in the Hearst newspapers, which had

a circulation of ten million.

What won the *Nation* its reputation among liberals was its coverage of the Paris Peace Conference at the end of World War I. Villard decided to cover the conference for the *Nation*. He arrived in France after a perilous ocean voyage and after overcoming difficulties in obtaining a visa because of his reputation as a liberal and pacifist. He was disdainful of the conference's secrecy and dubious of President Wilson from the very start.

He also covered the meetings of the Socialist Second International at Bern, then proceeded to Germany, defying an Allied prohibition against such travel. He reported on the bloodshed and starvation in Germany. As the only United States correspondent in Munich at the time of Bavarian president Kurt Eisner's assassination, Villard secured a major exclusive. He witnessed the ensuing riots, civil war, curfew, and censorship. His penetrating firsthand reports made him the envy of the press corps. He returned to France a celebrity. Instead of being reproached for violating the prohibition on travel to Germany, he was "sought after, much invited, and entertained" for his firsthand insights into the German situation, prompting him to quip, "Apparently it sometimes pays to defy the Presidential ukases."

Following his return to Paris from Germany, Villard continued to rail against the peace conference. Although the *Nation* had been among the first to endorse the concept of a permanent international organization for peace in 1916, and although it had backed President Wilson's well-known "Fourteen Points" speech on peace, the journal was a vehement opponent of the peace conference, which Villard wrote was a "palpable fraud upon the world"; the ensuing Versailles Treaty, which to him was a "covenant with death"; and the League of Nations, which was "only another Holy Alliance." The *Nation* also published a damning editorial by William MacDonald, "The Madness at Versailles" (17 March 1919), of which Villard later wrote, "No more powerful or prophetic editorial ever appeared in *The Nation* or, I sometimes think, in any other journal." In that editorial, which attracted international comment, MacDonald blasted Wilson: "The one time idol of democracy stands today discredited and condemned. His rhetorical phrases, torn and faded tinsel of a thought which men now doubt if he himself ever really believed, will never again fall on the ears of eager multitudes."

Members of a delegation that appeared before the New York State Senate and Assembly Codes Committee in 1930 to voice their opposition to the state's capital-punishment law. Villard is standing at center with Ruth Hale on his right and Arthur Garfield Hays and Dudley Field Malone on his left. Dr. Frederick L. Hoffman is seated at center.

Before long, considerable disillusionment developed within the country toward the treaty and the conference, vindicating the position of the *Nation*. Because of the consistency of the journal's opposition and its early prophetic warnings, in the eyes of many liberals it overtook the *New Republic* as America's preeminent liberal voice. The *Nation* was, in the words of *Atlantic Monthly* editor Ellery Sedgwick, "incomparably the best weekly paper in the country."

Back in America, Villard and the *Nation* campaigned against U.S. and Allied intervention in the Russian revolution and criticized the United States for withholding recognition from Russia. Villard denounced United States intervention in Haiti and Santo Domingo as the "blackest chapter in American history in the Caribbean." He waged courageous and unrelenting battles against intolerance and the suppression of dissent under the Sedition Act of 1918. He championed the release of Eugene Victor Debs, who was convicted and sentenced to ten years imprisonment under the Espionage Act for a speech condemning American involvement in World War I and exhorting socialists to destroy capitalism. In 1920 Villard backed Debs's candidacy for president on a Socialist ticket, saying Debs "in his character, his devotion to principle, and his readiness to perish if need be for his beliefs, towered even

in his prison cell head and shoulders above" the other candidates.

When Att. Gen. A. Mitchell Palmer, pursuant to an act of Congress, in January 1920 began deportation proceedings against alien communists, anarchists, and radicals, Villard railed in the *Nation* against "self-constituted mobs of uniformed men." He later lamented, "We had little aid from the press in this fight which was one after my heart since it enabled us to champion the oppressed, the tortured, the innocently convicted." He vigorously fought for the defeat of peacetime state and federal sedition laws and spoke out during the Red Scare of the 1920s, warning that the "radical reform of today is usually the accepted custom of tomorrow." He threw the *Nation* behind the movement to free Nicola Sacco and Bartolomeo Vanzetti, two Italian-immigrant anarchists and draft evaders sentenced to death for murder and robbery on the basis of what many liberals felt was dubious evidence. He wrote a leader titled "Massachusetts the Murderer," deriding the "injustice, corruption, maladministration, intolerance, and lack of progress in our public officials." He joined the Citizen's National Committee for Sacco and Vanzetti to denounce a "monstrous miscarriage of justice" and continued the fight even after the execution of

Villard speaking to students at Western Reserve University during an antiwar rally in 1935, the year in which he sold the
Nation *because its editors were softening their stand against American involvement in the events that led to World War II*
(Brown Brothers)

the two men as a "patriotic duty" to reform a "defective system."

For their championship of these unpopular causes, Villard and the *Nation* were targeted by several right-wing groups. In early 1921 an attempt was made to bar him from speaking before the Women's City Club of Cincinnati, and when that failed the meeting was stormed. He had to be spirited out of the city in an automobile because the railroad had been surrounded by patrolling American Legionnaires. The *Cincinnati Tribune* blasted his "damnable doctrines" and warned that there were "momentous occasions" when to tolerate anything other than "one universal opinion, conviction, judgment, is to tolerate treason."

In 1929 Villard's name made a blacklist of some of the most prominent liberals and pacifists of his times who were barred by the Daughters

of the American Revolution and the Key Men of America from speaking at their meetings. He lampooned the list in the *Nation*, organizing a "Black List Party" for one thousand people on the "Roll of Honor." In a more serious vein, however, he castigated his tormentors: "It is certainly entirely unAmerican not only to deny others the right to speak, but to seek to tarnish their characters merely because of differences of opinion. . . ."

He crusaded for civil liberties, an antilynching bill, and prison reforms, and against third-degree interrogation, capital punishment, and governmental intrusion into individual morals. He also opposed as discriminatory immigration-law reforms that sought to exclude alien anarchists and introduced a literacy test for new immigrants. "The modern Americanism wants a Chinese Wall around the United States," he complained, taunting those who sought to exclude "undesirable aliens" by saying that the greatest mischiefmongers and crooks it had been his duty to "scourge" had American names. He also protested a proposal for compulsory registration of aliens because it violated their civil rights.

He was sympathetic to labor, vociferously denounced attempts to break up unions, and exhorted workers to civil disobedience, even posting twenty thousand dollars bail for one labor leader arrested under the Riot Act. He launched a campaign in the *Nation* against Congress's refusal to seat Victor Berger, founder of the Socialist party, who was elected to the House of Representatives from Wisconsin.

Throughout the peace years he mocked the conservativeness of American leaders, ridiculing "the corrupt Administration of President Harding, the standstill Administration of Calvin Coolidge, and the do-nothing Administration of Herbert Hoover." He attacked President Hoover's rejection of proposals for governmental intervention to aid individuals caught up in the Depression and attacked government dole outs to corporations. He championed peace, liberty of thought and expression, minority and individual rights, equality, justice, political democracy, and responsive and responsible government. Simultaneously, the magazine began advocating national planning, unemployment insurance, and other welfare programs. Villard also opened the journal to revisionist historians probing United States involvement in World War I.

Concerned by increasing monopolization in the business sector, he advocated the nationalization of railroads and later water power, natural resources, and utilities, including radio, telephone, and telegraph. He rejected laissez-faire and called for price controls and public-works programs. His war experiences had profoundly changed him, he said, steering him to the left, causing him to lose his faith in the existing political order and in the ability of the capitalist system to redeem or reform itself. "In short," he wrote, "by 1919, I think that I had been emancipated from any merely smug liberalism and social blindness due to the ease and luxury of my upbringing. Never yet, however, have I been won for a doctrine or a system that requires bloodshed to introduce it or to maintain it once it had been adopted."

He advocated political reforms, observing that the Republican and Democratic parties were indistinguishable and the most conservative in the western world. He complained that the two

parties were even further to the right than the British Tories and that the United States was lagging fifty years behind modern democracy. He was active in several voluntary organizations. One partial list included thirty-one, ranging from the Anti-Imperialist League and the Citizen's Committee of One Hundred on Behalf of Pullman Porters and Maids, to the Friends of Freedom for India and the Women's International League for Peace and Freedom.

Throughout the 1932 presidential campaign he ran a series of articles titled "The Pot and the Kettle" (7 September-9 November) and in protest voted for Socialist Norman Thomas for president even though he steadfastly refused to adopt the Socialist party. For years the *Nation* agitated for a third party that would stake out the middle ground between conservatism and socialism. Villard participated in the convening in 1924 of a Conference for Progressive Political Action, which endorsed the independent candidacy of Robert M. LaFollette, who secured almost five million votes. The following year Villard, with a handful of liberals, established the National Progressive party and later the New York Progressive party. He even contemplated a run for the Senate on the party's ticket and continued to agitate for a third party through the 1932 elections, even though the party fizzled out in November 1927.

Villard turned over active management of the *Nation* to a board of editors in 1932 but stayed on as contributing editor and maintained his majority stock holdings. While promoting the full spectrum of liberal causes in his regular weekly column, "Issues and Men" (11 January 1933-29 June 1940), he warned of the dangers of excessive governmental control and of the concentration of power in the hands of the executive. Although initially lukewarm toward Pres. Franklin Delano Roosevelt, he warmly embraced the reforms of the New Deal.

As World War II approached, he advocated mandatory neutrality. He sold the *Nation* on 16 April 1935, partly for financial reasons, but also because the magazine was softening its stand against United States involvement in the events that led to the war. Although Villard continued as editorial associate, the divestiture was not easy for him, he said, because "I have repeatedly asserted that one who has had the joy of saying in print just what he thinks and feels, of breaking a lance on behalf of any cause in which his heart was enlisted, never relinquished this privilege hap-

Villard speaking to students at Princeton University in 1938, during a rally opposing Frank Hague, the controversial and powerful Democratic mayor of Jersey City, New Jersey. Norman Thomas is seated at far right.

pily but always with deep regret." About the same time Villard also divested himself of two yachting magazines, *Yachting*, which he founded in 1907, and the *Nautical Gazette*, which he had acquired in 1918. Little is known about the extent of Villard's editorial role in those magazines, in which he became involved because of his love for sailing.

In the 1936 elections Villard backed Norman Thomas for president, saying that war and peace were the paramount issues of the time and that Roosevelt was embarking upon the road to war. For him, the neutrality records of state and national candidates became the sole litmus test for his political support. He even teamed up with conservative isolationists and reactionaries to oppose United States involvement in World War II through an Emergency Committee to Defend America First. When his liberal critics pointed

out that the committee sought an impregnable defense for the United States, something Villard had resisted throughout his life, he defended himself by saying that his supreme objective was to keep the United States out of war. He argued that while the European democracies had an obligation to resist fascism, the United States did not share that obligation.

This one-time hero of liberals was accused in the later years of his life of becoming a conservative and isolationist himself. His die-hard insistence on United States neutrality in the war prompted the *Nation*, which had come out for collective security against Fascist expansion, to reject his manuscripts. He was so obsessed with the fear that Roosevelt would drag the country into the war that he began protesting in the *Nation* that a third term for Roosevelt presaged potential fascism for the United States, infuriating the editors to repudiate his columns in their editorial paragraphs.

In May 1940, after his contract with the *Nation* expired, he was told that he would be continued on a week-by-week basis. When the journal called for a broad military-aid program for Britain, including universal military training, Villard decided to terminate his association with the journal. He complained that the *Nation* had been "prostituted and had struck hands with all the forces of reaction," and he expressed the hope that it would either "die very soon or fall into other hands."

In his farewell column, "Valedictory" (29 June 1940), Villard wrote that his retirement was precipitated "by the editors' abandonment of the *Nation*'s steadfast opposition to all preparations for war, to universal military service, to a great navy, and to *all* war, for this in my judgment has been the chief glory of its great and honorable past." He predicted that "the present editors will some day awake to a realization that the course they are now proposing will inevitably end all social and political progress. . . , impose a dictatorship and turn us into a totalitarian state." Just as World War I had resulted in his break with the *Evening Post* in 1918, twenty-two years later World War II caused his alienation from the *Nation*.

But for Villard, his pacifism towered far above anything else, as is reflected in his stirring defense of his position: "You may glorify the struggle as you will, and supply it, if you please, with aims as lofty as you can possibly portray by pen or voice; you may attribute to yourself and your allies the purest motives, the noblest adjectives, the most humanitarian desires. You will inevitably fail to achieve those ends, and your beautifully cadenced words will turn to ashes because it is ordained by the way of the world that goodness and virtue, the safeguarding of human rights and what is called civilization can never be achieved by letting loose hell upon earth."

Villard walked through the war years with what the *Nation* called "the consciousness of a rectitude," living in a kind of "dream world." He continued his crusades against the war in increasingly intemperate and parochial speeches; appearances before congressional committees; and columns, which appeared for the main part in the *Christian Century* between 1942 and 1944, when he suffered a stroke. He also wrote for the *Progressive, Uncensored, Asia and the Americas, Human Events, Harper's,* and *Atlantic Monthly.* Almost all his writings dealt with war and peace,

but he also occasionally reported on food conferences, Puerto Rico, and the press. In some of his articles he expounded conspiracy theories accusing Roosevelt and the media of trying to whip up hysteria, hate, and fear to precipitate United States involvement in the war. By 1944 Roosevelt had replaced Wilson on Villard's list as "the greatest falsifier and prevaricator in American History." For a brief time Villard, dismayed perhaps at his waning influence, flirted with the idea of starting a new magazine to reach the disconnected antiwar groups in New England and the Midwest, but he abandoned the plan.

He did write several pamphlets denouncing the war and a book, *Free Trade, Free World* (1947), in which he condemned protective tariffs as "wicked," "robbery," and "extortion." Villard's books cover a broad range of subjects, including economics, history, the press, defense, and Germany. In *The Disappearing Daily* (1944), he lamented the decline in journalism from "what was once a profession but now a business." A strong believer in the marketplace of ideas, he insisted that a democratic society was "dependent for its health and its progress upon an informed and enlightened electorate, constantly exposed to new and, if need be, unpopular ideas by a free, a fearless, and untrammeled press." For that reason, he denounced press monopolies, chain ownership, the decline in daily newspapers, and the rise in single-newspaper cities.

He also criticized the Associated Press, whose board of directors he had joined in 1916 as "one of a very few liberals who ever joined the board," and he claimed to have had a "certain ameliorating influence upon the board." He complained that the cooperative nature of the Associated Press put it at the "mercy of the mass psychology of its members" and that the United Press was a more liberal news agency "with a wider vision, a more catholic taste, and far greater sympathy for the underdog and the oppressed and for the problems of labor in general."

Villard died on 1 October 1949, a bitter man, as is reflected in this epitaph he chose for himself in 1941:

He grew old in an age he condemned
Felt the dissolving throes
Of a social order he loved
And like the Theban seer
Died in his enemies' day.

Heywood Broun wrote in the *Nation* (2 January 1929), "It is a curious piece of casting which

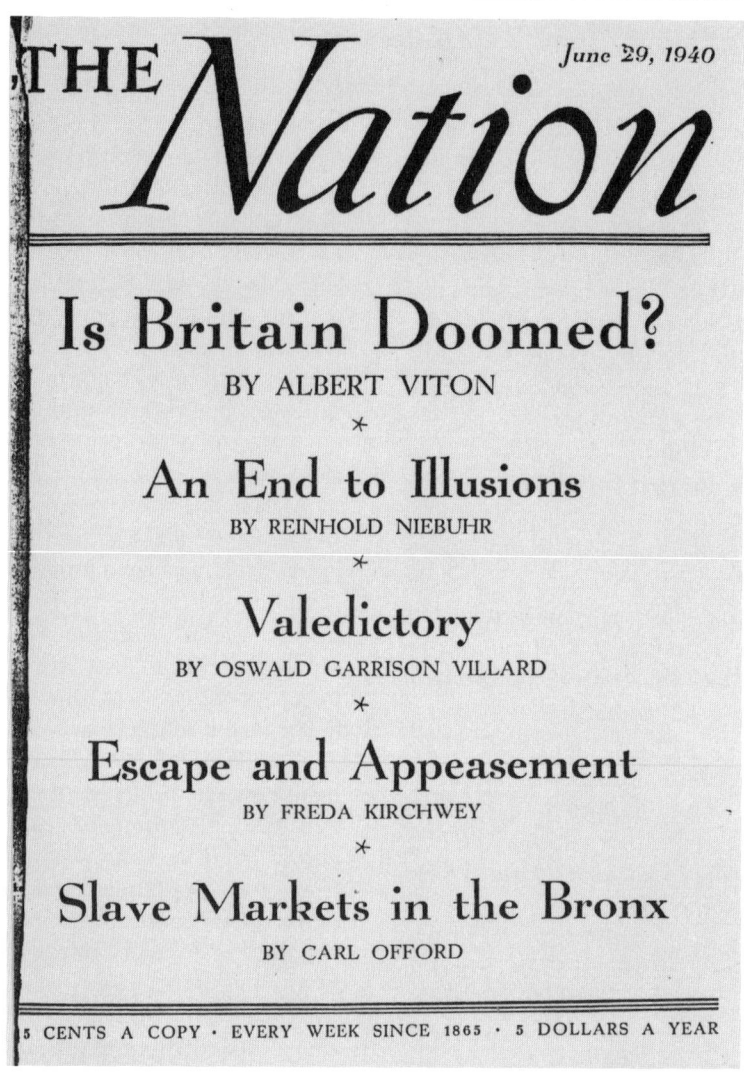

THE *Nation*

June 29, 1940

Is Britain Doomed?
BY ALBERT VITON

✳

An End to Illusions
BY REINHOLD NIEBUHR

✳

Valedictory
BY OSWALD GARRISON VILLARD

✳

Escape and Appeasement
BY FREDA KIRCHWEY

✳

Slave Markets in the Bronx
BY CARL OFFORD

5 CENTS A COPY · EVERY WEEK SINCE 1865 · 5 DOLLARS A YEAR

Cover for the issue of the Nation *in which Villard announced that, because of "the differences of opinion which have arisen between myself and the present editorial board as to the relation of the United States to the catastrophe in Europe," he would no longer write his weekly "Issues and Men" column for the magazine*

finds [Villard] head, and also body, of the most effective rebel periodical in America." Indeed, this son of a self-made capitalist, sometimes dubbed the "aristocrat of liberalism," is the unlikeliest of men to have become one of America's foremost reformers, who, in the words of one colleague, "made more acres of public men acutely miserable per unit of circulation than any other editor alive."

Even in defeat, Villard never lost his faith in the power of reason and justice over force and coercion. His self-righteous moralism, unrelenting idealism, uncompromising pacifism, and fanatical devotion to principles–the absolutisms, according to the *Nation* editor Max Lerner, of a "crusader for lost causes"–may have lost him his

causes, but they have immortalized the spirit with which he championed them. In his autobiography he asked to be remembered for the fact that "he did know how to fight and cared enough about the struggle to put into it all that he had to give during his fighting years. . . ." And unquestionably his innovativeness, courage, and perseverance endure to this day in the *Nation*, which, according to one staffer, was to journalism "What 'Main Street,' 'Winesburg, Ohio,' and 'Spoon River' were in other fields of literature."

In the *Nation* Villard left an enduring organ of American liberalism, imbued with his character, his deep and earnest convictions, and his fighting spirit, even though he may have despaired at some of its positions. Waldo L. Cook, editor of the *Springfield Republican*, said Villard and the *Nation* created "an everlasting moral upheaval that is without rest . . . a sharp prod to our lazy conscience . . . unsurpassed if not incomparable in the press of America."

Biographies:

D. Joy Humes, *Oswald Garrison Villard: Liberal of the 1920s* (Syracuse, N.Y.: Syracuse University Press, 1960);

Michael Wreszin, *Oswald Garrison Villard: Pacifist at War* (Bloomington: Indiana University Press, 1965).

References:

Lewis S. Gannett, "Villard and His Nation," *Nation*, 171 (22 July 1950): 79-82;

Gannett, "Villard's Nation," *Nation*, 150 (10 February 1940): 155-158;

W. E. Garrison, "Lone Eagle of Journalism," *Christian Century*, 56 (26 April 1939): 546;

Freda Kirchwey, "Oswald Garrison Villard," *Nation*, 169 (8 October 1949): 340;

Max Lerner, "Liberalism of O. G. Villard," *New Republic*, 98 (26 April 1939): 342-344;

R. M. Lovett, "Testament of a Liberal," *Nation*, 148 (15 April 1939): 437-438;

Randolph Radosh, *Prophets of the Right: Profiles of Conservative Critics of American Globalism* (New York: Simon & Schuster, 1975), pp. 67-117;

S. K. Ratcliffe, "Oswald Garrison Villard," *New Statesman and Nation*, 38 (15 October 1949): 426;

C. Rogers, "Villard and the Nation," *Outlook*, 151 (6 March 1929): 384-386;

Stephan Thernstrom, "Oswald Garrison Villard and the Politics of Pacifism," *Harvard Library Bulletin*, 14 (Winter 1960): 126-152;

C. G. Woodson, "Oswald Garrison Villard," *Journal of Negro History*, 35 (January 1950): 105-106.

Papers:

Villard's papers are held at the Houghton Library, Harvard University. The New York Public Library houses his annotated sets of the *Nation*.

Checklist of Further Readings

Aaron, Daniel. *Writers on the Left: Episodes in American Literary Communism*. New York: Harcourt, Brace & World, 1961.

Allen, Charles. "The Advance Guard," *Sewanee Review*, 51 (1943): 410-429.

Allen. "Regionalism and the Little Magazines," *College English*, 7 (October 1945): 10-16.

Allen, Frederick Lewis. "American Magazines, 1741-1941," *Bulletin of the New York Public Library*, 45 (June 1941): 439-445.

Anderson, Elliott, and Mary Kinzie, eds. *The Little Magazine in America: A Modern Documentary History*. Yonkers, N.Y.: Pushcart Press, 1978.

Arndt, Karl J. R., and May E. Olson. *German-American Newspapers and Periodicals, 1732-1955*. Heidelberg: Quelle & Meyer, 1961.

Atherton, Gertrude. "Literary Merchandise," *New Republic*, 3 (July 1915): 223-224.

Bakeless, John E. "Aristocrats of Publishing," *Vanity Fair*, 40 (August 1933): 42-44, 52.

Bakeless. *Magazine Making*. New York: Viking Press, 1931.

Baker, Harry T. "Periodicals and Permanent Literature," *North American Review*, 212 (December 1920): 777-787.

Baughman, James L. *Henry R. Luce and the Rise of the American News Media*. Boston: Twayne, 1987.

Berelson, Bernard, and Patricia J. Salter. "Majority and Minority Americans: An Analysis of Magazine Fiction," *Public Opinion Quarterly*, 10 (Summer 1946): 168-190.

Bixler, Paul. "Little Magazine, What Now?," *Antioch Review*, 8 (March 1948): 63-77.

Brainerd, Marion. "Historical Sketch of American Legal Periodicals," *Law Library Journal*, 14 (October 1921): 63-69.

Brown, Dorothy M. "The Quality Magazines in the Progressive Era," *Mid-America*, 53 (July 1971): 139-159.

Burgess, Gelett. *Bayside Bohemia: Fin De Siècle San Francisco & Its Little Magazines*. San Francisco: Book Club of California, 1954.

Canby, Henry Seidel. "Free Fiction," *Atlantic Monthly*, 116 (July 1915): 60-68.

Chenery, William L. "American Magazines, 1741-1941," *Bulletin of the New York Public Library*, 45 (June 1941): 445-448.

Chielens, Edward E., ed. *The Literary Journal in America, 1900-1950*. Detroit: Gale Research Company, 1977.

Colvert, James B. "The Function of the Academic Critical Quarterly," *Mississippi Quarterly*, 23 (1969-1970): 95-101.

Compaine, Benjamin M. *The Business of Consumer Magazines*. White Plains, N.Y.: Knowledge Industry Publications, 1982.

Compaine. "The Magazine Industry: Developing the Special Interest Audience," *Journal of Communication*, 30 (Spring 1980): 98-103.

Cook, Michael L. *Mystery, Detective, and Espionage Magazines*. Westport, Conn.: Greenwood Press, 1983.

Cort, David. *The Sin of Henry Luce: An Anatomy of Journalism*. Secaucus, N.J.: Stuart, 1974.

Daniel, Walter C. *Black Journals of the United States*. Westport, Conn.: Greenwood Press, 1982.

Davenport, Walter, and James C. Derieux. *Ladies, Gentlemen, and Editors*. Garden City, N.Y.: Doubleday, 1960.

Deats, Ruth Z. "Poetry for the Populace: Trends in Poetic Thought in American Popular Magazines," *Sewanee Review*, 50 (July-September 1942): 374-388.

Ditzion, Sidney. "The History of Periodical Literature in the United States: A Bibliography," *Bulletin of Bibliography*, 15 (January/April 1935): 110; (May/August 1935): 129-133.

Drewry, John Eldridge. *Some Magazines and Magazine Makers*. Boston: Stratford, 1924.

Drewry. "American Magazines To-Day," *Sewanee Review*, 36 (July 1928): 342-356.

Elson, Robert T. *Time, Inc.: The Intimate History of a Publishing Enterprise, 1923-1941*, edited by Duncan Norton-Taylor. New York: Atheneum, 1968.

Elson. *The World of Time, Inc.: The Intimate History of a Publishing Enterprise, 1941-1960*, edited by Duncan Norton-Taylor. New York: Atheneum, 1973.

Emmart, A. D. (Richel North). "The Limitations of American Magazines," *Modern Quarterly*, 1 (March 1923): 2-12; (July 1923): 18-30; (December 1923): 17-26.

Faxon, Frederick W. "Magazine Deterioration," *Bulletin of Bibliography*, 9 (April 1916): 34-35.

Felker, Clay S. "Life Cycles in the Age of Magazines," *Antioch Review*, 29 (Spring 1969): 7-13.

Ferguson, Marjorie. *Forever Feminine: Women's Magazines and the Cult of Femininity*. London & Exeter, N.H.: Heinemann, 1983.

Fletcher, Alan D. "City Magazines Find a Niche in the Media Marketplace," *Journalism Quarterly*, 54 (1977): 740-743.

Fletcher, D. and Bruce G. VandenBergh. "Numbers Grow, Problems Remain for City Magazines," *Journalism Quarterly*, 59 (Summer 1982): 313-317.

Ford, James L. C. *Magazines for Millions: The Story of Specialized Publications.* Carbondale, Ill.: Southern Illinois University Press, 1969.

Geiger, Louis G. "Muckrakers—Then and Now." *Journalism Quarterly,* 43 (Autumn 1966): 469-476.

Gillespie, Harris. "Magazine Mortality," *Magazine World,* 1 (October 1945): 27-30.

Goldwater, Walter. *Radical Periodicals in America, 1890-1950; A Bibliography with Brief Notes: With a Genealogical Chart and a Concise Lexicon of the Parties and Groups Which Issued Them.* New Haven, Conn.: Yale University Library, 1964.

Goodstone, Tony, ed. *The Pulps: Fifty Years of American Pop Culture.* New York: Chelsea House, 1970.

Goulart, Ron. *Cheap Thrills: An Informal History of the Pulp Magazines.* New Rochelle, N.Y.: Arlington House, 1972.

Greene, Theodore P. *America's Heroes: The Changing Models of Success in American Magazines.* New York: Oxford University Press, 1970.

Griffin, Max L. "A Bibliography of New Orleans Magazines," *Louisiana Historical Quarterly,* 18 (July 1935): 491-556.

Guenther, Paul, and Nicholas Joost. "Little Magazines and the Cosmopolitan Tradition," *Papers on Language and Literature,* 6 (Winter 1970): 100-110.

Hamblin, Dora Jane. *That Was the Life.* New York: Norton, 1977.

Hamilton, Ian. *The Little Magazines: A Study of Six Editors.* London: Weidenfeld & Nicolson, 1976.

Hamilton, William B. "Fifty Years of Liberalism and Learning," *South Atlantic Quarterly,* 51 (January 1952): 7-32.

Hamilton, ed. *Fifty Years of the South Atlantic Quarterly.* Durham, N.C.: Duke University Press, 1952.

Handbook of Magazine Publishing. New Canaan, Conn.: Folio Magazine, 1978.

Hausdorff, Don. "Magazine Humor and Popular Morality, 1929-34," *Journalism Quarterly,* 41 (Autumn 1964): 509-516.

Hausdorff. "Magazine Humor and the Depression Years," *New York Folklore Quarterly,* 20 (1964): 199-214.

Hirsch, Paul M. "An Analysis of *Ebony*: The Magazine and Its Readers," *Journalism Quarterly,* 45 (Summer 1968): 261-270.

Hoffman, Frederick J. "Little Magazines and the Avant-Garde," *Art in Society,* 1 (Fall 1960): 32-37.

Hoffman. "The Little Magazines: Portrait of an Age," *Saturday Review of Literature,* 26 (25 December 1943): 3-5.

Hynds, Ernest C. "City Magazines, Newspapers Serve in Different Ways," *Journalism Quarterly,* 56 (Autumn 1979): 619-622.

Ingraham, Charles A. "American Magazines, Past and Present," *Americana*, 15 (October 1921): 325-333.

Janssens, Gerardus Antonius Mario. *The American Literary Review: A Critical History 1920-1950*. The Hague & Paris: Mouton, 1968.

Jillson, Willard Rouse. *The Newspapers and Periodicals of Frankfort, Kentucky, 1795-1945*. Frankfort: Kentucky State Historical Society, 1945.

Johns-Heine, Patricke, and Hans H. Gerth. "Values in Mass Periodical Fiction, 1921-1940," *Public Opinion Quarterly*, 13 (Spring 1949): 105-113.

Johnson, Charles S. "The Rise of the Negro Magazine," *Journal of Negro History*, 13 (January 1928): 7-21.

Joost, Nicholas. *Ernest Hemingway and the Little Magazines: The Paris Years*. Barre, Mass.: Barre Publishers, 1968.

Kahan, Robert S. "Magazine Photography Begins: An Editorial Negative," *Journalism Quarterly*, 42 (Winter 1965): 53-59.

Kelly, R. Gordon, ed. *Children's Periodicals of the United States*. Westport, Conn.: Greenwood Press, 1984.

King, Alexander. "The Sad Case of the Humorous Magazines," *Vanity Fair*, 41 (December 1933): 26-27, 68, 71.

Klingberg, Frank J. "The Value of Regional Literature," *Historical Magazine of the Protestant Episcopal Church*, 10 (December 1941): 399-401.

Kosinski, Jerzy. "Packaged Passion," *American Scholar*, 42 (Spring 1973): 193-204.

Lazarsfeld, Paul F., and Rowena Wyant. "Magazines in 90 Cities–Who Reads What?," *Public Opinion Quarterly*, 1 (October 1937): 29-41.

Libbey, James K. "Liberal Journals and the Moscow Trials of 1936-38," *Journalism Quarterly*, 52 (Spring 1975): 85-92, 137.

Littlefield, Jr., Daniel F., and James W. Parins. *American Indian and Alaskan Native Newspapers and Periodicals, 1826-1985*, 3 volumes. Wesport, Conn.: Greenwood Press, 1984-1986.

MacMullen, Margaret. "Pulps and Confessions," *Harper's*, 175 (June 1937): 94-102.

Makosky, Donald Robin. "The Portrayal of Women in Wide-Circulation Magazine Short Stories, 1905-1955." Dissertation, University of Pennsylvania, 1966.

Manchester, Harland. "The Farm Magazines." *Scribner's Magazine* (October 1938): 25-29, 58-59.

Matthews, Brander. "American Magazines," *Bookman*, 49 (July 1919): 533-541.

Meyer, Susan E. *America's Great Illustrators*. New York: Abrams, 1978.

Mondello, Salvatore. "The Magazine *Charities* and the Italian Immigrants, 1903-14," *Journalism Quarterly*, 44 (Spring 1967): 91-98.

Moon, Ben L. "City Magazines Past and Present," *Journalism Quarterly*, 47 (Winter 1970): 711-718.

Mott, Frank Luther. "College Literary Magazines," *Palimpsest:* 44 (1963): 303-310.

Mott. *A History of American Magazines*, 5 volumes. Cambridge, Mass.: Harvard University Press, 1938-1968.

Mugleston, William F. "The Perils of Southern Publishing: A History of *Uncle Remus's Magazine*," *Journalism Quarterly*, 52 (Autumn 1975): 515-521, 608.

O'Brien, Edward J. "The Little Magazines," *Vanity Fair*, 41 (October 1933): 20-21, 58.

Oursler, Fulton. "American Magazines, 1741-1941," *Bulletin of the New York Public Library*, 45 (June 1941): 448-456.

Peterson, Martin Severin. "Regional Magazines," *Prairie Schooner*, 3 (Fall 1929): 292-295.

Peterson, Theodore. *Magazines in the Twentieth Century*. Urbana: University of Illinois Press, 1964.

Peterson. "The Role of the Minority Magazine," *Antioch Review*, 23 (Spring 1963): 57-72.

Porter, William. "The Quality Magazines and the New American Reader," *Gazette*, 6 (1960): 305-310.

Pound, Ezra. "Small Magazines," *English Journal*, 19 (1930): 689-704.

Regier, C. C. *The Era of the Muckrakers*. Chapel Hill: University of North Carolina Press, 1932; Gloucester, Mass.: Smith, 1957.

Repplier, Agnes. "American Magazines," *Yale Review*, 16 (January 1927): 261-274.

Reuss, Carol. "*The Ladies' Home Journal* and Hoover's Food Program," *Journalism Quarterly*, 49 (Winter 1972): 740-742.

Rice, Philip Blair. "The Intellectual Quarterly in a Non-Intellectual Society," *Kenyon Review*, 16 (Summer 1954): 420-439.

Riley, Sam G. *Index to Southern Periodicals*. Westport, Conn.: Greenwood Press, 1986.

Riley. *Magazines of the American South*. Westport, Conn.: Greenwood Press, 1986.

Riley. "The New Money and the New Magazines," *Journal of Regional Cultures* (Fall/Winter 1982): 107-115.

Riley. "Specialized Magazines of the South," *Journalism Quarterly*, 59 (Autumn 1982): 447-450, 455.

Riley and Gary W. Selnow, eds. *Index to City and Regional Magazines of the United States*. Westport, Conn.: Greenwood Press, 1989.

Rollins, Hyder E. "O. Henry's Texas Days," *Bookman*, 40 (October 1914): 154-165.

Root, Robert, and Christine V. Root. "Magazines in the United States: Dying or Thriving?" *Journalism Quarterly*, 41 (Winter 1964): 15-22.

Ryant, Carl G. "From Isolation to Intervention: *The Saturday Evening Post*, 1939-1942," *Journalism Quarterly*, 48 (Winter 1971): 679-687.

Sampson, Robert. *Yesterday's Faces: A Study of Series Characters in the Early Pulp Magazines.* Bowling Green, Ohio: Bowling Green University Popular Press, 1983.

Schacht, J. H. *A Bibliography for the Study of Magazines*, fourth edition. Urbana, Ill.: College of Communications, 1979.

Schoenfeld, A. Clay. "The Environmental Movement as Reflected in the American Magazine," *Journalism Quarterly*, 60 (Autumn 1983): 470-475.

Severance, Frank Hayward. "The Periodical Press of Buffalo, 1811-1915," *Buffalo Historical Society, Publications*, 19 (1915): 177-280.

Singerman, Robert. *Jewish Serials of the World: A Research Bibliography of Secondary Sources.* Westport, Conn.: Greenwood Press, 1986.

Sloane, David E., ed. *American Humor Magazines and Comic Periodicals.* Westport, Conn.: Greenwood Press, 1987.

Smith, C. Zoe. "Black Star Picture Agency: *Life*'s European Connection," *Journalism History*, 13 (Spring 1986): 19-25.

Smith. "Germany's Kurt Korff: An Emigre's Influence on Early Life," *Journalism Quarterly*, 65 (Summer 1988): 412-419, 424.

Smith, James Steel. "American Magazine Missionaries of Culture," *Journalism Quarterly*, 43 (Autumn 1966): 449-458.

Stephens, Ethel. "American Popular Magazines, A Bibliography," *Bulletin of Bibliography Pamphlets*, no. 23, 1916.

Stinson, Robert. "McClure's Road to *McClure's*: How Revolutionary Were 1890s Magazines?," *Journalism Quarterly*, 47 (Summer 1970): 256-262.

Stuntz, Stephen Conrad. *List of Agricultural Periodicals of the United States and Canada Published During the Century July 1810 to July 1910.* U.S. Department of Agriculture. "Miscellaneous Publication," no. 398. Washington: Government Printing Office, 1941.

Swallow, Alan. "The Little Magazines," *Prairie Schooner*, 16 (December 1942): 238-243.

Swanberg, W. A. *Luce and His Empire.* New York: Scribners, 1972.

Tassin, Algernon de Vivier. *The Magazine in America.* New York: Dodd, Mead, 1916.

Tate, Allen. "The Function of the Critical Quarterly," *Southern Review*, 1 (1936): 551-559.

Tebbel, John. *The American Magazine: A Compact History.* New York: Hawthorne Books, 1969.

Terwilliger, W. Bird. "A History of Literary Periodicals in Baltimore," dissertation, University of Maryland, 1941.

Thomas, Dana L. *The Media Moguls*. New York: Putnam, 1981.

Torrence, Clayton. "The Semi-Centennial of the *Virginia Magazine of History and Biography*," *Virginia Magazine of History and Biography*, 51 (July 1943): 217-225.

Towne, Charles Hanson. *Adventures in Editing*. New York & London: Appleton, 1926.

Towne. "The One-Man Magazines," *American Mercury*, 63 (July 1946): 104-108.

Wainwright, Loudon. *The Great American Magazine: An Insider History of Life*. New York: Knopf, 1986.

White, Helen, and Redding S. Sugg, Jr., eds. *From the Mountain*. Memphis: Memphis State University Press, 1972.

Whittemore, Reed. *Little Magazines*. Minneapolis: University of Minnesota Press, 1963.

Wolseley, Roland E. *The Changing Magazine: Trends in Readership and Management*. New York: Hastings House, 1973.

Wolseley. *Understanding Magazines*, revised edition. Ames, Iowa: Iowa State University Press, 1966.

Wood, James Playsted. *Magazines in the United States, Their Social and Economic Influence*. New York: The Ronald Press, 1971.

Zuilen, A. J. van. *The Life Cycle of Magazines*. Uithoorn, The Netherlands: Graduate Press, 1977.

Contributors

Robert E. Alber..Dakota State University
Harry Amana ....Clark Atlanta University
David L. Anderson..University of Northern Colorado
Donald R. Avery...University of Southern Mississippi
Maurine H. Beasley ....University of Maryland
James Boylan ....University of Massachusetts–Amherst
John C. Bromley..University of Northern Colorado
Hilbert H. Campbell ....Virginia Polytechnic Institute and State University
Carolyn Garrett Cline..Southwest Texas State University
Jack H. Colldeweih ....Fairleigh Dickinson University
Ralph Engelman ....Long Island University
Mark Fackler..Wheaton College
Ralph Frasca ....University of Iowa
Cynthia Goldstein..Los Angeles, California
Lloyd J. Graybar ....Eastern Kentucky University
Bert Hitchcock..Auburn University
W. Wat Hopkins.........................Virginia Polytechnic Institute and State Univerity
Robert L. Hoskins..Arkansas State University
Terry Hynes..California State University, Fullerton
A. J. Kaul ....University of Southern Mississippi
Kathleen Kearney Keeshen..Morgan Hill, California
Peggy J. Kreshel..University of Georgia
Bruce W. McKinzie ....University of Northern Colorado
Achal Mehra ....Asian Mass Communication Research
and Information Centre, Singapore
Michael D. Murray ....University of Missouri at St. Louis
Hank Nuwer..Bloomington, Indiana
Cathy Packer.. University of North Carolina
Judith Paterson ....University of Maryland
Paula Cozort Renfro..Southwest Texas State University
Janene Roberts............................Virginia Polytechnic Institute and State University
Nancy L. Roberts ....University of Minnesota
Gary W. Selnow ....Virginia Polytechnic Institute and State University
C. Zoe Smith ....Marquette University
J. William Snorgrass..Florida A. & M. University
James Glen Stovall..University of Alabama
Carolyn A. Stroman..Howard University
Bruce M. Swain..Ithaca College

Cumulative Index

Dictionary of Literary Biography, Volumes 1-91
Dictionary of Literary Biography Yearbook, 1980-1988
Dictionary of Literary Biography Documentary Series, Volumes 1-7

Cumulative Index

DLB before number: *Dictionary of Literary Biography*, Volumes 1-91
Y before number: *Dictionary of Literary Biography Yearbook*, 1980-1988
DS before number: *Dictionary of Literary Biography Documentary Series*, Volumes 1-7

A

B

I

J

K

L

N

P

Q

R

S

Y